MESSAGES OF THE
GOVERNORS OF TENNESSEE
1857–1869

Volume Five

MESSAGES OF THE

Governors of Tennessee

1857–1869

by

ROBERT H. WHITE, Ph.D.
STATE HISTORIAN

AUTHOR OF

*Development of the Tennessee State Educational Organization,
1796–1929* AND *Tennessee: Its Growth and Progress*

VOLUME FIVE

Published by

THE TENNESSEE HISTORICAL COMMISSION
NASHVILLE

TYPOGRAPHY, PRINTING, AND BINDING IN THE U.S.A. BY
BENSON PRINTING COMPANY, NASHVILLE, TENNESSEE

PREVIEW

OF

VOLUME V

1857–1869

Controversy and conflict comprise the major portion of Volume V of the *Messages of the Governors of Tennessee, 1857–1869*. This was the period in our National history wherein social and economic factors led to the "irrepressible conflict" that embroiled the Nation in a four-year internecine war in which over six hundred thousand lives were snuffed out. The first half of the volume portrays the significant steps leading up to Tennessee's withdrawal from the Union, while the latter half deals with the Reconstruction Era in Tennessee which increased and intensified the hostilities engendered by the war.

Seven months before Isham G. Harris became Governor, the United States Supreme Court in the Dred Scott case had sanctioned the expansion of slavery and vouchsafed its protection even in the North. Chief Justice Taney declared, in effect, that the Missouri Compromise was void and that Congress had no power to prohibit slavery in the territories of the United States. Two years later, 1859, the same Court upheld the Fugitive Slave Law along with the rigid provisions for its enforcement. These two fateful decisions frightened the abolitionists, some of whom professed to believe that freedom itself was in danger of being declared unconstitutional. These incidents emphasized the social and economic problems revolving around slavery that ere long led to the secession of eleven Southern States which set up the Southern Confederacy.

Without question the War Between the States was the most dramatic episode that has occurred in the life of the American Nation. This statement is supported by the fact that over one hundred thousand volumes and brochures have been written and published, related in some degree to the martial conflict. Heroes have been extolled, battles have been analyzed, maneuvers have been re-enacted, and memorials erected throughout the country. These phases of the war have overshadowed such basic factors as recommendations of Governors and responsibilities of State legislative assemblies dealing with the herculean tasks of raising funds and equipping military personnel with war materiel. This well-documented volume, drawing from official and authentic sources, resurrects and brings to light such fundamentals as floating bond issues, enacting draft laws, and providing means and methods of defense.

This volume brings into sharp focus the contrasts in character and attitude toward the war as displayed by Isham G. Harris, Andrew Johnson, and "Parson" Brownlow. Bitter clashes in the legislative sessions are presented in detail; the hate-laden years of Reconstruction are depicted; and the ultimate downfall of the Radicalism of the Brownlow regime provides a fitting conclusion of the most hectic experience ever undergone by Tennesseans.

The fateful years covered by this treatise mark the great transition period wherein Tennessee's economy was drastically changed. The heyday of slavery and the broad plantation were terminated. The iron-rule of Brownlow Radicalism, whereby a minority ran roughshod over the majority, resulted in the adoption of the Constitution of 1870 whereby the democratic process was again restored. Volume V constitutes a veritable storehouse of historical information with which all Tennesseans should become better acquainted.

Governor of Tennessee.

July 1, 1959

ACKNOWLEDGMENTS

Sincere appreciation is hereby expressed for the support and encouragement given by ex-Governor Frank G. Clement and the Eightieth General Assembly for providing funds for the research and publication of Volume V of the *Messages of the Governors of Tennessee*. Similar gratitude is due Governor Buford Ellington and the Eighty-First General Assembly for providing funds for the continuation of the series. Splendid cooperation has been given by the State Library and Archives, the Tennessee Historical Society, the Nashville Public Library, and the Cossitt Branch of the Memphis Public Library. Especial appreciation is expressed for the valuable assistance rendered by Dr. Philip M. Hamer, Executive Director, National Historical Publications Commission, Washington, D.C., who supplied pertinent information upon two or three exceedingly difficult situations. His contributions can be determined by consulting the Index.

It would be amiss not to express my deep and genuine thanks to Mrs. Ruth Kennedy and Mrs. Ruth Armstrong who rendered invaluable service in proofreading the entire volume.

R.H.W.

CONTENTS

VOLUME FIVE

Isham G. Harris

Courtesy of Tennessee Historical Society, Nashville.

ILLUSTRATIONS

VOLUME FIVE

MESSAGES OF THE GOVERNORS OF TENNESSEE
1857–1869

VOLUME FIVE

🐦

CHAPTER ONE

Isham Green Harris

Isham Green Harris was born in Franklin County, Tennessee on February 10, 1818, the son of Isham Harris and Lucy Davidson Harris. The father and mother were North Carolinians and of Revolutionary stock. Leaving the Old North State, the pioneer parents migrated to Tennessee and settled on a farm in Franklin County where they reared a family of nine children. The log house and country schoolhouse were familiar features in that time, but such an environment was too cramped and circumscribed for young ambition to vaunt itself. At the early age of fourteen, young Isham with the consent and blessing of his father pulled up stakes and went to Paris, Tennessee where he hired out as a clerk in a mercantile establishment. During his clerkship tenure, the young man visioned wider fields of activity and service and added to his daily work as a clerk a nightly vigil of studying that most jealous of mistresses, the law.

Divorcing himself at length from his clerkship, he entered the law office of Judge Andrew McCampbell for supplementary study. Close application soon paid off, for shortly thereafter he applied for and procured a license in May, 1841, to practice law. Two years later he married Miss Martha Travis of Henry County of which marriage there were born eight children. He was successful in acquiring a large clientele and forged rapidly to the forefront as a skillful practitioner and doughty competitor at the bar.

But a successful law practice did not blur a sort of prophetic vision that glimpsed another field of service in which distinction might be blended with destiny. His taste, tact, ambition, and ability fitted him pre-eminently for the political arena whose seductive gates opened wide its portals and lured him into its folds as naturally as steel filings are drawn by a magnet. Henceforth the political hustings became, as it were, his Penates and constituted the arena in which was enacted the life drama of ISHAM GREEN HARRIS.

In 1847 began the public career of the man who for fifty years, with brief interruptions, occupied public office without ever suffering defeat at the polls. As a Senator of the Tennessee General Assembly, his aptitude for political foresight and analysis of public questions stamped him early as a leader and able judge of men and measures. The following year he was selected as the Democratic elector for the Ninth Congressional District which honored him the next year with a seat in the Lower House of Congress, with re-election to the same post two years later. He declined to accept a third nomination, and moved his residence to Memphis where he immediately took high rank at a bar distinguished for the ability of its members. But his ruling passion for political activity brought him forth in 1856 as elector-at-large for the Democratic Party. His clear, cogent, and at times dramatic speeches in the campaign won State-wide attention, resulting in his unanimous nomination as the Democratic candidate for Governor in 1857. Three times in succession he was nominated and elected Governor, in 1857, 1859, and 1861.

It was during his third term that the long pent-up fury and fanaticism incident to the institution of slavery broke from the moorings and the country was plunged into a fratricidal war. To Governor Harris, state sovereignty involved the right of secession, and with the courage of his convictions he met the existing situation with the only remedy he conceived as being applicable. To President Lincoln's call for two Tennessee regiments to help coerce the seceded States, Governor Harris replied with clarity and conviction:

"Tennessee will not furnish a single man for purposes of coercion, but 50,000 if necessary for the defence of our rights and those of our Southern brothers."

Governor Harris never any more doubted on the day of his death than he did on the day of the Shiloh battle that the Southern States had a legal and constitutional right to do what they attemped to do—peaceably to dissolve their relations with the other States of the Union. With Isham G. Harris, conviction was decision and decision meant action. He never needlessly explored or deplored; he thrust in his sickle with an energy that never sagged and with a devotion that never fagged. Wholly saturated with the belief that a State had a *political* right to secede from the Union, he saw, heard, and knew nothing but the duty to exercise that privilege. Like an enchantress, this idea of *secession* greeted his earliest thoughts in the morning and gilded his latest dreams at night. He was never afraid of doing right for fear of doing wrong.

With a ceaseless and untiring energy, he equipped and turned over to the Confederate Government by July, 1861, a hundred thousand Tennessee troops, earning a well-merited and to him a most highly-prized soubriquet—the "War Governor of Tennessee." When driven by the events of the war from his post of Chief Executive of Tennessee, he immediately entered the field of conflict on the staff of General Albert Sidney Johnston and personally assisted that fatally-wounded chieftian from his horse at the battle of Shiloh. With the end of the war, the fierce passions of politics interposed and drove him into exile. Faced with a trumped-up charge of treason to the State which he had so bravely defended, plus a five thousand dollar reward for his capture, he was forced to seek safety in Mexico and await a returning sense of shame on the part of his political persecutors. From Mexico to England was for him a change from enforced idleness to business activity. One year in Liverpool completed the two and one-half years of exile, during which time the ill-founded charges of treason were abandoned and rewards for his capture withdrawn, leaving the former Governor free to return to the State and people he had served so faithfully and earnestly.

After eight years of successful law practice in Memphis, with a reputed annual income of twenty thousand dollars, the lure of politics once more drew Isham G. Harris into the battle of ballots. On January 9, 1877, he was nominated for the six-year term of United States Senator and was elected by the General Assembly by a vote of 77 to 23. The more than three-to-one vote was convincing evidence of the affection and esteem in which he was held by his fellow Tennesseans. He was re-elected Senator in 1883, 1889, and 1895, serving in that capacity until his death on July 8, 1897.

What were the basic characteristics of the man whose life-span exceeded the well-known Scriptural limitation of "three score years and ten," with most of those years spent in public service during the times of fierce anti-slavery agitation, four years of as intense military conflict as the world ever witnessed, and the tantalizing and demoralizing period of Reconstruction? Perhaps the answer is to be found in a statement made by him in his old age to a query as to what he attributed his continued success in politics. "I don't know," said Senator Harris, "unless it be to the fact that I early learned the difficult art of telling the truth." This sterling attribute of his was emphasized and repeated at the time of his death by personal friends and political enemies throughout the one hundred and eighty pages of *Memorial Addresses on the Life and Character of Isham G. Harris*. Without one dissenting opinion, friend and foe alike paid tribute to the courage, conviction, and integrity of the dead statesman. Duplicity, evasion, and equivocation were foreign to his nature, and he never once sought refuge by simulating the tricks of the Delphic oracle. His answer on all public questions was a clear-cut "Yes" or an emphatic "No." Unlike Janus, Isham G. Harris never faced two but opposite directions. He scorned to practice the sly hypocrisy of "convenience"; he never yielded to the "whining yelp of complaint"; unlike Hamlet, Harris never soliloquized about "taking arms against a sea of troubles"; he simply took them up and marched breast forward!

The death of Senator Harris was neither sudden nor unexpected. During the winter preceding his death in the summer, he had had a long bout with lagrippe whose aftereffects left him weak and debilitated. Digestive disturbances were added during the hot and humid summer months, and sapped his physical strength. On July 8, 1897, almost at sunset, the old warrior ceased to breathe. Immediately, the news of his death was flashed across the country, and countless tributes to his life and career flooded newspaper columns throughout the Nation. On July 10, funeral ceremonies were held in the Senate Chamber at the National Capitol. Around the casket stood grouped his fellow-Senators, among whom he had been long acknowledged the ablest parliamentarian of them all. Secession, war, bitter times, and biting words were all forgotten. A rare and perhaps an unprecedented honor was tendered the dead Senator in that the President of the United States and his Cabinet were in attendance.

After the funeral ceremonies in the National Capitol, the remains were conveyed to Nashville where the body lay in state for an entire day. The Hall of Representatives was gracefully decorated with a wealth of floral tributes, with a large flag of the United States at one end and a Confederate battle flag at the other. Near the Speaker's stand was displayed a picture of Senator Harris. Everything had been made ready for the silent visitor, even the clock being draped in black and the hands set at 5:20 o'clock—the exact time of the Senator's death. From 10:00 o'clock in the morning until 7:15 in the evening, thousands of persons viewed the remains. At the end of the ceremonies, a military escort of Confederate Veterans accompanied the hearse which bore the body of the "War Governor" to the depot for conveyance to his home at Memphis. In Memphis, the body lay in state at the First Methodist Church where thousands throughout the day viewed the dead statesman. A company of uniformed Confederate Veterans stood silent guard about the casket which was literally buried beneath a wilderness of flowers. At 4:00 o'clock, the Reverend R. D. Smart, pastor of the First Methodist Church, read the Ninetieth Psalm and delivered a brief but impressive discourse. At the conclusion of his remarks, Dr. Smart turned to Dr. W. F. Hamner, pastor of the Central Methodist Church and a longtime friend of Senator Harris, and requested him to say anything which might occur to him as being appropriate for the occasion. Dr. Hamner's eulogy deserves to be preserved and perpetuated:

"The history of great men is the history of great mothers. Every grand and successful life is a monument to some motherly spirit. Many years ago a noble Tennessee mother gave to her State four distinguished sons. The varied occupations of those boys indicate the catholic spirit of the mother. One chose agriculture as his life work and laid down his life on the consecrated field of Shiloh. One held the scales of justice and died in the enjoyment of the full confidence and esteem of his countrymen. One was a preacher and laid the foundations of the church in this Western country. His influence runs like a golden thread through the religious history of Tennessee. One, whose body lies before us, gave his life to the State, and was a Statesman. All of them won a name and wielded a power that will continue far beyond the generation in which they lived.

As a Tennessean and a personal friend of the family, I am proud of this vast assembly of Tennesseans and friends from other States attesting that this observance is in memory of no ordinary man. It may be said of him as of Wellington:

'O, iron nerve to true occasion true,
    O, fallen at length that tower of strength
Which stood four square to all the winds that blew.'

He brought to the altar of his country personal integrity, burning patriotism, resistless energy and fearless devotion to duty. Through more than a half century the stern traits of character were held by an indomitable will to the accomplishment of what he believed to be right in state. He had an eye to see and courage to tell what he saw. He saw afar off and spoke out his convictions, regardless of the popular sentiment of the hour. His fidelity to principle and his frankness were intolerant of fawning or deception. 'Dowered with the hate of hate, the scorn of scorn and the love of love, he hated the hateful, scorned the scornful and loved the lovable.'

We wait the verdict of the next fifty years as to whether Tennessee has another such leader or her flag another such friend.

There is something more than marvelous to me than his long unbroken hold upon the loyalty and confidence of the people, and that is the reverence and esteem in which he is held by the children of the third and fourth generations of his family. He has stood for years as the central shaft in that large and ever widening circle of relatives, beloved and honored by all, from the oldest to the latest born.

We are glad that his body is to rest in the bosom of his own Tennessee, whose honors he has worn with credit to himself and glory to her own fair name. Now we leave him to the future and the discoveries of the last great day.

    'Farewell to thee! illustrious statesman
        with a lion's heart;
    Farewell to thee! uncompromising patriot
        with a true soul;
    Farewell to thee! indefatigable worker
        with an iron frame;
    Farewell to thee! undaunted friend with a
        faithful breast;
    Farewell to thee! loyal citizen with
        patriotic impulses;
    Farewell to thee! stalwart politician, in-
        trepid counselor—
    Fearless adviser, genial companion.'
  We mourn thee—
    'A senator without reproach,
    A man true and brave,
    A soul of honest aim.' "

Upon the conclusion of Dr. Hamner's remarks, announcement was made that the final ceremonies would be concluded at the cemetery. When the pallbearers brought the casket to the grave, Dr. Smart read the burial service of the Methodist Church and the mortal remains of

Isham Green Harris were laid to rest in beautiful Elmwood Cemetery. Toward the setting sun, Company A Confederate Veterans fired the last salute of three rounds over the grave of him who had for a time been the active head of the army in which they first saw service.

Tennessee bowed in deep and genuine grief upon the death of its native son "For whom the bell tolled." Isham G. Harris was a true friend who never forgot his people; he was an intrepid leader who never outgrew his usefulness. Policy never sat above his conscience. His career had been long, distinguished, and beneficial. He had epitomized the prophecy of Job:

"Thou shalt come to thy grave in a full age, like as a shock of corn cometh in his season."

Tennessee has not developed such a natural party leader since Andrew Jackson. James K. Polk and Andrew Johnson attained positions of loftier eminence, but neither had such a hold upon the people of Tennessee as that possessed by Isham G. Harris for half a century. His tremendous will power did not desert him even at the point of death. His mind was clear up to the hour of his passing. Its casement gave way beneath the accumulated years. "Tell the boys that the old frame has about worn out" was his final message to his Senatorial comrades. He never yielded until Nature had withdrawn its support and Eternity had touched his eyelids to sleep.

It is fitting that this altogether too-brief biographical sketch should be concluded with the cameo-like tribute paid Senator Harris by a group of distinguished Tennesseans a few days after his death. Their names were as follows: Ex-Governor Peter Turney, John J. Vertrees, S. F. Wilson, W. K. McAlister, James M. Head, John K. Shields, John Thompson, T. M. McConnell, J. M. Dickinson, John Allison, and Horace H. Lurton.

"Great men are the jewels of the republic. In peace we proudly boast of their characters and their achievements. In the hour of danger we arouse to action by their names and heroic deeds. It is, therefore, the duty of the living in a republic, to pass down to posterity with truthful and fitting testimony, the name of every really capable, honest, courageous public man.

Senator Isham Green Harris was such a man. On the 8th day of this July, in the 80th year of his age, he passed away.

In 1847 he was elected State Senator, and introduced into public life. In 1897 he died a United States Senator, after fifty years of almost continuous public service. While his countrymen mourn his death, it was not untimely. Neither in length of days, nor in lofty bearing, was his death untimely. By reason of strength his years were four-score, and they were full of that worth which entitle his name to live. We do not mourn for him as citizens of a republic which has been deprived of the full harvest of a strong and useful life, but grieve for him as a friend, and lament that we are deprived of his leadership, his influence, and his strength.

It were idle for us to testify in phrase and speech, to the high esteem in which Mr. Harris was held by the people of Tennessee.

That he served them fifty years and died with the harness on, enjoying the highest distinction which it was within their power to bestow; that from 1847 to 1897 he repeatedly contested with our ablest men for public honor, and never once suffered defeat; that a nation mourns his loss, and for the first time drapes the Senate Chamber on the occasion of a Senator's death—proclaim the strong hold which he had upon the confidence and affection of his countrymen.

Mr. Harris had foes. He had a multitude of unflinching friends, and of course, had foes. He was not without faults, but the faults were as nothing to the virtues which were his. He who stands immediately by a mountain's side may here and there observe the irregularities which appear to mar the patch of surface which his vision may command; but he who views it sufficiently afar to see that mountain itself—to observe the grandeur of its sweep, its loftiness, its massiveness, and its reach, forgets the gnarled tree, and barren spot upon its majestic side. So it is with the character of a great strong man. So it was with Mr. Harris.

He knew little of books, but much of men. He was sagacious. He was wise. He had the resistless and self-sustaining power which is born of the union of courage and will. He was himself a power because of the fact that whenever responsibility was his, decision marked the act.

He was Governor of Tennessee during the critical period which marked the war between the States. He was emphatically a 'war Governor.' No Governor was more resolute, impetuous, and aggressive than Mr. Harris. He declined the proffer of a seat in the Confederate Senate, for the reason that it would deprive him of the companionship of Tennesseans in the field. He became an exile in foreign lands when the fates announced that the Union should be preserved. He never apologized or recanted. Nevertheless, he realized and patriotically accepted the consequences. For the last twenty years he was a Senator of and for that Union he had previously labored so ardently to dissolve. It was no merit to him, neither would it be meritorious in any Tennessean worthy of the senatorship, that every act, and word, and vote as Senator was loyal and patriotic, and delivered with an eye single to the preservation of the Union, strength and prosperity of the States. It was well understood by the people of Tennessee when he was elected that Mr. Harris could and would pursue no other course.

When he was elected, loyalty to the Union was what the people of Tennessee demanded, and when he accepted the senatorship the loyalty which never shrinks was the only thing they had any right to expect. It is not, however, to his loyalty that we would refer, but to the fact that this sagacious and patriotic man, whom those who knew him not are wont to describe as 'unreconstructed' and imperious, has exhibited a conservative and wise appreciation of conditions which many others, called wise, have not. Senators and Representatives from the South have often been goaded and taunted with the past. 'Rebel' and 'disunion' and 'disloyal' have been exasperating missiles which have been kept in political stock; and the Representatives from the South have often been provoked into retort. This is not true as to Mr. Harris. Courageous, resolute, and even at times imperious, he has borne in dignified silence all offensive allusions to the past. The past with him was truly a dear and cherished memory, but as a United States Senator he sought neither to vindicate nor to defend. His every word was of the present, and of the future of the people whom he served, and whose happiness he labored to promote. The silence of Senator Harris was like the silence of Gen. Lee; and reveals a greatness of spirit and patriotic purpose possessed by few.

In another respect Mr. Harris was conspicuous. He was a most candid, punctual and truthful man.

In him there was no deceit—no promises, broken, no pledges, unfulfilled. Mr. Harris, like other public men, was not exempt from aspersions of party rancor, and the malignity of defeat; yet the accusation was never even made, to our knowledge, that he had broken a promise or betrayed a friend.

Mr. Harris was always with the majority, yet he never followed them. He was too sagacious, wise and practical to be a mere follower. He was too independent, honest and brave to follow, or even seek to ascertain, the popular will. But he was a Democrat of the strictest sect. He had real faith in the people. He was one of the people himself. Consequently, his sagacity perceived at once what was for their good. He subordinated his opinions upon party questions to his deep-rooted views of government, and to his confidence and faith in the honesty of the people themselves. His common sense was so clear, so honest and extraordinary, that it not only commanded and secured him leadership, but it inspired to him an unusual confidence in the sense and judgment of his fellow-men."

Legislative Messages of
Governor Isham G. Harris 1857–1862

Before proceeding to deal with the administrations of Governor Isham G. Harris, it might be advisable to diagnose the political situation that existed in Tennessee in 1856, the year prior to the election of Governor Harris for his first term. Political contests, both in the Nation and in Tennessee, were centered around the slavery question. The Whig Party in Tennessee had favored a settlement of the slavery controversy in 1850 through what was denominated the Missouri Compromise, and had triumphed in 1851 by the election of William B. Campbell as Governor, the last Whig to be elected to that office. By the repeal of the Compromise in 1854, however, the highly inflammatory slavery question was reopened with increased vigor and even greater ferocity. Vociferous and vituperative attacks upon the "peculiar institution" by Northerners had served to weaken the Whig Party in Tennessee, thereby contributing to the defeat of the Whig candidate—Gustavus A. Henry, "The Eagle Orator"—by Andrew Johnson in the gubernatorial contest of 1853. Moreover, the split in the Whig Party over slavery was the dominant factor that doomed the Whig Party to political oblivion as a significant political party. Its offspring, the so-called American Party (widely acclaimed the Know Nothing Party) drew to its ranks a tremendous number of persons unwilling to cast their lot or their votes with pro-slavery Democrats or anti-slavery Republicans. In addition, the Know Nothings attracted thousands of persons who sincerely be-

lieved that Catholicism and foreign immigration threatened to engulf
and take over the reins of government, both civil and religious, in the
United States. Those factors gave the Know Nothing Party startling
strength in the elections of 1854 and 1855. But the slavery issue plus
terrific attacks upon the secret and oath-bound party's tenets produced
a yawning breach in the organization to such an extent that in the presidential election of 1856 its candidate, Ex-President Millard Fillmore,
carried only the single State of Maryland. This crushing defeat plus the
increasing sectional antagonism over slavery ushered the party into an
early political graveyard.

Like the Whig Party, the Know Nothing Party was destroyed as a
national party by the rising tide of sectional dispute over slavery. In the
presidential contest of 1856, the recently-born Republican Party had no
strength in Tennessee and the race was between the Democratic Party
and the Know Nothings. Of tremendous political significance in Tennessee was a switch-over from the Whig Party to the Democratic Party
of many former Whig leaders. For instance, United States Senator
James C. Jones, who had defeated James K. Polk twice for the governorship, openly announced that he would support James Buchanan the
Democratic candidate for President. "Lean Jimmy," who had been the
idol of the Tennessee Whigs, entered wholeheartedly into the campaign
and unquestionably aided the Democrats in carrying Tennessee for
Buchanan. This was the first time since 1832 that Tennessee cast its vote
for the Democratic candidate for President. The popular vote in Tennessee was 73,638 for Buchanan and 66,178 for Fillmore.

Despite the collapse of their party from a national standpoint, the
Know Nothings in Tennessee held most of their adherents in the organization and proceeded to wage a spirited contest in the gubernatorial and
legislative contests in 1857. Heartened by the return at long last of Tennessee to the Democratic fold, the Democrats were alert and saw to it
that their gubernatorial candidate be a man of ability and courage. The
opening gun in the forthcoming gubernatorial contest was fired on New
Year's Day by the strongest Democratic newspaper [1] in Tennessee:

"GOV. JOHNSON—THE NEXT CANVASS.

The convention which meets in this city on the 15th April next will
have to select a candidate for Governor of the State. This convention
should represent the people, and in its action, conform to their wishes. The
great service rendered by GOV. JOHNSON to the democratic party has
made him deservedly our strong man, and fixed the hopes of many democrats upon him for another contest. The herculean labor which he performed in the canvass of 1855 is still gratefully remembered.—The service
he then rendered the party has never been exceeded by that rendered by
any man since the organization of our party. The success of know-
nothingism here in that contest would have been its success in most of the

---

[1] *Daily Union and American* (Nashville), January 1, 1857.

southern States; as its overthrow, through the transcendent ability with which it was exposed by GOV. JOHNSON, followed its crushing out by the Tennessee democracy. The result of that contest confirmed the position in the confidence and affection of the people which GOV. JOHNSON had well earned by a life devoted to their service; and it is no less a compliment to the people than to GOV. JOHNSON to say that no servant of the State has ever rendered more patriotic service than the latter, and that the former have never more gratefully remembered and honored such service. The hope that GOV. JOHNSON will again be a candidate for the office of GOVERNOR, as it may prevent that canvass of the qualifications of others which should precede the meeting of the convention, makes it proper for us to say, as we do by his authority, that he neither expects nor desires the nomination. His determination not to be again a candidate has been frequently and freely expressed to his friends ever since the last election and he will be ready to labor in the ranks for the triumph of the principles of democracy, and of such one of their true representatives as the people, in their convention, shall designate as leader.

We trust that the announcement we thus make, as it renders the nomination of a new man necessary, will secure a representation of every county in the State at the Convention in April. Our candidate must be the representative of our principles; and while distinguished services are entitled to remembrance and honor, yet no man who has real *claims* upon the party will ever urge them.—The democratic party may use its best men; but no man may use the democratic party.

These remarks are quite as true, and perhaps still more necessary to be urged, when applied to candidates for the Legislature, as when used in connection with the nomination of a candidate for Governor. Doubtless every reader of this article can call to mind cases in which Senatorial or Representative districts have been lost, and the Legislature also, by the obstinacy of aspirants for seats in the Senate or House, in persisting in being candidates against the wishes of the party. These men talk of their 'claims,' with an impudence which, of itself, should prevent their receiving a single vote. It should be always remembered that Senators and Representatives should be the best men of their counties; and that an aspirant for office is a very unsafe judge of merit in his own case. The man who will not trust the people to choose for themselves cannot be a safe representative of the people. There may be cases where conventions are unnecessary; but in such cases they can do no harm. Those who decry conventions are generally those who are afraid to trust the people to pass on their merits, and who are so eager for office as to take it by being accepted as a choice of evils.

We have not hesitated frankly and plainly to tell our political friends that while, for Governor, a nomination by a democratic convention is equivalent to an election by the people, yet the Legislature may be lost by the loss of a single democratic county. We have the strength to secure both Houses, if we do not permit ambitious aspirants, thinking more of personal aggrandizement than of the success of the party, to defeat us. A good democrat will submit to injustice sooner than risk the defeat of his party. He will act out the patriotic saying of the revolutionary father, 'IT IS NO TIME TO INDULGE PRIVATE GRIEFS WHEN THE ENEMY IS IN FRONT!' We are secure of a majority when, and only when, the policy is recognized and acted upon, that, in cases of rivalry for the candidacy for political offices, the party in convention is to be the final judge in the matter. An experience of near twenty years in party contests in Tennessee enables us to say that our principles would have been represented by a democratic Legislature four-fifths of the time since 1837, but for mere personal conflicts. Men and brethren! We *must not* suffer such conflicts in 1857!"

Some two weeks later, the rather rampant Democratic organ[2] in a vein of sarcastic *éclat* sought to twit the opposition as to the difficulties it was allegedly experiencing in finding a suitable candidate for the forthcoming gubernatorial race. In a rather adroit editorial, various names were suggested followed by comments upon the shortcomings of some of the individuals and by the hopelessness of the situation regardless of the identity of the Opposition nominee:

"KNOW-NOTHINGISM IN SEARCH OF A CANDIDATE

Who shall be the know nothing candidate for Governor? *What* shall he be? *Where* shall he come from? and *who* shall he belong to? Shall he be a know nothing? up to all Sam's mysteries? possessor of the 'third degree?' 'in favor of Americans ruling America' with brass knuckles and incendiary torches? Or shall he be some man who can safely swear that he 'swore not at all,' at a time when 'true Americans' had to swear to be false to the chief glory of America? In short, to have seen, or not to have seen, *Sam*—that's the question!

Present indications favor the pretensions of some 'old line whig'—of some man who did Sam's work last summer without taking his oath. As, for instance, Mr. EDMUND COOPER, of Bedford county; a clever man, but hardly large enough to fill the seat; GEN. HASKELL who, *we* think, would more fitly represent know nothingism than any other man in the State. Other 'old line whigs' are spoken of, but it is doubtful if they could be prevailed upon to run. One such, at least, whose name has been mentioned, would, we are sure, answer the seductive appeals of know nothingism for a candidate in *his* person by a flat refusal:

'He would say he once heard of an amorous youth,
    Who was caught in his grand-mother's bed;
But declare *he* ne'er had such a licorice tooth
    As to wish to be there in his stead!'

—But to return—shall the candidate be a *whig* or a *know nothing?* We shall not try to answer the question. We only want to let our readers know that '*it exists,*' and is of hard solution by our opponents. If a *whig* is nominated, the fact is an admission of the powerlessness, the hopelessness, of know nothingism; and there are several people in the State who would object to this. There are democratic deserters in the know nothing camp who would fear the tomahawk of their ancient enemies, the whigs, as much as they dread the scalping knife of their ancient friends, the democrats. If know nothingism goes back to whiggery, what shall become of our ancient friend, Gen. AMENT, and our scarcely less distinguished friend, JAMES M. QUARLES? Surely *they* will not consent to be carried as trophies over to the ranks of whiggery!—*They* will not willingly agree to represent silver dollars sticking to the tarred heels of political gamblers, whose single idea is—*spoils!*

And so, after all, and notwithstanding contrary indications at present,

[2] *Ibid.*, January 17, 1857.

we judge that the candidate for Governor who will be defeated by something upwards of ten thousand votes next August, will be an out and out know nothing. It can't be helped!

—We see no class of citizens who are more amused at the dilemma of know nothingism in search of a candidate than those old-line whigs who voted for Mr. BUCHANAN. They will vote against a whig as the nominee of know nothingism with more pleasure than they would vote against an out and out know nothing. The trick is stale. And thus, the difficulties of know nothingism in selecting a candidate—or rather in fixing up its next trick—are laughable all round and laughable only. For the democratic majority, in any event, will be overwhelming."

With the Whig Party dead and buried, plus the fact that the Know Nothings also were moribund, there can be no denial of the fact that the opponents of the Democratic Party in Tennessee were hard put to work out any sort of combination that would offer any reasonable prospect of success in the oncoming gubernatorial contest. Confronted with this dilemma, various Whig newspapers throughout the State began to "sound out" the sentiment of the old line Whigs and its offspring, the Know Nothings. A resumé of the Whig press was set forth in an editorial of the leading Democratic organ:[3]

"WILL THERE BE A KNOW-NOTHING CANDIDATE FOR GOVERNOR?

This question seems to be exciting a good deal of anxiety with some, and interest with others. It is a question that *we* have no right to answer, but about which we are free to conjecture. We do not believe there will be a Know Nothing candidate for Governor, *upon fair and open ground.* So utterly hopeless are the fortunes of that party—so crushing has been the verdict of popular condemnation—so great the odium that attaches to it—that we cannot believe another candidate will ever be run in Tennessee *as the nominee* of that heterogeneous compound. They dare not so insult the sense of the sovereign people.

We are not to be understood, however, as supposing that the Know Nothings will fail to have a candidate or that that candidate will not be a Know Nothing. We only contend that they will deny his paternity and complexion. We find ourselves sustained in this impression by the tone of certain of the Know Nothing Journals. The *American Statesman*, published at Dandridge, East Tennessee, breaks ground in favor of Judge [Ebenezer] ALEXANDER after the following style:

'He is an able man in point of intellect, is *free from all party ties, owes no allegiance to any party or sect,* is what you might call a man of his own head, and would not forsake, under any circumstances whatever, any principle of honor, for all the party demagogues in the land.

'True, the Judge voted, and perhaps, used his influence for the election of Millard Fillmore, as an old-line Whig should have done under the circumstances, for which he is none the worse, this being a free country. *He did not canvass the State; he had, we suppose, official business to attend,* and unlike others, he thought proper to hold inviolate the trust imposed in

---

[3] *Ibid.,* January 13, 1857.

him. *He had no hard epithets to apply to those of his old line Whig* brethren who honestly opposed him in the late contest for the Presidency, but like a freeman he supported the man of his choice, and let the future control the past.

'Judge Alexander *is a genuine old line Whig* of the Clay school, and has not participated in the great political fights very extensively, since the death of the Whig party, though, like a man, however, always free in expressing his political preferences whenever called upon.'

A correspondent of the *Eagle and Enquirer* says:

'The subject of a candidate by the Whigs and Americans, for the office of Governor, is now being stirred in the papers. I am an East Tennessean, and will support, in good faith, any man the Americans and Whigs may agree upon.'

He then continues by asking the question, 'who shall be our candidate.' He says that among the persons spoken of is Judge ALEXANDER, who is physically unable to canvass the State; THO. A. R. NELSON, whose 'heavy practice' at the bar will prevent his acceptance; JOHN NETHER-LAND, whose health is in the way; O. P. TEMPLE, who could not be induced to accept; N. G. TAYLOR, who 'is a Methodist preacher and would array against him all the sectarians in the State of other churches;' W. G. BROWNLOW, who says:

'He will not be a candidate in any event, for that or any other office, and for two reasons, which, in my judgment, are valid. First, he is poor, and not able to undergo the expense of a canvass.—Next, he has been for a quarter of a century engaged in *religious controversies*—has no regrets on this account—takes back nothing he has said—and would be voted against by thousands of his own party, on this account.'

The writer then concludes by suggesting 'WM. H. SNEED, the able representative in Congress from the Knoxville district,' who, he says, if nominated '*would* run, and is a gentleman of wealth, spends his money freely, and *could well afford to bear the expense of canvassing the State.*'

We doubt very much whether Mr. Sneed will feel thankful for such a compliment. It is taxing a man's liberality a good deal to ask him to spend his money in a hopeless cause merely for the honor of being beaten. The expenses of such a canvass will be not only upon the pocket, but the reputation, and the man that has the least of the last named commodity to lose, can best afford the expense. What has become of Haskell? He would make a splendid candidate. And then there are a number of younger aspirants who would be honored even with so poor a compliment as being set up to be defeated as a candidate for Governor. It will be interesting to observe how they fix it up."

Some three months had passed and there had been no definite decision reached by the Opposition as to the selection of a candidate to oppose the Democratic candidate whoever he might be. Only four weeks remained until the Opposition would convene in Nashville for selecting its candidate for the gubernatorial race. Finally, one of the strongest Whig journals suggested the name of Edwin H. Ewing of Nashville, who had been elected as a Whig to Congress in 1845. In the opinion of his sponsor. [4]

---

[4] *Republican Banner*, April 2, 1857.

". . . We believe the Convention can select Mr. Ewing with the full assurance that whatever is attainable in the way of political victories in the canvass will be realized by the vigorous onslaughts of his trenchant blade. We believe that his nomination would be hailed throughout the State as the sure harbinger of success, that it would infuse new life into the breasts of the drooping and despondent, and that our ranks would close up with alacrity in anticipation of an old fashioned victory."

It should be borne in mind that the Democratic Party in Tennessee had taken a lot of drubbings by the Whigs. In the judgment of the Democratic leaders the man most responsible for their defeats was the "Great Apostate," John Bell. Now, that the political tide in Tennessee had turned in the recent presidential election and in the last two gubernatorial contests, the Democrats relished the opportunity of taking a whack at the man who had wrecked repeatedly their hopes in the past. Consequently, in a sanguine belief that the Democrats could and would win in the forthcoming battle, the leading Democratic organ [5] tauntingly challenged Bell to accept the gage of battle and thereby give the Democrats a chance to even up the score with him. Accordingly, two weeks before the Opposition would meet to select a gubernatorial candidate, a gratuitous suggestion was made in the following manner:

"THE APPROACHING STATE CANVASS.

". . . He [Bell] has now had a long and eventful political history in Tennessee. No one is better known or better understood by the people. Our State has again returned to her first love, and for three successive elections has voted, with increased majorities, the Democratic ticket. The leading papers of the opposition are loudly calling upon their forces to rally, and as an incentive, point to the proud spectacle of the Democratic hosts in 1841, after the overwhelming defeat of the year previous, marshalled under the lead of their great and gallant standard bearer, JAMES K. POLK. The occasion to which they refer is well worthy of admiration, but nothing but an earnest love of *principle*, imbedded in the hearts of the people can possibly inspire such a spectacle, which precludes the possibility of know-nothingism ever imitating our example.

Let them *try*, however. We are anxious to see the issues fairly made up before the people in the next contest. Let the know-nothing press cease, in the future, to magnify the importance of small-fry politicians—such as DOUGLASS, HASKELL, MARTIN, and a host of others mentioned as their probable candidates for Governor—and bring out their big-man, the great Mogul of their party, the founder and fashioner of all the opposition that Democracy has ever had in Tennessee, Mr. BELL. No other man can so fully and completely represent all the antagonisms to Democracy. If there are in our midst any who are tinctured with Black Republicanism, Mr. BELL would satisfy them. If there are any who are still bitter in their hostility to Democracy from other causes than the oaths and . . . . [*] of know-nothingism, Mr. BELL will suit them.

His entire acceptability to the Know Nothing party is freely admitted. There can be no question then, of the fitness of such a nomination.—Mr.

---

[5] *Daily Union and American*, April 18, 1857.
[*] Blanks represent illegible words in newspaper.

BELL, in addition to his age, wisdom and experience, retains ample vigor for the canvass.—We are gratified to say that it has been years since we have seen him looking so well. If pressed upon him he *could not* refuse, and probably would be happy to accept. Mr. BELL'S party friends have everything, in their power that he has   of them. They can make no de- mand on him now that he would be at liberty to refuse.—   might not seem contrary to his interest to   Governor. There is no other man so much interested in getting to the United States Senate as he is, and upon the result of the next contest depends his success. Every consideration is favorable to his nomination. The nomination of JOHN BELL is not only due to that gentleman himself and his party friends, but it is specially due the Democratic party, that they should have an opportunity of meeting him *fairly* on the field. We ask for his nomination. We plead for it as an act of justice to all parties and all interests. We are actuated by no improper party motive in making this appeal. We earnestly solicit the Know Nothing press to respond to it in a spirit of candor and fairness."

But the crafty John Bell, occupying the seat of United States Sena- tor, preferred to continue in that position rather than "take arms against a sea of troubles" that would involve canvassing the State instead of but- tonholing the one hundred members of the Legislature in whose hands alone would rest the outcome of his effort to remain United States Sen- ator.

On April 15, 1857, the Democratic State Convention met in Nash- ville for the purpose of selecting a gubernatorial candidate. Due in part to the highly favorable impression made upon the public by his strong and aggressive canvass in the preceding year as Democratic Elector for the State at large in the presidential race, in which Tennessee went Democratic in the National election for the first time since 1832, the Convention merely confirmed the consensus of opinion as widely ex- pressed by the Democratic press and leading men of that political faith. Without any opposition in the Convention, Isham G. Harris of Mem- phis was unanimously selected as the standard-bearer in the forthcom- ing gubernatorial contest. The thirty-nine year old candidate had served one term in the State Senate, two terms in Congress, and had been a Democratic Elector for the Ninth Congressional District and also for the State at large. His stand on the slavery controversy had been forcibly set forth during his term in the State Legislature in 1847 by his intro- duction of a resolution opposing the Wilmot Proviso.[6] That resolution left no doubt but that Harris was a strong pro-slavery advocate, and that position met with hearty approval on the part of pro-slavery sup- porters. In addition to his being "right" on the slavery issue, he had two brothers occupying at the time positions of wide influence. One brother, William R. Harris, was a Judge of the Supreme Court and the other brother, George W. D. Harris, was a Methodist minister widely known as "the unmitered Bishop of West Tennessee."

---

[6] See *Messages of the Governors of Tennessee,* Volume IV, 249–250.

On May 1, 1857, just two weeks after the nomination of Isham G. Harris as the Democratic gubernatorial candidate, the Opposition convened in Nashville for the purpose of nominating a candidate to oppose Harris. Before that decision was made, a platform [7] was adopted:

"KNOW NOTHING PLATFORM.

Resolved, By this Convention, that the abuses and ultra tendencies of the party in power, calling itself the democracy, merit the earnest opposition of every friend of the Union and the Constitution.

Resolved, That the best interests of the country, present and prospective, require a material modification of the naturalization laws, in order to guard against the evils of foreign influence in the administration of our Government.

Resolved, That we utterly repudiate the doctrine which concedes to *aliens* the right of suffrage, and places them on an equal footing with the native and naturalized citizens of the United States, in framing the organic laws of new States, as equally unjust and unwise, and a violation of the Constitution.

Resolved, That all the States of the Union are entitled to participation in the public bounty; and that the policy of the party in power, by which the public lands are appropriated, in large quantities, for the benefit of particular States, is unjust, unequal, and injurious to the old States, and ought not to be tolerated.

Resolved, That Tennessee, in her insulated position, heretofore omitted among the favorites in the distribution of the public lands, with her load of debt, incurred for the development of her resources, has a deep stake in that policy which shall do her justice, and supply the means of saving her people from taxation.

Resolved, That Congress has power, under the war clause of the Constitution, to aid in the construction of the Pacific Railroad, and that the extension of such aid is highly expedient.

Resolved, That the Federal Union being, the only safe guard of American liberty, every true patriot should devote his best energies to its preservation.

Resolved, That the systematic agitation of the slavery question has brought our Union into peril, and it is the duty of every American patriot not to interfere with the institutions of other States over which he has no legitimate control.

Resolved, That we are opposed to the interference of the General Government in the settlement of the question of slavery in the Territories, and we believe that the citizens of the United States, *bona fide* residents in the Territories, have the right to determine the question of slavery, when they come to the adoption of a State Constitution."

In a somewhat satirical vein, the following analysis [8] of the "Know Nothing Platform" was made:

"THE END.

The platform of the know-nothing order adopted at the meeting of the

---

[7] *Daily Union and American,* May 3, 1857.
[8] *Ibid.*

State Council last Friday, almost entirely ignores the distinctive features which originally characterized the organization. The address is simply an attack upon the democratic party, for, as it is charged, holding 'adverse opinions' on several prominent topics. The resolutions, which will be looked to as containing the principles of the order, attempt to galvanize into use for this canvass the dead and rotten carcass of distribution, but make no defence of the original creed of know-nothingism. A vague opinion in favor of 'a material modification of the naturalization laws' is expressed; and there is something against what is called 'alien suffrage.' And that is all there is of know-nothingism! We are not told what would be regarded as a 'material' modification of the naturalization laws, and 'aliens suffrage' is a weak invention to delude the silly. There is not one word nor one allusion to the Pope and the Catholic either in the address or the resolutions. All that part of the machinery of the society is abandoned; and the fanatics who, two years ago and last year, most distinguished themselves by preaching an anti-Catholic crusade, are discarded with contempt, and left to rot by the way-side. The result shows that our institutions are abundantly able to vindicate themselves, when the sober judgment of the people has time to act. It will be at least fifty years before demagogues, either in or out of the pulpit, will again dare to make a similar experiment.

. . . Those curious in the study of hybrids will see that the animal dressed up for defeat on this occasion is *coon*, and nothing else, in all its leading characteristics. It has hardly a trace of 'intense Americanism,' and sets up no farther claim as the special defender of the Protestant faith. The few men once democrats who remain in the order have been transformed, apparently without their own knowledge, into *bona-fide* coons. We don't think they are worth the cost of the tails which now decorate their persons; but that may be a matter of taste."

With the platform out of the way, the Convention proceeded to the selection of a candidate. The contemporary press discloses that some three or four men were in a receptive mood, among them being General Wm. T. Haskell of Jackson and General James Minor Quarles of Clarksville. The latter two gentlemen were called to the rostrum, but it seems that General Haskell "hogged" the temporary limelight and pushed General Quarles into the shadow.[9] General Haskell consumed quite a bit of time portraying his sacrifices and services for the party, for which he said he had been "eulogized by the press and had received ovations and honors by the people; . . . but . . . when *substantial* honors were to be distributed, others had been their recipients and not himself." Although he had, so he alleged, been "tricked out of the nomination by intrigue, he would support the nominee but would not forget the intriguers." At the conclusion of General Haskell's remarks, General Quarles, Joseph G. Pickett, and Jacob Holland "were permitted to occupy the stand," but the newspaper sketch dismissed them with the laconic statement that "We regret we have not time to give a synopsis of their remarks." The nominee, however, had been selected prior to the call for Generals Haskell and Quarles to come to the rostrum,

---

[9] *Ibid.*, May 2, 1857.

apparently for the purpose of healing their wounds and soothing their grievances.

The nomination of a candidate for gubernatorial honors went to a young man not quite thirty-one years old, Robert Hopkins Hatton of Lebanon. He was a graduate of Harvard University and of the Law Department of Cumberland University. In 1852, he was a Whig Elector for the Fifth Congressional District and in 1855 was elected to the Legislature from Wilson County as a Know Nothing. In 1859, he was elected to Congress. In early May, 1862, he was made Colonel of the Seventh Tennessee Volunteer Infantry, and was some three weeks later advanced to the rank of Brigadier General in the Confederate Army on May 23. Ironically enough, about sunset eight days later he was killed instantly by a Minié ball at the battle of Seven Pines.

Now, that the nominees of the two respective parties had been chosen, the remaining item on the political agenda was the arrangement of speaking dates throughout the State. As was the custom at the time, the campaign was a face-to-face discussion from the same rostrum. There was no "long-distance argufying" between opposing gubernatorial candidates, each having to face his man and take his medicine accordingly. The campaign was opened at Camden on May 25, and an immense throng was present to hear the opening gun fired. Lack of space will prevent the inclusion of any running account of the campaign. Suffice it to say that "the shouting and the tumult" were continued throughout the contest by the partisan supporters of each candidate. Newspaper reports of the speaking engagements were so partisan and highly prejudicial that perhaps little confidence ought to be placed in any of them. Each side was equally guilty of attempting to put into practice the saying of Milton in *Paradise Lost*

> ". . . his tongue
> Dropped manna, and could make the worse appear
> The better reason . . ."

Perhaps one sample of newspaper banter [10] of that era is apropos:

"THE CANDIDATES.

The letter-writers for the *Patriot* and *Banner* inform us—and through such channels we are by no means surprised to hear it—that the recent discussions between Messrs. Harris and Hatton at Camden and Huntingdon, resulted in each instance in an 'overwhelming defeat' of the former, and a 'glorious triumph' for the latter. No doubt our opponents believe there are many illiterate people in this country, swayed by the popular clamor, who will give credence to such reports. They are mistaken, however. The great masses of the country have a better fund of common sense than those who are continually presuming upon their ignorance. They have heard such ridiculous clap-trap from the opposition ever since the habit of canvassing

---

[10] *Ibid.*, May 31, 1857.

was introduced into Tennessee. According to these newspaper reporters the Democracy are always routed up to the day of the election. 'Great victories,' 'splendid triumphs,' and 'indescribable enthusiasm,' have attended their candidates in every political contest that has transpired in our State. There is no game at which Know Nothingism plays more freely—we cannot say successfully—than that of 'brag.'

To believe them, their smallest pretender is always superior in debate to our ablest champion.—Every newspaper reader in the State will remember how completely Andrew Johnson was 'crushed out' in his first canvass for Governor with the Eagle Orator. From Carter to Shelby was but one continual series of democratic reverses, and yet when the election came off Johnson was elected. Such as have files of Tennessee Know Nothing papers for 1855, will be entertained by turning them over and re-reading the eloquent descriptions that were given then of the 'brilliant victories' achieved upon every field by Gentry over Johnson. We know of no more elegant pieces of composition than some of these productions afford.

From Memphis the correspondent of the *True Whig* (now the *Patriot*,) wrote of the discussion there:

'So far as we can learn, the universal sentiment is that Gentry's victory here was signal and complete, and judging from the gladiation of to-day, if he makes enough such speeches, the 1st Tuesday in August next will place him in the Gubernatorial chair by an overwhelming majority.'

Even from the good old Democratic county of Hickman, it was written to the same paper:

He (Gentry) made such a statesman-like argument that the lion-hearted Democracy of old Hickman acknowledge that the hand-writing is plain on the wall—'that Gentry is the next Governor of Tennessee.' Johnson did not come up to the expectations of his friends by a good deal, and Gentry went so far over the expectations of his enemies, that you may rest assured that old Hickman will give a larger vote against the Democracy than she ever has before, and will show that she begins to think that 'Americans should govern America.'

At Trenton Col. Gentry was still more overpowering. The ladies came out and garlanded him with roses. The same correspondent, writing from that place, said:

'During the delivery of his speech beautiful bouquets were literally showered upon our noble and gallant chief by the ladies from the windows of the Court House, who seemed to be much interested in his address. But, not to weary you, I must say this has been a glorious day's work for the Whig party in Gibson. I mean what I say.'

And yet, after all the newspaper triumphs and rich trophies won from the leaders in the canvass, *the people* gave a different verdict on the day of the election. We can scarcely believe that 'our Bob' is the superior of either Henry or Gentry.

In conclusion we advise our Know Nothing friends who are in the habit of betting on elections, to give but very little credit to these reported triumphs that are to appear regularly from this out in the *Patriot* and *Banner.* How ever little you may value our opinion, we assure you they will not do to bet on, but are of apiece with similar statements that have appeared for the last three canvasses in these papers, begetting confidence and losing money."

The joint campaign pursued the usual course characteristic of such contests. Excited partisans of each candidate "whooped it up" on every appearance of the candidates and each partisan group boasted that his man had licked his opponent to a frazzle. There was, however, a departure from the routine procedure when the candidates spoke in Fayetteville, on June 13. Toward the conclusion of Hatton's speech, he lugged in what had been one of the basic doctrines of the Know Nothing Party —that "Americans should rule America." In the course of his speech, the word "*infamous*" was used to which Harris requested an explanation as to whether the word was being applied to him personally. Hatton's reply consisted of a repetition of his former statement, but he did not quite complete his "explanation" due to his being knocked off the platform by Harris. There was a big hullabaloo over the personal difficulty between the men by the newspapers supporting the respective candidates. So much bias and prejudice were injected into the newspaper accounts that a sort of arbitration committee was formed for the purpose of straightening out the fracas. Since the personnel of the committee contained friends of each candidate, perhaps their jointly-signed statement received more credence than any or all of the highly inflammatory newspaper blurbs that emanated from a highly partisan press. The statement [11] was as follows:

"A STATEMENT TO THE PUBLIC.

The undersigned, acting in the capacity of mutual friends of Gen. Isham G. Harris and Col. Rob't. Hatton, after having fully canvassed between themselves the circumstances originating and attending the unpleasant personal difficulty that occurred during their discussion at Fayetteville on the 13th inst., are satisfied that it resulted from a mutual misunderstanding between the parties—that each acted upon a misconception of the language and intention of the other, and that therefore both have occasion to regret the unpleasant altercation that took place.

The friends of Col. Hatton understand him to have declared, 'That the doctrine that the alien, the unnaturalized man from the old world, who has no claims upon our country, no rights here, shall come to our country and rule and govern it, is an infamous doctrine, an iniquity that smells to heaven;' and that when Gen. Harris enquired whether he intended to apply such language to him, after a short colloquy, he repeated nearly the same declaration, that the *doctrine* was infamous, and 'that those who advocated it, advocated a doctrine that is infamous and smells to heaven.'

The friends of Gen. Harris understood Col. Hatton as assuming that Gen. Harris favored the *policy* of allowing an unnaturalized foreigner to vote in Tennessee for members of Congress, &c., and that this policy he denounced as 'infamous, that it was rank and smelt to heaven,' &c. Gen. Harris then asked Col. Hatton if he intended to apply the term 'infamous' to him. His answer was, 'Do you expect to intimidate me by coming forward and asking this question? Gen. Harris answered, 'By no means. I do not wish to intimidate any gentleman, but I have a right to know whether you apply the term infamous to me or not.' To which Col. Hatton re-

[11] *Ibid.*, June 19, 1857.

sponded, 'Then it is an explanation that you want?' To which Gen. Harris replied, 'That is all that I want. I only desire to know whether you intended to apply that term to me.' To which Col. Hatton replied, 'Fellow citizens, I repeat that the policy is infamous, rank and smells to heaven, and those who advocate it are -------' At this point Gen. Harris struck him.

> F. K. ZOLLICOFFER,
> F. C. DUNNINGTON,
> JOHN D. KELLY,
> G. P. SMITH,
> A. P. [S.] COLYER,
> GEO. W. JONES."

The difficulty was ironed out, as Hatton himself stated in a letter to his wife a week after its occurrence:[12]

"Athens, June 21, 1857.

MY DEAR WIFE:—

I know, Sophie, you have felt a good deal of uneasiness about me, since we parted, both on account of my health, and on account of the difficulty General Harris and I had at Fayetteville. It has all been, however, satisfactorily adjusted, and the General is more friendly to me than he has ever been since we started. The thousand-and-one stories—lies—that have been circulated about it have troubled you. Pay no attention to them. . . . I continue to make the same speech that gave rise to the fight, and he takes no exception to it. . . ."

For two months the candidates had slugged it out with each other, toe to toe. The issues, in part, were the old controversies revolving around Catholicism, aliens, and slavery. Harris would not permit his opponent to dodge these salient points which Andrew Johnson had utilized so effectively in his gubernatorial campaigns. Hatton could not avoid meeting as best he could the sledge-hammer blows being delivered by Harris, but he was not a spell-binder on the order of either Gustavus A. Henry or Meredith P. Gentry. State issues were touched upon, but they played a minor role in the campaign. As a member of the 1855 Legislature, Hatton had introduced a bill to establish a Normal School for the training of teachers, but his bill went down to defeat in the Democratic Senate by the eye-lash margin of one vote. Harris argued that the money for such a school could be used to better advantage if expended for the education of the children in the public schools. Harris also attacked vigorously Hatton's support of the so-called Omnibus Bill in which State financial aid was promised to a number of railroads. But the crux of the campaign strategy was to keep Hatton linked with the Know Nothing Party of which he was an acknowledged member, and the Know Nothings were fast falling into disfavor and disrepute. Due to the arduous itinerary and the extreme heat, the two contestants mutually agreed on July 22 to call it quits. On that date the last joint speaking was held in Nashville, the other engagements being cancelled. There was

---

[12] Drake, James Vaulx: *Life of General Robert Hatton*, 121-122.

only one thing remaining, the casting of ballots on August 6. Out of a total vote of 130,985, the majority for Harris was 11,371. Hatton's defeat, according to his biographer,[13] was largely attributed to his having been identified with the Know Nothings whose "organization was secret, clannish, and 'loved darkness rather than light.' " Hatton's defeat marked the end of the Know Nothing Party in Tennessee, and its demise nationally calls to mind the satirical lines of a new England poet:[14]

> "Some canderdates air dead and gone, an' some hez ben defeated,
> Which 'mounts to pooty much the same; fer it's ben proved repeated
> A betch o' bread thet hain't riz once ain't goin' to rise agin,
> An' it's jest money throwed away to put the emptins in:
> But thet's wut folks wun't never larn; they dunno how to go,
> Arter you want their room, no more'n a bullet-headed beau;
> Ther' 's ollers chaps a-hangin' roun' thet can't see peatime's past,
> Mis'ble as roosters in a rain, heads down an' tails half-mast:
> It ain't disgraceful bein' beat, when a holl nation does it,
> But Chance is like an amberill,—it don't take twice to lose it."

The Thirty-Second General Assembly convened in Nashville on October 5, 1857, with a Democratic majority in each legislative branch. Governor-elect Harris, in that respect, was in better shape than had been Andrew Johnson who had had a divided Legislature during both of his administrations. With only one absentee, Senator Ambrose R. Reid, the other twenty-four Senators elected on the first ballot Senator J. C. Burch of Hamilton County as Speaker by a vote of 17 to 7.[15] With nine Representatives absent on opening day, the rest proceeded to elect a Speaker. By a vote of 37 to 29, Representative Daniel S. Donelson of Sumner County was victorious on the first ballot.[16] On the following day, Governor Andrew Johnson transmitted his final Message to the Legislature.[17] The out-going Governor listed the State indebtedness as some four million dollars, with a further liability of approximately eight million dollars in the nature of State bonds loaned to railroads and turnpike companies. He recommended a constitutional amendment that would inhibit any future Legislature from creating any public debt beyond a specified amount without first submitting the proposition to a vote of the people. In addition, he regarded the Bank of Tennessee as having failed to accomplish its basic purposes and accordingly recommended its abolishment. Inasmuch as these items will be dealt with as the legislative proceedings are reviewed, discussion of them will come later.

Since the term of United States Senator James C. Jones had expired

---

[13] *Ibid.*, 149-150.
[14] Lowell, James Russell: *The Biglow Papers.*
[15] *Senate Journal*, 1857, 4.
[16] *House Journal*, 1857, 5.
[17] This Message was duly incorporated in Volume IV of the *Messages of the Governors of Tennessee*, 671-697.

on March 3, 1857, the election of a successor was an item of great concern on the legislative agenda. Accordingly, Senator W. E. Travis on the second day of the session introduced the following resolution [18] which was passed:

"Resolved, That the Senate will meet the House in convention, in the Hall of the House of Representatives, on Thursday, the 8th instant, at 11 o'clock A.M., for the purpose of electing a Senator in the Congress of the United States in the place of the Hon. James C. Jones, whose term of office since has expired."

On the same day, an identical resolution was introduced in the House by Representative Hiram S. Bradford of Haywood County and was passed by a vote of 36 to 32. At the designated time, the Convention assembled and Representative W. C. Dunlap of Shelby County placed in nomination the name of Andrew Johnson for United States Senator. No other name was placed in nomination, but Ex-Governor Neill S. Brown received a substantial vote by the House members. Only one ballot was had, and the total vote was as follows: [19]

For Andrew Johnson . . . . Senators   17
                                  Representatives   40
                                                      Total 57.

For Neill S. Brown . . . . Senators   7
                                   Representatives   31
                                                      Total 38.

For the next two weeks the Legislature dealt with a few miscellaneous matters. Appointments of Standing Committees were announced, seventeen in the Senate [20] and twenty in the House.[21] Codification of the laws was considered desirable and a codification committee was announced.[22] Another routine item was on the agenda, namely, the determination and announcement of the official vote for Governor. That matter was attended to on October 20 at a joint meeting of the House and Senate, the matter having been held in abeyance several days until the belated vote of Jefferson County was received. The vote by counties was read and the figures tabulated, whereupon the Speaker of the Senate declared that Isham G. Harris had received a majority of the votes cast and was "duly and constitutionally elected Governor of Tennessee for the next two years ensuing." [23]

Inasmuch as the Legislature was largely just marking time until the

---

[18] *Senate Journal*, 1857, 7.
[19] *Senate Journal*, 1857, 38.
    House Journal, 1857, 36.
[20] *Senate Journal*, 1857, 35.
[21] *House Journal*, 1857, 37–38.
[22] *Senate Journal*, 1857, 57.
    House Journal, 1857, 55.
[23] *Senate Journal*, 1857, 58–60.
    House Journal, 1857, 61–63.

inauguration of Governor-elect Isham G. Harris and the transmission of his Message, there were both time and leisure to look around and ascertain whether or not there was any item that needed legislative attention. The Democrats, who enjoyed a majority in each legislative branch, decided to look into the matter of seeing to it that the successor of United States Senator John Bell be chosen. There was nothing so sure as "striking while the iron was hot." Already, Andrew Johnson had been elected to succeed James C. Jones in the United States Senate. Why not insure that he have a fellow-Democrat to keep him company in that august body? To be sure, the term of Bell did not expire until March 3, 1859, but the Legislature of that year would not convene until October. In the meanwhile, Tennessee would have but one Senator in case an extra session of Congress were called. This was the type of logic employed by the Democrats in analyzing the political situation. But underneath there seethed a deep and determined desire to get even with the man who had been a thorn in the side of Tennessee Democracy for more than twenty years.

It was decided that the time was ripe for dethroning the "Great Apostate," and the first legislative step in that direction was taken on October 10 when Senator W. C. Whitthorne of Maury County introduced the following resolution:[24]

"Providing for a joint convention of the two Houses on Tuesday, 20th., for the purpose of electing a Senator in the Congress of the United States, to serve from the 4th day of March, 1859, to the 4th day of March, 1865."

Temporarily, a monkey wrench was thrown into the works on October 19 when a motion to proceed to holding the joint convention failed by a deadlock vote of 12 to 12. On the following day, however, the resolution was called up and passed by a vote of 14 to 10.[25] On October 23, after a bit of jockeying around in an effort to postpone the date for holding the joint convention, the House by a vote of 39 to 29 adopted the resolution looking toward the election of a Democratic United States Senator to displace the Whig bellwether, John Bell.[26]

On October 27, the Legislature met in joint session for the above purpose. The official record discloses that one Senator and three Representatives were absent.[27] An effort was made by the firebrand Whig Representative from Rutherford County, Dr. J. W. Richardson, to postpone the election until November 3 in order to give Senator Bell and the prospective Democratic nominee, A. O. P. Nicholson, opportunity to reply to a questionnaire propounded by the minority. An adjournment for lunch was the best the rampant Whig devotee could procure. At the afternoon session, Nicholson's reply was read to the body, but

[24] *Senate Journal*, 1857, 43.
[25] *Ibid.*, 60.
[26] *House Journal*, 1857,74.
[27] *Ibid.*, 91.

apparently Bell made no reply, for none was presented to the convention.[28] At this juncture, Senator Whitthorne placed in nomination Honorable A. O. P. Nicholson of Maury County for United States Senator. Representative R. C. Saunders of Smith County did not like the look of things and proceeded to give vent to his feelings which were representative of Bell's supporters [29]

"We on this side of the House, were called upon the other day to dance to the tune of a vacancy occasioned by the expiration of a term of office. The tune, though no favorite of ours, owing to the circumstances was one which necessity required, one which the Constitution sanctioned, and to it we gave the best we had on hand. But we are called upon now, sir, to dance—no, to shuffle to a tune of an entirely different nature, and I for one most frankly confess I can't take the step."

Upon the conclusion of this exhibition of political spleen, he reached for his hat and stalked out of the Convention declaring that the whole thing was a farce and wholly unconstitutional.[30] Senator A. F. Goff of Davidson County had similar compunctions of conscience and was excused from voting. Likewise Representative Michael Vaughan of Davidson County was excused from voting on the ground that he believed "the election to be a party fraud." [31]

Although the official legislative *Journals* make no mention of any nominations other than that of Nicholson, yet John Bell received a substantial minority vote. The recorded vote was as follows: [32]

	Nicholson	Bell	Campbell
Senate	17	6	
House of Representatives	41	29	1
Total	58	35	1

On November 3, in accordance with the arrangements made by the Committee of Inauguration, Isham G. Harris was inaugurated as Governor. The order of the ceremonies was set forth in the official record as follows: [33]

"ORDER OF PROCEEDINGS
Music by Band—'Hail Columbia'
Prayer
Music
Gov. Johnson's Valedictory
Music—'Hail to the Chief'
Gov. Harris' Inaugural

---

[28] *Senate Journal*, 1857, 80.
[29] *Republican Banner and Nashville Whig*, October 29, 1857.
[30] *House Journal*, 1857, 92.
[31] *Ibid.*
[32] *Senate Journal*, 1857, 80–81.
House Journal, 1857, 92.
[33] *Senate Journal*, 1857, 99.

Oath of Office
Music
Concluding Prayer
Music—'Star Spangled Banner' "

According to a contemporary newspaper,[34] the exercises at the State Capitol were attended by members of the General Assembly and a large concourse of citizens. After music and a prayer by Reverend Dr. Howell of the Baptist Church, the valedictory and inaugural addresses were delivered and the oath of office administered by Judge S. D. Frierson. Retiring Governor Johnson's Valedictory Address and Governor Harris' Inaugural Address were as follows:

"GENTLEMEN OF THE SENATE, OF THE HOUSE OF REPRESENTATIVES, AND FELLOW CITIZENS:

It has now been four years since my inauguration as Governor of the State, embracing two gubernatorial terms. I entered upon the duties of the office with a firm and fixed resolution to perform every obligation imposed on me by law and the Constitution. And notwithstanding there has been much difficulty, and many perplexing questions have arisen during my administration of the State government, yet, I have the proud and conscious satisfaction to believe that they have been disposed of in such manner as will conduce to the solid advancement of the best interest of the State. I will, therefore, without further remark in regard to my own administration, submit all my official acts to the judgment of a free and unbiased people.

In retiring from the office I now hold, permit me to tender to you, and through you, to my fellow-citizens throughout the State, my profound thanks and grateful acknowledgments for their continued confidence and support of me as a public man.

On leaving my present position, and in assuming the new one, which has been assigned me by the sovereign people of the State, through their honored representatives, I can give no other or higher guarantee for my future course, touching the common weal, than my past public life, and will enter upon the duties of the office with a firm and unalterable determination to do my duty in compliance with those indissoluble ties, which bind me to an honest and confiding constituency and in accordance with the requirements of the Constitution of my country, to the people of the whole Union.

It is with pleasure and full confidence that I now pass to my

---

[34] *Daily Union and American*, November 4, 1857.

respected and worthy successor, the ermine of State, pure and un-sullied as it was when transmitted to me by my distinguished prede-cessor, and in doing so, I tender with it, my sincere prayer to the Giver of all good, for the faithful and successful administrations of the State government, during his gubernatorial term, and that His divine presence and blessing may be with and rest upon this favored people in all time to come.

I am no longer Governor of the State of Tennessee, and as be-fore stated, I pass the ermine to my honored and worthy successor."

Then Gov. Harris stood up and read his Inaugural Address to the General Assembly in the following words:

"GENTLEMEN OF THE SENATE AND HOUSE OF REPRESENTATIVES:

Having been called by the popular vote of the people of Ten-nessee to the Chief Executive Office of the State, I appear before you to take the oath of office prescribed by the Constitution, and to de-fine, to some extent, the principles and policy by which I expect to be governed during my official term.

Impressed with a profound sense of gratitude for the confidence implied in my selection for this important trust, I enter upon the discharge of its duties with an unaffected distrust of my ability to give full and entire satisfaction.

The long line of able and distinguished men who have preceded me in this position admonishes me that it will be difficult, if not im-possible, to equal them in the public administration.

Yet, I am encouraged by the reflection that they have left a lumi-nous record to guide and direct the steps of their more humble suc-cessor.

The present ceremony (a constantly recurring one in our form of government) presents a striking and favorable contrast with the installations into office in other and dissimilar governments, where an inaugural ceremony is but too often the concluding scene in the bloody drama of revolution, where position is attained through the blood of innocent victims, and the seat of power reared upon the crushed hopes and violated rights of an oppressed and suffering peo-ple.

But it is a characteristic and glorious feature of our governments that power is quietly transferred from one hand to another, accord-ing to constitutional forms, and in accordance with the voluntary will of the people as expressed by the silent and peaceable operation of the ballot box.

The excitement of a popular election subsiding so soon as the public will is declared, and the American citizen, whatever may have been his partialities or his prejudices, bows with genuine loyalty to the will of the majority of his countrymen, by which means our governments are made to promote and subserve the public interest, and their efficacy to depend in a great degree upon the public confidence.

The constitution requires me to take the oath which each of you have taken 'to support the Constitution of the State and the United States'—which imposes the duty of obedience to each, and of allegiance to two distinct governments.

This imposes the necessity of enquiring to some extent, at least, as to the relative position, rights, powers and duties of each.

Our whole system of government is based upon the simple and sublime truth that man has capacity to govern himself, and that supreme sovereignty rests with the people.

For their own convenience and security they formed State Governments, each of which was independent of the others, possessing all the attributes of a free sovereign and independent nation.

But subsequently, 'in order to form a more perfect union, establish justice, insure domestic tranquility, provide for the common defence, promote the general welfare, and secure the blessings of liberty to themselves and their posterity,' they confederated all of those States into one General Government, delegating to it, by the Federal Constitution certain powers therein specifically innumerated. 'And the powers not delegated to the United States by the constitution, nor prohibited by it to the States, are reserved to the States respectively or to the people.'

From which it is manifest that each of those Governments possesses powers which are denied to the other, and beyond the limits of which neither can go without encroachment upon the rights and legitimate functions of the other.

Yet so long as each confines its action within the scope of well defined authority it results in the most perfect harmony between the two, affording to the citizen all the blessings good government can confer.

But when either transcends the limits of its power and usurps the powers of the other, harmony is at once destroyed, and dangerous and alarming collisions arise, which inevitably weaken and may eventually destroy the bonds of Union.

It is, therefore, the highest duty of every public functionary, State or Federal, to confine his action within the boundary of well defined constitutional authority, abstaining from the exercise of all doubtful powers.

In addition, however, to those powers delegated in express terms, there is a class of implied powers properly claimed and exercised by the Federal Government, which involves by far the most serious and difficult questions of constitutional construction, the only safe solution of which is to be found in subjecting the implication to the following test:

Is it fairly and properly an incident to an expressly delegated power? and its exercise necessary to the execution of the same, and without the exercise of which the expressed power would be nugatory?

If it is, Congress may properly exercise it. But if it is not, it is one of those powers 'reserved to the States or to the people,' which Congress cannot exercise without usurping the legitimate powers of the State Government.

To carry this doctrine of implied powers further than this, upon any idea of expediency or 'general welfare,' is to make the powers of Congress depend upon the ever varying opinions of its members, as to what is expedient, or what will promote the general welfare— in effect making the Federal Government one of unlimited powers.

Under the doctrine of liberal or latitudinous construction of the Constitution, arising from the uncertainty of implied powers, the most extraordinary and alarming assumptions of Federal authority have originated. And it is to be regretted by all who earnestly desire the peace and perpetuity of our Government, that there is a class of politicians in some of the States, who claim for Congress the power to mould the domestic institutions of the Territories, and seek to degrade from the rank of equality one half of the States of the Confederacy, by prohibiting the introduction of a species of property common to those States.

The Federal Constitution recognises domestic slavery as an existing institution, and leaves the question to the exclusive jurisdiction and control of the several States and Territories, each having the unlimited power, to determine for itself by its Constitution, whether slavery shall or shall not exist within its corporate limits; and where it exists to be regulated and controlled by them, free from interference by the Federal or any other Government. Indeed it is placed by the Constitution beyond the pale of Federal legislation, except in the single instance of providing for returning the Fugitive to his owner.

And while I hold it to be our imperative duty to preserve and maintain the General Government in all of its Constitutional vigor, 'as the sheet anchor of our peace at home and security abroad,' it is equally our duty to watch with jealous vigilance, and guard with a strong hand against the encroachment of the Federal, upon the reserved rights of the State Government.

The formation of our domestic institutions and the administration of our domestic affairs, are amongst the highest and most important powers 'reserved to the States and to the people' the exclusive exercise of which by the States is the surest bulwark against anti-republican tendencies, and certainly affords to the citizens a greater amount of security for life, liberty, and property, and in the pursuit of happiness, than can be secured under any other Government that has ever existed.

And any attempt on the part of the Federal Government or a sister State to interfere with the domestic institutions or policy of a State Government, or the formation of the domestic institutions of a new State, would be a palpable usurpation of power and an officious intermeddling, fraught with the most serious dangers and resulting probably in the most disastrous consequences.

If we would preserve our institutions unimpaired and maintain our rights undiminished, it becomes the duty of all the States, and especially of those whose Constitution and laws recognise the existence of domestic slavery, to adhere with firmness and pertinacity to a strict construction of the Constitution, upon which rests the principle of 'non-interference by Congress with domestic slavery either in the States or Territories.'

Amidst the mutation and decay of parties, it is gratifying to know that there is, and has been from the beginning of the Government, a political organization co-extensive with the Union, which has ever stubbornly maintained and still maintains the doctrine of strict construction, as the cardinal tenet of its faith, and has resisted to the extent of its ability every attempt at Federal usurpation.

The present able and distinguished Chief Magistrate of the Confederacy, taken from and elected by that organization, stands pledged to the maintenance of all the reserved rights of the States, under a strict construction of the Constitution, and to the principle of 'non-intervention by Congress with slavery either in the States or Territories.'

To that organization, in my judgment, we are indebted for the prosperity of the past and the security of the present, and upon the great principles which it maintains, rest the brightest if not the only hopes of our Government for the future.

I shall, therefore, feel it to be my duty to co-operate cordially with the legislative and judicial departments of the State Government, by the use of all the constitutional and lawful means with which the Executive is invested, in their efforts to confine the action of the State Government within its well defined limits on the one hand, and upon the other, in resisting any encroachments upon her reserved rights of sovereignty.

One of the most serious objections to our Federal system, urged by some of the wisest and most patriotic of its founders, was the danger of its gradually attracting to itself the powers and functions of the State Governments, by assuming their burdens and lavishing its bounties upon them. Such means of overthrowing the independence and absorbing the sovereignty of the States is by far more dangerous than a bold and direct attempt at usurpation. A brave and generous people may be charmed by the allurements of a splendid munificence into concessions, which external foes or physical force could never wring from them.

The policy of distributing among the States the proceeds of the sales of the public lands is not in my opinion warranted by the Constitution.

To concede this power and adopt the policy would be to make the Federal Government the tax gatherer for the States to that extent, and accustom them to look to that source from which to supply the State Treasury and to defray the expenses of the State Government.

'It is manifest that this constituted no one of the objects in the creation of the Federal Government, and to permit its exercise would be to reduce the States to the degraded condition of subordinate dependencies upon that Government, tending to destroy their separate and independent sovereignty and to make the government of the Union, in effect, a consolidation.'

But if the power were conceded the policy is unwise, unequal and unjust, for every dollar that is abstracted from the Federal Treasury for this purpose must be replaced by means of a tariff of duties upon the necessities of life, and revenue thus raised must necessarily be collected in unequal portions from the people of the respective States. The agricultural and planting States must contribute much the larger proportion; while to distribute according to population, the manufacturing States being more populous, would receive the larger share.

The inevitable effect of the policy would be gradually, but certainly to transfer the wealth of the former to the coffers of the latter.

It would therefore be the most unwise policy in the agricultural States such as ours, to attempt to raise any portion of their revenues through the instrumentality of the Federal Government, or to encourage the raising of more revenue by the tariff system than the amount absolutely necessary to support the Federal Government economically administered.

Passing now, gentlemen, from these subjects, involving to some extent, the rights, powers and duties of both the State and Federal Government, I propose a brief exposition of my views touching domestic policy.

One of the highest duties devolving upon the State Government is the preservation of public credit.

Our citizens have embarked in an extensive, and in its inception, a wise system of Internal Improvement, to develop the immense resources of the State, and in aid of those works the public credit stands pledged to a large amount. Such steps should be taken as will insure the prompt and full redemption of that pledge.

And while the most liberal policy consistent with the preservation of the credit of State, should be pursued towards those companies, justice to them as well as to the State, forbids that the system of pledging its credits in aid of those enterprises should be further extended.

The present deranged condition of the currency of the State deserves serious consideration.

By the universal custom of civilized nations, gold and silver are recognized as the standard of exchange, and commercial balances are readily effected through their instrumentality.

Their intrinsic value is such that they never materially fluctuate, so as to destroy their utility as a universal circulating medium, and the uniformity in the amount of currency prevents those sudden and violent fluctuations in the value of property and labor, to which the country is subject under the expansions and contractions of a general banking system. Yet the present condition of the country demands that such reform as may be adopted, should be slow and gradual in its operations, giving to the commercial and all other interests in the country ample time to adapt themselves to the proposed change.

And while the system of banking is continued, it should be so regulated and restricted (where the Legislature possesses the power to do so) as to make their issues convertible into gold and silver on demand, at the place where it is put into circulation.

Bank issues expel from general circulation the coin of the country, locking it up in Bank vaults or employing it elsewhere in profitable exchange, and while these institutions are permitted to furnish the circulating medium of the country based upon a system of credit, they should be required to furnish one equally as good as that which they displace.

The policy of a general system of popular education, based as it is, upon the principle that every citizen of a Republic should possess sufficient intelligence to discharge, understandingly, the high duties devolving upon him, has justly received a large share of public consideration.

A more efficient system of common school education is imperatively demanded if we regard the wants of the present, and the highest interest of future generations. Such a system, to be efficient, should regard the moral as well as the intellectual training of the child. And he would be a public benefactor indeed, who would devise a plan of common school education, which would be adapted to our moral, intellectual and physical developments as a people.

The importance of the subject demands, and should receive early and earnest attention.

Having thus briefly indicated some of the principles that will control my action in discharging the high duties to which I have been called by the partiality of my countrymen, and earnestly invoking upon my own humble exertions, and upon our beloved State and country the Divine blessing, I enter upon the duties assigned me."

On the day of his inauguration, Governor Harris transmitted to the Legislature a minor Message* relating to the confirmation of his nominees for Directors of the Bank of Tennessee.

"EXECUTIVE DEPARTMENT,

November 3, 1857.

GENTLEMEN OF THE SENATE AND OF THE HOUSE OF REPRESENTATIVES:

In obedience to law, I nominate for your approval and confirmation, the following named gentlemen, for Directors of the Bank of Tennessee, viz:

> Cave Johnson, of Montgomery county.
> H. Douglass, of Davidson county.
> James Nichol, of Davidson county.
> M. Vannoy, of Davidson county.
> M. Burns, of Davidson county.
> F. R. Rains, of Davidson county.
> Frank McGavock, of Davidson county.
> John S. Hutchinson, of Robertson county.
> J. R. A. Tompkins, of Sumner county.
> L. H. Cardwell, of Smith county.
> D. D. Claiborne, of Macon county.
> F. G. Wood, of Cannon county.
> J. K. Howard, of Wilson county.
> J. W. Childress, of Rutherford county.
> John McGavock, of Williamson county.

ISHAM G. HARRIS."

On November 10, a week after the inauguration, Governor Harris transmitted to the Legislature a Message* of less importance than the preceding one:

"EXECUTIVE DEPARTMENT,

November 10, 1857.

GENTLEMEN OF THE SENATE:

I hereby nominate for your approval and confirmation for In-

---

*Senate Journal, 1857, 102.
  House Journal, 1857, 117–118.
* Senate Journal, 1857, 126.

spectors of the Penitentiary the following named gentlemen, viz:
   Dr. John D. Winston, Genl. William G. Harding, and John Overton.

ISHAM G. HARRIS."

Without any apparent wrangling and certainly by unanimous vote, all nominees for Bank Directors and Penitentiary Inspectors were formally approved and confirmed.

In the meanwhile, Governor Harris delayed transmitting his major Message until December 17. This hiatus of approximately six weeks since the inauguration date had left the Legislature relatively little to do, since the recommendations of the Governor were generally considered to be of paramount importance. Undoubtedly a lot of huddling was done, political animosities were reviewed and revived, and finally it was decided that the *bête noir* (black beast) to Tennessee Democracy needed another larruping. John Bell was still anathema in the eyes of most Democratic leaders in Tennessee, despite the fact that he had been soundly defeated only two weeks previously for re-election to the United States Senate. But the thing that galled the Democrats was that Senator Bell's term did not expire until March 3, 1859—a long spell of some fifteen months! Undoubtedly some of the Democratic leaders caught a whiff and a sniff of what was but thinly disguised in the Democratic organ [35] two days after Bell's decisive defeat for re-election. Doubtless the concluding paragraph of the blistering editorial was reread and rehearsed at length:

"Tennessee has, for years past, been grossly misrepresented by Mr. Bell. The popular voice of the State has been declared three times in succession against him. But notwithstanding this fact, and his expressed pledge to resign, he persists in holding on to his official station. It was rendered more important, therefore, that his successor should be elected by the present Legislature, that the country may correctly understand the true sentiments of the people of Tennessee. Mr. Bell may continue to occupy his seat in the Senate by virtue of the date of his commission, but it will be in the face of popular condemnation, and under circumstances that will take from the office all but the privileges it confers, and the salary it affords. As widely as we differ with the honorable Senator in politics, we have over-estimated his self respect if he shall continue to cling to his cushioned chair in the Senate under circumstances so disparaging."

The editorial provided the key to resolving the much-desired objective—"... his [Bell's] expressed pledge to resign...." And so, one of Bell's speeches in Congress in 1854 on his opposition to the passage of the Kansas-Nebraska bill which in effect repealed the Compromise Act regarding slavery, was resurrected and hailed with delight by the Democratic-laden Legislature. Whether or not lots were cast is unknown, but

---

[35] *Daily Union and American*, October 29, 1857.

at any rate Senator J. Knox Walker of Shelby and Fayette Counties introduced the following resolution [36] designed to embarrass Bell and perchance procure his immediate resignation, "a consummation devoutly to be wished" by the Democrats:

"Whereas, The act of 1820, commonly called the Missouri Compromise act, was inconsistent with the principles declared and laid down in the acts of 1850, better known as the Compromise acts of that year, and whereas, the Missouri Compromise acts were a palpable wrong done to the people of slave-holding States, and should have been repealed; and whereas, the principles of the Kansas-Nebraska bill meet our unqualified approbation, and should have received the cordial support of our Senators and Representatives in Congress.

Whereas, one of these Senators, Hon. John Bell, in a speech delivered against the Kansas-Nebraska bill, May 25, 1854, said:

A noble, generous, and high-minded Senator from the South, within the last few days, before the final vote was taken on the bill, appealed to me in a manner which I cannot narrate, and which affected me most deeply. The recollection of it affects and influences my feelings now, and ever will. I told that honorable Senator that there was one feature in the bill which made it impossible that I should vote for it, if I waived all other objections. I said to others who had made appeals to me on the subject, that while it would afford me great pleasure to be sustained by my constituents, yet if I was not, I would resign my seat here the moment I found any course upon this subject was not acceptable to them. As for my standing as a public man, and whatever prospects a public man of long service in the councils of the country might be supposed to have, I would resign them all with pleasure. I told that gentleman, that if upon this or any other great question, affecting the interests of the South, I should find my views conflicting materially with what should appear to be the settled sentiment of that section, I should feel it my imperative duty to retire.

*   *   *   *   *   *   *   *

I declare here to-day, that if my countrymen of Tennessee shall declare against my course on this subject, and that shall be ascertained to a reasonable certainty, I will not be seen in the Senate a day afterwards.

Whereas, the voices of his 'countrymen of Tennessee,' on three occasions—1855–56–57, has been pronounced adversely to the Senator's 'course' on that vital question to the South; therefore—

Be it resolved by the General Assembly of the State of Tennessee, That the Hon. John Bell be, and he is hereby respectfully requested to redeem the pledge so solemnly made by him, as set forth in the preamble to this resolution.

Resolved, That a copy of this preamble and resolution be forwarded to our Senators and Representatives in Congress, and that the Governor of the State be furnished a copy of the same."

Was the Walker resolution intended merely to humiliate John Bell? Any humiliation or embarrassment which the Democrats could heap upon Bell was exceedingly pleasing to the Democrats, and at first glance

---

[36] *Senate Journal,* 1857, 150–151.

the adoption of the Walker resolution would seem to have been a "bountiful plenty." But there was a deeper motive beneath the denunciation of Bell's opposition to the passage of the Kansas-Nebraska act. At that time, a long-observed custom was still kept in mind. Since United States Senators were elected by the Legislature, it was taught and thought that the Legislature had the right to "instruct" Senators as to how to vote upon measures pending before the Congress. If Senators felt that they could not obey such legislative "instructions," then the only decent thing to do was to resign. A dramatic precedent had been established in Tennessee in 1839 that resulted in the resignations of two Whig United States Senators, Ephraim H. Foster and Hugh Lawson White.[37]

Two weeks after the introduction of the Walker resolution, two members of the Committee on Federal Relations filed an objection to the Walker resolution,[38] to-wit:

"REPORT.

The undersigned members of the Committee of Federal Relations, to which committee were referred the preamble and resolutions, requesting the Hon. John Bell to resign his seat in the Senate of the United States, beg leave to submit the following minority report:

They have been unable to concur with the views of the majority of the committee, and feel that it is due to themselves, to present in brief form, the reasons for their difference.

They are unable to perceive any necessity or propriety in asking Mr. Bell to resign his seat, when the single question of the Kansas-Nebraska Act, upon which he is sought to be arraigned, has long since been settled, and neither he nor his political friends in Tennessee seek or intend to disturb its provisions. That act, whether wise or unwise, is now the law of the land upon the subject of slavery in the new State, and there let the agitating question rest forever: so says Mr. Bell, and so say we.

The point with Mr. Bell and those who voted with him in the South, in opposition to that act, involved no question of constitutional power, no sentiment inimical to the institution of slavery, but merely the peace and harmony of the country; and how that peace and harmony have been disturbed, and the two great sections of the Union brought into antagonism, let the whole country bear witness. The strife has been fearful, and the agitation not only alarming, but embarrassing to the administration of the Government. Such a state of things is deplorable, and that public man who anticipated it, and acted upon his convictions, deserves praise rather than censure at the hands of his political opponents.

All that we now experience as a nation, and all that we deplore of sectional discord, had its origin in the introduction and passage of the Kansas-Nebraska Act. It re-kindled the fires of opposing passions, that had been allayed by former compromises, and furnished a new occasion for all the enemies of the Union to precipitate themselves into the arena of sectional conflict.

---

[37] See *Messages of the Governors of Tennessee*, Volume III, 365 and 390.
[38] *Senate Journal*, 1857, 207–209.

Mr. Bell apprehended and foretold what we have realized. He opposed the bill because of the very evils which all good men now lament. And what has it accomplished for the South? Nothing but the assertion of the abstract principle of non-intervention, to which none but fanatics were ever opposed. It has added no new Slave State to the Union, and no man in his sober senses now believes it ever will.

But this act, which has been claimed by its Southern friends as a great measure for slavery, has at the same time been claimed by its Northern supporters as a measure of freedom. This generous family rivalry—this honest difference of opinion, has not been difficult to harmonize. We have seen these antipodes supporting the same men for office, shouting in the same host, and then in turn receiving, promiscuously, the showers of public patronage. Is it a measure for freedom or slavery? Its supporters are divided in opinion, and time alone will decide.

We respectfully urge, however, that those who are so tolerant of differences among themselves might esteem something of the same virtue towards their political opponents. But there are provisions in that act, according to the interpretation of a portion of its supporters, to which the undersigned can never assent. Squatter Sovereignty has been claimed under it, and boldly insisted upon—a doctrine utterly at war with Southern interests, and contrary to the professed views of Southern men who voted for the law. To admit such a doctrine is to wall up all the territories against the South.

Alien suffrage, too, has found place in this act, and has attained a baneful prominence under its administration. American citizenship and even permanent residence have been treated with contempt. No solid growth—no stable institutions—no permanent prosperity can be the offspring of such radical levelling doctrines.

But the undersigned deny that the Kansas-Nebraska Act has ever been approved by the people of Tennessee. Certainly not under the interpretation now put upon it. And the result likely to follow its administration will add but little to the approbation already given to it.

The elections that have transpired in the State since its enactment furnish no conclusive test.

That there is an overwhelming majority against its disturbance, so far as relates to the subject of slavery, is beyond all question. That sentiment is founded more in a desire to stop further agitation than in any fixed views of the law itself. Popular acquiescence has been mistaken for approbation. The people never demanded its passage, because they desired issue, and they are averse to its repeal for the same patriotic reason.

In all the recent elections, other questions have had a more decided prominence. The fierce antagonism between the North and South, irrespective of the merits or demerits of the act itself, has notoriously swayed thousands of our voters, and the deepest feeling which now occupies the minds of the people of Tennessee, is one of regret at the distractions which pervade the national public opinion.

The undersigned do not feel called upon to eulogize Mr. Bell. He needs no such tribute at their hands. His long services in behalf of the State, in different departments, and under the eye of the nation, are his best testimonials; and his elevated position in the Senate, is the monument of his greatness. All these ought to have shielded him from the carping censure contained in this preamble and resolution.

His future in the body of which he is a member has been circumscribed, and to permit him to close, unmolested, the remainder of his term, would neither impair the ascendency of the party in power nor jeopardize any favorite policy. More than all, the nation can ill spare the services of such a man upon other questions foreign and domestic, about which there are no party differences. For these and other reasons, we dissent from the views of the majority of the committee, and respectfully urge that the Resolution be not passed.

All of which is respectfully submitted.

W. LaFAYETTE McCONNICO,
JAMES B. HEISKELL."

Despite a prolonged period of haggling, the resolution with two minor amendments was finally adopted [39] on February 10, 1858.

Prior to the passage of the resolution, a fervent and irrepressible Whig, Dr. J. W. Richardson of Rutherford County, made an impassioned speech occupying portions of two days in behalf of John Bell and his public record. The concluding portion of Representative Richardson's plea was as follows: [40]

" . . . Mr. Bell is the oldest public servant now alive in Tennessee; I mean he has been in public life longer than any other man in Tennessee.

He was born in this (Davidson) county, and commenced the practice of law at a very early age in the adjoining county of Williamson.

In the year 1817, he was elected by the managers of a fourth of July celebration to deliver an oration, which he did, and before he left the ground he was nominated by public acclaim as a candidate to represent the county in the Senatorial branch of the General Assembly, which was to convene in the city of Knoxville on the 3rd Monday of Sept. following. And although Mr. Bell had only one month to canvass, and had also an opponent already in the field—a gentleman of tried abilities and high qualifications, yet he was elected by a handsome vote, and some say even before he was constitutionally eligible.

He served the session, returned to middle Tennessee—married, in my county, the daughter of a most excellent and worthy gentleman, and settled soon afterwards in Nashville to pursue the practice of the law, which he did, until the summer of 1827, when he made the memorable canvass for Congress against a man who was considered the ablest and shrewdest politician in the State—I allude to the Hon. Felix Grundy. It was indeed an exciting and able canvass. They canvassed the district, then composed of the counties of Davidson, Williamson and Rutherford, and everywhere the people rushed in crowds to hear the disputants. I shall never forget the scene in my country town, Murfreesboro. The people were wild with anxiety to hear, and a vast multitude convened, a thing then unusual, and unknown in our country.

I was but a school boy, and I recollect that many of us left and went to hear the young man meet the champion of many battles. It was the first political speech I ever heard, and I shall never forget the appearance of Mr. Bell on that occasion. As was perfectly natural, Mr. Bell being much the younger man, he had our sympathies. We rejoiced at the result of the debate, and all—everyone, I think, left Bell men.

---

[39] *Senate Journal*, 1857, 520.
[40] *Republican Banner*, February 20, 1858.

He continued to represent the people in Congress after the district was changed, and was once elected Speaker of the House of Representatives.

In 1840, he received the appointment of Secretary of war in Gen. Harrison's cabinet, and in 1842 resigned, having filled the office with distinguished ability and to the entire satisfaction of his friends.

He remained in private life until 1847, when he was elected by an overwhelming majority to represent the county of Davidson in the popular branch of the General Assembly, and during the session I had the pleasure of helping to elect him a Senator to the Congress of the United States.

In 1853 he was re-elected, and his term of office expires, by the Constitution, on the 4th of March, 1859.

And now, Mr. Speaker, here is a man who commenced public life *forty years ago*—who has spent the vigor of his manhood, and almost the whole of his life in the service of his country, and greatly too, as every public man knows, to his own private injury—who has now grown old in maintaining the character and dignity of Tennessee in the councils of the nation—whose term of service will expire, at furthest, in a little more than one year from this time. I say, sir, this man who stands now almost as the only link, if not the *only* one, which connects us of the present day to the heroes of the Revolution, and to the fathers of our glorious Constitution, is to be driven from the Senate, even before his time, by the party, calling itself Democratic! Well, sir, I have no favors to ask of you for Mr. Bell. Strike him down. We defy you; But remember, we shall take an appeal to Tennessee. Many of you hope that he will disobey your mandate—I know not. You succeeded once before in driving from the Senate that old patriot and statesman, Hugh L. White, and the people of Tennessee emptied the vials of their wrath on your heads for such an outrageous act. *It may be so again.*

But, Mr. Speaker, who is to succeed him? Where is your man to fill his place in the Senate? You may strike him down, but who is to fill the seat which he has occupied with such distinguished ability? Whom have you got that can stand as conservator of the peace in these perilous times? Who, of all your men, can stand in *his* place in the Senate, and command the respect and confidence of the conflicting sections now at work for the destruction of our Union? You have not got the man—he does not belong to your party—you may select, and doubtless will select someone to succeed him, but I imagine his successor, when he comes to occupy the seat which Mr. Bell has filled with so much credit to himself and honor to his country, will feel very much like Martin Van Buren looked when he was dressed in Gen. Jackson's regimentals and commanded to walk in the footsteps of his illustrious predecessor."

John Bell had been reprimanded sharply by the Legislature, but he did not resign his post. The net result of the scrap was that Tennessee's representation in the United States Senate until 1859 would be equally divided politically between Andrew Johnson, Democrat, and John Bell, Whig. By many, Bell was considered cold and phlegmatic and somewhat disdainful of adverse political criticism. Be that as it may, in this particular situation he did not obey his own pronouncement and perhaps considered the above legislative denunciatory resolution as being only

" . . . Words are words: I never yet did hear
That the bruis'd heart was pierced through the ear."

Bell's supporters thought that he bore the legislative castigation with much aplomb and dignity; his political opponents regarded his action as old-fashioned impudence. The crux of the whole matter boiled down to this—the Tennessee Democrats wanted to get rid of their arch enemy and were ready and eager to "kill him off" by any means which, in their eyes, would be justifiable political homicide! But Senator Bell did not resign, and the frequent clashes between Bell and Johnson during the two remaining years of Bell's tenure (1857–1859) were characterized by personal attacks upon each other that did not comport with the dignity ordinarily attached to such a distinguished position as that of United States Senator. Perhaps one such exhibit should be presented. Bell had argued that the excerpt from his speech of 1854, which had been used by the Tennessee Legislature of 1857 as the basis for reminding him of his promise to resign in case he were not supported by his constituency, had been garbled and mangled by his political opponents. On this point, Senator Bell spoke in a very positive and rather self-righteous air, to which Andrew Johnson replied in part as follows: [41]

Mr. Johnson. " . . . My honorable colleague said, in another portion of his speech, that he would not be seen in the Senate another day after it was ascertained that his course was not acceptable to the people of Tennessee. Why, then, should the Legislature be complained of? The honorable gentleman says he looks upon the resolutions as an insult. An insult to recite his own language and address it to him in respectful terms, and present it to the Senate of the United States! That is no garbled extract. It is the speech as it is in its context, and reads just as it is. There is the fair, unequivocal declaration, that if his course came in conflict with the views of the people of Tennessee, he would not be seen in the Senate another day. Where is there anything wrong or insulting in reciting that? It seems to me that it is an improper construction put upon the resolutions, and great injustice has been done to those who passed them."

*　　*　　*　　*　　*　　*　　*　　*

Mr. Bell. "I beg to correct my colleague again. I pray that he will do me justice. I said that I begged to differ in opinion with the Legislature on that subject, in the most courteous language that I was capable of using—not to disregard them."

*　　*　　*　　*　　*　　*　　*　　*

Mr. Johnson. " . . . I hope that I have succeeded in making myself understood by my competitor—"
Mr. Bell. "No competitor in any respect or in any way."

*　　*　　*　　*　　*　　*　　*　　*

Mr. Johnson. " . . . I have had competitors again and again, and many of them not inferior in ability and reputation even to the honorable Senator's own conception of himself. . . . I have had competitors who were foemen worthy of my steel, and they have met their fate like honorable

[41] *Congressional Globe,* 35 Congress, I Session, *passim,* 807–813.

men, and recognized me as such. A gentleman and well-bred man will respect me, and all others I will make do it:

> 'Upon what meat doth this our Caesar feed,
> That he is grown so great?'

Is he beyond the reach of popular sentiment? In rather a taunting and sneering manner he says he is not my competitor in any sense. If you have never been my competitor, your equals have; and in the conclusion of their contest they adjusted their robes and prepared themselves for their fate; and, I repeat again, fell like honorable men. . . ."

On December 17, 1857, Governor Isham G. Harris transmitted his main Message* to the Legislature:

"EXECUTIVE DEPARTMENT,
Nashville, December 16, 1857.

GENTLEMEN OF THE SENATE AND HOUSE OF REPRESENTATIVES:

At the commencement of the present General Assembly, we were met on every hand by the evidences of an unusual degree of prosperity, which prevailed throughout the whole country. Our fields, for a number of years, had yielded abundant crops, and the range of prices gave assurance of a full reward to each and every branch of industry and production.

But within the last sixty days, we have witnessed the suspension of specie payments by almost the entire banking institutions of our own State, as well as those of most of the States of the Union; the effect of which has been a sudden and wide-spread commercial revulsion—derangement of the exchanges and monetary concerns of the whole country—seriously crippling the operations of trade, and to a great extent paralysing the arm of industry and enterprise.

Whilst it is impossible for legislation to relieve the people of these evils and disastrous results, yet they may be, to some extent, ameliorated, and their recurrence prevented by wise and wholesome legislative provisions and restrictions.

In order that we may determine upon the proper remedy, it is

---

* *Senate Journal*, 1857, 288–296.

Author's note. Contrary to usual custom, the Governor's Message was not printed in both legislative *Journals*; only the *Senate Journal* carried it. Nor did the *Appendix*, 1857, carry the Message, although this separate publication carried a number of other Reports and State papers. The *House Journal*, 1857, carries this reference: "A message was received from the Governor. Mr. Rowles moved that the message be read; which was done. On motion of Mr. Stovall, seven thousand five hundred copies were ordered to be printed for the use of the House." Page 301.

necessary that we understand, if possible, the cause of the present panic and monetary derangement.

It is shown by the report of the Secretary of the Treasury of the United States, to the Congress just assembled, that on the 1st of January, 1857, the immediate liabilities of the banks of the several States were as follows:

Notes in circulation $214,778,822
Amount due depositors 230,351,352
Aggregate immediate liabilities $445,130,174

Against which they had in specie in their vaults, $58,349,838; making about ($7.66) seven dollars and sixty-six cents of immediate liabilities for one dollar in their vaults; showing, conclusively, that the system throughout the whole Union is unsound, unreliable, and fraught with a multitude of evils, many of which the country is now unfortunately experiencing.

The reports of the various banks in Tennessee show, that on the 1st January, 1857, their immediate liabilities were as follows:

Notes in circulation .... $ 9,021,475
Amount due depositors 5,051,256
Aggregate immediate liabilities $14,072,731

Against which they had in specie in their vaults, $2,325,823; making about six dollars of immediate liabilities, to one dollar of specie in the vaults.

And on the 1st day of July, 1857, as follows:

Notes in circulation .... $ 6,036,982
Amount due depositors 4,545,104
Aggregate immediate liabilities $10,582,086

Against which they had in specie in their vaults, $2,670,751; making about four dollars of immediate liabilites to one dollar in specie.

From these facts, it is evident that on the 1st of January, 1857, the banks of our own State had reached a point of expansion dangerous to themselves, and injurious to the best interests of the community; the effect having been to cheapen currency, and thereby greatly augment the prices of every species of property; to stimulate over-trading, by offering such inducements and facilities for that character of hazard as seldom fail to lure thousands of our citizens from the fields of labor and productiveness, to the more inviting, yet more dangerous fields of speculation; to encourage habits of luxury and wasteful extravagance, and to drive from circulation, if not from the country, the precious metals; for it is a well-established law of trade, that two classes of currency of unequal value cannot circulate together, the more valuable always retiring from the field of unequal competition, to seek a market where it is more properly appreciated, and can be more profitably invested.

But after having expanded this bubble almost to the point of explosion, and invited their victims far out upon the dangerous chances of speculation, between the 1st of January and 1st of July, 1857, they suddenly and violently contracted their circulation from nine to about six millions of dollars. Could the banks have stopped at this point, the effect might not have been so great as not to be overcome by the energies of our people, and the wonderful resources of the country, without serious and lasting injury. But so great an expansion must necessarily have a corresponding reaction: the contraction doubtless continued in the same ratio from July to the present period, reducing their circulation to a point not far above $3,000,000; in the meantime, having suspended specie payment, leaving, as the only alternative for the people, in their financial extremes, an irredeemable and depreciated paper as their only currency or medium of exchange, producing thereby a general and great depreciation in the price of every species of property, and almost universal panic and distress.

The history of our banking system has presented, from the beginning, one perpetual scene of expansions and contractions, producing periodically a flush in the monetary affairs of the country, which is invariably succeeded by contraction, panic, and pecuniary distress; and as long as the system is continued as at present organized, these scenes must be of frequent recurrence. A paper currency can never be safe—that is, not the actual representative of capital.

It may be confidently stated, upon the highest financial authority, that a paper currency of more than two of circulation to one of specie, or three of immediate liabilities to note-holders and depositors, to one of coin, cannot be sustained as a sound convertible currency. When the disproportion between their specie and immediate liabilities runs higher than this, the banks are, at all times, liable to be driven to suspension, if not to insolvency, and especially so where the circulation is local, as it is with all the banks in Tennessee.

Under the present system, bank notes do not represent coin or capital. Their issues are not limited by the amount of metal in their vaults; for we have seen many of our banks issuing as high as four, five, six, and in some instances, ten dollars of their circulation for one in specie. Their notes are the mere *substitute* for coin which they have not got, and their ability to redeem them is made to depend upon their collections from their customers. The ordinary transaction between them and their customers, being purely an exchange of credits, the customer paying a premium of from six to eight per cent per annum upon the credit of the bank.

Can this system furnish to the community what they so much need and desire, A SOUND, UNIFORM, AND CONVERTIBLE CURRENCY? for the amount of currency is of far less importance to the people than its uniformity and soundness. And to obtain this, is the great object to be accomplished, if your Legislature would remedy existing evils.

But can this important object be accomplished as long as bank notes can be multiplied at the mere discretion of the maker, and to any extent that his avarice or cupidity may prompt? and which is but too often multiplied, as we have seen, far beyond the limits of prudence and safety.

This currency may pass from hand to hand as a circulating medium, and for a time answer the ends of trade and commerce, but when the collapse comes, as come it must, the disastrous consequences are felt by every class of society; the laborer is thrown out of employment, the enterprising merchant is crushed, the wheels of the manufacturer are stopped, and thousands of industrious citizens involved in irretrievable ruin.

Shall we, by our policy, longer contribute to these fatal results?

The evil is upon us, however, and its recurrence in the future can only be prevented by eradicating the whole system, or imposing such restrictions upon it as will effectually and certainly check over-issues and violent expansions and contractions. Whether it be thought that the banks, by suspension, have forfeited their charters or not, no one doubts the authority of the sovereign power of a State to impose such additional restraints as may be necessary to secure an honest and faithful execution of the trust confided to them, or to provide such security as may be deemed necessary against the misuse and abuse of their privileges, provided these restrictions and provisions do not conflict with any fundamental right, or defeat the primary objects of the incorporation. The great end and aim of the charters conferred upon our banks was to secure a sound currency; and any legislation to this end, is beyond all question, within the legitimate scope and power of the Legislature.

It is, however, believed that no sudden and radical change of policy can be adopted without inflicting serious injury upon the country, and prolonging, if not increasing, the distress.

I respectfully recommend the passage of a law requiring:

1st. That the banks shall resume specie payment upon a day fixed, and as early as practicable; thus making our currency convertible, and re-establishing confidence to some extent at least.

2d. That from and after a given day, no bank or branch bank in the State shall issue any bill of the denomination of five dollars or under; and upon a given day, within a reasonable time thereafter, they shall issue no note or bill of the denomination of ten dollars or under; and upon a given day, within a reasonable time thereafter, they shall issue no note or bill of the denomination of twenty dollars or under.

3d. That upon a fixed day, within a reasonable time after the banks cease to issue notes or bills of the various prohibited denominations of twenty dollars and under, they shall cease to circulate, retiring them gradually—first fives and under, next tens, and lastly twenties.

The withdrawal of small notes from circulation, would not only secure a metallic one in their stead, for all the smaller operations of trade, thus lessening the evil with that class of community who are least benefited by bank accommodations, and yet are the most serious sufferers from a depreciated currency, but would tend to restrain the excessive issues of banks, and give to them, as well as to the public, a firmer basis to rest upon, in case of any unexpected revulsion in our commercial affairs.

4th. That no note or bill, issued by any bank not within the limits of the State of Tennessee, of a less denomination than our own banks are authorized to issue, shall circulate within the State. And that no banker, broker, corporation, revenue officer, or any person exercising a licensed privilege, shall pay out or circulate the notes of any other than the banks of our own State.

If private bankers are allowed to issue the notes of banks of other States, they might usurp almost the entire circulation, while our own, under a system requiring each bank to pay out its own issues only, would be driven home for redemption. The restrictions imposed upon our banks, for the purpose of securing a sound currency, might thus fail to attain the end in view.

5th. That no bank or branch bank in the State, shall issue or put in circulation, any note or bill that is not payable in specie at the counters where the same is issued or put in circulation.

The issue by each bank, of its counter notes only, would confine the circulation of each bank to the legitimate wants of the community, upon whose trade it is predicated. It would tend to secure a sound currency in each and every neighborhood in which a bank may be located, by affording to all an opportunity of converting into coin, without expense, whatever paper might not be needed as mere matter of convenience for our internal trade.

The facility for returning the notes thus issued upon the bank for redemption, would serve as a constant check upon them, and would do much towards keeping them within safe limits. It would put an end to that system of flooding the community with the depreciated or doubtful issues of our own or foreign institutions. In my opinion, such a provision is indispensably necessary to any wholesome legislation upon the subject.

6th. That no bank shall issue more than two of circulation for one of specie in its vaults, or incur liabilities to note holders and depositors of more than three dollars for one in specie in its vaults.

7th. That the President and Cashier of each and every bank in the State shall make a monthly report, upon their oaths, to some officer of the State Government, the real condition of their respective banks at the time of the report, and that the report be published at the expense of the respective banks, in some newspaper at Nashville; and that swearing falsely to any such report, shall be deemed perjury, and punished accordingly.

8th. Such penalties and forfeitures for the violation of any of these provisions, as will secure implicit obedience to them, should be provided.

Whilst it may be admitted that the Bank of Tennessee, under the control of its present able and efficient president and directors, has been managed with an amount of skill and ability unsurpassed, if indeed it has been equalled, by any preceding boards, both as regards profits, and the observance of those laws of banking, which tend to restrain the excessive issues of its own branches, as well as other banking institutions; yet it is by no means certain that the State will, at all times, be able to obtain either the same skill or integrity for its future management, even if it were deemed politic to perpetuate the institution. Indeed, it is fearful to contemplate the evil that might be produced, if the bank should ever fall into the hands of unskillful and dishonest men! What pecuniary loss to the State—what suffering to the people by the depreciation of its circulation! Great as these might be, they are yet as nothing compared with the injury inflicted by tampering with the freedom of the elective franchise, or the corruption, in other respects, of public morals—silently, unobserved by the world, but all the more dangerous to that high sense of integrity and morality, which are, after all, the only true safeguards to our republican institutions. It is also confidently believed that the State should not engage in banking, or any other business or speculation, in competition with her citizens, with a view to money-making, and that an institution of this character can never be so well or so successfully managed by the government, as in the hands of private enterprise, from the fact of the liability, under every new administration of the government, to an entire change of its directory and officers, resulting, very often, in an entire change in the policy of the bank. In addition to which, it may truly be said, that you rarely find the same amount of care and energy exercised in the execution of a public trust that is common to the prosecution of private and individual enterprise; and as an investment, it is confidently believed, that if the entire property of the bank was converted into money, and with the capital of the bank invested in the six per cent bonds of the State, that it would result, ultimately, in more profit to the treasury than our present, or any other system of State banking is likely to do. Thus furnishing, to that extent, a home market for our State securities, already depreciated for the want of it, and ridding the State of the expensive and demoralizing machinery of a banking institution, and of the hazards necessarily incident to the banking business.

The President and Directors, in their report to the present session, say 'that the true interests of the State will hereafter be best promoted by a dissolution of all connection with the banks or internal improvement companies, at as early a period as the finances of the State will admit of it, without unnecessarily oppressing the people, and with due regard to the public faith pledged to them.'

I recommend that you fix a day in the future, and as soon as it can be done, without distressing our people, upon which the Bank of Tennessee and her branches be put in gradual liquidation.

The time should be fixed far enough in the future, to give all classes of the community reasonable time to adapt themselves and their business to the inauguration of the proposed policy, and the liquidation should be slow and gradual in its operation, so as to do as little violence as possible to existing interests, by withdrawing the circulation of the bank, or rapidly collecting its debts.

My distinguished predecessor has already laid before you a full statement of the financial condition of the State, showing the actual indebtedness, present and prospective liabilities, &c. I fully concur with him in recommending the sale of all the stock owned by the State in the banks and internal improvement companies, and the appropriation of the fund to the payment of the actual indebtedness of the State, believing, as I do, that the State is never profited by associations or partnerships with corporations or stock companies, and that the sooner the connection is severed the better for the interest of the State.

I also fully concur with my predecessor in recommending an amendment of the constitution of the State, so as to fix a reasonable limit, beyond which the Legislature shall not go, in creating a debt or liability of the State, without first submitting the question directly to the people, except in cases of invasion, insurrection or rebellion. Such an amendment is certainly wise and proper in itself, securing to the people the right to be consulted, and to determine for themselves, by popular vote, whether they will take upon themselves the liability proposed or not; especially in view of the fact that our legislative elections are generally made to turn much more upon party considerations and federal politics, than upon local or State policy, and most of the questions, out of which have sprung these heavy liabilities, have been very little discussed, if, indeed, they have been discussed at all, before the people, previous to their enactment.

Another salutary effect following such an amendment is, that it would inspire confidence in such securities as the State has issued or may hereafter issue, throughout the money markets of the world; and to the extent that you convince capitalists that we have not issued, and will not issue bonds beyond our ability to pay, do you restore and appreciate the credit of the State. And in this connection, allow me earnestly to recommend, that the faith and credit of the State be no further pledged in aid of internal improvement or otherwise. The reasons for this recommendation are too palpable to require argument; a sufficient one, however, is found in the fact, that the actual indebtedness, present and prospective liabilities, of the State amounts to near twenty millions of dollars; and before we increase the aggregate liabilities of the State in aid of those works, we should see to what extent our internal improvement experiments are successful.

Under various acts of the Legislature, the State has, by the endorsement of the Governor, guaranteed the payment of the principal and interest of various bonds of certain corporations. There is no provision made for the payment of the semi-annually accruing interest, out of the State Treasury, in the event of failure to pay on the part of the corporations. The faith and credit of the State is certainly as much pledged for the prompt payment of the interest on these bonds, as it is upon the bonds of the State loaned to companies; and for the coupons to remain unpaid after maturity, is not only a breach of the good faith of the State, but it affects most injuriously her credit. I, therefore, recommend the passage of a law putting those bonds upon the same footing in this respect with the bonds of the State loaned to companies, and thus secure the payment of the interest, as well as the principal, with the same degree of promptitude.

Almost the entire indebtedness and liability of the State is evidenced by coupon bonds, a coupon being issued for each instalment of the interest. These coupons, when dissevered from the bond to which they belong, may pass from hand to hand, being good in the hands of the holder, against the Treasury for their amount; and after being paid and taken up, if by any accident they should be lost, or get out of the possession of the proper officer, they might be again presented and paid, and there are no means provided by existing laws to detect the error, so as to prevent the re-payment. I, therefore, recommend the passage of a law requiring all coupons, when paid, to be returned to the Comptroller of the Treasury, to be by him registered, with an accurate and full description of the same, in a well-bound book to be kept for that purpose, and that they be immediately defaced by some mark of cancellation, and, at stated periods, to be by him burned, in the presence of the Governor, Treasurer, and Secretary of State, or any two of them.

All of which recommendations are respectfully submitted to your favorable consideration.

Isham G. Harris."

Although the Legislature had convened on October 5, 1857, it will be noted that the above Message of Governor Harris was not transmitted to the Legislature until after the lapse of approximately six weeks. At the present time, the cause of the delay can be only speculative. Perhaps the second paragraph of the Message provides a clue, in that reference was made to the suspension of specie payments not only by the banks of Tennessee but "as well as those of most of the States of the Union." And this had come about "within the last sixty days." It is, therefore, highly probable that the impending financial crisis had been of such grave concern to the newly-installed Chief Executive that he was investigating and digesting whatever facts could be obtained in order to present a true picture of the situation to the Legislature.

At the outset of his Message, Governor Harris presented an analysis of the banking status throughout the country as disclosed in a Report by the Secretary of the Treasury of the United States. That the situation throughout the Nation was indeed alarming was disclosed by the fact that for every dollar in the bank vaults there were outstanding liabilities amounting to $7.66. In Tennessee, so Governor Harris reported, the situation was slightly better, the ratio being about four dollars in liabilities backed up by one dollar in specie. Small wonder that Governor Harris reached a conclusion that banks had

" . . . expanded this bubble almost to the point of explosion, and invited their victims far out upon the dangerous chances of speculation . . ."

Governor Harris, in his Inaugural Address, had referred in general terms to the banking system in vogue, leaving his specific recommendations for inclusion in his Message to the Legislature. Every member of the Legislature doubtless knew that the "banking business" would be the major problem confronting that body. The early introduction of banking bills was indicative of that fact, some seventeen [42] having been intro-

---

[42] *Senate Journal*, 1857, *passim*, 867–876.
House Journal, 1857, *passim*, 912–923.

duced prior to the inauguration of Governor Harris. With the suspension of specie payment, the banks had not only alarmed but had irritated the general public. A reading of the criticisms of the contemporary press concerning the monetary crisis that had been precipitated by the virtual closing of the banks warrants the conclusion that the banks had not quite mastered the fine art of plucking the fowl without making it squawk. There were plenty and to spare of "squawks" throughout the entire State.

During the first week of the session, Senator J. J. Jones from the counties of Franklin and Lincoln decided that some sort of punitive penalty should be visited upon the banking fraternity in case any "chicken feed" type of banking were invoked by the banks. To forestall any such toy-like "banking," the pertinent section of his proposed law read as follows:[43]

"A bill to suppress the circulation of small notes as currency in the State of Tennessee.

Be it enacted by the General Assembly of the State of Tennessee, That if after the first day of March next any person or persons, body politic or corporate, within the State of Tennessee shall make, emit, issue, utter, sign, draw, or endorse any bank note, promissory note, or any instrument of writing, for the payment or delivery of money or other valuable thing or of anything purporting to be a valuable thing, of a less denomination or amount than $5.00, to be used as a paper currency, or as a circulating medium, either as money or in lieu of money or of any other currency, every such person or persons and every member, officer, or agent of such body politic or corporate concerned in, or assenting to, such making, emitting, issuing, uttering, signing, drawing, or endorsing, as aforesaid, for any of the purposes aforesaid shall forfeit and pay the sum of $40.00 for each and every such bank note, promissory note, or instrument of writing so made, issued, emitted, uttered, signed, drawn, or endorsed, one half to the use of any person who shall sue therefor and the other half to the use of the State of Tennessee."

The hastily-introduced Jones bill was subjected to a cooling-off process and, on February 2, 1858, his proposal went down to defeat by a vote of 16 to 7.[44]

Senator W. E. Travis, representing the counties of Henry, Weakley, and Obion, proposed to deliver a solar plexus to those banks that had suspended specie payment. His knock-out blow was to be delivered in the following manner.[45]

"An Act entitled An Act to regulate the currency of Tennessee and compel the banks to pay their debts.

WHEREAS, the Bank of Tennessee, the different stock banks in the

---

[43] Senate Bill No. 21. Original manuscript in State Archives, Nashville.
[44] *Senate Journal*, 1857, 454.
[45] Senate Bill No. 37. Original manuscript in State Archives, Nashville.

State and the free banks thereof, with few exceptions, have suspended specie payments and refuse to pay their debts contracted with the people, and

WHEREAS, this has been done while large amounts of gold and silver remain in their volts which properly belong to there creditors, and

WHEREAS, this state of things has been brought about by them at an unprecidented period of prosperity and abundance, THEREFORE,

Section 1. Be it enacted by the General Assembly of the State of Tennessee that the charters of all the banks in this State that have suspended, and such others as may hereafter suspend, be and the same are hereby declared forfeited and that the Attorney General for the State is hereby required to take such steps as will put said banks in gradual liquidation and wind them up."

Apparently, the Travis bill was considered too drastic, for on February 10, 1858, its author was permitted to withdraw the bill from further consideration.[46]

Senator W. S. Munday, from the counties of Smith and Sumner, on November 30, 1857, proposed to loosen up a bit the tight clamp which the banks had fastened down in that they were refusing to pay out any specie. Senator Munday thought that a slight penalty upon such institutions might tend to cause them to relax their pressure somewhat. In accord with his feeling, he proposed the following lever with which to pry open the vaults:[47]

"A bill entitled An Act to regulate the banks and the business of banking in the State of Tennessee.

Section 3. Be it further enacted, That all the banks in this State which have already or may hereafter suspend specie payment shall forfeit and pay to the State of Tennessee at the rate of ½% per month, payable monthly, on all the issues of such bank then in circulation, for and during the period such bank or banks shall remain and continue in a suspended condition...."

Although Senator Munday's bill was set for special order on the following day, nothing transpired. On January 11, 1858, the Senate got around to consideration of the bill and rejected same by a vote of 13 to 8.[48] One week before adjournment an effort was made to reconsider the rejection of the bill, but the attempt went for naught.[49]

Examination of the above seventeen banking bills introduced before the Message of Governor Harris was transmitted to the Legislature discloses that most of them were shallow and illy-conceived. The general public, of course, was on the outside trying to look in, but their vision was cut off by the "suspension placard" posted on the bank doors. Most of the above alleged legislative panaceas are reminiscent of a quotation from the epitaph [50] on the gravestone of a Puritan locksmith:

---

[46] *Senate Journal*, 1857, 515.
[47] Senate Bill No. 117. Original manuscript in State Archives, Nashville.
[48] *Senate Journal*, 1857, 342.
[49] *Ibid.*, 765.
[50] *Remaines Concerning Britaine* (1637).

> "He stood without and would not knocke,
> Because he meant to picke the locke."

Among the medley of bank bills there was one, however, that received careful consideration, namely, Senate Bill No. 82, introduced on November 16, 1857 by Senator J. Knox Walker of Shelby and Fayette Counties. This bill unquestionably had had close attention, for it was the collective thinking of the Joint Committee on Banks. While the Senate was deliberating upon the question of considering amendments to the Walker bill, Senator Thomas Menees offered a bill in lieu which was adopted by a vote of 12 to 9.[51]

From time to time, various amendments to the substitute bill were offered in both branches of the Legislature resulting in conflicts and in the subsequent appointment of a conference committee composed of three Senators and five Representatives.[52] The principal point at issue was the date to be fixed for the resumption of specie payment. A number of other details in connection with the bank question had been outlined in the recommendations of Governor Harris, consisting of eight specific items, to-wit:

1. Resumption of specie payment at an early fixed date.
2. From and after a fixed date, no bank should issue bills of five dollars and under; "within a reasonable time thereafter" no bill of ten dollars and under should issue; and finally "within a reasonable time thereafter" no bill of twenty dollars or under should be issued.
3. After the cessation of issuance of notes or bills of twenty dollars and under, a fixed date shall be established for the prohibition of their circulation.
4. Out-of-State bank bills and notes, of less denomination than the authorized bills or notes of Tennessee banks, to be barred from circulation in Tennessee.
5. No Tennessee bank shall issue or put in circulation any bill or note that was not payable in specie by the bank issuing same.
6. No bank should issue more than two "circulating" bills or notes for one of specie in its vault, nor should bank liabilities to note holders and depositors exceed three dollars for each dollar in specie in its vault.
7. Each bank required to submit monthly reports, under oath, as to the actual condition of said bank, false reports to be deemed as constituting perjury and punished accordingly.
8. Legal provisions should be made for penalties and forfeitures for violation of any specified regulations and requirements.

Governor Harris concurred with his immediate predecessor, Gov-

---

[51] *Senate Journal*, 1857, 279.

Author's note. The vote as given in the Journal is in reverse order, as may be verified by counting the Senators voting *pro* and *con*.

[52] *Ibid.*, 424.

ernor Andrew Johnson, that the Bank of Tennessee and its Branch Banks should be "put in gradual liquidation" as soon as it could be done "without distressing our people."

With various bank bills in the legislative hopper, plus the recommendations of Governor Harris and ex-Governor Johnson, plus the clamor and the furore of the press and the people, the Legislature felt itself to be "between the Devil and the deep blue sea." Sharp criticism and barbed sarcasm were being hurled from all directions. In addition to public criticism, the spectre of partisan politics both within and outside the Legislature arose and exerted an influence upon the legislators themselves. A strongly partisan newspaper leveled the following barrage at a divided and bickering Legislature:[53]

"THE HARMONIOUS DEMOCRACY AND THE BANKS.

All the attempts of the General Assembly to frame a Bank Bill which would secure a majority in both houses had failed up to Friday night, though there were indications that the House would go back to the democratic caucus or 'conference' bill and take it up for another trial. On Friday in the House, Judge Rowles, one of the weather-beaten sentinels upon the locofoco outer walls, signalled the following warning to his unsuspecting fellow soldiers, peacefully reclining upon beds of political down within:

The votes of the minority, indicated to his mind, that it was their object to make the bill purely a party measure, and hence it became democrats to act unitedly and firmly.

The cheek of the above is amusing. After attempting through the entire session to frame and pass a *locofoco* Bank Bill—after caucusing and 'conferencing'—after executing innumerable marches and countermarches inside their own lines, and fighting twenty-five or thirty sham fights—in the vain hope of beating in the undisciplined, and presenting an undivided phalanx upon the question—to get up and say the minority wanted to force them to pass a party bill, is decidedly jolly. It is a joke worthy of the Judge.

The minority in the Legislature have at no time presumed that they could succeed in engrafting their own ideas as the leading features of any measure on this subject. But while they have stood back and waited the result of the operations of the official doctors, they have carefully weighed every proposition, and with an honest purpose to accomplish the greatest good to the greatest number, have endeavored to secure the best of a generally very undesirable set of projects. *The failure of the democratic party to unite upon any principle* is the cause of the ridiculous attitude which that party now occupies upon this subject before the people.—Every appliance has been used to soften the hards and harden the softs, so as to produce a medium consistency, but without success up to this writing. Smarting under a realization of the absurdity of their attitude, the leaders are attempting to frighten the refractory into the traces by pointing them to the minority —to what they have heretofore styled as 'the remains of Sam'—'the relics only of an opposition.' If it serve to scare recusants into ranks, even democratic leaders will acknowledge that it has not lived for nothing.

But while we have no objection to democratic leaders using any means

---

[53] *Republican Banner*, December 20, 1857.

which may come to their hands—as they will undoubtedly do—to get up a union of the harmonious upon the question of currency—we protest against the gentleman from Bradley, (Mr. ROWLES,) rolling out his misrepresentations of the position of the minority. ..."

The legislative brawl continued for a month, with no legislative action having been taken. Once more, the editor dipped his pen in acid and penned the following satirical thrust [54] as related to a personal fight between two unidentified legislators who represented opposing views on the bank bill:

"FIGHT AT THE CAPITOL—THE BANK BILL BILLETED.

The warmth of feeling engendered in the General Assembly in view of the immense responsibility resting upon that body, as the agent whose duty it is to relieve the people of the financial embarrassment which now envelopes them, has attracted the intense attention of the world, and thousands have been gazing upon the drama in breathless suspense, expecting every moment to hear something *drop*. Scene after scene and act after act passed before the public, and the impending climax has seemed ever and anon about to burst upon a startled constituency. But fortunately this event has been from time to time avoided, and the disastrous consequences apprehended have been indefinitely postponed. But we have the melancholy duty assigned us of announcing that the seething volcano has at length bursted, and the pent up lava has been scattered about in terrible profusion.

The unfortunate affair, the revolting details of which we are about to relate, provided our ink does not blanch upon the paper, and our pen refuse its melancholy office, whether considered in the light of the time, the place, the cause, the character of the difficulty, its process or its sanguinary climax, is one of the most intensely remarkable and remarkably intense that has occurred since the terrible pummeling which Mr. Sumner received at the hands of the lamented Brooks. The time was the Sabbath day. The sun rose bright and transcendently beautiful, and was quietly and unsuspectingly climbing the eastern hills. The church bells were mingling their welcome music with the joyous voices of exhuberant youth returning from their Sabbath lessons, and invoking the silent outpouring of matured manhood and womanhood, winding their way with grateful hearts to the various churches, to return thanks for the blessings of another week, and solicit a continuance of the same. It was at such a time that our tragedy opened.

The place was that splendid temple of the liberality and State pride of Tennessee—that magnificent edifice erected for the noble purpose of perpetuating and perfecting the rights and liberties and the sovereignty of the chivalrous and patriotic people of the Volunteer State. What a theatre for the performance of such a tragedy as the one which now overwhelms us with its stupendous enormity!

The occasion was the financial condition of a distressed and bankrupt country—sufficient, truly, to invoke the deepest interest and provoke the most unremitting labors of the representatives of the people, and the people themselves, to inaugurate measures of relief—not sufficient, however, to provoke a desecration of the Sabbath, the Capitol of a proud State, and the soil of Tennessee!

---

[54] *Ibid.*, January 19, 1858.

We approach the crisis. At the critical time which we have mentioned, two men, servants of the public, living upon the public treasure, one representing the Senatorial, and the other the popular branch of the Legislature, might have been seen, like our friend James' solitary horseman, wending their way along the beaten and ascending path which leads to the halls of legislation. Incidentally and very naturally, the all absorbing question of the Bank bill became the subject of conversation, and arriving in the lobby of the House, the argument waxed warm. B. the representative of the Senate alleged that the lower branch had pursued a revolutionary and unconstitutional course of legislation upon the subject of Banking.

After the democratic party had agreed upon a measure to relieve the country, and maintain their party supremacy, the Senate had passed it and sent it down to the House. It was the duty of that body to pass it at once, and send it back for enrollment. But they had presumed to *Amend* that bill, and had destroyed its efficacy. G. alleged in reply, with much warmth and indignity, that the lower branch, though technically lower, was composed of freemen, and they had the undoubted right to amend the bill. They had done so. Their amendments were of a salutary character, and calculated to relieve the country of the financial embarrassment under which it was now struggling.

We need not proceed to give the details of the discussion. It is sufficient to say that it was warm, spirited, able, and soon merged into a *darkly* personal character. Epithets followed insinuations, and hostile attitudes followed epithets, until G. put into practical operation his devotion to the individual liability clause by attempting to claw the cuticle of his opponent. Spectators stood aghast, and a ring was involuntarily thereby formed of trembling witnesses. The two combatants were unequally matched, physically, but B. made up for lack of altitude by a superabundance of pluck. The weapons were a billet of wood, first, which came in with felling effect upon the cranium of B. The latter returned the compliment with a ponderous broomstick, and his attack was followed by the casting of a patent spittoon, containing about half a bushel of sand, by which G. attempted to throw sand in the ocular developments of his antagonist. The contest continued for some time. The two gladiators, like their illustrious prototypes, who

> Fit and bled and bled and fit;
> And struggled in their mud,
> Until the ground for miles around
> Was covered with their blood.

Continued the conflict until want of breath, that great draw-back to heroic deeds, forced a suspension, and both parties retired with their usual indignity to change and renew their linen, G. finding himself minus his inner garment, and wash out the 'damned spots' which likened their faces to illustrated editions of the book of martyrs. Fortunately the niches which surrounded them, intended to receive the statues of great men who have made their lives sublime, were vacant, else the marble presentments of the heroes of the purer days of the republic would doubtless have bled at the nose, or manifested some other terrible evidence of their patriotic horror at the scene before them.

We feel a delicacy in giving the names of the parties who thus disgraced the Sabbath and the State, but justice to those who were not engaged in the affray makes it our imperative duty to imitate Gen. Jackson and take the responsibility. We therefore have to say that the party representing the Senate was *Buck*, chairman of the committee on fires, sweeping out, packing documents, and *ex officio*, chairman of the committee on *special* privileges. The party representing and defending the lower House was *George*, who occupies a corresponding relation to that august body. . . ."

The reading of the legislative *Journals* and the contemporary newspapers covering the larger part of the session up to the middle of January, 1858, will disclose that piddling and fiddling around constituted the major activities of the legislators. Time had been frittered away on buncombe speeches, profitless and ofttimes witless cross-firing, discussing and amending and amending and discussing rules of order of which there was but litle maintained. Even the time of meeting and adjourning the daily session consumed the better part of two days in argument. Very, very few general laws had been enacted, and for the most part they were of trifling nature. Nearly four months had passed since the convening of the Legislature, and no constructive legislation had been passed dealing with the most crucial matter confronting the general public—remedying the banking situation. Representative Hiram S. Bradford of Haywood County, upon a return from his constituency, uttered a palpable truth when he declared [55] that

"The people are *perfectly disgusted* with the way in which we have been frittering away the public time, and encroaching upon the public treasury."

Even the dyed-in-the-wool Democratic organ scented the discontent which had become State-wide, and decided to warn the Democratic-controlled Legislature by citing evidence of deep dissatisfaction pervading the length and breadth of the State:[56]

"SPIRIT OF THE PRESS.

If we may judge from the tone of our exchanges, the people are growing restive under the failure of the Legislature to adopt some wholesome reform in the Banking Policy of the State. From an article in the Chattanooga *Advertiser*, we make the following extract:

HAVE THE BANKS CONTROL OF THE LEGISLATURE.

It seems from the tardiness of action of the Legislature, that the people's representatives are muzzled by the influences of worthless rage, worse than usurious machines, and rotten corporations. Why the Legislature is so slow to act is an enquiry constantly made, and only solves itself into mystery. The

---

[55] *Ibid.*, January 26, 1858.

[56] *Daily Union and American*, January 28, 1858.

Author's note. Whether or not the editorial and newspaper excerpts exerted any influence can not, of course, be measured. It is interesting to note, however, that on the same day of the appearance of this article in a morning newspaper, the Banking Bill later that day was enacted into law!

course of the Banks, at present, is worse than ruinous; because it breeds illegal money lending, uncontrollable, sacrifices, opens up corruption and swindling attended with the most dire consequences, and places the man of small means entirely in the hands of the capitalists; or those who have control of paper thumb screws. That any people professing republicanism will longer submit to the enormity, we think would be an anomaly too hideous to conceive of. The banks now are in a state of suspension, but will not allow their creditors to partake of the same privilege. If you owe the Banks, you have got to fork over, or you are popped with a writ, but if you happen to have a little of their unlawful paper, you can't get the specie for it. So it goes. The Banks say: 'I will gouge you, but you shan't gouge me.' How long, then, will the people submit to such onorous usurpations? Always? No! We think the mutterings of the sovereigns are distinctly audible, and ere the cocatrice issues forth again from its safe retreat, the shell and its contents will be crushed under the indignant heel of an out-raged people.

The Memphis *Appeal,* in an article somewhat similar in tone, says:

THE BANKS AND THE PEOPLE.—We have had the satisfaction of being congratulated upon the course pursued by this paper and its corre-spondents, with reference to the banks, by numbers of our best citizens, and we have yet to meet with the first man, outside of the bankers themselves, who does not heartily approve of the general remarks we have made, touch-ing the ruinous policy now pursued by our banks. Those with whom we have conversed—feel no malice towards the gentlemen who conduct these establishments, but they see that the tendency of the present banking policy is to break down public and private credit, and finally to engulf themselves in the general ruin of credit.

We mention this fact, not through a spirit of egotism, but merely to show the general sentiment of the community. Our businessmen should be true to themselves, and hold a public meeting to protest against the action of the banks. They owe it to their own position and interest. Their credit abroad must go by the board, if the present policy should be pursued a few weeks longer. People abroad reason that there must be a collusion between businessmen and banks, when such high rates of exchange, as are now de-manded, are paid without an effort being made to prevent it.

A respectful and earnest protest, from the business men of this com-munity, would do more to remedy the evils that now exist, than any other thing, save prompt and efficient action by the Legislature.

One of two things are perfectly certain: either the banks of the State are hopelessly rotten, or else they are pursuing their present course of sus-pension and usury, through that grasping spirit which must sooner or later break down all credit. One of these conclusions cannot be evaded. When they suspended, they boasted that they did so because the suspension of the Eastern banks had created an artificial demand for coin, and they would be subjected to a heavy loss by a drain of coin from their vaults. They said they were sound and strong, and would be prepared to resume as soon as the Eastern and New Orleans banks resumed. All the Eastern banks, except those of Pennsylvania, have resumed thirty days ago, and the latter are preparing to do so. The New Orleans banks were the first in the Union to resume. And yet there is no talk whatever among the conductors of the Ten-nessee banks, of their resumption. Their friends in the Legislature oppose their resumption on the 1st of July. What do they mean? What is the mat-ter? We repeat, they are either unsound and cannot pay, or else they cannot resist the temptation to make heavy and illegal profits and draw the life-blood from the country, and are determined to grind down as long as they will be permitted to do so.

The Legislature ought to take action immediately, and compel the banks to resume payments.

They ought, at least, to force the Bank of Tennessee to resume. She is the institution of the State, and if she were to resume it would discredit the notes of all other banks in the State which refuse to obey the mandate of the Legislature.

The Memphis *Bulletin,* whose editor has always been an advocate of banks, in opposition to the Democracy, in defining its position in connection with our present financial troubles, frankly says:

'We are in favor of a thorough reform in the errors and abuses of the present banking system in Tennessee—to wit: that the banks shall redeem their notes at the place from whence they are issued, whether they be principal banks or branches, so that they may be conveniently *convertible* into gold and silver, at the will of the holder. They should be allowed to *receive* whatever they choose in payment; but should not be allowed to *pay out* anything but their own notes, which should not be of a less denomination than five dollars.' "

In considering the Bank Bill, the Senate passed its version on the very same day on which Governor Harris had sent his Message to the Legislature, December 17, 1857. When the measure went to the House, an amendment was tacked on fixing January 1, 1859 as the date for the beginning of specie payment by the banks. This amendment by the House was rejected by the Senate, the vote for rejection being 14 to 10.[57] The issue between the two legislative branches became a stalemate, and on January 26, 1858 a conference committee was appointed with a view of ironing out the differences. The Senate members of the committee consisted of Senators W. C. Whitthorne, A. F. Goff, and Thomas Menees.[58] The House members were Representatives G. W. Rowles, Michael Vaughan, W. V. Thompson, Hiram S. Bradford, and C. W. Beale.[59] The conference committee went into action immediately and, at an afternoon session of the Senate, the recommendations of the committee were agreed to by the Senate by a vote of 13 to 10.[60] On the next day, January 28, 1858, the House expressed its approval of the committee report by a vote of 36 to 33.[61] Thus ended the hectic battle that had been waged for more than a month.

Now that a banking law [62] had been enacted, what were its main provisions? The banks were required to resume specie payments by November 1, 1858; after July 1 of the same year, no bank notes of less than five dollar denomination were to be issued and no notes of less than ten dollars were to be issued after January 1, 1859. The banks were also

---

[57] *Senate Journal,* 1857, 350.
[58] *Ibid.,* 410.
[59] *House Journal,* 1857, 461.
[60] *Senate Journal,* 1857, 424.
[61] *House Journal,* 1857, 472–473.
[62] *Acts of Tennessee,* 1857, Chapter 25.

denied the privilege of paying any dividends during the period of suspension, and the rate of exchange was limited to two per cent. Other requirements called for quarterly reports to the State Comptroller who was directed to publish all such reports in the newspapers in order that the public might be advised as to the condition of the bank. The final section of the act provided that the rights of depositors and note-holders were not to be affected by the enactment of said statute.

On the whole, the recommendations of Governor Harris regarding banking were enacted into law, with one notable exception. Nothing was done toward providing "for the gradual liquidation of the Bank of Tennessee," although both Governor Andrew Johnson and Governor Harris had so recommended. This bank had been born in politics and was all along a political machine that wielded powerful influence in gubernatorial and legislative elections throughout the major portion of its existence, beginning from the date of its establishment in 1838.[63]

There is valid testimony [64] that the Bank of Tennessee and some of the more important private banks were not in as bad condition in 1857 as the public was led to believe. Two years later (1859), Cave Johnson, President of the Bank of Tennessee, reported to the Legislature on October 3 that the Union and the Planter's Banks had proposed to resume specie payment on July 1, 1858, *four months earlier* than required by the act of January 28, 1858. This action on the part of the private banks threw the Bank of Tennessee into a tizzy, for it was declared by President Johnson that

" . . . This difficulty between the Banks produced embarrassment in the business of the country for some weeks, and furnished additional grounds to those unfriendly to Banks to assail them, and their attacks were then mainly directed against the Bank of Tennessee. It was represented as a *swindling concern, unsound, unworthy of credit, and not to be trusted by the people . . .*"

Although the Bank of Tennessee was upset by this action of the private banks and was reluctant to fall into line by resuming specie payments, yet it was deemed the better part of wisdom to do so. Accordingly, the branches of the parent bank were advised to resume specie payments by August 1 which "was cheerfully complied with." And it was also declared that "the principal Bank had at no time refused payment of its notes in gold."

Actually, the Bank of Tennessee had been placed behind the eight ball by the passage of a law just four days before legislative adjourn-

---

[63] For sketches of the *political aspects* of this institution for the first twenty years of its existence, see index references in Volumes III and IV of *Messages of the Governors of Tennessee.* A more extended account appears in Robt. H. White's *Development of the Tennessee State Educational Organization, 1796–1929, passim,* 32–206.

[64] *Public Documents, Tennessee Legislature,* 1859, 79.

ment. That amendatory act [65] provided that the Bank of Tennessee would not be required to resume specie payment "until the Union and Planter's Banks shall file their acceptance of the provisions of this act." This, as already stated, was done and the Bank of Tennessee was forced to do likewise.

The final passage of the banking law did not give *immediate* relief, but there can be no doubt that the banking fraternity deemed it wise to put their houses in order. This they did by resuming specie payment before legally required to do so. What was perhaps more important was *guarding the future* against shady banking manipulations that had been characteristic of the past two decades.

Although the outgoing and the incoming Governors, Andrew Johnson and Isham G. Harris, had recommended the sale of all stock owned by the State in banks and internal improvement companies, the Legislature turned a deaf ear to such suggestions and failed to enact any such legislation. Governor Harris was very emphatic in his plea that this be done, inasmuch as he did not believe the State should be involved in such transactions and furthermore stated that "the sooner the connection is severed the better for the interest of the State."

The validity of the recommendation of Governor Harris, although unheeded by the Legislature, was supported later on in the legislative session by a factual report giving the entire history of the financial status of the Bank of Tennessee from the establishment of the institution in 1838. The information concerning the bank's history was supplied by the President of the Bank of Tennessee in compliance with a request from Governor Harris. The Legislature had called upon the latter for this information through the passage of a resolution [66] somewhat detailed and rather specific; introduced by Representative J. J. Turner of Sumner County:

"*Resolved by the House of Representatives,* That the Governor of this State is hereby required to furnish to this House, as soon as possible, the following information:

1st. The amount of the capital stock of the Bank of Tennessee at this time.

2d. The amount paid in of its capital when first created, and how much has been paid since, and when.

3d. How its capital stock was raised; how much was in it by a deposit of money by the General Government, and how much by State loans, and how much from other sources, if from any.

4th. The amount of State bonds issued to raise its capital; how much they sold for; when they fell due, and the interest they drew.

5th. The amount of money she has paid into the Treasury of the State, and all amounts of money that she has in any way paid out by order of the Legislature, or otherwise.

---

[65] *Acts of Tennessee,* 1857, Chapter 73.
[66] *House Journal,* 1857, 610–611.

6th. The amount of profits made by the Bank for the various years it has been in operation.

7th. The amount of its capital that has been lost.

8th. What per cent. the State has realized upon the capital furnished the said Bank.

9th. And all such other information as he may have in regard to its management, profit, and the necessity of its continuance as a fiscal agent of the State."

The reply of Governor Harris was based upon the detailed statements submitted by Cave Johnson, President of the Bank of Tennessee. The thorough analysis of the Johnson report, as made by Governor Harris and reported by him to the Legislature, warrants its inclusion in this treatise, for this clear-cut statement was perhaps the most informative of any such report ever submitted to any Tennessee Legislature upon this particular topic. Here was what * Governor Harris reported:

"EXECUTIVE DEPARTMENT,
Nashville, March 2, 1858.

GENTLEMEN OF THE HOUSE OF REPRESENTATIVES:

Having no record in my office containing the information sought by House Resolution, No. ——, I transmitted a copy of the same to the President of the Bank of Tennessee, with a request that he would report to me such information as the books of the bank would furnish. In answer to which I have received from him a communication with tabular statements, marked A, B, C, D, E, and F, which I herewith transmit to the House. From these tables, and a thorough examination of the various reports of the Comptroller of the Treasury, I am enabled to answer the various questions propounded by the resolution:

The Capital Stock of the Bank of Tennessee, with the date when paid into the Bank, as shown by table 'B', is composed of the following items:

July 1, 1838.

Proceeds of one million of dollars of 6's State Bonds, payable 30 years after date, and dated 7th May, 1838, interest payable semi-annually in New York,
$1,000,000 00

School Fund,	$266,299 05	
School fund from Ocoee lands,	$600,406 42	
		866,705 47

July 1, 1839, *to July* 1, 1840.

Surplus revenue deposited with the State by act of Congress,	1,353,209 45
1845. Proceeds of sales of public lands,	11,703 32

Aggregate of cash capital actually paid into the Bank,		$3,231,618 24
1856. State stock in the Union Bank,	$625,600 00	
School fund stock in same,	38,894 00	
School fund stock in Planters' Bank,	232,700 00	
		897,194 00

* *Appendix,* 1857, 365–370.

Total amount of capital stock paid in,   4,128,812 24

By reference to table 'A', it will be seen that the Bank reports her capital on 1st January, 1858, including stock in the Union and Planters' Banks, to be, $3,367,737 32

Which, when taken from the amount actually paid in, shows that she has sustained a loss of her capital, amounting to   761,074 92

PAYMENTS MADE BY THE BANK.

By act of the General Assembly, passed 9th February, 1850, the bank was relieved from the payment of interest on the State debt, and the annual payments to schools and academies, and was required to pay her profits, semi-annually, into the Treasury.

The books of the Comptroller of the Treasury show, that from the passage of this act, up to the 1st of October 1851, there was paid into the Treasury, as the profits of the Bank. $332,170 43

For next two years ending 1st October, 1853, 394,818 54

  " " " " " 1st October, 1855, 175,000 00

  " " " " " 1st October, 1857, 500,000 00

   Total amount paid into Treasury, $1,391,988 97

It will be seen by examining table 'C', that from the organization of the bank, up to July, 1849, she had paid for the use of schools and academies, $1,298,000 00

Also interest on State debt, $1,377,529 20

Interest on State debt, which accrued from 1st July, 1849, to 9th February, 1850, and which should have been charged to the account of interest on State debt, instead of to the Treasury, as stated by the Bank report of 1851, 94,628 75

Total amount of interest on State debt paid out by the bank, $1,472,157 95

The same table shows that the Bank paid appropriations for the improvement of rivers,   68,375 66

Total payments by the Bank from its origin to 1st January, 1858, $4,230,522 58

PROFITS OF THE BANK.

Table 'A' shows that the aggregate profits of the Bank, from its origin to January 1, 1858, are $4,266,088 73

And that, within the same period she has reduced her capital by the loss of bad debts, &c.,   761,074 92

Which, when taken from the profits to restore her capital, leaves a balance of profit of $3,505,013 81

This amount includes the dividends received upon the Union and Planters' Bank stock, amounting to $ 146,314 10

Which, taken from the profits, leaves as the result of the operations of the Bank of Tennessee for nineteen and a half years, a nett profit of $3,358,699 71

Table 'A' also shows the rate per cent per annum, ranging from 3 68-100 to 15 per cent., which the Bank has made upon her capital.

It is proper, however, to remark, that the calculations which produced this result, are based upon what is termed *'actual capital,' and not upon the amount of money actually paid into the bank as capital.* This table shows that the 'actual capital' of the Bank has, for several years, been fluctuating, being diminished by the failure of their debtors, &c., and increased by the collection of debts which had been charged off as lost.

As it seems to be the object of the House of Representatives to ascertain to what extent the funds of the State have been profitably invested in the business of banking, and whether or not it would be good policy for the State to borrow money at six per cent per annum, payable at New York semi-annually, to increase her banking capital, I have made an accurate calculation of the simple interest upon each item of the cash capital of the Bank of Tennessee, from the date it was paid in, as shown by table 'B', up to the 1st of January, 1858, excluding the stock in the Union and Planters' Banks from this interest calculation, and find that if the same funds had been invested in State bonds, bearing an interest of six per cent per annum, it would have yielded a profit of $3,609,133 00

While the same funds used in banking, have
　　yielded, as shown above, *a nett profit of only*　　　3,358,699 71
Showing that at six per cent the fund would have
　　yielded　　　　　　　　　　　　　　　　　　　　　250,433 29
more profit to the State than the Bank has made upon it.

But a more important consideration than that of the amount of profit to be realized, will be found in the fact that the investment in State or Government securities is much more safe, involving less, vastly less danger of the loss of the capital invested; and the profit, while it is larger, is a sum fixed and certain, which the State can calculate and confidently rely upon, and the whole operation is simple and easy of comprehension, and equally easy of management, requiring a very small proportion of the time and attention of the Comptroller or Treasurer for its entire management, without incurring the expense of keeping up the machinery of a banking establishment and the risk of losing the original capital by failures, defalcations, insolvencies, &c., &c.

The statement of the profits of the Bank, as shown by table 'A', is based on the supposition that the $8,207,187 82 of the present means of the bank (as shown by the report of the 1st of January, 1858, consisting of discounted notes, bills of exchange, bills and notes in suit, State bonds, real estate, specie, &c., &c.,) are of par value and will be realized, and just to the extent that losses are sustained in collecting or converting those means into money, will the profits, as shown, be reduced.

On the 1st of January, 1858, the bank had been in operation nineteen and a half years, and the amount of profits shown above, proves that she has realized less than six per cent per annum upon the actual cash capital which she received. With this, as the result of an experiment of nineteen and a half years in the business of banking, is it good policy for the State to borrow money, paying an interest of six per cent per annum, semi-annually in New York with exchange, say one per cent, to raise money to increase our banking capital? If the bank has failed to realize six per cent upon her capital heretofore, what assurance have we that she will make it hereafter?

But one of the most serious evils to be apprehended from the policy of issuing State bonds, to increase her capital, is the depreciation of our State securities, which is a result that must follow as inevitably, as that supply and demand control the price of property. Why is it that Tennessee six per cent bonds are now selling in New York at from 88 to 90 cents, while Kentucky six per cent bonds, are selling in the same market for from 102 to 103 cents on the dollar.

Has Kentucky been more punctual in the payment of her liabilities than Tennessee? This will not be pretended; for no State has paid her liabilities more punctually than Tennessee. Are the resources of Kentucky superior to those of Tennessee? The last census report shows that they are not. Why this difference then, in the market value of the securities of the two States? The answer is to be found in the fact, that Kentucky has issued very few State bonds; while we, by our system of legislation, have issued and authorized the issuance of near twenty millions—an amount so large, that we have to some extent, shocked the confidence of capitalists in our ability to meet our heavy and constantly increasing liabilities.

Our State securities have, however, within the last few months advanced from about 70 to 88 or 90 on the dollar, and this too, during a period of the severest financial derangement and pecuniary pressure. Is it not apparent that the reason of this appreciation, is to be found in the fact of the distinct and unequivocal declarations of both political parties in the State prior to, and about the commencement of your present session, that the liabilities of the State should not be increased?

But let the Legislature require the issuance of $1,250,00 State bonds, to be hawked and peddled upon the money markets of the world to raise capital to invest in the uncertain and hazardous enterprise of banking, and all the confidence which our pledges and declarations have inspired, is at once destroyed. Although the amount is comparatively small and not sufficient of itself to produce any great amount of evil, yet, capitalists will regard it as a violation of our pledges against an increase of State liabilities, and just in proportion to the doubts that they may entertain as to when and where we will stop this increase of liabilities, just in that proportion will all our State securities depreciate.

The bonds cannot be sold except at a ruinous discount, and the fact of your having authorized their issuance, will depreciate the bonds now held by the various Internal Improvement Companies, thus crippling and retarding their progress, if not defeating their enterprises.

As to the necessity of the Bank of Tennessee, as a fiscal agent, I have only to say that I do not consider it at all necessary to the successful management of the financial affairs of the State.

Under the present system, if the State has to make a payment within her own limits, the Treasurer makes the payment, by checking upon the funds of the Treasury on deposit in the Bank; so the only agency the bank has in that payment is to pay the check of the Treasurer, just as she pays the check of every other depositor; and if the payment is to be made beyond the limits of the State, *it is made out of the money of the Treasury, with the current rate of exchange, and in many instances half per cent commission, to the 'Correspondent' of the Bank in New York;* so the only agency the bank has in this case is simply to transmit the fund to the place of payment.

In making the payment within the State, the Treasurer could count the money due the creditor and pay it to him, as easily as he can count out his deposits to the bank, and then check for the amount due each creditor. And in making a payment in New York or elsewhere, beyond the limits of the

State, he could purchase the exchange and forward it himself. It would only cost him the current rate of exchange, (and the State pays that under the present system,) or he could ship the coin if necessary.

The only agency the bank has in the first case is to pay the check of one of her depositors, (the Treasurer,) and in the second case to transmit the funds provided by the Treasury, to the place of payment, and this could certainly be done as well by the accounting officers of the Treasury, as by the officers of the Bank.

With regard to the payments which our several Railroad Companies have to make semi-annually in New York, the Companies are bound to furnish to the bank the money, with the current rate of exchange, fifteen days before the interest falls due in New York; and if they fail to do so, it is the duty of the Bank to report the Company in default. As none have been reported, it is fair to presume that they have, up to this time, complied with the law in this respect. Now, if the Railroad Companies furnish the Bank with the money, and the current rate of exchange with ½ per cent commissions, fifteen days before the interest falls due in New York, could they not within that fifteen days just as easily purchase the exchange and transmit it themselves? It would cost them very little trouble to do so, and not one cent more than it costs them to make the payment through the instrumentality of the bank.

Therefore, in no point of view that I can conceive, is the bank necessary to the State, and from the foregoing it is evident that its capital could have been more profitably invested in any reliable six per cent securities, in the winding up of which there would have been no risk; but when you come to wind up the bank, and restore to the State the capital invested, it will require the work of years to accomplish it, and of course her depositors, note holders, &c., must be first paid, taking the most available of her assets; leaving the State to look to the most doubtful of her means with which to re-pay the capital.

For these and other reasons assigned, I am satisfied that it is impolitic for the State to issue bonds to increase the capital of the bank.

All of which is respectfully submitted to your consideration.

Isham G. Harris."

Each of the above Governors fared better in regard to recommending to the Legislature a call for a Constitutional Convention for amending the existing State Constitution, for a law [67] was passed authorizing the people to vote "Convention" or "No Convention" on the first Thursday in September, 1858.

Apparently there was little interest on the part of the people in the above election for the total vote polled amounted to only 27,619.[68] The vote was as follows:

For Convention—4,204
Against Convention—23,415

The contemporary newspapers gave scant comment on the election returns, some of them being content with a blanket statement to the effect that the call for a Constitutional Convention had been overwhelmingly

---

[67] *Acts of Tennessee*, 1857, Chapter 76.
[68] *Daily Union and American*, September 26, 1858.

defeated. Whether the call for a Constitutional Convention was defeated on account of the recommendations of Governor Harris must remain a mooted point. Governor Harris was alarmed at the size of the State debt, most of which had been incurred by State aid to private railroads and turnpike corporations. Though conjectural, it is highly probable that those vested interests pooled their strength in helping defeat the movement for a Constitutional Convention, for some of those corporations were in hard financial straits and doubtless did not desire to be prohibited from stretching their hands toward the Legislature for more financial soothing syrup.

As already indicated in this chapter, Governor Harris in his main Message to the Legislature restricted his recommendations to one single issue—that of dealing with the financial crisis that arose at the beginning of his administration. With the passage of a law dealing with the Bank of Tennessee, a State institution, the Legislature was left without further suggestions on the part of the Governor as to what additional legislation was deemed advisable. However, Governor Harris undoubtedly surmised that legislative consideration would be given to some of the recommendations offered by out-going Governor Andrew Johnson. Among Governor Johnson's numerous recommendations, one stands out pre-eminently as being near and dear to his heart—that of Law Reform. In his major Message of 1853, Johnson went into minute detail as to what he thought ought to be done in regard to revising the judicial system of the State.[69] Two years later, he repeated his former recommendation in almost the exact language of his former statement.[70] In his final Message to the Legislature in 1857, just a few days before the expiration of his term of office, once more he referred to "Law Reform" as being a highly desirable object, and expressed the hope that the Legislature would "conform their action to the popular will. [71]

But Governor Johnson had been faced with *political* handicaps during both of his administrations, in that he never had a Legislature *in toto* of his own political faith. But now (1857), the picture had changed. Both branches of the Legislature were Democratic, and further ignoring of judicial reform on the part of the Legislature would place the onus of failure on that party. With the Democrats in control of both the Executive and the Legislative branches of State Government, it behooved the Democrats to take action on the much-recommended issue. Any further dillydallying or pussyfooting would likely raise a political question of embarrassing nature. Some simplification and clarification of the Judicial System were almost universally admitted desirable by each political party. If nothing were done to effect judicial reform, the tantalizing query could and would be—"If not, *why* not?"

---

[69] See *Messages of the Governors of Tennessee*, Volume IV, 553–557.
[70] *Ibid.*, 642–646.
[71] *Ibid.*, 693.

With the prestige of two terms as Governor and his recent eleva-tion to the United States Senate, Andrew Johnson's continued insist-ence upon some improvement in the Judicial System could not easily or safely be brushed aside. The masses viewed Johnson as somewhat the embodiment of what later on Bliss Carman set forth in poetic form:

> "No fidget and no reformer, just
> A calm observer of ought and must."[72]

Inasmuch as there was nothing of "the lunatic fringe" in Johnson's judicial reform recommendation, the Legislature wisely and speedily decided to take some type of affirmative action. Three days after the delivery of Governor Johnson's Message to the Legislature, on Octo-ber 6, 1857, Senator J. B. Heiskell introduced the following resolution [73] which was passed immediately:

"Resolved, That a joint committee of both Houses shall be appointed, to consist of three members from the Senate, to meet such members as the House may appoint, to whom shall be committed the 'Code of Laws,' to be reported by the revisors heretofore appointed, with authority to examine the same in conjunction with said revisors."

On October 15, the House accepted the Senate Resolution and pro-vided for the appointment of five House members to serve with the Senate members.[74]

One reason for the long-overdue revision of the general laws of the State was on account of "an agreement to disagree" between Return J. Meigs and William F. Cooper who had been appointed by the Legis-lature in 1852 to revise and digest the general statutes. On October 12, 1857, Mr. Meigs submitted to the Legislature what he called "A Report to the General Assembly on the Revised Statutes." [75] In the introduction of the Report, Mr. Meigs stated that he and Mr. Cooper

" . . . had an interview and partitioned the work between us.
In conformity to that arrangement, I have revised the general Statutes belonging to my department, and digested them under the following heads. . . .
. . . I beg to conclude by saying that I shall hold myself in readiness, at all times during your session, to wait upon any committee to whom the revisal may be referred, and to perform any work or duty which it may be your pleasure to assign me."

But there was another "precinct to report!" On October 19, 1857, Mr. Cooper also submitted a "Report on the Revisal of the Statutes," [76]

---

[72] Carman, Bliss: *The Joys of the Road.*
[73] *Senate Journal*, 1857, 39.
[74] *House Journal*, 1857, 52.
[75] *Appendix*, 1857, 31–34.
[76] *Ibid.*, 187–196.

and his statement discloses that there had been a deep breach between the two eminent lawyers. According to Mr. Cooper, he had yielded to a plan proposed by Mr. Meigs who was "the elder and better head," and Mr. Cooper had spent fifteen months doing his allotted part of the work. Mr. Cooper advised Mr. Meigs that he (Cooper) was ready "to unite with him (Meigs) in throwing our material into a joint work." Mr. Meigs said that his engagements had been such that he had not prepared his part of the work and that it would be impossible for him to do so in time to submit the result of their labors to the General Assembly then about to convene.

Mr. Meigs, so it seems, had decided upon another plan of revisal in the meantime. Final agreement, however, was reached upon this revised plan and Mr. Cooper during the two ensuing years completed his part of the assignment. Mr. Meigs was notified by Mr. Cooper that the latter was ready with his part of the job and that it was time to get together and prepare the report for the General Assembly convening in 1855. Again, according to Mr. Cooper,

"Mr. Meigs assured me that his professional labors . . . his duties as State Librarian, and in other public capacities, had prevented him from proceeding with his part of the digest as fast as he had hoped, and that he could not cooperate with me until after the legislative session of that year. . . ."

Thereupon, Mr. Cooper, with full justification, let the cat out of the bag as to the difficulties encountered by him in an effort to work with Mr. Meigs upon the legislatively-assigned task. Let Mr. Cooper's own words state the situation as viewed by him:

" . . . During the next eighteen months I rewrote my part of the digest, and prepared material with a view to Assist Mr. Meigs in his part, should his engagements still prevent him from progressing so as to ensure the completion of the digest for the present General Assembly. Early this spring I proposed to him that we should spend the summer together in the joint work, and offered to aid and assist him in any part of his task, if he required it. For the first time, he intimated that he felt it was his duty to go over the whole of the statutes in the manner first proposed by him, and that he hoped to be able to complete this task sometime during the month of September, if he could get rid of the September courts, which he hoped to do through the courtesy of the bar; and that, until he had thus gone through with the statutes, he would not be prepared to cooperate with me in a joint work. I deeply regretted this view taken by Mr. Meigs of his duty, because it necessarily destroyed all hope of submitting to the present General Assembly a digest produced by our joint labors. It did more, it imposed upon me the task of going over the whole body of our laws; for, if it was his duty, it was mine also. Accordingly, I quit my business, retired into the country, and by writing from ten to twelve hours a day, succeeded in completing the digest which I now submit to your body. Mr. Meigs has not advised me of his progress, nor of his intentions, but I have felt it my duty no longer to delay a work so much needed by the profession and the people. I would gladly have been spared one half of the mere mechanical labor of preparing so large a work, and was anxious to share the responsibility with one so well qualified as the gentleman with whom I was associated. He will, doubtless, submit the result of his labors to the General Assembly."

On October 20, 1857, the Senate appointed three members to serve with five House members as a Joint Committee to confer with Messrs. Meigs and Cooper whose separate reports on codification had been filed with the Legislature. Inasmuch as this Joint Committee was called upon to perform a tremendous amount of highly important work, it seems fitting that their names should be handed down to posterity.

Senators	Counties Represented
Davis, W. P.	Bedford and Marshall
Heiskell, Joseph B.	Hawkins, Hancock, and Jefferson
Whitthorne, W. C.	Maury, Lewis, Hickman, and Dickson

Representatives	Counties Represented
Bate, Humphrey R.	Fayette, Tipton, and Shelby
Bicknell, S. T.	Blount
Bullock, Micajah	Carroll, Gibson, Madison, and Henry
Dunlap, W. C.	Shelby
Vaughan, Michael	Davidson

At an afternoon session on November 17, 1857, Senator Heiskell introduced Senate Bill No. 86, the same being a bill to revise the statutes of Tennessee. The Joint Select Committee on the Code, of which Senator Heiskell was Chairman, consulted from time to time with Messrs. Meigs and Cooper and then submitted to the Legislature in sections what eventually turned out to be the 1858 Code of Tennessee. From November 17, 1857 till March 22, 1858, the final day of adjournment, the proposed Code in some form or another was before the Legislature for consideration. With the frequency and monotony of circulating decimals in a table of logarithms a stereotyped expression was sprinkled during those four months throughout the pages of the two legislature *Journals*, to-wit:

" . . . Proceeded to the consideration of the special order, the reading of the Revised Code to revise the Statutes of Tennessee."

The *Senate Journal* alone carries eighty separate references to "the reading of the Revised Code!" The revisers and the Code Committee met practically every night, but the bulk of the Code was the work of Messrs. Meigs and Cooper. Less than one hundred sections of the Code were suggested or written by the members of the Joint Code Committee.[77] Two days before final adjournment of the Legislature, the Senate concurred in a House resolution to the effect that the names of Messrs. Heiskell, Bullock, and Bicknell should appear on the title page of the printed Code in recognition of the gigantic task performed by them. At length, the 1150 page tôme came from the press and, for the first time, Tennessee had adopted an official Code. Several compilations of the statutory laws had been printed prior to 1858, but that year marked the advent of the first official Code of Tennessee, there being a significant difference between a *compilation* and a *codification*. Perhaps the conservatism of Tennessee is nowhere more markedly etched in its entire history than in its reluctance to codify its statutory laws. Tennessee was sixty-two years old before its first official Code appeared in 1858; seventy-four more years were to pass before a second codification was approved, that of 1932.

For the past twelve years, 1845–1857, building of the State Capitol had been on the agenda of each legislative session. Usually, it was a question of more money being appropriated for carrying on the work. At long last, this session of 1857 proved to be an exception in that no appropriation was sought or deemed necessary, in that there was a considerable residue left over from the appropriation made in 1855. In order that the Legislature might be fully informed as to the exact status of the project, a detailed Report was filed near the beginning of the session. That Report, dated October 1, 1857, gives the completest figures of any report as to the cost of the Capitol Building, although determination of exact cost is impossible, in that the Report contains a considerable variable relating to the value of the convict labor that was employed. The Report [78] itself is, however, self-explanatory and extremely specific as to other details, to-wit:

---

[77] Letter of William F. Cooper, dated December 17, 1893, and quoted in the *History of Codification in Tennessee* by Samuel Cole Williams, 23.

Author's Note. In reality, the Code of 1858 was not a "Revised" Code, as was erroneously indicated by the caption of Chapter 177, Acts of 1858, reading as follows, "An Act to provide for the printing of the Revised Code." Mr. Cooper concluded his letter with the following interesting comment, to-wit:

"At first there was an impression among the members of the Legislature that I had not adhered closely to the wording of the existing statutes and had made many changes and additions in my revisal, and this impression has come back to Heiskell in his old age. For this reason frequent objections were made by members of both Houses when the sections of the revisal as read struck them as new, and, not being very familiar with the laws, much of it appeared strange to them. But when it was found, as soon it was, that both revisers had adhered rigidly to the existing statutes—Mr. Meigs almost literally, and I in substance; and when, moreover, some of the sections most fiercely objected to by particular members, were shown by Heiskell and Major Bullock to be literal copies, much to the confusion of the objectors and the amusement of their fellow-members, all discussion ceased, and the Code was merely read continuously, and passed nem. con.

Truly yours,
W. F. Cooper."

[78] *Appendix*, 1857, 275–280.

"Office of the Commissioners ⎫
For the Erection of the State Capitol. ⎬
October 1st, 1857.

To the Honorable the Legislature of Tennessee:

The undersigned, in behalf of the Board of Commissioners for the erection of the State Capitol, has the honor of Reporting

That at the date of his last statement of the expenditures and means of the Commission, there remained in the Treasury

An unexpended balance of	$ 54,337 96
Since which there has been received from the Bank of Tennessee proceeds of 80 State Bonds	73,100 37
Interest received on amount due the Board from Oct. 1st, 1855, until expended	1,039 37
And for surplus materials, tools (no longer useful) for Old Buildings sold, &c.,	2,238 98
Making a total of Receipts,	$130,716 31

Of which has been expended as follows:

Paid special appropriation to T. Shelton	$ 600 00	
To Penitentiary for work done	21,222 30	
Real Estate purchased to extend the Capitol grounds	42,150 00	
Furniture, fixtures, &c.,	7,431 66	
To Labor, Materials purchased, and Salaries	48,584 19	
And for incidental expenses not properly coming under either of the foregoing heads	3,329 88	
		123,318 03

Leaving unexpended from that portion of the last appropriation which has come into the Treasury of the Board, this Balance,	$7,398 28

By reference to the act of the last Legislature (chap. 268, page 555, Acts of 1855-6,) making an appropriation for the use of the Capitol Commissioners, it will be seen that the sum so appropriated was one hundred and fifty thousand dollars, for which the Bank of Tennessee was directed to pay the checks of the Commissioners; the Governor of the State being authorized to issue to the Bank, six per cent Coupon Bonds of the State to reimburse it for the amount thus paid to the Commissioners.

In the preceding statement of assets is found the following: 'From the Bank of Tennessee proceeds of 80 Bonds $73,100.' From statements by the Bank of Tennessee, it appears that this amount only has been allowed as a credit to the Board for 80 State Bonds deposited by the Governor, and from which it will be readily seen that by this process of scaling the value of Bonds, the appropriation has already been cut down in this one item to the extent of $6,900, and to what further extent the appropriation is liable to reduction must depend entirely on the value which the Bank may deem it expedient to place on the seventy State Bonds yet to be delivered.

So far as the pecuniary interest of the State is involved in this transaction it matters not—as what is lost to the Treasury of the Commissioners is made by the Bank.

The only objection this Board has to the process is, that it renders the amount of the appropriation unfixed and precarious, whilst it also seemingly swells the cost of work they have in charge.

The undersigned would, therefore, in behalf of his Board, respectfully suggest to your honorable body that by Resolution or otherwise, you give a fixed money value to the last appropriation, in order that the Commissioners may know to what extent they are authorized to contract for work yet to be done, and so relieve them from their present state of uncertainty as to the amount they have at command.

If the last appropriation be fixed by you as a cash one, then the means of the Commissioners may be thus stated:

Balance on hand as per statement,	$ 7,398 28
Amount of reduction made by Bank on 80 bonds,	6,900 00
(Which it is suggested to have refunded to the Commissioners.)	
Portion of last appropriation yet uncalled for	70,000 00
Making a total of	$84,298.28

applicable to the completion of the building, enclosing, and grading grounds, &c.

As regards the Capitol building proper, there remains comparatively little to be done for its final completion; the fitting up the Library Room; iron ballustering and hand rails to the private stairways, and to the top of the tower; together with some work yet to be done on the crypts, and the promenade, constitute the principal items of much cost; some further outlay in furniture for the offices, and for the Representatives' Hall, will be necessary.

For the heavy iron work necessary for the completion of the Library Room, for stairs, &c., I have asked for and received several bids, but none at prices which I deemed at all reasonable, and of course refused to accept either of them; hence the delay in having this part of the work executed.

I am inclined to the opinion, that, taking into view the large amount of this kind of iron work, including that necessary for enclosing the grounds, that has yet to be done, and the almost utter impossibility of having it satisfactorily executed by contract, it would be better to have it done on the spot by employing competent workmen at home, rather than give it out to contract, and especially to those living at a distance, who, in addition to their profits, would have to be paid a heavy amount for freights, and other charges of transportation. However, this is a subject on which more mature deliberation and consultation will be proper before determining what course will be most advantageous to be adopted for economically accomplishing the object in view.

Since the adjournment of the last Legislature, the public grounds on the north of the building have been extended by purchasing from several parties to the extent of 258 feet on High Street, (east,) the same number of feet on Vine Street, (west,) and 538 feet on Gay Street, (north;) making the present area of the public grounds a parallelogram of about 766 feet in length, with a breadth of 540 feet. Between the building, including the portico, the terrace, and the promenade on the west, there is less than 100 feet clear to the western boundary of the public grounds. This, it will be apparent to all, is a very contracted space for so large and so fine a building to stand in, and is a difficulty which I would respectfully commend to the consideration of your honorable body, as worthy of being remedied by the purchase of the half square immediately west of the Capitol, provided it can be procured on fair and reasonable terms, as most likely it can be at present. Should it be your pleasure to order the purchase of this land, or other grounds for the public use, an appropriation for that purpose will be necessary, as will be one for enclosing and grading the same. As to the amount necessary for the latter purpose, much will depend on the rapidity with which you may desire it to be done. I feel satisfied, however, that the grounds cannot be economically and properly graded until the enclosure is partially completed, nor until the city finally determines on the grade of the streets surrounding the Capitol enclosure.

Finding that the services of an Architect were no longer necessary, the Board, on the 1st of May last, dispensed with the services of that officer, and now retain as salaried officers only a Secretary, (who also performs the duties of General Superintendent,) and one Superintendent of work; to each of these officers an annual salary of $1,200 is paid.

With the Secretary of the Board will be found ready for inspection, at all times, a detailed statement, showing each item of expenditure made by the Board from its first organization to the present day, to which your Committee is referred for more minute information than properly can be put in this report: an examination of the same is respectfully asked for.

It affords the undersigned no small degree of satisfaction to be able to report that every individual in the employment of the Board, has honestly, industriously, and faithfully performed his whole duty to the State. For the entire cost of the building, up to the present day, including work performed by the convicts, I refer you to the annexed statement, furnished by the Secretary of the Board.

In making his estimate of the value of the convicts' labor, it may be well to state that the cost of keeping and supporting the convicts is arrived at from a statement furnished by the late Dr. John S. Young, who, at the time of making the report alluded to, was one of the inspectors of the prison.

All of which is respectfully submitted by

S. R. MORGAN,
President, &c."

"To SAMUEL D. MORGAN, ESQ.,
    President of the Board of Commissioners of State Capitol:

Sir:—In reply to your interrogatory: 'What is the entire cost of building the Capitol, from its commencement, Jan. 3, 1845, to this date, October 1, 1857,' I would respectfully state:

There has been received from all sources, by the Board of Commissioners from its commencement to the present day the sum of

$835,262 60

Disbursed as follows:

On the Capitol Building	$711,367 59
T. Shelton Special Appropriation	600 00
Real Estate purchased	42,150 00
Interest account paid Bank of Tennessee	8,822 99
Furniture and Decoration	23,701 44
Penitentiary	41,222 30
Balance on hand	$ 7,398 28

$835,262 60

Above we find expended on the Capitol Building proper $711,367 59
Add to which the actual cost to the State of the Penitentiary labor employed, say for 120 Convicts, to which
   we were entitled by Acts of 1845–6, chap. 49, say 120
   hands at $76 00 per annum for ten years, is   91,200 00
                                                   ————————
                                             $802,567 59

And we find the entire cost of the Capitol Building to be $802,567.59.

You will perceive a very material discrepancy exists between the charges made by the Penitentiary for work done on the Capitol, say $363,072 12, and the credit which I give that Institution for the same work, say $91,200.

In estimating the actual cost to the State of erecting the Capitol, I contend that the State should be charged by her own institution, (the Penitentiary) only with the cost of the labor thus employed, and not with quadrupled profits thereon.

The estimate of that labor in this calculation is one made by a former inspector of that institution, who from its books and vouchers ascertained the actual cost to the State for maintenance of each Convict, together with his pro rata of the entire general expenses of the Institution, and such in my opinion should be the charge against the State for the labor of the Penitentiary expended on the State Capitol.

                                      Respectfully, Sir,
                                      Your ob't servant,
                                      JAMES PLUNKET, *Secretary*.
Nashville, Oct. 1st, 1857.
The Board of Commissioners consists of
                    Samuel D. Morgan, *President.*
                             Gov. I. G. Harris,
                             Allen A. Hall,
                             Jacob McGavock,
                             James P. Clark,
                             James Woods,
                             Return J. Meigs,
                             John Campbell,
                             Dr. J. D. Winston."

The ever-recurring liquor question bobbed up in the 1857 Legislature in the form of nine liquor bills in the House of Representatives and seven in the Senate. Curiously enough, and quite in contrast with many previous legislative sessions, not a single petition was filed before the 1857 Legislature on the liquor problem. Scrutiny of the 1857 legislative *Journals* and contemporary newspapers discloses that the usual emotional and near-hysterical pleas were absent. The various bills, as a rule, dealt with some projected change in rates of taxation and methods of distribution. The only bill to run the legislative gamut was Senate Bill No. 55, introduced by Senator John C. Burch, Speaker of the Senate. The caption of the bill [79] was entitled "An Act to establish the Tippling Law."

—————
[79] *Senate Journal*, 1857, 100.

Tennessee's liquor-legislation is a bit complicated and perhaps an explanatory word is apropos. In the two generations from her admission to the Union till the outbreak of the War Between the States, Tennessee tried out a number of solutions of the vexatious liquor problem. None of the remedies proved entirely satisfactory. From 1796 to 1831, the retailing of spirituous liquors was restricted to "places of public entertainment"—variously described as ordinary, tavern, inn, hotel. From 1831 to 1838, so-called tippling houses after payment of a small licensing fee were also permitted to sell liquor. From 1838 to 1846, an effort was made to abolish retailing altogether, the legal provision being that it was unlawful to sell in quantities less than a quart which liquor could not be consumed on the premises where the liquor had been sold. From 1846 to 1856, a return was made to the former general licensing system with the licensing fee increased. For two years, 1856-1857, a return was made to the "quart law," but late in 1857 the State restored the former general licensing system by reviving the law [80] of 1845-46. Reliable statistics are not available to support any one of the above provisions governing the sale of spirituous liquors as to which statute was the more effective. It is perhaps safe to say that none of the various laws was particularly effective in curbing the sale of intoxicating beverages, for no law at the time had the backing of a powerful public sentiment. The continuous agitation of the liquor question during the above period of more than half a century is at least evidence of the growing consciousness that there existed the belief that the sale and use of liquor constituted a "social evil" that needed restraining influences.

In full support of the position taken by his predecessor, Andrew Johnson, Governor Harris strongly recommended that a halt be made in the matter of lending State aid to Internal Improvements consisting largely of railroads and turnpikes. In concurrence with that recommendation, the 1857 Legislature refrained from making any appropriations for such purposes, contenting itself with merely modifying the existing charters of some thirty-eight railroads and one hundred and twenty-six turnpikes.[81] Those modifications related in part to extension of time, change in name of corporation, consolidations of actual or projected lines, and changes in rates of toll. But in all the legislation pertaining to these agencies not one dollar of State aid was voted at that legislative session—a radical departure indeed from preceding sessions. On the final day of the session, the following self-explanatory Report [82] of the Committee on Internal Improvements was submitted, to-wit:

"MR. SPEAKER:

I beg leave to submit the following report from the Committee on Internal Improvements, showing the amount of State aid saved by the present

[80] *Acts of Tennessee*, 1857, Chapter 16.
[81] *Acts of Tennessee*, 1857, Index, 441–445.
[82] *House Journal*, 1857, 889–890.

Legislature, by cutting off aid from Railroad Companies that have not commenced work, and by the consolidation of various companies that have commenced work:

By consolidating the Memphis and Ohio with the Memphis, Clarksville and Louisville Railroad Company, 130 miles of State aid is cut off, at $10,000 per mile,	$1,300,000
By consolidating the latter company with the Nashville and Northwestern Railroad Company, distance cut off 45 miles, at $10,000 per mile,	450,000
By repealing the law granting State aid from Paris to the mouth of Sandy, on the Tennessee river, 20 miles,	200,000
Bridge aid cut off from Memphis, Clarksville, and Louisville Railroad Company	100,000
By stopping the Tennessee and Alabama Road, at Mount Pleasant, 89 miles, including the branch to Lawrenceburg, at $10,000 per mile; including also $130,000 bridge aid,	1,020,000
The Nashville and Cincinnati Company, length of road in Tennessee, 100 miles, with aid by State at $10,000 per mile,	1,000,000
Bridge aid across Cumberland,	100,000
By transferring State aid from the North to the South side of the Tennessee river, between Stevenson and Chattanooga,	195,000
By reducing State aid on Tennessee Central Railroad, one thousand dollars per mile for 35½ miles,	35,500
By refusing to extend the time to commence the Atlantic, Tennessee and Ohio Railroad Company, which cuts off the State liability, 47 miles, at $10,000 per mile,	470,000
By refusing to extend the time to the Mississippi Central, and Tennessee extention from Jackson to Tennessee river, 61 miles, at $10,000 per mile,	610,000
	$5,480,500

Showing that the gross amount saved by the present session of the Legislature, to be five million four hundred and eighty thousand five hundred dollars, (5,480,500,) which should be deducted from the prospective State liabilities. Not one dollar of new aid for Internal Improvements, has been granted at the present session; nor has one new State bond been authorized to issue for any purpose whatever; and at the same time, while this immense amount of saving has been done by consolidations, many parallel roads have been cut off, making all the roads of importance, main lines, which will insure success to the one road, while if left separate, as provided heretofore, would have created much confusion and annoyance, not only to the companies, but to the State.

And your committee think that much has been done to reform your system of Internal Improvements, and to check the issuance of additional bonds for any purpose whatever.

All of which is respectfully submitted,

TAZ. W. NEWMAN,

Chairman Committee on Internal Improvements."

With some hope of keeping better tab on the railroad business, especially as relating to the financial status of the roads receiving State aid, a law [83] had been enacted providing for the appointment of a Commissioner of Railroads whose duty it was to check carefully into the financial condition of such roads as had been recipients of financial aid from the State. In his Report [84] on October 19, 1857, Road Commissioner R. G. Payne advised the Legislature of the difficulties encountered by him in trying to get reports from the various railroads. Although the law required all such companies to submit reports sixty days prior to the convening of the Legislature, "in no instance has this been done," according to Mr. Payne's statement. In the same report, the Road Commissioner pointed out that State aid and obligations granted or pledged to Railroads exceeded nineteen million dollars, but that there were at the time only 635 miles of finished railroad lines in the entire State. For a number of years the clamor had been for railroads, and various Legislatures had complied by making the necessary means largely available through State aid in the form of coupon bonds. It seems that not a great deal of thought had been given to the "pay-off" which would eventually have to be faced. Lavish State appropriations had been apparently voted on the basis mentioned in 1876 by "Marse Henry" in his famous editorial [85] on *Financial Bugaboos*. Marse Henry reminded his readers of the old "Georgia Cracker" who wanted "to stamp as much money as folks could spend." When asked how it could be redeemed, the naive reply was: "That's just what I'm coming to: I'm ag'in redemption."

Return Jonathan Meigs, the State's first librarian, submitted a concise but definitive report [86] to the Legislature regarding the status of the State Library which had been in existence only three years. With an appropriation in 1854 of five thousand dollars, Mr. Meigs had purchased a nucleus of books for the beginning of a Library which was badly needed at the time. In his report, Mr. Meigs made a number of interesting observations. While the Library was not of the "circulating" variety, yet it seems that the members of the Legislature viewed the matter differently. At any rate, the Librarian stated that during the preceding session of the Legislature twenty-six volumes had been taken out by legislators and had not been returned, necessitating their repurchase. Meticulous detail regarding the expenditure of the appropriated fund was gone into, even including such items as freight on books and maps, insurance on books amounting to $2.48, and two registered letters amounting to forty cents. According to the Biennial Report, the Librarian had left on hand in 1857 the sum of $6.92.

Mr. Meigs pleaded for a larger appropriation for the support of the

---

[83] *Acts of Tennessee*, 1855, Chapter 58.
[84] *Appendix*, 1857, 37–46.
[85] Krock, Arthur: *The Editorials of Henry Watterson*, 50–51.
[86] Appendix, 1857, 241–251.

Library "so as to forestall the sneers of visitors from some of our sister States who look upon our collection with contempt, on account of its diminutive size." One of the most interesting observations made by Mr. Meigs was his idea as to how books in a library should be classified. He reduced the whole subject of books to three categories as regards classification. "Let the first division comprise books that relate to the earth; the second division, books that relate to man here; the third division, those that relate to man hereafter!"

The plea for an increased appropriation of funds met with a legislative response [87] that was not only disgraceful but positively insulting, to-wit:

"Be it enacted, That the unappropriated tax, levied in the act for the benefit of the Lunatic Asylum, passed at the present session of the Legislature, be, and is hereby given to the Librarian of the State for the next two years, for the purpose of increasing the collection of books in the State Library."

When Mr. Meigs glued his optics upon the act [88] passed "for the benefit of the Hospital for the Insane" he was greeted with this bonanza:

"Be it enacted by the General Assembly of the State of Tennessee, That the annual tax of one and a half cents, allowed by the act passed February 7, 1856, chapter 146, be reduced to nine-sixteenth of a cent on the hundred dollars, annually for the next two years; and that eight-sixteenths of the proceeds of said tax be applied by the trustees of said institution to finishing said institution and improving the grounds attached thereto, and for such other purposes as the majority of said trustees may direct for the benefit of said institution."

Two years later, in his Biennial Report [89] for 1857-59, Mr. Meigs reported that the provisions of the above act had produced the sum of $3,882.34 for the two-year period. This was far short of the $15,000 which he had originally requested for the purchase of additional books for the State Library.

A lengthy and detailed report [90] on the Penitentiary was submitted for the biennial period, 1855-1857, by the Agent and Keeper, Richard White. Statistical data in the report set forth various facts regarding the number of prisoners in confinement, amounting to two hundred and eighty-six; number of prisoners discharged by expiration of term, twenty-nine; number of convicts pardoned by the Governor under the provisions of the Act of 1836, Chapter 63, amounting to eighty-one; number of prisoners pardoned under other provisions of law, including three prisoners pardoned by President of the United States, twenty-four; and number of deaths, amounting to sixteen. Table Number 6

---

[87] *Acts of Tennessee*, 1857, Section 14, Chapter 151.
[88] *Ibid.*, Chapter 54.
[89] *Public Documents, Tennessee Legislature*, 1859–1860, 146.
[90] *Appendix*, 1857, 73–117.

exhibited statistics on the entire prison population regarding name, nativity, age, place where convicted, term of sentence, nature of crime committed, occupation prior to conviction, and the occupation in prison. The ages of the convicts ranged from fifteen years to seventy. One hundred and thirty of the convicts had been married; thirty-two were either widows or widowers; and one hundred and twenty-four had never married. Fifty-six could neither read nor write, while four had received a "classical education." One hundred and twenty-eight were classified as having been "moderate drinkers," and one hundred and twenty-five were listed as "intemperate." Thirty-three were denominated "temperate." Crimes ranged all the way from murder, larceny, and "Negro stealing" down to bigamy, forgery, counterfeiting, and "drawing an 'Arkansas Toothpick'." Prison terms were from life to one year. Shelby County led off with having contributed fifty prisoners, while Davidson County had sent up thirty-one. Among the occupations prior to conviction, one hundred and five gave "no occupation"; the next largest number had been laborers, amounting to eighty-one; fifteen had been shoemakers; fourteen were blacksmiths, and twelve had been carpenters. Among the convicts were four physicians, three brick masons, and one each of jeweller, stage driver, saddler, butcher, sailor, and sugar refiner.

The Penitentiary official called attention to the inadequacy of the prison facilities, stressing the over-crowded condition. Dr. Felix Robertson, the prison physician, stated that proper ventilation of the cells was impossible, and that the over-crowded conditions constituted a health menace. The cells, or "dormitories" as they were called by Dr. Robertson, were seven feet and six inches long, three feet and six inches wide, and seven feet high. Into some of these cells two prisoners were at times thrust. Small wonder that the physician urged remedial work on the prison situation without delay. Strong recommendations were submitted by the Agent and Keeper of the Penitentiary that the old nine-acre site be salvaged and that a suitable location of two hundred acres be purchased along the Cumberland River somewhere in the neighborhood of three or four miles from Nashville. His position was supported by the following report,[91] one member of the committee being Governor Isham G. Harris himself:

"Nashville, March 4, 1858.

GENTLEMEN OF THE SENATE AND HOUSE OF REPRESENTATIVES:

The undersigned having had under consideration the questions submitted by joint resolution, No. 135,

REPORT:

That from such information as they have been able to elicit, the nine acres of land upon which the State Prison is located, with the buildings

---

[91] *Senate Journal*, 1857, 677–678.

and building materials thereto belonging, would command upon the market $25,000.

That lands on the South side of Cumberland River, ranging from two to three miles of the city of Nashville, will cost from two hundred and fifty to four hundred dollars per acre. And on the North side of the river, about the same distance from the city, from eighty to two hundred and fifty dollars per acre.

It is impossible for the undersigned to report the probable cost of constructing suitable buildings and walls, &c., for a new prison, without submitting a general plan to an Architect, and having estimates, &c., and as the resolution indicates no general plan, we have been unable to fix an estimate.

We are of opinion that the labor of constructing new Prison Buildings or enlarging the present buildings can be performed by the convicts without materially interfering with the mechanical trades in the Prison, as now carried on, especially so soon as the labor of the 120 hands now appropriated to the work of the State Capitol, can be made available.

The undersigned all concur in the opinion, that the enlargement of the present Prison, or the building of a new one is indispensably necessary.

The present number of convicts is 308, while there are only 232 cells, each cell suited to the accommodation of only one person; and the number of convicts is constantly and rapidly increasing.

The convicts cannot be so profitably employed as they might be, if additional shops were built, &c.

All of which is respectfully submitted.

ISHAM G. HARRIS,
W. G. HARDING,
JNO. D. WINSTON."

As was the usual custom, biennial reports from other State departments were transmitted to the Legislature, among which were Reports from the School for the Blind, School for the Deaf and Dumb, Hospital for the Insane, Bank of Tennessee, State Geologist, State Comptroller, State Treasurer, and three institutions of higher learning, namely, East Tennessee University, West Tennessee College, and University of Nashville. In addition, there were included in the 1857 *Appendix* 588 printed pages representing the *Second Biennial Report of the Tennessee State Agricultural Bureau*. Unfortunately, space limitations prohibit inclusion of detailed items as set forth in these official reports.[92]

---

[92] *Appendix*, 1857.

Author's note. The *Appendix* contains overall 988 pages, of which 588 pages deal with the transactions of the State Agricultural Bureau, the State Fair, Division Fairs, and County Fairs. Ten thousand copies of the Agricultural Report were ordered to be printed and distributed at State expense. By studying these various official Reports, a comprehensive bird's-eye view of the State's economic, industrial, and agricultural condition may be procured. For example, the following summary from the State Comptroller's Report throws a world of light upon certain basic factors in the State's economy:

	Acres of Land	Value of Land	Value of Town Lots	Number of Slaves	Value of Slaves
East Tennessee	8,369,787	$31,860,018	$ 2,895,223	11,862	$ 7,480,920
Middle Tennessee	10,425,842	69,871,674	12,798,812	63,407	42,069,296
West Tennessee	6,567,097	37,646,650	11,345,530	44,019	32,769,507

The Thirty-Second General Assembly concluded its deliberations on March 22, 1858, after having been in session almost six months. The prolonged length of the session was largely due to the tremendous amount of time necessary for the reading and consideration of the Code, the first codification of laws ever made in Tennessee. Examination of personal data [93] regarding the membership discloses the following interesting facts. Of the seventy-five House members, forty-eight were married, twenty-four were single, and three were widowers. The average age was thirty-six years, with a range from twenty-two to fifty-nine. Two members were fifty-nine, W. C. Dunlap of Shelby and Joseph L. Ewing of Davidson. Three members were just twenty-two, their names being James Fulton of Lincoln, E. E. Harney of Giles, and James G. Rose representing Hancock, Hawkins, Jefferson, and Greene. With regard to occupations, the odds were even, with thirty lawyers being offset by the same number of farmers. There were six merchants and four physicians. The remainder of the ranks was filled by one each as follows, tanner, dentist, tailor, school teacher, and bricklayer.

Of the twenty-five Senators, twenty were married, three were single, and two were widowers. The average age was thirty-seven years, Mr. Speaker Burch, who was thirty, being the youngest member. The oldest member, who was fifty-three, was Senator F. H. Bratcher of Campbell County. As to occupations, the lawyers led off with thirteen members, followed by the farmers who numbered ten. The remainder consisted of one merchant and one physician.

The three major legislative measures enacted by the 1857 Legislature were (1) the Act of January 28, 1858, whereby the Free Banking System was repealed to such an extent as to deny any future banking organizations to be operative under this law that had ushered in a lot of "wildcat" banks; (2) the passage of the legislation approving the "Code of 1858"; and (3) the refusal to appropriate any further State aid to Internal Improvements, the latter action being based upon the pre-election pledges of candidates for the Legislature. This latter movement put an end, for the time being, to the orgy of voting State aid to numerous unnecessary and unsound enterprises that had placed the State in a precarious financial condition.

There is a dearth of contemporary evidence, in the official *Journals* and newspapers, relating the "horse-play" tactics on the part of the Legislature. Most of the members appear to have been substantial citizens with a minimum of personal and political axes to grind. Perhaps the following excerpt [94] from the official records constitutes valid testimony that Representative W. P. Kendrick of Wayne County yearned for a bit of head-line publicity in the contemporary press:

---

[93] *Legislative Union and American*, 1857, 32–33.
[94] *House Journal*, 1857, 248–249.

"Whereas, all forms of business and rules of order for the great principles of freedom and reform as promulgated at this day and time, manifestly have a tendency to prevent and impede the giant strides of Young America, and that the same operates often as a check upon the talent and genius of members of this House, which for their own future prospects, and the enlightenment of the country, should be allowed

'To stray unbidden forth.'

Whereas also, that the time taken up by members of this House, in frequent discussions, although costing the State a large sum of money daily, is insignificant, compared with the incalculable benefits resulting to the country from the light that these luminaries throw forth upon this benighted land of ours. Therefore, be it,

Resolved, That the aforesaid forms of business, and rules of order, be, and the same are hereby abolished; and that hereafter a petition, resolution or bill may be taken up, and acted upon by this House at any time they may see proper.

And be it further resolved, That the right of free speech is an inalienable right, and a fundamental doctrine of our glorious government, and the opposite, in the language of another, is a fundamental absurdity; and that, hereafter, each and every member of this House shall be permitted to speak as often as he desires upon any and all subjects, and shall not be confined to the subject under discussion, should he be disposed to 'loom out.'

Further resolved, That not more than two members shall be allowed to occupy the floor at one and the same time, except when in Committee of the Whole, when all shall be allowed to speak."

On Monday morning, March 22, 1858, after certain routine measures had been carried out, the legislative wheels came to a stop. Mr. Speaker of the House, D. S. Donelson of Sumner County, bade his comrades adieu, concluding his valedictory with the following:[95]

"We have, at length, after an unusually long and laborious session, reached a point when we must separate; the bosom of every member present, is buoyant with joy, at the bare mention of the fact, that the time is close at hand when he will join family and friends; but, this joyous feeling cannot be altogether unmixed, when the mind recurs to the fact, that we shall never *all* meet again; though now in fine health, the grave will shortly close over the forms of some of us. In a short time this Hall, where all has been excitement in the conflict for favorite measures, will be hushed, these seats will be vacated; some will doubtless return to occupy them two years hence; others obtain higher political positions; perhaps the greater portion seek repose in private life, where alone is to be found that true happiness, which may be looked for in vain in political life. Such is the destiny of man.

I now pronounce this House adjourned, *sine die.*"

Youthful Speaker of the Senate, John C. Burch, representing the counties of Rhea, Bledsoe, Bradley, Hamilton, and Marion, regaled his hearers with this graceful parting word:[96]

---

[95] *House Journal,* 1857, 894–896.
[96] *Senate Journal,* 1857, 848–849.

"SENATORS: The hour has come when we must part. How pleasing the anticipation of again mingling with a confiding constituency, and participating in the endearments of the domestic circle. And yet how painfully, mournfully sad the reflection, that this parting will forever sever the bonds which have so pleasantly bound us together.

Long years of joy or sorrow may come, but so agreeable has been the intercourse of the individual members of this Senate, that no Lethe in life can drown the happy recollections of our association. When your partiality assigned me this distinguished position, I placed my reliance for the successful discharge of my duties upon your cordial co-operation. The result has shown the full realization of my most exacting anticipations. Whatever of success has followed my efforts in preserving harmony, and properly enforcing the rules adopted to govern in your deliberations, is due more to your own intelligence and amenity of disposition, than to any ability of mine. It was natural to expect that in the conflict of opinion which would arise in the discussion of measures, both of local and general legislation, and particularly in the discussion of questions of a political caste, that there would be some manifestations of excited feeling. In the excitement of debate, some momentary evidences of bitterness would not have been unnatural. But our session has passed like the May-month, all brightness, rather than like an April day, commingling sunshine and storm.

Some of us may again set within these massive walls, clothed in the robes of office, but many Senates will meet and many Senates will adjourn, before there will be a legislative session more agreeable to its members than I feel the present has been to each and all of us. The kindest wish that I could express for the people of Tennessee, would be that the laws which we have enacted, may prove as beneficial to them as our intercourse has been agreeable to us.

Our State, 'the land of beauty and of grandeur,' possesses all the elements to make her great in manufactures, and great in commerce—elements which need but the fostering care of discreet legislation, to make her the proudest of a sisterhood of equals. Whether our labors here shall prove to be for her weal or woe, I feel assured that each and every Senator will concede to his associates purity and patriotism of purpose. If the test of time shall demonstrate that there are errors in our legislation, let them be attributed to the erring judgment of man, not to the absence of proper impulses in the Senator.

Our session has been something longer than either of the last two, but the revisal of our entire Code of Laws, the Herculean labor of the session, which has been so long and so much needed, and which will stand a monument of the industry and energy of those who have superintended the revision, and the unusual importance of the measures disposed of by us, it is to be hoped, will prove a satisfactory apology to a generous constituency for our protracted stay.

For the kind and courteous manner in which you have yielded to the decisions of the Chair, and for the flattering testimonial of your appreciation of my official conduct, which you have placed upon the Journals of the Senate, I tender you the assurances of my unceasing gratitude. The fact that there has not been during the entire session an appeal from a decision of the Chair, (which you have so kindly alluded to in your complimentary resolutions) while it is the highest compliment which could be paid to a presiding officer, is attributable to your urbanity rather than to the universal correctness of those decisions. While memory dwells within the chambers of my brain, your energy and watchfulness as Senators, your kindness and courtesy as gentlemen will live fresh within my recollection.

> 'Let fate do her worst, there are relics of joy,
> Bright dreams of the past she cannot destroy,
> Which come in the night time of sorrow and care
> 'And bring back the features which joy used to wear.'

In after years, may the scenes through which we, as a Senate, have passed, be to us individually such 'relics of joy,' such 'bright dreams of the past.'

And now with saddened heart, I make the last announcement: THE SENATE STANDS ADJOURNED *sine die*.

                                        J. C. BURCH,
                                Speaker of the Senate.
C. STONE,
Clerk of the Senate."

With the Thirty-Second General Assembly out of the way and its deliberations a matter of history, there was a political armistice for approximately one year from the day of its adjournment on March 22, 1858. During that year, Governor Harris attended to the routine duties of the office and unquestionably girded his loins for another forthcoming political contest with the opposing forces which desired to place in the executive chair a man of different political faith.

On February 18, 1859, a rampant Whig journal expressed high approval of the "remarkable unanimity in many counties with reference to the approaching State Convention." [97] The State Convention alluded to would be composed of those who opposed the incumbent Democratic regime, including of course Governor Isham G. Harris. The "outs" were hard pressed for a suitable name, inasmuch as the Whig Party was to all intents and purposes dead, and its offspring, the Know Nothings, had been all but annihilated in the preceding gubernatorial race in Tennessee. They were confronted with the dilemma that puzzled Romeo and Juliet:

"What's in a name?"

The down-and-outers, remembering the political defeats of the recent past and the emergencies of the present, were in the same category as Bunyan's pilgrims who halted at Doubting Castle. Under *what name* should the opposing political forces be resurrected, mustered, organized, and pepped-up for the oncoming gubernatorial and congressional battles in Tennessee? In a rather exultant manner, a strong Democratic party organ [98] chided the efforts of the anti-Democrats to dig up some sort of name that would act as a talisman to lure the strays and malcontents into their fold. At the same time, it was pointed out that the personnel of any new-fangled party would be in its essence composed of

---

[97] *Republican Banner*, February 18, 1859.
[98] *Nashville Union and American*, February 20, 1859.

the remnants of the Whigs and the more recent Know Nothings. In keeping with that line of reasoning, the following diagnosis was proffered:

"THE OLD PARTY WITH ITS NEW NAME.

It is really amusing to read the proceedings of the so called 'Opposition' meetings that the Know Nothings are now holding in the different counties in Tennessee to appoint delegates to their State Convention.

First, who is it that are holding these meetings? This is a matter so plain to the understanding of every one that it would be useless to ask such a question; and yet it is evident that those who get them up are guilty of the egregious folly of endeavoring to conceal the fact, and cheat the public as to their own identity. For instance, for the last two canvasses there have been but two parties in Tennessee, Democrats and Know Nothings. They marshalled under their respective banners, and were thus designated. No change in the organization of parties in this State has taken place since that time. In politics we are now just what we were then. There may be some who, disappointed in their expectations of getting favors with the Democracy, will in another election vote with their opponents. There may be Know Nothings who, disgusted with so contemptible a cheat, are ready to join the Democrats. Some changes in the membership of parties are constantly taking place. But the two parties that divide the people of the State are, in fact, the same to-day that they were in the last election, except that Know Nothingism has grown wonderfully less and Democracy proportionably stronger. But the Know Nothings would fain create a different impression; not by open declaration so much as by indirect action. In proof of this, we no longer hear of 'the great American party,' about which they boasted so lustily in the last canvass. They are as loth to speak of it as a man is of his disreputable ancestors. They would be glad to have the world believe they sprung from a different race—that they never knew Sam. They have ceased to call themselves 'Americans'; Their newspapers speak only of the 'Opposition.' It is customary about this time, preceding every State election, for Conventions to nominate candidates for Governor. The Democrats have called theirs, and *another* party have called theirs; but one may look through all the papers in the State and see no reckoning of an *American Convention*. Meetings are being held in the various counties of the State to appoint delegates to attend these two Conventions, but we see no account of 'American' meetings. In Shelby, Monroe and some other counties they designate themselves as a meeting of the *Whigs*. In all the rest they are called 'Opposition' meetings. These, the Whig and Opposition, are new parties—the last a bran new party. When 'Americanism' was ushered into existence they told us the Whig party was dead. Now we are informed that old fashioned Whiggery is alive, and that Know Nothing is dead.

But what of this other part of the new party, the 'Opposition?' What is it, and where did it come from? Who fathers it, or does it belong to that unfortunate class of bantlings who never know their fathers? What credentials does it bring as evidence that it is worthy of credit? May it not be an imposter or a clown? These are questions that should be answered; and we call on gentlemen who are now trying to introduce it into genteel society to answer them. The entire public are willing to hear.

In the mean time, we will indulge in some speculations about this new party, that puts itself forward with such arrogant pretensions, under the convenient cognomen of 'the Opposition.' In our opinion it is a humbug; a silly pretense; a clownish disguise; a questionable character in borrowed clothes, that instead of concealing, serve only to expose the hideous deformity beneath. In other words, the new party is nothing but the old party—Know Nothingism under an assumed name. The only thing about it new is its *tricks*. We shall hear no more of the blue book—the rituals, the oaths, and *the dollar* that was paid in. In future it will be an insult to mention these. Nor will we hear much of their intense love for the 'native born,' and their earnest appeals to 'put none but Americans on guard.' The Pope still sits upon the Vatican and thunders forth his bulls, but we will hear no more of the dangers of his inquisitorial power in this country. Oppressed humanity in the old world still keeps an anxious look to the beacon of hope which beckons them across the waters; and pilgrims and emigrants are still landing by thousands on our shores, but we shall no longer hear them spoken of as the 'paupers and criminals of Europe unworthy the privileges of freemen.' These were the old tricks and they have served their turn. New ones must take their places. What they are to be the future will develop; but the motive that influences the change of name is two-fold; First, to escape the odium which justly attaches to the old ones, and makes its very touch contamination. Secondly, to deceive the unwary with the idea that there is in Tennessee a class of voters opposed to Democracy, other than those who have heretofore marshalled under the banner of the so called American party.

The name itself has a foreign origin. Like Know Nothingism, it was coined by the Abolitionists of the North. There it was used, with some propriety, as representing the combined forces of Abolitionism and Know Nothingism, in their joint efforts to beat down the National Democracy. It can be used for no such purpose here, unless similar elements exist at the South. There is but one other reason we can conceive of, which is, that Know Nothingism in the South may be regarded as joined to, and an integral part of that same combination of Abolitionists and Know Nothings at the North that have been making common cause of late to break down the only party in that fanatical section who are loyal to the Union and willing to observe the rights and honor of the slave-holding States.

Away with such a party. It is unworthy of any age or country. It is an insult to the intelligence of the people. It can only serve to encourage the hope of fanaticism at the North, increase the dissentions in the country, and be a political lazar-house for disaffected, reckless and adventurous politicians. The people will trample it under their feet."

The Democratic State Convention met in Nashville on March 17, 1859 for the purpose of adopting a platform and nominating a candidate for the gubernatorial chair. If the delegates upon their arrival in Nashville read the newspaper that day, their eyes fell upon the following editorial [99] which characterized the Democratic Party as being the *Imposition* Party:

"DEMOCRATIC STATE CONVENTION.

The 'white spirits and black' which constitute the motley, hybred and many-faced Imposition party, formerly known as Democracy, are to assemble in State Convention in this city to day, to put GOV. HARRIS upon

---

[99] *Republican Banner*, March 17, 1859.

the track for a second race, and attempt to reconcile the conflicting opinions among their people, to whitewash the glaring corruptions and frauds, the responsibility of which rests upon their shoulders, and generally seek to mingle and commingle antagonistic elements, in order to make one more fight for the spoils. The work will tax even the resources of the Imposition, so fertile in expedients to humbug the people and secure place and position. The distractions are so palpable, the feuds so apparently irreconcilable, and the separating chasm so wide and fearful, that the work of closing up will be found a herculean labor.

We expect to find nothing in their platform to approve. In a national point of view, as the friends and representatives of the present inefficient, corrupt and wasteful Administration, they must necessarily take grounds which the people cannot sustain. The condition of the country during Mr. FILLMORE'S Administration, and at its close, as contrasted with its condition since the accession of PIERCE and BUCHANAN—its bankrupt condition now—are enough to satisfy every reflecting man that the Imposition party have neither the ability nor the integrity, the patriotism or the policy, to manage the affairs of this Government. And, therefore, we say we expect nothing from them, in a national point of view, that will physic the disease of the times.

In State politics, the leading issue of the canvass will be the currency. We are interested deeply in what they will say on this question. We beg of them to take a position upon principle; one susceptible of a fair definition and explanation, and one which the people can understand. Let it be either fish, or flesh, or fowl. Anything but a two-faced specimen of imposition, to ring like gold in one place and fold up like a bank note in another. Such a position is unworthy of a 'great party,' and if our friends in this Convention are induced to pursue it, they will doubly disgrace themselves, commit political suicide, and deprive us of the pleasure of killing them in a genteel, sportsmanlike way. . . ."

The Democratic Convention was all set for a calm and frictionless meeting. The list of county delegates was unusually large and appeared quite enthusiastic. Colonel John K. Howard of Wilson County was elected Chairman without opposition, and two delegates from each Congressional District composed the committee to draft the platform. The forenoon was taken up largely in pronouncing eulogies upon the life and services of Aaron V. Brown whose death was formally announced to the Convention by Andrew Ewing. In the afternoon, the Platform Committee proposed the following resolutions which were unanimously adopted, to-wit:[100]

"Resolved, That the Democratic party adhere with unchanging faith to the principles heretofore adopted in their conventions in regard to a strict construction of the language of the Constitution, giving powers to the different departments of our Federal Government, and that they believe most of the evils developed in our system of Administration have arisen from a failure in the practice of this fundamental rule in its interpretation.

Resolved, That a tariff for revenue alone is the true policy of the country and a correct exposition of the power of Congress on the subject

[100] *Nashville Daily Gazette*, March 18, 1859.

of indirect taxation. The amount necessary for revenue will vary with the necessities of the Government, but the principle itself is immutable.

Resolved, That the acquisition of the Island of Cuba is, in our opinion, eminently desirable for the safety, happiness and prosperity of our Republic, and we should hail with pleasure any measure consistent with justice, that would accomplish this object. We can never consent to its appropriation by any of the powerful States of Europe, and would incur all the danger of war, rather than acquiesce in such a result.

Resolved, That we are satisfied with the views announced by the Supreme Court of the United States in the celebrated case of 'Dred Scott,' on the rights of slaveholders and the statute of slavery in the Territories, and are willing to abide by the principles announced in that decision. Slavery and the rights of slaveholders are protected by the Constitution of the United States, and by an appeal to the action of the judicial tribunals of the Union, until the formation of a Constitution by the people of a Territory, and then the State must decide for itself on that, as well as other legitimate subjects of government.

Resolved, That it was intended by the framers of the Constitution that gold and silver should be the legitimate currency of our people, and we deeply regret that Banking institutions and paper circulation should ever have been so deeply engrafted into our pecuniary relations; but being so engrafted we are compelled to legislate under the circumstances by which we are surrounded. In view of which, as a remedy for existing evils, we will insist that our present banking system shall be so reformed as to enforce invariable redemption at their counters of their circulation by every Bank in the State, and a limitation on their issues to notes of a large denomination, increased protection to the noteholder, the right of supervision upon the part of the State, and a forfeiture of their charters—for abuses of their privileges—and by these and such other steps as experience may demonstrate to make as near an approach to a Constitutional currency as may be found wise and proper.

Resolved, That it is essential to the welfare of the State, that in all charters of incorporation, granted by the Legislature, that the power should be reserved in all cases to change, modify or abolish these private and privileged incorporations as the public good shall demand.

Resolved, That we have an abiding confidence in the ability and patriotism of the President of the United States, and that we approve generally the ideas contained in his messages and the acts of his administration. We therefore renew our pledges to his support, and our faith in his adherence to the principles of our party.

Resolved, That we feel undiminished confidence in the present Chief Magistrate of the State, his energy and talents shown as our candidate in the former election, the signal triumph he achieved in that race, his ability, dignity and frank bearing as Governor of the State, alike entitle him to our gratitude and warmest support."

Only one other item remained on the agenda, that of nominating a candidate for the gubernatorial chair. This matter was attended to in rapid fire order. Colonel Jo. C. Guild of Sumner County introduced a resolution [101] to the effect that

"Honorable Isham G. Harris, the present incumbent, be nominated by

[101] *Ibid.*

acclamation as the Democratic candidate for Governor. The resolution was adopted amidst great enthusiasm..."

Approximately two weeks after the meeting of the State Democratic Convention, the Opposition State Convention held forth on March 29. Ex-Governor Neill S. Brown was elected Chairman of the Convention. After two whoop-em-up speeches by Colonel Jere Clemens, Editor of the Memphis *Eagle and Enquirer*, and Ex-Governor H. S. Foote of Mississippi, the Committee on Resolutions headed by Felix K. Zollicoffer presented the following "declaration of principles," to-wit:[102]

"The people of Tennessee opposed to the Democratic party declare:

I. That the Union, as established by the Federal Constitution, is the surest guaranty of the rights and interests of all sections of the country, and should be preserved.

II. That while we will maintain with unwavering firmness, our constitutional rights in relation to slavery, we believe that the further agitation of the question tends to no practical good to any portion of the country, and should therefore cease; regarding the principle as settled, that the people, when they come to form a Constitution and establish a State Government, shall decide the question for themselves.

III. That we are opposed to direct taxation and in favor of the adoption of a tariff adequate to the expenses of an economical administration of the general government, with specific duties where applicable, discriminating in favor of American industry.

IV. That the United States should accept the Island of Cuba at any time when it can be acquired consistently with the national honor, and should oppose, to the last extremity, its transfer to any foreign power.

V. That in the disposition of the public lands, otherwise than for governmental purposes, Tennessee and all the old States are equally entitled to receive a proportion with the States and Territories where they are located.

VI. That we are in favor of a reasonable extension of the period of probation now prescribed for the naturalization of foreigners, and a more rigid enforcement of the law upon that subject—the prohibition of the immigration of foreign paupers and criminals, and the prevention of all foreigners not naturalized from voting at elections.

VII. That the recommendation of the President that Congress shall confer upon him the war-making power, and subject the Army and Navy to his control, with the demand for enormous appropriations out of the public Treasury, to carry out his views; coupled with the reckless extravagance, waste of the public money, and corruption practiced under the present Administration, deserve the unqualified condemnation and rebuke of the whole country.

VIII. That we are in favor of a sound and well-regulated banking system, the issues whereof shall, by being payable on their face at the place whence issued, be convertible, at the will of the holder, into the precious metals.

IX. That we favor the maintenance, inviolate, of the public faith, by the prompt payment, at whatever sacrifice, of the public debt, and no further increase of it unless for some object of indispensable public necessity.

[102] *Republican Banner*, March 30, 1859.

X. That we here pledge ourselves to use our earnest exertions and united influence to overthrow that party, which, having brought the Government to bankruptcy and filled the whole land with discord, have now, themselves, caught the contagion, and agree in nothing but a desire for dominion and are bound together by no tie except 'the cohesive power of public plunder.' "

After the "spontaneous ratification" of the above "principles," Colonel J. H. McMahon of Shelby County reminded the Convention that there remained "one more small bit of work to be done." Thereupon, he proposed:[103]

"That we recognize the unmistakeable preference of the Opposition party all over the State for John Netherland, and hereby ratify that preference by nominating him as our candidate for Governor of Tennessee."

The Convention closed on this optimistic note: "Let the Opposition rally to the contest, and there can be no doubt of the result."

Ridicule and a tangy bit of sarcasm were interspersed in the analysis of the Opposition Party and their vociferous gentry by a dyed-in-the-wool Democratic editor of a partisan organ. With all the crossed-up and messed-up personnel composing the Opposition Party, one is reminded of Henry Watterson's famous description of John Pierpont Morgan who was alleged to have been a cross between a mountain daisy and a cockle burr! With biting satire, Editor Eastman pulled no blows:[104]

"THE OPPOSITION CONVENTION.

When the lost spirits found themselves groping amidst the darkness of the nether world, we are told they 'held council together.' The fallen powers of the political pandemonium have done the same thing. In the depth of their despair, in the gloom of their disappointment and discontent, the leaders of the opposition have assembled in caucus. Hopeless of preferment in the parties they deserted, these political bankrupts have met to console each other in their misfortunes and take measures to regain the forfeited favor and confidence of the people. It was, indeed, a singular assembly. Men who had acted with all parties and who had betrayed them all, Old Whigs, apostate Democrats, disguised Know Nothings, fire-eaters and freesoilers— all were there, consulting and conspiring together to overthrow the Democracy and elevate themselves to power. Orators occupied the same stand who had never held a sentiment in common except a desire for office. The most adverse and inconsistent opinions were announced and advocated, amidst the unbounded enthusiasm of the Convention. The first speaker was a former Democratic Senator from Alabama, who had been long enough in the Know Nothing ranks to become naturalized among his new associates. He had lost the emoluments of office and declaimed loudly against the corruption of office-holders. He felt an intense disgust for the wild hunt after office, having himself broken down in its pursuit. He could 'pay the debt of nature' with much more 'confidence in the future' since the as-

---

[103] Ibid.
[104] Nashville Union and American, March 31, 1859.

sembling of this Convention than he could have done a week ago. He thought it a great shame that Mr. Avery, the member from the Memphis district, should repose on a seventy-five dollar sofa and smoke a twenty-five cent cigar. He denounced the Cincinnati Convention, and abused the Administration because it had not adhered to the platform which that corrupt Convention had adopted. He closed with a martial flourish of trumpets, drank nearly a pitcher of water, and sat down amidst tumultuous applause. We did not hear Mr. Clemens allude to the foreigners or the Pope. These hobgoblins have ceased to haunt his imagination, and he has found new causes of complaint against the Democratic party which he deserted some time after they refused to re-elect him to the Senate.

The convention then adjourned. When it reassembled the committee brought in a series of Resolutions which were received with avidity by the hungry office-seekers, who were willing to swallow anything that would fill the aching void within, and supply their party with nutriment to live on for the next four months. Col. Netherland was then nominated by acclamation. Mr. Thomas J. Campbell responded to the nomination. Col. N. had fought, bled and died in the service of the Whig party, and *would do it again*, of which we have no doubt. The information did not seem to be very palatable to the crowd, and especially to General Quarles and Col. Clemens, who have fought, bled and died in opposition to the Whig party.

Governor Foote then addressed the convention.

Politically, the Governor has been *regenerated* several times, but since the rise of the Opposition, has thought it necessary to be *'born again.'* The process seems to have improved his appearance and renewed his youth. We should scarcely have recognized the grey-haired Senator who was rejected by the Democracy of Mississippi some years ago in the rejuvenated individual who addressed the convention. He is really a very hopeful scion of the Opposition, and displays much *new-born* zeal in the cause. He has not forgotten his ancient attachments, however, and still professes to love the old Democratic party and its principles; but don't like the modern kind. That is, Governor Foote loves the Democracy that elected him to the Senate, but is disgusted with the Democracy that defeated him. He abused Mr. Nicholson and Gen. Pierce a good deal, because they opposed his election.

Gen. Quarles then took the stand and ventilated his vocabulary. His speech if written out would be equal to a copy of Aesop's Fables, and would amuse the children on account of its highly colored illustrations. He swallowed the candidate with all his whiggery, endorsed the platform and said he had his own election 'wrapped up in a rag.' The Genl. then told the crowd that he had said all he intended, whereat the crowd applauded and the General retired. John F. House followed in a short speech which was warmly applauded by the audience. After this, the Convention adjourned, to reassemble after tea for the purpose of hearing a speech, from the great god-father of the Opposition bantling—Hon. JOHN BELL. . . ."

Somewhat comparable to the duties of "seconds" who arranged the details of "an affair of honor" when the Code Duello held sway, Honorable Andrew Ewing and ex-Governor Neill S. Brown worked out an agreed-upon schedule of speaking engagements for the two candidates which included sixty-five towns and cities. The speaking dates, at which time toe-to-toe and face-to-face political slugging matches would be the order of the day, ranged from May 2, at Nashville, to and including August 2, at Loudon.[105] Governor Harris was assigned the task of opening the argument at the first engagement, and thereafter the opening speech would be on an alternative basis. No other speaking appointments were to be made, and the "usual rule as to division of time in their addresses" was to be observed throughout the contest.

Having exposed to public view the "innards" of the Opposition Party, Editor Eastman deemed it expedient and politically beneficial to dissect their gubernatorial candidate's past political history. With keen relish and, at times, a bit of gusto, Mr. Eastman sketched in the following editorial [106] the chameleon-like political changes of Mr. Netherland:

"COL. NETHERLAND AND HIS ANTECEDENTS.

It has been the uniform practice of the Opposition to characterize Democratic candidates as 'Demagogues.' No single instance can be found to which this remark will not apply, from the days of Thos. Jefferson to the present time. We will not imitate their example by thus characterizing their candidate for Governor, Col. Netherland, but will briefly sum up his history as a public man, and leave the public to determine what word will most correctly portray the kind of politician he is.

We have always been earnest and unsparing in our strictures upon the misconduct of public men, but we have chosen to deal in *facts* rather than *assertions*, and would scorn to do injustice for a party purpose.

Colonel Netherland started out in public life claiming to be a Democrat, and as such advocated with great zeal all the distinctive doctrines of the Democratic party, and argued with earnestness against the creed of their opponents. In 1836, he abandoned the Democratic party, denying, however, that he was a deserter, but expressly declaring in an address, which he published to the State, that he had in view the success of Democratic principles. This is change No. 1.

A few years later Colonel Netherland ranked himself with the more ultra school of Whigs, a party whose distinctive creed was a United States Bank, a high Protective Tariff, Internal Improvements by the General Government, Distribution of the proceeds of the Public Lands, and the Bankrupt Law, and Opposition to the annexation of Texas. Col. Netherland and his party were defeated in 1844. In 1848, the Whig Convention which assembled in Philadelphia to nominate a candidate for the Presidency, was taken possession of by a set of political adventurers, who threw Mr. Clay overboard, and nominated a *no-party* candidate in his place. Col. Netherland

---

[105] *Nashville Daily Gazette*, April 20, 1859.

Author's note. The *Gazette* held itself aloof from highly colored reports of the forensic efforts of the two opposing candidates. The paper observed this caution to such an extent that little can be gleaned from its columns regarding the contest between Harris and Netherland. The *Gazette's* position was made clear about a week after the speaking schedule started:

". . . As the Conductor of a journal, attached not more to one political party than the other, we have, we hope and believe, sufficient philosophy to exclude any matter calculated to give our paper a party complexion."

[106] *Nashville Union and American*, May 12, 1859.

went upon the electoral ticket in Tennessee, as the advocate of this no-party candidate, General Taylor. Notwithstanding the want of honesty in such a position, Colonel Netherland continued a Whig, and supported General Scott in 1852, one of whose peculiar merits was his love for 'the rich Irish brogue and the sweet German accent'; and the belief that the present naturalization laws ought to be reduced in time.

But the next thing that is heard of Col. Netherland, he has ceased to be a Whig, having united himself with a secret, oath-bound society, known as the 'American Order,' which claimed to have risen upon the ruins of the two old parties, and would not be responsible for 'the obnoxious acts or violated pledges of either.' This was change No. 2.

Col. Netherland having abandoned the old Whig party—having paid his admission fee into the new order, and taken its oaths and degrees, continued zealous in its support from 1855 to 1857, during which time the Northern wing of the new order had triumphed over the Democracy, secured a majority in Congress, elected Banks, an Abolition Know Nothing, Speaker; Cullum as Clerk, and spent more money than any other Congress that ever assembled before or since. The next that we hear of Col. Netherland, he makes his appearance as one of the orators before the Convention which assembled in Nashville, in 1857, to nominate a candidate for Governor, styled the 'American *and Whig*' Convention. Col. Netherland was professing to have discovered then that the old Whig party was *not* dead; which profession carried with it the necessary inference that he, with others, had been engaged in a dishonest fraud upon such democrats as had been deluded into the new order with them. This was change No. 3.

The new device fixed up for 1857, was a more complete failure than the trick of 1855. One thing was now clearly demonstrated, that the only possible means of defeating the Democratic party was in successfully combining into one party all the hostile elements, North and South. Political tricksters in Congress seized hold of the application of Kansas for admission into the Union as a *slave* State as the rallying point for this coalition of the isms, and immediately the cry was raised: 'In the stand taken against the admission of Kansas under the Lecompton Constitution, we have the undoubted germ of a great national party!' This new party in Tennessee wanted a candidate. Where was there a man so well suited for such an emergency as Col. Netherland! Nature seemed to have fashioned him for the purpose. As the representative of Democrats he has only to point to the time when he was the eulogist of Andrew Jackson, and endorsed every principle of his administration—opposing banks, opposing tariffs, opposing distribution, &c. As the representative of old Whigs he has only to point to the time when he fought under their banner—favoring banks, favoring tariffs, favoring distribution, &c. As the representative of no party men, he has only to point to the time when he deserted Mr. Clay and took a place on the electoral ticket of Gen. Taylor—who was known at the time as opposing nothing and favoring nothing. As the representative of the Know Nothings, imitating the example of Mr. Fillmore, he can point to some second Scroggs, who will certify to having sworn him into all the degrees, mysteries and obligations of the order—to persecute Catholics and proscribe foreigners. As the representative of the foreigners he can point to the fact that he is himself the son-in-law of a foreigner, and in 1852, supported for the Presidency a man who favored the policy of increasing their facilities for naturalization, rather than restricting them. Therefore, Col. Netherland accepted. This was change No. 4.

Thus it appears—and let the reader bear in mind that it is a matter of public record and will not be controverted by the Opposition—that Col. Netherland has been a member of *every* party and the advocate of *every* creed known in the history of the country. What such a fact argues— whether it argues duplicity on his part, or honest dealing; whether it argues manly patriotism or the mere tricks of a political mountebank; whether it argues high statesmanship or the arts of a mere huckstering, bartering politician—we leave the public to determine. We do so in the confident belief, however, that with the impartial mind there can be but one conclusion—that John Netherland is worse than a demagogue."

For three months, May through July, Governor Harris and his opponent went the rounds from the opening date at Nashville to the closing of the joint speaking engagements at Loudon. The farewell shot at Loudon was fired just two days before the battle of ballots on August 4, 1859. The campaign, according to the contemporary newspapers, seems to have been conducted on a rather dignified plane, all personalities and ill-flavored taunts having been eliminated by the two principal actors. Even the erratic and acid-tongued "Parson" Brownlow, who was doing a bit of political "reporting" for the Opposition press, could find nothing to condemn at the joint meeting at Athens between the two candidates.[107]   There had been, of course, a lot of ballyhoo on the part of local supporters of each candidate, but matters had calmed down considerably since the hectic days of Polk and "Lean Jimmy" Jones who largely originated the clownish tactics that characterized each of their gubernatorial races. But even so, an ultra-conservative newspaper thought there were still too much banter and ballyhoo in the political contests of the day:[108]

"ELECTION DAY.

The first Thursday in August is with us. The freemen of Tennessee to-day determine who shall be their next Chief Magistrate, and who shall represent them in the State and Federal Council Chambers. In the busy contest now terminating, the people have had ample opportunity of judging as to the personal merits of the various candidates before them, and they have had also abundant opportunity of acquainting themselves with the nature of the political questions upon which the two parties have joined issue. The stump and the press have labored with sleepless zeal in simplifying those things which seemed difficult to be comprehended, and in bringing political aspirants prominently before listeners and readers. To get the favor and support of that class of people controlled in their political action more by parade and display than by reason and argument, all manner of musical instruments, fire-works and explosive material have been brought into requisition, and most industriouly employed; 'armies with banners' have been marshalled valiantly through our public thoroughfares; and an almost measureless quantity of spirituous and malt liquors have gone the way of

---

[107] *Republican Banner*, July 14, 1859.
[108] *Daily Gazette*, August 4, 1859.

all the earth. The seeming necessity for the employment of such vain, meaningless claptrap in our popular elections is of course a matter of regret with many thinking men in each of the two political parties, but it is now 'a time-honored custom,' and we yield to it with as much complacency as we usually submit to 'the force of circumstances.' Therefore we marvel not that we occasionally see in our party papers such exhortations as 'Once more to the breach, oh ye braves!' 'Hang out our banners on the outward wall; the cry is still they come!' 'Remember that eternal vigilance is the price of liberty!' 'Up, Guards, and at them!' 'To your tents, oh Isreal!' 'Give one day to your country!' 'A long pull, a strong pull, and a pull altogether, and the victory is ours!'

> 'Strike till the last armed foe expires,
> Strike for your altars and your fires,
> Strike for the green graves of your sires,
> For God and our native land!'

Such trashy expedients as the above have been most profusely employed in the canvass which closes with this day, and for this reason we are heartily glad that the present occasion for their use is about to cease."

Governor Harris, a rather strict "party man," stood by the Democratic platform which expressed satisfaction with the decision of the United States Supreme Court in the famous Dred Scott case; opposed a protective tariff; and somewhat "hedged" on the currency question by insisting that "the framers of the Constitution intended that gold and silver should be the legitimate currency of our people" but that the right of State supervision of the banks should be inculcated. Over and above these questions towered the slavery issue, with Harris championing the viewpoint that the Democratic Party constituted the only instrument that would and could protect the South against the anti-slavery fanaticism of the North. John Bell was lambasted by the Democrats throughout the campaign for his having "harloted with the North" on the Kansas question, and the charge was hurled time and again that the Opposition Party planned to join the "Black Republicans."

Despite Netherland's admitted ability as a speaker and entertainer, the defense of his political position was rather weak. Most of his argument consisted of his assertion that slavery should not be made an issue in the State campaign, and that Governor Harris was a "hard money man" and strongly opposed to banks.

Governor Harris emerged as a victor from the August election, but by a much-reduced majority when compared with his election two years before. The Opposition Party, although losing both gubernatorial and legislative battles, had on their side seven of Tennessee's ten Congressmen. The Democrats had planned a mammoth celebration for October 1, just three days before the convening of the Legislature. An all-day downpour of rain all but broke up the celebration, the much-publicized giant barbecue in Watkins' Grove having to be abandoned. A constant critic of the Democratic Party dashed off a lengthy editorial [109] regarding the contemplated Democratic jubilee:

"WHAT IS IT ALL ABOUT?

This question is in the mouth of every body, in reference to the great Democratic Jubilee to come off in this city to-day.—What can Democrats find to rejoice over in the result of the late election in Tennessee! We will undertake to answer the question.

But first, let us see what they are *not* expected to rejoice over. They are not expected to manifest any very decided feeling of joy or exultation over the diminution of the majority this year for Governor Harris by one third of his majority two years ago. They will find nothing in that circumstance to cause them to rejoice, for Governor Harris is a very popular man with his party, and anything that has the appearance of a 'letting down' in their champion, would be a source of sorrow, rather than joy.

In the next place, they are not expected to rejoice over the whittling down of the democratic majority in the State Legislature fifty per cent. on the majority of the last Legislature. These two 'results' of the last election bode no good to the Democracy in 1860 or 1861. The work commenced in '59, will be continued next year and the year after, when the large majority against the Opposition now, so handsomely reduced in the last campaign, will entirely disappear and leave them masters of the whole field.

These important circumstances are not of a nature to afford much pleasure to the Democratic jubilants—unless they are inclined to be happy because it is no worse. They may be in a condition to receive small favors with large thanks and rejoice that they saved their Governor and the Legislature at all, without the least fastidiousness about the size of their majorities.

Since, in these respects, the result of the late election is not a matter of jubilation, we are forced to the conclusion, that our democratic friends are to rejoice to-day over the result of the Congressional elections. This view affords the only satisfactory response to the question we set out to answer. We have no doubt that the Administration is as unpopular with Democrats as it is with the Oppositionists, and it was only in the Congressional elections that the merits of the Administration could be brought fairly and squarely in issue. The result was such as might have been expected. The Administration was not only rebuked, but effectually 'killed off,' and our Democratic friends have abundant cause of rejoicing because they will never more be troubled with it—at least they think so—and this, in our view of the case, is the whole secret of their jubilee. They are relieved of the 'Buchanan Gripes' —a disease which has prevailed as an epidemic for the last two years throughout the United States and has generally proved fatal to all who have been attacked by it. Our Democratic friends in Tennessee have suffered in common with their brethren in other States, but it has only occasioned death in seven instances.

In the first district, Landon C. Haynes, the gallant Murat of Tennessee, fell before the ravages of this terrible epidemic. In the third district the clever and amiable Smith, not John, but Samuel A., was the next victim. In the second district, the 'Buchanan Gripes' killed Ramsay so quickly, he did not know what hurt him. In the fourth district, the great Tecumseh, bowed

---

[109] *Republican Banner*, October 1, 1859.

his head and yielded up the ghost, all efforts to prolong his life having proved vain and futile. In the fifth district, it was hoped that Ready would escape, as he, like Naaman of old, had bathed himself seven times in the Jordan of Know Nothingism. But he, too, is gone, and the 'places' that once knew him, know him now no more forever. In the eighth district, the 'Family Physician' was considered equal to the emergency. All the remedies known to the political dispensary were as familiar to him as 'blue mass' and 'ipecac.' But his skill was all in vain. 'Physician heal thyself.' He exerted himself with all his energy, but the 'Gripes' were too many for him and he took up his journey to that bourne, to which he had sent so many before him. And Atkins too, the Ajax Telamon of the ninth district—he 'walked with Buchanan and was not, for the "Gripes" took him.'

Thus seven Richmonds were slain on the 4th of August. One inscription will serve for all their tomb-stones—'Died of the Buchanan Gripes.' With these seven victims, the monster, Death, was satisfied, and because he demanded no more, our Democratic friends rejoice. Let them rejoice and be exceeding glad, for Buchanan is defunct and his supporters are dead; henceforth the survivors may live in conscious security from a return of the 'Buchanan Gripes.' "

The Opposition's query was not allowed to go unanswered. The very next day after its appearance in the Opposition press, the editor of the Democratic organ replied as follows:[110]

"The *Banner* wants to know what the Democrats are rejoicing about. We have just eight thousand one hundred and three reasons for rejoicing, having given Gov. Harris the largest vote ever polled for any candidate in Tennessee, and secured a majority in the Legislature, in spite of the infamous and iniquitous apportionment, by which the *Banner's* party sought to fix the yoke of their decision upon the necks of an unwilling people."

In retrospect, it can be easily determined that the Opposition Party, composed almost wholly of the fragmentary remains of the Whigs and Know-Nothings, lacked solidarity, cohesion, and political *finesse*. The Whigs and Know-Nothings as PARTIES were *dead*, but their immediate successor attempted to masquerade under the nonentity of OPPOSITION and preferred a *post mortem* effort at political success rather than sink into oblivion. In other words, the Opposition chose to be dissected rather than be buried; the result was that it was first dissected and afterwards buried.

On October 3, 1859 the Thirty-Third General Assembly convened in Nashville. From a political standpoint, the Democrats had a majority of three in the Senate and seven in the House of Representatives. A Democratic organ [111] pointed out,

"As the majority is with the Democracy, our party
will fairly be held responsible for what is done.
If they will act upon this motto

[110] *Union and American,* October 2, 1850
[111] *Ibid.*

'In essentials, unity; non-essentials, liberty;
and in all things, has [cash?] money,
they will have no occasion, when the session closes,
to shirk this responsibility."

Without delay or difficulty, a Speaker of the Senate was elected on the opening day of the session. Democratic Senator Tazewell W. Newman representing the counties of Franklin and Lincoln was named Speaker over Opposition Senator John W. Richardson, who had been an irrepressible Whig and a member of numerous preceding legislative sessions. The speakership issue in the House was settled likewise on the first ballot. Representative W. C. Whitthorne from the counties of Maury, Williamson, and Lewis was elected over Representative James W. Gillespie representing the counties of Rhea, Bledsoe, and Hamilton.

With the Legislature organized for business, Governor Harris transmitted to that body his main Message on October 5, to-wit:

Legislative Message*, October 4, 1859

"EXECUTIVE DEPARTMENT,
Nashville, Oct. 4, 1859.

GENTLEMEN OF THE SENATE, AND HOUSE OF REPRESENTATIVES:

Charged, as I have been, for the last two years with the administration of the State Government, and the execution of its laws, I proceed to the performance of the duty assigned me by the Constitution, of submitting to your consideration such information as I may have as to the state of the government, and such recommendations as I deem best calculated to promote the interests and protect the rights of the people of Tennessee.

THE FISCAL CONDITION OF THE STATE

Is as follows:

Received into the Treasury from all sources, from
1st October, 1857, to 1st October, 1859 . . . . $1,848,094.88
Add to this balance remaining in the Treasury on
the 1st October, 1857 . . . . 36,496.06

Which makes the total receipts $1,884,590.94

---

* Public Documents, Tennessee Legislature, 1859, 107–133.

Author's note. This is the first instance in the history of Tennessee's legislative proceedings in which the Governor's primary Message was not printed in either the Senate or the House Journal. Five thousand copies of the Message in pamphlet form were ordered printed "for the use of the Senate," and "the usual number ordered printed for the use of the House."

Disbursements for all purposes, from 1st October,
   1857, to 1st October, 1859 .... 1,704,287.61

Which leaves balance in the Treasury on 1st
   October, 1859, of ....$ 180,303.33

For a full and detailed account of all the sources and various items of receipts and expenditures, you are respectfully referred to the full and lucid reports of the Comptroller and Treasurer.

By reference to the Comptroller's report, it will be seen, that the aggregate expenditures of the two years, ending 1st October, 1859, have been increased to the extent of $341,609.71, by various extraordinary expenditures required by law to be paid out of the Treasury, within that period, for the items of which you are referred to the Comptroller's report.

Take this amount from the gross aggregate expenditures of the two years, and it leaves, as the actual expenditures for the ordinary purposes of government, including the payment on actual indebtedness of the State, the sum of $1,362,677.90.

The most rigid scrutiny into all the expenditures of the government is invoked, in order that they may be reduced to the lowest point consistent with public justice and sound public policy.

It will be seen from the Comptroller's report, that the aggregate taxable property of the State amounts to $377,208,641.00, being an increase of taxable property, since the 1st October, 1857, of $76,-849,830.00; and that the receipts into the Treasury for the last two fiscal years have been considerably more than sufficient to meet the expenditures of the same period.

In this connection, it is proper that I call your attention to the fact, that sixty-six thousand six hundred and sixty-six dollars and sixty-six cents of the bonds of the State, issued for State stock in the Nashville, Murfreesboro' and Shelbyville Turnpike Company, fall due on the 25th July, 1861, the duty of providing for the payment of which devolves upon your present session.

THE ACTUAL INDEBTEDNESS OF THE STATE

Is as follows:

5 per cent. Bonds, issued for State
   stock in Turnpike Roads ......$ 1,091,190.00

5 ¼ per cent. Bonds, issued for
   same purpose 137,166.66

                                           $1,228,356.66

Total for stock in Turnpike Roads,
5 per cent. Bonds, issued for State
   stock in East Tenn. and Georgia
   Railroad ....$ 650,000.00
5 per cent. Bonds, issued for State
   stock in the Memphis and La-
   Grange Railroad 83,250.00
5 ¼ per cent. Bonds issued for same   102,000.00

Total for State stock in Railroads.. $ 835,250.00
5 per cent. Bonds, issued for State
   stock in the Union Bank, yet unpaid 125,000.00
6 per cent. Bonds, issued to raise
   Capital of the Bank of Tennessee 1,000,000.00

Total for Bank Stock, yet unpaid,   1,125,000.00
6 per cent. Bonds, issued for the
   construction of State Capitol,
   yet unpaid,   608,000.00
6 per cent. Bonds, issued for the
   purchase of the Hermitage   48,000.00

Total actual indebtedness of the
   State $ 3,844,606.66
Upon which an annual interest is paid of $209,388.25.

THE LIABILITIES OF THE STATE

On account of bonds loaned to Internal Improvement Companies, are as follows, to wit:
6 per cent. Bonds of the State,
interest payable semi-annually,
   loaned to Railroad Companies ..$10,348,000.00
6 per cent. Bonds of the State
   loaned to Turnpike Companies .   57,000.00

6 per cent. Bonds of the State
    loaned to Agricultural Bureau .   30,000.00

Total amount of Bonds loaned $10,435,000.00

Bonds of Internal Improvement Com-
    panies, the payment of the
    principal and interest of which
    is guaranteed by the State are as
    follows, to wit:

The Bonds of Railroad Companies. . $2,014,000.00

The Bonds of the City of Memphis for
    the benefit of Memphis and Little
    Rock Railroad Co. 350,000.00

Total amount of endorsed Bonds $ 2,364,000.00

Total present liabilities of the State
    exclusive of actual indebtedness   12,799,000.00

Add actual debt of the State   3,844,606.66

Which makes the total liabilities of
    the State of every character, $16,643,606.66

As most of the Internal Improvements to which the aid of the State is pledged by existing laws, are completed, or far advanced towards completion, it is confidently believed that the prospective liabilities of the State in aid of those works, will not far exceed three millions of dollars.

The indomitable energy and enterprise of our people, and the very liberal policy pursued by the State government, have secured to the State a splendid system of Railroads and Turnpikes, which give to every section of the Commonwealth easy access to the markets of the world.

It is gratifying that I am able to state to you that up to this time our Railroad Companies have paid each installment of interest upon their State bonds promptly at maturity. The fact that they have been able to do so, through a period of commercial revulsion and general financial derangement throughout the whole country, while most of their roads were in progress of construction, with only short and disconnected lines in operation, necessarily earning very little compared with what their earnings must be when completed and important commercial connections are formed, and through trade established, encourage the confident belief that now, as the various roads are being completed, penetrating every commercial locality within the Atlantic States, greatly increasing their business and profits, that they will in future be able to pay, as they have done heretofore, all of their liabilities promptly as they fall due.

The act of 1856, chapter 120, requires all Railroad Companies, which have received the aid of the State, either by the loan or endorsement of bonds, at the expiration of five years from the date of issuance, and annually thereafter, to pay into the treasury of the State a sinking fund of 2 per cent. upon the amount of said bonds, and makes it the duty of the Governor, Comptroller, and President of the Bank of Tennessee, as a Board of Sinking Fund Commissioners, to invest said fund in 6 per cent. bonds of the State, and annually re-invest the accruing interest, &c.

The first instalment of this fund fell due in 1858, since which time we have collected from the various Companies $82,840.95, which we have invested, with the interest accruing on the same, in the 6 per cent. bonds of the State and those endorsed by the State, amounting in the aggregate to $109,750, having purchased said bonds at the current rate of discount; upon which we will hereafter collect an interest of $6,417.50 annually.

These bonds are deposited in the Bank of Tennessee and the receipt of the President of the Bank for them is on file in the Comptroller's office.

The Commissioners have deemed it proper to keep the account of each Company separate, and to invest the funds of each for its own benefit. For a statement of their various accounts you are referred to the Comptroller's report.

The time fixed by the act referred to, for the payment of this fund, is, 'at the expiration of five years from the date of issuance or endorsements.'

The general internal improvement act requires all bonds to bear date the 1st day of January of the year in which they are issued, under which, all bonds issued within the year must bear the same date, though in point of fact, portions of them are being issued and delivered to the companies every month in the year.

To avoid the necessity of frequent settlements with the various companies, and the collection of sums too small for investment in a bond, and inasmuch as the bonds all bear date the first day of January, I have fixed that as the day upon which the annual instalment is due and payable. Some of the companies contend with plausibility, if not indeed, correctly, that the first instalment of the sinking fund upon each separate lot of bonds received by them, falls due five years from the day upon which the bonds were received.

If this be the proper construction of the act, it imposes the necessity of a number of settlements with each company every year, necessarily resulting in the collection of a small portion of this fund, each settlement, and balances too small for investment, thus produced, lying idle in the hands of the Commissioners, to the injury of the company.

I therefore respectfully recommend the passage of a law fixing a day upon which the entire sinking fund of each year shall be paid. This will obviate the necessity of more than one settlement with each company annually, and secure the collection of sums sufficiently large for investment.

If the companies continue to pay their sinking fund as they have done heretofore, of which I have no doubt, the present mode of investment will extinguish the entire Railroad debt of the State before maturity.

It is to be regretted, however, that notwithstanding the entire success of our internal improvement enterprises thus far, and the fact that the interest upon our bonds, and the bonds themselves as they have matured, have been in every instance punctually paid, yet Tennessee bonds are selling in the market at a discount of near ten per cent., owing in a great measure, as I believe, to the large number of them thrown upon the market, which has a tendency to shock the confidence of capitalists who know the extent of our liabilities, and know very little of our immense resources. And the manner in which they are but too frequently sold by inexperienced holders who know little or nothing of the stock market, at just such prices as they will command upon forced sale, is well calculated to depreciate the credit of the State, and has unquestionably had that effect to some extent.

In view of which facts I cannot too earnestly recommend that the liabilities of the State be not increased.

Under the present revenue laws, it is held that the bonds of the State in the hands of individuals are taxable, the policy of taxing our own bonds may well be doubted, as it is certain that to the extent they are taxed their value will be diminished, and certainly we should adopt no policy which would tend to discredit or depreciate them at home.

The Comptroller's Report shows that $1,228,356.66 of the actual indebtedness of the State was contracted for stock in Turnpike roads, upon which amount the State pays an annual interest of $61,760.75, while the dividends upon the stock paid into the treasury the last year, amount to the sum of $20,844.76, which shows an excess of interest paid over the amount of dividends received, of $40,915.99, annually, to say nothing of the principal, which must be provided for and paid, at maturity. Governments are never profited by investments of this character, or partnerships with individuals, corporations or stock companies. They never manage such enterprises, or interests in them, successfully, or so well as individuals, and in my opinion, the sooner the connection of the government with those corporations is dissolved the better for the people of the State.

I therefore recommend the passage of a law authorizing the Commissioner of Roads, or Secretary of State, by and with the consent of such other officers of the government as may be deemed advisable, to sell the stocks owned by the State in all internal improvement companies, and appropriate the proceeds to the extinguishment of that much of the actual indebtedness of the State.

The Act of 27th February, 1854, Ch. 44, Sec. 1, provides 'that after paying the interest on the bonds of the State, issued for stock in the Union Bank, the balance of dividends and bonus shall be paid on the order of the Governor and Comptroller for 6 per cent. bonds of the State.'

The 3d section of the Act requires the Governor and Comptroller to cancel the bonds purchased with this fund, until the amount shall equal the sum paid out of the Treasury for the redemption of Union Bank bonds.

Under this Act my predecessor and Comptroller Crozier, received of this fund the sum of ....$156,376.94.

Which they invested as follows:

20 Capitol Bonds, $250 each, due 1st

of April, 1958 ....$ 5,000.00
Interest paid on same 126.16

56 Capitol Bonds, $250 each, due 1st
  of April, 1858 .... 14,000.00

32 Capitol Bonds, $250 each, due 1st
  November, 1859 .... 8,000.00
Interest paid on above 88 bonds 568.00

59 Capitol Bonds $1000 each, due
  July, 1886 .... 59,000.00
Interest on same, ...   590.00

50 Capitol Bonds, $1000 each, due
  March, 1876 .... 50,000.00

19 Capitol Bonds, $1000 each, due
  March, 1871 .... 19,000.00

Total paid for the above $155,000 of
  bonds including interest paid on them . $156,284.16

Which left to the credit of the
  Governor and Comptroller 92.78

    The above described bonds were cancelled by Governor Johnson and Comptroller Crozier, and are now on file in my office.

The present Comptroller and myself received
  from the Union Bank in 1858, the balance
  of dividends and bonus for the year 1857,
  the sum of $13,681.08

Add to this the balance to the credit of
  Johnson and Crozier 92.78

Which makes the total receipts in 1858 ....$13,773.86

With which we purchased three 6 per cent Capitol
  Bonds, $250 each, and fourteen 6 per cent.
  Bonds of the State, of $1000 each, for all
  of which we paid the sum of 13,635.00

Which left to our credit a balance of 138.86

The bonus due from the Union Bank for the year
  1858, we received in 1859, amounting to 9,965.54

Premium received in exchanging ten bonds for ten
    other bonds having less time to run 200.00

Total receipts in the year 1859 ....   10,304.40

With which we purchased eleven 6 per cent. Bonds of
    the State, of $1000 each, at 90c 9,900.00

Which left to our credit a balance of 404.40

Add to this the proceeds of the above described three
    Capitol Bonds, of $250 each, which fell due in
    1859, and were paid 750.00

And it makes the sum of .... $ 1,154.40

With which we purchased one 6 per cent. Bond of the
    State, of $1000, at 90c 900.00

Which leaves to our credit in the Bank of Tennessee
    a balance of .... $ 254.40

The bonds thus purchased by Comptroller Dunlap and myself
are deposited in the Bank of Tennessee, and the receipt of the President of the Bank for them is on file in the Comptroller's office.

The Act of 1856, Ch. 62, Sec. 3, requires the President and Directors of the Bank of Tennessee to invest the interest accruing upon
the bonds purchased with this fund; we therefore deemed it proper
to deposit them there.

I am unable to see any desirable object which is to be accomplished by keeping this as a separate fund. The stock owned by the
State in the Union and Planters' Banks having been sold, we no
longer receive dividends, and the only item composing this fund in
future, will be the bonus paid by the Union Bank, which, by the
charter of the Bank, is appropriated to the Common School Fund.

I therefore recommend that the Acts of 1854 and 1856, above
referred to, so far as they relate to this fund, be repealed, and that
the fund be paid directly into the treasury, and distributed as other
school funds.

BANKING.

Currency being the measure by which the value of labor and
property is determined, its amount, uniformity, certainty and char-

acter, become matters of deep interest and importance to the whole people.

The Constitution of the United States provides that, 'No State shall coin money, emit bills of credit, or make anything but gold and silver coin a tender in payment of debts.'

The Supreme Court of the United States has decided, that the States are not prohibited from incorporating companies to issue bank notes and conduct the business of banking. And upon the authority of the decisions of that court, the States have assumed the same power to incorporate companies for this purpose, that they have to incorporate them to manufacture iron, domestics, or any other commodity. Yet they have no more power to give *currency* to a bank note than to the iron, domestics, or any other commodity upon the market. No power 'to make anything but gold and silver coin a tender in the payment of debts,' or to compel any man to use anything but coin in any of the varied transactions between men. Every individual being left perfectly free to use or reject a paper currency, as he may see proper, the Constitution recognizing nothing but gold and silver as the standard of value and medium of exchange.

The Constitution of Tennessee prohibits your 'passing any law for the benefit of individuals, inconsistent with the general laws of the land; or any law granting to any individual or individuals, rights, privileges, immunities, or exemptions other than such as may be, by the same law, extended to any member of the community who may be able to bring himself within the provisions of such law: Provided always, the Legislature shall have power to grant *such charters of incorporation as they may deem expedient for the public good.*'

This clause of the Constitution forbids the passage of any act of incorporation, except such as are *'expedient for the public good.'*

The primary, leading, and controlling object must be, to promote the interests of the *public*—not those of the *individuals* incorporated.

Yet the effect of the charter is, to clothe the individuals with powers and special privileges usually highly beneficial to them, and from which the balance of the community are excluded. One of which is, in banking corporations, the privilege of issuing two or more dollars in paper for every dollar of their actual capital, with the whole amount of which they discount the notes of individuals at the rate of six per cent, thus realizing from twelve to twenty-five per cent per annum upon their actual capital in this, the least profitable part of their business, for they realize yet much larger profits in the purchase of bills of exchange. To illustrate which, take the case of the Planter who draws his bill upon New Orleans at thirty days; the bank discounts the bill at the rate of six per cent per annum, as interest, in addition to which it takes one per cent from the whole amount of the bill as exchange, thus making the simple item of exchange equal to twelve per cent per annum: add the items of interest and exchange together and it makes eighteen per cent per annum as the profit which the bank charges upon the loan of its *notes,* and if it issues only two dollars of its notes for one specie, it makes the round sum of thirty-six per cent per annum, which the bank realizes upon its *actual capital,* while individuals who do not enjoy similar privileges, can only realize six per cent per annum upon theirs.

But the profits of this transaction do not stop here, for at maturity, the bill of exchange is paid by the planter in New Orleans, and the fund placed to the credit of the bank, upon which it draws its check, which is sold to the home merchant at a premium of one per cent, which if repeated monthly, makes another item of profit of twelve per cent per annum; add this to the items of interest and exchange originally taken from the bill, and it swells the profits upon the *actual capital* of the bank to forty-eight per cent.

Now when the public part with these privileges by conferring them upon individuals, *the good of the public* is the sole object to be accomplished, according to the plain rule laid down by the Constitution, and the greatest care should be taken at all times, that this should be secured; and certainly it will not be contended that this can be done by anything less than securing to the people a convenient, sound, uniform, and convertible currency; and all must agree that the larger the specie basis in all banking corporations, and the more complete the control which the people have over them for the purpose of checking their excesses, the sounder and more uniform their currency, and consequently, the greater the probability of their promoting the public good: and surely the corporators cannot object to any restrictions and reservations necessary to the accomplishment of this object. For they are bound, not only by the plain letter and spirit of the Constitution, but by every consideration of sound policy, public justice and common honesty, to furnish to the community a currency as sound, uniform, and reliable as the one which they displace, a currency which is at least the representative of, and not the mere substitute for, specie, one which is at all times convertible into coin at the will of the holder.

But has such been the history of banking under the present system in Tennessee?

They have, in many instances, issued as high as four, six, eight and even ten dollars of their paper for one in specie.

They have made their notes payable at points the most remote from the place of putting them in circulation, for the purpose of retarding their return upon the bank for payment, thus depreciating their paper and making it less valuable to the holder.

They have expanded and contracted at will, causing injurious and disastrous fluctuations in trade, and affecting the price of every man's labor and property.

And not unfrequently, actuated by a spirit of selfish avarice and cupidity, they have flooded the country with their circulation, by which they have stimulated overtrading—wild and reckless speculations—habits of luxury and extravagance, and induced thousands of our population to abandon the fruitful fields of production, for the more fascinating, yet more hazardous fields of speculation; and when they have reaped the full benefit of a large business, and the bubble can be expanded no farther, public confidence becoming shocked, and the country threatened with commercial revulsion as one of the legitimate fruits of their conduct, they have quietly closed their doors and said to the victims of their policy: We extend no farther accommodations; we have suspended, and will not even pay the notes you hold upon us. Thus leaving in the hands of the people a depreciated and irredeemable paper, as their only currency—the losses by the depreciation of which, fall upon the industrial classes, who are usually the note holders; while the banks avail themselves of the depreciation by transmitting their available means to some one of the commercial cities of the North, and charging their note holders from 3 to 10 per cent. premium for exchange, or in other words, they first depreciate their own paper by refusing to pay it, and after having depreciated it, they buy it up at from 3 to 10 per cent. discount, paying for it in a check on New York instead of gold.

Now, when Banks redeem their paper in gold, you can never be under the necessity of paying higher than about ¼ of one per cent. for exchange upon any point within the Atlantic States. For exchange is always worth just what it will cost to transmit the gold to the place of payment, and gold can be transmitted from Tennessee to any commercial point within that limit at a cost of about ¼ of one per cent.

The country is now just recovering from a period of about ten months suspension of specie payments, upon the part of all the banks in Tennessee, in which every bank in the State was selling exchange at a premium of from three to ten per cent., except the Bank of Tennessee, which furnished exchange to the extent of her ability throughout the whole period of suspension at a premium of one per cent.

These are some of the evils of our *present* banking system, under the practices of our most solvent banks, to say nothing of the millions of dollars which have been lost to the people of Tennessee by the failure and insolvency of others, not sufficiently guarded and restricted; evils to which the community have been compelled to submit, because those corporations are clothed with, and fortified by, irrepealable charters, which enable them thus to outrage the public interest with impunity, and to defy the whole people and the' Legislative authority of the State. For under the *present* system, when you have passed a bank charter, and the company has organized under it, it is held by the courts, that there is no power in the government to abolish, no power to add a single restriction or safeguard, however necessary and important further restrictions may be for the security of the interests of the public; and when the individual citizen appeals to the courts of the country for relief, they may say to him, it is clear that you are wronged and oppressed by these institutions, but they are clothed with vested rights under their charters, over which we have no power, and therefore, can give you no relief.

Can institutions which engage in practices like these, so selfish and antagonistic to the general prosperity of the country; institutions, whose only object seems to have been the realization of the largest possible profits, regardless of the great injury or ruin which they bring upon the balance of the community, clothed with power to go on in their career of reckless speculation, defying any legislative enactment intended so to reform them as to protect the best interests of the people for whose benefit they were established, be *'deemed expedient for the public good?'* When so far from promoting the public good, they have, under this unrestricted system, been vampires upon the public interest, fattening upon the misfortunes of the people, which their own policy has produced.

That a paper currency is a convenience to the public, no unprejudiced mind can deny; but that it is a convenience, which, under our *present* system, has cost the people vastly more than it is worth, is equally clear. And the only means of preserving this convenience, so as to make it beneficial to the people, is by radically reforming the whole system, and throwing around it such stringent restrictions and safeguards as will secure uniformity, and perfect certainty as to the convertibility of the paper into coin at all times, at the will of the holder.

And as a means of accomplishing this, it is, in my opinion, indispensably necessary that upon the face of every charter you should expressly reserve to the people, through their Legislature, the power to modify or abolish such charter, when in their opinion the public interest demands it.

Indeed, to deprive the people of the power to control or abolish institutions created by their authority and alone for their benefit, is inconsistent with the great and fundamental principle of self-government.

I maintain that the people are at all times capable of determining for themselves, and are the best judges, as to what will promote their own interests. That they have a right to determine for themselves the number and character of banks they will have, and to restrict and guard them, as the lights of experience may prove to be necessary, and to abolish them when they fail to perform their functions fully and properly, and cease to be a public benefit. And for one Legislature to fasten upon the State a number of banking institutions for a period of thirty or fifty years, the charters of which cannot be amended, modified or repealed, is an usurpation of the rights of future Legislatures, contrary to the principles of self-government, and an outrage upon the rights of posterity.

It is, in effect, denying to those who shall come after us the rights which we claim and exercise for ourselves. And not only for ourselves; for, by this policy, we undertake to penetrate the dark and distant future, and decide for our successors, for the next quarter or half century, the character of institutions which they shall have, withholding from them the power to mould or modify them to suit their necessities or convenience, or to protect themselves against the wrongs which they may perpetrate, or to abolish them, however pernicious and prejudicial to the public interest they may become; thus denying to the people, in the future, the privilege of profiting by the wholesome lessons taught by the experience of an entire generation.

I will never assume the responsibility of denying to the people, in the future, the right of deciding for themselves as to the character of institutions which will 'be expedient for the public good,' aided, as they will be, in determining the question, by the lights of experience, and the facts and circumstances which time will have developed.

If the people of the present day need and desire banks, they have a right to make such as the Constitution contemplates, and to manage and control them for themselves; but they have no right to forestall the popular will and tie the hands of their successors. For the experience of every man proves that the policy which may be highly expedient at this time, and under present circumstances, may become the very reverse in the course of a few years, when circumstances have changed. And the great distinguishing feature of our Government, which commands the love of its citizens, and the respect and admiration of the civilized world, is that it is purely a Government of the people, who have the capacity and the right to mould and modify their institutions and their laws to suit their own interest and convenience, and the circumstances which may surround them from time to time; but if you adhere to the policy of irrepealable charters, the result is the establishment of sovereignties within our midst, invested with powers to affect materially the interest of every man in the community, with regard to which the people have no power except that of patiently enduring such wrongs as may be perpetrated upon them.

There is no dissenting voice in this country, and I trust there never will be, to the proposition that the people, through their Legislature, may at all times make, modify, or repeal the laws upon which the life, liberty, and property of every man in the State depend; yet this policy of irrepealable charters and 'vested rights' denies to them the power to modify or repeal the law upon which the special privileges and franchises of a soulless corporation depend. Are these to be held more sacred by the people of Tennessee than the life, liberty and property of the citizen?

Let the banking system of the State, like all other measures of public policy, be placed under the control of the people, and then just so long as the banks perform their functions fully and in good faith; just so long as they make themselves advantageous and beneficial to the public; just so long as they are 'expedient for the public good,' they will be fostered and sustained; and when they fail in these respects, they ought to be abolished.

The fact that their continued existence is made to depend upon their promoting the public good, by a full and fair performance of duty, would furnish the powerful incentive of self preservation as a motive to banks to avoid excesses, however much tempted by the prospect of large profits, and to perform, with perfect fidelity, their whole duty to the people.

It seems to me that you had as well expect a rational people to shut themselves in from light, air, and the genial warmth of the sun, as to expect them to strike down institutions which are promotive of their interests, and beneficial and convenient to them; and the Constitution forbids your chartering any corporation which is not of this character. Hence, corporators who intend to make a bank which will furnish to the people, at all times, and under all circumstances, a sound, uniform, and convertible currency, need have no fear of the reserved power; and it would be unwise and impolitic in the extreme, as well as unconstitutional, to give them the privilege of creating one of a different character.

About half the States of the Union, and amongst them New York and Pennsylvania, two of the largest commercial States in the Government, guided by the lights of long experience in banking, have been forced to adopt the policy of reserving complete legislative control over their banking institutions. New York adopted this policy by legislative enactment in 1829–30, and after testing it by a trial of sixteen years, it was incorporated into the constitution of that State, and there is not a single instance upon record, where it has been adopted by any State that the reserved power has been abused by the people.

Indeed, I cannot see why they should be expected to abuse this power any sooner than any other or every other legislative power which they possess.

I therefore earnestly recommend the following restrictions, as indispensably necessary to any system of banking which is expected to furnish a sound, uniform, and convertible currency:

First.—The power reserved to the people, through the Legislature, to amend or repeal the charter when *'deemed expedient for the public good'* to do so.

Second.—That no bank shall be permitted to issue more than two dollars of paper for one of specie, or to permit its entire liabilities to note holders, depositors, and others, at any time, to exceed the specie in the vaults more than three for one.

The experience of the financial world has demonstrated, beyond controversy, that the convertibility of a paper currency cannot be maintained, at all times, when the disproportion between their specie and liabilities runs higher than this.

Third.—That no bank be permitted to issue any note of less denomination than twenty dollars. This will secure a specie currency for all the smaller business transactions of the country, and at least a partial exemption from losses by bank failures and a depreciated currency, of that class of the community who are least benefitted by bank accommodations, and yet are generally the most serious sufferers by their failures or depreciation. And the large amount of specie necessarily retained in the country in constant circulation under this policy, would go far to relieve, if it did not prevent the commercial revulsions and financial derangements which have been of but too frequent recurrence.

Fourth.—That no bank or branch bank in the State shall issue or put in circulation any note or bill that is not payable in specie at the counter where the same is issued or put in circulation.

The issue by each bank of nothing but its counter notes, would confine the circulation of each bank to the legitimate wants of the community, upon whose trade it is predicated. It would tend to secure a sound currency in each and every neighborhood in which a bank may be located, by affording to all an opportunity of converting into coin, without expense, whatever paper might not be needed as a mere matter of convenience for our internal trade.

The facility for returning notes thus issued upon the bank for redemption, would serve as a constant check upon the banks, and would do much towards keeping them within safe limits. It would put an end to that system of flooding the country with the depreciated or doubtful issues of our own or foreign institutions.

Fifth.—The individual property of each stockholder to be liable for the debts of the bank, but as between themselves, their liability to be in proportion to the amount of stock taken by each, and this liability to the creditors of the bank to continue for the term of four months after public notice of any transfer of stock, so that the creditor may proceed against the original stockholder, if he prefers doing so to relying upon the solvency or management of the purchaser of the stock. This will prevent solvent stockholders from relieving themselves from liabilities to creditors by transferring their stock to insolvent parties.

Stockholders establish banks and invest their capital in them for their own pecuniary benefit; they have the management and control of them; if profits accrue they are the beneficiaries; if losses are sustained, they are bound, by every consideration of honesty and fair dealing, to bear them; but without some provision making them individually liable, the stockholders will pocket the profits, and when, through their mismanagement or fraud, the bank fails or its paper depreciates, the note holders are forced to sustain the losses. Banking is purely the speculation of the stockholders, and they must incur its hazards if they would realize its profits.

Indeed, where the managers of a bank are disposed to act fraudulently, they may enrich themselves, by getting in circulation the largest amount of their paper possible, suspend payment, discredit the paper, and buy it up at mere nominal rates, or pocket the assets and leave their creditors to look to the empty vaults of the corporation for satisfaction of their claims. Make them individually liable to the creditors, and they will have no motive to discredit their own paper, for they will be bound to make it good to the holder, and you will thus secure a much more prudent and safe management of these institutions, than we have had under the present system.

Sixth.—Require the registration and countersigning of every note to be issued by a bank, by the Secretary of State, or some officer of the government, by which means the public can, at all times, know the maximum circulation of every bank in the State, and it would go far to prevent over issues.

Seventh.—The creation of a Board of Supervisors, consisting of three competent men, who shall have the power to enter and examine the condition of every bank in the State, at any time, and whose duty it shall be to do so at least quarterly, and report, through the columns of some newspaper at Nashville, their true condition, so that the public may know the real condition of the various banks, and to what extent they are worthy of confidence.

The only information the public has as to the condition of banks, under the present system, is through the reports of their officers, who are interested in making the most favorable report possible, and whilst, in a great majority of cases, these reports are honestly and fairly made, yet, in some, they are not; and the people are deeply interested in, and have a right to know, the true condition of every bank in the State.

Eighth.—Make the suspension of specie payment for the term of twenty days, or the violation of any provision of the act of incorporation a forfeiture of charter, and give the supervisors the power, when they shall be satisfied by a full examination that any bank has thus suspended or violated its charter, and that the security of the public interest demands it, to attach the assets of the bank for the benefit of creditors, and to proceed at once to prosecute the bank to a judgment of forfeiture. Make it also their duty to report to each session of the Legislature, and to recommend such reforms as they may deem necessary to the perfection of the system.

Ninth.—Such penalties and forfeitures as will insure a strict observance of, and conformity to, all of the above, and such other restrictions as you may see proper to impose.

With these restrictions imposed upon the banking system of the State, our currency must become much more uniform, sound, and reliable, than it has been heretofore under the present banking system, and, under these restrictions, stockholders have an ample margin for legitimate and highly remunerative profits.

While it is indispensably necessary to the security of the public, that the people should hold Legislative control over, and have the power to protect themselves from injury resulting from improper practices of these institutions, by guarding, restricting, or abolishing such banks as they may see proper to charter, yet it is confidently believed that the State should not engage in banking, or any other business or speculation in competition with her citizens, with a view to money making. In addition to which, it may truly be said, that you rarely find the same amount of care and energy exercised in the execution of a public trust that is common to the prosecution of private and individual enterprise; and as an investment, it is confidently believed that if the entire property of the Bank of Tennessee was converted into money, and with the capital of the bank invested in the six per cent. bonds of the State, that it would result, ultimately, in more profit to the Treasury than our present, or any other system of government banking is likely to do. Thus furnishing, to that extent, a home market for our State securities, already depreciated for the want of it, and ridding the State government of the expensive and demoralizing machinery of a banking institution, and of the hazards necessarily incident to the banking business.

The President and Directors of the Bank in their report to the last session of the Legislature, say, 'that the true interest of the State will hereafter be best promoted by a dissolution of all connection with the banks or internal improvement companies, at as early a period as the finances of the State will admit of it, without unnecessarily oppressing the people, and with due regard to the public faith pledged to them.'

In this opinion I fully concur. One million of dollars of the capital of the bank was raised by the issue and sale of that amount of the bonds of the State. These bonds fall due in 1868, and must be paid either by taxation or out of the capital of the bank.

I have no doubt that the true policy of the State will be found in winding up the Bank of Tennessee at the expiration of its charter, and leaving the business of banking to private enterprize, under such guards and restrictions as the Legislature may, from time to time, see proper to throw around it.

For a statement of the business, profits and condition of the Bank of Tennessee, you are respectfully referred to the report of the President and Directors.

In this connection I earnestly recommend the adoption of resolutions, proposing so to amend the Constitution of the State, as to prohibit the Legislature from chartering banks or other speculative corporations, without reserving the power to amend, modify, or repeal the same.

Without such constitutional prohibition, a single session of the Legislature favorable to the policy, may fasten upon the State any number of corporations of this character, for half a century, depriving the people of the power to control or to abolish them, however much every member of the community may feel the absolute necessity of doing so.

The importance of the subject demands that I repeat to you a recommendation which I had the honor of submitting to the Legislature at its last session, of an amendment of the Constitution of the State, so as to fix a reasonable limit, beyond which the Legislature shall not go, in creating a debt or liability of the State, without first submitting the question directly to the people, except in cases of invasion, insurrection, or rebellion. Such an amendment is certainly wise and proper in itself, securing to the people the right to be consulted, and to determine for themselves, by popular vote, whether they will take upon themselves the liability proposed or not; especially in view of the fact that our legislative elections are generally made to turn much more upon party considerations and federal politics than upon local or State policy, and most of the questions, out of which have sprung these heavy liabilities, have been very little discussed, if, indeed, they have been discussed at all, before the people, previous to their enactment.

Another salutary effect following such an amendment is, that it would inspire confidence in such securities as the State has issued, or may hereafter issue, throughout the money markets of the world; and to the extent that you convince capitalists that we have not issued, and will not issue bonds beyond our ability to pay, do you restore and appreciate the credit of the State.'

THE PENITENTIARY.

It will be seen from the Report of the Inspectors and Agent of the Penitentiary, that there has been a gradual and constant increase in the number of convicts received at the Prison for the last two years. The number, however, is constantly fluctuating by the receipt of new convicts and the discharge of others. The average may be safely set down at about four hundred.

The institution is laboring under some serious disadvantages, which the best interests of the State, as well as the laws of humanity, require should be speedily remedied.

It is impossible to employ the labor of the average number of convicts profitably within the area of the present prison walls. In my opinion it is absolutely necessary that the walls be extended north to the northern boundary of the property owned by the State, so as to include the entire property. There is not within the present inclosure sufficient shop room for the hands, shelter room for the necessary stock of material, or ware room for the articles manufactured. If you would employ the labor of the convicts profitably, additional shops must be built, or every shop in the prison enlarged. In addition to which a ware and sale room in front of the prison, where every article shall be deposited so soon as completed, and where all sales shall be made by one salesman, is indispensable to the success of the institution in a pecuniary point of view. The last Legislature appropriated the sum of ten thousand dollars ($10,000) for the purpose of building additional cells; and under the supervision of the present very efficient Board of Inspectors and Agent, a new wing, containing one hundred and twenty cells, has been constructed, which I am satisfied, will, in point of security, neatness, convenience, and comfort, compare favorably with any prison in the United States. But the old building had only two hundred and thirty-two cells, and the new wing has one hundred and twenty, which makes the whole number only three hundred and fifty-two, while the number of convicts almost constantly considerably exceed the number of cells. More cells are indispensable to the health and comfort of the convicts, and should by all means be provided for without delay.

There is at present no place of deposit for the excrement from the prison. The practice heretofore has been to haul it out and deposit it near the walls upon adjacent lots owned by individuals, but the country around the prison is being rapidly settled up and becoming densely populated, and the community will not, and should not be expected to submit to the creation of a nuisance of this character in their midst. The only remedy for this evil will be found in the construction of a subterranean sewer, which will carry off all of this excrement, without injury or offence to any one.

It is believed that much the greater portion, if not all the work in the construction of the improvements necessary, can be done by the convicts, if the Legislature should see proper so to employ their labor. In that event, however, appropriations from the Treasury will be necessary, for the purchase of material and the support of the institution while their labor is thus employed.

For full and accurate information as to the business and condition of the Penitentiary, you are referred to the report of the Inspectors and Agent. From which it will be seen that the available assets for the last two years are about equal to the liabilities incurred for the same period, and the labor of the convicts in the construction of the new wing, is estimated at about ($27,000) twenty-seven thousand dollars, and the stone cut for the Capitol is estimated at about ($17,000) seventeen thousand dollars more than they receive for it, which makes a total of ($44,000) forty-four thousand dollars, about which amount, it is believed by the Agent, would have been realized from the prison, if the entire labor of the convicts had been employed in manufacture instead of improvements.

The general management of the prison, as regards discipline, subordination, cleanliness, and the observance of all rules necessary to the preservation and promotion of health and comfort, will compare most favorably with any prison in the Union.

Governments, however, are never good financiers—never manage pecuniary interests successfully or well—and ours forms no exception to the general rule in this respect.

In view of which fact, I do not doubt that the best interests of the State would be promoted by leasing out the entire labor of the prison annually. The State, through her agent, feeding, clothing, and controlling the convicts, as at present, except as to the character of work within the various shops, which would be determined and controlled by the lessee. The Legislature prescribing, with precision, the rules which are to regulate the leasing of the various shops, and the government of the convicts, so as to secure to them the best treatment, and the highest degree of comfort consistent with their position.

There can be no doubt that, in a pecuniary point of view, the State would be greatly profited by the adoption of this policy. In the States where it has been tried, it is said to have worked remarkably well, and I cannot doubt it would do so here.

THE STATE AGRICULTURAL BUREAU.

The report of the State Agricultural Bureau, which will be laid before you by the Secretary, on the first of December, will inform you of the progress made since the last report, in the formation of County Agricultural Societies, and of the results accomplished by these Societies in agricultural improvements. There have been chartered in the State, forty-two County Societies. Most of these are in operation, acting under the general law, and reporting annually to the State Bureau. Division Fairs are held each year, at Knoxville and Jackson, for the Eastern and Western divisions of the State, and in the Middle division with some one of the County Societies of that division. County Fairs are, also, annually held by nearly all the County Societies, at which a very commendable emulation in excellence of stock, agricultural products and mechanical skill is excited. A noticeable advance in improved methods of farming, as well as in the products of the farm and the implements of cultivation, has been made within the last few years. The products of the soil have been increased, and the soil itself protected against exhaustion, by more intelligent and scientific culture; while the invention and gradual introduction of improved machines for the cultivation and husbandry of crops, and the yearly increased facilities for transporting those crops to the best markets, by making production cheaper and enhancing value, is rapidly advancing the wealth of the State and of her citizens. The leading business of the people of Tennessee is agriculture and its attendant interest—the production of domestic animals. It has been a policy adopted by your predecessors in legislating for the State, with great unanimity, to encourage and foster this interest. Many of you have been witnesses of the effect of this legislation in your own counties and districts, and bring to your duties as legislators, personal experience of the benefits of past legislation in stimulating the industry and developing the resources of the State. A continuance of the policy which has proved of so much benefit will, therefore, I am confident, accord with your own judgment, as well as with the expectations and wishes of your constituents.

The framers of the act establishing a State Agricultural Bureau, evidently intended and expected that its provisions would apply equally to the agricultural and mechanical interests of the State, and it has been the earnest desire of the Bureau so to execute their duties as to secure such a result. In 1855–6 an act was passed providing for an appropriation of $10,000 each to East, Middle and West Tennessee, to purchase and fit up Fair grounds, in the event that the delegates to the Division Fairs of those divisions should think it expedient to locate the Division Fairs. Under this act, the Division Fair for East Tennessee was located at Knoxville, and that for West Tennessee at Jackson, and the appropriation of $10,000 for each fair was drawn from the Treasury. The Middle Division Fair was not located: the delegates deciding that they preferred the plan of holding the fair for that division, as originally provided, alternately in the different counties. Application was therefore made by the Mechanical Association at Nashville, for a transfer to their Association of the ten thousand dollars which had been thus contingently appropriated and not used, to aid them in building a hall for their purposes in Nashville. The Legislature, at its last session, passed an act consenting to the transfer, provided the consent of the delegate members to the Bureau from Middle Tennessee should first be obtained. The members in question have taken no final action in the matter. I refer the subject to you for further action, if you deem such action necessary and proper, adopting for myself the language of my immediate predecessor, speaking of the subject in his last message to the Legislature.

The Mechanics' Institute of Tennessee, said Gov. JOHNSON, has done much, it is believed, by its annual fairs, to stimulate the mechanical and manufacturing interests of the State, and to develop much talent peculiar to the successful prosecution of these branches of industry. The leading principle upon which this institution is established, is paramount, in directing the mechanical genius of the young men of the country, in that branch of mechanism to which it is best adapted. In brief, it is designed to stimulate and bring out the latent mechanical talent and excite a laudable ambition among mechanics, manufacturers, artizans, and inventors, to excel, to foster and to encourage the arts in every way, and ultimately to establish a school of design for the benefit of the youth of the State, whose opportunities are limited for the want of pecuniary means, or otherwise. The institution is not established upon such a basis as desired by the Directors; though they have been struggling against many difficulties, it is believed they will ultimately succeed in its permanent establishment. They desire to erect a Hall suitable for the institution, and have already leased a lot of ground convenient and favorably located for the erection of suitable buildings.

The Legislature with great liberality has aided other important interests in the State, such as Railroads and Agriculture. Will it not therefore extend similar aid to manufacturers and mechanics, and in so doing place these great interests on an equal footing with the other industrial pursuits of the country, and thereby exonerate the Legislature from the charge of invidious and partial legislation? *If you legislate for one, legislate for the whole.*

STATE LINE COMMISSION.

Being informed by His Excellency, Henry A. Wise, Governor of the State of Virginia, of his readiness to send a commission to the field, to meet commissioners from Tennessee, for the purpose of running and re-marking the line between the States of Tennessee and Virginia:—In obedience to the act of 1858, chap. 43, I appointed Gen. Samuel Milligan, of the county of Greene, and Col. George R. McClellan, of the county of Sullivan, Commissioners on the part of Tennessee.

The joint commission has been in the field for some considerable time, and I am informed by the commissioners that they have completed the work; their engineer being now engaged in the preparation of the necessary maps, &c., which, when completed, will enable me to lay their final report before you.

The second section of the act authorizes the Governor to pay one-half of all the expenses incurred in running and marking the line, and two dollars per day to each Tennessee Commissioner, and ten cents per mile for all necessary travel going to and returning from the line, &c.

I have, at the request of the Commissioners, ordered the Comptroller to issue his warrants upon the treasury to them, amounting in the aggregate to the sum of $1,697.68.

In this connection, it is proper that I call your attention to the fact that the compensation allowed the Commissioners by the act above cited, is wholly inadequate to the service required. The duties devolving upon this commission involve weighty responsibilities, and much labor and exposure.

I respectfully recommend that their compensation be made equal to the importance of the service required at their hands.

The act of January, 1858, chap. 26, provides for the appointment of two Commissioners by the Governor of Tennessee to meet such Commissioners as may be appointed on the part of the State of Kentucky, 'to run and re-mark the line established by the compact between the States of Tennessee and Kentucky.' The 2nd section makes it the duty of the Governor to transmit a copy of the act to the Legislature of Kentucky, then in session, with a request that said Legislature take such action as may be necessary to effect the object. I transmitted a copy of the act to His Excellency, Charles

S. Morehead, Governor of Kentucky, immediately after its passage, with a request that he would lay the same before the Legislature of that State, accompanied with such recommendation as he might see proper to make. Very soon after which, I was informed by a communication from Gov. Morehead, that the Legislature of Kentucky had passed an act very similar to our own, and that Kentucky was ready to proceed with the work. Whereupon I appointed, as Commissioners upon the part of Tennessee, Dr. Benjamin Peeples, of the county of Henry and Col. O. R. Watkins, of the county of Jefferson.

They proceeded to the field some time in the month of November, 1858, and have been progressing with the work since that time. The information derived from correspondence with the Commissioners, justifies the belief that they will complete the survey in time to enable me to lay their final report before you during your present session.

The 4th section of the act appropriates the sum of three thousand dollars to the purchase of necessary instruments and the cost of making the survey. This sum being exhausted, and there being no authority to furnish the Commissioners such funds from the treasury as was absolutely necessary to complete the work, we procured for them, from the Bank of Tennessee, upon the individual credit of myself, Col. J. E. R. Ray and Gen. J. T. Dunlap, the sum of two thousand dollars, for which the Bank holds our note.

It will devolve upon your present session to provide for the payment of the balance of the expenses of the Tennessee Commission in making this survey, and also to fix the rate of compensation to the Commissioners, as the act is silent upon that subject; and I respectfully recommend that it be made fully commensurate with the toil, exposure, privations, and responsibilities which the duties of the position impose.

THE STATE LIBRARY.

I beg to commend the State Library to your favorable consideration. It may now be regarded as an institution of the State, having been founded by your predecessors of 1855, and liberally provided for by the last General Assembly. An efficient method of discharging your constitutional 'duty to cherish literature and science,' is by extending your aid to this interesting department of our government. But besides enumerating it among the objects of legislative solicitude and care, I have another motive for giving it a place in this communication,—that of informing the young men of the State, that even now, they may find on its shelves much important aid to investigation and research in almost every branch of knowledge; and of suggesting to them that a few months spent within its walls, in diligent study, before entering upon the pursuits to which they intend to devote their lives, would be an evidence of their resolution to make themselves useful citizens. You will learn, from the Librarian's report, its present condition and its operations for the past two years. It is hoped that the work of fitting up the room, appropriated to the reception of the books, may be completed by the commissioners of the capitol before your adjournment, in accordance with the act of 1855, so as to enable you to see more clearly what has been and what remains to be done, to place the library upon a footing of utility and efficiency.

WEIGHTS AND MEASURES.

The 11th section of the act of March, 1858, chap. 55, authorizes the Governor to have made, under the direction of the Superintendent of Weights and Measures, for each county in the State, a set of substitutes, or copies of the standard weights and measures, and such other apparatus as may be necessary to their use.

On the 28th of March, 1858, I addressed a note to the Superintendent, directing him to proceed at once to their manufacture. He has completed eighty-five sets, samples of which are now in the office of weights and measures, subject to your inspection. About half of them have been delivered to such counties as have, through their County Courts, applied for them, and the balance are ready for delivery upon proper application.

They have been gotten up by the Superintendent with a precision and accuracy, and in a style of workmanship, which, I doubt not, will be found entirely satisfactory to the public, and highly creditable to that officer.

They have cost in the aggregate $4,250.08, which makes the cost of each set $50.00. Nothing has been done in the manufacture of the standard weights and measures for the several counties of the State since your last session; the entire time and attention of the

Superintendent having been devoted to preparing the substitutes above referred to.

PUBLIC ARMS.

The act of March, 1858, chap. 81, authorizes the Superintendent of Weights and Measures to collect and keep in good order the public arms of the State. The Capitol Commissioners have set apart and had fitted up the north basement of the Capitol as a State Arsenal, and upon my order the public arms, heretofore deposited at Knoxville, Jackson and the State Prison, have been removed to the Arsenal and placed in the keeping of the Superintendent. A full and accurate report, as to their number, character and condition will be laid before you during the present session.

REPORT OF THE JOINT SELECT COMMITTEE.

The Joint Select Committee, appointed by the Legislature at its last session, to examine and report, in vacation, the condition of the books and accounts in the offices of the Comptroller and Secretary of State, after a laborious investigation of the manner in which the business of these offices had been conducted, eliciting many facts and conclusions of importance and general interest to the public, submitted their report to me, six thousand copies of which have been printed in pamphlet form by the public printer, some of which have been distributed amongst the people and the balance are in the possession of the Secretary of State, subject to any order which you may see proper to make respecting them. A copy of the Report is herewith transmitted. The facts developed by this investigation, demonstrate the necessity of a more effectual system of checks upon the accounting officers of the Treasury, so as to place it beyond the power of any one of them, to defraud the Treasury, without the complicity of another. While I have the utmost confidence both in the integrity and entire competency of the present incumbents, I deem it a matter of the highest importance that such a system of checks should be adopted, as will put it out of the power of any public officer to practice frauds upon the Treasury, without the certainty of immediate detection and punishment.

CHARITABLE INSTITUTIONS.

For full and accurate information, as to the present condition and business of the Hospital for the Insane, and the Institutions for the education of the Blind and the Deaf and Dumb, you are respectfully referred to their several reports.

The establishment and support of these institutions, do honor to the philanthropy and liberality of the people of the State, and in this enlightened age, it requires no argument to prove, that we are bound, by every consideration of justice and humanity, to those most unfortunate classes of our citizens, to continue to yield a liberal support to these institutions, which contribute so much to their comfort and the alleviation of their misfortunes. Such information as I receive respecting them, justifies the belief, that the present condition and management of each of those institutions will compare favorably with those of a similar character anywhere.

Your favorable consideration of all just claims, in aid of these praiseworthy efforts in behalf of the cause of humanity, is respectfully invoked.

SECRETARY OF STATE.

Since the adjournment of the last session of the Legislature, a vacancy in the office of Secretary of State was occasioned by the resignation of Dr. F. N. W. Burton, which I filled on the 28th day of May, 1858, by appointing to said office John E. R. Ray, Esq., of the county of Shelby.

The duty of filling this vacancy, by election, devolves upon the present session of the General Assembly.

THE GREAT SEAL OF THE STATE

Is, by law, in the custody of the Governor, and can only be used by his order; it is that which gives authenticity to every official document coming from the Executive Department. There is at present no law prohibiting individuals from making and using a facsimile, which might be done greatly to the prejudice of the State and the injury of individuals; to prevent which, I respectfully recommend the passage of a law containing such prohibition, and prescribing such penalties as may be considered necessary to accomplish the object.

SALARIES.

Whilst I hold it to be the duty of all governments to pursue the strictest economy in the expenditure of public money, consistent with the efficiency of the public service and sound public policy, I hold that it is equally the duty of governments to pay their public officers such salaries as will defray all expenditures which are necessarily incident to their respective positions, with a reasonable compensation for their services. A contrary policy will, in effect, exclude all men from the honors of public position except such as have estates sufficient to justify them in sacrificing their time to the public service, and it requires no argument to show the gross injustice of such a policy.

Under the present law the Secretary of State receives a salary of $800, and as Internal Improvement Commissioner $500, with some inconsiderable perquisite; and the Treasurer a salary of fifteen hundred dollars per annum, with three-fourths of one per cent. upon all monies received and disbursed by him as Treasurer of the Insane Hospital, which amounts to about four hundred dollars.

The duties of each of these offices require the constant presence of the officer at the Capitol, and it is a fact, easily demonstrated, that they cannot bring their families to Nashville and support them upon their respective salaries.

These salaries were fixed at a time when the necessary expenses of living were not more than half as much as they are at present, nor the responsibility connected with these offices much more than half as great as they are at this time.

The salary of the Agent of the Penitentiary was reduced by the last Legislature to the sum of one thousand dollars. The duties of this office impose weighty responsibilities, great vigilence and constant attention, and require a high order of business qualifications.

I respectfully recommend a full investigation of the matter, and the fixing of such salaries for the officers referred to as may be deemed fair and just, both to them and the public.

THE HERMITAGE.

The act of February 11th, 1856, chapter 96, authorized and directed the Governor to purchase, for the State of Tennessee, five hundred acres of the late residence of Gen. Andrew Jackson, deceased, including the mansion, tomb, and other improvements, known as the Hermitage. This duty, as was reported to the Legislature at its last session, was performed, at a cost of forty-eight thousand dollars. The same act directed that a tender of the property should be made to the Federal Government, on the express condition that it should be used for a branch of the Military Academy at West Point, and that if it should not be accepted for that purpose, within two years from the expiration of that session of the Legislature, it was made the duty of the Governor to have laid off fifty acres, including the tomb, the mansion and the spring and spring-houses, and expose the balance to public sale. The tender having been made by my predecessor, and not acted on by the Federal Government, the Legislature, at its last session, passed an act (chap. 52) giving the further time of two years from the 6th of February, 1858, during which the Federal Government might signify its acceptance of the tender. By the original act, Mr. Andrew Jackson was allowed the possession of the property for the term of two years, unless applied for by the General Government within that time; and by the act of 1858, it was made the duty of the Governor to see that the property was taken care of, until the Federal Government should determine the question of its acceptance. The Federal Government having failed to signify its acceptance of the property on the terms provided in the act of 1856, and Major Jackson having notified me of his intention to remove from it during the coming winter, further legislation will be necessary at your present session.

If it be deemed advisable to sell a part of the property, I recommend that the part reserved by the State be laid off in a square, so as to include the mansion, tomb and spring and spring-houses, and extend out to the Nashville and Lebanon Turnpike, which would probably embrace about one hundred and fifty acres. You cannot preserve the harmony and beauty of the property without including at least this much; and that specific instructions for its preservation and care be provided by law.

The most appropriate custodian of the estate would seem to me to be the State Agricultural Bureau; and, in the event of its willingness to accept, and preserve, and beautify the property, the whole should be retained, if preferred by the Bureau. This body, composed of gentlemen, eminent alike for their enterprise, intelligence, public spirit and patriotism, would, I am confident, undertake the management of the property, and so direct it as not only to preserve, but to beautify and adorn it.

The farmers of the State would feel constant pride in decorating with their choicest care the fields which the hero loved so well, and which are sacred to them as holding the ashes of the patriot. I refer the matter to your consideration, confident that you will do all in the premises which the Representatives of the people of a great State can do, to protect as the shrine of patriotism, and to decorate, as the resort of beauty and taste, the beloved resting-place of him who will be regarded, by all coming generations, as one of the purest patriots, and as having been at once the hero and the statesman, the captain and the sage.

Invoking the blessings of Divine Providence upon your deliberations, this great Commonwealth, and our whole country, I commend to your care and favorable consideration the foregoing recommendations, with all other questions which affect the prosperity and well-being of the people of Tennessee.

ISHAM G. HARRIS."

One of the early formalities of every legislative session has been the official counting of the votes for the respective candidates in the gubernatorial race. At an afternoon session on October 17, the House and Senate met in joint session and the following result [112] was announced, to-wit:

"VOTE FOR GOVERNOR IN THE ELECTION OF 1859.

Counties	For Isham G. Harris	For John Netherland
Anderson	382	793
Bedford	1,435	1,585
Benton	740	393
Bledsoe	343	486
Blount	734	1,267
Bradley	1,096	749
Campbell	625	363
Cannon	1,009	420
Carroll	1,029	1,687
Cocke	584	965
Carter	281	880

[112] Senate Journal, 1859, 38–39.
House Journal, 1859, 56–57.
Author's note. The vote of Sequatchie County was omitted from the total vote cast for Governor. Quite a squabble developed over the question as to whether or not the Sequatchie vote should be included and counted. The hassle was occasioned by the establishment of Sequatchie County after the Reapportionment Act of 1851 but prior to the enactment of the next reapportionment law, due to be made in 1861. As a matter of fact, the inclusion or exclusion of the Sequatchie County vote did not affect the outcome of the gubernatorial race between Harris and Netherland, as the differential far exceeded the Sequatchie vote.

Counties	For Isham G. Harris	For John Netherland
Claiborne	765	684
Coffee	995	395
Davidson	2,412	3,463
Decatur	487	359
DeKalb	845	745
Dickson	861	432
Dyer	681	712
Fayette	991	913
Fentress	538	148
Franklin	1,443	315
Gibson	1,392	1,953
Giles	1,472	1,295
Grainger	791	1,141
Greene	2,102	1,022
Grundy	401	56
Hamilton	1,056	1,121
Hancock	553	448
Hardeman	1,148	580
Hardin	890	585
Hawkins	1,289	1,103
Haywood	902	781
Henderson	811	1,290
Henry	1,868	978
Hickman	1,071	195
Humphreys	693	272
Jackson	1,155	1,339
Jefferson	641	1,611
Johnson	200	565
Knox	926	2,603
Lauderdale	422	458
Lawrence	794	539
Lewis	253	19
Lincoln	2,578	477
McMinn	1,122	1,031
McNairy	1,109	999
Macon	471	535
Madison	909	1,355
Marion	414	462
Marshall	1,302	640
Maury	1,916	1,379
Meigs	643	124
Monroe	1,107	911
Montgomery	1,043	1,353
Morgan	335	218
Obion	1,118	611
Overton	1,457	347
Perry	523	329
Polk	750	366
Rhea	446	339
Roane	851	1,031
Robertson	1,077	1,274

Counties	For Isham G. Harris	For John Netherland
Rutherford	1,515	1,504
Scott	264	225
Sevier	266	1,046
Smith	801	1,486
Shelby	2,231	2,026
Stewart	827	521
Sullivan	1,575	566
Sumner	1,736	776
Tipton	616	365
Van Buren	197	131
Warren	1,222	392
Washington	1,355	982
Wayne	582	679
Weakley	1,709	1,043
White	844	968
Williamson	801	1,601
Wilson	1,255	2,240
Total	76,073	68,042

Majority for Harris ....8,031"

In accordance with the arrangements of the Committee on Inauguration, plans for the ceremonies were scheduled for the forenoon of November 3, 1859. Governor-elect Isham G. Harris was escorted to the speaker's stand by the Speaker of the Senate and the Speaker of the House, after which the band played *Hail Columbia*. Prayer was offered by Reverend J. B. McFerrin and followed by more music. Governor Harris arose and then delivered the following brief Inaugural Address:[113]

"GENTLEMEN OF THE SENATE AND THE HOUSE OF REPRESENTATIVES:

I am here for the purpose of taking the oaths required by the Constitution, of the Governor of Tennessee. Having discharged the duties of that office, for the last two years, to the extent of such poor abilities as I possess, the highest guarantees that I can offer for the future are to be found in the history of my past administration. Believing, as I do, that the highest reward ever meted out to public servants, is found in the approval of those whom they have labored to serve, I am the better prepared to appreciate deeply the compliment and the honor found in the fact of being again called, by the

[113] *Legislative Union and American*, 1859, Volume II, 132.

people of Tennessee, to this high position, and the discharge of the high duties that devolve upon it.

As my position and opinions are known by all who have any desire to know them, with regard to all the questions of public policy, through my messages and my public addresses, I deem it unnecessary to enter upon the discussion here, and shall, therefore, decline doing so.

I have, in conclusion, to tender to the people of Tennessee, through you, their representatives, the deep sense of gratitude with which I am impressed, for the honor they have conferred and evidenced in their continued confidence, in calling me again to the discharge of the high duties of this position.

I am now ready to take the oath of office, prescribed by the Constitution, and enter upon the position assigned me."

At the conclusion of the Inaugural Address, the oath of office was administered by Judge Nathaniel Baxter of the Davidson County Circuit Court. Then came more music followed by the benediction pronounced by Dr. McTyeire.

It will be observed that a significant portion of the Message of Governor Harris, transmitted to the Legislature on October 4, 1859, dealt extensively with the banking question. All along, the problem of handling the banking situation had puzzled and worried public officials charged with legislating and administering the laws and regulations governing this very vital and sensitive business. Gradually, the policy of regarding originally banking as a monopoly, to be exercised by capitalists, had given way to the more democratic idea that government should not encourage or support monopolistic enterprises. In harmony with the popular idea that exclusive rights should not be granted to capitalistic organizations, political parties attempted to frame their platforms so as to offend as few voters as possible. Perhaps there have been few political platforms adopted by any party in Tennessee at any time that better exemplify the above statement than that portion of the Democratic platform on banking adopted at the time Governor Harris was renominated as the Democratic candidate for Governor, in 1859. The fifth "resolve" of the State Democratic Convention's platform, herein cited on page 90, *straddled* the bank issue by declaring both *for* and *against* paper money. On this point, a contemporary Opposition newspaper commented somewhat sarcastically as follows:[114]

". . . They were prepared to act understandingly. They had seen that their party had declared *for* and *against* paper money, in almost an equal

[114] *Tri-Weekly Whig* (Knoxville), March 24, 1859.

number of counties, according to the interest of the banking facilities of the different counties, and the assembled wisdom and patriotism of the State very prudently *took both sides. . .*"

Just why was the "banking business" such a potent issue in the gubernatorial campaign of 1859? Well, the United States as well as other stable governments exercises the exclusive right of regulating the medium of exchange. Specifically, the Constitution of the United States declares that Congress has the power "to coin money [and] regulate the value thereof" and that no State shall coin money or make anything but gold and silver coin a tender in payment of debts. As business seems to move in cycles, it has been noted that in "hard times" money is difficult to lay hold of and that any appreciable lack of "the coin of the realm" produces a general cause of complaint. Hard times and money scarcity seem to walk hand in hand, and small wonder that one is charged as being the cause of the other, though determining just which is the cause and which the effect may remain a matter of interesting speculation. Tennessee had just undergone the throes of a "money panic" in 1857, and the bitter experiences of that regime were too recent not to be remembered and lugged into the political campaign only two years hence. Consequently, each political party in Tennessee deemed it advisable to "stand up and be counted" on the money question. At the time, neither party seems to have produced a leader who could dispose of the troublesome "money question" in as adroit but unsound method as was employed by the incomparable "Bob" Taylor whose facetious remedy was, "I am for more gold, more silver, more greenback—and a *leetle* more counterfeit." Once again, "Our Bob's" sense of humor enabled him to parry the thrusts of his political opponent!

In general terms, the reforms proposed by the State Democratic Convention had specified a specie basis for bank circulation; that the State reserve the right to modify or abolish bank charters; and that stockholders be made liable individually for obligations assumed by the banks.

In compliance with the platform planks and his campaign promises, Governor Harris analyzed at length the past policies of the banking fraternity in his major Message to the Legislature. He scored relentlessly some of the past practices of the banks, such as the high rates of interest upon their *paper* medium that sometimes exceeded ten times the actual amount of specie involved. In such instances, it was insisted that the banks were reaping a large per cent of their earnings upon a *fictitious* capital, a thing that Governor Harris strongly and emphatically opposed. With sledge-hammer blows, Governor Harris pounded away at the unrestricted and vested rights enjoyed hitherto by the banks as provided in their charters, and he demanded that the Legislature enact only such laws as would enable the people to be protected from the past policy of "irrepealable charters and vested rights" on the part of "soulless corporations."

After enumerating nine specific recommendations for the improvement of banking conditions, Governor Harris was particularly emphatic in regard to his support of a proposed constitutional amendment on what he considered the most important point in the whole bank question, namely:[115]

"In this connection I earnestly recommend the adoption of resolutions, proposing so to amend the Constitution of the State, as to prohibit the Legislature from chartering banks or other speculative corporations, without reserving the power to amend, modify, or repeal the same.

Without such constitutional prohibition, a single session of the Legislature favorable to the policy, may fasten upon the State any number of corporations of this character, for half a century, depriving the people of the power to control or to abolish them, however much every member of the community may feel the absolute necessity of doing so...."

The series of restrictions proposed by Governor Harris to be imposed upon the banks, all of which were set forth in his Message, may be briefed and catalogued as follows:

First.—The power reserved to the people, through the Legislature, to amend or repeal the charter "*when deemed expedient for the public good*" to do so.

Second.—That no bank shall be permitted to issue more than two dollars of paper for one of specie, or to permit its entire liabilities to noteholders, depositors, and others, at any time, to exceed the specie in the vaults more than three for one.

Third.—That no bank be permitted to issue any note of less denomination than twenty dollars. This will secure a specie currency for all the smaller business transations of the country, and at least a partial exemption from losses by bank failures and a depreciated currency of that class of the community who are least benefited by bank accommodations, and yet are generally the most serious sufferers by their failures or depreciations. And the large amount of specie necessarily retained in the country in constant circulation under this policy, would go far to relieve, if it did not prevent the commercial revulsions and financial derangements which have been of but too frequent recurrence.

Fourth.—That no bank or branch bank in the State shall issue or put in circulation any note or bill that is not payable in specie at the counter where the same is issued or put in circulation.

Fifth.—The individual property of each stockholder to be liable for the debts of the banks, but as between themselves, their liability to be

[115] See that specific portion of Governor Harris' Message dealing with this point, pages 119–120.

in proportion to the amount of stock taken by each, and this liability to the creditors of the bank to continue for the term of four months after public notice of any transfer of stock, so that the creditor may proceed against the original stockholder, if he prefers doing so to relying upon the solvency or management of the purchaser of the stock. This will prevent solvent stockholders from relieving themselves from liabilities to creditors by transferring their stock to insolvent parties.

Sixth.—Require the registration and countersigning of every note to be issued by a bank, by the Secretary of State, or some other officer of the government; by which means the public can, at all times, know the maximum circulation of every bank in the State, and it would go far to prevent over issues.

Seventh.—The creation of a Board of Supervisors, consisting of three competent men, who shall have the power to enter and examine the condition of every bank in the State, at any time, and whose duty it shall be to do so at least quarterly, and report, through the columns of some newspaper at Nashville, their true condition, so that the public may know the real condition of the various banks and to what extent they are worthy of confidence.

The only information the public has as to the condition of banks, under the present system, is through the reports of their officers, who are interested in making the most favorable report possible, and while, in a great majority of cases, these reports are honestly and fairly made, yet, in some, they are not; and the people are deeply interested in, and have a right to know, the true condition of every bank in the State.

Eighth.—Make the suspension of specie payment for the term of twenty days, or the violation of any provision of the act of incorporation a forfeiture of charter, and give the supervisors the power, when they shall be satisfied by a full examination that any bank has thus suspended or violated its charter, and that the security of the public interest demands it, to attach the assets of the bank for the benefit of creditors, and to proceed at once to prosecute the bank to a judgment of forfeiture. Make it also their duty to report to each session of the Legislature, and to recommend such reforms as they may deem necessary to the perfection of the system.

Ninth.—Such penalties and forfeitures as will insure a strict observance of, and conformity to, all of the above, and such other strictions as you may see proper to impose.

Contemporary newspaper editorials, exhibiting bias and prejudice in matters political, were clearly divided upon the more salient points embraced in the Message, the Democratic papers supporting and the Opposition press opposing the recommendations submitted by Governor Harris. As a rule, the Opposition papers maintained that the banking recommendations of Governor Harris, if put into execution, would "restrict the banks out of existence." A summary of the objec-

Section N° 2:   Amendments offered to S.B. 106:

M° Neill₂ moves to strike out five and insert "Ten" in Sec. 2:
Stokes – amends said Section by a Proviso as follows – Carried

Section 5: Stokes am.ᵗ adopted –

Section 9: M° Neill₂ moves to strike out 20 & insert 15 ₂

Section 12: Stokes – moves to strike out all after   Carried

Section 13 Steakly amends as follows, withdrawn

Section N°. 14 – M° Steakly amends as follows – Laid on Table

Section 15: Stokes – offers one in Lieu – Adopted

Section 18: after the word Gov.ʳ "insert" and to be Confirmed by the Sena
and hold his office for 2. years – added to the Section
as follows –

Section 20. M° Lane offers amendment as follows

Section 23 = Stokes movs after the word "Bill" – Insert in the name of
the Supervisor

Section 24 – Stokes – moves after Word "Bank" & Certify

Section 31: – offered by Mickle₂ as follows – Rejected

32 M°. Lane – offered Sect. 32 as follows – Adopted.

Sec. 33 – M° Steakly – Offers amendment as sec: 33:
        Stokes moves to Lay on the Table – Carried
Stovall moves to Reconsider the vote laying on Table amendment N° 33
                        Refused to Reconsider
Sec: 34: M° Hildreth offers amendment to Sec. 19: as follows
        Stokes moves to Lay on the Table – Laid on Table
M°. Peters offers am.ᵗ to Sec. 26: by adding all the Stockholders

A sample of legislative hocus-pocus *re* banking bill.
Extract is from the Senate Clerk's memorandum.
Original in Tennessee State Archives, Nashville.

tions raised by the Opposition press was expressed, rather crudely it must be confessed, by a strong pro-Harris organ:[116]

"... The Opposition papers are trying their teeth upon the Governor's Message. It seems not to be of a material very favorable to mastication, as they have not as yet attempted any division or separation of its constituent parts, but content themselves with swallowing it whole, and spitting it up again, a good deal altered by the digestive menstruum it got mixed up with, and then calling attention to the not very attractive mass, saying 'here's a message from a Democratic Governor,' when they would say with more truth, 'Here's an Opposition attempt at digestion.'"

Perhaps there was one appraisal of the Message, as free from any partisan slant as could have been made, which appeared in the only significant newspaper published in the State that refrained from sponsoring some political party or indorsing some specific candidate. That non-partisan organ [117] commented, in part, as follows:

"Governor Harris occupied all the ground which can be well converted into an argument against chartered banks, while on the other side he recommends restrictions, some of which have been tried and found good— others that have been found to be worthless, and still others that it has been reserved for him to be the originator; or, in other words, those which are good are not new, and those which are new are not good....

We venture to glean from the Message that a bank is not an unconstitutional thing 'per se,' and we think that it will bear this tremendous significance of interpretation, and though this opinion has been safely arrived at by many public men, yet the Message shows that the writer has gone through 'deep waters' in order to find the constitutional terra firma upon which to place himself....

But the business community, with whom we have to deal the most—the planter, who probably cannot count interest as fast as the Governor—the farmer, who may or may not have a bill to sell at 30 days, are interested in some of the deductions drawn in the Message...."

With banking and currency constituting the major issues in the recent gubernatorial and legislative campaigns, it was but natural that legislators as well as Governor Harris should "rise, stand, and be counted." Governor Harris had indulged in no shirking or straddling in his Message, and had devoted a large part of his Message to the banking and currency topics. As partial evidence that the Solons in the other Department of State had their ears to the ground, nineteen bills on "banking" in some shape or fashion were dropped into the legislative hoppers.

To trace each of these individual bills through the legislative session would be tedious and not altogether profitable. Out of the welter and conflict, there emerged nine banking laws of which there was one of

---

[116] *Nashville Union and American,* October 12, 1859.
[117] *Nashville Daily Gazette,* October 12, 1859.

positive and meritorious nature whose caption was entitled "An Act to reform and regulate the business of Banking in Tennessee."[118] In the Act of thirty-three sections, the most pertinent provision of all was contained in the opening sentence of section 3, to-wit:

"... The capital stock of each Bank in this State shall be paid in coin, and no substitute or equivalent shall be received in lieu thereof ...."

A further safeguard was that no bank could commence business with a capital stock of less than Three Hundred Thousand Dollars. These two prerequisites put a stop to the "wildcat" banks which had multiplied like the ancient plagues of Egypt under the Free Banking Act of 1851 and whose two chief "assets" were fictitious capital and highly ornamental bank notes of beautiful design and engraving. A Bank Supervisor, to be appointed by the Governor and confirmed by the Senate, was vested with broad powers in regard to whether or not any bank had violated any of the regulations governing banking as provided in the sweeping statute. The War Between the States, however, followed too closely upon the reforms provided in this and other banking laws of that session for any far-reaching effects to have been accomplished.

In support of a previous recommendation by the President and Directors of the Bank of Tennessee, Governor Harris left no doubt in his Message as to his attitude regarding the liquidation of this State agency:[119]

"I have no doubt that the true policy of the State will be found in winding up the Bank of Tennessee at the expiration of its charter, and leaving the business of banking to private enterprize...."

On the surface, it looks as though the strong recommendation of Governor Harris for the winding up of the Bank of Tennessee was destined for easy sailing through the Legislature. One of the most militant and able Senators, Dr. John W. Richardson, a dyed-in-the-wool Whig and later a Know Nothing, on March 7, 1860, introduced Senate Bill No. 317 "to wind up the Bank of Tennessee."[120] The bill routinely passed first and second readings in the Senate. The bill was set for special order on March 14 and, without argument or wrangling, was called up for third and final reading. The vote stood: Ayes, 7; Noes, 15, with three Senators either absent, or present and not voting. This adverse action on the part of the Senate ended the matter, for the bill was never transmitted to the other legislative branch.

---

[118] *Acts of Tennessee*, 1859, Chapter 27.

Author's note. The other eight laws, dealing with minor points, were Chapters 13, 14, 26, 57, 98, 107, 122, and 132.

[119] See further extracts from the Message of Governor Harris, page 119.

[120] *Senate Journal*, 1859, 611.

It is a matter of interesting speculation as to why this bill, backed by the Democratic Governor and the strongest Opposition member of the Senate, met such decisive defeat. The political and geographical distribution of the Senators and their respective votes on the measure were as follows:

Senators	Political Affiliation	Counties Represented
For Liquidation		
Allen, V. S.	Opposition	Gibson, Carroll, Dyer.
Bumpass, R. W.	Opposition	Madison, Haywood, Lauderdale, Tipton.
Lane, James T.	Democrat	Meigs, McMinn, Polk, Monroe.
Richardson, Dr. John W.	Opposition	Rutherford, Williamson.
Stokes, Jordan	Opposition	Wilson, DeKalb.
Stokely, D. V.	Opposition	Greene, Cocke, Sevier, Blount.
Trimble, John	Opposition	Davidson.
Opposed to Liquidation		
Boyd, James S.	Opposition	Knox, Roane.
Bradford, W. M.	Opposition	Hawkins, Hancock, Jefferson.
Hildreth, Reese T.	Democrat	Morgan, Scott, Fentress, Overton.
Horn, Judson	Opposition	Robertson, Montgomery, Stewart.
Hunter, H. W.	Democrat	Giles, Lawrence, Wayne.
Johnson, James M.	Democrat	Bedford, Marshall.
Mickley, James E.	Democrat	Humphreys, Perry, Decatur, Henderson.
Minnis, J. A.	Democrat	Rhea, Bledsoe, Bradley, Marion, Hamilton.
McClellan, George R.	Democrat	Johnson, Carter, Washington, Sullivan.
McNeilly, Thomas	Democrat	Maury, Lewis, Hickman, Dickson.
Nash, M. V.	Opposition	Claiborne, Grainger, Anderson, Campbell.
Newman, Tazewell W.	Democrat	Franklin, Lincoln.
Stanton, S. S.	Opposition	White, Jackson, Macon.
Stovall, B. L.	Democrat	Henry, Weakley, Obion.
Ward, Ed J.	Democrat	Warren, Cannon, Coffee, Grundy, Van Buren.

	Political	
Senators	*Affiliation*	*Counties Represented*

Either Absent or "Present and Not Voting"

Payne, R. G.	Democrat	Fayette, Shelby.
Peters, Dr. George B.	Democrat	Hardin, Hardeman, McNairy.
Thompson, James L.	Democrat	Smith, Sumner.

The *location* of the ten Branch Banks does not appear in every instance to have been a determining factor as to how the Senator of that community voted on the retention or liquidation of the Mother Bank at Nashville and of the various branches. For example, Senator Allen, of the Opposition, voted to wind up the Bank of Tennessee and its branches, although a Branch Bank was located in Trenton, one of his counties being Gibson. The same was true of Senator Trimble, representing Davidson County in which was located the Mother Bank. On the other hand ten Senators, namely, Hildreth, Hunter, Johnson, Mickley, Minnis, McClellan, Newman, Nash, Stovall, and Ward voted against liquidating the Bank of Tennessee, although no Branch Bank was located in their respective Senatorial Districts. Geography and politics were so mixed up in the issue that it seems impossible at this faraway time to determine with any degree of accuracy as to just *why* who voted for or against liquidation of the "political engine" that had played an important role in partisan politics ever since its establishment in 1838.

At every legislative session from 1838 to 1866, inclusive, biennial bank reports and legislative investigations of the Bank of Tennessee constituted a considerable part of legislative action. Statements, bank reports, and arguments *pro* and *con* concerning the Bank of Tennessee consumed a lot of time and space in the various legislative *Journals.* Perhaps no more detailed analysis of the record of this institution can be found than that of Senator John W. Richardson of Rutherford County whose speech in favor of liquidation justifies its inclusion in this treatise. In support of his bill to wind up the Bank of Tennessee, Senator Richardson regaled his fellow Senators as follows:[121]

"BANK OF TENNESSEE

Speech of
MR. RICHARDSON.
of Rutherford,
On his Bill to Wind up the Bank of Tennessee,
In Senate, March 14, 1860.

MR. RICHARDSON said he desired to present to the Senate and the country the history of State Banking in Tennessee. The State was organized

---

[121] *Legislative Union and American,* Volume II, 1859, Appendix, 606–609.

in 1796, and in 1807 the Legislature chartered the 'Nashville Bank,' the State
reserving to herself the right of taking stock in it to the amount of twenty
thousand dollars ($20,000.) This was the first bank chartered in Tennessee,
and the following comprises the list up to 1817—the dates of their charters
and their durations—

Names of Banks.	Capital.	Date.	Term of years.
Nashville Bank ....$	20,000	1807	30
Bank of State of Tennessee.........	400,000	1811	30
Fayetteville Bank	400,000	1815 till	1840
Jonesboro' Bank	400,000	1815 "	"
Franklin Bank	400,000	1815 "	"
Gallatin Bank	400,000	1817 "	1841
Carthage Bank	400,060	1817 "	"
Rogersville Bank	400,000	1817 till	"
Farmers and Mechanics' Bank at Nashville	400,000	" "	"
Winchester Bank	400,000	" "	"
Kingston Bank	400,000	" "	"
Columbia Bank	400,000	" "	"
Maryville Bank	400,000	" "	"
Shelbyville Bank	400,000	" "	"
Murfreesboro' Bank	400,000	" "	"

Fifteen Banks with $5,800,000 capital—stock to be raised,
and the Banks authorized to issue ten millions of dollars in paper for a
population of three hundred thousand souls!

In 1819 the whole of them that had gone into operation suspended
specie payment, with the exception of the Knoxville Bank, of which Judge
White was the President.

The history of this monetary crisis, although the State was flooded with
paper money, shows from public documents, that the notes of those suspended Banks were at a discount of from 30 to 40 per cent; and gold and
silver were at 30 per cent premium.

Bankruptcy, ruin, and general distress pervaded the whole State, and
Gov. McMinn in his message recommended, in order to relieve the distress
on the country,—first, The staying of judgments for two years; or to compel
creditors to take Bank notes. Second, A general redemption law. Third,
The exemption of certain property from execution—and lastly, he recommended a valuation law. In 1820, he said that general distress still pervaded
the country and was marked with permanence.

In 1821, Governor Carroll, in his message to the Legislature, protested
and advised against State Banking, and exposed the ruinous policy of the
State engaging in the business of banking.

To relieve all this distress of 1820, produced by *excessive* State banking, the Legislature chartered the old Bank of Tennessee with a capital of
one million, ($1,000,000,) a branch at Knoxville and a loan agency in each
county in the State.

Now commenced a splendid and popular scheme of State Banking to relieve the people from the injuries of injudicious banking, and the excessive
issues of paper money.

Take the period from 1816 to 1826, during this system of State banking,
and you will find that 'shinplasters' reigned the whole time, and some of

these swindling machines sold their gold and silver at a premium of 30 per cent., while their own notes were at 40 per cent. discount!

In 1823 the notes of the Fayetteville Bank, and the Farmers' and Mechanics' Bank, at Nashville, were worth only 25 cents in the dollar!

In 1829 Gov. Carroll warned the Legislature against the policy of *State* banking and protested against employing the funds of the State in banking.

He recommended an investigation of the Bank. Everything looked well. The accounts all balanced—the Bank's liabilities were put down at $1,070,849 84½, and its assets the same, $1,070,849 84½—all looked well. The investigation was perfected, and in 1833, when the Bank was wound up, the actual loss to the State stood, as reported by the investigating committee, $252,784 85-⅛—one single individual being himself a defaulter to the amount of $49,338 06.

The whole of these facts and figures are copied from the public records, and can be found on file in the State Capitol.

The Union and Planters' Banks are *stock* Banks. They were chartered in 1832.

The State had stock in both of these Banks, from which it derived good dividends. Two years ago the stock was handed over to the State Bank, and will be examined after awhile.

In 1837-38 the Legislature chartered the Bank of Tennessee, providing that its capital should be $5,000,000. This amount, however, was never procured for the Bank, and the first report made to the General Assembly in 1839, shows a capital of $2,148,706. This amount has been added to from time to time, as I will explain in the sequel, until the capital ought now to be over $4,000,000.

The capital, in October, 1847, made up of one million of State Bonds, the surplus revenue and School funds, amounts as by report to $3,191,215. The operations of the Bank—its liabilities and means, after about ten years of existence, may be seen from the following analysis of the report made up to October, 1847, and to this analysis I direct the attention of the Senate and invite the closest scrutiny:

Condition of the Bank of Tennessee from Report of the President, made up to the 1st of July, 1847.

LIABILITIES.

*Capital Stock	$3,186,421 65
Treasurer of Tennessee	106,341 60
Discount on State Bonds	50,816 55
Internal Improvement Fund	11,703 32
Sinking, or Contingent Fund	287,672 36
Dividend Account	556,726 70
Exchange Account	68,338 25
Discounts Received	66,062 72
Interest Account	27,080 71
Damages	3,779 48
Internal Improvement Dividend	5,256 00
Profit and Loss Account	62,281 73
Common School Land Districts	130,685 82
Due to Banks	338,770 18

*The statements as to amount of capital disagree somewhat.

Circulation 1,556,282 00
Certificates of Deposit............................ 888 00
Individual Depositors 317,147 67

Total Liabilities $6,776,254 74

MEANS.

Discounted Notes $1,771,168 78
Domestic Bills 942,957 40
Bills and Notes in suit 606,512 24
State Bonds discounted 333,890 00
Common School Bonds 90,793 60
Expense Account 22,970 45
Real Estate 200,605 07
Interest on State Bonds 1,051,012 00
Due from Banks 649,002 51
Appropriation to Rivers 163,269 54
Ocoee School Fund 10,313 50
Notes of State and City Banks 249,537 48
Gold and Silver 684,042 17

Total Means $6,776,254 74

The above statement taken from the Report, shows a complete ability on the part of the Bank to meet its liabilities so far as *figures* are concerned. But let us go into a searching examination of the Report and see the result.

The *liabilities consist* of two classes, viz: *Funds* which have been conferred upon the Bank from other sources to bank upon, and *funds* which have been created by the banking operations of the institution itself.

The *means* also consist of two classes, viz: *Assets* now available to meet liabilities, and *expenditures* that are merely indications of what is forever lost to the Bank.

1. Funds which have been *conferred* upon the Bank from other sources to bank upon, and which constitute its *actual liabilities,* are the following, viz:

Capital stock $3,186,421 65
Treasurer of Tennessee 106,341 60
Internal Improvement Fund 11,703 32
Sinking, or Contingent Fund 287,672 36
Internal Improvement dividend 5,256 00
Common School Land Districts 130,685 82
Due to Banks 338,770 18
Circulation 1,556,282 00
Certificates of Deposit 888 00
Individual Depositors 317,147 67

Actual Liabilities $5,941,168 60

1. Funds now in the Bank which constitute the available means to meet the preceding liabilities, are as follows, viz:

Discounted Notes $1,771,168 78
Domestic Bills 942,957 40
State Bonds discounted 333,890 00

Common School Bonds	90,793 60
Due from Banks	649,002 51
Notes of State and City Banks	249,537 48
Gold and Silver	684,042 17
Bills and Notes in suit	606,512 24
Real Estate	200,605 07

Actual Means	$5,528,509 25

The deficit in the Means to meet the Liabilities is $412,659 35.
Let us now examine the second class of Liabilities and Means; and first the *liabilities* created by the Bank in its banking operations:

2. Funds created by the Bank are

Discount on State Bonds	$ 50,816 55
Dividend Account	556,726 70
Exchange Account	68,338 25
Discounts received	66,062 72
Interest Account	27,080 71
Damages	3,779 48
Profit and Loss	62,281 73

Total by banking	$ 835,086 14

2. Expenditures—lost to the Bank, and which constitute the *second class of Means*, are as follows, viz:

Expense account	$ 22,970 45
Interest paid on State Bonds	1,051,012 00
Appropriation to Rivers	163,269 54
Ocoee School Fund	10,313 50

Total Expenditures	$1,247,565 49

The deficit is shown here also to be $412,479 35. The difference between this deficit and the one made under the calculations of the *first class* of Liabilities and Means, is $180, which may have been produced by some typographical error in the Report.

But there are other losses of the Bank's capital

besides the	$412,479 35
viz: E. W. Dale's defalcation (see Bank Rep, p 7)	33,800 17
Suspended Debt, '*bad*,' (see Bank Rep, p 5)	212,573 00
One-half of the 'doubtful debt' (see Bank Rep, p 5)	51,896 00
Probable loss on Real Estate	50,000 00

Apparent Deficit	$760,748 52

The President of the Bank states in his Report page 10, that the loss of the Bank is $222,573 from bad debts; and this is the only loss so presented by him; but the above analysis shows very conclusively to me that the loss is much greater.

From this analysis it will be seen that the loss of the Bank up to October, 1847, amounted to $760,748. From a nice examination of a report made to Governor Harris, by the President of the Bank, two years ago, in answer to a resolution of inquiry from the Legislature, the Governor comes to the conclusion, and I think correctly, that the Bank has lost $761,074.

From this report it also appears that there has been paid into the Bank by the State, in actual cash, at various times, $4,128,812.

For the facts here presented, the Senate is referred to a message of Governor Harris sent to the Legislature March 2, 1858, which may be found in the Appendix to the Journals of 1857-8, and in the Legislative Union, page 168. I beg leave to read a paragraph from this message. The Governor says: 'On the 1st day of January, 1858, the Bank had been in operation nineteen years and the amount of profits shown above proves that she has realized less than 6 per cent upon the actual cash capital stock which she received. With this, as the result of an experiment of nineteen years in the business of banking, is it good policy for the State to borrow money, paying an interest of six per cent per annum semi-annually, in New York, with exchange, say one per cent, to raise money to increase our banking capital?'

Let us briefly examine the report made by the Bank to the present General Assembly. On page 31, statement P of the report, you will find, 'Loss and debts deducted from the capital' to stand thus:

Loss at	Nashville	$124,551 90
"	Rogersville	45,833 62
"	Knoxville	new branch.
"	Athens	114,952 89
"	Sparta	13,774 10
"	Shelbyville	14,553 63
"	Columbia	63,257 93
"	Clarksville	57,983 16
"	Trenton	31,132 41
"	Somerville	26,757 24
"	Memphis	new branch.
Loss deducted from capital		$492,786 88

If you deduct this loss from the actual capital which the Bank ought to have from the report two years ago to Gov. Harris, which was $4,128,812, you will have $3,636,026, making only a small difference from the capital as stated in the last report, October, 1859, to this General Assembly. Here, then, you see a loss of nearly half a million, and if you will examine the report critically, and try it by the analysis made in 1847, you will be convinced that the loss is nearer one million than half a million.

The history of State banking in Tennessee shows conclusively that it has always been impolitic for the State to engage in banking at all. Not one of the experiments has succeeded, and it has been the opinion of nearly every Governor whom we have had since the present Bank was chartered that it would not and could not answer the purposes for which it was created. Almost all the Presidents of the Bank have recommended the Legislature to wind it up. The late President (Hon. C. Johnson) has been decidedly of this opinion, and only opposed it in his report to the Legislature of 1857, on account of the then monetary crisis which existed in the country. His opinion, as I understand him, is that the State should do *all* the banking for the State, or do *none*. And as the present Legislature has renewed the charters of the Union and Planters' Banks—chartered a new Bank in Memphis, one in East Tennessee, one at Clarksville, besides several others of minor importance, there certainly can be no necessity of renewing the charter of the Bank of Tennessee—and if it is to go out of existence at the expiration of its charter, it is time that a Bill was passed to put it into gradual liquidation. I do not propose now, nor will I go into an examination of the manner in which the Bank has been conducted by the different Boards of officers which have had control of its affairs. It is enough for me to know, and to announce to the Senate and the country that the Bank and its management have been a bone of political contention almost ever since its organization. It has been under the control from time to time, first of the one political party and then of the other—not long at a time under the control of either, and the party out of power invariably complaining at its management, and charging those in power with using the funds of the Bank for electioneering purposes in order to perpetuate their own existence. Whether those charges have had any foundation in truth, I know not. It is enough to state them, and every Senator will endorse the truth of the assertion.

No man will for a moment contend that the State has made any money by banking. It will not be contended by any one that the Bank has made more than 6 per cent on its capital, while many believe (the present Governor included) that it has not made so much.

I am frank to confess that I do not believe the Bank has been either wisely or profitably conducted, nor do I believe it can be while organized as at present. I do not believe any set of officers would use the same precaution and care in the management of a Bank in which they have no pecuniary interest as they would of one in which they had an interest.

It could scarcely be expected that they would; and when we see the policy of the bank continually changing, according to the whims and notions of the Legislature—making laws for its government at one session and changing them at another—cutting the Branches loose from all control of the parent Bank, as far as they possibly can—changing the officers almost at every session, or as often as the one party or the other may have the majority, sometimes selecting men for political purposes as officers, rather than from any other considerations, I am constrained to believe that the Bank is corrupting rather than beneficial to the people.

The capital of the Bank of Tennessee, as reported to the present General Assembly, consists of:

Proceeds of State Bonds	$1,000,000
School Fund	803,373
Common School Fund	45,621
Surplus Revenue	932,879
Union Bank Stock	664,494
Planters' Bank Stock	232,700
	$3,679,068

The Bank Report says that the School Fund, which constitutes a part of the capital, amounts to $1,120,589.

The statutes of the State affirm that the School Fund amounts to $1,500,000, making a difference in their estimates of $379,410 86. Instead, then, of the capital of the Bank being $3,679,068, it seems to me that it ought to be over four millions of dollars.

If you take the capital as reported to the General Assembly of 1847, you will find it to be $3,191,215. Add to this amount the stock in the Union Bank $664,494, and the stock in the Planters' Bank $232,700, which were added to the capital of the Bank of Tennessee by the last Legislature, and the amount will be $4,088,409.

Again: If you take the surplus revenue, which I understand to be

$1,353,209, and add it to the capital instead of the $932,879, as reported by the Bank, you will still have over $4,000,000 of capital in the Bank.

If I am correct in these estimates and calculations, (and I think I am certainly correct as to the surplus revenue,) it appears that a much larger amount has been lost by the bank than is supposed. The liabilities and assets of banks, as made out on paper, always equal each other. They are made to do so by the rules of the bank; and it is one of the duties of their clerks to *make* the means always equal the liabilities. And I suppose if a clerk in a bank could not, or did not, make his books *prove*, that he would very soon be dismissed. It will not do then to conclude that a bank is solvent and doing well merely because the assets equal the liabilities as made out in its reports, because a broken bank will make the same exhibit. This may be easily enough understood when we recollect that the term assets or means in Bank Reports include the bad and doubtful notes as well as the good.

In offering this bill to wind up the Bank of Tennessee I do not wish to be understood as opposing banks. I am the friend and advocate of banks —believe that they are essentially necessary to carry on a healthy and prosperous commerce, and that no country can prosper without banks. But certainly no man will contend that it is wise policy in a State to set herself up as a trader in the commerce of the country—a dealer in exchanges, and a shipper of produce in competition with her citizens.

If the bank of Tennessee had been under the control and management of those who had a pecuniary interest in its well being, it would in all probability have done as well as any other bank. But whilst other banks have made large dividends for their stockholders, the Legislature have been under the necessity from time to time of assisting the State Bank, in order to enable it to keep up. Every advantage which could be extended to it has been extended, and still it suffers by comparison with some others, and no one who understands its operations believes that it can maintain a safe or even respectable status in competition with its rivals.

The parent Bank has but little control over the Branches, and some of the latter have been so badly managed that the notes payable at their counters have accumulated in the parent Bank, at one time, to more than half a million on account of their inability to redeem them. Still, the Legislature refuses to give the parent Bank control of the Branches while it continues to hold her responsible for the forthcoming of the entire capital of the Bank. It is understood here, and I suppose will not be denied, that without the support of the parent Bank some of the Branches would not be able to maintain their credit a month. If the Branches, or any one of them fail, the whole concern suffers, and the parent Bank is compelled in order to preserve its own credit, to preserve the credit of its Branches also. And as our Governors, Bank officers, directors, and all who are conversant with its operations, declare that it ought to be put into a state of liquidation, I have introduced this Bill and urge its passage.

The objection heretofore made against winding up the Bank of Tennessee was, that we did not have banking capital enough. This objection can not be urged now. There have been banks enough chartered by this Legislature to answer all the purposes of trade and commerce. *Banking* is the business of individuals and should not be engaged in by the State, and certainly it should not be done, when the State borrows the money to bank with. There is no inducement for any man to seek a position in the State Bank except for the salary paid him for his services. Positions in the Bank are sought after by men, not to make money for the State, but to make money for themselves, and consequently there are often and repeated applications to the Legislature to increase the pay of its officers, and to increase the number. Every man almost seems to be influenced by the principle, that as the State owns the capital, she can afford to pay large salaries and ought to pay them, and all try to see how much they can get for themselves rather than how much they can make for the State. This, however, is nothing more than a natural propensity, and if the State loses her money she ought to attribute it to her own foolish policy rather than to the mismanagement or dishonesty of the Bank officers. Nothing better could be expected from the system.

The Bill on your table, Mr. Speaker, proposes to wind up this Bank. It effects its object by an easy, safe and certain process—no debtor of the Bank need be oppressed—all, with the exception of drawers of bills payable out of the State, have five years to pay their liabilities, interest included, in ten equal semi-annual instalments, by securing the debt. This will ensure the collection of many bad debts, and of some which would otherwise be eventually lost. The expenses of the Bank are stopped almost at once, and the Bank will go out of existence so gradually that no one will feel the loss. It will expire like the flickerings of a candle in its socket, or go down like a summer's sun beneath the western horizon, leaving I trust, not a cloud behind it, and none to mourn its departure but those who are fattening on its substance."

Despite the bipartisan support of Governor Harris and Senator Richardson, the Bank of Tennessee was not finally put out of business until the Brownlow regime in 1866.[122] Thereafter ensued one of the longest and most bitterly contested lawsuits in the annals of Tennessee. In a volume of 566 pages, in a case entitled the *State of Tennessee and Samuel Watson, Trustee, vs. President and Directors of Bank of Tennessee*, the Supreme Court of Tennessee in 1875 wrote *finis* to one of the most controversial issues ever determined by that tribunal.[123]

It is a bit singular that none of the Nashville newspapers carried any significant editorial comment upon the defeat of the bill to wind up the business of the Bank of Tennessee. A strong Democratic organ [124] contented itself on this matter by merely inserting the following sentence without comment:

"In the Senate on Wednesday, Mr. Richardson's bill to wind up the Bank of Tennessee was rejected."

In its issue of March 21, 1860, this same newspaper carried in full Senator Richardson's speech favoring the liquidation of the Bank of Tennessee.

The only editorial [125] in any Nashville newspaper that carried even a *hint* as to the newspaper's attitude on this highly controversial measure appeared in an Opposition newspaper:

[122] *Acts of Tennessee*, 1866, Chapter 28.
[123] *Tennessee Reports*, Baxter 5, 1–566.
[124] *Nashville Union and American*, March 18, 1860.
[125] *Republican Banner and Nashville Whig*, March 22, 1860.

"We call especial attention to the able speech in this morning's paper, by the distinguished Senator from Rutherford, Dr. John W. Richardson, in support of his bill to wind up the Bank of Tennessee. It is as full of facts and arguments in support of his proposition as it could well be, and they are presented with a force and logical effect which is irresistible. No one can rise from its perusal with any doubt in his mind as to what *ought* to be done with the Bank of Tennessee.

The speech referred to is very valuable as containing a succinct and reliable history of Banking in Tennessee from the beginning, prepared with no little labor and research. It is well worth filing away carefully."

Although Governor Harris "earnestly recommended" the adoption of a resolution proposing to amend the Constitution in such manner as to prohibit the State from assuming financial liability, especially in the issuance of bank charters, unless and until such items were submitted to and approved by popular vote, yet the Legislature failed to enact such legislation. Early in the legislative session, on October 28, 1859, the Democratic Speaker of the Senate introduced a resolution [126] to that effect, but the official record discloses no further action on the matter. Representative John J. Williams of Hickman County, likewise a Democrat, tried his hand on the same proposition. The Williams resolution carried a proviso to the effect that the Legislature should and would have power at all times to alter or amend charters of incorporation when "deemed expedient for the public good."[127] The resolution was held in a state of suspended animation until February 11, 1860, when it was rejected by a vote of 34 to 25.[128] And so, the recommendation of Governor Harris went down the drain.

But Governor Harris had better luck with a recommendation that all State stock in turnpikes be sold and the proceeds applied toward the extinguishment of the State debt. Under the provisions of the law [129] the Governor, Secretary of State, and the State Comptroller were authorized to advertise and sell all such investments and apply the proceeds to the reduction of the State debt. As of that date, the State debt proper was reported to be $3,844,606.66,[130] whereas the amount loaned by the State to Turnpike Companies was reported to be $57,000. But the State's financial picture was not quite so roseate as the above figures, at first glance, would indicate. A recapitulation of State *liabilities*, as reported by the State Comptroller on October, –, 1859, mounted to the peak of $16,643,606.66 of which amount State bonds "loaned to Railroad Companies" exceeded ten million dollars!

From a voluminous Report consisting of fifty printed pages in the

---

[126] *Senate Journal*, 1859, 83–84.
[127] *House Journal*, 1859, 58.
[128] *Ibid.*, 695.
[129] *Acts of Tennessee*, 1859, Chapter 55.
[130] *Public Documents, Tennessee Legislature*, 1859, 41 and 46.

official proceedings of the Legislature,[131] Governor Harris was able to obtain specific information regarding the operations of the Penitentiary for the preceding biennium, 1857-1859. The Report proper was based upon the several reports from the Inspector, the Superintendent, the Agent, the Architect, the Chaplain, and the Prison Physician. The prison population had shown a gradual increase, numbering at the date of the report 378 inmates. The age range was from thirteen years to seventy years, there being thirteen in the former category and six in the latter. In the group from eighteen years to twenty-five, there were one hundred and twenty-three convicts. One hundred and thirty-seven were married, one hundred and seventy-three unmarried, with the balance consisting of two widows, forty-seven widowers, and nineteen divorcees. Two hundred and ninety-one of the inmates could "read and write," seventy-six were illiterates, while eleven were listed as having a "classical education." Two hundred and seventeen were listed as intemperate, one hundred and forty-four as "common drinkers," and seventeen as being temperate. The crimes committed consisted, among others, of larceny, murder, robbery, passing counterfeit money, bigamy, and "giving a pass to Slaves." By grand divisions, East Tennessee had contributed one hundred and twenty-two of the prison inmates, Middle Tennessee, one hundred and five, while West Tennessee had sent up one hundred and fifty-one. By counties, Shelby had contributed the largest number, eighty-four; Davidson, forty-five; and Knox, twenty. Each of the sixty-eight counties had at least one representative. Three hundred and eighteen of the convicts had been born in America, while foreign countries had furnished sixty, the "Sons of Erin" having the banner number amounting to thirty.

Space is lacking for the inclusion of statements regarding the overcrowded conditions at the Penitentiary, the poor sanitary conditions which bordered upon "slow murder," and the grossly underpaid personnel managing the institution. With inadequate sanitary facilities and with two prisoners, at times, jammed into the extremely small cells, it seems almost miraculous that only twenty-seven deaths had occurred during the biennium. In accord with the suggestions of various officials connected with the Penitentiary, Governor Harris recommended the enlargement of the prison grounds, an increase in the number of cells, and the construction of a subterranean sewer.

Just why Governor Harris recommended rather strongly the leasing of the prison labor to private individuals or incorporated concerns is difficult to comprehend. Perhaps he was influenced by a statement

[131] *Ibid.*, 227-277.

Author's note. From both intensive and extensive research among State records, beginning with the establishment of the Penitentiary in 1831, no other State Department or State Agency has provided as *complete and detailed* reports as has the Penitentiary.

in the State Comptroller's Report to the effect that since its establishment the Penitentiary "had been a vampire upon the public Treasury."[132] Whatever may have been the basis, at any rate the Governor
emphatically stated in his Message that

"Governments, however, are never good financiers—never manage
pecuniary interests successfully or well—and ours forms no exception to the
general rule in this respect.
    In view of which fact, I do not doubt but that the best interests of the
State would be promoted by leasing out the entire labor of the prison annually . . ."

What makes the Governor's above recommendation appear un-
realistic was a statement by the Penitentiary Inspectors, namely, J. D.
Winston, W. G. Harding, and J. Overton, that the financial condition
of the prison "showed a profit to the State of over fifty thousand dollars, including the work on the new wing and the Capitol."[133]
    About one week after the transmission of the Governor's Message
to the Legislature, Democratic Representative George V. Hebb of
Lincoln County

"Introduced House Bill No. 53 to be entitled An Act to Lease out the
Penitentiary."[134]

On February 7, 1860, Representative Hebb withdrew his bill and that
was the end of his proposal.[135]
    Over in the Senate, Democratic Senator B. L. Stovall from a tier of
West Tennessee counties, Henry, Weakley, and Obion, introduced a
bill to lease out the Penitentiary.[136] Inasmuch as this was the first attempt to lease out the convict labor, it may be advisable to ascertain
the conditions and provisions under which such arrangements would
operate. The original Stovall bill is herewith incorporated verbatim:

"A Bill To Lease out the Penitentiary.

    Be it enacted by the General Assembly of the State of Tennessee, That
the Governor of the State of Tennessee is hereby authorized and directed
to lease out the Penitentiary for the term of four years, twenty days after
the adjournment of the present Legislature. And that the Governor be directed to give notice of the same through two or more newspapers, published in Nashville, for the time of twenty days; and that all the tools,
engines, and everything appertaining to the same be turned over to the
said Lessee; and an inventory of the same shall be taken, and the said

<hr>

[132] Ibid., vi.
[133] Ibid., 228.
[134] House Journal, 1859, 34.
    Author's note. Unfortunately, the original bill could not be located in the State
Archives.
[135] Ibid., 643.
[136] Senate Journal, 1859, 198.
    Author's note. Original manuscript bill is in the State Archives, Nashville.

Lessee shall, on the expiration of his said term—the tools and implements shall be delivered to the State in as good fix as when received by the said Lessee or Lessees. The buildings, machinery, fixtures and tools to be kept in good order; unavoidable accidents, as respects the buildings and machinery, only excepted.

First. In the event a fire should occur in said institution, without any fault of the keeper, his assistant or guards, the General Assembly, if in session, if not, the Governor shall cause to be erected as soon as practicable, other permanent and suitable buildings, as they may deem for the best interest of the State, not exceeding $12,000, to be paid for out of any money in the Treasury, to the credit of the State. The Governor of the State may make such deduction from the rent as he may deem just and equitable, on account of loss of the buildings by fire, and his decision in the premises is to be subject to the ratification of the Legislature.

Second. If the rent due at the close of any one year, shall remain unpaid for the period of ten days, it shall be the duty of the Governor to cause a judgment to be rendered against said Lessee and their or his security, at the next or any succeeding term of the Davidson Circuit Court, by motion.

Third. The said Keeper or Lessee, as aforesaid, in addition to the said amount which he and his security agrees to pay, shall furnish at his or their own expense, the necessary guard, and pay the same for their services, feed and clothe the convicts; furnish all the necessary bed and bedding for the cells; pay the liberating money to the convicts, and pay a regular physician, whose duty it shall be to examine into the health and situation of each convict, and report to the Governor whether any convict is engaged at any work which is injurious to his health, if so, the Governor shall cause such convict to be changed to other work; and shall, in all other respects, pay all the necessary expenses in maintaining said institution, and shall save the State harmless from all expenses connected with the management of the same during the existence of said lease.

Fourth. The Governor shall appoint three Inspectors, and one Keeper, whose duty it shall be to see that the said convicts are humanely, kindly, and properly treated; and see that the food and clothing of said convicts are the same as now allowed by the State; one or more of said Inspectors or Keeper are to visit said Prison every other day or oftener; all four are to make a report every month of the condition of said institution, or oftener if need be, to the Governor. Said Inspectors are to receive $2.00 per day *each*, for their services, for each day they attend as now and the Keeper $1,000 per annum, and to be paid by the State, and to hold their appointment for two years, unless dismissed by the Governor or resignation, in that case the Governor is directed to appoint other persons in their places. No inspector of the Penitentiary shall become personally interested, directly or indirectly in the profits thereof, or in its management.

No laws are to be enacted which may impair, substantially, the right of the lessee or lessees. The Legislature may, however, pass such laws as may be deemed necessary for the welfare and the reformation of the convicts.

The said lessee shall execute a bond for $30,000, with sufficient security, conditioned for faithful compliance with the contract and provisions of this act, which bond shall be approved by the Governor.

That should the Lessee or Lessees of the Penitentiary fail or refuse to comply with the obligations imposed upon him by this act, and his or their contract as set forth, or should be guilty of any misfeasance or malfeasance in office, then, and in that event the Judge of the Davidson County Circuit

Court shall have power to try the same before twelve legal jurors of the State of Tennessee; and if convicted, to be punished as any other misdemeanor, and to be removed forthwith: *Provided*, the jurors so agree.

Be it further enacted, That all the articles which they may now have on hand, shall be sold for the benefit of the State; and that all articles remaining unfinished shall be sold to the highest bidder; and all material on hand to be sold to the highest bidder, for cash; and the mules, &c. be sold.

Be it further enacted, That the said Lessee shall have the free use of the stone quarry owned by the State during said lease.

Be it further enacted, That any improvements made by the said Lessee in the way of a sewer and hospital, the State will make an allowance for the same—what the said work may be valued at by three disinterested workmen—Provided that the said work does not amount to more than what said Lessee obligates himself to pay to the State for the Lease of the same."

After routine first and second readings, the bill on third reading was rejected on February 17, 1860, by a vote of twelve to nine.[137] Apparently, the Legislature was influenced in its action by the favorable financial report concerning the Penitentiary, as reported by the duly constituted authorities, namely, the Penitentiary Inspectors. And so, another of Governor Harris' recommendations went down to defeat. Unfortunately, many years later the leasing out of the convict labor of the Penitentiary went into effect with the result that some of the most shocking scandals in the history of Tennessee ensued. It is regrettable that Isham G. Harris, one of the strongest of all Tennessee Governors, should have been the first Chief Executive to recommend such a procedure. For some unknown reason, his usually keen and incisive vision had become blurred on this occasion.

With regard to Agriculture, Governor Harris reviewed the progress and benefits that had accrued as a result of legislation enacted during the past three or four years. A previous appropriation of ten thousand dollars had been allocated to the Middle Division Fair, but the funds had not been utilized for that purpose. In the meanwhile, the Mechanical Association at Nashville had requested that these funds be transferred to that organization for the purpose of building a hall. Governor Harris left the matter in the hands of the legislators who failed to enact any law upon the subject.

In compliance with previous statutes, Governor Harris made arrangements for re-running and re-marking the State lines between the State of Tennessee and the States of Kentucky and Virginia. Exhaustive reports were prepared and submitted to Governor Harris by the Commissioners who ran the lines. Suffice it to say that these lines, thus established, constitute the permanent boundary lines since recognized by the respective States. The previous appropriations for performing this service became exhausted before the work was completed, and

---

[137] *Ibid.*, 505.

it became necessary for Governor Harris to borrow upon his personal note the sum of two thousand dollars for continuing the work. By special act,[138] he was reimbursed for this amount.

If any one is intrigued by reading the "field notes" of a surveyor, he is respectfully referred to the twenty printed pages of the act [139] that fixed the permanent boundary line between Tennessee and Kentucky. Nineteen of the twenty printed pages of the law follow without deviation the "style" exhibited on the first page of the law, to-wit:

". . . Beginning on the east bank of the Mississippi river, near Compromise, Kentucky, in north latitude thirty-six degrees, twenty-nine minutes and fifty-five and seven-tenth's seconds, (36° 29′ 55."7,) and running south eighty-nine degrees, fifteen minutes and eighteen seconds, east, (S. 89° 15′ 18″ E.,) passing a large set rock at station four hundred and fifty-six feet, (0..456,) and passing a small set rock at station twelve thousand eight hundred and forty feet, (12..840,) to station thirteen thousand two hundred and fifteen feet, (13..215,) the west bank of the Mississippi river.

Beginning on the east bank of the Mississippi river, at station thirty-five thousand three hundred and sixty-three feet, (35..363,) in latitude thirty-six degrees, thirty minutes and twenty-nine hundredth's of a second, (36° 30′ 00."29,) and running south eighty-nine degrees, thirty-five minutes and fifteen seconds east, (S.89° 35′ 15″, E.,) passing a set rock at station thirty-five thousand eight hundred and seventy-seven feet, (35..877,) to a set rock at station forty thousand and fifty-five feet, (40..055); thence north eighty-three degrees, forty minutes and nineteen seconds, east, (N. 83° 40′ 19″, E.,) passing stone No. 1, at station fifty-two thousand and eight hundred feet, (52..800) to station sixty-six thousand seven hundred and fifty-one, (66..751,) to a mulberry post; thence south, eighty-eight degrees, thirty-five minutes and fourteen seconds east, (S. 88° 35′ 14″, E.,) to stone No. 2, station seventy-nine thousand five hundred and fifty ft., (79..550,) thence south eighty-eight degrees, fifty-seven minutes and forty seconds, east, (S. 88° 57′ 40″, E.,) to station ninety thousand seven hundred and twenty-three ft., (90..723); . . ."

The above legislation was enacted in light of the recommendation of Governor Harris as set forth in a special Message, to-wit:

Legislative Message*, December 17, 1859.

"GENTLEMEN OF THE SENATE AND HOUSE OF REPRESENTATIVES:

I herewith transmit the Joint Report of the Commissioners heretofore appointed by the Governor of the State of Kentucky and myself, under the authority of the law of our respective States, to run and re-mark the line established by compact, between the States of Tennessee and Kentucky. And also the supplemental report of

---

[138] *Private Acts of Tennessee,* 1859, Chapter 8.
[139] *Public Acts of Tennessee,* 1859, Chapter 79.
* *Senate Journal,* 1859, 269–270.
  House Journal, 1859, 432–433.

the Tennessee Commissioners, correcting some clerical errors which were committed in copying said joint report.

It will be seen by reference to this report, that the commissioners commenced their survey upon the east bank of the Mississippi river, from which point they have run the line to the eastern boundary of the State of Kentucky; thence to the southwestern corner of the State of Virginia; marking the same by planting stone posts, marked as monuments of boundary, every five miles upon it, as well as by marking the timber all along the line where timber was to be found.

The report and accompanying maps containing an accurate description of the line, as run and marked, and the large map required by the act of 1858, to be deposited in the office of Secretary of State, I am assured by the commissioners is in progress of preparation and will be ready at an early day. I respectfully recommend the passage of a law establishing the line reported, run and marked, as above stated, as the true boundary between the States of Kentucky and Tennessee, providing, however, that land titles of any description whatever acquired under the authority of either of said States, shall not be affected or prejudiced by the establishment of said line, but that the same shall be, and remain as valid as though said line had not been established, and provided, further, that said act shall take effect only on the express condition, that the legislature of the State of Kentucky, shall pass an act establishing said line as the true boundary between the two States, and also providing, that land titles shall not be affected by the establishments of the same.

The report shows that the expenses of the party under the control of the Tennessee Commissioners amount to $16,617 34, of which amount they have already

Received from the Treasury the sum of . . $5,000 00
And the proceeds of the sale of property
sold by commissioners when they completed
the work 952 78 $5,952 78

Which leaves a balance of $10,664 59
still due to the various employees of the Tennessee Commissioners.

This amount does not include any compensation to the commissioners; the law under which they were appointed being silent upon the subject, the duty of fixing their compensation will devolve upon you. I see from the report that the Joint Commissioner suggest the rate $350 00 per month, as a fair compensation for their services, and in view of the weighty responsibility, to-wit: exposure and privation necessarily involved in the performance of the duty assigned them, I do not regard that amount as unreasonable. I therefore, respectfully recommend, that the sum of $10,664 59, be appropriated for the purpose of paying off the balance due their various employees, with such additional sums as may be necessary to fully compensate the Commissioners for their services in the premises.

Which report and recommendations are respectfully submitted to your favorable consideration.

ISHAM G. HARRIS."

The State Library was commended to the favorable consideration of the Legislature with reference to appropriation of funds sufficient for a continuation of the service begun by previous administrations. The Library's source of funds consisted of an appropriation of five hundred dollars per annum and one-sixteenth of a cent on each one hundred dollars of taxable property. For the preceding biennium, 1857–1859, the Library was the beneficiary of a total of $4,382.34.

According to the Report [140] of the State Librarian, Return Jonathan Meigs, all but $286.79 had been expended for the purchase of books and operating expenses during the preceding biennium. The book collection had been increased by 1,643 volumes, through purchase, and by means of exchanges and donations a little over two thousand additional volumes had been procured, giving an overall total of 8,250 volumes in the State Library. As to the nature of the books in the Library, Mr. Meigs assured the public that

"No mere curiosity of literature has been purchased, nor any books but those of acknowledged reputation and value; and I feel confident there is not a volume in the collection which a competent judge would desire to see excluded from the shelves. . . ."

With commendable attitude and vision, Governor Harris in his Message stressed the value of building up a representative Library that would offer facilities and advantages for the young men of the State who might the better prepare themselves for being useful citizens by utilizing the resources of the Library "through research and investigation in almost every branch of knowledge." In harmony with the general recommendations of Governor Harris, the Legislature passed a law [141] appropriating twenty-five hundred dollars annually for the

[140] *Public Documents, Tennessee Legislature*, 1859, 145–150.
[141] *Private Acts of Tennessee*, 1859, Chapter 53.
Author's note. Just why this law was placed under PRIVATE ACTS rather than the Public Acts can not be determined.

"And Curst be he yt Moves my Bones."
From Epitaph on Shakespeare's Tombstone at Stratford-on-Avon.

support of the Library and raised the salary of the Librarian to eight hundred dollars per year.

No specific recommendations were made by Governor Harris with reference to Weights and Measures mentioned by him in his Message; he submitted in reality only a skeleton report dealing with the situation as then existing. The only legislation enacted bearing upon the subject was the repeal of Section 1834 of the 1858 Code, and making in the law "*a half-barrel*" refer to *capacity* rather than to *dimensions*.[142] Incidentally, the salary of the Superintendent of Weights and Measures, who also was designated as the Keeper of the Public Arms, was increased fifty dollars, making his total annual salary six hundred dollars.[143]

Six thousand copies of the Report of the Joint Committee to investigate the offices of the State Comptroller and Secretary of State were reported by Governor Harris to have been printed, but no copy of same seems to be extant. Apparently, the Legislature was not impressed with the necessity or desirability of passing any legislation bearing upon the subject, contenting itself merely with providing for payment of the investigators [144] and raising the salary of the Secretary of State fifty dollars annually.[145] Likewise the recommendation of the Governor regarding the protection of the Great Seal of the State failed to receive any type of legislation whatsoever.

The status of the Hermitage was fully set forth in the concluding paragraph of the Executive Message. As pointed out by Governor Harris, the Federal Government had failed to accept the property upon the terms designated by a previous Legislature, and the then present occupant had served notice that he would vacate the property at an early date. Governor Harris urged that proper action be taken in order to

". . . Protect as the shrine of patriotism and to decorate as the resort of beauty and taste the beloved resting-place of him who will be regarded, by all coming generations, as one of the purest patriots, and as having been at once the hero and the statesman, the captain and the sage."

Doubtless with the best of intentions but with poor judgment, Senator John Trimble of Davidson County introduced a bill [146]

"To erect a monument to Andrew Jackson on Capitol Hill, in the City of Nashville."

Senator Trimble's proposal [147] is herewith reproduced in facsimile:

---

[142] *Acts of Tennessee*, 1859, Chapter 48.
[143] *Ibid.*, Chapter 117.
[144] *Ibid., Private Acts*, Chapter 48.
[145] *Ibid.*, Chapter 92.
[146] *Senate Journal*, 1859, 388.
[147] Manuscript bill in State Archives, at Nashville.

On February 13, 1860, Senator Trimble's bill came up on third reading and passed unanimously,[148] and was ordered to be engrossed and transmitted to the House of Representatives. On February 16 the bill routinely passed first reading in the House. Before the bill reached second reading, however, the following Message* was received from Governor Harris accompanied by a letter from the adopted son of Andrew Jackson:

Executive Department
Feby 27th 1860

Gentlemen of the Senate
And House of Representatives

As there is a bill now pending in the House of Representatives, having already passed the Senate, directing the removal of the remains of General Andrew Jackson and those of Mrs. Jackson from the Hermitage to Capitol Hill, and the erection of a suitable monument &c &c I deem it proper to lay before you a communication which I have just received from Maj. Andrew Jackson remonstrating against the passage of the same, By reference to which, it will be seen that upon his death bed, Genl. Jackson expressed the hope that the remains of himself and wife, should in no event be taken from the Hermitage, I therefore respectfully recommend that said bill be not passed, and that you will pass a law directing the disposition of such parts of the Hermitage property as it is deemed advisable to dispose of and directing specifically as to the manner of preserving and taking care of the remainder, which will of course include the tomb and mansion &c,   Respectfully

Isham G. Harris

"Sea-Long, Bay of St. Louis
Shieldsborough, Feb. 22, 1860.

HIS EXCELLENCY GOV. HARRIS:

My Dear Sir:—I was called from my old home, the Hermitage, a few weeks since, to the South, my present residence, on some business, and expected to return before the adjournment of the present Legislature, which perhaps I cannot do. I now write you, sir, for the purpose of expressing the dying sentiments of my venerated father to me, and Mrs. Jackson, just before his decease, as I perceive a movement has been made in the Legislature, to have his and Mrs. Jackson's remains removed to the State Capitol

---

[148] *Senate Journal*, 1859, 479.
* *House Journal*, 1859, 811–812.

grounds at Nashville. He called me and my wife up to his bed-side and said: 'My son and daughter, it may become necessary for you to sell or dispose of the Hermitage grounds hereafter, but I beg of you to let my remains, and those of my dear wife, remain together at the Hermitage, a sacred spot to me, there to rest in peace and quiet until the final day of judgment, when our Lord and Master will call for us, &c., &c., &c.'

I have written you rather hastily, Governor, upon the subject, and will you do me the favor to present the expressions I have here used, of the dying request of my father, to the members of the Legislature generally. Perhaps they may, under the circumstances, reconsider the matter. I trust so. I, nor any member of my family, have been consulted in the matter; therefore, we all earnestly and respectfully protest against it. Oh, let his bones and ashes repose at his own chosen and loved Hermitage. Do plead with the members about it; and oblige your distressed friend and

Obedient servant,
ANDREW JACKSON."

The above communications caused the House of Representatives to end any further action on the measure "without a dissenting voice." [149] But there remained the question as to what to do in regard to preserving the mansion and the premises from falling into disuse and consequently into decay. Appropriately enough, Democratic Senator James T. Lane on March 15 (Jackson's birthday) introduced a bill

"To protect the Hermitage and the tomb of General Jackson."[150]

When the bill reached third and final reading, an Opposition Senator, D. V. Stokely, moved to amend the bill by

". . . Directing the Governor to sell the entire Hermitage tract of land to the highest responsible bidder, except three acres of ground on which the tomb of General Jackson is situated, the proceeds of said sale to be invested in the purchase of the bonds of the State sold to raise money to buy said lands."

Another Opposition Senator, M. V. Nash, was a bit more generous than his political confrère and moved to strike out three acres and insert fifty acres. Fortunately, the mole-like vision of the two Senators was not allowed to prevail, inasmuch as both amendments were voted down. The original bill was then passed on final reading by a vote of 22 to 0.[151] The act in its entirety was as follows:[152]

"CHAPTER 204.

An Act to protect the Hermitage and tomb of Gen. Jackson.

WHEREAS, it is understood the grounds and fixtures of the Hermitage, and that the tomb of Gen. Jackson are in a dilapidated condition, and that suitable repairs and improvements are absolutely necessary; therefore—

Section 1. *Be it enacted by the General Assembly of the State of Tennessee,* That the Governor and Secretary of State are hereby requested and authorized to make, or cause to be made, such repairs and improvements

---

[149] *House Journal,* 1859, 1046.
[150] *Senate Journal,* 1859, 680.
[151] *Ibid.,* 706–707.
[152] *Acts of Tennessee,* 1859, Chapter 204.

as in their judgment are necessary and proper, and that they employ, if necessary, such a laboring force as will keep the houses, yards, gardens, tomb and surrounding grounds in a neat and perfect state of repair, and for the payment of any expenses which may be incurred for such improvements as may be ordered by the Governor and Secretary, the Comptroller is hereby directed to issue his warrant on the treasury, upon the order of the Governor for the same.

Sec. 2. *Be it further enacted,* That this act take effect from its passage.

W. C. WHITTHORNE,
Speaker of the House of Representatives.

TAZ. W. NEWMAN,
Speaker of the Senate.

Passed, March 24, 1860."

On the whole, the most important recommendation of Governor Harris to the Thirty-Third General Assembly related to the banking and currency question. In compliance with his request, remedial legislation was enacted that put an end to the "wildcat" banks that had sprung up under the so-called Free Banking law. The remedy consisted in the repeal of that law and a stringent requirement that all banks substitute for "paper capital" the real coin of the realm. This prerequisite shattered the roseate dreams of the plundering "wildcatters" who had robbed and raped the honest yeomanry of untold savings. If no other wholesome legislation had been enacted, this one action was sufficient to have reflected glory and merited credit upon both the Executive and Legislative Departments of State. The other recommendations of Governor Harris were of a rather minor nature and most of them were allowed to fall by the wayside. Some of the issues that caused the Legislature to bypass a number of the Governor's suggestions will be noted and recorded forthwith.

Towering above all other National and State issues at the time (1859) was the slavery question. At the bottom of the controversy lay the question of *political ascendency* in the Federal Government. The pivotal point involved the equal representation of States in the United States Senate, for a majority in the Senate amounted substantially to political control of the Federal Government. The faster the free States increased in population, with a consequent importance in an increased membership in the Lower House of Congress, the more essential it was to the Southern section to multiply States below the slave line, and to push up the slave line so as to include more States when admitted to the Union. Hence arose the bitter and prolonged battles in Congress over the Missouri Compromise, the Compromise of 1850, the Kansas-Nebraska Bill, the plight of "bleeding Kansas," *et cetera*.

Aiding and abetting the slave interests were the downward revision of the tariff, the withdrawal of the ship subsidies, and the celebrated Dred Scott decision, all of which served to open up the territories to the advancement of slavery. Thirteen days after the convening of the 1859

Legislature, a bomb-shell was exploded by the fanatical John Brown who selected a strategical point of attack at Harper's Ferry, the site of the United States armory and arsenal and offering an easy gateway to the South. On Sunday night, October 16, 1859, heading up his force of seventeen white men and five Negroes, Brown moved to the assault which collapsed. Two days later, the survivors were hemmed up in a fire engine house whose doors were battered down and the insurgents captured by a force of United States Marines under the leadership of Colonel Robert E. Lee and Lieutenant J. E. B. Stuart. Ten of the raiders were killed, and Brown along with six of his companions were adorned with hemp neckties on December 2.

This appalling episode resounded throughout the land with the clangor of a fire alarm, accentuating the fears of a people whose raw nerves were already excited by threats of a race war. Nine days after the Harper's Ferry incident, Democratic Representative William M. Bayless of Washington County dropped the following resolution into the legislative hopper: [153]

"WHEREAS, a most dangerous epoch has arisen in the history of our country, based upon the fanatical aggressions of Northern Black Republicans, on the reserved rights of the States and the institutions of the South, seeking to abolish slavery by preventing the extension into common territory, and rendering it insecure and hazardous in our midst; *And, Whereas,* in the recent insurrection at Harper's Ferry, as well as in the revolutionary scenes in Kansas, we recognize the legitimate fruits of that treasonable policy avowed by the acknowledged head of the Black Republican party, Wm. H. Seward, in his famous Rochester speech, in which he said:

'These antagonistic systems (free and slave labor) are continually coming into closer contact, and collision results. Shall I tell you what the collision means? They who think that it is accidental, unnecessary, the work of interested or fanatical agitators, and therefore ephemeral, mistake the case altogether. It is an irrepressible conflict between opposing and enduring forces, and it means that the United States must, and will, sooner or later, become either entirely a slave-holding nation, or entirely a free-labor nation. Either the cotton and rice fields of South Carolina and sugar plantations of Louisiana will ultimately be tilled by free labor, and Charleston and New Orleans become marts for legitimate merchandize alone, or else the rye fields and wheat fields of Massachusetts and New York must again be surrendered by their farmers to slave culture, and to the production of slaves; and Boston and New York become once more markets for trade in the bodies and souls of men. It is the failure to apprehend this great truth that induces so many unsuccessful attempts at final compromise between the slave and free States, and it is the existence of this great fact that renders all such pretended compromises, when made, vain and ephemeral.'

And, Whereas, Henry Wilson, another Black Republican Senator from Massachusetts has declared:

'Let us remember that more than three millions of bondsmen, groaning

---

[153] *House Journal,* 1859, 98–100.

Author's note. This resolution, with very few minor changes, became Resolution Number 5 in *Acts of Tennessee,* 1859, 653–656.

under nameless woes, demand that we shall reprove each other, and that we labor for their deliverance.' I tell you here to-night, that the agitation of this question of human slavery will continue while the foot of a slave presses the soil of the American Republic.'

And Mr. Wade, another Black Republican Senator from Ohio, has said:

'There is really no union now between the North and South, and he believed no two nations upon the earth entertained feelings of more bitter rancour towards each other than these two nations of the Republic. The only salvation of the Union, therefore, was to be found in divesting it entirely from all taint of slavery.'

And, Whereas, Senator Seward, addressing Southern Senators from his place in that body, proclaimed to the world that:

'At last a new voice issues from your own region, from the South, from the slave States, and protests against your further persistence in this mad enterprise, (of extending slavery,) and admonishes you that it must and will fail. The cohorts are gathering from the South; the men of moderation and conservatism, who as they have heretofore moderated in favor of slavery and against freedom, will now be obliged, in consistency with their just and well established character and their habitual patriotism, to moderate against you in favor of freedom, and rise up unanimously against slavery.'

And again, at Rome, in New York:

'It will be the show of the next two years to witness the organization of this same Republican party within slave States, under the lead of brave and true men, such as Frank P. Blair, of Missouri, and Cassius M. Clay, of Kentucky. What remains of organization as a national party to be effected is as sure and certain as what has already occurred, and is now so distinctly seen.'

Therefore,

Resolved by the General Assembly of the State of Tennessee, That we recognize in the recent outbreak at Harper's Ferry the natural fruits of the treasonable 'irrepressible conflict' doctrine put forth by the great head of the Black Republican party, and echoed by his subordinates; and that it becomes the imperative duty of national men of all parties throughout the Union, to announce to the world their sense of its infamy, and to unite in crushing out its authors, as traitors to their country, and as deadly enemies to the public peace, the rights of the States, and the preservation of our Republican institutions.

Resolved, That we record it as the sense of the Tennessee Legislature, that the declaration of Mr. Seward that a respectable portion of the Southern people, under the lead of such men as Cassius M. Clay and Francis P. Blair, will unite with the Black Republican party to prevent the extension of slavery, and will eventually 'rise up against slavery,' is a libel upon the honor and loyalty of the Southern people, and will but serve to make them more watchful and exacting of their public servants in the national councils.

Resolved, That it is the duty of our Representatives in Congress, to recognize as enemies to the Union, and especially to the slave States, all who favor in any way or affiliate with this sectional Black Republican party; and that any action on their part which favors a co-operation with the Black Republicans in organizing the House, and thus placing the officers and important committees of that body under their control, would be false to the sentiment of the people of Tennessee, an insult to their constituents, and disgraceful to themselves.

Resolved, That we acknowledge our appreciation of the promptness with which the National Administration took steps to check the recent conspiracy before it obtained the huge dimensions of a revolution.

Resolved, That our Senators and Representatives in Congress be furnished with a copy of these resolutions."

When the Bayless resolution came up for consideration on November 25, Representative William Brazelton, Jr., of Jefferson County, who was of the Opposition party, offered a toned-down substitute [154] which failed of passage by a vote of 35 to 27.

Next followed two proposed minor amendments by Democratic Representative George Gantt of Maury County and Opposition Representative W. H. Wisener of Bedford County, both of which were defeated. In an afternoon session on the same day, December 1, 1859, Representative William Ewing of Williamson County, an adherent of the Opposition party, tried his hand with the following lengthy resolution: [155]

"*Resolved,* That the members of this General Assembly look upon the recent silly and wicked attempt of John Brown and his seventeen misguided followers, to excite an insurrection among the slaves at Harper's Ferry, as mainly the result of the gross delusion (gotten up and fostered by fanatical agitators,) which prevails at the North in regard to the condition of the slave population in the South. Assuming it to be so grievous as to inspire constant discontent among the slaves, and disposing them to eagerly embrace any project which may be held out to them to effect their escape from bondage—a delusion which it would be unwise and of mischievous consequences on the part of the South to confirm or strengthen, by exaggerating for party effect, or for any other purpose, the danger to be apprehended from such outbreaks as that of John Brown and his followers at Harper's Ferry; in which they utterly failed to excite an insurrectionary spirit in a single slave, so far as we are informed.

Resolved, That while it is manifest from the number and the cost of the arms collected by Brown and his followers, that they must have received direct aid and encouragement in their wicked enterprise, from many abolition leaders, besides such monomaniacs as Gerritt Smith and Dr. Howe; and whilst it is further manifest that they acted in perfect harmony of purpose with the teachings and sympathies of the whole abolition faction at the North; nevertheless we do not believe the great body of the Republican party encourage or sympathise with such wickedness and folly. But it must be conceded by all reasonable men, that the existence of such a party at the North, no matter under what circumstances of provocation it had its origin —a party based upon the single idea of hostility to slavery, powerful in the number of its members and in the ability of its leaders—a party upheld by numerous public journals, daily teeming with exaggerated pictures of the oppression endured by the slaves, with inflammatory invectives against the South, against slavery and the slaveholders—inevitably tends to incite the

[154] *Ibid.,* 285–286.
[155] *Senate Journal,* 1859, 200–203.
House Journal, 1859, 302–304.

weak-minded and fanatical to engage in such desperate and preposterous schemes; and that if such a party shall be long upheld at the North, it must in the end engender such a degree of alienation and bitter hatred between the people of the North and South as will prove to be incompatible with the existence or continuance of a common government.

Resolved, That the idea or theory that the existence of slavery in some States or communities, and the absence of it in other and adjoining States or communities, is incompatible with the existence of a union of such States and communities under one Federal head or General Government, was refuted by the judgment and conclusions of the founders of the Republic, and the framers of the Federal Constitution, and has been clearly disproved by the experience of more than half a century of a successful, harmonious and prosperous career of the whole country under the present confederated Union.

Resolved, That in the opinion of the members of this General Assembly, there is no necessary conflict between free and slave labor in any well regulated community, and least of all in a country like the United States, embracing such a variety and extent of soil, climate and production; that in this country, so far from being in conflict, free and slave labor may coexist in perfect harmony, and to the mutual advantage and convenience of both —the African race being by nature endowed with powers of endurance and a capacity for labor and enjoyment in climes which soon impair the energies of the white race, may be appropriately and profitably employed in the culture of such staples as rice, sugar and cotton, products so necessary to the comforts of the white race, while the latter, in climes more congenial to their physical constitution, may find profitable employment on the farm and in the workshop, in supplying products adapted to the consumption and wants of both races, of the slave as well as of the free white race.

Resolved, That the theory of an 'irrepressible conflict,' is a startling and mischievous invention and is well calculated, if held to be true, to reconcile the minds of men, both North and South, to a separation of the Union, under the apprehension that in no other way can the multiplied mischiefs of perpetual strife on the subject of slavery between the two sections be avoided.

Resolved, That in the opinion of this General Assembly, all the evils growing out of the present intense slavery agitation—all the discord, alienation, and bitter hatred now growing up and extending between the North and the South, are the legitimate fruits not of any necessary and 'irrepressible conflict' between free and slave labor, but of a conflict between rival aspirants in the race of ambition North and South, urged on by an inordinate greed of official power and plunder—a conflict which can only be repressed by a powerful and successful effort by the friends of the Union, to arouse the people to a conviction of the reality and magnitude of the impending dangers to its existence.

Resolved, That the declaration of Wm. H. Seward to the effect that a respectable portion of the South, under the lead of such men as F. P. Blair, of Missouri, and Cassius M. Clay, of Kentucky, are prepared to unite with the Republican party against the extension of slavery, 'and will eventually rise up against slavery,' we aver to be unfounded in fact, at least as far as the people of Tennessee are concerned. But we think it due to truth and candor to state that Mr. Seward and others who have falsely asserted the contrary, have had high Democratic authority to sustain them in their assertion, since it is well known that leading politicians and the public journals in this State have proclaimed to the world that a large proportion of the people of the State of Tennessee, under the lead of prominent men of the Opposition party, were preparing to unite with the Republican party; and some of them have gone so far as to assert that some of the leaders of the Opposition were abolitionists in sentiment.

Resolved, That we have full confidence in the conservative members of Congress from this State; and that they will regard as enemies to the Union and will have no affiliation with any party or faction, or with the members of any party or faction who have given encouragement or countenance to the wicked outrage perpetrated by John Brown and his followers at Harper's Ferry; and further, that they will co-operate with the conservative men North and South in so organizing the House of Representatives, that the offices and important committees of that body may be placed in the hands of those who will cherish the union of the States as a national blessing and expose the corruptions of the present administration of the General Government; and in doing this, they will, in our opinion, represent the sentiment of the people of Tennessee and reflect honor on themselves and their constituents."

At the conclusion of the reading of the Ewing resolution, Democratic Representative John J. Williams of Hickman County jumped to his feet as if

"Stung by the splendour of a sudden thought."

Catching the eye of the sympathetic Speaker of the House who gave instant recognition, Mr. Williams "demanded the previous question" which request was granted by a vote of 41 to 27.[156] Then came the test on the Bayless resolution which was passed by the following vote:[157]

	Aye	Nay
Preamble	43	25
Resolution 1	56	13
Resolution 2	57	12
Resolution 3	40	29
Resolutions 4 and 5	51	17

Through a lightning-like legislative maneuver, Representative Williams had succeeded in preventing any vote whatsoever upon the Ewing resolution.

Over in the Senate, on the following day, that body was informed that the House had adopted the Bayless resolution. Thereupon a veteran legislator, Dr. John W. Richardson of Rutherford County, who had been a life-long Whig and thereafter a Know Nothing, a man skilled in legislative legerdemain and who was conversant with a lot of hocus-pocus in political battles, bobbed up with a resolution in lieu of the Bayless resolution that had just run the gauntlet of the House of Representatives. The Richardson resolution, upon examination and com-

---

[156] *House Journal,* 1859, 304.
[157] *Ibid.,* 305–307.

parison, was almost an exact duplicate of the Ewing resolution (with the exception of an introductory paragraph) which had just been given "the brush off" the day before by the House of Representatives. Perhaps the old warhorse thought that his exordium might sidetrack the Senate and lead to the rejection of the House-adopted resolution. At any rate, Senator Richardson's Preamble [158] was as follows:

"WHEREAS, the Democratic members of the House of Representatives have introduced into the General Assembly a preamble and resolutions, known as the 'Harper's Ferry Resolutions,' conceived, we believe, for party purposes, and drafted with the special design to throw the organization of the House of Representatives of the Congress of the United States into the hands of the friends of the administration, whereby all the investigation into the abuses, extravagance and corruption of the present Administration will be strangled and defeated: and, whereas, said resolutions and preamble having been passed by the House, and are now presented for our action—and as we do not intend to commit ourselves to any such project; nor to abuse the trust committed to us by a common constituency, by instructing their servants in one department of the Government what they may, or what they may not do, when we, too, are only servants in another department of the Government. But as the democrats have embodied *their* views in the preamble and resolutions, and forced them into the General Assembly, it will be expected that the Opposition also, will embody their views in some form. Condemning, as we do, the Harper's Ferry riot and all those engaged in it, their aiders and abettors, most unqualifiedly, yet we do not think the Democratic view of the subject should be presented by the General Assembly to the country. Therefore, we prefer the following resolutions, and offer them in lieu, as expressing our opinions in our own language. Therefore. . . ."

Senator Richardson's strategy failed, for the Senate rejected his resolution by a vote of 13 to 8.[159] Without further delay or maneuvering, the Bayless resolution was thereupon passed in the Senate by a vote of 13 to 8, a complete all-about switch from the preceding vote.

But the passage of the Bayless resolution on December 2, 1859, did not end the agitation of the slavery question in the 1859 Legislature. For decades, the Nation had witnessed the Titantic struggle between the two sections of the country over the slavery issue; great and powerful advocates on each side of the issue had thundered forth their views in Congress and State Legislatures; liberty of speech and of the press had become guarded and restricted; churches were divided, and the social temper had soured and become exasperated. In a word, the two great sections of the Union were alienated by deep suspicion which culminated in a hatred unparalleled in intensity and in violence of expression. No wonder the Harper's Ferry episode provided fuel for the flames that soon were to engulf the Nation in a fratricidal struggle for four long and dreary years.

[158] *Senate Journal*, 1859, 200–201.
[159] *Ibid.*, 203.

Unmistakeable evidence that the slavery question in Tennessee was a current and burning issue was vouchsafed by the transmission to the Legislature of the following Message from Governor Harris, accompanied by the legislative action of two sister States:

Legislative Message*, February 28, 1860.

"GENTLEMEN OF THE SENATE AND HOUSE OF REPRESENTATIVES:

I herewith transmit resolutions adopted by the Legislatures of South Carolina and Mississippi, upon Federal Relations.

Whilst I do not concur in their recommendations—not seeing the necessity or propriety of a convention of the slaveholding States of the Union at this time—I nevertheless deem it proper that I should communicate, and that you should respectfully consider the suggestions of our sister States.

Believing, as I do, that the people of Tennessee are loyal to the Constitution in all its parts, and with each and all its guarantees; possessing a jealous regard for the rights of the States, and feeling justly apprehensive of encroachments upon them, they would feel and demonstrate, when necessary, their identity with any of her sister States in resisting any unjust and unconstitutional warfare upon them or their institutions.

This resistance should be, first, by the use of all the constitutional means in our power, to the end that the Union may be preserved as it was formed, and the blessings of a government of equality, under a written constitution, perpetuated. But if the hope of thus obtaining justice shall be disappointed, and the Federal Government, in the hands of reckless fanatics, shall at any time become an engine of power to invade the rights of individuals and of States, to follow the example of our fathers of 1776 will be the only alternative left us.

Whilst there is much in the present attitude of parties, States and public men in the northern portion of the Confederacy to cause apprehension as to the security of our rights and the continuance of fraternal feeling, yet there is a probability, and I hope a strong one, that wise, temperate, and firm councils may avert the impending evils. Therefore, before widening the breach in the manner

---

* *Senate Journal,* 1859, 562–563.
  House Journal, 1859, 832.

designated in the resolution herewith submitted, our policy should be to exhaust every means, consistent with honor and the Constitution, in an earnest effort to check the tide of aggression, and restore the era of good feeling and fraternity throughout the whole country.

Respectfully,

ISHAM G. HARRIS."

"Executive Department,
Unionville, S. C., Feb. 15, 1860.

HIS EXCELLENCY GOV. HARRIS:

Dear Sir:—I have this moment noticed an extract from the Nashville News, (in one of our newspapers,) giving the information that the resolutions passed by the Legislature of this State, in relation to Federal Affairs, had not reached you. I sent a copy to each Executive of the slaveholding States, on the same day, and by the same mail, and regret that it has miscarried. I hope this will reach you in time to lay the resolutions before the Legislature of your State, and that Tennessee will not hesitate to confer with her southern sisters.

With great respect and consideration,

I am yours, &c.,
WM. H. GIST.

RESOLUTIONS IN RELATION TO FEDERAL AFFAIRS.

WHEREAS, The State of South Carolina, by her ordinance of A. D., 1852, affirmed her right to secede from the Confederacy whenever the occasion should arise justifying her in her own judgment in taking that step, and in the resolution adopted by her convention, declared that she forebore the immediate exercise of that right, from considerations of expediency only.

And whereas, More than seven years have elapsed since that convention adjourned, and in the intervening time, the assault upon the institution of slavery, and upon the rights and equality of the Southern States have unceasingly continued, with increasing violence, and in new and more alarming forms; Be it therefore,

1st. *Resolved unanimously,* That the State of South Carolina, still deferring to her Southern sisters, nevertheless, respectfully announces to them, that it is the deliberate judgment of this General Assembly, that the slaveholding States should immediately meet together to concert measures for united action.

2d. *Resolved unanimously,* That the foregoing preamble and resolutions be communicated by the Governor, to all the slaveholding States, with the earnest request of this State, that they will appoint deputies, and adopt such measures as in their judgment will promote the said meeting.

3d. *Resolved unanimously,* That a special commissioner be appointed by his Excellency the Governor, to communicate the foregoing preamble and resolutions to the State of Virginia, and to express to the authorities of that State, the cordial sympathy of the people of South Carolina with the people of Virginia, and their earnest desire to unite with them in measures of common defense.

4th. *Resolved unanimously*, That the State of South Carolina owes it to her own citizens, to protect them and their property from every enemy; and that for the purpose of military preparations for any emergency, the sum of one hundred thousand dollars ($100,000) be appropriated for military contingencies.

In the House of Representatives, ⎫
December 16, 1859. ⎭

Resolved, That the House do agree to the resolutions.
Ordered, That they be sent to the Senate for concurrence.
By order,   JOHN T. SLOAN, C. H. R.

In the Senate, ⎫
December 22, 1859. ⎭

Resolved, That the Senate do concur in the resolutions.
Ordered, That they be returned to the House of Representatives.
By order,   WM. E. MARTIN, C. S.

Executive Department ⎫
Jackson, Miss., Feb. 20, 1860. ⎭

SIR: I herewith transmit a copy of the resolutions upon Federal Relations, passed by the Legislature of this State, agreeably to the requirements of the fifth of said resolutions.
Very respectfully,
JOHN J. PETTUS,
Governor of Mississippi.

RESOLUTIONS UPON FEDERAL RELATIONS.

1st. *Resolved by the Legislature of the State of Mississippi*, That the Constitution of the United States recognizes property in slaves, and the government created by it cannot, nor can any tribunal acting under its authority, whether it be executive, legislative, or judicial, within its appropriate sphere, justly withhold from the owners of slaves that adequate protection for their slave property to which the owners of property of other kinds are entitled, or which, from its nature, they may further require to secure them in its possession and enjoyment.

2d. That the election of a President of the United States by the votes of one section of the Union only, on the ground that there exists an irreconcilable conflict between the two sections in reference to their respective systems of labor, and with an avowed purpose of hostility to the institution of slavery as it prevails in the Southern States, and as recognized by the compact of Union, would so threaten a destruction of the ends for which the constitution was formed, as to justify the slaveholding States in taking counsel together for their separate protection and safety.

3d. That in order to be prepared for such a contingency, Mississippi accepts the invitation of South Carolina to her sister slaveholding States to meet in convention, and proposes the first Monday in June next, and Atlanta, Georgia, as a suitable time and place to meet to counsel together, and recommend the action they should take in such an event, which shall be reported to the Governor, who shall convene the Legislature, if, in his judgment, it may be required; and that this Legislature, at its present session, proceed to elect seven delegates to the convention at Atlanta.

4th. That a commissioner be appointed by the Governor to proceed to the capital of Virginia, and express to the people of that commonwealth, through her executive, the indignation that Mississippi feels at the outrage committed in the recent invasion of her soil, and the readiness and determination of Mississippi to unite with her, or any other slaveholding State, in repelling any assailment of their people, or their rights; and that said commissioner also present to her executive a copy of these resolutions, and invite her co-operation in the proposed convention.

5th. That the Governor of this State be requested to transmit a copy of these resolutions to the Governors of each of the slaveholding States of the Union, to be laid before their Legislatures, and invite their co-operation.

JOHN J. PETTUS, Governor.

A. B. DELWORTH, Secretary of State.
Approved Feb. 10, 1860."

Ardent Southerner and later an "unreconstructed rebel," Governor Harris advised moderation and deliberation in the premises. On the day following the Message of Governor Harris, two Democratic Representatives introduced measures in harmony with same. Representative W. N. Baker from the counties of Perry and Decatur proposed the following:[160]

"*Be it resolved by the General Assembly of the State of Tennessee,* That while the State of Tennessee will defend and maintain her rights under the Constitution at all hazards, and to the last extremity, we do not think it politic to have a Convention of Governors of the slave States alone, as we do not think the exigency of the times demand such a step. We, however, promise our sister Southern States, that when such an emergency does arise, Tennessee will lend a powerful support in their behalf. We respectfully recommend to our sister slave States a system of direct commercial intercourse with Europe as the better means of protecting ourselves from Northern aggression and securing Southern rights and independence."

On the heels of the Baker resolution, Representative George Gantt of Maury County offered the following:[161]

"*Resolved,* That the General Assembly of the State of Tennessee, recognizing in our present relations with the non-slaveholding States an imperative necessity for decisive measures, does not yet distrust the capacity of the Southern States, by a wise and firm exercise of their reserved powers, to protect the rights and liberties of the people, and preserve the Union. For this purpose, we earnestly desire the concerted action of the Southern States; but the General Assembly respectfully submit for the consideration of South Carolina and her sister States of the South, that the most efficient policy for preserving our liberties and the Union will be found in such direct legislative action upon the part of the Southern States as may be nec-

[160] *House Journal,* 1859, 839.
[161] *Ibid.*

essary, and by offering united opposition at all times to the sectional party known as the Black Republican party, and that such a line of policy is more likely to attain the great end in view, than the agency of an assemblage which can exercise no powers except to debate and advise.

Resolved, therefore, That in the opinion of the General Assembly, it is inexpedient to appoint deputies to the Conference proposed by South Carolina.

Resolved, That the Governor of this State be requested to communicate the foregoing resolutions to the Governor of the State of South Carolina, and to the Governors of the slaveholding States."

On March 12, the Baker resolution was laid aside and that of Mr. Gantt was passed by a vote of 44 to 20.[162]

On March 21, the Gantt resolution came up for consideration in the Senate. The ubiquitous Senator from Rutherford, Dr. John W. Richardson, though of the Opposition party, offered in lieu a resolution largely in harmony with the suggestions communicated by Governor Harris:[163]

"WHEREAS, It is proposed by South Carolina to hold a convention of the Southern States, and the proposition has been submitted to this State to send delegates to said convention, for the taking into consideration certain contemplated grievances, and adopt a course of policy for the South in view of certain anticipated events; *And, whereas,* we do not believe there is any necessity for such a convention, and do believe that all such assemblages are calculated to weaken rather than strengthen the ties of the Federal Union; therefore,

Resolved, That we ought to 'frown upon the first dawning of every attempt to alienate any portion of our country from the rest, or to enfeeble the sacred ties which now link together the various parts.'

Resolved, That the right of the people of one or more of the States of this Confederacy to absolve themselves at will and without the consent of the other States from their most solemn obligations, and hazard the liberties and happiness of the millions comprising this Union, cannot be acknowledged by this General Assembly. Such authority is believed to be utterly repugnant both to the principles upon which the General Government is constituted and to the objects which it was expressly formed to attain.

Resolved, That a State or any portion of the people suffering under long and intolerable oppression, and having tried all constitutional remedies without the hope of redress, may have a natural right when their happiness cannot be otherwise secured, and when they can do so without greater injury to others, to absolve themselves from their obligations to Government, and appeal to the last resort, need not and cannot be denied, but that such a state of things does not now exist.

Resolved, therefore, That it is inexpedient to appoint deputies to the Conference proposed by South Carolina, of the Southern States.

Resolved, That the Governor of this State be requested to communicate the foregoing resolutions to the Governor of the State of South Carolina, and to the Governors of the other slaveholding States."

[162] *Ibid.,* 968.
[163] *Senate Journal,* 1859, 727.
      Legislative Union and American, Volume II, 1859, 583.

By the narrow squeak of one vote, the proposed substitute resolution of Dr. Richardson went down to defeat [164] by a strictly party vote of 12 to 11. Two Democratic Senators, Hunter and Thompson, were not recorded as voting. The question then recurred upon the original Gantt resolution which was passed by the following vote: [165]

	Aye	Nay
First resolve	13	11
Second resolve	24	0
Third resolve	13	11

The passage of the Gantt resolution served notice that Tennessee felt keenly and deeply the issues involved in the slavery question. In Tennessee, as throughout the Nation, a half century of haggling over the slavery problem, the two-year old Dred Scott decision, and the current outbreak at Harper's Ferry riveted the attention of the 1859 Legislature upon slavery factors in general and upon certain local phases involving the Negro's status in Tennessee. Aiding and abetting the war of nerves was the publication of a book, called *The Impending Crisis*, in 1857. Its author was a twenty-seven year old North Carolinian by the name of Hinton R. Helper whose vitriolic attack upon the "haughty cavaliers of shackles and handcuffs and the lords of the lash" infuriated the South which was in no mood to listen to such criticism.

Sixteen bills affecting the Negro were introduced in the 1859 Legislature. Some of the bills were frivolous; others were drastic indeed. The captions dealt with such items as payment for slaves who had been executed; to better secure slave property; to prevent the emancipation of slaves; to prevent the assembling of Negroes; methods of punishment of runaway slaves; to prevent the education of slaves and free Negroes; to prevent preaching by Negroes; and to prevent tampering with slaves.[166]

On the fourth day of the legislative session, Democratic Representative William H. Barksdale, representing Smith, Sumner, and Macon counties, introduced House Bill No. 19 which kept the Legislature on needles and pins until near the end of the session. The bill [167] was

"To be entitled an Act for the expulsion of Free Negroes from the State."

It is well to bear in mind that there were two classes of Negroes in Tennessee, slaves and Free Persons of Color. As of the year 1859, there were in Tennessee in round numbers two hundred and seventy-five

---

[164] *Senate Journal*, 1859, 733.

[165] *Ibid.*, 733–734.

Author's note. Resolution Number 42 in the *Acts of Tennessee*, 1859, pages 681–682, is identical with the original Gantt resolution with the exception of inserting the word "other" before the two concluding words of the resolution.

[166] *House Journal*, 1859, 1205–1220.

[167] *Ibid.*, 18.

thousand slaves and seven thousand Free Persons of Color. The monetary value of the slave population was reckoned at one hundred eleven million dollars constituting about thirty per cent of the wealth of the State. The 1796 Constitution of Tennessee recognized the Free Negro—those who had been emancipated by their owners or who had purchased their freedom—and granted them the privilege of suffrage. The slow but gradual increase of this class produced alarm among many slave owners who alleged that the Free Negro was a menace to the welfare and contentment of the slave. Politicians also became disturbed, for the Free Negro might not follow dictation at the ballot box. After a hectic time in the 1834 Constitutional Convention, the privilege of voting was denied to him.

There seems to be little doubt but that the Free Negro occupied a rather anomalous and unenviable position. Describing his status in 1834, Chief Justice John Catron of the Tennessee Supreme Court in a famous lawsuit cogitated as follows: [168]

" ... He is a reproach and a by-word with the slave himself, who taunts his fellow slave by telling him 'he is as worthless as a free negro' . . . The free black man lives amongst us without motive and without hope . . . He is a degraded outcast, and his fancied freedom a delusion . . . With us the slave outranks him in character and comfort. . . ."

In early Tennessee there was considerable anti-slavery sentiment. But radical abolitionists in the North coupled with the Nat Turner insurrection in 1831 strengthened the pro-slavery forces in the South. In that year, Tennessee passed a law [169] prohibiting any Free Negro outside the State to come into and remain in Tennessee more than twenty days, and all courts were denied the power to emancipate slaves unless they be "immediately removed from this State . . ." In 1854, a law decreed that any freed slave was to be sent to Africa.[170]

The idea, of course, behind the Barksdale bill was to get rid of the Free Negro in Tennessee. Some of the pertinent provisions of the original measure [171] embodied the following:

(1) No Free Negro between the ages of twenty-one and fifty would be permitted to remain in Tennessee after January 1, 1862.

(2) The Sheriff was empowered to arrest any Free Negroes found in the State after the above date who were then to be sold at public auction.

(3) A mother with children under five years of age was to be kept by the purchaser of said mother and the children were to be hired out as soon as they were old enough to work.

(4) The Sheriff was directed to take into custody any Negro chil-

[168] "Fisher's Negroes vs. Dabbs and Others," *Tennessee Reports*, Yerger VI, 131.
[169] *Acts of Tennessee*, 1831, Chapter 102.
[170] *Ibid.*, 1853, Chapter 50.
[171] Manuscript bill in State Archives, Nashville.

dren from seven to twenty-one who had no mother and hire out said children, whose earnings were to be deposited in the county treasury and turned over to said children when they reached the age of twenty-one, provided they agreed to leave the State.

(5) The prosecuting attorneys were allowed five dollars for each presentment or indictment rendered under the provisions of this proposed law.

Representative Barksdale must have been comforted by the fact that on the day following the introduction of his bill he was appointed Chairman of the Committee on Free Negroes and Slave Population,[172] and a few days later the Barksdale bill was referred to this committee. There is internal evidence in the official proceedings tending to show that Representative Barksdale experienced difficulty with his committee in the consideration of his bill. The bill was placed in the hands of the committee on October 15, but a month passed before Chairman Barksdale made any report concerning the action of his committee. During this interval, numerous reports were made by various and sundry Standing Committees, but not a peep was heard from the Committee on Free Negroes and Slave Population. At long last, Chairman Barksdale reported on November 16 that

"The committee have considered House Bills Nos. 19, 30, and 136 upon the subject of free persons of color, and have instructed me to recommend the passage of the bill in lieu which is herewith submitted."[173]

The substitute bill by the committee was as follows:[174]

"A bill for the expulsion of free persons of color from this State.
Section 1. *Be it enacted by the General Assembly of the State of Tennessee,* That no free person of color, between the ages of twenty-one and fifty years, shall reside within the limits of this State after the 1st day of May, 1861.

Sec. 2. *Be it further enacted,* That it shall be the duty of the sheriffs and constables of the several counties in this State, to arrest and to commit to the jails of their respective counties any free person of color suspected and believed to be between the ages of twenty-one and fifty years, and report the fact to the Attorney General of the Circuit in which said arrest and commitment shall have been made, at the next term of the Circuit Court holden thereafter for the county wherein the said arrest and commitment were made. And it shall be, thereupon, the duty of the Attorney General to prefer indictments *ex-officio* against such free person or persons of color, for residing within the State of Tennessee, contrary to the provisions of the first section of this act. Which being done, the Court shall, without delay, empanel a jury to try such free person or persons of color, and if found guilty of residing within this State contrary to the provisions of the first

[172] *House Journal,* 1859, 23.
[173] *Ibid.,* 236.
[174] *Ibid.,* 237–238.

section of this act, the Court shall render judgment, that such free person or persons of color shall be sold at auction to the highest bidder.

Sec. 3. *Be it further enacted*, That immediately after the adjournment of said Court, the Clerk of said Court shall, after giving twenty days notice, proceed to sell to the highest bidder for cash, such free person of color against whom such judgment was rendered, and the purchaser shall acquire a good and valid title to the same, which shall be recognized in the courts of law and equity. *Provided*, In no case shall a free person of color who resides in this State, under this act, be a lawful purchaser at such sale, or be allowed thereafter to acquire such persons as property. *Provided further*, That if any free person sold under this section, shall be the mother of a child or children under the age of ten, the purchaser shall be required to take and keep such child or children shall arrive at age of ten, when the same shall be delivered over to the sheriff to be hired out under the provisions of this act.

Sec. 4. *Be it enacted*, That all costs necessarily incurred in the execution of the provisions of this act shall be paid out of the proceeds of the sale of such free persons, and the remainder shall be paid by the Clerk into the common school fund of the county where such sale may be made.

Sec. 5. *Be it further enacted*, That it shall be the duty of the sheriffs and constables of the several counties in this State, to seize and take into custody all free persons of color found in their respective counties, after the 1st day of May, 1861, between the ages of ten and twenty-one years, and hire such minor free persons till they are twenty-one years of age, and the proceeds of their hire shall be paid to the county Trustee, who shall loan the same at interest, upon bond and good security, renewable annually, until such minor free persons are twenty-one, at which time said fund shall be paid over to such free persons; *Provided*, they give bond and security in a sum equal to the amount of the fund so paid them, conditioned to leave the State within the time prescribed by the sixth section of this act. *Provided*, That if any minor shall be the mother of any child or children, the hirer of the mother shall be required to take the same until the mother arrives at the age of twenty-one.

Sec. 6. *Be it further enacted*, That if any of the free persons of color described in section five of this act, shall be found in this State three months after they arrive at the age of twenty-one, unless detained by sickness, they shall be subject to the provisions of the first, second, and third sections of this act; and that all free persons of color bound or apprenticed in this State, who shall be found in this State three months after they arrive at the age of twenty-one, unless detained by sickness, shall be subject to the provisions of this act.

Sec. 7. *Be it further enacted*, That nothing in this act shall be held to prohibit free persons of color from going into voluntary enslavement, as provided by the Code of Tennessee; but when any free person of color elects to go into voluntary enslavement, the person chosen as owner shall pay into the Clerk's office one-half the value of such free person of color, instead of one-tenth as prescribed by the Code.

Sec. 8. *Be it further enacted*, That the Attorney General shall be allowed the sum of ten dollars for each conviction under this act, and that sheriffs and constables shall be allowed five dollars for each arrest, and clerks shall be allowed the same commissions on the proceeds of each sale as the law now provides in sales made by clerks under the decree of any Court in this State."

According to the *House Journal*, the committee bill was adopted [175] on December 5, the official record stating that

"The bill in lieu of Nos. 19, 30, and 136, recommended by the Committee on Free Negroes and Slave Population, was adopted by the House."

In the afternoon of the same day,

"The House again proceeded to the consideration of bill in lieu of House Bill No. 19, and passed same on its second reading."[176]

Apparently Mr. Barksdale was dissatisfied with the action of his committee which had recommended a substitute bill instead of his own. Therefore, he prepared a substitute of his own which was presented on January 6, 1860, and was as follows: [177]

"SECTION 1. *Be it enacted by the General Assembly of the State of Tennessee,* That from and after the 1st day of January, 1861, it shall not be lawful for any free person of color to reside within the State of Tennessee.

SEC. 2. *Be it further enacted,* That it shall be the duty of the justices of the peace, after the 1st day of January, 1861, to report all free persons of color in their respective civil districts, to the Clerk of the Circuit Court of their respective counties. This report shall show the age and sex of such free persons, whether married or unmarried, and if married, whether to a slave or free person. It shall also show the age and sex of the children of free persons of color, in connection with the parent or parents of such children, so as to present by itself each family.

It shall, in like manner, show the property owned by such free persons of color, and the nature of the same. It shall be the duty of the said clerks to present their reports to the Judges of their respective Courts, at the first term after the same are made; by whom the same shall be examined, and an order made, directing the clerk to issue a capias for the arrest of such free persons of color, who, when arrested, shall be brought before the Judge making the order. Thereupon, it shall be the duty of the Judge to direct the clerk to take proof, and report instanter, if practicable, what estate is owned by the families of free persons of color, or those who have no families. And if it shall appear that said families of free persons of color have, respectively, property sufficient to pay the expenses of their transportation to the Republic of Liberia, and six months support thereafter, it shall be the duty of the Judge, forthwith, to decree a conversion of such property into money, in as short a time as the same can be done without a sacrifice, to such free persons of color. It shall be the duty of the clerk to make such sale, and it shall also be the duty of the clerk, to hire out such free persons of color until their property can be converted into money, as contemplated by this act; the proceeds of hire to be added respectively to the fund of those hired. As soon as the said property is converted into money, the Judge shall order the clerk to pay it into the Treasury of the State, and notify the Governor; and the Governor shall, by himself, or such agent as he may appoint, make the necessary arrangements for conveying such free

---

[175] *House Journal*, 1859, 327.
[176] *Ibid.*, 329.
[177] *Ibid.*, 456–458.

persons of color to some sea-port town of the United States, for transportation to the Western Coast of Africa, and for providing for their comfort six months, for which purpose the Comptroller of the Treasury shall issue his warrant, upon the requisition of the Governor.

Such free persons of color, and families of free persons of color, as have no property, or an insufficient amount to transport them to Africa and support them for six months, as may be embraced in the report of the parties, it shall be the duty of the Judge by his order, to direct the clerk to hire out until a sufficient fund accumulates for that purpose; and as fast as that may be the case with said free persons of color and families of free persons of color, the Judge shall order it paid into the Treasury for the removal and support of such free persons of color, and the same shall be done by the Governor, as above provided. *Provided,* That where any free person of color, or family of such persons, may have an insufficient amount of property for their removal and support, that the same shall be converted into money as above provided, and loaned by the clerk at interest, until it is made sufficient by the addition of the proceeds of hiring; that families shall be sent together; but the provisions of this act shall not apply to free persons of color over forty-five years, if they elect to remain in Tennessee.

SEC. 3. *Be it further enacted,* That free persons of color may, at any time, elect to go into slavery before removal, and in the event of such election, the election of the mother shall bind her children under six years of age, and their condition shall be that of slavery. Children over the age of six years, shall not be bound by the election of the mother, but shall be hired out by order of Court, in accordance with the provisions of this act, and the proceeds placed at interest for their benefit, until such of them as are males, shall reach the age of eighteen years; and such as are females, shall reach the age of sixteen; at which time their fund shall be paid into the Treasury, and steps taken as provided by this act, to transport them to Africa. *Provided, however,* at the age above stated, they may elect to go into voluntary enslavement, and the provisions of this section shall apply to all free minor children of color, who may have no mother, as to the age at which they shall be transported, or elect to go into slavery. Voluntary enslavement shall be effected as now provided by the Code, except that the purchaser shall pay one-half instead of one-tenth of the value of the free person so enslaved.

SEC. 4. *Be it further enacted,* That all monies that shall arise from voluntary enslavement, as well as the estates of those entering into voluntary enslavement, shall, including the heirs, be paid into the Treasury of the counties where the enslavement is effected; and the same shall be a fund under the control and direction of the County Court, to be applied to the support of the aged, infirm, and helpless free persons of color of such counties respectively, embracing women and children who may be unable to support themselves.

SEC. 5. *Be it further enacted,* That the provisions of this act shall not apply to such free persons of color as from age, disease or infirmity, are unable to go to Liberia.

SEC. 6. *Be it further enacted,* That the provisions of this act shall not only apply to free persons of color, but also to those colored persons who have a right to freedom by deed, will, contract or purchase.

SEC. 7. *Be it further enacted,* That it shall not be lawful for any person to buy any free person of color for the benefit of such free persons of color, with intent to evade the provisions of this act; and whoever shall be guilty of the same shall, upon conviction, be fined not less than five hundred dollars, and imprisoned for a period of not less than six, nor more than twelve months.

SEC. 8. *Be it further enacted*, That if any free person of color shall remove from the State, and return and remain for the space of twenty days, after notified in writing by any white citizen to leave, such free person of color shall be arrested by the sheriff and lodged in jail, and advertised for sale for the space of ten days, at some public place, and sold into slavery, the proceeds of sale to be paid into the treasury of the county where the sale is made, as provided by the 4th section of this act; and all free persons of color coming to this State from other States, shall, upon receiving a similar notice, be sold into slavery under the provisions of this act, and the proceeds paid into the county treasury. And it shall be the duty of sheriffs, constables, and justices of the peace, to give the notice provided by this section, in all cases where they may be aware of any such free persons being in the State of Tennessee.

SEC. 9. *Be it further enacted*, That the costs of executing the provisions of this act, shall be paid out of the transportation fund, hire or proceeds of sale, as the case may be.

SEC. 10. *Be it further enacted*, That it shall not be lawful for any owner of slaves to confer upon them the rights of freedom in Tennessee, unless he at once removes them, or causes them to be removd from this State. All last wills and testaments for the emancipation of slaves, shall be invalid, and so shall every gift of freedom or contract for that purpose, unless it is executed by the immediate removal of the slaves in whose favor it is made, by the person making it."

After considerable haggling by various members and the addition of minor amendments, Mr. Barksdale had the satisfaction of seeing his substitute bill adopted [178] a week later by a vote of 40 to 28.

The bill was then transmitted to the Senate and was passed routinely on first and second readings. On third reading, Senator George B. Peters from the counties of Hardin, Hardeman, and McNairy succeeded in tacking on an amendment, but the amended bill failed of passage [179] by a tie vote of 12 to 12. On February 20, the Senate by a vote of 12 to 8 reconsidered its action in rejecting the bill and the whole matter was again up for consideration.[180] If we may rely upon contemporary sources of information, the fireworks were really set off. Democratic Senator John A. Minnis participated in the barrage with a lengthy speech [181] in which he explained, expostulated, and analyzed the situation as he viewed it. Although Senator Minnis expressed considerable reluctance at speaking a second time on the expulsion of Free Negroes from Tennessee, the length of his speech seems to indicate that he was not especially "reluctant."

[178] *Ibid.*, 486.
[179] *Senate Journal*, 1859, 458.
[180] *Ibid.*, 519.
[181] *Legislative Union and American*, Volume II, 1859, Appendix, 609–615. *Nashville Union and American*, April 5 and 6, 1860.

"FREE NEGROES

————

Speech of

JOHN A. MINNIS,

OF HAMILTON,

On the Bill for the Expulsion of Free Persons of Color

from this State.

In Senate, February 20, 1860.

MR. SPEAKER:—Having already detained the Senate, on a former occasion, with a few remarks on this subject, I had not designed or intended
again to trouble this body with anything more on the subject; but it seems
to be the desire of the friends of the bill that I shall address the Senate before the vote is taken. And, as I believe the question under consideration
involves principles of far more importance than any that has or will be before this Legislature—of as vital importance as can, in fact, well be brought
before the Legislature—I yield my own inclinations and wishes to the desire
of my friends, and ask the serious attention of Senators whilst I attempt, in
my feeble manner, to show what I think the important principles in this
controversy.

Now, sir, let Senators be not mistaken; I do not regard it of such vital
importance to the State of Tennessee, whether the free negroes are immediately expelled from the State; or even whether they shall be at any future
time. As a question of mere policy, there are most unquestionably, arguments for and against it. I, for one, believe it is good policy that they
should be expelled; that it should not be done too hastily; it should not be
done harshly; it should not be done rashly, or inhumanely, but should be
done certainly, as a question of policy, of humanity, and as to time and
mode, we can discuss this question without attaching to it the vital importance the question has assumed by the course of the argument. Those who
oppose the measure, maintain it is unconstitutional, and upon that, mainly
rest the argument. Yes, sir, it is insisted that the passage of a law expelling
Free Negroes, is unconstitutional, and refer especially to sec. 8, art. 1. of our
bill of rights, as well as many others, but this will illustrate the whole argument, and therefore, I need not refer to others. This section is as follows:
'That no freeman shall be taken or imprisoned, or disseized of his freehold,
liberties or privileges, or outlawed, or exiled, or in any manner destroyed
or deprived of his life, liberty or property, but by the judgment of his
peers, or the law of the land.' Now, sir, the whole question is involved in
this, are free negroes or any portion of the African race, protected by
the above, and other similar provisions in our Constitution, the Constitution
of the State of Tennessee. Was the Declaration of Independence, our Federal Constitution, or the Constitution of the State, made by, or for the protection of the African race, or do they or any portion of them constitute
any portion of the sovereignty or sovereign people of our government? I
maintain the negative, and if I am right, there, sir, is an end of the constitutional question, but those who maintain the other side of this question, insist
free negroes are embraced by the term 'freemen' in our bill of rights. In my
opinion, upon the principles involved in this question, depend the rights of

slave property, the very rights of slavery itself. The Declaration of Independence, the very foundation of our government, declares, 'We hold these truths to be self-evident, that all men are created equal, that they are endowed by their Creator with certain unalienable rights, that among these are life, liberty, and the pursuit of happiness.'

Now, I appeal to every Senator, to every candid man, if 'freemen' in our bill of rights embraces free negroes, or freemen of the African race, if 'all men' in the Declaration of Independence, by the very same reasoning does not embrace all men of the African race; if so, then by the Declaration of Independence, an instrument sacred to every American heart, the principles of which will ever be held in the greatest veneration by every patriot in the land: 'All men are created equal,' &c., all men, including all races, includes the African race; and slaves being men of the African race, are included; and being created equal, 'are endowed by their Creator with certain unalienable rights, among which are life, liberty, and the pursuit of happiness.' These rights being unalienable—that is, such as cannot be sold, disposed of, or of which a party cannot, in any manner, be deprived, then, according to the argument of those who hold this law unconstitutional, because a violation of the 8th Sec. Art. 1 of our bill of rights, Constitution of Tennessee, and similar provisions in our Constitution, because, as they insist, by the term 'freeman,' is embraced free negroes, of course, 'all men,' in the Declaration, includes those men held in slavery; and if this argument is true, every slave held in the South is held in violation of the fundamental doctrines of that sacred instrument, the Declaration of American Independence. This is the argument, yea, sir, the very foundation of the argument of political abolitionists; it is, sir, the very foundation upon which they build. In the celebrated Dred Scott case, and to which I shall allude and adduce as an authority to show that the Supreme Court of the United States have settled this direct question, Justice Curtis gave a dissenting opinion, and in which he reviews this identical question, and uses this language: 'I shall not enter into an examination of the existing opinions of that period respecting the African race, nor into any discussion concerning the meaning of those who asserted in the Declaration of Independence that all men are created equal; that they are endowed by their Creator with certain unalienable rights; that among these are life, liberty, and the pursuit of happiness. My own opinion is, that a calm comparison of these universal abstract truths, and of their own individual opinions and acts, would not leave these men under any reproach of inconsistency; that the great truth they asserted on that solemn occasion they were ready and anxious to make effectual whenever a necessary regard to circumstances, which no statesman can now disregard without producing more evil than good, would allow; and that it would not be just to them, nor true in itself, to allege that they intended to say that the Creator of all men had endowed the white race, exclusively, with the great natural rights which the Declaration of Independence asserts.' [See this entire opinion, in Clusky's Political Text Book, page 173, second edition.] I quote the opinion of Judge Curtis to show the Black Republican or Abolition view of this case, as held by members of the Supreme Court, and which is the view taken by the entire Abolition or Black Republican party. In that same case, Chief Justice Taney, who delivered the opinion of the Court, upon this very point, after quoting the language of the Declaration of Independence, says: 'But it is too clear for dispute, that the enslaved African race were not intended to be included, and, formed no part of the people who framed and adopted this Declaration'; and goes on to show conclusively the reasons from the history of the times, that the men making this Declaration were, many of them, slaveholders, high in literary and legal attainments, &c., &c.

But, Mr. Speaker, to avoid the force of this argument, the Senator from Wilson insists the Declaration of Independence, nor the Constitution of the United States, has anything to do with the question. The Senator from Rutherford asserts the Declaration of Independence is not true. Now, I appeal to every candid man, if language of the precise same import used in the Declaration of Independence, in the Constitution of the United States, and in the Constitution of the State of Tennessee, is not to, and should not, be construed to mean the same; I will show before I take my seat that such is the opinion of our own Supreme Court. But is the Declaration of Independence untrue? If you take the construction of Judge Curtis; the construction of the Abolitionists; if you construe it upon the same principles, that those who insist the word 'freeman' in our constitution, embraces free negroes; if you construe it to mean, all men are equal in mental, moral, and physical stature, then it is untrue. But if you construe it as it was intended by those who made it, as the Supreme Court of the United States construe it, and which is unquestionably the true and correct construction, then it is true—that is, 'all men,' all men of the class, who are of the class constituting the sovereign people, that people who were entitled to political rights under the British Government—the colonies up to the time of the Declaration of Independence, belonged to the British Government; were subjects of that Government—it was that people who declared their independence, and it was for themselves, and those entitled to like rights for whom this Declaration was made and an independent Government was organised. Did the African race constitute any portion of these people? It is but necessary to look to the history of the times, to see most conclusively that it did not. The white race came to and settled this continent, freely and of their own accord, bringing with them all the rights and privileges of citizens or subjects of the mother country. How was it in relation to the African race; there was probably not one then in the country, that himself or ancestry came here of their own accord,—not one whether free or slave that himself or ancestry had not been brought here as a slave. Judge Taney in delivering the opinion of the Court in the Dred Scott case, says: 'No one of the race had ever emigrated to the United States voluntarily; all of them had been brought here as articles of merchandise. The number that had been emancipated at the time were but few in comparison with those held in slavery; and they were identified in the public mind with the race to which they belonged, and regarded as a part of the slave population rather than the free. It is obvious they were not in the minds of the framers of the Constitution,' and of course not in the minds of those who made the Declaration of Independence. This same learned Judge, says: 'It is difficult at this day to realise the state of public opinion in relation to that unfortunate race (the negro race) which prevailed in the civilized and enlightened portions of the world at the time of the Declaration of Independence, and when the Constitution of the United States was framed and adopted. But the public history of every European nation displays it in a manner too plain to be mistaken. They had for more than a century before been regarded as beings of an inferior order, and altogether unfit to associate with the white race, either in social or political relations; and so inferior, that they had no rights, which the white man was bound to respect; and that the negro might justly and lawfully be reduced to slavery for his benefit. He was bought and sold as an ordinary article of merchandise and traffic, whenever a profit could be made by it.' Such, Mr. Speaker, was the light in which the negro race was then viewed. Such was the light in which he was viewed by the various States of the Confederacy, now constituting the free States, as their history and public statutes, made at the time, abundantly show—then can it for one moment be supposed, that the convention which framed the Declaration of Independence, having partaken of and being fully imbued with these feelings and opinions, and many of whom were slaveholders, even thought of making a declaration that these slaves were born their equals, and had unalienable rights to liberty, &c? Nothing but the veriest fanaticism could ever lead a sensible mind to such a conclusion. Then the Declaration of Independence, embracing as it did, those belonging to the class making the declaration, and who were understood and admitted to belong to that class, is true, so far as the term 'all men' is concerned, and does not embrace the African race, and the very foundation of Abolitionism as a political question fails. But to confine it to this class, are all men equal, &c. The Declaration of Independence was declaring men's political rights—all men of this class have equal political rights, such as are enumerated, and hence the doctrines set forth in the Declaration of Independence are true, however men may be unequal in size, in mental and moral capacities, &c. &c.

Having, Mr. Speaker, examined the status of the negro race, under and in relation to our Declaration of Independence, I propose now to examine this question under the Constitution of the United States. The preamble of the Constitution of the United States shows by whom, and for whom, and for what purpose this Constitution was made, 'We, the people of the United States, in order to form a more perfect union, establish justice, insure domestic tranquility; provide for the common defence, promote the general welfare, and secure the blessings of liberty, to ourselves and posterity, do ordain and establish this Constitution for the United States of America.'

Now, who was 'the people of the United States?' upon the very same reasoning that asserts that 'freeman' in our State Constitution, 8th section, 1st art., Bill of Rights, embraces free negroes—'the people of the United States' would embrace all who, in the general acceptation, are included in the general term, people: free negroes and slaves, are both people, in the general and common acceptation of the term—and, therefore, upon this argument, are a portion of that people by whom and for whom and their posterity this constitution was made. But we have but to look to the history of the times, the position occupied by the African race, the manner in which this race was regarded and treated by not only the people of the United States, but by the civilized world, to see, conclusively, this race did not constitute a part of the people making or for whom and for whose posterity it was made. At the formation of the Constitution of the United States, many of the States now free were slave States, a large number of the delegates were owners of slaves; and, as already shown, the whole civilized world regarded the African race as an inferior race, unfit for social or political relations with the white race, and that the negro might justly and lawfully be reduced to slavery by and for the benefit of the white race—the very Constitution itself regarding slaves as property—then, sir, what can be more preposterous than to suppose these slaves, this race thus degraded, constituted any portion of the people making the Constitution, &c.; and if not constituting any portion of the sovereign people, then, as a necessary consequence, they are not embraced in the provisions of that Constitution. But this direct point has been recently before the Supreme Court of the United States, most elaborately discussed, and carefully and thoroughly examined by the Court, and so far as a question of this character can be settled by the courts, it has been conclusively settled that the African race, whether free or slave, are not 'citizens,' in the meaning of our Constitution, are not a portion of the political body, constitute no portion of 'we, the people,' or 'the sovereign people,' and that 'people of the United States,' and 'citizens' are synonymous terms. This was in the celebrated case of Dred Scott. This case originated in the Circuit Court of the United States for the district of Missouri. This declaration, amongst other things, alleged that the plaintiff, Dred Scott, was a citizen of the State of Missouri—the defendant pleaded in abatement in substance, that the plaintiff, Dred Scott, was not a citizen of the State of Missouri as alleged in his declaration, because he is a negro of African descent, &c. To this plea there was a demurrer. And the question directly presented was as to the rights of free negroes under Art. 4, Section 2, of the Constitution of the United States, and which is as follows:

'The citizens of each State shall be entitled to all privileges and immunities of citizens in the several States.' No case before the Court ever excited more interest or was more carefully, and elaborately considered; Chief Justice Taney delivered the opinion of the Court, which was concurred in by the others, (except Justices Curtis and McLean; who gave dissenting opinions) the judges all, I believe, delivering written opinions. C. J. Taney in delivering the opinion of the Court, says, 'The words "people of the United States" and "citizens" are synonymous terms and mean the same thing. They both describe the political body, who according to our Republican institutions, form the Sovereignty, and who hold the power and conduct the Government through their representatives. They are what we familiarly call the "Sovereign people," and every citizen is one of this people, and a constituent member of this Sovereignty. The question before us, is whether the class of persons described in the plea in abatement compose a portion of this people, and are constituent members of the Sovereignty? We think they are not, that they were not included, and were not intended to be included, under the word "citizens" in the Constitution, and can therefore claim none of the rights and privileges which that instrument provides for and secures to citizens of the United States.' In support of this opinion, this learned judge refers to a case in Kentucky in 1822, to the case of Claiborne vs. the State of Tennessee, Meigs' Reports 331, to the opinions of the Attorneys General of the United States, of the Secretary of State, and some other cases in the Supreme Court of the United States. In this case Judge Curtis in giving a dissenting opinion, maintains that free negroes are citizens of the United States under the Constitution; and relies greatly on the case of 'the State vs. Manuel 4 Dev. and Bat. N. C. Reports.' Senators will bear in mind this is the very identical authority so much relied on by Senators to show the bill now under consideration is unconstitutional, and if Senators will take the trouble to examine this opinion of Judge Curtis, they will find, to say the least of it, a great similarity between the reasons and arguments of Judge Curtis, and the arguments of Senators on this floor. But without taking up the time of the Senate to pursue this branch of the subject further, when we look to the history of the times, the condition of the African race; to the action of the colonies, to the Declaration of Independence, the articles of Confederation, the legislation of the various States, and to the formation of the Constitution of the United States, the various actions and opinions of the various officers and departments of the Government, and adjudications of the courts; it is incontrovertibly true that the African race are not included in the term 'all men' in the Declaration of Independence, are not included in the terms 'people' &c., &c., in the Federal Constitution, constitute no part of the Sovereign people, no part of the body politic; and are not entitled to the various provisions in the Constitution of the United States, made for the protection of the Sovereign people or citizens.

Now, having, as I think, conclusively shown the status of the African race under the Government, I come to consider it under the Constitution of the State of Tennessee. It is argued that the bill for expelling the free negroes from the State, is a violation of Art. 1, Sec. 8, of the Constitution of Tennessee, which is as follows: 'That no free man shall be taken or imprisoned, or disseized of his freehold, liberties or privileges, or outlawed, or exiled, or in any manner destroyed, or deprived of his life, liberty or property, but by the judgment of his peers, or the law of the land.' Also Art. 1, Sec. 14, which provides, 'that no freeman shall be put to answer any criminal charge, but by presentment, indictment or impeachment.' Also, Art. 1, Sec. 11, which declares, 'that laws made for the punishment of acts committed previous to the existence of such laws, and by them declared criminal are contrary to the principles of free government, wherefore, no *ex post facto* laws shall be passed. Also, the 20th sec. of the Declaration of Rights, which declares, 'that no retrospective law, or law impairing the obligation of contracts, shall be passed.'

And now, do any of these provisions embrace free negroes? Most clearly they do not, and in the argument of this question, I shall more particularly confine myself to the first, as the same argument will pretty much apply to all.

The first Constitution of Tennessee was made in 1796, and was made by 'We the people,' &c., &c. Now, by what people? A portion of that very sovereign people who made the Constitution of the United States, a portion of that very people who declared their independence from Great Britain; who maintained that independence; who formed an independent government, and of whom Chief Justice Taney in the case already referred to, says the African race constituted no portion, and therefore, not protected by the provisions of the Federal Constitution; then does it not follow beyond question, that there being in the old constitution no express provisions for the protection of free negroes, that they were not entitled to the protection of its provisions? It is argued, that under the old constitution of North Carolina, which I have not before me, and I deem unnecessary to notice, and under the old constitution of Tennessee, free negroes were allowed to vote, to muster and to exercise many other privileges, and therefore the argument seems to be made, they were under these constitutions secured in these rights. It is true, at an early day in North Carolina and in Tennessee, the proportion of free negroes being very small, being principally those who had been emancipated for meritorious services, they by mere permission enjoyed many privileges that belonged to citizens, but it will not be pretended they were citizens, or entitled to the rights and privileges of citizens; but I deny these rights were secured by the constitution; they were not constitutional rights, but mere privileges enjoyed by the consent of the sovereign power, the people of the State, who constituted the sovereign people, either expressed through the Legislature, by the Courts, or merely by a sort of tacit consent. Article 3, section 1, of the old Constitution of Tennessee, provided, 'Every free man of the age of twenty-one years and up-wards, possessed of a freehold in the county wherein he may vote, and being an inhabitant of this State, and every free man being an inhabitant of any one county in the State six months immediately preceding the day of election, shall be entitled to vote for members of the General Assembly, for the county in which he shall reside.' Under this provision free negroes were permitted to vote—for it is argued 'free men' embraced free negroes under the old constitution; and the framers of the constitution under the same term in that section of the bill of rights embraced free negroes.

Now for one moment let us examine the soundness of this argument; whilst free negroes, were under the old constitution permitted to vote for members of the Legislature, they were also permitted to muster and vote for military officers; the old constitution provides: 'captains, subalterns and non-commissioned officers, shall be elected by those *citizens* in their respec-tive districts who are subject to military duty.' Art. 7, sec. 1. Now if the argument is worth anything, these officers being required by the constitu-tion to be elected by *citizens*, free negroes being permitted to vote, there-fore free negroes under the old constitution were citizens of the State, this is not pretended and cannot be without overturning the adjudication of the Supreme Court of the United States, the action of the general govern-ment and all its departments—the adjudications of Tennessee, North Caro-lina, Kentucky, and probably all the States in the Union, and the entire legislation of Tennessee on the subject. The truth is, as before stated, these were privileges not expressly forbidden by the constitution, nor prohibited by an act of the legislature, and enjoyed by the mere permission, and at the will of the sovereign power of the State. The declaration of rights was pretty much the same under the old as under the new constitution, and thus as to constitutional provisions the matter stood until 1834, when the new constitution was made.

The new constitution, so far as it bears on this subject, is very nearly the same as the old, except it in express terms confines the right of voting to 'free white men,' this is the declaration of the sovereign power of the State, expressed through its delegates in convention as a fundamental law, that in future no consent shall be given either by the legislature, by the courts, or by common consent, for any but free white men to exercise the high prerogative of the elective franchise. But it is argued that because the convention in framing the constitution in relation to the qualification of voters used the term 'free white man' and in the 8th sec. art. 1, they use the term 'free white man' that they understood, and intended 'free man' to include free negroes, and to sustain this, the journal of the convention is appealed to, and the views of two of the members, to-wit: Mr. Allen, who said, 'I am also against inserting the word white before the word freeman in this clause of the constitution, because it goes to exclude a description of persons from the right of voting, that have exercised it for thirty-eight years, under the present constitution, without any evil ever having grown out of it. This will be the effect, unless a clause is added, extending the privilege to men of color in certain cases as provided in some of the amend-ments on your table.'

Mr. Loving and others advocated the measure, and seemed to think there was nothing in the constitution to prevent a free negro from being Governor, member of the Legislature, &c., &c. There was nothing in the old constitution expressly in terms prohibiting free negroes from holding the highest office known to the State Government, and if the arguments of

Senators on this floor are true, they are eligible to the highest offices in the State; and yet, who for a moment believes that one, if elected, would have been permitted, or held by the Courts, eligible to the most inferior office, and most certainly he would not have been. And why? Because he was not one of the race, class, or caste that constituted the sovereign power, who made the Government, to whom it belonged, and who had a right to control and administer it. No stronger case could be given to demonstrate what I have already said, that the privileges exercised by free negroes under the old Constitution were not constitutional rights, but merely permitted privileges; but, it is said that 'free white men' was inserted in the new Constitution to prevent free negroes from voting. I admit it. I have already shown it was the declaration of the sovereign power, expressed in a fundamental law, that they would no longer suffer any such permission to free negroes. This whole argument, attempted to be drawn from the convention's journal, is what politicians would call a handsome dodge of the main point in question, and what lawyers would call astute special pleading.

The new Constitution of Tennessee, the old Constitution of Tennessee, the Constitution of the United States, the old Articles of Confederation and the Declaration of Independence, were all made by the same people, by the sovereign people of this Government; and who, in the Declaration of Independence, are included by 'all men,' who are included in the preamble to the Constitution of the United States, in the expression of 'we, the people,' who are included in the preamble to the old Constitution of Tennessee, in the expression of 'the people of the Territory,' &c., and are included in the preamble to the new Constitution of Tennessee by the expression of 'the people of the State of Tennessee,' the declaration of rights, art. 2 of the old Constitution of Tennessee; 'that all power is inherent in the people' means this precise same sovereign people, 'freeman,' in section 8 of the bill of rights in this old Constitution means the same thing, includes precisely the same people. The term 'freemen,' in the new Constitution, bill of rights, art. 1, section 8, means precisely the same thing, includes the same men, does not, nor ever was intended to include any portion of the African race. This direct question, under the new Constitution of Tennessee, has been before the Supreme Court and received its solemn adjudication, and in which, the Court, Judge Green, delivering the opinion, says: 'It is contended that this act is in derogation of the bill of rights of this State. We think the word "freeman," as used in the bill of rights, is of equally extensive signification with the word "citizen," as used in the Constitution of the United States; and that although the defendant, by his emancipation in Kentucky, obtained a qualified freedom, he did not, become a "freeman" in the sense of Magna Charta, or of our Constitution.' [Meigs' Reports, 344, State vs. Claiborne, in 1833]. This identical case, is referred to and recognized as sound law by the Supreme Court of the United States, and the Dred Scott case.

The whole legislation of Tennessee, under the old and under the new Constitutions, shows conclusively that the legislature has always taken this view of the rights of free negroes. By the Act of 1806, all free negroes and mulattoes are required to be registered, &c. And if found loitering about without a copy of the register of his or her freedom, to be arrested &c. By the Act of 1819, negroes, bond or free, upon due proof or pregnant circumstances, appearing before any County Court, be found to have given false testimony, should, without further trial, be ordered by said County Court to have one ear nailed to the pillory, &c. This legislation in relation to any portion of the white race would have been a palpable violation of the old

Constitution of Tennessee, and would have been a palpable violation if the free negroes had been included in its various provisions. By the Act of 1831 it is made a felony for any free negro to come into this from any other State. The act was held by the Supreme Court to be constitutional in the case referred to, of Claiborne vs. the State. And by various acts since, all free negroes have been required to enter into bonds, &c. Again, our statutes make it a capital felony for a negro or mulatto, whether bond or free, to commit an assault on a white woman with intent to have carnal knowledge without her consent; whereas, this offence, committed by a white man, subjects him only to penitentiary punishment. If negroes were included in the term 'free man' in our bill of rights, this whole legislation would most unquestionably be a violation of that Constitution; and whatever may be the opinion of any as to the constitutionality of these and other similar provisions of our statutes, it shows most conclusively the construction that was placed on the Constitutions by our Legislatures, frequently composed in part, of members who had been members of the Conventions that framed these Constitutions.

It is most conclusively shown, that upon principal from the action of the government; from the circumstances under which the various Constitutions above referred to were formed; from the history of times at which they were formed, the condition of the African race and the manner in which they were regarded, by adjudications of the Supreme Court of the United States, and of the State of Tennessee, that the terms 'people of the United States' and 'citizens' under the Federal Constitution, are synonymous terms, that describe the political body known as the sovereign power, and that free negroes do not belong to this class and are not included in its terms, and are not protected by its provisions; that the term 'freeman' in our bill of rights, and other similar terms are of equal extensive signification with the word 'citizen' as used in the Constitution of the United States, and do not embrace free negroes; this is as clearly settled as such a question can be settled by reason and authority.

Then, whilst the General Government, being one of limited powers, can only exercise the powers expressly given—the sovereign power of a State being in the Legislature, clothed with full power to pass any law not prohibited by the Constitution of the United States, or the State of Tennessee; and as I believe it is most conclusively shown that free negroes are not embraced in any of the above provisions of the Constitution of the United States or of the State of Tennessee, there is no constitutional prohibition against the passage, by the Legislature, of a law expelling free negroes from the State.

But it is insisted in argument, that in the emancipation of slaves, the State in the act of emancipation entered into a contract, by which the negroes have a right to remain; and a law now expelling them is a violation of the 20th section of the bill of rights, which is 'That no retrospective law, or law impairing the obligation of contracts shall be made.' For the sake of argument admit that there is a contract between the State and the emancipated negro, and admit that this Constitutional restriction upon the legislature is a restriction upon the action of that body, upon the subject matter of the contract, and not upon the person of the negro; and this is an extreme admission—then Sir, what is the contracts. Up to 1801, what few negroes that were emancipated, were emancipated by the legislature, and the act of emancipation would constitute the contract. In 1801, the legislature passed a law conferring on the County Courts the right to emancipate, describes the manner by which it shall be done, and upon all the requisitions therein being complied with, enacted: 'Such slave shall be held and deemed free, and entitled to all the privileges and immunities that other free people of color in this State are.' Then to give the argument all the possible benefit that can be claimed, and the contract of the State was they should have just such privileges and immunities that other free persons of color in the State were entitled to. I have already fully shown what that was, and if as I think I have conclusively shown, those already free might be constitutionally expelled, then those emancipated occupy precisely the same condition by the contract itself, and hence to expel them is no violation of contract. But it is argued that the provision in the second section of this act where emancipated slaves be rendered incapable of providing for themselves, they shall be provided for by the county, and may be removed from any other county to the county where emancipated; gives them a right to remain; whatever right they may have had under this law whilst it remained in force, it cannot be pretended that the legislature at any time had not the right to repeal it, as any other law. It did not, and could not confer any constitutional rights if it did most unquestionable it was not only the right to remain, but also to be supported, and I presume no man will argue that free negroes are now entitled to any such right. It was a right given to emancipated free negroes, and was by them held by the same tenure of the many privileges enjoyed by them, and other free negroes, at various times; it was not held by the tenure of the constitutional right, but by the mere permission of the sovereign people, the permission in this case being given by the legislature, and which the legislature might at any time take away, and which they have long since taken away, which they never could have done if it had been a constitutional right. Then from every point in which you can view this case it is most manifest the legislature has the constitutional power to expel the free negroes from the State. And now the question is, is there any necessity for such a measure? Is it good policy, and is it consistent with the principles of humanity to pass such a law? Every Senator who has addressed the Senate, and every man who I have heard speak on the subject at all, admit, free negroes as a class, are a great nuisance to society, that they are injurious to the slave population, and that it would be a great blessing if we were clear of them. I maintain that the existence of a class of inferior and degraded beings as they are, and still free, living among men of a superior class, yielding to them no rights, is totally inconsistent with the best interest of both, and that when we take into consideration our slave population being of their class with whom they associate, it is still more inconsistent, and must, in the very nature of things work mischief; but, as I before stated, all admit they are a nuisance, and that it would be a great blessing to be freed of them. I need not pursue this part of the argument further. What does the house bill propose? It proposes to give them choice of going into voluntary slavery, or to expel them from the State. And Senators talk most pathetically about the inhumanity of the measure, and at the same time say they believe the free negroes would be better off in slavery. Strange inconsistency. What, I ask, is the condition of the free negroes among us—I speak of the mass—a poor degraded set, permitted to enjoy scarcely any of the privileges of a citizen, kicked and cuffed about without even the protection of a master. The act of our legislature passed in 1831, and our entire legislation since show conclusively the feelings and opinions of the people as expressed through the legislature, that this population is an evil, that it is necessary to remove. But when Senators become so horrified at the inhumanity of this act, I ask them where are your feelings of humanity, where are your tears of sympathy for the poor slave, if it is so inhumane to require a worthless free negro to select his own master, or to leave the State. I ask where is the humanity of holding in slavery without his consent, a good and honest negro, who has never committed any crime. I ask gentlemen to answer me, how they reconcile slavery with their notions of humanity. I maintain that if you go to Africa and examine the condition of the negro race in his own native country, at his own home—follow him into Europe and England, where he is free, and examine his condition there; go, sirs, to the Islands of St. Domingo and Jamaica, examine their conditions before and since their emancipation; come sir, to the United States, the free States, and to Canada, and examine the condition of the negro there; come with me to the Southern States and examine their condition here, and all demonstrate, that the negro is an inferior race, not capable of the enjoyment of freedom, and the rights enjoyed by the sovereign people. Yes, sir, examine the negro himself, in his moral, mental, and physical organization, and it is demonstrated that his true condition is that of slavery—that he absolutely needs a master to look after, control, and direct him. I assert that the slaves of the South are more elevated in the scale of civilization; are every way in a better condition, more happy and contented than the same number of the negro race in any other portion of the known world; demonstrating beyond cavil that such is the condition for which he is fitted. For what purpose they have been organized, it is not for me to inquire, but unquestionably it has been so ordered by the inscrutable providence of an all-wise and beneficient Creator for good and wise purposes of His own. This being the admitted condition of the negro race—every where their emancipation having proved a failure, demonstrates the wisdom of our fathers in excluding them from a participation in the formation of our Government, in not including them as any portion of 'the sovereign people.' And upon this rest securely in law, in morals, in humanity, in Christianity, the right of African slavery; then, where is the inhumanity of even reducing free negroes to slavery, especially when you extend to them the right to leave the State. Whilst I know and fully admit that those who oppose this bill on constitutional grounds, on grounds of humanity, are as strong pro-slavery men as I am; yet, I do maintain that the very same reasons, that would construe the constitutional rights of free negroes, so as to deprive the Legislature of the power to expel free negroes from the State, would destroy the right to hold slaves. The very same argument that shows it a measure of inhumanity, will prove that it is inhumane to hold slaves. But, entertaining the opinions I do in relation to the African race, I believe slavery is lawful, humane and right —that the African race constitute no part of the body politic, no portion of the 'sovereign people,' are not included in the provisions of the Constitution of the United States—or of the State of Tennessee—are entitled to just such rights and protection as 'the sovereign people,' through their Legislature, courts, &c., are willing to permit them to enjoy—that the Legislature being the representative of that sovereign power, have the right to expel— that this bill is for the best interest of the citizens, for the free negroes and slaves—that it is demanded by the people, and is necessary in view of our condition. I shall give it my most hearty support, and hope it will become a law."

But, bearing in mind Shakespeare's maxim, as depicted in *Hamlet*,

"Look here, upon this picture and on this,"

Senator Jordan Stokes of the Opposition Party presented the other side of the proposition that had kept the Legislature on the *qui vive* throughout most of the session. Senator Stokes, in a restrained but illuminating discussion, must have impressed his hearers with the extent of his knowledge and research into the vexatious problem: [182]

"Speech of

JORDON STOKES,

of Wilson,

On the Bill for the Expulsion from the State of Free Persons of Color.

In Senate, February 20, 1860.

MR. SPEAKER:—I had concluded not to trespass on the time of the Senate with any remarks of mine; but the course of argument indulged in by honorable Senators this morning has changed my determination. I deeply regret that this extraordinary measure has been forced into our deliberations by the action of the other House. I do not regret it on account of anything personal to myself. I have no political aspirations to foster and promote by my course on this or any other subject. It has been said that the people demand the passage of this bill, and that their hot displeasure will fall on the authors of its defeat. I have not permitted myself, in my investigations, to look to the right or to the left to find out the soft places or the hard places in the popular sentiment. I have endeavored honestly and faithfully to banish all selfish ends and views and to follow the light of truth and justice wherever it may lead me; and I am willing to abide the judgment of an upright and intelligent people when they shall have heard the reasons for my course.

It is conceded, Sir, on all sides, that few subjects of greater interest or moment could claim the attention of this body. We have had free persons of color in our midst ever since the Territory of Tennessee was detached from North Carolina. They came along with the pioneers who cut the cane and cleared up the first settlements; they were arm to arm with that band of hardy settlers who drove back the Indian tribes and prepared a wilderness for the arts and comforts of civilized life; they have been permitted down to this day to enjoy many of the blessings of our civil and religious institutions. How natural it is that a proposition now to expel them from the State should awaken deep concern! It would have received in the early days of our history an indignant rebuke. What new discovery has made it necessary or proper to drive them from the state? It is not pretended that there is any great State necessity for their expulsion. No Senator has had the hardihood to place himself upon any such ground. They are too few in number, too equally dispersed over the State, and too feeble in moral, mental and physical power, to form even the nucleus of a conspiracy or combination that could endanger or disturb the safety or peace of our political, civil or social institutions. Senators would make Tennessee a laughing stock among her sister States, if they were to rest their support of this measure on such grounds.

---

[182] *Legislative Union and American,* Volume II, 1859, Appendix, 615–623.
Republican Banner and Nashville Whig, March 16, 1860.

But, Sir, we are told that free negroes are degraded and vicious; that they are indolent, unthrifty and immoral; that they contaminate our slaves, and annoy every community with their thievish habits and evil practices; in a word, that they are, as a class, a public nuisance—a curse to the white and black population. It may be true that this gloomy picture does not in the main too deeply color their moral and social condition; but all will admit that there are many among them who are industrious, religious and orderly, pursuing upright avocations for an honest livelihood. Do gentlemen expect to justify or excuse the expulsion of these persons in this way? They cannot do it, Sir. Will they maintain that the evil habits and crimes of any individual members involve justly the whole class in equal criminality? Can they find in any system of just laws a warrant for visiting the crimes of the wicked upon the heads of the innocent? No such odious principle can be found in the laws of enlightened and well-regulated governments; if it can be found anywhere on the face of the earth, it will be where the whim of the despot is the law to his subjects.

I have stated, Sir, that this was an extraordinary measure. How it found its way from a sister State into the halls of this Legislature, it is not my purpose to inquire. It is here without material change, and we must deal with it on its own merits or demerits. Its paramount object is the expulsion from the State of all free persons of color—men, women and children under forty-five years of age. It allows them until the first day of the next year to hunt new homes and to get away; and all found here after that day are to be taken into custody and transported to Liberia. The Senator from Shelby [Mr. Payne] and the Senator from Hamilton [Mr. Minnis] have boldly asserted that the Legislature has power under the Constitution to expel them, and that it is expedient and proper to do so at this time. I take issue with those Senators on both propositions. I deny that we have the constitutional power, or that it is expedient or proper. I will discuss these questions calmly and fairly. We should let reason and judgment, not passion or prejudice, control our conclusions. When Queen Elizabeth directed Lord Coke to prosecute, not for Her Majesty, the Queen, but for Her Majesty, Truth, she uttered a noble and generous sentiment, worthy to be followed by this investigation.

I will speak, Sir, in the first place, to the question of constitutional law. I admit that the Legislature can enact any law within the scope of State legislation not prohibited by the Constitution, and that it devolves on the opposers of this measure to show some constitutional prohibition. I might well argue that there are exceptions to this general principle, founded chiefly in the nature and objects of government. It is said that parliament is omnipotent in England, yet statutes grossly repugnant to reason and public morals, are held to be void although enacted by this omnipotent Parliament. A distinguished Judge of our Supreme Court, in a well considered opinion, uses this language: 'It does not follow, therefore, because there may be no restriction in the Constitution prohibiting a particular act of the Legislature, that such act is therefore constitutional.' But I do not intend to rely upon any such exceptions or distinction. I will meet the question on the broad admission just made. The principles embodied in the Declaration of Rights are so many restrictions on the powers of the Legislature: they are expressly declared to be a part of the Constitution; and that no doubt might arise as to their inviolability, they are excepted out of the general powers of legislation. Judge Mills, of the Court of Appeals of Kentucky, in commenting on the Bill of Rights and the powers of the Legislature and other departments of Government, says: 'The powers which they are therein forbidden to exercise, they do not possess, and cannot exercise over any man or class of men, be they aliens, free persons of color, or citizens.' A free people cannot too highly estimate these wholesome safeguards; they cannot construe them too liberally against the demands of the Legislature; nor can they too promptly resist attacks upon them, come from whatever quarter they may. Are free persons of color embraced in these restrictions? Are they known in any guaranty of the Constitution? Have they no rights or privileges that the Legislature cannot take away or impair? Have we, Sir, a race of freemen living in every community, whose lives, liberties, and property depend alone for their preservation on the wisdom or caprice of each General Assembly? The framers of our Constitution could not have intended to leave these persons so dependent and unprotected, and it will abundantly appear from various provisions of that instrument that they have not so left them.

Mr. Speaker: the Constitution, by the first section of the fourth article, declares that 'all free men of color shall be exempt from military duty in time of peace, and also from paying a free poll tax.' Several important deductions may be logically drawn from this simple declaration. Free persons of color are recognized by this clause as a class of 'free men,' rightfully and lawfully residing in the State without limitation as to the duration or continuance of that residence. These persons are positively protected from the passage of any law requiring them to muster in time of peace or to pay a free poll tax. How long are they exempted from mustering and paying a poll tax? Just as long as they are lawful residents of the State. How long are they entitled to reside here? The Constitution prescribes no limit, nor does it empower any department of government to fix the time. Will gentlemen tell us how these persons can be expelled without violating the spirit and true meaning of this clause? Can the Legislature terminate this right of residence and make their presence here afterwards a crime, punishable with expulsion from the State? That would be exercising a power nowhere conferred, and declaring an act to be criminal which the Constitution pronounces right and lawful. It would involve necessarily a double violation of the same instrument. Why, Sir, we cannot make them muster in time of peace, yet we can collect them together in gangs and drive them from the country of their birth, peace or no peace! We cannot force them to pay a cent on the head as a poll tax, yet we can compel them to sell their homes, abandon the graves of their kindred, and pay their own way across the ocean to Liberia! We cannot be so insensible to reason and argument as to believe that the framers of the Constitution would have protected them in the most positive terms from being forced to muster and pay a poll tax, yet resign their lives, their liberties and their property to the mercy of the Legislature, without restriction or limitation. Such are the ridiculous absurdities to which gentlemen are driven, who undertake to maintain the constitutional right of the Legislature to expel free persons of color.

I desire, Sir, to call the attention of the Senate to the eighth section of the Declaration of Rights. It declares, 'that no freeman shall be taken or imprisoned, or disseized of his freehold, liberties or privileges, or outlawed, or exiled, or in any manner destroyed, or deprived of his life, liberty or property, but by the judgment of his peers or the law of the land.' It is admitted in argument, and cannot be controverted, that we have no power to exile free persons of color, if they are included in the term 'freemen' in this section. The question is then narrowed down to an inquiry as to the extent and scope of meaning to be given to the term 'freemen;' and a review of the political and civil *status* of free persons of color, under the old Constitution of North Carolina and Tennessee, will reflect much useful light upon the subject.

The people of North Carolina formed their first Constitution in the year 1776, after the Continental Congress had declared the Colonies free and independent. What were the rights and privileges of free negroes before the adoption of this Constitution, it is difficult and not very important to ascertain. By the 7th and 8th sections, it is declared that all 'freemen of the age of twenty-one years with the property qualifications therein mentioned, shall be entitled to vote for members of the Senate and House of Commons.' The context will give us no aid in construing the term 'freemen;' it stands here to be measured by its own import and signification. It is, however, well known as a part of the political history of that State, that, under this designation of qualified voters, free persons of color exercised the great right of the elective franchise down to the formation of a new Constitution in the year 1836, when it was taken from them. Sir, the term 'freemen' was transplanted from Magna Charta in the beginning of our great struggle; it was interpreted while the humble soldier of color was following our flag through the smoke and dust of battle; when he was weary and worn down, the glittering hope of political freedom beamed in the future and cheered him on to new toils and labors; and after the struggle ended, the people, the Legislature and the Courts confirmed the just interpretation and awarded to him the great right of suffrage for sixty long years.

It would violate the principles of sound reasoning to hold that freemen of color were entitled under the 7th and 8th sections of the Constitution to the highest political blessing of a free government, yet deny them blessings of inferior grade and dignity, secured in the Declaration of Rights. The Courts of North Carolina have met and refuted the ridiculous absurdity that they were entitled to vote under the term 'freemen' but were not secured in life, liberty and property by such sections in the Declaration of Rights as the one now under consideration. In the case of the State *vs*. Manuel, a free person of color, reported in the 1st Bat. & Dev. L. Rep., 20, Judge Gaston after reviewing the rights of these persons under various sections, concludes by saying: 'We understand all the sections which interdict outrages upon the person, liberty and property of a free man, as securing to that extent for all amongst us who are persons entitled to liberty, and permitted the enjoyment of property. They are so many safeguards against the violation of civil rights and operate for the advantage of all by whom these rights may be lawfully possessed.'

Such, Sir, was the well defined and well understood construction of the term 'freemen' in our mother State, under her old Constitution. The people of Tennessee called a Convention and framed a Constitution in the year 1796, and were soon afterwards admitted into the Union as a State. In all respects bearing upon the civil and political rights of free persons of color, it was an exact copy of the first Constitution of North Carolina. The members of the Convention had seen and understood its workings while they were citizens of the mother State; they knew perfectly well what construction had been placed on the term 'freemen' in the sections where it occurs, and they no doubt intended that it should have a significance equally broad and comprehensive wherever they used it.

It is a speaking fact, that when Mr. Henderson moved an amendment, the effect of which would be to confine the elective franchise to 'citizens of the State' and 'persons who had done duty in the militia,' the Convention voted it down, and purposely left the right of suffrage as broad as 'all freemen of the age of twenty-one years and upwards.' It is, Sir, within the memory of persons still living, that free men of color were permitted to vote in all popular elections and to keep and bear arms in their common defence, from the admission of the State into the Union down to the adoption of our present Constitution. Judge Catron in the case of Fisher vs. Dabbs, 6 Yer. Rep. 126, correctly describes the political condition of these persons under the old Constitution. In speaking of the gift of freedom and the effects of the State's assent, he says: 'It is adopting into the body politic a new member; a vastly important measure in every community, and especially in ours where the majority of freemen over twenty-one years of age govern the balance of the people, together with themselves; when the free negroes vote at the polls, it is of as high value as that of any man. * * * * It is an act of sovereignty, just as much as naturalizing the foreign subject. The highest act of sovereignty a government can perform is to adopt a new member with all the privileges and duties of citizenship.'

We see, Mr. Speaker, that, when the Convention assembled in this city in the year 1834, to 'revise and amend' the old Constitution, the two States, the Mother and the Daughter, had uniformly held the one for the sixty, and the other for thirty-eight years, that 'freemen,' in their organic law, in their Constitutional dialect, meant freemen, white and black. Whatever may have been the defects and blemishes in the old structure, it is manifest that it was to the ground-work of the new fabric. I hold it, Sir, to be undeniably true, as a rule of common sense as well as of legal sanction, that the whole machinery of government, that the civil and political rights of individuals and classes, remain the same, except so far as the Convention may have changed or modified them; and that words and phrases which had definite and known meanings under the old, carry the same meanings with them into the new Constitution. Such rules have been often applied in construing amendatory Statutes, and they are equally applicable to the interpretation of Constitutions.

What changes or modifications were made; and do they affect the right of freemen of color under the 8th section of the Declaration of Rights? I have carefully compared the two constitutions, and I have not been able to find more than four changes, bearing upon this class of persons. They are deprived of two privileges or immunities, and they are relieved from no burthens or duties. It is highly probable that the members of the Convention had in their minds some idea of compensation when these changes were made. Whilst these persons are prohibited from keeping and bearing arms for their common defence, they cannot be forced to perform military duty in time of peace; whilst they are not allowed to exercise the great privilege of voting, they are in the same section relieved from paying a free poll tax. So far from these changes having the effect to destroy or impair any civil rights, they serve to fortify and strengthen my construction of the section under discussion.

It will be seen, Sir, on examination of the proceedings, that the Convention considered and amended the Declaration of Rights in committee of the whole. Each section, as it stood in the old Constitution and as it is in the new one, was read and agreed to without amendment, until the committee came to the 26th section, when this was read as follows; 'that the freemen of this State have a right to keep and bear arms for their common defence.'

Mr. John A. McKinney moved this amendment in lieu: 'That the free white men alone of this State shall be permitted to bear arms for their common defence,' and it was adopted. Why, Sir, was this section in lieu adopted, if 'freemen' did not in the opinion of members of the Constitution include free persons of color? Why substitute 'free white men alone' in the place of freemen, if they did not think that free negroes would be embraced in the one and not in the other expression? While the amendment is the specification of the one class, it is also an exclusion of the other; and view it in whatever light you may, it is a refutation of the restricted construction of the term 'freemen.'

But, sir, the action of the Convention on the subject of free negro suffrage is perhaps more in point. Various propositions were offered early in the session. Mr. Leadbetter proposed 'that the right of suffrage be taken from free persons of color;' Mr. Green, that it be limited to 'every free white man of the age of twenty-one years and upwards;' Mr. Carter, that it be restricted to free white men over twenty-one years of age, who are citizens of the United States,' and Mr. Purdy proposed, in lieu of Mr. Carter's proposition, to give it to 'every freeman of color, possessing a free hold or personal property worth $200.' When these various amendments were considered, a pretty fierce and extended debate sprung up, as to whether the right of suffrage should be taken from free persons of color. I will read to the Senate two extracts taken from the speeches of Mr. Allen and Mr. Loving.

Mr. Allen said:

'I am also against inserting the word white before the word freemen in this clause of the Constitution, because it goes to exclude a description of persons from the right of voting, that has exercised it for thirty-eight years under the present Constitution, without any evil having grown out of it. This will be the effect, unless a clause is added, extending the privilege to men of color in certain cases as provided for in some of the amendments on your table.'

Mr. Loving said:

'Who, sir, could indulge the thought of seeing a free person of color Governor of our State, member of the Legislature, and filling civil offices of government? Such, however, could be the case for anything in the Constitution to prohibit it, and although there is no probability of such a thing at present, or for some time to come, yet it is not prohibited by the Constitution and such a thing was possible.'

I read these extracts to the Senate for the purpose of showing what the members of the Convention understood to be the constitutional import of the term 'freemen'. While in committee of the whole, the draft of a new Constitution was agreed upon, and afterwards reported to the Convention for its action. By the first section of the third article, the right of suffrage was given to 'every free man of the age of twenty-one years and upwards, being a citizen of the United States.' Mr. Weakly moved to amend by inserting the word, 'white', after the word 'free', in the first line of the section, and it was determined in the affirmative by a vote of 33 ayes, to 23 noes. Mr. Stephenson moved further to amend the section by adding thereto the following: 'Provided that no free man who is now a resident of this State, and who has heretofore exercised the right of voting shall hereafter be debarred from that privilege,' and the amendment was rejected; ayes 23, noes 34. I will not read the name of the members voting on these propositions for fear that some clever gentleman, who has grown so much Southern in sentiment and feeling, that he doubts the soundness of every body else, may be found voting for perpetuating free negro suffrage.

I must not omit to give the Senate another piece of history, reflecting the views of the members of the Constitution on the rights of the free persons of color. A number of memorials were sent to the Convention from different counties, praying that some system of gradual emancipation might be agreed upon; these memorials were referred to a special committee, of which Mr. John A. McKinney was made Chairman; and he submitted a written report on behalf of a majority of the Committee, recommending the rejection of the prayer of the memorialists. Mr. McKinney displays great ability and research in the report, and enters elaborately into the reasons why the prayer should not be granted. I will read from it an extract which presents one of the strongest reasons. Mr. McKinney says:

'But some of the memorialists pray, that when made free, the people of color may be sent from among us and colonized. Have they counted the cost of such an enterprize? Would a million of dollars be sufficient to send the free people of color to Africa? Where else could they be sent? Where could the money be procured? Could it be raised by taxation; and would the people pay it? But suppose the money could be procured, would the people of color consent to go to Africa? AND BEING THEN FREE, THEY COULD NOT BE COMPELLED TO GO WITHOUT THEIR OWN CONSENT.'

Mr. Kincaid moved to strike out a portion of the report, which gave rise to a debate, in which the reasons and arguments for the recommendation of the Committee were freely canvassed. Mr. Kincaid's motion was rejected by a vote of ayes 12, noes 42; and the report, with its reasons and conclusion, was adopted by a vote of ayes 44, noes 10.

I will not, sir, detain the Senate long with any comments of mine on the weight and importance to be given to this mass of evidence drawn from fountain sources. Gentlemen can make their comments and draw their own deductions. It is difficult to understand how any investigating mind can hesitate as to what meaning the framers of the amended Constitution intended should be attached to the word, 'freeman,' in the sections in which it occurs without an explanatory context. We have here a construction unbroken in uniformity for sixty years in North Carolina, and for near forty years in Tennessee; we have the people and all the departments of government adopting or acquiescing in the broad and comprehensive meaning, and we have the members of the convention actually engaged in conforming the various sections of the amended Constitution to the construction and meaning thus impressed on the term. We cannot, will not err in coming to a correct conclusion, if we will read this instrument in the clear and steady light diffused over it from these sources.

I deem it proper, sir, to remark just here, that the disfranchisement of free men of color does not affect in any way their civil rights under the Constitution. The right of suffrage does not constitute a necessary element in citizenship; an individual may be a citizen of a State, yet have no voice in its government. Persons convicted of infamous crimes are disqualified from voting, yet they do not forfeit thereby their civil rights and immunities. Judge Gaston, in the case I have already mentioned, says, 'the possession of political power is not essential to constitute a citizen;' and Chief Justice Taney, in the opinion of the Court in the Dred Scott case, says, 'undoubtedly, a person may be a citizen that is not a member of the community who form the sovereignty, although he exercises no share of the political power, and is incapacitated from holding particular offices.'

Sir, the advocates of expulsion refer us to the case of the State vs. Claiborne, (Meigs' Rep. 331,) with an air of complacent triumph. They tell us correctly that the venerable and learned Judge, in delivering the opinion of the Court in that case, says that the term 'freeman,' in the section in dispute, does not include free persons of color. I undertake to show that this part of the opinion cannot be fairly relied on as a judicial decision, and that it is not sound in argument as the mere conclusion of a learned lawyer and judge. It is not authoritative as a judicial decision, and would not be so regarded in the same Court, for the reason that it is a mere *obiter dictum* of the Judge. Was the point properly before the Court, and was it necessary to decide it? The defendant, a free person of color, was indicted for coming into this State from Kentucky and remaining here more than twenty days, in violation of the act of 1831, chap. 102, and it was insisted in the defense, that the act was unconstitutional and void. It is laid down in the opinion as an indisputable principle of law that 'every free State has a right to prevent foreigners going to it, and to punish those who violate such laws,' and it would follow from this principle that the act of 1831, prohibiting free persons of color from coming in this State, was constitutional, unless they were protected under the clause of the Federal Constitution which declares, that 'The citizens of each State shall be entitled to all the privileges and immunities of citizens in the several States.' The Court upon full argument of this point, decides that free persons of color cannot be citizens of any State in the sense of this clause, and the correctness of this decision has been confirmed by the Supreme Court of the United States in the late Dred Scott case. Right here, the whole matter of the defense was fully refuted, and the constitutionality of the act put to rest. The Court further decided that the 8th section, be its true construction whatever it may, did not apply to foreigners, and it would follow necessarily that, as Claiborne was here in violation of a Constitutional statute prohibiting his coming, he could not claim the benefit of that section. It is thus clear that the learned Judge had to pass over these two points, each conclusive on the constitutionality of the act, before he could get to the meaning of the term, 'freeman.' Does the opinion rest upon a process of sound reasoning, or upon a train of judicial decisions? It rests mainly, if not solely upon one prop, and that will be found on careful examination to be a broken reed. It is stated that 'freeman,' in Magna Charta, only embraced those persons 'who were entitled to all the privileges and immunities of the most favored class,' and upon this assumption the opinion is based mainly, and freemen of color placed without the pale of the Constitution and its solemn guarantees. Lord Coke, than whom no greater authority can be produced on Magna Charta, in commenting on the very clause, now under examination, says that '*Nullus liber homo,* no freeman, extends to no villeins, saving against their lord, for they are free against all men, saving against their lord.' Coke's second Inst. chap. 29. Chancellor Kent says, that a villein as to all persons except his lord was a 'freeman, and as against them he had rights of property,' 2 Kent's Com. page 251. Villeins did not belong to the most favored class in England; they were to all intents and purposes vassals, slaves, menials to their lord or master, and were inferior in respect to civil rights and privileges to free persons of color under our laws; yet the term, 'freeman,' was comprehensive enough to bring them under the broad shield of Magna Charta.

I might, Mr. Speaker, here close my argument on the question of constitutional power, and defy successful refutation from any quarter, but there is another clause that deserves consideration before passing from the main purpose of the bill. By the 20th section of the Declaration of Rights, it is declared, 'that no retrospective law or law impairing the obligation of contracts shall be made.' I do not know that a learned disquisition on the terms, 'obligation' and 'contract' as they are used in this section, would aid us much in the present inquiry. A plain, practical common-sense view will better elucidate the subject. I shall confine my remarks to the rights of those free persons of color under this section, who have been emancipated by virtue of the act of 1801, chap. 27. This act was in full force without material change, until passage of the act of 1831; and the great body of these persons, including their offspring, now in the State, were set free under its provisions. By the first section it is provided that the owners of slaves, where they are desirous of setting them free, shall prefer a petition to the County Court, stating the intention and motive for such emancipation; that the Court may grant the prayer of the petition if 'consistent with the interest and policy of the State'; but it can not be granted until the petitioner gives bond and security to indemnify the county against such slave becoming chargeable, and then they are free and 'entitled to all the privileges and immunities that other free persons of color are.' By the second section it is provided that when such liberated persons shall by any ways or means be rendered incapable of providing the necessaries of life, they may be taken back to the county where emancipated, and the Court shall provide for them.

Now, sir, does the 20th section just read interpose no barrier to the expulsion of these 'liberated persons' from the State? Have they no such right to country or residence as the Legislature can not annul or violate? The right of the master to set his slaves free is an essential element of ownership; and the power of the State to prescribe who shall become members of the community or body politic, is an indispensable part of its sovereignty. In the emancipation of a slave under the act of 1801, the right of the master and the power of the State meet and unite in producing one result—the investing him with the privilege and immunities of a freeman of color. It will be seen, on examination, that the act of the owner communicates to the slave a right to freedom, which this section protects, inviolate as a contract, while the assent of the State only fixes the locality where the freeman may use and enjoy his freedom. In the case of Lewis against Simonton, 8 Humphrey's Rep. 189, Judge McKinney says that 'the owner may part with his right of property in the slave as fully as at common law, and thereby vest him with an imperfect right to freedom,' and by virtue of such contract, 'the legal character and condition of the slave is changed.' He continues: 'His relation to his former master and to the community are likewise changed. By the act of the master imparting to him an imperfect right to freedom, he ceases to be in the state and condition of slavery—ceases to have an owner or master within the meaning of the law.' Why, sir, does this learned Judge call it 'an imperfect right to freedom?' Can the master do anything more to make it perfect and complete? No. He has parted with his ownership and dominion as perfectly as if he had conveyed the slave to a third party. He has no right or power to reduce him again to slavery. He cannot, on any pretence annul or impair the obligations of this contract. The slave has no master—he has no owner—he is not a slave in the eye of the law. The right to freedom was imperfect under the act of 1801, because the slave could not enjoy it here without the consent of the County Court.

Prior to the passage of the Acts of 1777 and 1801, the mere act of the master made his slave a freeman, and invested him with all the privileges and immunities of his class in the community. It was the purpose of these two Acts to take away from the owners of the slave the sovereign power of introducing new members into the body politic, and give it to the County Court, that its abuse and perversion to evil might be prevented. Now, Sir, what was embraced or included in the assent of the County Court? What benefit or privilege did it confer on the slave? It did not affect intrinsically the right of the slave to freedom, or give any additional validity to the contract; for in legal contemplation, the master and the slave were in court, and the validity of his right to freedom was not and could not be questioned. It imparted to the slave all that the sovereign power could give—the right of residing in the State as a free person of color. Judge Catron defines it correctly when he says: 'It is adopting into the body politic a new member—it is an act of sovereignty adopting a new member with all the privileges and duties of citizenship.' It is deducible from the face of the Act, that a right of residence is the specific thing which the assent of the court confers upon the liberated slave; and it is alike deducible that this residence was to continue during life. Why require a bond of indemnity securing the county against the slave becoming a charge before the assent is given, if residence is not the thing to be granted? Why provide that the county in which the slave is set free shall support him when he is rendered 'by any ways and means' incapable of providing the necessaries of life, if he was not entitled to remain in the State during life? Having ascertained what was granted, did it impose on the State the obligation of contract? Call it what you may—a compact, grant, agreement, privilege—(names are nothing)—it has all the elements of contract, reduced to writing in solemn form, and attested by a court of record. The master parts with his ownership of the slave, and undertakes that he shall never become a county charge; the court, on behalf and in the name of the State, invests him with the right of residence and membership in the community; the county agrees to maintain him when too old or infirm to maintain himself, and to look to the bond of the former owner for indemnity; and the manumitted slave parts with the protecting care and support of a kind and provident master to take upon himself the rights and duties of a free man of color. The State gets what her laws and policy then regarded as worthy, in the language of Judge Catron, 'the highest exercise of sovereignty—a new member in the body politic with all the privileges and duties of citizenship.' It will not do to say that the County Court, as agent, could not thus bind the State; for it had as plenary power over the whole subject as the Legislature could confer. It cannot be said that the slave was incapable of entering into such a contract, for we have seen that he could make a valid contract for his freedom. If for his freedom with his owner, why could he not contract with the State for the right of residence and membership in the community? I deny Sir, utterly, deny, that the Legislature can stride into courts, cancel all the decrees of emancipation, disregard its solemn compacts or agreements with liberated slaves, and drive them as a herd of cattle out of the State.

But, sir, I wish to look at this matter in another point of view. Gentlemen admit that free persons of color may lawfully acquire property by all the modes of conveyance known to the law. They may acquire land by grant from the State, or by deed from individuals; and it is well known that many of them had lands granted to them, in the early settlement of the State, for military services in the war of the revolution. By a grant of land the State conveys all its title and authorizes the grantee to take possession. It does more—it expressly secures to the grantee and his heirs forever the use and enjoyment of the land. Now, sir, a grant is issued to a free person of color; he goes into possession under it, and he is now in possession. Can the State annul the grant and take back the land? That cannot be done; for the grant is a contract, rendered inviolate by the section under examination. Can the Legislature drive off and force a sale of the land? That would destroy the assurance given the owner of the free and full use and enjoyment of it by himself and his heirs. No such power is reserved in the grant; it forms no part of the right of eminent domain; it cannot be found in the letter or spirit of the Constitution; it nowhere exists save in the wild assumption that the life, liberty and prosperity of such persons are subject to the unbridled will of the Legislature.

It must be admitted Sir, that these persons are human beings, endowed with mind, moral feelings, and capacity to enjoy happiness and suffer pain, however much their habits, color, their caste, may have degraded and lowered them in the scale of human life. It must be true that they have a right to live somewhere on the earth, to breathe the air of heaven in some latitude, to die and be buried in some quarter of the globe. But let us determine that they have no right to live and die in this State, although they may have violated no penal law, and it follows necessarily that they have no country, no right of residence or burial anywhere. Many of them are the creatures of our policy; whether wise or unwise, it is too late to inquire. They have been clothed with their existence as freemen by our laws and courts; they have resided here for many long years with our permission, and have gathered around their hearthstones several generations who are free born. Where else, Sir, have they any such high claims?—Where else have they any claims whatever?—Can we ask or expect any other State or country to receive and take care of them? We cannot rightfully force them upon any other government. Every free State has the indisputable power to prohibit their coming into its territory: it may meet them on the boundary and resist their entering to the death; and if they were to succeed in entering, it could drive them out by all the means proper or necessary to the end. Don't tell me, Sir, that there are countries that will receive them. Those countries may change their policy the next day, and drive them out from their limits, and make them wanderers, exiles, outcasts, with no country for a home and no barren spot for a grave.

I rejoice, Sir, that no incident in our past history can be found to sanction any such wanton act of barbarity, or to feed and sustain the unhallowed fires of such a persecution. I rejoice that no such power as that of expulsion can be found imbedded like a volcanic crust, in the bosom of the Constitution. I rejoice that the framers of that instrument had clearer conceptions of a well regulated government than to leave a whole class of freemen under a despotism of unchecked passion and prejudice. I have shown that this class can find in its solemn guaranties a calm and secure refuge from the storm that now threatens nearly all its members with destruction. We have seen, Sir, that they are protected by the distinct recognition of them as a class, that their right of permanent residence is founded on no less firm and steady foothold than an inviolable grant of the State, and that its continued enjoyment is amply protected in that restriction against exiling freemen. When anchored within either of these constitutional harbors, they may say to wind and wave, Peace! Peace!

I will now, Mr. Speaker, direct the minds of Senators to another feature of this bill, which is obnoxious to constitutional objection. It is most manifest that its author did not have clear conceptions of our Supreme law, or that he had regarded free persons of color as utterly undeserving and incapable of having any rights that the Legislature ought to respect. By the 6th section of the Declaration of Rights it is declared 'That the right of trial by jury shall remain inviolate,' and by the 9th section, 'That in all criminal prosecutions the accused hath a right to demand the nature and cause of the accusation against him,' and 'to a speedy public trial by an impartial jury of the county or district in which the crime shall have been committed.' Now, Sir, in the face of the great right of trial by an impartial jury, thus guaranteed to the accused in all criminal prosecutions, this bill provides that free persons of color may be sold into perpetual slavery without any trial or hearing whatever.

I do not see how a more open and direct attack could be made upon the inviolability of that invaluable right which underlies our whole system of criminal law. I will state the provisions of the bill on this point more distinctly. It provides that, if a free person of color come into this State, any person may give him notice to leave, and if he remains twenty days after the notice, it is made the duty of the Sheriff to seize and lodge him in the county jail, and after giving ten days' notice of the time and place of sale, to sell him into slavery. How do gentlemen on the opposite side meet my objections to these harsh provisions? They assert that this class of persons cannot be criminals in the sense of the 9th section, and cannot, therefore, claim as a matter of right a trial by jury. Do they expect us to credit this assumption on their declarations alone? Will you not, Sir, demand some authority for so gross a departure from our criminal law? I anxiously expected them to give us some great name, some distinguished Judge, but they have failed even to do this. I refer again to that most excellent opinion of Judge Gaston, from which I have read extracts, as a complete vindication of my position. I have here another case directly in point, decided in the Court of Appeals in Kentucky. Two freemen of color were arrested for emigration to that State in violation of the Act of 1808, and the County Court, before which they were carried, ordered them to enter into recognizances to leave the State, and on failure to do so, 'they were to be sold for the term of one year.' The defendant failed to enter into recognizance, and carried the case to the Court of Appeals by a writ of error. Chief Justice Robertson, in delivering the opinion of the Court quotes the section of the Constitution of Kentucky which secures to the accused a speedy public trial by an impartial jury of the vicinage, and interpreting the Act of 1808 as dispensing with a jury, he declares 'it is so far in conflict with the supreme law of the land.' He adds: 'The Act cannot be constitutionally enforced without the intervention of a jury. A free man cannot be sold, even for an instant, unless a jury of his peers shall have passed condemnation upon him.' [See Dana's Rep., 332]. I think this excellent Judge asserts the true doctrine as to the relation existing between the trial by jury and the liberty of all freemen. I may overestimate the value of the right of trial by the jury, and reverence too highly its inviolability; I may err by being too liberal in its application, but I declare here to-day that I would not deny it, in any case involving life or liberty, to the meanest free negro that ever lived.

Mr. Speaker, there is another feature in this bill that demands a brief notice. It is provided that free women of color, who prefer remaining in the State, may elect to go into slavery, and that their election of slavery shall

make slaves of all their children under the age of six years. And this provision applies to free women of color who have been set free by their
owner, but have not obtained the assent of the State. It is wholly beside my
purpose to inquire whether or not any free person of color can by contract
transform himself into a slave. How far the great principle underlying the
fabric of the English Common Law, that no freeman can by contract make
himself a slave, may be modified or changed by the institution of slavery
in the South, it is unnecessary to notice for any object of my argument.
However this may be, can we give a free woman of color the right and
power to enslave her children?

I do not think that the Legislature can enslave free children of color
in any such way. I do not believe that we can communicate to the mother
the power to do so. I have shown that free persons of color are entitled to
all the guarantees of life, liberty and property contained in the 8th section
of the Declaration of Rights. I have shown that the act of the master, freeing a slave, communicates a vested right of freedom which is protected by
the 20th section. Under the latter the right to freedom is made inviolable,
and under the former the liberty of the freeman is amply secured. Can the
election of the mother to go into slavery destroy or impair the Constitutional rights of her offspring? No one can or will maintain any such false
position. The same restrictions that prohibit the legislature from destroying
their liberty, protect them from wrongs and outrages on the part of the
mother. Their civil rights do not depend upon any discretion the Legislature may give the mother, but they must stand or fall on their own footing.
Why, Sir, the Legislature once attempted indirectly to take away the right
to freedom, given to certain slaves under the will of their deceased master,
but the effort received from an enlightened and independent court an
indignant rebuke.

I have been, sir, a slaveholder from my cradle and expect to remain one
during my life. I have been reared with the institutions of slavery surrounding me. I am ready to do all in my power that is just and honorable
to maintain and preserve it; but I can not and will not inflict the great
wrong on the inviolable rights of helpless infancy. Give to the mother the
right and power to enslave her free children! No, Sir, no! I know of no
country in Christendom where the mother can lawfully do such a thing,
and Tennessee shall not be, by my vote, the first Christian State to clothe
her even in name only with such power.

I have deemed it my solemn duty to submit these remarks on the question of constitutional law. I have endeavored to vindicate the truth of my
position in the opening. I am now firm and clearer in the conviction that
this measure starts out with an egregious error which pervades all its parts.
You cannot plant your foot on any prominent feature in it, and feel that
you have a steady rock to rest upon. You cannot pass it without making
fearful inroads on forbidden grounds—without obliterating old landmarks.
Let us do our duty faithfully and fearlessly under our solemn oath to the
Constitution, and intrust our vindication to a free and intelligent constituency.

I will not, Sir, detain the Senate long on the question of expediency. I
am truly thankful for the patience and kind attention with which you have
listened to me. The subject is deeply important and interesting in all its
phases. We cannot, if we wished to do so, prevent friends as well as enemies
from looking into the motives and main springs of our actions; and enlightened Christian governments are subject to the same law of human so-

ciety. Can we satisfy our own minds and consciences that the expulsion of free negroes from the State is wise, politic and just? Will we be able to justify or excuse it as a proper remedy for any malady existing in the body politic? Will we stand uncondemned before the bar of enlightened public opinion? We have seen, Sir, that these persons were permitted, for nearly forty years, to worship with our fathers at the same altar in the temple of civil and political liberty. Have we any sufficient reason for denying to them now the light that gushes from its windows? They have been suffered for a quarter of a century more to rest securely in the shadow of that temple and feed upon the crumbs that fall from the festive board within. Have we on this day adequate cause for driving them away from their homes and the country of their birth, to find early graves in an inhospitable climate? I do not believe that any sufficient justification or excuse for their expulsion can be found in any or all the evils existing in consequence of their presence in our midst.

Down to the year 1831, it was a part of the policy of our legislature to foster and encourage the spirit of emancipation. We held out to benevolent masters an assurance that their slaves, when set free, should be allowed to remain here and have permanent homes. The Courts, in assenting to their freedom on behalf of the State, embodied this assurance in the decrees; and many a master emancipated his slave and went down to his grave, believing that the plighted faith and honor of the State thus given would be kept inviolate. More, Sir, we have allowed these persons to engage in the pursuits of industry, to acquire and hold real and personal property, to contract marriages with their own color, bond and free, and under the sanctions of our law many of them have farms, comfortable homes and dependent wives and children. Can we now in justice and good faith repudiate the fruits of that policy, disannul the solemn decree of the Courts, violate the plighted faith of the State, break up their homes and families, and send these unfortunate persons adrift on the world like waifs on the ocean? Such an act of cruelty could not be reconciled with the moderation and clemency which has heretofore characterized our legislation; it could not be reconciled with that noble and pure Christianity which constitutes the cornerstone of our political as well as our moral institutions; nor could it be reconciled with that spirit of genial humanity which fills and swells the great heart of our people.

I have, Sir, too much confidence in the intelligence of the people, and their sense of justice, to believe that gentlemen are correct when they tell us that the country demands the passage of such a measure. I have mingled with them enough to know that they will denounce such a wholesale injustice and wrong. They will not open out our public domain for homes to penniless wanderers from the Old World, yet deny to the humble free negro a place whereon to lay his head; they will not give to prosecuted fugitives from other governments all the blessings of our free institutions, yet refuse free persons of color, resident here from their birth, the privilege of breathing the air that sweeps over our hills and valleys. Why, Sir, the people do not enforce the law prohibiting free negroes from coming and residing here from our sister States. Will they execute one tenfold more harsh and severe? Some laws are so repugnant to natural justice and enlightened humanity, that they are a dead letter on the statute-book. How many persons were prosecuted under the odious Alien and Sedition Law, and how few were willing to defend or excuse its enormities, when it was attempted to be enforced? Pass this bill, Sir, into a law, and like results will follow. Many of those who are to be its victims will doubtless be here when the Sheriff starts on his mission under it to hunt them out and mark them for the sacrifices. Can Senators contemplate without emotion the scene that will transpire in many counties in the State? Look on that motley group of men, women and children, with saddened hearts and streaming eyes: they are the victims of the law, on their way to hear its penalty pronounced against them. They are led by the Sheriff and followed by a gray-headed father or grandfather, who cannot stay behind; they are huddled together and crowded into court; the Judge pronounces the sentence of expulsion from the State against all under the age of forty-five years and transportation to Liberia; and they are now ready to be started on their journey whose end can only be equalled in horror by what preceded the Exodus of the Jews. Ah, Sir, parental feelings will have the mastery. That gray-headed sire is seen hobbling forward, his scars received in the storm of battle, perhaps at King's Mountain, Talladega or New Orleans, pleading in his behalf. He makes one simple request: 'Let me go along with my children and grandchildren, that their hands may close my eyes in death.' Oh! Sir, there will be present crowds of brave and generous Tennesseans whenever and wherever such scenes may transpire, and there will not be a heart among them that will not throb and beat with wild indignation. I sincerely hope that no such scene may transpire; but let it transpire whenever it may, under such a law, the condemnation of the people will descend as in 'dilated flakes of fire' on the heads of its authors and champions.

I have done, Sir, what appeared to me to be my duty to myself and my country. I shall have no remorse, no stings of conscience, whatever may be the fate of this measure. I desire to record my vote against each one of its provisions to which I have directed my remarks. Some future historian will gather up the events and incidents of this day, and this measure will no doubt have a page in that work. I trust that my humble name will be associated with those who have been firmest in opposition to it. I wish this vote to be transmitted as a rich legacy to my children and grand-children as a testimonial of my faithfulness to the Constitution and the impulse of a common humanity. In conclusion, I entreat Senators, in the name of that Constitution which embraces the rights and liberties of these unfortunate persons in its solemn guarantees, in the name of the plighted faith of the State, which held out to them the hope of permanent homes, and in the name of our common Christianity, to pause, pause long before they enact this measure into a public law. May a high sense of Truth, Justice and Mercy lead you all to such a conclusion as will plant no thorn on your pillow in the hour of death!"

On the day following "the shouting and the tumult" of the preceding day, Senator Peters withdrew his former substitute bill whose principal provisions [183] were:

(1) That the free persons of color should leave the State before the first day of October, 1860 "and forever thereafter remain beyond the limits thereof."

(2) Any free person of color violating the above requirement was deemed guilty of a felony and was to be transported to the west-

[183] Manuscript bill in State Archives, Nashville.

ern coast of Africa "or sold into perpetual slavery according to the choice of the person thus convicted."

(3) Any free Negro convicted in order to be sold was to remain in custody of the sheriff until the day of sale.
(4) No free Negro permitted to marry any slave.
(5) No free Negro permitted to assemble at meetings with slaves.
(6) All free Negroes electing to be transported to Africa must pay their own expenses and be provided with funds sufficient for six months support after their arrival.
(7) County court given power to hire out all children of free Negroes who have no living parents.
(8) All judges directed to explain the law to grand juries of their courts.

On February 3, 1860, Senator Peters introduced for the second time a substitute bill [184] entitled:

"A bill to amend the laws in force, in relation to emancipated slaves and free persons of color."

The principal provisions of this second substitute bill [185] included the following:

(1) Unlawful for any person by will, deed, or in any other manner to dispose of a slave for the purpose of emancipating such slave unless the owner provided sufficient funds to transport the slave to the western coast of Africa and provide him with funds for six months subsistence.
(2) Any slave of fifteen years or older permitted to choose a master and remain in slavery.
(3) All laws authorizing courts to emancipate slaves were repealed.
(4) Free persons of color failing to comply with the conditions of proposed law deemed guilty of a felony and upon conviction were confined to the penitentiary not less than one year or more than five years.
(5) No free person of color living in another state permitted to come into Tennessee.
(6) The law was to go into effect on April 1, 1860.

After the rejection of a minor amendment, Democratic Senator James T. Lane moved to postpone the bill indefinitely,

". . . so that the whole subject may go back to the people for their action."

By a vote of 15 to 5, this legislative effort to dodge the issue was turned down with a resounding whack. After a bit of more jockeying around,

---

[184] *Senate Journal*, 1859, 522.
[185] Manuscript bill in State Archives, Nashville.

the bill was passed [186] on second reading by a vote of 14 to 6. At an afternoon session on February 28, with the acceptance of a minor amendment by Senator Stokes, the bill was put on third and final reading and was passed [187] by a vote of 16 to 6. The net result on the bill for the expulsion of Free Persons of Color, after FIVE months of batting the bill back and forth from one legislative body to the other, was as follows: The House had passed its bill on the subject, and the Senate had also passed its own bill. But the two bills differed materially, and agreement somewhere was necessary if there were to be a law enacted on the touchy subject.

Less than two weeks before the date for *sine die* adjournment, Mr. Speaker Whitthorne of the House called up on special order the Senate-approved bill which had been substituted for the House bill. After more legislative maneuvering, involving efforts to amend the Senate bill, Democratic Representative R. A. Bennett of Sumner County decided to end the misery by moving that the House concur with the Senate bill. The motion to concur failed [188] by a vote of 38 to 23.

On March 16 the Senate acknowledged that it had been informed of the non-concurrence of the House in the Senate bill. Senator Stovall, determined and unyielding, insisted on the Senate's bill. His motion to that effect was approved [189] but, legislatively speaking, there was a gulf separating the House and Senate bills as wide as that which separated Dives from Lazarus. FINIS had been written upon the most controversial and bitterly contested measure that came before the 1859 General Assembly. Since no law had been enacted on the topic, the opponents of the two bills had won a hard-fought battle.

As heretofore pointed out, the Thirty-Third General Assembly labored under an almost unprecedented tension which had been induced largely by the slavery question. Throughout the entire session, the "peculiar institution" hung like the sword of Damocles over the heads of the legislators. Subjected to terrific pressure, it would have been well-nigh miraculous had not the Legislature done some foolish things. One such act of folly was the abolishment of the office of State Geologist and Mineralogist. In 1831, the General Assembly took a forward step by appointing Dr. Gerard Troost State Geologist, though the meager salary of five hundred dollars a year was almost an insult to a man of his energy and knowledge. For nineteen years he labored in season and out of season, compiling scientific data which were published in nine biennial Reports submitted to the State Legislature. For profound research and intelligent interpretation, these Reports have never been equalled by any similar publications dealing with the soils and minerals of Tennessee.

[186] *Senate Journal*, 1859, 523.
[187] *Ibid.*, 562.
[188] *House Journal*, 1859, 1033.
[189] *Senate Journal*, 1859, 689.

His death occurred in 1850, and for four years the office remained vacant.

In 1854, the office was restored by the election of Dr. James M. Safford as "Geologist and Mineralogist of the State." His tenure of office lasted only five years, being terminated by the passage of a three-line statute [190] to the following effect:

"Be it enacted by the General Assembly of the State of Tennessee, That the office of Geologist and Mineralogist of the State be and the same is hereby abolished, and sections 253 to 259 of the Code are repealed."

Apparently, there was an agreed-upon plan to abolish the office of State Geologist from the very outset. The Legislature had been in session only one week when Democratic Representative Robert Johnson from a tier of Upper East Tennessee counties introduced a bill [191] to be entitled

"An act to abolish the office of Geologist and Mineralogist of the State."

Within less than a week thereafter, a companion bill was introduced in the Senate by Democratic Senator Reese T. Hildreth representing the counties of Morgan, Scott, Fentress, and Overton. The movement for the abolition of the office moved merrily along, but was halted momentarily on November 1 by a resolution [192] introduced by Democratic Representative H. C. Lockhart of Stewart County:

"Whereas, A bill is pending in the House of Representatives to abolish the office of State Geologist;
And Whereas, It is desirable that the Report of the State Geologist should be received before action is taken on said bill; therefore,
Be it resolved by the General Assembly of the State of Tennessee, That the present incumbent be requested to submit his report to the General Assembly at as early day as practicable."

On November 8, Representative William L. Martin of Wilson County, who was of the Opposition Party, "presented the Report of the State Geologist" to the House of Representatives,[193] which ordered 150 copies to be printed. The Report [194] was as follows:

"REPORT of the STATE GEOLOGIST, to the
General Assembly of the State of Tennessee.

November 8, 1859.

REPORT.

To the General Assembly of the State of Tennessee:
GENTLEMEN:—It becomes my duty, as State Geologist, to present to

[190] *Acts of Tennessee,* 1859, Chapter 24.
[191] *House Journal,* 1859, 28.
[192] *Ibid.,* 149.
[193] *Ibid.,* 192.
[194] *Public Documents, Tennessee Legislature,* 1859, 297–302.

you my Biennial Report upon the progress and condition of the work under my charge. This would have been done sooner, but a desire to complete my survey in the section of the State in which I have recently been, (the southwestern part,) in connection with the unusually favorable weather, has kept me in the field. The present Report will be made as brief as the circumstances appear to require, and as a clear presentation of the subject will admit.

It affords me pleasure to state, at the outset, that, at the expiration of my present term, I shall have completed the fundamental portions of the survey, and, that I shall then have in preparation, (a work, in fact, already commenced,) a systematic and *Final Report* upon all that has been accomplished.

My term expires in March next. It will then be six years since, in an official capacity, I first entered upon the Geological and Mineralogical survey of the State. Up to this time, the work has been carried forward with all the energy that the means placed at my disposal would permit. It has engrossed all my thoughts; every thing has been made subservient to it; no reasonable labor has been spared. Every county in the State, without exception, has been visited and examined. In many cases, where the geology of the counties has been intricate and difficult to work out, they have been visited again and again, until all anomalies have been cleared up, or the ends sought after obtained.

In addition, I beg leave to state that, at intervals, during the four years preceding my first election as State Geologist, I explored, at my own expense, no inconsiderable portion of the State, the result of which explorations are freely given to the State; they have been, in fact, already incorporated in the general results. Altogether, the labor has been indeed great, and has involved an amount of traveling within the State, equal to more than seventeen thousand miles.

PLAN PURSUED.

In the prosecution of the Survey, the same *plan* has been constantly kept in view. It has been, as stated in my former reports, the *first* consideration to develop the geological structure of the State—to make out its formations, to trace out their limits, to ascertain their thickness and composition, for this is the foundation of the whole work. The formations are the great storehouses which contain our mineral wealth, and a knowledge of them is indispensable to a systematic and economical development of that wealth. In the development of the position and quantity of our stone-coal, as an example, it was first necessary to ascertain the existence and 'whereabouts' of that particular group of rocks, or, in other words, of that formation in which the coal beds are always found, and to which they are confined. This done, we know where to look for coal—we know, too, (a matter of great economical importance,) where not to look for it—where research in that direction would be worse than useless. Definiteness and system are thus given to the development of this mineral. So it is with iron-ores, copper-ores, and all that constitutes our mineral wealth.

After making out the formations, or, so far as practicable, in connection with this work, the *second* consideration has been (as already implied) to discover, examine, and determine, both as to quality and quantity, the minerals and valuable products that these formations afford the ores, coal, marble building materials, &c.

A *third* consideration has been the examination and classification of the *soils* of the State with reference to their improvement and greatest production. Here, again, the making out of the formations is the foundation of the work. The formation determines, almost universally in Tennessee, the character of the soil which rests upon it. The farmer speaks of 'limestone-soils,' 'sandstone-soils,' 'slate-soils,' &c. To understand well then the character of the soils, we must know something about the limestone, the sandstone, and the slate. Such is the connection between the soil and the rock, that a geological map is a map of the soils. Such a map is the basis of an agricultural survey. It exhibits the natural agricultural districts of the State for the soils of each of which the necessary analyses and experiments can be instituted. Much more might be said with reference to this feature of the survey; but I cannot here enlarge. Reference may be made to my former reports for further information on this subject.

WHAT HAS BEEN ACCOMPLISHED?

Such is the plan, which, from the first, I have had before me; and now the question arises, What has been accomplished?

In the *first place*, the ground-work of the survey is finished. The State has been traversed from Shelby to Johnson. All the great formations have been worked out and their limits ascertained. They can now be accurately represented upon a map to serve as a guide to the miner, or as an agricultural chart to the farmer. To make these out, to have this part of my work, in connection with what Dr. Troost had done before me, complete, has been a leading object with me. Hitherto I have been desirous of remaining in the field, for the reason, that having once commenced, I was unwilling to retire without having completed some principal part or parts of the survey. Now this reason no longer exists.

In the *second place*, the examination of the mines and minerals of the State has been general and elaborate. The coal and iron-ore beds have been traced out with care. The localities of all other mineral products have been examined and many discoveries have been made. I trust I shall be able to present a full and satisfactory report upon our entire mineral wealth as at present known to me, either through my own discoveries, or those of others.

In the *third place*, the ground-work of an agricultural survey has been secured. The making out and the mapping of the formations will give us an agricultural chart. The soils have been classified. Much information in regard to their composition and adaptions has been obtained, and will be presented in my Final Report.

It is in this department of the survey, however, that the most remains to be done. Should the work be continued, it ought, henceforth to take, in the main, an agricultural direction, and by what has been done, the way is clearly open for its easy prosecution.

FINAL REPORT.

Having thus stated, in general terms, what has been accomplished, I beg leave now to speak more particularly of the *Final Report* to which reference has been made.

As my official connection with the survey will terminate in a few months, I desire to present to the State a full digested account of all the results that have been obtained—to *post up* all that has been done in as clear and as systematic a manner as lies within my power. This will constitute my

Final Report. Such a work is necessary in order that the State may secure what has been done, and in order that the same ground may not be traveled over again by those who may succeed me.

The Report when published, will form a book of five or six hundred ordinary octavo pages. To complete it will cost much labor and time. Nearly 100 pages are already written, but to write what remains, and to make the report as practical, as useful, and as reliable as I desire, will require nine or ten months. This time will extend beyond the expiration of my term, but beyond that, all I ask is simply the publication of my report.

In order that you may be further informed as to the character of this work, I add a synopsis of its contents.

It will be divided into four parts. The *First Part* will be *Introductory*, and will include a description of the leading, external physical features of the State. The different natural divisions of Tennessee will be described as to form, elevation above the sea, river system, climate, &c. Such divisions, as examples, are the great Smoky Mountain range; the great and beautiful Valley of East Tennessee; the Cumberland Mountain, or Table-land, as it should be called; the fertile and wealthy limestone basin of Middle Tennessee; the Mississippi plain, or slope, and the Mississippi bottom of West Tennessee. This first part or introduction will be necessary to what follows, and will contain much practical and important geographical information which has never yet been published.

The *Second Part* will be a description of the geological structure of the State, and of its formations. The formations will be enumerated and described as to their extent, thickness, composition, practical importance, the minerals they contain, &c. The number of the great formations which are found in the State, and which constitute its mass, form its mountains and underlie its valleys, are twenty in number. These will be described in the text, and their geographical extent represented upon a map.

The *Third Part* will be devoted to the mines and minerals of the State. It will describe our coal-beds, as to their number, position, thickness, the quality, availability, present production and prospective value of the coal. The iron ores, the mines and ores of copper, lead, zinc, manganese, and gold, will all be described in the same manner. In this part, too, all useful rocky products, such as marble, building materials, roofing slates, hydraulic limestones, and marls, will be reported upon. In addition, other minerals, such as salt, alum and nitre, will be treated so far as may be necessary.

This part will be made as plain and as practical as possible. It will be the largest part of the Report. All that precedes may be regarded as introductory to it. The localities of all minerals will be indicated upon the map, which will accompany the Report.

The *Fourth and Last Part* will be devoted to the soils and the general agricultural results of the survey. The soils of the different agricultural districts will be treated of separately, with reference to their capabilities, defects, &c. This part will truly present the ground-work of an agricultural survey. The map, as stated before, will be necessarily a map of the soils; and this, with the text, will constitute the basis, not to be constructed again, from which all future researches of this kind may start, and upon which they may rest.

In addition, and by way of supplement, I shall treat of all the counties separately; in each case giving a full annotated index of all the formations, minerals and soils found in the county. By this means, the geological features and products of any county can be at once determined, and all parts of the Report referring to it consulted, without the necessity of looking over the entire report.

SPECIMENS COLLECTED.

Finally, during the progress of the survey, I have at all times, whenever there was occasion for it, collected such specimens of ores, minerals, rocks, and fossils as were considered desirable for the elucidation of a final report, and for the establishment of a cabinet illustrating the geology and the mineral wealth of Tennessee. A great number of specimens have thus been collected. A few of these are in the hands of the Librarian; the mass of them, however, are in my own hands, no place having been provided for them. These specimens are valuable, and it would be well for your honorable body to provide suitable room for them somewhere in the Capitol, and to make provision for the necessary case, or cases, in which to exhibit and preserve them.

All of which is respectfully submitted.

J. M. SAFFORD,
State Geologist."

On November 22, the bill to abolish the office of Geologist was passed in the Senate by a vote of 17 to 3, and ordered to be transmitted to the House of Representatives.[195] For some undisclosed reason, the Senate-passed bill was allowed to languish in the House, but on February 1, 1860, the bill was passed on third and final reading by a vote of 35 to 31. A motion to reconsider the action in passing the bill was called up on February 28, but the attempt failed by the same vote.[196] And so, for the time being, the State was without a State Geologist.

The abolition of the above office smacks somewhat of "politics." Two Democrats introduced the bills for abolishing the office. While the vote in the Senate was heavily in the affirmative, the vote in the House was close, with a majority of the Democrats voting to abolish the office. When the bill was pending in the Senate, Senator John Trimble of Davidson County and a member of the Opposition Party introduced a resolution [197] calling upon the State Librarian

". . . To report the States of the Union in which surveys, by authority, on Geology and Natural History, have been made and published; . . . and report the best mode of procuring or publishing such a survey of the State of Tennessee."

Return J. Meigs, the State Librarian, complied with the request embodied in the Senate resolution. His report [198] was concise but highly informative, and he recommended the publication of the findings mentioned by Dr. Safford in his Report to the Legislature. Herewith is the Report submitted by Mr. Meigs:

[195] *Senate Journal*, 1859, 165.
[196] *House Journal*, 829.
[197] *Senate Journal*, 63–64.
[198] *Legislative Union and American*, 1859, Volume II, 319–321.

"To the General Assembly of the State of Tennessee:

By resolution of the Senate, No. ——, I am directed to make a report embracing the following particulars:

I. The States of the Union in which surveys by authority, on Geology and Natural History, have been made and published.

II. The best mode of procuring and publishing such a survey of the State of Tennessee.

III. A statement of the advantages of such a work.

In complying with this resolution, it ought to be premised that I do not pretend to any geological knowledge, and that whatever I state, upon any of the points of inquiry, is drawn, almost entirely, from such sources of information as are open to all who will take the trouble to consult the proper repositories. I am aware, indeed, that nothing more is expected of me, upon such a topic, but to abbreviate the labors of the members of the General Assembly, who, looking to the development of the resources of Tennessee, merely desire to be informed what has been done in our sister States in this direction, how it has been done, and what valuable results are attainable by means of such a work.

1. Geological surveys, more or less complete, have been made by legislative authority, in the States of Alabama, Arkansas, California, Connecticut, Delaware, Indiana, Iowa, Kentucky, Maine, Maryland, Massachusetts, Michigan, Minnesota, Mississippi, Missouri, New Hampshire, New Jersey, New York, North Carolina, Ohio, Pennsylvania, Rhode Island, South Carolina, Vermont, Virginia, and Wisconsin. And the General Government has caused geological explorations to be made and reports published of Iowa, Illinois, Wisconsin, the Sierra Nevada and of the Coast Range, and, in all the explorations of our Western territories, under the authority of the General Government, the geology of every district has been made a capital object for the most obvious reasons. By individuals, also, reports have been published on the geology of particular districts in various sections of the Union, in the scientific journals of the country. Of the State surveys, we have in the State Library those of Alabama, Arkansas, California, Connecticut, Iowa, Kentucky, Massachusetts, Missouri, New Jersey, New York, North Carolina, Pennsylvania, and Vermont.

Among them, those of Massachusetts, Pennsylvania, and New York seem to be the most complete .

The New York publication is entitled, 'Natural History of New York,' and consists at present of nineteen quarto volumes. Of these, four volumes are on Zoology, two volumes on Botany, one volume Mineralogy, four volumes on Geology, five volumes on Agriculture, and one volume on Meteorology: on Palaeontology two volumes have been published, and three remain to be published; so that when the series is completed, it will consist of twenty-two volumes. Each department has been assigned to separate chiefs—the Zoology to DeKay, Botany to Torrey, Mineralogy to Beck, Geology to Mather, Vanuxem, Emmons and Hall, Agriculture to Emmons, Meteorology to Hough, and Palaeontology to Hall.

The first appropriation to this great work was made by an act of the 15th of April, 1833, by which the sum of twenty-six thousand dollars was appropriated annually for four years, to defray the expenses. By an act of May 8, 1840, the Governor was authorised to cause the work to be continued; and by an act of the 9th of April, 1842, another appropriation of twenty-six thousand dollars was made to pay for the materials furnished and services rendered under the act of 1840. By an act passed on the 8th of

April, 1843, the Governor is authorised to continue the work, and the Treasurer is directed to pay, on the Comptroller's warrant, the costs and expenses already incurred, or afterwards to be incurred in the completion of the work. Every branch of it is most elaborately executed, and illustrated by engravings when necessary.

It may be that the unequalled prosperity of this great State is in part due to the clear knowledge of its resources, imparted to its inhabitants by this elaborate exposition of its Natural History.

2. As to the best method of procuring and publishing such a survey of this State, as is contemplated by the Senate's resolution, perhaps the reference already made to the laws of New York may be regarded as pointing out a safe pattern. The splendid results obtained in that State, however, are due to the intelligence of those to whom the execution of the work has been entrusted, seconded by the liberal appropriations made, more than to the scheme of the survey itself, proposed in the original law. For it is true, in regard to such a work, as well as to every other branch of the public administration, that good results are obtained from even imperfect legislation, if integrity and knowledge preside over the execution of the law.

The laws of several of the States have been examined, and it has been found that good suggestions are contained in some of them, where comparatively unimportant reports have been published. The work of thoroughly examining the Natural History of a State, and of preparing it for publication, in a manner becoming its importance, requires great and varied talents and acquirements, such as are rarely, if ever, combined in a single individual. And, indeed, if an individual could be found possessed of the requisite knowledge, it would require a life time of assiduous labor to achieve what could be done in a few years by the combined abilities and industry of a few competent persons.

Twenty-three years have elapsed since New York set on foot the preparation of her Natural History, and it is not yet completed. The labor of such a vast amount of original research is far beyond the power of any single individual. We have seen that the Geology alone is the work of four different hands; while what has been done in Tennessee for this important department of knowledge, has been the work of two individuals, without assistants, and for an annual compensation scarcely equal to the earnings of a day laborer.

Dr. Troost was appointed Geologist, Mineralogist and Assayer of the State by the act of 1831, chapter 28, which required him to make a Geological survey, with a view, as far as practicable, to develop its mineralogical resources;—to examine into those mineral and metallic regions believed to exist in the different formations found in the different sections of the State; —to make the proper analyses of such substances as he believed to be of value;—to examine the soils of different parts of the State, and the rocks of those parts, and report upon the same, accompanying his report with such remarks as might lead the citizens to an estimate of comparative value and use, as well as to enable them to judge understandingly of its metals and minerals.

All this, that accomplished mineralogist, geologist and chemist, was to do for five hundred dollars a year, which salary increased for 1838-9 to one thousand dollars, was, with great difficulty continued to him until the session of 1847-8. His first report was presented to the legislature on the 14th of November, 1838, and we have an analysis of it in the House Journal of that year, page 303–5. His last report, the ninth, may be found in the Appendix of the House Journal of 1847, p. 143-168. These reports are all full of important information; but they present only an imperfect view of the geology of the State, and of the kindred topics, because it was impossible to make the requisite explorations for a full development, without means to defray the expenses of it, and to procure the aid of assistants.

These remarks are applicable to the case of Mr. Safford, the present Geologist, from whom, as from Dr. Troost, more has been expected than can be accomplished by any unaided individual, whatever his abilities and acquirements.

The scheme that is best adapted to procure a thorough geological survey of the State, is that which the most accomplished geologist would devise, and of course it must be left to him; and if we would have the work done, we must devote to it such an amount of money as will secure the services of such a head, and must furnish him with all the aid which his arduous work makes necessary. A bill accompanies this report, which, if passed, will attain the end in view.

3. As to the third point:—the advantages of a thorough geological survey of our State,—let us reflect that the scope of geology is to teach us the constituents of the crust of the Earth, to whatever depth it is possible to penetrate;—not merely to gratify curiosity, which, however, would be no mean object, considering who made this planet,—but to enable the inhabitants of any district to subdue the part of the Earth on which they dwell, and to have real control over it;—to appropriate to their use, and make subservient to their wants, the various materials which constitute the external surface, the producer of vegetation, and the interior, where lie concealed the metals and minerals, without which human life, except in its most savage state could not be maintained in any climate liable to the great vicissitudes of heat and cold.

This being so, what material science can compare with Geology in importance; what other branch of human knowledge so clearly demands attention at the hands of the representatives of the people? It may safely challenge comparison with any other.

If we could cut our globe, like an apple, into halves, there would be exhibited to our sight, beginning at the surface, a succession of layers, each layer extending around the entire circumference, of uniform composition in every part of its extent, and differing from the layer below it, until descending towards the center, we should come to a nucleus, around which the other layers would have the appearance of having been wrapped or folded. In some of these layers, especially the uppermost, we should see the remains of vegetable and animal life; and we should see that each layer wherever it occurred, had its own peculiar vegetables and animals differing from those of the layer below, so that we could follow each around the globe and identify it in every locality. We should see that the soils, upon which the crops of the tiller of the ground are grown consist of the ruins of the more recent of these layers, washed to their present position by rains and torrents; and, of course, that each soil partakes of the nature of the layer from which it was separated; and from this we should plainly see the necessity, to successful agriculture, of the knowledge of the composition of each soil, of the analysis of each, and of that branch of science called agricultural chemistry. We should see that after passing through these alluvial deposits, we should in certain places called basins, find clays and limy and sandy matters, and 'imbedded in them remains of marine animals blended with fresh water species, quadrupeds, and even birds.' We should see that these lie upon chalk, that this is succeeded by certain varieties of sand and sandstone, these by freestone mingled with lime, and limestone mingled with clay or magnesia, this by coal, this by mountain limestone, old red sandstone, &c.

As all this would appear to the eyes to be perfectly uniform, we should make no extravagant expenditures in search of coal or metallic ores where such are not to be found. We should be taught that, as in the British Isles, so in every other country, 'not a single mine of any metal has ever been worked in any layer more recent than the magnesian limestone'; that, as a general truth, 'rich veins of lead, copper, tin, silver, &c., abound only in and near to districts which have been greatly shaken by subterranean movements,' as in the vicinity of New Madrid, Missouri, where gold, silver and copper have been recently found, and in geological proximity to which the celebrated Iron Mountain is situated; and in California, where gold being discovered by accident in Capt. Sutter's mill race, was traced to the quartz veins in the mountains, from which it had been disintegrated by the action of natural causes; and in Australia, where, when the geological structure of California becomes known to scientific geologists, Murchison declared gold would be found to be as abundant as in California; and it was this vaticination that led to the discovery of the gold deposits of that far-off land. We should see from our imaginary section of the globe, where lines of railroad, canals and common roads should be located; what materials most perfectly resist atmospherical changes, and are therefore best adapted for architectural purposes; we should have a perfect knowledge of springs and the subterranean distribution of water, and should plainly perceive the best methods of draining from the surface the superabundant moisture where it exists; and exactly to what stratum a well must be sunk to obtain a supply of water.

All this, and much more, would be manifested to our eyes if we could have before us such a section of the globe; and indeed all this, and much more, geology, even with our imperfect means of penetrating into the depths of the earth, has already taught. What is needed in Tennessee, is a complete development of our strata, so that we may not grope in the dark and be misled by deceitful promises and superstitious notions to seek for subterranean treasures, at a very great expense, in strata where no such wealth can exist.

In England, eminent practical men of the great northern coal field, denied the existence of coal under the magnesian limestone; yet now, in consequence of Smith's geological report of 1822, there is annually sent to the London Market, from beneath that stratum, enormous quantities of excellent coal. So, in regard to draining: it can never be done, upon good principles, unless the geological structure of the district be known. Where porous rocks alternate with strata impervious to water, the springs will commonly issue at several points on the surface line of the junction of the strata; and by making a deep drain along the line of junction the complete desiccation of wet lands in certain districts in England, have been effected, which had been in vain guttered in all directions by the usual hollow drain. At Scarborough, in England, under the direction of Dr. W. Smith, a subterranean reservoir was found in the sandstone rock; on the site of a little spring, closed with a dam, into which he conducted the superabundant water of the winter, and regulated its discharge for the supply of the town in summer.

That the abstract truths of geology may become of general interest or public value, maps and sections of particular districts, representing the extent, thickness and superpositions of the several layers, are indispensable, and until the whole of the land be thus surveyed and described, geological inferences are insecure, and are utterly destitute of practical value.

While such a survey, for geological purposes and results, is being carried forward, it ought to be connected with a complete triangulation of the State, and the construction of a perfect topographical map, representing the surface with accuracy. This done, the location of a road or canal, anywhere in the State, could be made upon the map with infallible accuracy.

Such are some of the advantages of an adequate geological survey of the territories of a State. They are not a whit exaggerated but are greatly underrated in this report, owing to my imperfect acquaintance with the subject, and the want of time to devote to it, and the absence of the materials to which reference ought to be made. Such as it is, I submit it to the Senate with the hope that it may lead the Legislature to render this session illustrious by taking steps to set on foot a geological survey of Tennessee which shall be prosecuted, without faltering, until whatever is attainable in regard to our agricultural and mineral resources shall be completely developed and set before the public mind.

With this geological survey, an investigation of the other branches of the Natural History of the State ought to be connected. Nothing should be left unexplored; for nothing that God has made, nothing that inhabits the region in which we dwell, can be without its interest and use to man. The insect world is generally passed unheeded, by the unreflecting multitude; but, is it not important to us to know the times of generation and duration of the life and the habits of those insect tribes that are injurious to crops? In Massachusetts and New York, and perhaps in other states, books have been written on this topic, and certainly not without manifest advantages to the commonwealth. By means of the information such books contain, the cultivator is instructed how to prosecute his labors so as to avoid or prevent the ravages of these little enemies, and in the adoption of measures for their destruction. Instead of barbarously destroying birds, without discrimination, an intelligent study of the habits of some tribes would teach that they are among his best friends, preying, as they do, upon the secret depredators of the seed he has deposited in the ground.

These utilitarian views seem to recommend the work contemplated; but there is a higher motive surely for the study of the creatures of the Author of Life,—the motive of divining the scheme of creation, and of assuring ourselves that the universe emanated from and is sustained by Divine Love.

R. J. MEIGS."

On November 15, 1859, Senator Jordan Stokes of Wilson County succeeded in getting passed his resolution approving the publication of Dr. Safford's *Final Geological Report* in the number of twenty-five hundred copies.[199] There can be little doubt but that the able report of Return Jonathan Meigs had exercised considerable influence on the Senate in this matter. A week later, however, the resolution encountered trouble in the House and was rejected by a vote of 29 to 24.[200] But a bit of repentence is in evidence for such action, because the matter was again taken up on February 7, 1860, and the

[199] *Senate Journal*, 1859, 141–142.
[200] *House Journal*, 1859, 262.

"motion to reconsider prevailed, and the resolution was adopted."[201]

It should be borne in mind that the battle for the publication of the Safford Report was led by two members of the Opposition Party, Senator Jordan Stokes and Representative William L. Martin, both of whom were from Wilson County.

Before Dr. Safford's *Final Geological Report* was made ready for the press, the War Between the States began and put a stop to the whole project. A year after the termination of the war, a resolution [202] was adopted on November 22, 1866, calling upon Dr. Safford to inform the Legislature as to what remained to be done in order that there might be carried out the intent of the legislative "resolution adopted February 7, 1860." After two more years, in which Dr. Safford completed the work on his Report, final approval and authorization were given for the publication of the document.[203] In 1869, there came from the press, by legislative authority, a volume of 450 pages accompanied by a Geological Map of Tennessee.[204] Dr. Safford was voted fifteen hundred dollars as his compensation for the work done toward completing the report. This monumental work, based upon twenty years of observation and research, constitutes the most important work of the sort that has ever been published on the geological resources of Tennessee.

Although Governor Harris made no mention of the State Capitol in his major Message to the Legislature, yet it was a project of importance not yet completed. At various times, the Legislature displayed a bit of complaint at what was regarded tardy progress toward completing the Capitol. Knowing full well that a report as to the status of the work would be expected by the Legislature, the Capitol Commissioners submitted a Report on October 20 through Representative Edward H. East of Davidson County.[205] The Report,[206] setting forth the financial situation which involved certain difficulties, and explaining other factors in detail, was as follows:

"REPORT.

Office of the Commissioners.
For the Erection of the State Capitol.
Nashville, October 1, 1859.

To the Honorable, the Legislature
Of the State of Tennessee:
In behalf of the Board of Commissioners for the erection of the State Capitol, the undersigned has the honor to

[201] *Ibid.*, 635.
[202] *Acts of Tennessee*, 1866, Resolution 20, 265.
[203] *Ibid.*, 1867, Resolution 130, 367.
[204] Safford, James M.: *Geology of Tennessee.*
[205] *House Journal*, 1859, 74.
[206] *Public Documents, Tennessee Legislature*, 1859, 137–142.

REPORT:

That at the date of his last statement of the means at the disposal of the Board, there remained in its Treasury the sum of......................	$ 7,398 28
Since when, there has been received into it as follows, viz:	
Amount allowed by the Bank of Tennessee for $45,000 of 6 per cent. coupon Bonds deposited with it by the Governor, the sum of..........	$39,900 00
And from sales of surplus materials, tools, &c., no longer needed or useful, ...	242 80
	$47,541 08
And the expenditures of the Board have been for the same time as follows, viz:	
Paid Penitentiary for dressed stone furnished, etc., etc., ... $ 8,728 06	
And for materials, labor, salaries, furniture, fixtures, and incidental expenses, ... $35,990 82	
	44,718 88
Leaving in the Treasury unexpended, ...	$ 2,822 20

My last Report showed that of the appropriation made in 1855-6, there remained unused, seventy Bonds of $1,000 each, out of which the Governor has handed over to the Bank of Tennessee forty-five, for which it has passed to the credit of the Board only $39,900, or $5,100 less than their amount, notwithstanding the Act granting it (1855–6, ch. 268, p. 555,) made the appropriation a specific one of $150,000 cash, as it directed the Bank to honor the checks on the Commissioners for *that sum,* not making the amount to be received at all dependent on the assumed or real value of State Bonds.

This reduction of the amount of the appropriation, added to a similar one previously made, and noticed in my last Report, has thus far reduced the assets of the Commission to the extent of $12,000. And as there remains yet to be handed over to the Bank $25,000 more of Bonds, there will be a still further reduction, dependent on the price the Bank places on them—most probably decreasing the appropriation to the extent of $15,000 in all.

This uncertainty as to the sum to be realized from an appropriation of this character, causes great embarrassment to the Board, inasmuch as it leaves entirely undetermined what amount it can safely calculate on having at command, or to what extent it may prudently enter into contracts predicated on it.

It may be argued, that in a pecuniary point of view, it matters not, as both the Bank and the Capitol building are the property of the State.

This is in the abstract true; still, the Commissioners feel embarrassed in making contracts in advance of the means they have *actually in their treasury;* because, in so doing, they are liable to incur obligations beyond what the Bank may allow them as a credit for any future deposit of Bonds to be made by the Governor; and, beside this inconvenience and perplexity, they feel a reluctance to having the amount of State Bonds charged against the construction of the Capitol thus swelled twelve or fifteen thousand dollars, beyond the amount actually received by the Board.

Beside other work of less importance since the date of my last Report—
There has been erected around the building an extensive cut stone promenade, of the most substantial and durable character.

The southern crypt has been substantially paved with heavy stone flagging, resting on solidly cemented masonry.

The northern crypt has been fitted up in good style, with all conveniences for the reception and safe custody of the public arms of the State.

A large amount of blasting around the public grounds has been done, preparing them for receiving the contemplated enclosure, besides grading on the surface, together with the accumulation of a considerable amount of dressed stone, intended for the foundations of the enclosure.

In addition to which, the Board has contracted for the iron balustering of all the stairways of the building, including also, iron stairs from the base to the roof of the tower, for fitting up and shelving the Library room, together with suitable gas posts and lamps for the four main entrances to the building—all in the most substantial manner, and in a style corresponding with the other parts of the building.

The balustering of the stairways and the tower stairs are very nearly completed; and a portion of the balustrades, cornices, shelving, and fixtures for the Library are already received, and are now being put up in a satisfactory manner by the contractors.

In fitting up this apartment, no material whatever but iron, will be used —thus securing against the possibility of danger from fire the valuable works it is destined to contain. For the iron work thus alluded to, there will have to be paid some $25,000, or about the sum remaining unexpended of the appropriation of 1855-6, leaving the Commissioners without means to progress with the enclosure of the grounds, etc.

In consequence of the temporary occupancy of the room intended as a State Cabinet—having been granted to the United States Courts—no shelving or cases adapting it to the purposes it is intended for, have as yet been provided.

The State Geologist being desirous of having some safe repository for the many mineralogical and other specimens of value collected by him, has made application for some suitable apartment; but having none such vacant, his request could not, of course, be complied with. If, however, possession of this room is resumed by the State, it will require but a few weeks time, and a very inconsiderable expense to prepare it for the reception and safe keeping of any specimens or objects of interest which your Geologist may have to put in it. And I doubt not he already has many such, and which, without some such place for their safe keeping, will be lost or destroyed.

At its last session, the undersigned did not ask of the Legislature any appropriation whatever.

If, however, it is the intention of your Honorable body to have the work of enclosing, grading, and ornamenting the grounds proceeded with, an appropriation for that purpose will be desirable at an early day; and should it be deemed advisable to further extend the public grounds on the west, I would suggest that an additional appropriation be made for that purpose— the sum of which, to be fixed after the probable worth of half the square fronting the western face of the building be ascertained and reported on by a committee of your own body.

Of the stone work necessary as a foundation for the iron superstructure of the enclosure around the building, I would suggest that the State convicts are, in all respects, competent to dress and prepare it for setting.

And should it be the determination of the Legislature to have the stone prepared by the prison, I would respectfully suggest, that the present arrangement by which it furnishes it to the Commissioners at a fixed price, and for which it receives payment of them in cash, is the very best plan that can be adopted, by which to save money to the State; a plan, as experience has fully demonstrated, superior to that of having set apart the labor of a given number of the convicts. The State owns the quarries, and has at command a cheaper and more available force of laborers than can be found elsewhere; and, as previously stated, in all respects capable of executing the work required of them.

In order to preserve the building from damage, and it and the public grounds from being made the resort of vicious, unruly, or evil-disposed persons, the Commissioners have found it necessary to keep employed a watchman during a part of the day and night; but as he is supposed to be unclothed with official or legal authority, his efforts to carry out the intentions of the Board, are in a great measure, unavailing.

I would, therefore, respectfully suggest to you the passage of a law, giving to such watchmen or custodians of the public grounds and building, as may be appointed by the President of the Board of Commissioners, such powers as are possessed by police officers of the city of Nashville, and also subjecting depredators on the building and grounds to such punishment as, in your judgment, you may deem fitting.

In an appendix to my last Report, will be found a statement showing the actual cost of the Capitol building, including purchase of grounds, interest paid, furniture and fixtures, and also inclusive of penitentiary labor, to have been, up to the 1st October, 1857, $835,262 60; since when, as per this Report, there has been expended the further sum of $44,718 88. Thus making the entire cost of it, including furniture, etc., etc., to be $879,981 48, up to this date.

For every item of expenditure made by the Board of Commissioners since its organization, there will be found on file in its office full and complete vouchers, showing for what each and every expenditure has been made.

To an examination and investigation of these vouchers, they invite such committee as you may appoint, and of which committee the appointment is respectfully asked.

Should other or fuller information in relation to the undertaking confided to the management of the Commissioners be deemed necessary, it will at all times afford pleasure to the undersigned to respond to any inquiries made of him.

All of which is respectfully submitted, by

SAM. D. MORGAN,

President of Board of Commissioners for the Erection of the State Capitol."

But the above report, though detailed and specific in all essential matters, did not quite satisfy some captious members of the House of Representatives. Just who they were will perhaps remain unknown, for the name of the author of the following resolution and the vote thereupon were not disclosed in the official proceedings:[207]

---

[207] *House Journal*, 1859, 113.

"House Resolution, No. 55: Asking information as to the number of workmen employed on the Capitol.
Was taken up, read and adopted."

In compliance with the above request, the Chairman of the Commissioners for Erection of the State Capitol submitted the following statement:[208]

> "Office of the Commissioners for the
> erection of the State Capitol
> Nashville 10 th Decr. 1859.

To The Honorable,
    The Speaker of the House of Representatives
The undersigned has just been furnished with a resolution adopted by the honorable body over which you preside, asking of the Commissioners for the erection of the State Capitol information as regards the number of men in the employment of the Board and the salary or wages of each.

To which I reply—That in consequence of no appropriation having been made since the session of 1855-56 the Commission finds its treasury exhausted of means beyond an amount barely sufficient to pay for the iron-work now being put up in the Library room and elsewhere; consequently it became necessary some weeks since to discharge all the mechanics and laborers previously employed, except only such as were indespensably necessary to assist in putting up the Library work previously alluded to, to receive and unload stone prepared by the Penitentiary, to take care of, and drive the wagon teams and carts, and to keep in order and preservation the building. For these purposes it was deemed essential to retain *eight* men: viz, two stone-cutters, at wages of $2.50 and $2.25 respectively per day, and six others as laborers, teamster, watch-men etc. etc., to each of whom $1.25 per day is paid.

Besides these mechanics and laborers the services of the Secretary and Treasurer, Mr. Plunket and those of Mr. Creighton the general superintendent are retained. The duties performed by the first named of these is to receive and pay out on the order of the President all monies received by the Board, to keep the books of the Commission, to audit and settle all accounts, and to perform such other and various duties as are required of him. The duties of the latter are to direct and superintend all mechanics and laborers employed on the grounds, or building, to furnish drawings and prepare patterns for the dressed stone and other materials needed. In a word, to perform all the labor and duties appertaining to one having charge of the construction of such a building.

To each of the above officers a salary of One Hundred Dollars per month is paid.

Presuming it to be the intention of the Legislature to have the Capitol grounds enclosed and improved, the retention of the services of these gentlemen was thought advisable, inasmuch as these offices could not be better, if as well filled by others, certainly by none having more deserved characters for probity and high qualifications for the posts they have both so long and so satisfactorily filled in the service of the Board.

All of which is most respectfully submitted.
                        Sam D. Morgan
                        President of the Board of Commissioners
                        for the erection of the State Capitol"

---

[208] Manuscript document in State Archives, Nashville.

In an effort to acquaint the members of the Legislature with the pertinent facts regarding the size and boundaries of the Capitol grounds proper, the Capitol Commissioners drafted and submitted the following:[209]

"To the General Assembly of the State of Tennessee.

The undersigned, Commissioners of the State Capitol, beg leave to present to the Legislature, the following facts and suggestions in regard to the building and the grounds, belonging to it.

The appropriation of $150,000 made by the General Assembly of 1855-6 (See Acts of that session, p. 555) will probably only net the sum of $135,000, for the reason stated in our Report at the present session. This appropriation has been expended in purchasing ground on the north side of the Capitol; by which the Capitol square has been extended to Gay Street, and in work already done, or now in progress, under contracts heretofore made.

No ground on the west side has been purchased as was contemplated by the Act of 1855-6, for the reasons stated in the report at last session; and of the work ordered by that Act, we have still remaining to be done the enclosing of the grounds and improving them in the manner then directed.

To accomplish these objects, an appropriation must be made, and we think ought to be made at the present Session.

The present grounds front on the North 538 feet.

South 542 feet 6 in.
East 777 feet 11½ in.
West 766 feet 10½ in.

and embrace about nine acres.

The building stands in the Southwestern angle of the Square, 180 feet from Cedar Street its Southern boundary, and only 80 feet from Vine Street its Western limit. . . .

Owing to the steepness of the ground on the West, when the Street comes to be brought to the grade necessary to make it passable, it will be, for a considerable distance, more than twenty feet below the present surface of the Capitol Square, and will present, on that side, a perpendicular precipice, against the face of which, a wall must be erected, at great expense, to enclose the Square and shut it out from so dangerous a neighbor.

Besides, the ground on this side is so contracted as to be totally disproportioned to the building, and the rest of the square, and cannot be improved in a manner becoming the style and character of the edifice.

It is an important consideration, too, that Vine Street occupies the site most suitable, or rather, the only suitable position, for the fixtures necessary for warming the house.

By running a street from Cedar to Gay between Vine and Spruce Streets, equidistant from both, a plot of ground would be cut off, fronting the present grounds of the Capitol along its western boundary, and about   feet wide, as shown by the dotted line on the diagram.

This plot, if added to the present grounds, would make the enclosure a square; and it would be susceptible of graduation in a convenient manner; could be tastefully and appropriately embellished; have good and sufficiently level streets around it, and suitable and commodious approaches on every front, which last is totally impracticable at present on the west side.

---

[209] Manuscript document in State Archives, Nashville.

For these reasons; but chiefly on account of the manifest inadequacy of the present grounds, the undersigned pray your Honorable Body to authorize the purchase of the ground referred to, and to make the necessary appropriation for that, and for the enclosure and improvement of the square.

SAML. D. MORGAN
R. J. MEIGS
J. P. CLARK
JOHN D. WINSTON
JACOB McGAVOCK
JAMES WOODS"

On the back of the last page of the document appears the following notation:

"I fully concur with the Capitol Commissioners in the opinion that the Capitol Grounds should be extended farther west than the present western boundary.
Decr. 7th 1859
ISHAM G. HARRIS."

With the foregoing reports before the Legislature, two days before *sine die* adjournment Section 32 of the General Appropriation Act provided the following:[210]

"*Be it further enacted,* That the Comptroller and Secretary of State shall be added to the Board of Capitol Commissioners; that the Board shall employ a competent engineer, who shall not be a contractor or interested as such in the work, to estimate the necessary cost of making excavations and fills, and doing other work to reduce to proper grade, and complete the capitol grounds as contemplated by the act of 1855-56, and report the same to the Board, who shall have said report published, and that then the Board shall let or have said work done upon the best terms practicable for the interest of the State; and it is provided hereby, that in order to pay for said work, the Governor of the State shall issue coupon bonds of the State, bearing six per cent. interest, and having thirty years to run to maturity, which shall be cashed upon the application of the Board, at par by the Bank of Tennessee: *Provided,* That nothing herein contained, shall authorize the Governor to issue an amount of bonds exceeding in all, one hundred thousand dollars, nor shall the contracts of the Board for work exceed that sum: *And provided, further,* That if the said work can be completed for a less sum than one hundred thousand dollars, that only so many bonds shall be issued as will cover that sum."

With the beautiful State Capitol nearing completion, the idea seems to have occurred to a member of the House of Representatives that the Chief Executive should have a residence provided for him while serving in that capacity. Imbued with such a notion, Representative John Patrick Farrelly of Shelby County introduced on November 7, 1859, the following resolution:[211]

[210] *Acts of Tennessee,* 1859, Chapter 130, 125–126.
[211] *House Journal,* 1859, 182.

"*Resolved*, That the Speaker appoint a committee of five to act in conjunction with such committee as may be appointed on the part of the Senate, whose duty it shall be to enquire into the propriety and expediency of purchasing an 'Executive Mansion' for the Governor of Tennessee, and that said committee report their action as soon as practicable."

A second effort by a member of the Legislature to provide a residence for the Governor of the State met with success in the House.[212] Next, the resolution was transmitted to the Senate where favorable consideration was given on November 17. A committee, suggested by the resolution, was composed of the following:

SENATE	HOUSE
McNeilly, Thomas	Farrelly, John Patrick
Stovall, B. L.	Gillespie, James W.
Trimble, John	Johnson, Robert
	Porter, James D., Jr.
	Sheid, J. M.

On February 10, 1860, Senator R. W. Bumpass introduced a bill [213] as follows:

"A Bill to be entitled

An Act to provide for a permanent residence for the Governor of Tennessee.

Sec. 1. Be it enacted by the General Assembly of the State of Tennessee, That the building known as the old Lunatic Asylum, and at present used as a hospital in the city of Nashville, be and the same is hereby appropriated as a residence for the Governor of the State.

Sec. 2. Be it enacted, That the Secretary of State and Comptroller for the time being, together with John Kirkman, W. T. Berry and Granville C. Torbett, shall constitute a Board of Commissioners, with authority and for the purpose of making such alterations, repairs and improvements on said building and grounds as shall adapt them for a convenient and comfortable residence for the Governor and to this end they may have torn down the wings of said building, and repair and refit the center building, and make such new erections of out buildings as they deem necessary.

Sec. 3. Be it enacted, That said Commissioners shall lay off and attach to said residence not less than two acres of said ground, in proper and convenient shape for garden and other purposes, with substantial enclosures, and shall have surveyed and laid off the remainder of the ground owned by the State, into lots, streets, and alleys, to the best advantage, so as to bring the highest price, and after giving thirty days notice, they shall sell said lots at public auction for cash or on credit, and with the proceeds of said sale or sales, the said Commissioners shall defray the expenses of the alterations, repairs and improvements provided for in the 2nd Section of this Act, and shall also furnish in a suitable manner for occupation said buildings.

Sec. 4. Be it enacted, That should the proceeds of the sales of lots aforesaid be more than sufficient to defray the expenses aforesaid, then and in

---

[212] *Ibid.*, 221.

Author's note. The first effort was made in 1850. See *Messages of the Governors of Tennessee*, Volume IV, 391.

[213] Original manuscript in State Archives, Nashville.

that event the said Commissioners shall pay into the Treasury of the State any surplus that may remain.

Sec. 5. Be it enacted, That nothing herein contained shall authorize said Commissioners to call upon the State for any money to accomplish the foregoing purposes, or make the State in any manner liable for the same.

Sec. 6. Be it enacted, That the Commissioners aforesaid shall use all proper diligence in the preparation of said building, so that, if possible, it shall be finished and completed, ready for occupancy, by the Governor who shall be inaugurated in the fall of the year eighteen hundred and sixty one.

Sec. 7. Be it enacted, That nothing in this act shall be so construed as to take away or impair any of the rights heretofore granted to the medical faculty of the University of Nashville, by an act entitled 'An Act to provide for the future management of the State Hospital, and for other purposes,' passed 29th February, 1856.

Sec. 8. Be it enacted, That the Commissioners appointed by the first Section of this Act, be and they are hereby empowered to acquire, upon such terms as they may be able, all the rights so granted to said medical faculty, and procure a relinquishment of the same for the purposes of this bill, and to this end they may use any surplus of the proceeds of said property not necessary to be used for the other purposes of this bill.

Sec. 9. Be it enacted, That if the Commissioners deem it best, they may have the entire building taken down, and a new one built, using such of the old material as may be suitable, and dispose of the balance, with the stone in the walls around said property, and all other property about the place, so as to procure a suitable residence for the Governor; Provided, no claim against the State, beyond the proceeds of this property, shall ever be incurred for the building and furnishing a Governor's residence."

With the passage of the bill on second reading, the bill then was referred to a Select Committee composed of Senators V. S. Allen, R. W. Bumpass, Thomas McNeilly, J. A. Minnis, and B. L. Stovall. On February 20, 1860, the above committee came up with the following recommendation:[214]

"Mr. Speaker:

The Joint Select Committee on the part of the Senate, to whom was referred the subject of taking into consideration the propriety of purchasing a residence for the Governor, have had the same under consideration, and have examined the residence of Mrs. Brown, and learned the price of the same, and have also learned the price of other property; and we are of the opinion that if the Legislature intends purchasing a residence for the Governor, that the residence of Mrs. Brown would be far preferable to any they have examined, and her price in their opinion is reasonable enough. But taking into consideration the large appropriation to be made necessary to finish the Capitol and Capitol Buildings, Grounds, &c., the committee is of the opinion that it would be inexpedient at this session of the Legislature to purchase a residence for the Governor.

Respectfully submitted,
B. L. STOVALL, Chairman."

The bill, having been set for special order on March 6, two amend-

---

[214] *Senate Journal*, 1859, 516.

ments [215] were added by two of the committee members. Senator Allen's amendment provided protection for the medical faculty of the University of Nashville, involving the use of the facilities of the Old Lunatic Asylum for medical teaching and nursing care of the indigent. Senator Stovall's amendment related to the wrecking of the old building and using the materials in any contemplated new buildings. The amended bill then passed third and final reading by a vote of 14 to 7.

The Senate-approved bill passed first and second readings in the House routinely. At this juncture, considerable concern was manifested by the Medical Faculty of the University of Nashville, and is evidenced by the presentation of the facsimile memorial [216] on February 17 by Senator Trimble of Davidson County.

Despite the strong protest by the physicians, the Senate rode roughshod over the objections set forth in the memorial and passed the bill by a two to one majority. But the memorial undoubtedly slowed down action in the House, and not until three days before final adjournment did the House consider the bill on third and final reading. [217] Representative D. W. C. Senter (later Governor of Tennessee) offered the following bill [218] in lieu of the original bill:

"*Be it enacted by the General Assembly of the State of Tennessee*, That the Governor, be and he is hereby authorized to appoint three commissioners, whose duty it shall be to sell the property belonging to the State, known as the old Lunatic Asylum, and the proceeds arising from such sale shall be applied to the discharging of the State debt, and any remainder, if such there be, shall be applied to the use of the Common Schools in this State.

Sec. 2. *Be it further enacted*, That such property shall be sold on time, or for cash in hand, as such commissioners may deem best for the interest of the State."

Representative Senter's idea did not appeal to his fellow members who quashed his effort by a vote of 35 to 25. Thereupon, Representative George Gantt of Maury County, in what must be regarded as a facetious move, proposed the following as an amendment to the original bill: [219]

"*Provided*, That without cost to the State, the Commissioners shall be bound, at all events, to furnish the State a mansion in accordance with modern taste and style, and conveniently adapted for the mansion of a Governor, and supply the same with suitable furniture. The house thus furnished, including the furniture, to be worth at least thirty-five thousand dollars, and to be on the best site for the purpose on the ground, and to have

[215] *Ibid.*, 605.
[216] *Ibid.*, 503–504.
Author's note. The memorial itself which is reproduced is in printed form in the State Archives at Nashville.
[217] *House Journal*, 1859, 1148.
[218] *Ibid.*, 1148–1149.
[219] *Ibid.*, 1149–1150.

To the Honorable Legislature of the State of Tennessee:

THE undersigned petitioners, honorably in charge of a great trust, are constrained by a high sense of duty to the public, to appear before your honorable body, as they have had to appear before your predecessors, and, in all probability will have to appear before your successors, to explain as follows, to-wit:

That the Trustees of a State institution, viz., the University of Nashville, did in the year 1851 organize a Medical Department, and then, and subsequently, appoint the undersigned as teachers in said Department.

That said Trustees, and said Faculty of Medicine, thus appointed, did jointly expend upon said Department more than Fifty Thousand Dollars, in order to make it a first class institution of the kind.

That subsequently, to enrich its cabinets and museum, that no less than three members of its Faculty have been sent to Europe, at different times, and at other times the services of private agents procured, in securing for the college means for medical teaching not surpassed, if equaled, by any medical college in the United States.

That by the energy and faithfulness of the Faculty, this Medical College, in the "backwoods of America," within six years after its organization, rivalled in the means of instruction and the magnitude of its classes the great institutions of the North, being far in advance of any attempt to teach medicine in the slaveholding States.

That it has thus secured the admiration of the unprejudiced medical public wherever upon the habitable globe medicine is cultivated as a science.

That it is now closing its ninth session with the largest class it has ever enjoyed, drawn almost exclusively from the slaveholding States, and, deducting the recent losses from northern colleges by the secession of southern students, it now has the largest class, and is in a more prosperous condition than any similar institution in the United States.

That it is but natural that this extraordinary development of a new power in the South, depriving the North of what from long enjoyment she regarded hers of right, should awaken and stimulate within her an active vigilance in search of means that will insure its ruin.

That in this attempt, under various pretexts, allies should arise, will not appear strange to those conversant with the history of human events.

They would further represent to your honorable body:

That your predecessors did establish the old Asylum Buildings and appurtenances a State Hospital for her unfortunate citizens.

That subsequently the Medical Faculty of the Univ. of Nashville were constituted its governors for a definite period.

That they have faithfully discharged their duty to the afflicted in said Hospital.

That they have expended five hundred dollars in money in repairs.

That they have paid the salaries of the resident physician out of their private funds.

That in order to secure the only proper nurses for the sick, they did (having full faith and confidence that the arrangement made with the State would not be interfered with,) bargain and agree with the Sisters of Charity to break up their own hospital arrangements and take charge of the State Hospital for the entire time.

That the said Sisters of Charity did in consequence take possession, under the law, for the entire term of years secured to the Faculty, and that they and their successors have faithfully discharged the duties assigned them.

That such an institution at the capital of the State of Tennessee is an indispensable provision by a christian people for the afflicted poor.

That by the present arrangement it does not cost the State anything, but enables a great commonwealth to do good without taxing her people.

That prior to the wise provision of the State in appointing the Faculty of a flourishing medical college the governors of this institution, whose interest it was to conduct it properly, the Legislature appropriated at one term seven thousand dollars for its support for two years, during which it accomplished infinitely less than it has any two years since it has been governed by the Faculty, without the appropriation of a cent for its support.

That the medical colleges at the North make annually a great parade of hospital advantages to medical students, in order to seduce them from the South, and with astonishing success.

That through this Hospital as an arm of the college, Tennessee has been enabled to check this annual exodus of southern medical students northward. For while comparatively a small hospital, her surgical cliniques surpass in variety, extent and brilliancy those of any hospital in the United States, as the statistics will show. A single year in this hospital exhibits an extent of operative surgery that the great General Massachusetts Hospital at Boston does not equal in two years, and it is the brilliant surgical clinique that attracts students. Ordinary medical cases in a Hospital they care little or nothing about. Six States at one time have been represented in this Hospital by persons demanding great surgical operations. Students who attend lectures here and in the North at different sessions know and declare that our surgical clinique here is infinitely superior. But in addition to this we can always keep the medical wards as full as we desire. In the summer, when we desire it, we have often sixty or seventy patients in the Hospital at a time. They are not all paupers there.

That it is now seriously proposed to the Legislature of a great State, and a bill introduced for that purpose, to break up this great charity, sell a part of the grounds upon which it stands, erect a palatial residence on the remainder at public expense, that this public adornment of the grounds *may increase the value of property in the neighborhood*, and enable a few speculators in corner lots to profit by the transaction.

That a great Southern State should break her plighted faith with her own citizens, and demolish an institution of scientific learning, which next to the resplendent glory of her arms, and her civic triumphs, has served to make lustrous her annals, for the attainment of no higher an object than to benefit rival institutions at the North, and enrich speculators in town lots, is, in effect, proposed by the bill before you; for that it seriously contemplates the establishing of the "Old Lunatic Asylum" a St. Helena, for the banishment of future Governors of the State, exceeds all rational belief.

We would represent to your honorable body that there were in attendance during the present session of lectures in the Medical Department of the University of Nashville, no less than two hundred and sixty of your constituents, besides one hundred and ninety-three from other Southern States, and from the North, making an aggregate of four hundred and fifty-four, and that there have been educated in part or in whole in this institution during the nine years of its existence, more than 1,600 Tennesseans, and in all 2,798 young men, nearly all from the South.

We therefore pray your honorable body to reject the bill concerning the State Hospital of Tennessee, now before you.

And your petitioners, etc.,

THOMAS R. JENNINGS,	J. BERRIEN LINDSLEY,
C. K. WINSTON,	A. H. BUCHANAN,
JOHN M. WATSON,	PAUL F. EVE,
W. K. BOWLING,	WILLIAM T. BRIGGS.

Medical Sense Triumphed over Legislative Folly

at least two acres of said ground: *And provided, further,* That the commissioners shall so obligate themselves, before they undertake to carry out the provisions of this act."

A bit of jockeying thereupon ensued in which an effort to postpone indefinitely the bill and amendments failed by a vote of 31 to 26. Next, Representative Robert Johnson proposed another substitute bill naming the Governor, Secretary of State, Comptroller, and Treasurer as a Board of Commissioners to take charge of the buildings and grounds, survey same, lay off streets and alleys, sell the same at public auction and turn over the proceeds to the State. This movement was approved by a vote of 35 to 23, and the following were added as additional commissioners: W. G. Harden [Harding], John M. Lea, S. R. Anderson, and E. H. Ewing. An effort by Representative Senter to table the bill and amendments failed by a vote of 32 to 24. At this stage of the game, Representative A. Caldwell of McMinn County demanded the previous question which request was sustained by a vote of 34 to 24. The question then was on the passage of the original bill which was rejected by a vote of 32 to 27. A motion to reconsider the vote first failed, then later prevailed. The final act in the somewhat farcical scene then took place when, upon reconsideration, the action to reject the bill triumphed by a vote of 30 to 25.[220] If the Thirty-Third General Assembly had been, like Hamlet, blessed with a "prophetic soul," it would have discerned that more than one-half of a century would roll by before provision was made for a "permanent Mansion for the Governor." But who would be so rash as to contend that the medical faculty of the University of Nashville did not make a significant contribution toward saving Tennessee from being the laughing stock of the Nation with its Governors domiciled in what had been the "Old Lunatic Asylum?"

In his major Message to the Legislature, Governor Harris pinpointed a truism that was then true and still is, namely, "The leading business of the people of Tennessee is Agriculture and its attendant interest. . . ." The recently-established State Agricultural Bureau had deepened the interest and spurred to beehive activity the citizenry of the State in that most basic of all activities—Agriculture. Governor Harris, like his predecessor, Governor Andrew Johnson, realized the importance and necessity of encouraging further advancements in that vocation which "makes all, pays all, and supports all." Agriculture supplies food, the shortage of which neither State statutes nor city ordinances can supply. Small wonder, then, that statesmen and forward-looking citizens have always lent aid, encouragement, and stimulation to this indispensable occupation. The call of Agriculture has interested and intrigued some of our greatest statesmen. Andrew

---

[220] *Ibid.,* 1153.

Jackson was conducting personally the planting of his crops when summoned to the command of his troops that won triumph for his country. The great triumvirate—Webster, Clay, and Calhoun—strolling amid their crops, flocks, and herds exhibited as much nobility of character as when pouring out their eloquence on the forum or in the Senate Chamber of the Congress. It is understandable, then, that the Thirty-Third General Assembly of Tennessee paused amid its labors to listen to discussions on Agriculture. On the morning of October 11, 1859, the Speaker of the House, W. C. Whitthorne,

"...Presented an invitation from the State Agricultural Bureau to attend at the fair Grounds today to hear the address of Commander M. F. Maury;
Which, on motion, was accepted."[221]

On the above day, Commander Matthew Fontaine Maury of the United States Navy delivered at the Sixth Annual State Fair the following remarkable address [222] which should not be allowed to drop into oblivion:

"LADIES AND GENTLEMEN:
It is usual for all of us who have the good fortune to enter upon a career that is upward and onward, to pause as we gain height after height, that we may see the progress that we have made, and contemplate the difficulties we have overcome. The retrospect inspires to new resolution and gives fresh courage. It is therefore profitable.
Farmers of Tennessee, let us here, from the eminence which you have gained in your glorious march of agricultural improvement, take such a view, not so much of the difficulties you have met and conquered, as of the progress you have made—the distance you have put between farmers and farming now, and the farming and farmers of former times.
Where were you in the days of my boyhood? Drifting your crops down the Mississippi river in flat-boats, and footing it back with your young men through the Indian nation. In a commercial sense you could make but one crop in two years; for the rule was, a year to grow and to gather, and a year for market and the return. It was hard work poling up the Mississippi, and slow business drifting down. I can recollect when in winter it took the farmer of Williamson two weeks to make a trip from Franklin to Nashville—18 miles—with a load of tobacco. Wagons went in pairs, so they might 'double teams,' and help each other out of the mud holes by the way. The fences on the road-side were literally used up in prying wagons out of those mud holes. Indeed the road hence to Franklin was in winter almost literally one long mud hole, and after struggling through it, twenty cents the bushel for corn could not always be got; but

---

[221] *House Journal*, 1859, 32.
[222] *Public Documents, Tennessee Legislature*, 1859, 575–585.
    Author's note. The inclusion of the addresses of Commander Maury and Governor Harris in this volume is in keeping with a statement in the Preface of Volume I of the *Messages of the Governors of Tennessee*, to-wit: "Much additional documentary material outside the title of the volumes is included. In a sense, the volumes will be semi-documentary in nature."

twenty-five cents the pound for common brown sugar, was sure to be charged.

Now contrast your present condition as farmers with that of your fathers, and compare with theirs, your manner of life, your modes of tillage, the results of one man's labor, your conveniences to market, the time it took them then and the time it takes you now to come and go,—and when you have drawn the picture faithfully and true, you will be surprised to see how wide is the difference in the condition of the farmers of Tennessee now, and the condition of the farmers of Tennessee then.

The people of East Tennessee were worse off even, than they in this part of the State. After their groceries were poled up the rivers to Nashville, they had to wagon them to Knoxville. Their dry goods, they hauled from Baltimore. Their wagons went away on their catapillar gait, for the most part empty, for the country produced nothing for them to carry but a few feathers and dried fruits,—a little honey, ginseng, and bees-wax. Their grain had to be put upon the hoof before it could be got to market, and driven away beyond the mountains for sale.

The condition of the people of East Tennessee in those days, reminded me as I passed through their country on my way to join the Navy, of the good old patriarchial times, when Joseph's brethren went trading down into Egypt, carrying 'a little balm and a little honey, spices and myrrh, nuts and almonds' in their hand.

Really, had Providence chosen in those days to send famine upon any portion of this goodly land, the people in one end of the State might have perished with hunger while those in the middle had enough and to spare.

In those 'homespun' times—and it has not been a very long time ago, for it was when I was young, and I am not yet old—such a spectacle as Nashville this day presents was simply an impossibility.

Now, and then! What a contrast!

I do not intend to weary you with platitudes, or to bore you with common place about railways and steamboats. But give me, I pray, your attention for a little while that we may consider the influences to which this great improvement in the agricultural and social condition of the State is owing.

Agriculture is reciprocal in its influences. If railways have helped it, it has built, and it sustains the railways. If the State in its prosperity has encouraged agriculture with a generous hand, agriculture has given the State that prosperity. Railways have stimulated the farmer to work, and they help him to get his crop to market, but railways do not till the earth. The truth is, the farmer himself has improved; and as you improve him, everything else is improved along with him. In the progress of the age, the farmer and the man of science have been brought closer together, and with the resulting acquaintanceship commenced those discoveries, inventions, and improvements, which have brought the agriculture, not only of Tennessee alone, but of the civilized world, to its present high state. It is high, but it is bound to be higher, for it is but just getting fairly under good *head*-way. More comely than an army with banners, the farmers of this State have entered upon a line of march by which they are destined to reach heights still more commanding, and to plant their flag of agricultural progress on eminences still more glorious than any which they have yet attained.

There are some callings in which it is hard to make innovations.

Architecture as a science, and sculpture as an art, remain at this day very much as ancient Greece and Rome left them. To this day, the potter uses the wheel described in the Bible; and for a long time the husband-man was as anti-progressive as he; but they have parted company, for where now is the *threshing-floor* on which the ox treadeth out the corn? *We* know that there has been innovation with progress and improvement, in this, the noblest calling that ever drew sweat from the brow of man.

And though the farmer has been slow to move, he is now thoroughly awake; his tramp on the march of improvement strikes the earth with a steadiness, a solidity, and a sound that has startled the world.

Nevertheless, he was amazingly like the potter in his antipathies; and for a long time; for the invention of printing and the revival of letters which exercised such marked influences upon the industrial pursuits generally, seem for centuries to have exercised them sparingly upon agriculture.

You recollect that when Captain Smith came to Virginia he made prisoners of two Indians whom he describes as 'most exact villains.' These he compelled to teach his people to cultivate Indian corn. The rows must be so wide, and the hills so far apart—exactly of that distance and width, to an inch, were the rows and hills planted when I followed the plow in an adjoining county, and it may be so yet. All innovation is not improvement, and like the potter with his wheel, so let this Indian rule remain, unless you can find a better one. The crop depends far less on the distance of an inch more or less between your rows, than it does in the preparation of the soil and the treatment of the plant.

Up to the beginning of the present century, the agriculture of England remained very much as the Romans left it. The crusades and the discovery of America enriched it with new staples, and pointed out new modes of culture; but they were for the most part simple and rude. When Henry VIII ascended the throne, neither carrots nor any other of the edible roots were known in England.

The first time we hear of turnips as food for sheep, is from Haughton in 1681. He tells us, moreover, that the failure of the corn crop then, compelled the Irish to dig up the ground and almost sift the dirt for a 'bacciferous herb with esculent roots' which he had been informed was first brought out Virginia by Sir Walter Raleigh, who, stopping in Ireland, caused some to be planted there, which in this famine stood the people in such good stead.

'It is an ill wind that blows nobody good,' for one of the results of the European wars which ushered in the present century, was to give to agriculture almost its first great impulse.

For the twenty years preceding 1795, the average price of wheat, in England, was $1,50 the bushel. Wheat then began to rise and went up, up with Napoleon's wars until 1812, when it reached the enormous rate of $3,80 the bushel. These high prices stimulated industry; and the soldiers bringing home from the wars, their observations concerning agriculture in foreign lands, enabled England,—which at that time set us the example and showed us the way in most of the industrial pursuits,—to commence that system of agricultural improvements which acting and re-acting, has added so much to the prosperity and true glory of the two nations.

This also was the period of cotton, and the cotton gin, of the steam engine, the spinning-jenny, and the famous loom. In 1825, cotton in this country went up to 25 or 30 cents the pound, and that price produced the effect here that had been produced in England by the price 126 shillings and sixpence the quarter for corn.

In 1823, Commodore Stewart brought home some bags of guano from the Chincha Islands. He had observed its fertilizing effects upon crops in Peru. Explaining its virtues to his friends in Maryland, he presented it to them. They made no use of it, however, for the farmer in those days trusted more to the virtues of hard labor than to the application of anything like chemistry to the art of husbandry.

Finally, in 1840, Liebig took the farmers fairly by storm with his book on 'Chemistry in its application to Agriculture and Physiology,' which, in the course of a few years, was improved by Boussingault's 'Rural Economy.'

It was now that farmers and men of science began to shake hands cordially with each other. It was now perceived that there was such a thing as scientific farming, and farmers began to rotate their crops according to the behests of chemical science. They had been taught to separate the silica plants from the potash plants, and to give them in cultivation, tripartite rotation with lime plants.

Until about twenty years ago, it may be said that agriculture was not ripe for science nor was science sufficiently advanced materially to benefit agriculture. But now they are every day acting and re-acting upon each other. Never was there a time when agricultural societies were as numerous or as flourishing. Steam on road and river has enabled the farmer to go abroad and see what the farmers are doing in other neighborhoods than his own. The effect of this is not only to stimulate but to cause every improvement in tillage to spread rapidly. No one who will consider the increasing number of Agricultural Societies, the numbers and excellence of agricultural journals,—the legislation of the States for the encouragement of agriculture, and the tone with which the people at large begin to call for agricultural schools, and colleges, and information, can fail to perceive the progress that agriculture has been and is making.

To have a proper appreciation of this progress, go back to the state of agriculture in the 16th century, when it was the business of the farmer's wife to make clothes for herself and husband, to winnow all 'manner of cornnes,' to brew, to go to market, to sell the crop and bring home the money to her lord and master. Nay, the relics of that rude state have not entirely disappeared yet, for even in some of the States of Christendom, the spectacle of a woman and an ox pulling a plow together is still not uncommon.

But though much has been done by you, much remains to be done and as long as this is the case we should not content ourselves with the drawing of contrasts, but rather survey our ground ahead, gird ourselves up for further progress, and push on to fresh conquests.

In what direction shall we march for the greatest of these conquests? Almost in any direction, for they lie right and left in our way. The public mind seems, however, to be very much impressed that mighty things are to be done through agricultural schools and colleges. We are pointed to them as a field upon which great achievements are to be won, but all such institutions seem to be planned upon the idea that they are to be a sort of expletive—a supplement to a finished education. It is well to have them of this sort. I'll huzza with the utmost enthusiasm for the establishment of richly endowed colleges and splendid schools of agriculture, but I'll toss my cap and give my halloo with a hearty good will also for something more humble; for the men who have the most to do with agriculture in a practical way at the South are not planters nor men of letters, but rather, the overseer—your man of but little book-learning; cannot something be done for his improvement?

It is well to have agricultural colleges to make the education of farmers complete, but it was suggested by a friend on my way hither, whether we might not have a school of practical agriculture for overseers also—something plain and unpretending, and such as every county may have by the expenditure of a very trifling sum of money. Overseers are peculiar to the slaveholding States; they form a highly useful, important, and respectable portion of the community. They give energy to your industry; they add to your prosperity, and indirectly they do much to advance social intercourse, to refine society, and enhance the hospitalities of the South, for they are 'careful about many things' while planters play the host. As a class they are peculiar, but as a class little or nothing has been done for them. Farmers have their clubs, Merchants their Guilds, Manufacturers their societies, Seamen their nautical schools, Sailors their horns, and Mechanics their associations; but I have never yet heard of any institution in this country for the especial improvement or benefit of overseers.

Labor is scarce, and produce sells at remunerative prices. Never were the industrial energies of the people so strained; and with this strain the duties and responsibilities of overseers have been greatly enhanced. The overseer of the present day has to consult the principles of hygiene as closely in the treatment of the working force under his control, as in the cultivation of his crop, he has to study the character of the soil and the habits of the plants which yield to his care their increase.

As a rule, the industrial force of the South is under the effective control of the overseer. It is a vast interest; and how to make him altogether equal to it—how to qualify him for giving it the most intelligent direction day by day, and hour after hour, is the question I wish to present for your consideration. Is it not worthy of it?

I do not know how you may best accomplish his improvement, and it hardly becomes me even to make a suggestion; but I may be permitted to give, by an illustration, an idea of how, in my judgment, something may be done.

Some ten or fifteen years ago, the statesmen of Great Britain were startled at the discovery that the shipping of the United States was fast overtaking and about to surpass that of Great Britain in the amount of its tonnage. The inquiry was made in Parliament, 'To what was this great difference owing? why is it that American ships can generally in foreign ports have the preference over British ships for freights?' The answer was, the Americans generally make shorter passages and deliver their cargoes in better condition—why? The reason was obvious,—as a rule, the American shipmaster is a better educated man than his English rival. The American, moreover, often has a personal interest in his ship, and therefore knows what he is about. English statesmen took the hint, and said, we must make our ship-masters as clever and intelligent as are the Americans, if we would hold our own in the commercial race. Accordingly, the British Government established a Bureau in the Marine Department of the Board of Trade, for the purpose of encouraging education among mates and masters. This Department is under the control of some of her cleverest Navy officers. It has, in the principal seaport towns of the realm, a local Marine Board, consisting of ship-owners, navy officers, merchants, and others. When a young man thinks himself qualified to be a mate, or a mate deems himself fit for a master, he is examined by one of these Boards, and if found qualified, a certificate is given to that effect.

This certificate does not entitle him to go on board the ship of the merchant, for the merchant can employ whom he pleases as mate or master, as the planter may employ whom he pleases as overseer,—but it serves as a recommendation, and it is a powerful one, for ship-owners have found these certificates to be the best of recommendations. Experience has proved that the best men count these examinations into their qualifications, and consequently when the owner wants a mate or master for his vessel, he inquires for one with a certificate.

On the other hand, if a mate or master, having a certificate, be guilty of any neglect, carelessness, or mismanagement on board his vessel or in the line of his duty, the Board inquires into the circumstances, and if he be 'caught tripping,' his certificate is cancelled; whereupon owners generally discharge him.

The effect of this system has been marvelous, and the English ship-master is now considered to be in a fair way of becoming as skilled and as accomplished as is his American competitor. His improvement has been wonderful.

It devolves upon you to run the parallel between the British ship-master and the Southern overseer; between your agricultural societies and the local Marine Boards of the British Government; between the nautical schools of England, and the schools of practical agriculture, to which I have alluded; and when you have done this, it is then for you to decide whether the planters of the South may not establish some system for the agricultural education and improvement of overseers, or some Board for the examination of them and the giving of certificates.

No State in the Union is superior to yours in the agricultural advantages which nature has given it. To develop these is the main object of this gathering together of the farmers of the State, the purpose and aim of your Agricultural Bureau. With soils as fine as any in the world, and geographically situated between parallels the most favorable to variety and excellence of production, Tennessee offers to her husbandmen a double set of climates—the climates due difference of latitude, and the climates due difference of elevation. So that the farmer of this State, may find diversity of climate—of soft or gentle climate—by going up or down the mountain, as well as by traversing the State from North to South.

The agricultural meteorologist, when he comes to contemplate the [topography] orography of your State, will not only admire the beautiful relief which your mountains, hills, and valleys give to the landscape, but he will recognize among your mountains, sites with climates for the finest vineyards; on your plantations he will see all the conditions that are requisite for good sheep-walks, and the most profitable wool growing, and as for fruits, no country in the world that lies between the parallels 36° 30′ and 35° can on account of your rare advantages of climate in altitude, surpass your State for abundance of yield, beauty of form or richness of flavor. Your hills, and knobs, and mountains afford every variety of sub-climate and site that the most fastidious fruit-grower can desire. Your very distance from the sea-board gives you advantages of climate, which they, even in the same latitude, near the sea, may sigh for in vain.

I do not know how it is now, or how it may have been in other parts of the State, but when I was a boy, the peach crop in Williamson county generally failed every other year—only with Mr. Brown, our neighbor, who lived in the knobs, it never failed. Mr. Brown, was a plain man, but Mr. Brown was a philosopher. He built his house on a knoll in the valley, but his orchard he planted on the knob, and in the years of failure with his neighbors he would have a most abundant crop, which he sent to town by the wagon load and sold for from $1,00 to $2,00 the bushel. 'What is the reason that Mr. Brown's orchard never missed' was a question that exercised the neighborhood.

Years after, when I was conducting a series of observations upon the radiation of heat, I stumbled upon the solution, and in this wise: I made, out in the open air, in the yard as if a hen's nest of wool; put a thermometer in it, and laid another as if on a mole-hill on the edge of it—and on a clear, calm, hot night in the month of August, with the thermometer in the house at 80°, that on the mole-hill at 70°, the temperature in the nest of wool—the hollow—was 42°. In the heat of the day with the sun upon them, the thermometer in the wool stood at 150°, that on the mole-hill at 110°. In windy nights and cloudy weather, the two thermometers stood alike. The explanation was simple enough. In the clear night, as the earth was cooled down by radiation it abstracted fresh supplies of heat from the air in immediate contact. This cooled the air on the ground, and that on the hill being thus cooled, became heavier than that on a level with it over the hollow below; consequently, it rolled down the sides of the hill, displacing an equal volume of warmer and lighter air below, and entering the nest of wool, caused the air on the top to rise and come in contact with the surrounding ridge, again to be cooled and to roll down into the hollow below for further cooling by further radiation there. So that the coldest air was not on the hill but in the bottom of the nest.

Now the hen's nest of wool was the valley; the mole-hill, the knob. Nights favorable for a powerful radiation and the process I have described, are comparatively rare. The rest of the time, as by day and of cloudy or windy nights, unfavorable to radiation, the valley is the warmer. This pushes forward the vegetation in early spring, and when the cool, calm and clear night happens to come with the tender buds in this stage, the vegetation in the valley is nipped, while that on the hills escapes by being neither so much chilled by radiation, nor so far advanced by the genial warmth of cloudy nights and sunny days.

In late fall, the same phenomenon is repeated. It is in the low grounds, not on the knolls and knobs, that you go to seek for the first signs of frost in autumn, and every farmer has noticed that his cotton and other tender plants will be touched in the valleys sometimes ten days or two weeks before it is on the hills. So likewise but conversely, in spring; the frost will appear in the low grounds ten days or two weeks later than on the ridges and knobs, and this ten days is enough to save the peach crop where the orchard is properly located.

There my young friends of Pomona, in planting your orchards, whether among the knobs or in a rolling country, recollect Mr. Brown, the thermometer, and the nest of wool; and never select low grounds and valleys, but go to the ridges and hills to plant your young fruit trees.

Your Bureau—will, no doubt, furnish you with statistics and information upon this subject which will enable the fruit-growers of Tennessee, at no distant day, to put her in her true place, which is in the very front ranks, of the fruit-growing States of this Union.

Tennessee possesses also superior advantages as a grazing State. Her soil and climate are likewise admirably adapted to the cultivation of flax, hemp, and tobacco. Cotton is one of her staples; and as for wheat and corn, she cannot be surpassed. Tennessee wheat is just beginning to be known in the markets abroad, and it has at once been classed among the finest of the land. Like the 'south side' wheat of Virginia, the flour from it can stand transportation on the longest sea voyages, and like that, it commands the highest price in distant markets.

Besides all this, your rivers afford inexhaustible sources of water-power with the most choice mill-seats, and excellent of manufacturing facilities. Your mountains are filled with iron, and coal, and copper, and marbles, and minerals, each of superior quality, some world renowned, and all very accessible.

With such boundless and various sources of individual prosperity to call forth the energies and the enterprise of the people and to reward their labors, the difficulty with them is what to choose; for in a wilderness of undeveloped wealth like this, where mining, and milling, and grazing, and farming, and planting are all profitable, there is danger of instability in the industrial pursuits of men. I think I have myself observed something like signs of this instability, at least in Williamson, however it may be in other parts of the State. I can recollect when, next to Indian corn, tobacco was the staple there, and when Ohio flour was sold in the groceries of Franklin to the farmers of the county. After that, tobacco gave way to cotton; then many farmers gave up cotton, took to grazing, and returned to cotton again. Such is my recollection. Now I believe wheat is in favor. In my young days, there was no such thing as a wheat field in that county, there were some 'wheat patches,' but no fields.

Steamboats and railways penetrating the rivers and mountains of a country are well calculated to change its industrial pursuits, and wise are the people who can promptly and without inconvenience change their avocations and adjust their labor to any new order of things. I speak not of that, for it is excellent; but an individual who is first at one thing and then at another, is generally looked upon by his friends as one who is not in the royal road to wealth—and I speak of the drawbacks growing out of the like instability in the occupation of communities.

The railroads have called for an entire change in the industrial pursuits of many parts of the State, and the change has been made with admirable facility and effect. So much so, that within a few years, millions and tens of millions have been added to the value of the property of the commonwealth. But while you keep pace with the improvements of the age, and apply your industry according to the demands for your various staples, beware of running riot in the multitude of blessings with which bountiful nature has endowed your climate and soil, your hills and water-courses.

To collect statistics and digest them so as to assist the people in giving the most effective direction to their labor, is one of the most important duties of your Agricultural Bureau.

To determine this direction after having procured the data, is not so difficult as it would seem, for there are principles to guide us which are as certain in their operation as are the laws of supply and demand in the business of trade. Principles, which our political economists in their speculations are unfortunately too apt to ignore, but which, nevertheless, are as sure to exert influences upon the growth of wealth in a State, as the light and heat of the sun are to influence its vegetable growth.

With lavish hand, Providence has grouped these principles together for you; it has lodged them in your hills, imparted them to your never failing streams, or given them to your soil and climates. In assisting to give direction to the industrial pursuits of your State, therefore, consider the principles which govern the geographical distribution of labor, and shape action accordingly.

But this is not all. There is a work to be done more difficult still. It concerns deeply not only the western tier of counties of this State, but also the river counties of all the States below. I do not know that it comes within the province of the Tennessee Bureau of Agriculture to look after it, or in any way to take cognizance of it; but it touches agriculture and concerns the common prosperity of several States most deeply, and therefore seeing representatives from these States here, I venture to allude to it. It is the restraining of the floods of the Mississippi, and the bringing of that river under the control of man, at least to a certain extent. A difficult task, and a Herculean, I admit; but in my judgment, it by no means comes within the category of things impossible.

The difficulties that have occurred, and the mischief that has happened from the attempts to levee that river were foreseen and pointed out to the friends of the measure at the time the 'swamp land bill,' as it is called, was under consideration in Congress.

Unless the levee system was properly planned, it was not difficult to foresee that without answering their purpose at home, the levees of one State, would, in spite of Commissioners, be found operating seriously to the injury of the people of another State, and such has been the case.

Last winter, the citizens of Shelby, Tipton, Lauderdale, Dyer, and Obion counties, in this State, came up to Washington, with their memorial, setting forth that in consequence of the levees in Arkansas, the waters of the Mississippi had been thrown over upon them, overflowing and damaging plantations in Tennessee that had always been before above high-water mark.

Many planters in Mississippi and Louisiana have been drowned out in consequence of insufficiency of embankments, and we all know that plantations there have suffered an incalculable amount of damage by reason of the resulting overflow.

Which of you, having a friend with the cachexy would think of calling in numbers of doctors, and of requiring each one to 'go ahead and physick away on his own hook,' without regard to the course of treatment the others might be pursuing? And yet it would be almost as reasonable to expect a patient so treated to recover, as it is to expect the Mississippi river to be controlled and its floods restrained by several independent corps of engineers, each acting 'on his own hook.' I don't care how able and skillful, and accomplished they may be, but without a common head—without concurrent action up and down the river, and with an organization which necessarily requires the commissioners of each system or district to treat their part of the river without regard to what those above or below or on the opposite side may be doing, or may intend to do,—you will find all the science in the world of but little avail. I fear it is not in the power of your engineers, as capable as I know some of them to be—but being so controlled —I fear it is not in their power to control the Mississippi with any reasonable expenditure of money.

Your levees on one side of the river may be never so wisely placed and judiciously constructed, yet a single mistake on the opposite side, or for some distance above or below, or the placing of another without regard to yours, may prove fatal to you, and your engineer can't help it.

Running water has its laws, and according to these laws must the improvements on both sides of that river, above and below, be carried on, else disappointment and failure will be sure to overtake you in your attempts to control the Mississippi.

The riparian interests of this stream have become vast and valuable, and though there was a time when cut-offs might be made and the river tampered with in various ways without regard to the caving of banks or overflow, and with comparative impunity; and though vast sums have been expended upon improvements of various sorts upon that river, the question now begins to present itself to the minds of reflecting men: 'Upon the whole, would it not have been better had these improvements never been made?' It may be a question whether it would not cost much less and be far more easy for the Hydrographic Engineer to take that river, were it now as it was 50 years ago, and subject it to discipline, than it will now cost for him to take it in the condition it actually is, and bring it under proper restraint.

That river gives expression to a majestic and a mighty flow of waters, we all know, and in its anger, it is terrible. But vast are the powers of man and wonderful the resources of modern science. Invoke these, give them sway, and they will, I doubt not, master that mighty river for you.

Pardon me for dwelling so long, and for speaking so earnestly and plainly upon this subject. I feel an especial interest in the Mississippi river, and all that concerns the people who live by its waters. In the days of my youth, I drank of its fountains. My friends are among them. In later years I studied its habits, and believe them to be such as the science of the day can control. I was an early and an earnest advocate of the swamp land bill. I thought the riparian States would be largely benefited by it. I believed it would contribute in the most signal manner to the general welfare, and I believe so still. Wherefore I could not say less—but I will not say more.

I have heard with satisfaction of the introduction into this State of the 'Cashmere goat, and the Brahmin cattle,' both of which I am told thrive well and promise to add not a little to the resources and wealth of this favored State. But the field in this direction is by no means exhausted, for there are other domestic animals which I think would do well in almost all parts of the State, but particularly in the hill country of this and the adjoining States. If I be right in this opinion, these animals would vie in value with the sheep and the cow. I refer to the camel of the new world, especially to those varieties of the Lama known as the Alpaca and Vicuna. Their geographical range in the southern hemisphere is from Patagonia to the Equator. They live where sheep would perish, and their meat is excellent. Their fleece is a fibre between wool and silk. That of Alpaca brings in England from 50 to 60 cents the pound, that of the Vicuna from $1,00 to $1,25, and sometimes as high even as $2,00 the pound. The Alpaca yields at a single clipping two or three times as much as an ordinary sheep. Indeed, I have heard of their yielding as much as 30 pounds.

A friend who is extensively engaged in the woollen manufacture is of opinion that the growth of Alpaca and Vicuna wool, would, upon experiment, prove a most profitable source of industry to the farmers of the country, particularly to those who live in the mountains. It is only in recent times that this animal could be brought here with a chance of outliving the voyage. Before the railroad was completed across the Isthmus of Panama, they had to be brought around Cape Horn. Now, in three weeks from Peru, they may be in Tennessee.

This is a subject worthy the consideration of your stock raisers, as well as of your Legislature. It may be well for your Bureau to inquire whether some encouragement should not be given for the introduction of these animals, and for making experiments with exotics.

But suppose the Mississippi river to be in leading strings, the Alpaca to be introduced, a good system for the education and training of overseers to be established, and the State to have been brought to the highest stage of agricultural improvement that it is possible to attain, is there nothing more for this Bureau to do? Yes, the crowning work of all.

After the harvest has been gathered, then comes the sale. Prices are now to be regulated according to supply and demand. It is the business of the merchant to know what the demand is, and it *ought* to be the business of the producer, one would think, to know the extent of the supply. But do they? No, they look to the middle-man for that also.

Now clearly, his interest and theirs are antagonistic. The rumor of short crops would sustain prices, but the report of large ones will bring them down; and then, if after the crop begins to come forward, there be a rise, the speculator gets, perhaps, the largest share of it. This is so well-known and understood, that, as a rule, report makes the growing crop larger than it generally turns out to be, for the greater the exaggeration the greater the margin for speculation. The instances of this are of common occurrence. As a case in point, I quote from a morning paper:

'The total receipts of cotton at all ports, (the New York Post says,) now amount to exactly 3,700,000 bales, which will be further increased about 50,000 by the first of September, making the crop nearly a quarter million in excess of the largest previous yield. The prospect for the coming crop is much finer than last, and with a similar picking season four millions and a half is considered possible.'

Last May or June there was a cold 'snap.' Wheat growers said the crop was much injured thereby. But presently, New York had its agents out upon the ground, who represented it to be a false alarm, that the crops were never looking better, and that the yield of wheat was to be unprecedented. But after about one-half the farmers have sold their wheat, merchants begin to say, and farmers to find out, that the crop is not so large after all.

Now is it so difficult to obtain correct information as to the promise and the yield of crops, that producers must go to the middle-man in the city to learn how their crops are in the country?

Suppose the effect of these exaggerated reports about crops be to diminish the price to the producer on the average ¼ cent. the pound on cotton, and five cents a bushel only on so much grain as reaches tide-water —you saw grain fall, not long since in Chicago, eight or ten times as much— what difference would it make in the aggregate annual receipts of producers? Only about eight million dollars, namely: four for the grain grower, and four for the cotton planter. This is irrespective of the collateral advantages of the plan such as stability of trade, a more wholesome demand, and the like; which in commercial affairs always attend accuracy of estimate and correctness of information.

It appears to me that in this Bureau you have already at hand all the organization requisite for obtaining such information without cost and with but little trouble; and all that is wanting is only to put the machinery of a statistical department in motion.

Let the Legislature make it the duty of the sheriffs and their deputies in all the counties, to make monthly reports to the Agricultural Bureau of the crop or the preparation therefor, according to the season. Is the breadth of land in preparation for any particular staple greater or less than usual? How has the weather been during the month—favorable or unfavorable?

At another season, the reports would tell of the appearance and promise of the crops, the ravages of insects, the damage from unseasonable weather, and its extent from that or any other cause. In short, the reports for each month would give exactly that sort of information which would enable the Bureau to state in monthly bulletins, the general result. Every newspaper would be glad of such a paragraph.

Now, if this were done regularly, both planters and merchants would soon perceive that these returns, coming from the Bureau, would contain the most reliable accounts to be had of crops; and both merchants and farmers would go by them, and both, but especially the latter, would gain by them.

In a little while, and as soon as the plan was fairly understood by farmers generally, the compulsory reports of the Sheriffs might be dispensed with; the Bureau substituting therefor the reports of its own correspondents, and affiliated societies—other States would follow.

It is said, concert of action among farmers is difficult. True, but it is not so difficult to get farmers together as it is to have combined action among sailors; and yet, sailors have shown the utmost readiness to come forward with *daily* reports of wind and weather at sea. The results obtained, and the value and importance of the information derived from these simple reports, have astonished all who use the sea. Make your plan general; press it upon the attention of other States; solicit the co-operation of their societies; and my word for it, these monthly reports will prove as valuable and as interesting to the farmers, as the abstract logs have been to mariners.

I dwell upon the importance of every State Agricultural Society, having its statistical department, because the farmer is not interested in the crop of his neighbor alone, but as a seller, he is interested in crops in all parts of the country that meet him in market as competitors—and I attach great importance to *simple* returns,—to formularies for co-operators which shall be of the most simple character, calling at first for information only upon such points as will enable your statistician to answer monthly, or quarterly, the simple question, 'What of the crops?'

Let the beginning be by little and little, contenting yourselves first with a few things, and they of the most obvious importance. Afterwards, as you make progress, the scope and aim of the plan may be enlarged so as to include statistics generally, and finally, perhaps, to embrace a system of agricultural meteorological observations in the States also.

There is here a convocation of planters from the cotton growing States. The object of their assemblage is to take into consideration just such measures as the one I am now advocating; and I hope this planter's convention will signalize its first meeting by the inauguration of a Planter's Bureau, or some other establishment which will keep their constituents posted up as to the promise and state of the cotton crop, at least, if upon no other of the great staples.

Cotton will beautifully demonstrate the benefits of the system; for it may be carried out with cotton better and more conveniently than with any other staple. Cotton growers from all parts of the country are here; therefore, I say, make it general with cotton at once, leaving it to this gallant State through her admirably organized Bureau to bring up the rear with regard to the other staples and other States.

I say, moreover, to this Planter's Convention now in the act of its first assemblage, look to your commercial conventions, and take warning. Keep men from the political commons out of your meetings, and prefer acts to resolutions.

By resolutions, your commercial conventions have ransacked the world for statistics; but the statistics would not come; nor will they come for you unless you will put your shoulders to the wheel and your hands to your pockets. Do that, and you may get whatever you choose to call for.

As for these statistical returns, and monthly reports, tell me the amount of cotton that is to be produced in the United States next year, and I will tell you pretty nearly what the price will be next season. This cannot be said of any other of our great staples, because they are met in the market abroad by foreign staples of like kind. Thus, a short crop of wheat in England and on the Continent will give us high prices for breadstuffs. But England and the Continent compete not with us in cotton. India, Egypt, and Brazil, are our only competitors in that staple; and their competition is almost too feeble to be felt, for we greatly surpass them both in quantity and quality.

The annual production and consumption of cotton have attained such proportions, that the ratio between that consumption throughout the world and the production here in this country, determines the price of the raw article in all the markets of the world.

We may lay it down as a rule, that if, when the cotton crop is coming forward, its amount be overestimated, the producers have to pocket a loss in the aggregate nearly equal in value to the number of bales by which the estimate may prove to exceed the actual crop.

It is to the interest of the speculator to buy low and sell high. By representing the crop to be shorter than it really is, he is not enabled to buy cheap; but by representing it to be larger than it really is, he may be enabled so to buy. His interests and those of the planter, in this respect, are, therefore, antagonistic. Why should planters leave it to the speculator to collect statistics about the growing crop, and then when selling time comes, go to him for information and leave it to him to fix the prices? If the broker's estimates be a hundred thousand bales or so too high, the aggregate receipts of planters, will be in money about the value of a hundred thousand bales or so too low.

I hope that gentlemen will not separate without having provided for an organization—call it a Committee, call it a Bureau—call it what you please, but let it be a working concern, which, as the season draws on, will enable the planter to answer the merchant well and truly, next March, and monthly thereafter every year, till the cotton is all picked, the question that is ever on your tongue and his lips—What of the crop?

M. F. MAURY."

Exactly one year before Commander Maury's Address, Governor Isham G. Harris opened the Fifth Annual State Fair with the following address [223] which exhibits a phase of the "War Governor's" nature practically unheralded and unknown. The citations by Governor Harris to certain famous agricultural triumphs of Tennesseans should serve the lofty purpose of helping "Keep Tennessee Green."

"First Day—Monday, October 11, 1858.
Opening Address of Gov. Isham G. Harris.

Ladies and Fellow-Citizens: As Governor of Tennessee, I am, by law, made President of the Agricultural Bureau, whose Annual Fair we this day

[223] *Ibid.,* 585–588.

inaugurate. Owing my position here, and the honor of addressing the industry of the State through its assembled representatives, to the kindness of my fellow-citizens, in calling me to another office, rather than to eminent attainments in those pursuits, which it was the wise policy of the State, in the establishment of the Bureau, to foster; it would be presumptuous in me to attempt to instruct the experienced and eminently successful agriculturists and mechanics who surround me, in their respective pursuits. I come here equally a curious learner of the arts by which many of you have illustrated your noble callings, and to pay the homage of my ardent admiration to the signal success which is attending the general interest lately awakened in our State in the great cause of agricultural and mechanical industry. I address you, not so much as a matter of choice, as in the performance of official duty, yet almost shrinking from that duty, in the certainty that your time would be much more profitably employed in listening to the narrative of the long observation and actual experiments of some one of the many scientific or practical agriculturists who compose my audience, than the mere suggestions or theories of an individual like myself, who cannot justly claim eminence in either theory or practice.

There are, however, some popular errors, which have taken possession of the public mind, which need only to be pointed out and maturely considered, to be corrected, a brief notice of which is deemed not inappropriate to the present occasion.

The first of these errors is a want of proper appreciation of agriculture and mechanics art, as vocations in life.

It may be set down as an axiom throughout the world, that man never excels, if indeed, he succeeds in any vocation, where he does not feel that his pursuit in life is in every way worthy of his respect, interest, energies, and highest efforts. He may rest assured that there is no industrial pursuit—no vocation in life—to which the undivided energies of the best of the species may not be profitably applied.

Hence, the agriculturist or mechanic who feels degraded by his pursuit, or thinks that his position in society is compromised by it, can never enter upon its duties with that singleness of purpose, united energies, and fixed resolve, absolutely necessary to success in every department of the business of life; and the effort which may be made by this character of hesitating, or reluctant hand, must result in the failure of the enterprise, and the degradation of a position which the individual is unworthy to fill.

The origin of the evil is to be found in the fact that too many fathers of the present day, instil into the minds of their children, the idea that there is more dignity, respectability and worth to be found in the professions of law, medicine, &c., than in those of planting, farming, mechanism, or manufacturing; the result of which is that in almost every family you find one or more candidates for preferment in those professions, while the latter pursuits are adopted as the dernier resort of those who are supposed to be too dull to succeed in the former; and when thus driven to this department of labor, they reluctantly adopt it temporarily, until some employment shall present itself which they regard as more reputable, and hence more congenial to their taste, in which they hope to do better.

Silly errors! Fatal to the individual who entertains them, and injurious to the highest and best interests of the country. Will such a man honor the calling of agriculture or mechanics? Never. If you would excel, or even succeed, you must give to your business, whatever it may be, the undivided energies of both mind and muscle, and act upon that old adage, which is certainly as true as it is homely, 'Whatever is worth doing at all, is worth doing right, and doing well.'

If you would honor your calling, you must resolve to equal, if you do not excel, the most successful in your respective departments of labor.

What employment is more dignified or worthy, than that department of labor by which God has decreed that all of his children shall eat bread? Palsy the hand of agriculture, and the merchant's doors are closed, the wheels of the manufacturer are stilled, the tools of the mechanic rust in his shop, the sails which whiten every avenue of commerce are furled, and business in every department is hopelessly prostrated, to be reviewed only by the revival of that class of labor which ALONE PRODUCES the wealth of the world.

The lawyer, the physician, the merchant, and the teacher are all absolutely and indispensably necessary to the well-being of organized society. Yet, however useful each may be to the community, and however successful each may be in his profession, *he produces nothing*—adds nothing to the aggregate wealth of the country; but is a tax—a necessary tax, it is true, yet he is a tax to the extent of his consumption upon the productive industry of the nation; while he who produces one pound of cotton, wool, iron, sugar, or tobacco—a single grain of wheat, rye, or corn, or even one sprig of grass, or from the raw material has produced a fabric which contributes to the comfort of man, has added something to the aggregate wealth of the world, and is to that extent a benefactor.

Then where is the vocation in life more honorable, more dignified, more important, and the votaries of which are more independent than those of agriculture and mechanics? Another, and very serious of those errors, is the employment of almost the entire agricultural labor of Tennessee in the production of a few crops, such as cotton, tobacco, and the cereals, to the exclusion of grasses, stock, and choice varieties of fruits and flowers which contribute so materially to the profit, health, comfort, and luxury of man. East Tennessee should recollect that her mountain sides, however precipitous, can be made to smile in the verdure of the cultivated grasses, supporting large flocks and herds, rivaling in profit and surpassing in beauty, her fertile and productive valleys. Middle Tennessee should learn that there is scarcely a cedar glade or hill-top within her limits, that will not produce blue grass and clover luxuriantly, however near the surface the rock may approach, each acre of which will support its number of sheep, cattle, mules, or horses, costing the husbandman little or no labor, while the land is being improved every day, and yielding a larger return in pecuniary gain as well as in ornament, than the same amount of toil would yield in any other department of agricultural labor. And experience will very soon teach the planter of the west, that the swamps of that section, though too wet for cotton, tobacco, or the cereals, will produce herdsgrass and timothy in great perfection, the products of each acre of which in hay and stock, will pay a larger profit than his best acre in cotton or tobacco.

These improvements, so important, if not indispensably necessary to the success, health and beauty of the farm, may be made, by the judicious employment of such leisure as occurs between the employment of crops, at comparatively very trifling cost of labor or capital.

The time has come when Tennesseans should learn the importance of a variety of crops and diversifying their labor, thereby improving, instead of impoverishing, a soil so generous and fertile as almost to tempt our people into a system of careless and slovenly farming, especially when this lesson may be learned and practiced with so much profit in every point of view to the farmer. Let each grand division, nay, every hamlet of the State, learn that our soil and climate are admirably adapted to the successful cultivation of very choice varieties of fruit. The grape, the apple, the peach, the pear, the plumb, and the cherry, may all be grown to perfection in any portion of the State, and certainly there is no investment which pays the husbandman better in pecuniary profit, physical comfort, luxury and beauty than that which is employed in the cultivation of choice fruits. In view of these very important considerations, and the small amount of labor or capital necessary to the accomplishment of fruit growing, he who disregards it in the economy of the farm or plantation is not only blind to his own interest and comfort, but guilty of a most culpable neglect.

In this connection I may be permitted to appeal to the mothers and daughters of the State, to persevere in the cultivation of choice flowers. Though they may never succeed in the production of one so beautiful or so attractive as their own smiles, yet the well cultivated and tastefully arranged flower garden adds a charm to the homestead which is always appreciated and never forgotten by the visitor or the inmate; and it stands prominent amongst the myriad of fond and pleasing memories which the son or brother carries with him when he goes out into the world to engage in the battles and struggles of life, causing him to look back to that old homestead as the dearest spot on earth.

Let these crude suggestions be adopted by our farmers and planters, and we will have the gratification of seeing our State unrivaled in all the elements of prosperity as well as beauty, and may soon congratulate ourselves upon the fact that the *American* manufacturer is supplied with wool from AMERICAN *flocks*, and that the people of Tennessee will buy no more Irish potatoes, apples, mules or hay from sister States.

Tennessee has already assumed a high and proud position in the rank of agricultural States; she has successfully competed with and triumphed over the agriculturists of the civilized world in the two great and indispensable staples of wool and cotton. It may not be invidious, (for it is certainly no disparagement to others,) to remark, that Mark R. Cockrill, Esq., of the county of Davidson, at the world's fair in London, wrung from the assembled wool growers of the civilized world, the reluctant confession that Tennessee produces the finest fleece known to man. Thus establishing, beyond controversy, (and contrary to the almost universal opinion previously entertained,) the fact that wool, superior in quality and equal in quantity, can be grown in low latitudes as well, or indeed better than in a more rigorous climate. While, at the same fair, our not less distinguished citizen and agriculturist, Col. John Pope, of the county of Shelby, received the premium for the best cotton known to the world.

These were great triumphs, of which Tennessee, as well as those distinguished individuals may well be proud.

But will Tennessee maintain the high stand she has taken in the line of agricultural States? Blest as she is, with a soil generous and almost inexhaustible, susceptible of almost every variety of crops, with a climate at once free from the rigors of the North, and the discomforts and epidemics of the South; with bone, sinew, and muscle, which has the ability and knows how to labor—with intelligence sufficient to direct that labor into the most profitable channels of production—with railroads and navigable streams, giving easy and prompt access to the markets of the world, stimulating us to renewed efforts and increased production; will she make the necessary effort to maintain this proud position? Let the results of the future answer! If she fails to do so, however, she will have the humiliation of knowing that with all of those great natural advantages, owing to a want of a proper energy and effort upon the part of her people, she is retrograding and failing to keep pace with the improvements, spirit and progress of the age.

But I flatter myself with the fond hope that, in the future, as in the past, her progress will be steady, onward, and upward, in every department of productive industry and improvement, and that her future may be even more brilliant than her past has been successful. Let each one of us who compose the junior class of agriculturists, earnestly resolve, that from this day, we will strive to improve upon the lessons of the past, and each year we will become better farmers. Let us emulate the brilliant achievements of our successful seniors; the field is large and ample for improvement and laudable competition, and there are laurels yet to be won as green and as attractive as those so worthily worn by our fathers in this noble vocation.

Our State, in the establishment of the Agricultural Bureau, and providing for County Agricultural Societies, and State, Division, and County Fairs, has taken an important step in the right direction. I do not know of any other State in the Union, which has been equally liberal, or to use a better word, equally just to the great industrial interests. And if the design of the act creating the Bureau is fully carried out, each county in the State will have its annual fair, at which all branches of industry will be represented, comparisons of excellence instituted, new theories tested, and eminent success in every department of labor secured and acknowledged.

This should be so. I would have these fairs a week's holiday for the people, at which all classes should be proud to compete, and the awards of which should be as eagerly sought, and as highly prized, as was the palm of the Olympic Games, or the laurel of the Roman conqueror.

The farmer should by all means fully appreciate the importance and dignity of his vocation and position. They were farmers who wrested these beautiful lands from savage sway. They were farmers from the Holston and Watauga who fought the battle of King's Mountain, and checked the progress of British power in the South. They were farmers—aye! Tennessee farmers!—who, at Talladega, Emuckfaw, and the Horseshoe, saved the feeble and helpless from the whetted tomahawk of the Creek Indian. They were Tennessee farmers who were foremost in protecting the beauty and booty of New Orleans from the ravages of the enemy, giving to the second War of Independence its most brilliant victory.

But I will not pursue these themes. It is unnecessary here, where all around me is full of them. The presence of this vast concourse is in itself a tribute, more eloquent than any I could utter, to the cause of agriculture and mechanical industry. It remains for me only, as the organ of the State Agricultural Bureau, to welcome to these grounds, the people of Tennessee. To the dwellers among the romantic mountains and smiling valleys of the east; to the cultivators of the prolific soil of the Middle Division; to the planters of the fertile west; to the mechanics and manufacturers of the whole State; to every man who honors useful labor; and last in the list, though first in our affections, to the mothers and daughters of the State, without whose presence the first 'garden was a wild,' and in whose absence there could indeed be no *fair*—to all, a cordial welcome!"

There can be no doubt but that Commander Maury's allusion to the desirability of flood control of the rivers of Tennessee was responsible for the Legislature's consideration of that important matter. Representative Stith Richardson from the counties of Dyer and Lauderdale knew from direct observation and experience something of the havoc of the Mississippi River floods which overflowed time and again portions of the counties represented by him. Unquestionably impressed by the facts set forth in the Maury address on flood control measures, Mr. Richardson introduced the following resolution:[224]

"WHEREAS, Under the operation of laws passed by Congress, granting lands to Missouri and Arkansas, and to companies for the building of levees along the western bank of the Mississippi river: *And, whereas,* The construction of said levees has caused the waters of said river to inundate large and valuable tracts of land in Tennessee, hitherto above the overflow of said river, and also covered to a much greater depth large and rich bodies of land that were inundated by the natural overflow of said river: *And, whereas,* It has been provided by the constitution of the State of Tennessee, that if at any time a division of the public lands of the United States or of the money arising therefrom, shall be made among the individual States, the part of such lands or money coming to this State, shall be applied to the purposes of education and internal improvements, and shall never be applied to any other purpose: *And, whereas,* The Congress of the United States have always shown a very liberal spirit in granting lands to the different States for such purposes, and that the State of Tennessee has never been an equal recipient with her sister States in sharing the munificence of the General Government: *And, whereas,* Knowledge, learning and virtue are essentially necessary to the perpetuity of our republican institutions, and the continuation of that prosperity and happiness, and even liberty itself, which our country and State now enjoy, depends much upon the general diffusion of knowledge among all classes of society: *And, whereas,* The State of Tennessee is now desirous of establishing a good and thorough system of common schools, such a system as will place it in the power of every man to give his children a thorough education in those branches of learning which are necessary to develop the mind, and fit the individual for the various pursuits of life, and to act well the part of a citizen of a free Republican Government; therefore,

Be it resolved by the Legislature of the State of Tennessee, That our Senators be instructed, and our Representatives requested to secure, if possible, an act of Congress appropriating out of any monies in the National Treasury, not otherwise appropriated, or a donation of land, not otherwise disposed of, sufficient to levee the eastern bank of the Mississippi River, from Hickman, in Kentucky, to the mouth of Wolf River, so as to prevent any further overflow, and to establish a system of common schools, ample in all its dimensions to meet the intellectual wants of the State.

Resolved, That this appropriation or donation would be nothing more than justice to the State of Tennessee demands, in restoring to the use of our citizens large bodies of valuable lands, and restoring us to the condition in which we were formerly placed, and not cast upon us burdens which nature refused to do. That the General Assembly relies with implicit confidence upon the justice of Congress in the restoration asked for, and that Congress will at least show as much liberality to Tennessee as it has

[224] *House Journal,* 1859, 317–318.

done to other States, and especially when their liberality is asked for the purpose of diffusing knowledge.

Resolved, That his Excellency, I. G. Harris, is most respectfully requested to forward a copy of this preamble and resolutions to each of our Senators and Representatives in the Congress of the United States."

On February 25, 1860, an effort to substitute another resolution for that of Representative Richardson failed by a vote of 28 to 27, whereupon the resolution of the latter squeezed through by a margin of one vote, the actual vote being 30 to 29.[225] Three days later, when the measure came up in the Senate, quite a battle ensued. Efforts were made to adopt the original resolution and next the substitute resolution, but both failed by an identical tie vote, 11 to 11.[226] The matter was revived a few days later, and a reconsideration of the rejection of the resolution was carried. Thereupon, the substitute resolution was adopted in the Senate by a vote of 17 to 5.[227] The House, on March 12, non-concurred in the Senate-approved substitute resolution and so notified that body.[228] The Senate was a bit stubborn and "decided to insist on the resolution adopted in lieu," and notified the House of the action taken by the Senate.[229] Apparently faced with defeat of the measure, the House receded from its action and accepted by a vote of 29 to 27 the resolution in lieu as adopted by the Senate.[230] The resolution finally adopted was as follows:[231]

"RESOLUTION NO. 38.

Joint Resolution instructing our Senators and requesting our Representatives in Congress assembled, to use all constitutional means to procure an act, granting appropriations from the National Treasury, or a donation of Lands, to Levee the Eastern Bank of the Mississippi River from Hickman, in the State of Kentucky, to the mouth of Wolf River, in the State of Tennessee.

WHEREAS, under the operations of a Law passed by Congress, granting large donations of lands to the States of Missouri and Arkansas, and to companies for the building of Levees along the Western bank of the Mississippi River; and whereas, the construction of said Levees have caused the waters of said river to inundate large and valuable tracts of land in Kentucky and Tennessee hitherto above the overflow of said river, and also covered to a much greater depth large and rich bodies of fertile lands, thereby rendering the same useless and untenable that were not so by the natural overflow of said river; as an act of justice to the citizens of Kentucky and Tennessee, therefore,

Be it resolved by the General Assembly of the State of Tennessee, That

---

[225] *Ibid.,* 805.
[226] *Senate Journal,* 1859, 557–558.
[227] *Ibid.,* 567–568.
[228] *House Journal,* 1859, 974.
[229] *Senate Journal,* 1859, 681.
[230] *House Journal,* 1859, 1062.
[231] *Acts of Tennessee,* 1859, Resolution 38, 679.

our Senators be instructed, and our Representatives in Congress be requested to secure by all constitutional means, by an act of Congress, an appropriation of money out of the Public Treasury, not otherwise appropriated, or donation of lands out of the public domain, not otherwise appropriated, of sufficient amount to Levee the Eastern Bank of the Mississippi River, from Hickman, in the State of Kentucky, to the mouth of Wolf River, in the State of Tennessee, so as to prevent more damages from the overflow of said river than would have occurred from the natural overflow of the same, and that the application be placed on the express ground that the lands or money bestowed is given as compensation for injury done to the lands of Kentucky and Tennessee by action of the Federal Government.

W. C. WHITTHORNE,
Speaker of the House of Representatives.
TAZ. W. NEWMAN,
Speaker of the Senate."

Adopted, March 19, 1860.

For the third time, a Tennessee Legislature considered the passage of a law requiring the registration of births, deaths, and marriages. The first effort was made in the 1847 legislative session during the administration of Governor Neill S. Brown. The bill, upon second reading in the Senate, encountered stiff opposition in the person of Senator John W. Richardson, a physician, whose influence with his lay members succeeded in sounding the death knell of an important measure.[232] The second effort was made two years later, but the bill was rejected by the House of Representatives without being even considered by the Senate.[233]

After a lapse of ten years, Senator George B. Peters, a physician, initiated for the third time a movement looking toward the enactment of a law that would enable the citizenry to learn something about the vital resources of the State. What was not recognized by the public at the time was that vital statistics, regarding births and deaths, comprise the alphabet of sanitary science. Dr. Peters, of course, was cognizant of that fact and desired to enact a statute that would institute a system of "bookkeeping" that related to the three most important events in the life of an individual—birth, marriage, and death.

In accord with his belief, he introduced on February 10, 1860, a bill [234] entitled

"An Act for the establishment of a general system of registration of births, marriages, deaths, &c., in this State."

The bill had the support of the medical fraternity, as it bore the indorsement of the organized profession which transmitted to the Legislature the following memorial: [235]

---

[232] *Messages of the Governors of Tennessee,* Volume IV, 255.
[233] *Ibid.,* 388.
[234] *Senate Journal,* 1859, 454.
[235] *The Nashville Patriot,* March 2, 1860.

"MEMORIAL.

Of the 'State Medical Society,' to the Tennessee General Assembly, 1859-60. 33rd Session.

To the General Assembly of the State of Tennessee: At the last Annual Meeting of the State Medical Society, the undersigned were appointed a committee under the following resolution, to which we most respectfully call your attention:—

Resolved, That the President of this Society appoint a committee to memorialize the next General Assembly on the subject of a Registration of Births, Deaths, and Marriages, of the State.

Your memorialists most respectfully ask that your honorable body will take into consideration the propriety of such a law. That there is a *necessity* for such a law, is too palpable to admit of controversy. We therefore submit the subject by simply saying, that we earnestly desire that you will pass such a law at this present session.

W. R. HURLEY,
JOHN P. FORD,   } Committee"
J. E. MANLOVE,

A brief summation of the important points in the thirteen sections of the bill [236] discloses that the most important provisions were:

1. Tax collectors of each county required to procure with the general tax returns a separate return regarding the births, marriages, and deaths, and causes of deaths during the year in each respective taxing district, these returns to be transmitted to the County Court Clerk of the county.
2. All clergymen or persons performing the marriage ceremony required to keep a register of all marriages performed by them and return such data to the County Court Clerk of the county within thirty days after the marriages had been consummated.
3. All surgeons, physicians, clergymen and midwives called upon to keep a register of all births and deaths at which they had attended.
4. All parents required to give notice to the County Court Clerk of the births and deaths of their children, and of every birth or death happening in their home.
5. All records of births were to include the date, name of child, sex, color, free or slave, place of birth, plurality births, stillborn, illegitimate or not, if a slave the name of owner, if of free colored persons full names of parents, residence, and occupation; in recording deaths, the name, date of death, color, slave or free, married or single, sex, nativity, occupation, place of death, age at death, cause of death.
6. Any person refusing to give the above information or neglecting

---

[236] *Ibid.*
Author's note. The original bill was not located in the State Archives.

to discharge the duties above mentioned within six months after each event subject to a fine of five dollars.

7. County Court Clerk required to keep a record of all vital statistics data, a duplicate copy of which was to be prepared and sent to the State Comptroller on or before the 15th day of February each year.

8. Governor empowered to appoint a Registrar whose duty was to issue an annual report based upon the statistics collected from the various counties of the State and to publish three thousand copies of the report for public distribution.

As is perfectly obvious, there were many defects in the above bill, the principal ones being: The notification of births, marriages and deaths to be given by the parents or owner of slaves; calling upon lay persons to state the cause of death which, of course, was practically without value since a lay person is not qualified by training or experience to determine in many cases the actual cause of death; and the inadequate compensation provided for the performance of the specified duties, namely, the State Register was to receive an annual salary of five hundred dollars, County Court Clerks five cents for each record of birth, marriage or death, and the County Tax Collector entitled to retain out of tax money five cents for each entry made by him.

As viewed by modern criteria, it is quite obvious that the bill sponsored by Dr. Peters was extremely deficient in many vital particulars. And yet, incomplete and inaccurate as the records would necessarily have been, still a residue of valuable information would have been collected and preserved for posterity.

When the bill reached third reading in the Senate, some modifications were made by Senator Peters and the substitute bill passed third and final reading by a vote of 11 to 8.[237] After routine passage on first and second readings in the House, the bill reached third reading on March 23, just three days before *sine die* adjournment. A laconic but desultory reference in the official records reveals the fate that was meted out to a relatively advance movement:[238]

"Senate Bill No. 278, to establish a registry of births, marriages, and deaths in this State, was rejected."

Alas and alack! With the exception of an exceedingly poor law that remained on the statute books only a few months in the 1880's, no Vital Statistics law was enacted in Tennessee until 1909.

In all candor, the Thirty-Third General Assembly left a mediocre record. The membership was without strong and aggressive leadership in State affairs, although the House numbered among its personnel two

[237] *Senate Journal,* 1859, 609.
[238] *House Journal,* 1859, 1157.

men who later served as Governors of Tennessee, namely, DeWitt Clinton Senter and James D. Porter. On the very brink of the most devastating war the Nation has ever encountered, frustration and stand-patism characterized largely the attitude of the lawmakers in regard to legislation affecting the welfare of the State. Time was found, how-ever, to enact laws against sheep-killing dogs,[239] empowering Justices of the Peace to hold inquests,[240] inspecting whiskey,[241] exempting mil-lers and school commissioners from working on the road,[242] amending the law regarding the killing of red foxes, wolves, and wild cats,[243] and the licensing of shooting galleries and tenpin alleys.[244] It is a somewhat sad commentary that out of the passage of 132 public acts, 216 private statutes, and 48 resolutions, no worthwhile legislation was enacted deal-ing with such basic things as the promotion of public education and public health.

The slavery issue was paramount throughout the entire session, and its implications and actualities overshadowed all else. Perhaps no better criterion could be cited to show the intensity, not to say the bulldog determination, of a majority of the legislative membership than to record their sentiments as expressed by the enactment of the following resolution:[245]

"RESOLUTION NO. 5.

WHEREAS, A most dangerous epoch has arisen, in the history of our country, based upon the fanatical aggressions of Northern Black Repub-licans on the reserved rights of the States and Institutions of the South, seeking to abolish slavery by preventing the extension into common terri-tory, and rendering it insecure and hazardous in our midst. *And whereas,* in the recent insurrection at Harper's Ferry as well as in the revolutionary scenes in Kansas, we recognize the legitimate fruits of that treasonable policy avowed by the acknowledged head of the Black Republican party, Wm. H. Seward, in his famous Rochester speech, in which he said: '*These* antagonistic systems (free and slave labor) are continually coming into closer contact, and collision results. Shall I tell you what that collision means? They who think that it is accidental, unnecessary, the work of in-terested or fanatical agitators, and therefore ephemeral, mistake the case altogether. It is an irrepressible conflict between opposing and enduring forces, and it means that the United States must and will, sooner or later, become either entirely a slaveholding nation, or entirely a free-labor na-tion. Either the cotton and rice fields of South Carolina, and the sugar plantations of Louisiana will ultimately be tilled by free labor, and Charles-ton and New Orleans become marts for legitimate merchandise alone, or else the rye fields and wheat fields of Massachusetts and New York must again be surrendered by their farmers to slave culture, and to the produc-

---

[239] *Acts of Tennessee,* 1859, Chapter 45.
[240] *Ibid.,* Chapter 112.
[241] *Ibid.,* Chapter 81.
[242] *Ibid.,* Chapter 18.
[243] *Ibid.,* Chapter 78.
[244] *Ibid.,* Chapter 80.
[245] *Ibid.,* Resolution 5, 653–656.

tion of slaves, and Boston and New York become once more markets for trade in the bodies and souls of men. It is the failure to apprehend this great truth, that induces so many unsuccessful attempts at final compromise between the slave and the free States, and it is the existence of this great fact, that renders all such pretended compromises, when made, vain and ephemeral.' *And whereas*, Henry Wilson, another Black Republican Senator from Massachusetts, has declared: 'Let us remember that more than three millions of bondmen, groaning under nameless woes, demand that we shall reprove each other, and that we labor for their deliverance. I tell you here to-night, that the agitation of the question of human slavery will continue while the foot of a slave presses the soil of the American Republic.' And Mr. Wade another Black Republican Senator from Ohio, has said: 'There is really no union now between the North and South, and he believed no two nations upon the earth entertained feelings of more bitter rancor towards each other than these two nations of the Republic. The only salvation of the Union, therefore, was to be found in divesting it entirely from all taint of slavery.' *And whereas*, Senator Seward, addressing Southern Senators from his place in that body, has boldly proclaimed to the world, that–'At last a new voice issues from your own region, from the South, from the slave States, and protests against your further persistence in this mad enterprise of extending slavery, and admonishes you, that it must and will fail. The cohorts are gathering from the South, the men of moderation and conservation, who, as they have heretofore moderated in favor of slavery and against freedom, will now be obliged, in consistency with their just and well-established character, and their habitual patriotism, to moderate against you in favor of freedom, and rise up unanimously against slavery.' And again, at Rome, in New York: 'It will be the show of the next two years, to witness the organization of this same Republican party within slave States, under the lead of brave and true men, such as Frank P. Blair, of Missouri, and Cassius M. Clay, of Kentucky. What remains of organization as a national party to be effected, is as sure and certain as what has already occurred, and is now so distinctly seen.'

Therefore, Resolved by the General Assembly of the State of Tennessee, That we recognize in the recent outbreak at Harper's Ferry, the natural prints of this treasonable *'irrepressible conflict'* doctrine, put forth by the great head of the Black Republican party, and echoed by his subordinates; and that it becomes the imperative duty of national men of all parties throughout the Union, to announce to the world their sense of its infamy, and to unite in crushing out its authors as traitors to their country, and as deadly enemies to the public peace, the rights of the States, and the preservation of our Republican Institutions.

Resolved, That we record it as the sense of the Tennessee Legislature, that the declarations of Mr. Seward, that a respectable portion of the Southern people, under the head of such men as Cassius M. Clay and Francis P. Blair, will unite with the Black Republican party to prevent the extension of slavery, and will eventually 'rise up against slavery' as a libel upon the honor and loyalty of the Southern people, and will but serve to make them more watchful and exacting of their public servants in the National Councils.

Resolved, That it is the duty of our Representatives in Congress to recognize as enemies to the Union, and especially to the slave States, all who in any way favor or affiliate with this sectional Black Republican party; and that any action on their part which favors a co-operation with the Black Republicans in organizing the House, and thus placing the offices and important committees of that body under their control, would be false to the sentiment of the people of Tennessee, an insult to their constituents, and disgraceful to themselves.

Resolved, That we acknowledge our appreciation of the promptness with which the National Administration took steps to check the recent conspiracy before it obtained the hugh dimensions of a revolution.

Resolved, That our Senators and Representatives in Congress be furnished with a copy of these resolutions.

W. C. WHITTHORNE,
Speaker of the House of Representatives.
TAZ. W. NEWMAN,
Speaker of the Senate.

Adopted, December 2, 1859."

And now, let the 1859 Legislature and its activities be dismissed in the words [246] of its Speaker of the Senate, Tazewell W. Newman,

"Nothing is left for me to do—except to announce that the Senate stands adjourned *sine die.*"

As a general rule, the adjournment of a Legislature affords a sort of "occupational vacation" to the Governor. But such was not the case with Isham G. Harris during his second term of office. Within a few months after the *sine die* adjournment of the Legislature on March 26, 1860, political events changed what usually would have been a comparatively quiet tenure into a storm whose fury soon burst with unparalleled destruction upon the Nation. In the fall of 1860, the election of a sectional President of the United States, Abraham Lincoln, was the signal that initiated the secession steps of Southern States that marked the beginning of four years of martial conflict known as the War Between the States.[247]

From a political standpoint, the paramount question soon raised was whether the South should secede from the Union. South Carolina answered that query promptly and decidedly. On December 20, 1860, its Legislature passed by unanimous vote an ordinance of secession, to be followed within a few weeks by similar action on the part of Georgia, Florida, Alabama, Mississippi, Louisiana, and Texas. Tennessee was then faced with a momentous decision, whether to join hands with her sister States or to remain in the Union. Sentiment was sharply divided and, as a means of determining the status of that question, Governor Harris called the Legislature into extraordinary session on January 7, 1861. On the day of convening, Governor Harris transmitted the following bristling Message to the Legislature:

---

[246] *Senate Journal,* 1859, 788.

[247] For obvious reasons (lack of space and the publication of countless books and articles dealing with details) such factors as the 1860 Presidential election and the immediate reaction by the slave-holding States will be omitted in this volume.

Legislative Message*, January 7, 1861.

"GENTLEMEN OF THE SENATE, AND HOUSE OF REPRESENTATIVES:

The ninth section of the third article of the Constitution, provides that, on extraordinary occasions, the Governor may convene the General Assembly. Believing the emergency contemplated, to exist at this time, I have called you together. In welcoming you to the capitol of the State, I can but regret the gloomy auspices under which we meet. Grave and momentous issues have arisen, which, to an unprecedented degree, agitate the public mind and imperil the perpetuity of the Government.

The systematic, wanton, and long continued agitation of the slavery question, with the actual and threatened aggressions of the Northern States and a portion of their people, upon the well-defined constitutional rights of the Southern citizen; the rapid growth and increase, in all the elements of power, of a purely sectional party, whose bond of union is uncompromising hostility to the rights and institutions of the fifteen Southern States, have produced a crisis in the affairs of the country, unparalleled in the history of the past, resulting already in the withdrawal from the Confederacy of one of the sovereignties which compose it, while others are rapidly preparing to move in the same direction. Fully appreciating the importance of the duties which devolve upon you, fraught, as your action must be, with consequences of the highest possible importance to the people of Tennessee; knowing that, as a great Commonwealth, our own beloved State is alike interested with her sisters, who have resorted, and are preparing to resort, to this fearful alternative, I have called you together for the purpose of calm and dispassionate deliberation, earnestly trusting, as the chosen representatives of a free and enlightened people, that you will, at this critical juncture of our affairs, prove yourselves equal to the occasion which has called for the exercise of your talent and patriotism.

A brief review of the history of the past is necessary to a proper understanding of the issues presented for your consideration.

Previous to the adoption of the Federal Constitution, each State was a separate and independent Government—a complete sovereign-

---

* *Acts of Tennessee*, First Extraordinary Session, 1861, 1–13.
  Senate Journal, First Extraordinary Session, 1861, 6–19.
  House Journal, First Extraordinary Sessions, 1861, 4–17.

ty within itself—and in the compact of union, each reserved all the rights and powers incident to sovereignty, except such as were expressly delegated by the Constitution to the General Government, or such as were clearly incident, and necessary, to the exercise of some expressly delegated power.

The Constitution distinctly recognises property in *slaves*—makes it the duty of the States to deliver the fugitive to his owner, but contains no grant of power to the Federal Government to interfere with this species of property, except 'the power couples with the duty,' common to all civil Governments, to protect the rights of *property*, as well as those of *life* and *liberty*, of the citizen, which clearly appears from the exposition given to that instrument by the Supreme Court of the United States in the case of Dred Scott *vs.* Sandford. In delivering the opinion of the Court, Chief Justice Taney said:

'Now, as we have already said in an earlier part of this opinion, upon a different point, *the right of property in a slave is distinctly and expressly affirmed in the Constitution.*'

'And no word can be found in the Constitution which gives Congress a greater power over slave property, or which entitles property of that kind to less protection than property of any other description. *The only power conferred, is the power coupled with the duty, of guarding and protecting the owner in his rights.*'

This decision of the highest judicial tribunal, known to our Government, settles the question, beyond the possibility of doubt, that slave property rests upon the same basis, and is entitled to the same protection, as every other description of property, that the General Government has no power to circumscribe or confine it within any given boundary; to determine where it shall, or shall not exist, or in any manner to impair its value. And certainly it will not be contended, in this enlightened age, that any member of the Confederacy can exercise higher powers, in this respect, beyond the limits of its own boundary, than those delegated to the General Government.

The States entered the Union upon terms of perfect political equality, each delegating certain powers to the General Government, but neither delegating any power to the other to interfere with its reserved rights or domestic affairs; hence, there is no power on earth which can rightfully determine whether slavery shall or shall not exist within the limits of any State, except the people thereof acting in their highest sovereign capacity.

The attempt of the Northern people, through the instrumentality of the Federal Government—their State governments, and emigrant aid societies—to confine this species of property within the limits of the present Southern States—to impair its value by constant agitation and refusal to deliver up the fugitive—to appropriate the whole of the Territories, which are the common property of all the people of all the States, to themselves; by excluding therefrom every Southern man who is unwilling to live under a government which may by law recognize the free negro as his equal; 'and in fine, to put the question where the Northern mind will rest in the belief of its ultimate extinction,' is justly regarded by the people of the Southern States as a gross and palpable violation of the spirit and obvious meaning of the compact of Union—an impertinent intermeddling with their domestic affairs, destructive of fraternal feeling, ordinary comity, and well defined rights.

As slavery receded from the North, it was followed by the most violent and fanatical opposition. At first the anti-slavery cloud, which now overshadows the nation, was no larger than a man's hand. Most of you can remember, with vivid distinctness, those days of brotherhood, when throughout the whole North, the abolitionist was justly regarded as an enemy of his country. Weak, diminutive and contemptible as was this party in the purer days of the Republic, it has now grown to colossal proportions, and its recent rapid strides to power, have given it possession of the present House of Representatives, and elected one of its leaders to the Presidency of the United States; and in the progress of events, the Senate and Supreme Court must also soon pass into the hands of this party—a party upon whose revolutionary banner is inscribed, 'No more slave States, no more slave Territory, no return of the fugitive to his master'—an 'irrepressible conflict' between the Free and Slave States; 'and whether it be long or short, peaceful or bloody, the struggle shall go on, until the sun shall not rise upon a master or set upon a slave.'

Nor is this all; it seeks to appropriate to itself, and to exclude the slaveholder from the territory acquired by the common blood and treasure of all the States.

It has, through the instrumentality of Emigrant Aid Societies, under State patronage, flooded the Territories with its minions, armed with Sharp's rifles and Bowie knives, seeking thus to accomplish, by intimidation, violence and murder, what it could not do by constitutional legislation.

It demanded, and from our love of peace and devotion to the Union, unfortunately extorted in 1819-'20, a concession which excluded the South from about half the territory acquired from France.

It demanded, and again received, as a peace offering in 1845, all of that part of Texas, North of 36° 30′ North latitude, if at any time the interest of the people thereof shall require a division of her territory.

It would submit to nothing less than a compromise in 1850, by which it dismembered that State, and remanded a territorial condition a considerable portion of its territory South of 36 30.

It excluded, by the same Compromise, the Southern people from California, whose mineral wealth, fertility of soil, and salubrity of climate, is not surpassed on earth; by prematurely forcing her into the Union under a Constitution, conceived in fraud by a set of adventurers, in the total absence of any law authorizing the formation of a Constitution, fixing the qualification of voters, regulating the time, place, or manner of electing delegates, or the time or place of a meeting of such Convention. Yet all these irregular and unauthorized proceedings were sanctified by the fact that the Constitution prohibited slavery, and forever closed the doors of that rich and desirable territory against the Southern people. And while the Southern mind was still burning under a humiliating sense of this wrong, it refused to admit Kansas into the Union upon a Constitution, framed by authority of Congress, and by delegates elected in conformity to law, upon the ground that slavery was recognized and protected.

It claims the constitutional right to abolish slavery in the District of Columbia, the forts, arsenals, dock-yards and other places ceded to the United States, within the limits of slaveholding States.

It proposes a prohibition of the slave trade between the States, thereby crowding the slaves together and preventing their exit South, until they become unprofitable to an extent that will force the owner finally to abandon them in self-defence.

It has, by the deliberate legislative enactment of a large majority of the Northern States, openly and flagrantly nullified that clause of the Constitution which provides that—

'No person held to service or labor in one State under the laws thereof, escaping into another, shall, in consequence of any law or regulation therein, be discharged from such service or labor, but shall be delivered up on claim of the party to whom such service or labor may be due.'

This provision of the Constitution has been spurned and trampled under foot by these 'higher law' nullifers. It is utterly powerless for good, since all attempts to enforce the Fugitive Slave Law under it, are made a felony in some of these States, a high misdemeanor in others, and punishable in all by heavy fines and imprisonment. The distempered public opinion of these localities having risen above the Constitution and all other law, planting itself upon the anarchial doctrines of the *'higher law,'* with impunity defies the Government, tramples upon our rights, and plunders the Southern citizen.

It has, through the Governor of Ohio, as openly nullified that part of the Constitution which provides that—

'A person charged in any State with treason, felony or other crime, who shall flee from justice and be found in another State, shall, on demand of the executive authority of the State from which he fled, be delivered up, to be removed to the State having jurisdiction of the crime.'

In discharge of official duty, I had occasion, within the past year, to demand of the Governor of Ohio, *'a person charged in the State (of Tennessee) with the crime of slave stealing,'* who had fled from justice and was found in the State of Ohio. The Governor refused to issue his warrant for the arrest and delivery of the fugitive, and in answer to a letter of inquiry which I addressed to him, said: 'The crime of negro stealing, not being known to either the common law or the criminal code of Ohio, it is not of that class of crimes contemplated by the Federal Constitution, for the commission of which I am authorized, as the executive of Ohio, to surrender a fugitive from the justice of a sister State, and hence I declined to issue a warrant,' &c; thus deliberately nullifying and setting at defiance the clause of the Constitution above quoted, as well as the act of Congress of February 12th, 1793, and grossly violating the ordinary comity existing between separate and independent nations, much less the comity which should exist between sister States of the same great Confederacy, the correspondence connected with which is herewith transmitted.

It has, through the executive authority of other States, denied extradition of murders and marauders.

It obtained its own compromise in the Constitution to continue the importation of slaves, and now sets up a law, higher than the Constitution, to destroy this property imported and sold to us by their fathers.

It has caused the murder of owners in pursuit of their fugitive slaves, and shielded the murderers from punishment.

It has, upon many occasions, sent its emissaries into the Southern States to corrupt our slaves; induce them to run off, or excite them to insurrection.

It has run off slave property by means of the 'under-ground railroad,' amounting in value to millions of dollars, and thus made the tenure by which slaves are held in the border States so precarious as to materially impair their value.

It has, by its John Brown and Montgomery raids, invaded sovereign States and murdered peaceable citizens.

It has justified and 'exalted to the highest honors of admiration, the horrid murders, arsons, and rapine of the John Brown raid, and has canonized the felons as saints and martyrs.'

It has burned the towns, poisoned the cattle, and conspired with the slaves to depopulate Northern Texas.

It has, through certain leaders, proclaimed to the slaves the terrible motto, 'Alarm to the sleep, fire to the dwellings, poison to the food and water of slaveholders.'

It has repudiated and denounced the decision of the Supreme Court.

It has assailed our rights as guaranteed by the plainest provisions of the Constitution, from the floor of each house of Congress, the pulpit, the hustings, the school room, their State Legislatures, and through the public press, dividing and disrupting churches, political parties, and civil governments.

It has, in the person of the President elect, asserted the equality of the *black* with the *white race*.

These are some of the wrongs against which we have remonstrated for more than a quarter of a century, hoping, but in vain, for their redress, until some of our sister States, in utter despair of obtaining justice at the hands of these lawless confederates, have resolved to sever the ties which have bound them together, and maintain those rights out of the Union, which have been the object of constant attack and encroachment within it.

No one will assert that the Southern States or people have, at any time, failed to perform, fully and in good faith, all of the duties which the Constitution devolves upon them.

Nor will it be pretended that they have, at any time, encroached or attempted aggression upon the rights of a Northern sister State. The Government was for many years under the control of Southern Statesmen, but in originating and perfecting measures of policy, be it said to the perpetual honor of the South, she has never attempted to encroach upon a single constitutional right of the North. The journals of Congress will not show even the introduction of a single proposition, by any Southern Representative, calculated to impair her rights in property, injure her trade, or wound her sensibilities. Nor have they at any time demanded at the hands of the Federal Government, or Northern States, more than their well defined rights under the Constitution. So far from it, they have tolerated these wrongs, from a feeling of loyalty and devotion to the Union, with a degree of patience and forbearance unparalleled in the history of a brave and free people. Moreover, they have quietly submitted to a revenue system which indirectly, but certainly, taxes the products of slave labor some fifty or sixty millions of dollars annually, to increase the manufacturing profits of those who have thus persistently and wickedly assailed them.

To evade the issue thus forced upon us at this time, without the fullest security for our rights, is, in my opinion, fatal to the institution of slavery forever. The time has arrived when the people of the South must prepare either to abandon or to fortify and maintain it. Abandon it, we cannot, interwoven as it is with our wealth, prosperity and domestic happiness. We owe it to the mechanic whose shop is closed, to the multiplied thousands of laborers thrown out of employment, to the trader made bankrupt by this agitation. We owe it to ourselves, our children, our self-respect and equality in the Government, to have this question settled permanently and forever upon terms consistent with justice and honor, and which will give us peace and perfect security for the present and the future.

Palliatives and opiates, in the character of legislative compromises, may be applied, affording momentary relief; but there will be no permanent safety, security, or peace, until Northern prejudice has been eradicated, and the public sentiment of that section radically changed and nationalized. To attempt the application of effective remedies before this great object has been accomplished, is like cleansing the stream while the fountain itself is poisoned.

The consequences and immense interests which are involved in the proper solution of the difficulties that surround us, the deep, lasting and vital importance of settling them upon principles of justice and equality, demand the most serious consideration of the whole people, as well as that of the public functionaries of the State. Whilst I cheerfully submit to your discretion the whole question of our federal relations, having no doubt myself as to the necessity and propriety of calling a State Convention, yet I respectfully recommend that you provide by law for submitting to the people of the State, the question of *Convention,* or *No Convention*, and also for the election of delegates by the people, in the ratio of legislative representation, to meet in State Convention, at the Capitol, at Nashville, at the earliest day practicable, to take into consideration our federal relations, and determine what action shall be taken by the State of Tennessee for the security of the rights and the peace of her citizens.

The question of *Convention* or *No Convention*, can and should be determined and the delegates chosen at the same election, which can be very easily accomplished by heading one set of tickets Convention, and another set No Convention. If a majority of the people vote for Convention, then the persons receiving the largest number of votes in their respective counties and districts, to be commissioned as delegates.

This will place the whole matter in the hands of the people, for them, in their sovereignty, to determine how far their rights have been violated, the character of redress or guaranty they will demand, or the action they will take for their present and future security.

If there be a remedy for the evils which afflict the country, consistent with the perpetuity of the Union, it will, in my opinion, be found in such constitutional amendments as will deprive the fanatical majorities of the North of the power to invade our rights or impair the security or value of our property.

Clear and well defined as our rights are, under the present Constitution, to participate equally with the citizens of all other States in the settlement of the common Territories, and to hold our slaves there until excluded by the formation of a State Constitution, yet every organized Territory will become a field of angry, if not bloody, strife between the Southern man and the Abolitionist, and we shall see the tragedies of Kansas re-enacted in each of them, as they approach the period of forming their State Constitutions.

Plain and unmistakable as is the duty of each State, to deliver up the fugitive slave to his owner, yet the attempt to reclaim, is at the peril of the master's life.

These evils can be obviated to a great extent, if not entirely, by the following amendments to the Constitution:

1st. Establish a line upon the Northern boundary of the present Slave States, and extend it through the Territories to the Pacific Ocean, upon such parallel of latitude as will divide them equitably between the North and South, expressly providing that all the territory now owned or that may be hereafter acquired North of that line, shall be forever free, and all South of it, *forever* slave. This will remove the question of existence or non-existence of slavery in our States and Territories entirely and forever from the arena of politics. The question being settled by the Constitution, is no longer open for the politician to ride into position by appealing to fanatical prejudices, or assailing the rights of his neighbors.

2d. In addition to the fugitive slave clause provide, that when a slave has been demanded of the Executive authority of the State to which he has fled, if he is not delivered, and the owner permitted to carry him out of the State in peace, that the State so failing to deliver, shall pay to the owner double the value of such slave, and secure his right of action in the Supreme Court of the United States. This will secure the return of the slave to his owner, or his value, with a sufficient sum to indemnify him for the expenses necessarily incident to the recovery.

3d. Provide for the protection of the owner in the peaceable possession of his slave while in transit, or temporarily sojourning in any of the States of the Confederacy; and in the event of the slave's escape or being taken from the owner, require the State to return, or account for him as in case of the fugitive.

4th. Expressly prohibit Congress from abolishing slavery in the

District of Columbia, in any dock yard, navy yard, arsenal, or district of any character whatever, within the limits of any slave State.

5th. That these provisions shall never be changed, except by the consent of all the slave States.

With these amendments to the Constitution, I should feel that our rights were reasonably secure, not only in theory, but in fact, and should indulge the hope of living in the Union in peace. Without these, or some other amendments, which promise an equal amount and certainty of security, there is no hope of peace or security in the government.

If the non-slaveholding States refuse to comply with a demand, so just and reasonable; refuse to abandon at once and forever their unjust war upon us, our institutions and our rights; refuse, as they have heretofore done, to perform, in good faith, the obligations of the compact of union, much as we may appreciate the power, prosperity, greatness, and glory of this government; deeply as we deplore the existence of causes which have already driven one State from the Union; much as we may regret the imperative necessity which they have wantonly and wickedly forced upon us, every consideration of self-preservation and self-respect require that we should assert and maintain our 'equality in the Union, or independence out of it.'

In my opinion, the only mode left us of perpetuating the Union upon the principles of justice and equality, upon which it was originally established, is by the Southern States, identified as they are, in interest, sentiment and feeling, and must, in the natural course of events, share a common destiny, uniting in the expression of a fixed and unalterable resolve, that the rights guaranteed by the Constitution must be *respected*, and *fully* and *perfectly* secured in the present Government, or asserted and maintained in a homogeneous Confederacy of Southern States.

Mere questions of policy may be very often properly compromised, but there can be no compromise of cardinal and vital principles; no compromise between *right* and *wrong*. Principle must be vindicated, and right triumphant, be the consequences what they may. To compromise the one, or abandon the other, is not only unmanly and humiliating in the extreme, but always disastrous in its final results.

The South has no power to re-unite the scattered fragments of

a violated Constitution and a once glorious government. She is acting on the defensive. She has been driven to the wall, and can submit
to no further aggression. The North, however, *can* restore the Constitutional Union of our fathers, by undoing their work of alienation and hate, engendered by thirty years of constant aggression, and
by unlearning the lessons of malignant hostility to the South, and
her institutions, with which their press, pulpit and schools have persistently infected the public mind.

Let them do this, and peace will again establish her court in the
midst of this once happy country, and the union of these States be
restored to that spirit of fraternity, equality and justice, which gave
it birth.

Let them do this, and the vitality which has been crushed out of
the Constitution may be restored, giving renewed strength and vigor
to the body politic.

But can we hope for such results? Two months have already
passed, since the development of facts which make the perpetuity
of the Union depend, *alone*, upon their giving to the South satisfactory guarantees for her chartered rights. Yet, there has been no proposition at all satisfactory, made by any member of the dominant and
aggressive party of that section. So far from it, their Senators and
Representatives in Congress, have voted down and spurned every
proposition that looked to the accomplishment of this object, no
matter whence emanating; and the fact, that their constituents have,
in no authoritative manner, issued words of rebuke or warning to
them, must be taken as conclusive proof of their acquiescence in the
policy.

In view of these facts, I cannot close my eyes to the conclusion,
that Tennessee will be powerless in any efforts she may make to
quell the storm that pervades the country. The work of alienation
and disruption has gone so far, that it will be extremely difficult, if
not impossible, to arrest it; and before your adjournment, in all
human probability, the only practical question for the State to determine, will be whether she will unite her fortunes with a Northern
or Southern Confederacy; upon which question, when presented,
I am certain there can be little or no division in sentiment, identified
as we are in every respect with the South.

If this calamity shall befall the country, the South will have the
consolation of knowing that she is in no manner responsible for the

disaster. The responsibility rests alone upon the Northern people, who have wilfully broken the bond of Union, repudiated the obligations and duties which it imposes, and only cling to its benefits. Yet even in this dark hour of responsibility and peril let no man countenance the idea for a moment, that the dissolution of the Federal Union reduces the country to anarchy, or proves the theory of self-government to be a failure. Such conclusions would be not only erroneous but unworthy of ourselves and our revolutionary ancestry while our State governments exist possessing all the machinery, perfect and complete, which is necessary to the purposes of civil government, just as they existed before the Union was formed.

The sages and patriots of the revolution, when in the act of severing their connection with the mother country, and establishing the great cardinal principles of free government, solemnly declared that governments were instituted among men to secure their rights 'to life, liberty, and the pursuit of happiness; deriving their just powers from the consent of the governed; that whenever any form of government becomes destructive of these ends, it is the right of the people to alter or abolish it, and to institute new government, laying its foundations on such principles, and organizing its powers in such form, as to them shall seem most likely to effect their safety and happiness. * * * * But when a long train of abuses and usurpations, pursuing invariably the same object, evinces a design to reduce them under absolute despotism, it is their right, it is their duty, to throw off such government, and to provide new guards for their future security.'

Recognising these great principles, the people of Tennessee incorporated in their declaration of rights, as a fundamental article of the Constitution of the State, 'That government being instituted for the common benefit, the doctrine of non-resistance against arbitrary power and oppression is absurd, slavish, and destructive of the good and happiness of mankind.'

Whatever line of policy may be adopted by the people of Tennessee, with regard to the present Federal relations of the State, I am sure that the swords of her brave and gallant sons will never be drawn for the purpose of coercing, subjugating, or holding as a conquered province, any one of her sister States, whose *people* may declare their independence of the Federal Government, for the purpose of being relieved from 'a long train of abuses and usurpations.'

To admit the right or policy of coercion, would be untrue to the example of our fathers and the glorious memories of the past, destructive of those great and fundamental principles of civil liberty, purchased with their blood; destructive of State sovereignty and equality; tending to centralization, and thus subject the rights of the minority to the despotism of an unrestrained majority.

Widely as we may differ with some of our sister Southern States as to the wisdom of their policy; desirous as we may be that whatever action taken in this emergency, should be taken by the South as a unit; hopeful as we may be of finding some remedy for our grievances consistent with the perpetuity of the present Confederacy, the question, at last, is one which each member of that Confederacy must determine for itself, and any attempt upon the part of the others to hold, by means of a military force, an unwilling sovereignty as a member of a common Union, must inevitably lead to the worst form of internecine war, and if successful, result in the establishment of a new and totally different Government from the one established by the Constitution—the Constitutional Union being a Union of *consent* and not of *force*, of *peace*, and not of *blood*—composed of sovereignties, free, and politically equal. But the new and coercive Government, while it would 'derive its powers' to govern a portion of the States '*from the consent of the governed*,' would derive the power by which it governed the remainder, from the *cannon and the sword*, and not from their *consent*—a Union, not of equals, but of the victors and the vanquished, pinned together by the bayonet and congealed in blood.

I devoutly trust that a merciful Providence may avert such a calamity, and believe that there is no respectable portion of our people, whatever may be their differences of opinion upon other questions, who are so blind to reason, or so lost to patriotism and every sentiment of civil liberty, as to give countenance to a policy so fatal in its results, and so revolting to every sentiment of humanity.

While I sincerely trust that Tennessee may never be driven to the desperate alternative of appealing to arms in defence of the rights of her people, I nevertheless deem it proper, in view of the present excited state of the public mind and unsettled condition of the country, to call your attention to the fact that, with the exception of a small number of volunteer companies, we have no military organization in the State, the militia having disorganized immediately after the repeal of the law which required drills and public parades. Independent of the impending crisis, I regard a thorough reorganization of the militia as imperatively demanded by every consideration of prudence and safety. I therefore submit the question to your consideration, with the earnest hope that you will adopt such plan of organization as will secure to the State at all times, and under all circumstances, an efficient and reliable military force.

I am unable, in the absence of full reports from the clerks of the several counties, to inform you as to the military strength of the State. Such reports as have been made to this department shall be laid before you. I do not doubt, however, that the military strength of the State may be safely estimated at one hundred and twenty thousand men.

It is proper, in this connection, that I call your attention to the report of John Heriges, Keeper of Public Arms, herewith transmitted, showing the number, character and condition of the public arms of the State, and respectfully recommend that you provide for the purchase of such number and character of arms, for the use of the State, as may be necessary to thoroughly arm an efficient military force.

I regret that I cannot close this communication with the foregoing recital of facts pertaining to the all-important political crisis of the day.

But a comparative failure of crops for two successive years, with the destruction of commercial confidence, resulting in the suspension of commercial transactions, general stagnation of trade and financial embarrassment which pervade the whole country, with its ever attendant evil of general pecuniary distress at the beginning of which many of the banks in the State suspended specie payment, thereby incurring the penalties prescribed by the banking code of the last session.

It is asserted, and I suppose truly, that the condition of the banks was such as not to make suspension necessary on their own account; that by the adoption of a purely selfish policy, they could have weathered the storm and sustained themselves, but to have done so they must have cut off all discounts and enforced the collection of their debts from the people, which would have increased the general distress. It is also urged with great earnestness, by a very large number of the people, that you should pass laws for relief, and in order to enable the banks to afford the greatest possible assistance to the people until another crop can be made, that the penalties incurred by the suspension of the banks should be released.

While I am confident in the opinion that the suspension of specie payment by the banks is wrong in principle and tends to depreciate the currency and unsettle the standard of value, I am equally confident that the policy of relief laws, to which this general pecuniary distress has driven the public mind, is, to say the least of it, of doubtful policy, and generally injurious in their ultimate effects upon the community. The idea of freeing a people from pecuniary distress by legislation is, to my mind, an impossibility. Yet so universal is the anxiety expressed, and so confident the hope of relief from the adoption of the policy suggested, that while I cannot concur in the truth of the argument, or recommend the adoption of the policy, I do not feel at liberty obstinately to stand between the people of the State and their chosen Representatives to prevent the adoption of such legislation connected with these questions as they may think will promote their interest and general welfare.

I therefore submit to your consideration these questions for such action as you in your discretion may see proper to take with regard to them.

I am aware that there are many questions of a general character with regard to which the constituents of many of you desire legislation, but having convened you in extraordinary session, upon what I conceived to be an extraordinary occasion in the history of the country, and feeling the necessity of prompt and immediate action upon the absorbing questions connected with the political crisis of the day, I have intentionally avoided submitting any others than those to which I have especially called attention, trusting that no material interest will suffer by being postponed until the next regular session of the General Assembly.

With the earnest hope that your session may be short and agreeable, and devoutly trusting that an All Wise Providence may watch over your deliberations and guide and direct you in the adoption of such measures as will redound to the general welfare, peace, prosperity, and glory of our State and country, the questions, fraught as they are with weighty responsibilities and fearfully important consequences, are respectfully committed to your hands.

ISHAM G. HARRIS."

During the months of November and December, 1860, President James Buchanan stood hesitant and shrunk from taking positive action in the crisis facing him; Horace Greeley told the people of the North to "let the erring sisters depart in peace"; and Unionists in Tennessee declared their opposition to secession as a remedy for the issue dividing the Nation. However, there were strong advocates in Tennessee for a Southern Confederacy. The *Nashville Gazette* in lengthy articles stood for "an independent South." The *Union and American* warned that any attempt of the Federal Government to use force against South Carolina would result in a disruption of the Union. The *Memphis Avalanche* spurned the idea of a call for a Union meeting as constituting a "traitorous document." The day following South Carolina's declaration that she was out of the Union, Andrew Johnson rose in the United States Senate and delivered what was perhaps the most important speech of his long and colorful political career. When news of Johnson's Union speech reached Memphis, he was burned in effigy and denounced as a traitor to the South.

Tennessee's attitude on the issue dividing the North and the South was, at first, one of relative neutrality. This attitude was characterized at the Democratic Convention of Charleston in 1860. Her delegates voted against the Southern proposition to give slavery *carte blanche* leeway in the territories, and later met with the Northern delegates at Baltimore. When the Baltimore Convention refused to receive the Tennessee delegates who had withdrawn at Charleston, the Tennessee delegates then lined up with the other Southern delegates in nominating John C. Breckinridge for President. In the Presidential election that fall, Tennessee cast her electoral vote for John Bell who ran as the candidate of the Constitutional Union Party. This electoral vote cast by Tennessee was but additional evidence of her neutrality, being opposed as she was to both the extreme parties.

The popular vote was as follows: [248]

Party	Candidate	Vote
Constitutional Union	John Bell	69,274
Democrat	John C. Breckinridge	64,709
Democrat	Stephen A. Douglas	11,350
Republican	Abraham Lincoln	no votes

This brief backdrop presents the political situation in Tennessee at the time Governor Harris called the Legislature into extraordinary session on January 7, 1861. There was strong Union sentiment in Tennessee, especially East Tennessee, but pro-Southern sentiment was rapidly increasing in proportion as the secession movement developed in neighboring Southern States.

---

[248] Miller, Charles A.: *Official Manual of Tennessee*, 42.

Governor Harris, a man who never hesitated to do what he believed to be right for fear he might be wrong, was ready with his Message upon the day the Legislature met in extra session. After a brief address to the Senate by its Speaker, Tazewell W. Newman, word was received that the House had convened and was "now ready for business." A joint committee was appointed to inform the Governor that there was a quorum present of both branches of the General Assembly and had

". . . convened agreeably to his proclamation, and are ready to receive any communication he may have to make."[249]

The Message was decidedly pro-Southern in tone and content, carrying with it a catalogue of "crimes" attributed to the anti-slavery adherents. With cameo-like sharpness, Governor Harris sketched in brief but lucid phraseology the grievances thrust upon the Southern States by

"The systematic, wanton, and long continued agitation of the slavery question, with the actual and threatened aggressions of the Northern States and a portion of their people, upon the well-defined constitutional rights of the Southern citizen. . . ."

After a recital of the wrongs, as he viewed the situation, Governor Harris recommended the calling of a special election for the purpose of ascertaining the will of the people on the question of secession and the election of delegates to a convention to be held by the Southern States. After a bit of haggling over phraseology, the offering of substitute resolutions, and an effort to postpone action, an Act[250] was passed on January 19 "providing for a Convention of the people of Tennessee." Substantially, the law provided for an election to be held on February 9 at which time the voters were to cast their ballots for "Convention" or "No Convention." Before this law was passed, the conservative element in the Legislature forced the adoption of an amendment[251] to the original bill whereby

"No ordinance or resolution, which may be adopted by said Convention, having for its object a change of the position or relation of this State to the National Union or her sister Southern States, shall be of any binding effect or force until it is submitted to and ratified and adopted by a majority of the qualified voters in the State, taking as a basis the vote cast in the last election for Governor and members of the General Assembly."

The passage of the above law in a relatively short time after the reception of the Governor's Message filled the Union people with alarm. Typical of the sentiment of the Unionists was the voice[252] of the *Nashville Daily Banner* which warned all citizens to beware of a

[249] *Senate Journal*, First Extraordinary Session, 1861, 5.
[250] *Acts of Tennessee*, First Extraordinary Session, 1861, Chapter 1.
[251] *Ibid.*, Section 8.
[252] *Nashville Daily Banner*, January 26, 1861.

treacherous conspiracy to dissolve the Union. For the ensuing fortnight prior to the election on February 9, the State witnessed a beehive activity on the part of each faction. Newspapers teemed with approvals and disapprovals of the Harris Message and the action of the Legislature which, in the main, supported the position taken by the Governor. Two ex-Governors, Neill S. Brown and William B. Campbell, maintained that no valid cause existed for a dissolution of the Union. In East Tennessee a fervid campaign was launched in which some of the ablest men in that section participated.

In the election on February 9, old *Vox Populi* spoke emphatically. On the plain question of Secession, the vote was heavily pro-Union, the returns showing a vote of 88,803 for Union candidates and 22,749 for Secession candidates.[253] In regard to the calling of a Convention, the movement was rejected by a vote of 69,675 to 57,798. The decision by the people was a significant one, in that the action of both Governor Harris and the General Assembly was rebuked. The result was surprising in view of the fact that seven Southern States had already seceded and had organized a Provisional Government at Montgomery, Alabama.

The result of the election of February 9 indicated that Tennessee, under the then existing circumstances, would remain in the Union. For approximately two months after the above election, much of the previous excitement had subsided and matters moved along without any significant outbreaks of passion or threats of disunion. It is highly probable that the results of the recent election and the comparative quiet throughout the State were received as conclusive proof that the secession movement in Tennessee had been killed. But then came the news of the attack on Fort Sumter! With the force and suddenness of a lightning stroke, the Sumter bombardment became the all-absorbing topic of the day. Practically every town and city in Middle and West

---

[253] Author's note. Various authorities give different figures about the number of votes cast. Charles A. Miller, the Secretary of State, gave the following:

For Convention	57,798
No Convention	69,675
Union delegates	88,803
Disunion delegates	24,749

Dr. James W. Fertig, in a dissertation on the *Secession and Reconstruction of Tennessee*, gives a slightly different figure on the vote for delegates:

Union delegates	91,803
Disunion delegates	24,749

The gigantic difference between the majority vote for Union delegates and Disunion delegates and that of Convention and No Convention is somewhat of an enigma. Oliver Perry Temple, a strong Union man and a participant in the contest of February 9, suggested in his *East Tennessee and the Civil War*, page 176, that "While the Union leaders generally took decided ground against a convention, some Union men and possibly a great many others voted for a convention."

Regardless of the discrepancies in the vote as given by various writers, the fact remains that Tennessee, at the time, was not for Secession.

Executive Department
Nashville Tennessee
April 15 1861.

Hon Simon Cameron
Secretary of War.
Washington
D.C.

Sir

Your dispatch of 15th Inst.
informing me that Tennessee is called
upon for two Regiments of Militia for
immediate Service, is received

Tennessee will not furnish a
Single man for purpose of Coercion
but 50,000 if necessary for the
defence of our rights and those of
our Southern brothers,

Isham G. Harris
Governor of
Tennessee

Clarity, Brevity, Finality!

Tennessee became the scene of intense and enthusiastic demonstrations. Petitions and loud demands poured into the Governor's office for immediate alignment with the Southern States. Newspapers flamed with passionate editorials, while many influential citizens hitherto opposing secession as a remedy now became outspoken advocates of cooperation with the Confederacy. In response to President Lincoln's call for two Tennessee regiments to help quell the rebellion, Governor Harris felt in view of aroused public sentiment amply justified in dispatching his famous telegram.[254]

The bombardment of Fort Sumter and President Lincoln's call for Tennessee troops settled the controversial issue in Tennessee. It had now become certain that the Federal Government would attempt to coerce the South; Tennessee would be compelled to line up with one side or the other. Bound by social and economic ties, there could be little or no doubt but that Tennessee would unquestionably side with the Southern States and expend her energies in behalf of the Confederacy. For a short time, influential conservative Union leaders attempted to check the rising tide of excitement that was sweeping the State. Twelve prominent men, including ex-Governor Neill S. Brown, John Bell, Cave Johnson, Balie Peyton, Andrew Ewing and E. H. Ewing, in a published address to the people, indorsed the Governor's refusal to send troops in response to Lincoln's call, but disapproved of secession as the proper course to pursue. But their appeal for neutrality was practically nullified by their closing statement that if the Union undertook to subjugate the seceded States then Tennessee must resist such action, even by force of arms. This concluding statement of their address bound the conservative element to help resist Federal force, thereby forming an alliance with the Confederacy in the forthcoming conflict. After a few days, the conservatives were crowded into a tight corner. In a public meeting in Nashville on April 22, John Bell and the Ewings stated that the time had come for Tennessee to join up with the South. They no longer clung to the idea of neutrality, but advocated entering a league with the Confederacy and urged the people to enlist and arm immediately.[255] Aligned with the above three men was ex-Governor Neill S. Brown, a leader of the conservatives, who in a public letter stated that the policy of the Federal Government was to subjugate the South by force, that the border States would constitute the battleground, and that the first duty of Tennessee was to arm and make ready for the inevitable clash of arms.[256] Felix K. Zollicoffer, who was later killed in the early part of the war, sided with the above conservative leaders.[257]

---

[254] Original telegram in holdings of the Tennessee Historical Society, Nashville.
[255] *Nashville Daily Banner*, April 23, 1861.
[256] *Ibid.*, April 24, 1861.
[257] *Ibid.*, April 25, 1861.

John Bell, the ablest and most widely-known of the conservatives, had for many years in public life contended for the preservation of the Union and was opposed to disunion agitation in the South. In a personal interview with Lincoln, Bell had warned that the use of force against the Southern States would drive Tennessee out of the Union. And when war came, a thing that Bell dreaded and hoped to avert, he made the choice that Robert E. Lee and many other prominent Southern leaders made—he went with his State. Bell's turning to the South brought down upon him the curses and maledictions of many of his former friends and associates. Horace Greeley shrieked that "there is no name whereon will rest a deeper, darker stigma than that of John Bell." Oliver P. Temple, an East Tennessee Unionist, was more charitable. In discussing Bell's "defection," Temple said of Bell:[258]

". . . His heart revolted at the alliance he there made with his old enemies, but a fierce, an omnipotent, an overpowering Southern sentiment was around him and he yielded . . ."

If (but it is a big IF) Temple's conjecture be true, John Bell from a political standpoint made the supreme sacrifice when he espoused the Southern cause. Said Temple:[259]

"Suppose Mr. Bell . . . had remained firm and submitted to be driven out of his city and state, as a fugitive and an exile . . . how grandly he would have appeared in history. He would have been the most eminent citizen of the South who had remained true to the Union. His recent prestige as the candidate of the Constitutional Union party for the presidency would have received additional lustre from his patriotic sacrifice. He would have become the most popular as well as the most conspicuous statesman in the country, next after Mr. Lincoln. Honors would have fallen on him without stint. In 1864, he would almost certainly have been placed on the presidential ticket with Mr. Lincoln, and on the assassination of the latter, would have become president—the dream of his life. . . ."

It will be recalled that Governor Harris had ordered the General Assembly to convene in extraordinary session on January 7, 1861. That body remained in session until *sine die* adjournment on February 4, approximately four weeks. During its session, predictions, conjectures, and prophecies constituted largely the *pabulum* handed out to the public. Abraham Lincoln had been elected President but had not been inaugurated. His position on the slavery issue was alluded to in his first Inaugural Address on March 4, 1861, when he quoted from a former speech of his to the following effect:[260]

"I have no purpose, directly or indirectly, to interfere with the institu-

---

[258] Temple, Oliver Perry: *East Tennessee and the Civil War*, 232.
[259] *Ibid.*, 233.
[260] Richardson, James D.: *Messages and Papers of the Presidents*, Volume 6, 5.

tion of slavery in the States where it exists. I believe I have no lawful right to do so, and I have no inclination to do so."

But this and other pacific statements of Lincoln were drowned out by utterances thundered forth for more than four years past by such firebrand fanatics as William Lloyd Garrison, William H. Seward, Henry Ward Beecher, Charles Sumner, and others. Through the columns of newspapers, published speeches, and other media, Southern people had read or heard of the incendiary blast of Garrison [261]

"Independence Day. This is the Eightieth Anniversary of American Independence. That Independence began in a spirit of compromise with the foul spirit of slavery; it ends with every seventh person in the land a chattel slave,—the universal mastery of a slave-holding oligarchy,—the overthrow of all the rights of Northern citizens,—the reign of Lynch Law and Border Ruffianism throughout the entire South,—the subversion of the National Government by a clique of desperate and unprincipled demagogues,— . . . the reign of violence, tyranny, and blood, on a frightful scale. So much for disregarding the 'Higher Law' by our fathers! So much for entering into 'a covenant with death, and an agreement with hell.' Truly, God is just, and our national retribution another striking proof that, as a people sow, so shall they reap. A NEW REVOLUTION HAS BEGUN,—ANOTHER SECESSION is to take place,—and FREEDOM FOR ALL secured upon a sure basis. 'NO UNION WITH SLAVE-HOLDERS.' "

But there were firebrands in the South as well. Flashes of temper and invective served to intensify the mounting ill-will, and ere long reason and all attempts at arbitration were eclipsed in the maelstrom of sectional hatred that ushered in a fratricidal war on a gigantic scale. For a generation and more after the war, most historians attributed the tragedy of the War Between the States to slavery. True enough, slavery was in everybody's mind. But a more accurate view is emerging; geography, topography, soil, and climate were factors responsible for a wide divergence between the North and the South. A radically different type of life had developed in the agrarian South and the industrial North. The slave was the working capital of the Southerner, while cash and credit constituted the working capital of the North. Bitter cold winters and rocky soil did not and could not contribute to the utilization of slave labor in New England. But climate, soil, slave labor, plus the invention of the cotton gin, began to enrich the South as if by magic. Hence, economic jealousy and rivalry crept into the situation, and false concepts and mercenary motives soon became dominant. By 1859, due to the admission of new States into the Union, there were eighteen free States arrayed against fifteen slave States. This meant that the South had become a minority party in both branches of Con-

---

[261] Cluskey, Michael W.: *The Democratic Handbook,* 1856, in article entitled "Constitution and Union, Stand or Fall?" 6. Quotation is from Garrison's *Liberator,* July 4, 1856.

gress. And, with the election of Lincoln in 1860, there was added the Executive Department also. In political control of these two departments of government, the Abolitionists began to scream for immediate and total emancipation of slaves. The titanic struggle was on.

At the extraordinary session of four weeks duration, the Legislature enacted only thirteen Public Acts. By far the most important was the first act passed, providing for a Convention of the people regarding Secession or No Secession. Another act [262] was in compliance with the recommendation of Governor Harris in a special Message on January 16, advocating the relieving of railroads from paying "any part of the principal of a debt which does not fall due for thirty years."

In the belief that amicable settlement between the North and the South had now become impossible, a Joint Resolution [263] was passed for the election of delegates to a Convention of the slave-holding States. On January 25, the Legislature met in joint session and elected the following delegates: [264]

District	Delegate	County
First Congressional District	Samuel Milligan	Greene
Second Congressional District	Alvin S. Cullom	Overton
Third Congressional District	Josiah N. Anderson	Sequatchie
Fourth Congressional District	William Hickerson	Coffee
Fifth Congressional District	Robert L. Caruthers	Wilson
Sixth Congressional District	George W. Jones*	Lincoln
Seventh Congressional District	Thomas Martin	Giles
Eighth Congressional District	Felix K. Zollicoffer	Davidson
Ninth Congressional District	Isaac R. Hawkins	Carroll
Tenth Congressional District	William H. Stephens	Madison
State at Large	A. O. W. Totten	Madison
State at Large	Robert J. McKinney	Knox

The most pronounced example of "wishful thinking" on the part of Governor Harris was the proposal in his Message of five amendments

---

[262] *Acts of Tennessee*, First Extraordinary Session, 1861, Chapter 10.

Author's note. This Message was of minor import and is not incorporated in this volume. The Message may be found in *Senate Journal*, First Extraordinary Session, 1861, 57–58, and in *House Journal*, 92–93.

[263] *Ibid.*, Resolution 14, 52.

[264] *Senate Journal*, First Extraordinary Session, 1861, 98–107.

* Mr. Jones declined to serve as delegate, basing his decision upon the fact that of the eleven counties embracing the Sixth Congressional District the Senators and Representatives from only two of those counties had voted for him. To him, this meant that he was not the choice of a majority of such legislative members. Furthermore, in his letter of declination, he said that one of those supporters protested against the right of the Legislature to make such elections. *Senate Journal*, First Extraordinary Session, 1861, 141–142. The official records fail to show that any successor was elected. Apparently, the Sixth Congressional District was without representation to the Convention.

to the Federal Constitution. Underlying the five proposed amendments was the idea that if the Northern States would accept these amendments then friendly relations between the North and South could be maintained. In substance, the amendments would establish a line to the north of which slavery could not be extended and south of which slavery would *forever* be permissible; any State refusing to deliver up a fugitive slave to the owner would pay double the value of the slave; a slave owner would be protected while travelling through any State in the Confederacy, in that his slave should he escape, would be returned to the owner, or that State would indemnify the owner as in case of a fugitive slave; prohibit Congress from abolishing slavery in the District of Columbia, or in places such as naval docks and arsenals located in slave States; and that none of these amendments could be changed without the consent of all the slave States.

It is self-evident that Governor Harris did not place too much faith in having his proposals accepted. He undoubtedly knew that the long and tedious process of amending the Federal Constitution would be but another example of being "too late with too little." It looks as though the Governor had scanned all the "signs" in the political zodiac, and happened to fall upon amendments to the Federal Constitution as a sort of defense mechanism. Even the Governor, later on in his Message, frankly admitted that his belief was that

"The only practical question for the State to determine will be whether she will unite her fortunes with a Northern or Southern Confederacy; upon which question, when presented, I am certain there can be little or no division in sentiment, identified as we are in every respect with the South."

On January 22, the resolution proposing amendments to the Federal Constitution was passed in the Senate by a vote of 21 to 3,[265] the negative votes being cast by Senator M. V. Nash representing the counties of Anderson, Campbell, Claiborne, and Grainger; Senator D. Van Dyke Stokely from the counties of Blount, Cocke, Greene, and Sevier; and Senator John Trimble of Davidson County. Previous to the action of the Senate, quite a hassle had developed in the House of Representatives in regard to the consideration of the proposed amendments. On January 17, Representative R. B. Cheatham from the counties of Cheatham, Davidson, Montgomery, and Robertson introduced a resolution that expanded the five proposals of Governor Harris to nine categories.[266] A shower of proposed amendments to Mr. Cheatham's resolution flooded the Clerk's desk, most of which were defeated. However, Representative George Gantt of Maury County, a member of the Joint Committee on Federal Relations, later on advised the House that agreement had been reached by the Committee to offer a resolu-

---

[265] *Ibid.*, 83.
[266] *House Journal*, First Extraordinary Session, 1861, 98–101.

tion in lieu of the original.[267] Upon a demand for roll call, the Committee's resolution was adopted by a vote of 56 to 7. The seven opposing Representatives were: Samuel Baker of Weakley; H. C. Lockhart of Stewart; J. G. McCabe of Cannon; A. J. Vaughan of Monroe; W. H. Wisener of Bedford; and Speaker W. C. Whitthorne representing the counties of Williamson, Maury, and Lewis.[268]

The resolution,[269] as finally adopted, merely expanded the proposals of Governor Harris without materially altering their basal objectives. The passage of the resolution, however, amounted to absolutely nothing; it was only so much jetsam cast upon the stormy waters.

On February 4, 1861, the First Extraordinary Session of the Thirty-Third General Assembly adjourned. As has been shown, the people had defeated the secession movement in the February 9 election by a ratio of 4 to 1. But within sixty days thereafter, due to the bombardment of Fort Sumter, the collapse of the Washington Peace Conference, President Lincoln's call for troops, and plus a natural sympathy for those Southern States which had seceded, public sentiment in two-thirds of Tennessee underwent a radical change. Numerous former leaders in the cause of anti-secession withdrew their support and urged that Tennessee make ready for the conflict that was sure to come. Now, that many of the most valiant defenders of the Union had "changed signals" and had become pronounced in their support of the Southern cause, Governor Harris saw an opportunity for welding the State's forces into a "fighting machine" in aid of the Confederacy. Without hesitation, he called the General Assembly into a second extra session by the following proclamation:*

"WHEREAS, an alarming and dangerous usurpation of power by the President of the United States has precipitated a state of war between the sovereign States of America:

Therefore, I, ISHAM G. HARRIS, Governor of the State of Tennessee, by virtue of the power and authority in me vested by the Constitution, do hereby require the Senators and Representatives of the two Houses of the General Assembly of said State, to convene at the Capitol in Nashville, on Thursday, the 25th day of April inst., 1861, at 12 o'clock M., to legislate upon such subjects as may then be submitted to them.

---

[267] Ibid., 125–128.

[268] Ibid., 128–129.
Author's note. The tabulated vote shows seven negative votes, but in the recording of the names of the voters only six names were included. William Ewing from Williamson County was excused from casting his ballot, and it is probable that he was regarded as being in the negative and so recorded in the *tabulated* vote.

[269] Acts of Tennessee, First Extraordinary Session, 1861, Resolution 13, 49–52.

* Senate Journal, Second Extraordinary Session, 1861, 4.

In testimony whereof, I have hereunto set my hand and
(   ) caused the great seal of the State to be affixed at the Depart-
(LS) ment at Nashville, on this 18th day of April, A.D. 1861.
By the Governor: ISHAM G. HARRIS.
J. E. R. RAY, *Secretary of State."*

Ardent and indefatigable Secessionist as he was, Governor Harris allowed only seven days between the dates of his Proclamation and the day for the convening of the Legislature. He was waiting for neither time nor tide; he wanted action, and he wanted it NOW! Accordingly, his Message was ready for transmission the minute he was officially notified that the Legislature was in session and "ready for the transaction of public business." Here was the Message that was fraught with momentous consequences:

Legislative Message, April 2, 1861.*

"EXECUTIVE DEPARTMENT
Nashville, April 2, 1861

GENTLEMEN OF THE SENATE AND HOUSE OF REPRESENTATIVES:

The President of the United States—elected according to the forms of the Constitution, but upon principles openly hostile to its provisions—having wantonly inaugurated an internecine war between the people of the slave and non-slave holding States, I have convened you again at the seat of Government, for the purpose of enabling you to take such action as will most likely contribute to the defence of our rights, the preservation of our liberties, the sovereignty of the State, and the safety of our people; all of which are now in imminent peril by the usurpations of the authorities at Washington, and the unscrupulous fanaticism which runs riot throughout the Northern States.

The war thus inaugurated is likely to assume an importance nearly, if not equal, to the struggle of our revolutionary fathers, in

---

* *Acts of Tennessee*, Second Extraordinary Session, 1861, 3–11.
  Senate Journal, Second Extraordinary Session, 1861, 5–13.
  House Journal, Second Extraordinary Session, 1861, 4–11.
  Author's note. In each *Journal*, the date of the Message is given as April 2, 1861. This is a typographical error, the "5" having been omitted. The Message itself clearly indicates that it was prepared *after* the bombardment of Fort Sumter; otherwise Governor Harris would not have referred to the Federal Government as "having wantonly inaugurated an internecine war . . ." The date of the Message, as it appears in the above Acts, is correctly given, April 25, 1861.

their patriotic efforts to resist the usurpations and throw off the tyrannical yoke of the English Government; a war the duration of which and the good or evil that must result from it, depends entirely, in my judgment, upon the readiness with which the citizens of the South harmonize as one people, and the alacrity with which they respond to the demands of patriotism.

I do not think it necessary to recapitulate, at this late hour, the long train of abuses to which the people of Tennessee, and our sister States of the South have been subjected by the anti-republican spirit that has for many years been manifesting itself in that section, and which has at last declared itself our open and avowed enemy. In the message which I addressed to you at your called session in January last, these things were somewhat elaborately referred to, as constituting, in my judgment, the amplest reason for considering ourselves in imminent danger, and as requiring such action on the part of the Legislature as would place the State in an attitude for defence, whenever the momentous crisis should be forced upon us; and, also, as presenting to the North the strongest argument for peace, and if possible, securing a reconstruction of the Union, thus already dissolved by the most authoritative, formal, and matured action of a portion of the slaveholding States. Minor differences upon abstract questions— the ardent devotion of our people to the preservation of the Union, originating with their great loyalty to the Government—and a more hopeful view of the subject than I had been able to take, coupled with the supposed peaceful intentions of the authorities at Washington, have resulted in leaving the State poorly prepared for the sad realities which are now upon us.

But unfortunate as this may be, I am nevertheless encouraged with the belief that we are at last, practically, a united people. Whatever differences may have heretofore existed amongst us, growing out of party divisions, as to the right of Secession as a Constitutional remedy against Federal usurpation, all admit the moral right asserted by our fathers, of each and every people to resist wrong, and to maintain their liberties by whatever means may be necessary; 'that Governments derive their just powers from the consent of the governed, and that whenever any form of government becomes destructive of the ends for which it was created, it is the right of the people to alter and abolish it, and to institute a new government, laying its foundation on such principles, and organizing its powers in such form as shall to them seem most likely to effect their safety and happiness.' Standing by this common sentiment, with the bloody and tyrannical policy of the Presidential usurper fully before us; in the face of his hordes of armed soldiery, marching to the work of Southern subjugation; the people of the proud Commonwealth of Tennessee—true to their honor, true to the great principles of free institutions, true to the lessons of their fathers, and true to their brethren of the South, the subjects of a common oppression—have united, almost with one voice, in declaring their fixed resolve to resist the tyrant; and in pledging their lives, their fortunes, and their sacred honor to the maintenance of their rights, and the rights of their sister States of the South.

It cannot be overlooked that, in assuming an attitude of this character—forced upon us by the remarkable exigency of the times—we are, in effect, dissolving our connection with the Federal Union. As established by our fathers, that Union no longer exists. However much we may have cherished it heretofore, no intelligent and candid man can deny that it has ceased to be a blessing, and has become a curse; that it is no longer a high and sacred means of protection, but an engine of oppression; that it has ceased to be a bond of brotherhood, and has become a hateful connection between communities at war. It would be idle, therefore, to speak of ourselves any longer as members of the Federal Union; and while it is believed by many, whose opinions are entitled to the highest respect, that, by reason of the subversion of the Constitution by the authorities in power, inaugurating a revolution between the States thereof, each and every individual is already released from his former obligations to that government, yet, as best comporting with the dignity of the subject, and also from a due regard to those who may hold a different opinion—and farther still, that all the world may be advised of our action—I respectfully suggest that our connection with the Federal Union be formally annulled in such manner as shall involve the highest exercise of sovereign authority by the people of the State, and best secure that harmony, so much to be desired, in times like the present, upon questions even of mere detail. Until this is done many conscientious citizens may feel embarrassed in their action from their supposed relation to the General Government. In emergencies like the present, while it is our duty to act with due deliberation and prudence, unbiased as far as possible by excitement or prejudice, it is nevertheless of the highest importance that we should act with promptitude and decision.

Whatever grounds of hope may have been supposed to exist heretofore for an adjustment of the difficulties between the two sections of the Federal Union; however anxious we may have been to continue members of the same common family with the people of the North, such hope and expectation no longer exist in the mind of any rational man, who desires to maintain the honor and equality of the State, and the inviolability of her peculiar institutions.

The present administration, elected upon avowed purposes of hostility to the South—purposes which all knew then as well as now, could not be carried into effect, without an internecine war and a dissolution of the Union—has exerted every energy, resorted to every strategy, and disregarded every constitutional barrier, in order to hasten the accomplishment of the unholy mission for which the people of the Northern section had elevated it to power. They have lost no time—they have neither hesitated or faltered. The low duplicity in which their Administration was inaugurated—trusting, while conceding nothing, to lull the South into a fatal security, furnishing ground for divisions in the border slave States, while constant though secret preparation for the work of subjugation was going on, is now exposed and leaves us no alternative but independence out of the Union, or subjugation in it. The dishonorable and treacherous practices which have so far characterized the authorities at Washington, admonish us, that in the impending struggle we are scarcely to expect the rules of honorable warfare. Having its origin in a disordered moral sentiment of the North—not finding the ordinary restraints of patriotism among their people—deriving its power from a usurpation and perversion of the functions of government—having no middle-ground short of positive subjugation of the South, or a defeat which exposes its disgrace to the civilized world—I fear the time has passed when peace can be hoped for by the more moral force of a united South, without a trial of arms. Having succeeded in confusing and dividing the border slave States, they have had ample time for military preparations. The veil which concealed their recent movements has been thrown aside. The note of war has been sounded, and in the imperial proclamation, recently issued, the people of the Confederate States and all who sympathize with them are treated as rebels, and twenty days is allowed them to 'disperse' and return to their allegiance to the authorities at Washington. Without waiting for the expiration of the twenty days, in addition to the regular army and naval forces, a militia force of seventy-five thousand has been called into the field to execute this edict, by the power of arms. As if purposely intended to add additional insult to the people of Tennessee, I have been called upon, as their Governor, to furnish a portion of these troops. I have answered that demand as in my judgment became the honor of the State, and leave the people to pass upon my action.

The Federal Union of the States, thus practically dissolved, can never be restored; or if ever thus restored, it must, by the very act, cease to be a Union of free and independent States, such as our fathers established. It will become a consolidated, centralized Government, without liberty or equality, in which some will reign and others serve—the few tyrannize and the many suffer. It would be the greatest folly to hope for the reconstruction of a peaceful Union, upon terms of fraternity and equality, at the end of an internecine war. There can be no desirable Union without fraternity. And if we could not have that, before the unholy crusade which is now being waged against us, we cannot have it after they shall have wantonly imbrued their unholy hands in the innocent blood of our people, from no worthier motive than a desire to destroy our equality and subvert our liberties.

Therefore, I respectfully recommend the perfecting of an Ordinance by the General Assembly, formally declaring the independence of the State of Tennessee of the Federal Union, renouncing its authority, and re-assuming each and every function belonging to a separate sovereignty; and that said Ordinance, when it shall have been thus perfected by the Legislature, shall, at the earliest practicable time, be submitted to a vote of the people, to be by them adopted or rejected.

When the people of the State shall formally declare their connection with the remaining States of the Union dissolved, it will be a matter of the highest expediency,—I might almost say of unavoidable political necessity—that we shall at the same time, or as soon thereafter as may be, connect ourselves with those with whom a common interest, a common sympathy, and a common destiny identify us, for weal or for woe. That each of the Southern States, as they throw off their connection with the Federal Government, should take an independent position in the contest, without that concert of action which alone can be secured by political unity, is a proposition which surely no one will assent to, who anticipates the dangers of the hour and the necessity for perfect harmony in the work of our general defence.

Such a political Union with the people of the Confederate States is rendered essential, by the fact, that we have made no provision for arming, organizing, provisioning, and embodying our military forces, while the Government of the Confederate States, foreseeing this invasion, has had an eye to the necessities of the emergency, and stands prepared generously to lend us its assistance in this unprovoked and cruel struggle. If we accept that assistance, we should do it in a spirit of mutual trust and confidence, prepared to share its burdens equally, while we avail ourselves of its advantages. A Government thus perfectly organized can more thoroughly command the resources and aggregate the revenues of the country than isolated States, fighting without unity, and moving without a common and responsible head. These resources, being thus concentrated, because it is natural intuition to rally round such a Government, in such an emergency, for self-preservation and defence, can be disbursed with more efficiency, and with less cost to the people than when the revenues, necessary to support the war, are scattered by divided counsels and not controlled by a common bureau. The same may be said with regard to military operations. Unity of movement, to secure unity of purpose in attack or defence, is absolutely necessary to success. The people of the whole South, thus united by a firm political compact, moving under the direction of one Government, and animated by the sense of common perils and by a unanimous determination to maintain their rights, liberties, and institutions, are invincible, and must speedily conquer an honorable peace. The war must necessarily be protracted or brief in proportion to the union among themselves.

I, therefore, further recommend that you perfect an ordinance, with a view to our admission as a member of the Southern Confederacy, (which, it is evident, must soon embrace the entire slaveholding States of the South,) to be submitted in like manner, and at the same time, but separately, for adoption or rejection by the people; so that they may have the opportunity to approve the former and reject the latter, or adopt both, as in their wisdom may seem most consistent with the future welfare of the State. However fully satisfied the Executive and Legislature may be, as to the urgent necessity for the speedy adoption of both these propositions, it is our duty to furnish the amplest means for a fair and full expression of the popular will.

In the opening of a revolution, fraught with such consequences, and the close of which no one can foresee, it is a matter of the highest moment that we determine, as speedily as possible our future political relations, delaying only long enough to reach the will and voice of the people. Under existing circumstances, I can see no propriety for encumbering the people of the State with the election of delegates, to do that which it is your power to enable them to do directly for themselves. The most direct as well as the highest act of sovereignty, according to our theory, is that by which the people vote, not merely for men, but for measures submitted for their approval or rejection. Since it is only the voice of the people that is to be heard, there is no reason why they may not as readily and effectively express themselves upon an ordinance framed and submitted to them by the Legislature, as if submitted to them by a Convention. The Southern States, all of whom are now engaged in resistance to the encroachment of Abolition power, will necessarily encounter embarrassments, arising from a want of unity of action, until such time as they shall all be united under a common Government.

The mode of action suggested, in addition to the advantage of its being the speediest of all others, will be attended with less expense to the State, which is of far greater importance now than at any former period of our history, owing to the general embarrassment of the people, which must continue at least during these troubles, and to the heavy appropriations that you will have necessarily to make to defray the expense of our defences.

If, however, it should be deemed advisable that a Convention, representing the sovereignty of the people, should be called by the General Assembly, in preference to submitting an ordinance of independence directly to them, though I deem the latter measure more expedient, under the circumstances, I am not prepared to say that harmony and unanimity will not thus be effected. The Senators and Representatives, coming, as they do, directly from their constituents, are the best judges of this measure. It cannot be regarded other than a question of detail, inasmuch as a very large majority of the people regard themselves as being forever absolved from all obedience to a Government that has developed the coldest and most deliberate purpose to inaugurate a civil and sanguinary war among them.

I deem it proper to remark in this connection that the Constitution of the Confederate States, while it retains all that is valuable of the Constitution of the former United States, is an improvement in many essential points upon that instrument, as conceded by those even who were unfriendly to the mode and manner in which it originated.

The only additional matter to which I shall call your attention—and first in importance—is the necessity of such legislation as will put the State upon war footing immediately. I will not insult your intelligence or question your patriotism so far as to resort to argument to prove the necessity of this measure, but content myself by recommending the passage of a law regulating the raising and thorough organization of an efficient volunteer force for immediate service, in any emergency which may arise, and a thorough and perfect organization of the militia, so that in case of necessity the whole force of the State can be speedily brought into action.

In my message to your extra session in January last, I laid before you the report of the Keeper of Public Arms, showing the number, character, and condition of the arms of the State, to which I refer you for information on that subject. Since that report was made, I have ordered and received at the arsenal, fourteen hundred rifle muskets. If upon this subject further or more accurate information is desired, it shall be laid before you by the report of the proper officer.

It requires no argument from me to prove the absolute necessity of an immediate appropriation of a sum sufficient to thoroughly arm and equip such military force as the State may probably need in the prospective difficulties which lie before us. In addition to which, I respectfully recommend that you appropriate a sum sufficient to provision and maintain such force as is intended for the field, and an ample contingent military fund, to be subject to the order and disbursement of a Military Board, under such restrictions as you may see proper to impose.

The establishment of a Military Board, to consist of at least three persons, and invested with power to make all needful rules and regulations for organization and maintenance, I regard as indispensably necessary to a perfect military organization and equipment in the State, and the fact that the Legislature cannot foresee and provide for the various contingent expenses necessarily incidental to a state of war, justifies and makes necessary the contingent military fund referred to.

I trust, gentlemen, that I have not so far mistaken your intelligence and patriotism, as to render necessary that I should invoke you in the name of all that is sacred and dear to us as a people—even the sanctity of our domestic firesides—to forget past differences, and whatever may tend in the least to distract your counsels in the present momentous crisis, in which we have been involved by the unprovoked and tyrannical usurpation of a people who, forgetting the lessons of their fathers, have overthrown the fairest government upon earth, in the mere wantonness of an unnatural sectional prejudice amounting to a sectional hate, and a disregard of those great principles of justice and equality upon which the Federal Union was based. I trust that to-day there are in Tennessee no Whigs, no Democrats; but that we are one people—all patriots, all brothers, recognizing a common interest and a common destiny; and that we will stand as one man in defence of our honor and of our rights. I pray you to cultivate a feeling of this kind, and to disseminate it amongst your constituents. It is only by such united and determined action, on the part of the people of the whole South, that we can hope to avoid the calamities of the bloodiest and most devastating civil war that has afflicted any nation in the history of the civilized world.

I trust that a few days will be amply sufficient to dispose of the business which I have laid before you. Your presence may soon be needed in the field, and if not, will be required at home for counsel among your constituents.

Trusting that an All Wise Providence may watch over your deliberations, and direct you in the adoption of such measures, as may most subserve the maintenance of the rights and liberties of the people, I submit the determination of these matters to your hands.

ISHAM G. HARRIS."

Immediately after the reading of the Governor's Message, both branches of the Legislature by resolution went into secret session. The ban against public hearings, however, was lifted before the end of the session. But it was in secret session that most all of the proceedings relating to secession and the preparations for war were made. The Gov-

ernor's Message was not released for publication until nearly a week
after its delivery.[270]

One of the bases upon which Governor Harris issued the call for
an extraordinary session, so he explained, was "the bloody and tyrannical policy of the Presidential usurper [Lincoln] fully before us" who
had "wantonly inaugurated an internecine war between the people of
the slave and the non-slave holding States." One main objective for the
Legislature to consider was "to take such action as will most likely
contribute to the defence of our rights, the preservation of our liberties, the sovereignty of the State, and the safety of our people." "The
Federal Union," Governor Harris further asserted, "as established by
our fathers no longer exists." Under the present circumstances, that
Union was such that

"No intelligent and candid man can deny that it has ceased to be a
blessing, and has become a curse; that it is no longer a high and sacred
means of protection, but an engine of oppression; that it has ceased to be
a bond of brotherhood, and has become a hateful connection between communities at war."

By examination of the Governor's Message, it becomes self-evident
that he had given strict attention to details of procedure whereby his
recommendations might be enacted into law and implemented without
unnecessary delay. Instead of providing for a convention, involving the
election of delegates, the Governor proposed the adoption by the Legislature of an Ordinance of a Declaration of Independence to be submitted to a vote of the people. Coupled with this recommendation was
another providing for the admission of Tennessee into the Southern
Confederacy, a measure likewise to be submitted to a vote of the people. It was the Governor's reasoning that "the voice of the people"
could be as readily heard by voting upon an Ordinance framed and
submitted to them by the Legislature as if submitted by a Convention.
Furthermore, said he, such a procedure would decrease both delay and
expense.

On April 30, the Legislature in joint session was addressed by Henry
W. Hilliard of Alabama who had been appointed by Jefferson Davis
as a special agent to visit Tennessee. A lawyer, author, Congressman,
and diplomat with foreign experience, Mr. Hilliard regaled the legislators with a spirited address in which he expressed a decided opinion
that the pro-slavery government established at Montgomery, Alabama,
was the only possible government that could be maintained.[271] Apparently much impressed by Mr. Hilliard's plea, the Legislature on the
next day adopted the following resolution:[272]

[270] *Nashville Republican Banner*, April 30, 1861.
[271] Fertig, James W.: *The Secession and Reconstruction of Tennessee*, 24.
[272] *Senate Journal*, Second Extraordinary Session, 1861, 35.
   House Journal, Second Extraordinary Session, 1861, 42.

"*Resolved by the General Assembly of the State of Tennessee*, That the Governor be, and he is hereby authorized and requested to appoint three Commissioners on the part of Tennessee, to enter into a Military League with the authorities of the Confederate States, and with the authorities of such other slaveholding States as may wish to enter it, having in view the protection and defence of the entire South against the war that is now being carried on against it."

In compliance with the provisions of the above resolution, Governor Harris appointed Gustavus A. Henry, A. W. O. Totten, and Washington Barrow who met with Hilliard and drew up an agreement which was submitted to the Legislature for approval. Just prior to the submission of this agreement to the Legislature, the latter had enacted a law [273] submitting to a vote of the people a Declaration of Independence couched in the following phraseology:

"CHAPTER 1.

An Act to submit to a vote of the people a Declaration of Independence, and for other purposes.

SECTION 1. *Be it enacted by the General Assembly of the State of Tennessee*, That immediately after the passage of this act, the Governor of this State shall, by proclamation, direct the sheriffs of the several counties in this State to open and hold an election at the various voting precincts in their respective counties, on the 8th day of June, 1861; that said sheriffs, or in the absence of the sheriffs, the coroner of the county, shall immediately advertise the election contemplated by this act; that said sheriffs appoint a deputy to hold said election for each voting precinct, and that said deputy appoint three judges and two clerks for each precinct; and if no officer shall, from any cause, attend any voting precinct to open and hold said election, then any justice of the peace—or in the absence of a justice of the peace, any respectable *freeholder* may appoint an officer, judges and clerks to open and hold said election. Said officers, judges and clerks shall be sworn as now required by law, and who, after being so sworn, shall open and hold an election, open and close at the time of day, and in the manner now required by law in elections for members to the General Assembly.

SEC. 2. *Be it further enacted*, That at said election the following Declaration shall be submitted to a vote of the qualified voters of the State of Tennessee, for their ratification or rejection:

DECLARATION OF INDEPENDENCE AND ORDINANCE DISSOLVING THE FEDERAL RELATIONS BETWEEN THE STATE OF TENNESSEE AND THE UNITED STATES OF AMERICA.

First. We, the people of the State of Tennessee, waiving any expression of opinion as to the abstract doctrine of secession, but asserting the right, as a free and independent people, to alter, reform, or abolish, our form of Government in such manner as we think proper, do ordain and declare that all the laws and ordinances by which the State of Tennessee became a member of the Federal Union of the United States of America, are hereby

---

[273] *Acts of Tennessee*, Second Extraordinary Session, 1861, Chapter 1.

abrogated and annulled, and that all obligations on our part be withdrawn therefrom; and we do hereby resume all the rights, functions, and powers, which by any of said laws and ordinances were conveyed to the Government of the United States, and absolve ourselves from all the obligations, restraints, and duties incurred thereto; and do hereby henceforth become a free, sovereign and independent State.

Second. We furthermore declare and ordain that Article 10, sections 1 and 2 of the Constitution of the State of Tennessee, which requires members of the General Assembly, and all officers, civil and military, to take an oath to support the Constitution of the United States be, and the same are hereby abrogated and annulled; and all parts of the Constitution of the State of Tennessee, making citizenship of the United States a qualification for office, and recognizing the Constitution of the United States as the supreme law of this State, are in like manner abrogated and annulled.

Third. We furthermore ordain and declare, that all rights acquired and vested under the Constitution of the United States, or under any act of Congress passed in pursuance thereof, or under any laws of this State, and not incompatible with this ordinance, shall remain in force, and have the same effect as if this ordinance had not been passed.

SEC. 3. *Be it further enacted*, That said election shall be by ballot; that those voting for the Declaration and Ordinance shall have written or printed on their ballots, 'Separation,' and those voting against it shall have written or printed on their ballots, 'No Separation'; that the clerks holding said election shall keep regular scrolls of the voters as now required by law in the election of members to the General Assembly; that the clerks and judges shall certify the same, with the number of votes for 'Separation,' and the number of votes 'No Separation.' The officer holding the election shall return the same to the sheriff of the county, at the county seat, on the Monday next after the election. The sheriff shall immediately make out, certify, and send to the Governor the number of votes polled, and the number of votes for 'Separation,' and the number 'No Separation,' and file one of the original scrolls with the Clerk of the County Court; that upon comparing the vote by the Governor, in the office of the Secretary of State— which shall be at least by the 24th day of June, 1861, and may be sooner if the returns are all received by the Governor—if a majority of the votes polled shall be for 'Separation,' the Governor shall by his proclamation make it known, and declare all connection by the State of Tennessee with the Federal Union dissolved, and that Tennessee is a free, independent Government—free from all obligation to, or connection with the Federal Government. And that the Governor shall cause 'the vote by counties' to be published, the number for 'Separation,' and the number 'No Separation,' whether a majority votes for 'Separation,' or 'No Separation.'

SEC. 4. *Be it further enacted*, That in the election to be held under the provisions of this act, upon the Declaration submitted to the people, all volunteers and other persons connected with the service of this State, qualified to vote for members of the Legislature in the counties where they reside, shall be entitled to vote in any county in the State where they may be in active service, or under orders, or on parole, at the time of said election; and all other voters shall vote in the county where they reside, as now required by law in voting for members to the General Assembly.

SEC. 5. *Be it further enacted*, That at the same time, and under the rules and regulations prescribed for the election hereinbefore ordered, the following ordinance shall be submitted to the popular vote, to-wit:

AN ORDINANCE FOR THE ADOPTION OF THE CONSTITUTION OF THE PROVISIONAL GOVERNMENT OF THE CONFEDERATE STATES OF AMERICA.

We, the people of Tennessee, solemnly impressed by the perils which surround us, do hereby adopt and ratify the Constitution of the Provisional Government of the Confederate States of America, ordained and established at Montgomery, Alabama, on the 8th day of February, 1861, to be in force during the existence thereof, or until such time as we may supersede it by the adoption of a permanent Constitution.

SEC. 6. *Be it further enacted,* That those in favor of the adoption of said Provisional Constitution, and thereby securing to Tennessee equal representation in the deliberations and councils of the Confederate States, shall have written or printed on their ballots the word *'Representation';* those opposed, the words *'No Representation.'*

SEC. 7. *Be it further enacted,* That in the event the people shall adopt the Constitution of the Provisional Government of the Confederate States, at the election herein ordered, it shall be the duty of the Governor, forthwith to issue writs of election for delegates to represent the State of Tennessee in the said Provisional Government; that the State shall be represented by as many delegates as it was entitled to members of Congress to the recent Congress of the United States of America, who shall be elected from the several Congressional Districts as now established by law, in the mode and manner now prescribed for the election of members of the Congress of the United States.

SEC. 8. *Be it further enacted,* That this act take effect from and after its passage.

W. C. WHITTHORNE,
Speaker of the House of Representatives.

B. L. STOVALL,
Speaker of the Senate.

Passed May 6, 1861."

It will be noted that Governor Harris, in laying the foundation for the enactment of the above law, avoided making any recommendation for Secession. He was too keen a political diagnostician to inject such a controversial issue as the *right* of Secession, for he well knew that many Tennesseans had long and loudly denied the *Constitutional* right of any such action. He, therefore, adroitly and effectively laid before the Legislature a portion of the Preamble to the 1776 Declaration of Independence wherein it was declared that

"Whenever any form of government becomes destructive of these ends, it is the right of the people to alter or abolish it, and to institute a new government, laying its foundations on such principles, and organizing its powers in such form as to them shall seem most likely to effect their safety and happiness."

Had the Governor thought it expedient or necessary, he could also have referred the Legislature to the Tennessee Constitution which declared in its opening paragraph

"That all power is inherent in the people, and all free governments are founded on their authority, and instituted for their peace, safety, and happiness; for the advancement of those ends, they have, at all times, an unalienable and indefeasible right to alter, reform or abolish the government in such manner as they may think proper."

It was the *right* to REVOLT that Governor Harris advocated, and this keen analysis of *constitutional procedures* at that critical time marked him as a man of exceptionable ability. In his long and eventful political career, it is doubtful whether he ever displayed a more discerning judgment than in this Message to the Legislature on April 25, 1861. He had put out much of the fire of the anti-secessionists, because he was not advocating secession! On May 6, the Senate concurred in certain House amendments, and the bill providing for a popular vote on a Declaration of Independence became a law.

June 8 was the day fixed by the law for the election. In reality, that election was mere shadow boxing, for the terrific change in public sentiment made the outcome sure and certain.

On the day following the enactment of the above law, the Legislature received a Message from Governor Harris recommending the adoption of a Military League entered into by and between the Commissioner of the Confederate States and the Tennessee Commissioners appointed by Governor Harris. Three quick, successive steps were taken on May 7, namely: (1) acceptance of the terms of the Military League; (2) the Governor's recommendation that the Military League be adopted; and (3) the enactment of a law [274] in compliance with the Governor's request.

Curiously enough, the Governor's Message, the Military League, and the Resolution ratifying the League were consolidated into one bill and enacted into law in that manner. Here they are: [275]

"CHAPTER 2.
MESSAGE OF THE GOVERNOR.

Executive Department, ⎫
Nashville May 7, 1861. ⎭

GENTLEMEN OF THE SENATE AND HOUSE OF REPRESENTATIVES:

By virtue of the authority of your joint resolution, adopted on the 1st day of May inst., I appointed Gustavus A. Henry, of the county of Montgomery, Archibald O. W. Totten, of the county of Madison, and Washington Barrow, of the county of Davidson, 'Commissioners on the part of Tennessee, to enter into a Military League with the authorities of the Confederate States, and with the authorities of such other slaveholding States as may wish to enter into it, having in view the protection and defence of the entire South against the war that is now being carried on against it.'

---

[274] *Acts of Tennessee,* Second Extraordinary Session, 1861, Chapter 2.
[275] *Ibid.*

The said Commissioners met the Hon. Henry W. Hilliard, the accredited representative of the Confederate States, at Nashville on this day, and have agreed upon and executed a Military League between the State of Tennessee and the Confederate States of America, subject, however, to the ratification of the two Governments; one of the duplicate originals of which I herewith transmit for your ratification or rejection. For many cogent and obvious reasons, unnecessary to be rehearsed to you, I respectfully recommend the ratification of this League at the earliest practicable moment.

Very respectfully,

ISHAM G. HARRIS.

CONVENTION BETWEEN THE STATE OF TENNESSEE AND THE CONFEDERATE STATES OF AMERICA.

The State of Tennessee looking to a speedy admission into the Confederacy established by the Confederate States of America, in accordance with the Constitution for the Provisional Government of said States, enters into the following temporary Convention, Agreement and Military League, with the Confederate States, for the purpose of meeting pressing exigencies affecting the common rights, interests, and safety of said States, and said Confederacy.

First. Until the said State shall become a member of said Confederacy according to the Constitution of both powers, the whole military force, and military operations, offensive and defensive of said State, in the impending conflict with the United States, shall be under the chief control and direction of the President of the Confederate States, upon the same basis, principles and footing, as if said State were now, and during the interval a member of said Confederacy, said force, together with that of the Confederate States, to be employed for the common defence.

Second. The State of Tennessee will, upon becoming a member of said Confederacy under the Permanent Constitution of said Confederate States, if the same shall occur, turn over to said Confederate States, all the public property acquired from the United States, on the same terms, and in the same manner as the other States of said Confederacy have done in like cases.

Third. Whatever expenditures of money, if any, the said State of Tennessee shall make before she becomes a member of said Confederacy, shall be met and provided for by the Confederate States.

This Convention entered into and agreed, in the city of Nashville, Tennessee, on the seventh day of May, A. D., 1861, by Henry W. Hilliard, the duly authorized commissioner, to act in the matter of the Confederate States, and Gustavus A. Henry, Archibald O. W. Totten, and Washington Barrow, commissioners duly authorized to act in like manner for the State of Tennessee—the whole subject to the approval and ratification of the proper authorities of both Governments respectively.

In testimony whereof, the parties aforesaid have herewith set their hands and seals, the day and year aforesaid, in duplicate originals.

HENRY W. HILLIARD, [Seal.]
Commissioner for the Confederate States of America.

GUSTAVUS A. HENRY, [Seal.]

A. O. W. TOTTEN, [Seal.]

WASHINGTON BARROW, [Seal.]
Commissioners on the part of Tennessee."

It will be observed that the Military League in three brief paragraphs provided that said League was to continue in effect until Tennessee was admitted into the Southern Confederacy. In the meanwhile, Tennessee was to turn over its entire military and military operations to the direction of the President of the Confederate States. Upon becoming a member of the Confederacy, Tennessee also agreed to turn over to the Confederacy all property acquired from the United States. Whatever expenses were incurred by Tennessee during the transition period were to be reimbursed by the Confederacy. This agreement, in practical effect, made Tennessee a part of the Southern Confederacy, although its people were yet to go through the motion of an election a month later for the purpose of signifying its approval or disapproval of the legislative action.

As a means of implementing the actual and prospective war legislation, the Legislature on May 6 passed an act for raising, organizing, and equipping a provisional army of fifty-five thousand volunteers "for the defence of the State." [276] The Governor was directed to take charge of the military forces, the support of which was to be provided by the sale of five million dollars of State bonds. The State was obligated to pay eight per cent interest on the bonds, the payment of interest to be raised by an eight-cent tax annually on each one hundred dollars of taxable property and one-half cent on each dollar of merchandise "whether bought in or out of the State of Tennessee." The Governor, as Chairman of a Military and Financial Board which he was authorized to appoint, was the agency authorized to administer the military fund. Other and numerous duties were outlined and authorized in the 41-Section law.

There is internal evidence that the members of the Legislature were aware that unprecedented steps had been taken by them, one of which consisted of holding *secret* sessions. In order to explain such action and the reason therefor, resort was had to the appointment of a joint committee to prepare an address to the people of Tennessee. On April 30, the resolution providing for the appointment of the committee was adopted, and on May 9 the address was adopted by both branches of the General Assembly.[277] The address, of which ten thousand copies were ordered to be printed for distribution, was as follows:[278]

"LEGISLATIVE ADDRESS TO THE PEOPLE OF TENNESSEE.

Fellow-Citizens: The extraordinary legislation forced upon the General Assembly, by the necessities of the times, makes it not inappropriate that

---

[276] *Ibid.*, Chapter 3.
[277] *Senate Journal*, Second Extraordinary Session, 1861, 91.
     House Journal, Second Extraordinary Session, 1861, 97.
[278] *Senate Journal*, Second Extraordinary Session, 1861, 83–91.
     House Journal, Second Extraordinary Session, 1861, 97-105.

your Representatives should present some of the reasons which have influenced their action.

The Joint Select Committee, under the direction and with the approval of the Assembly, beg leave to submit the following statement to the calm judgment and consideration of their constituents:

The present session was called for by the Executive authority to dispose of more important questions than ever had engaged the attention of a Tennessee Legislature; the members of the two Houses could but feel most sensibly the responsibilities of their positions, well knowing that their action would not only affect the present, but the future destinies of the State. They had no interest to subserve apart from those of their constituents, and whatever may be the result of their labors, whether for good or evil, it will fall alike upon themselves and those whom they represent.

The election of a sectional President by an unreasoning appeal to numerical superiority, precipitated a crisis in the Government which many wise men anticipated and patriots would have gladly adjourned to another and far distant period. Several of the slaveholding States, upon the happening of this event, commenced preparations for leaving a Union which in their judgments, promised to become an instrument of destruction to the constitutional rights of the South. The excitement consequent upon the action of these States produced a necessity for the last extra session of this body, and the proposition for calling a Convention was submitted to the people. It was by them determined that no Convention should be held, thus giving the assurance of a fixed purpose to abide by the Union so long as a hope of safety or protection remained to them. A peace Congress was called for, and anxious to give every evidence of a sincere desire to settle existing difficulties, prudent and discreet men were sent to confer with delegates from other States. The Congress resulted in a failure, as did the faithful efforts of Southern men in the Congress of the United States. To every proposition a deaf ear was turned by the party in power. These ominous failures to come to an adjustment, while they weakened, did not dispel altogether the hope of a peaceable solution of existing troubles. It was believed that the masses of the Northern people would do justice to the demands of the South, if not prevented by the arts of their politicians. Subsequent acts prove that the masses are, if possible, more bitter in their hostility to the South than their leaders.

The inaugural address of the newly-elected President, however doubtful in its terms, was charitably construed into a message of peace. It was considered absurd to suppose that any President of a free country would ever venture upon the mad experiment of holding sovereign States together by means of the bayonet. No one not blinded by fanaticism, can fail to recognize the fact that a government based upon the popular will can only be maintained in its integrity by appealing to that powerful and controlling influence. Force, when attempted, changes the whole character of the Government; making it a military despotism, and those that submit become the abject slaves of power. The people of Tennessee have fully understood this important fact, and hence their anxiety to stay the hand of coercion. They well know that the subjugation of the seceded States involved their own destruction, and that, however plausible the pretext, an enforcement of the laws against an unwilling people had been the exercise of tyrants in every age of the world. That the people of the South were, many of them, deceived in the pretended peace policy of Lincoln, is not a matter of surprise or astonishment. The duplicity and double-dealing of this miserable tyrant, finds no parallel save in the corrupt governments of the dark ages, and would disgrace the diplomatic policy of a barbarian chieftain. A few facts will suffice to make good our assertions. To Southern Senators that approached him, he verbally construed his own inaugural into a peace document.

He caused it to be given out that he would abandon Fort Sumter, when at the very time he was privately preparing a powerful armament for its relief.

Under false pretences, he introduced an officer into Fort Sumter, who took advantage of the privilege to concert a plan of relief with the commandant of that fortress.

Congress refused to vote a dollar for the prosecution of hostilities against the people of the South; he and his agents got the appropriation by falsehood, pretending that it was needed to pay off the Government debts, and instead of so using it, fails to pay even the maimed and wounded soldier his pension, or the hard-working census-taker his salary, but scatters it among a brutal soldiery, whom he has hired to murder Southern freemen and to desecrate Southern soil.

Congress refused to pass a coercion bill, yet this contemptible usurper proclaims war against the South in defiance of the Constitution, in violation of his oath and his oft-repeated and positive pledges to the contrary.

Congress would not authorize the call for a single soldier, yet, in the face of the laws and the Constitution, this petty tyrant calls for armies of immense magnitude to march against peaceful and unoffending citizens.

He assured Tennessee members of Congress that his policy would be peaceful; his Premier, W. H. Seward, announced such to be the purpose of his Cabinet on every occasion; and yet, after lulling the people to repose, he impudently called upon the Governor of Tennessee for troops to follow his standard in a war of subjugation against their own native section.

The Mississippi river is declared to be free by the Constitution of Tennessee, and yet this vile usurper stations troops at Cairo to obstruct the navigation of this great highway and its tributaries, and these miserable instruments are now engaged in making war upon the commerce of non-seceding States.

Tennessee, ever loyal to the Constitution, has been an advocate for peace, and has struggled to bring together the broken fragments of the Union, yet in the midst of her well meant efforts, a war is made upon her; every avenue of trade is closed up, and the people are suffering all the privations of a blockade. Not even provisions, demanded by the necessities of the people, are allowed to be shipped into the State, and property of private individuals is made subject to piratical and illegal seizure. Boats have been plundered of their cargoes by authority of the Government, and when called on for an explanation by the Governor of Tennessee, even the honor of a reply is refused.

The States that desired to live in the Union, and to be on terms of friendship with all, are insultingly told that neutrality is impossible, and that they must aid in this ungodly war of subjugation, or else suffer the penalties. Had Tennessee ever desired to remain neutral, the miserable and degrading privilege is denied to her by the tyrants that assume to rule in the name of the Constitution.

The Confederate States sought for peace, and sent their agents to the Federal capital to consummate that object. They were assured that peace would be made, and while resting under the belief that they were dealing with honorable men, Lincoln and his Cabinet were secretly collecting an immense armament for the relief of Fort Sumter. It is a matter of no importance who fired the first gun in the attack on Fort Sumter, the war commenced when a hostile fleet set sail upon its mission of death.

Lincoln pretends in his inaugural that his only object is to protect the property of the nation, yet he organizes immense armies all along the lines of the border slave States, commissions them to seize and take the property of private citizens, holds Maryland in subjugation by the aid of her treacherous Governor and his armed hirelings, and converts the Federal capital into an entrenched camp, and subjects it to all the rigors of martial law.

We ask, if a man marked by every attribute that can disgrace a usurping tyrant and a false hearted hypocrite, should be permitted to control for a day, or an hour, the destinies of a free people? In this state of affairs the Legislature assembled at Nashville. The Governor had defiantly refused to call out a man to prosecute a war of subjugation, and had also refused to issue a writ of election for members to Congress. We were bound to recognize the fact that war had been already made upon the State, that for all practical purposes Tennessee was out of the Union, and every act of legislation has been based upon that palpable state of affairs. The Legislature endorsed and approved the action of the Executive. He could have pursued no other course without disgrace to himself and dishonor to his State. These resolutions are submitted along with this report.

Tennessee is unarmed, and the first great object was to organize the military and adopt every means of defence within our power, menaced as our county is by armies of alarming magnitude. Our western borders exposed to attack, with life, liberty and property staked upon the issue, it is no time to think of half-way measures. The money and the blood of Tennessee will be called for in no stinted quantities, if it be necessary to protect the priceless heritage of freedom that we possess, and which we hold as a sacred trust for our children. The military bill is also submitted with this address to the judgment of our constituents. Tennessee is now politically isolated from all of her sisters. She has no voice in any of their counsels. She will not disgrace her fair escutcheon by sending delegates to a Government that has made war against her, and where they are compelled to vote and speak with the glittering bayonets of a brutal soldiery gleaming around them. Our proud State will never seek to be represented in the counsels of its enemies and where wild fanaticism holds its infernal orgies over the mutilated and mouldering corpse of a once noble Republic. In the present dangerous attitude, we felt it to be due to ourselves, to the honor and safety of the State, and to the imperious demands of our constituents, that an opportunity should be promptly furnished for cutting loose every real or supposed tie that binds the people to the Lincoln Government, and to enable them by a vote at the ballot box to form other political relations, if it were so desired. In conformity with these obligations of duty, the Legislature has prepared two instruments to be voted upon by the people, on Saturday, the 8th of June.

Upon the first proposition the people will vote for or against separation from the old Confederacy. By the second proposition you will decide for or against a political union with the Confederate States. Both are submitted along with this address. The proposition for a union adopts the provisional, and *not* the permanent Constitution of those States; this Constitution is also submitted to the people. The Legislature has done what has already been done by Virginia, and will no doubt be the policy of North Carolina, and in the company of these time honored Commonwealths, Tennessee need entertain no fears for her own safety. If objections are found to the permanent Constitution, they can be removed as a condition of continued union with those States.

In submitting these two grave questions to the popular judgment, the Legislature dispensed with all intermediate agencies, preferring to go at once to the great source of all political power—*the people themselves*. The delays, embarrassments and expense of a convention are thus avoided. Nothing is left to trickery or political management. You can say whether you desire to separate from the old Government; you can also declare at the ballot box whether you desire to unite the fortunes of the State along with Virginia, North Carolina and Arkansas to the new Confederacy. By two words—*'separation'* or *'no separation,'* 'representation' or 'no representation,' you will decide the whole question and fix the future destinies of the State. A convention can do no more, though in session for weeks or months. Whatever be your decision it will be conclusive, and from it there *can be no appeal*. The Legislature has no power to put Tennessee out of the Union, nor to place it among the Confederate States; that body has the authority to order an election, which it has done, and it is to be sincerely hoped that *every voter* in Tennessee will be found at the polls on the day appointed by the Legislature.

We remark before passing from this subject, that while differences of opinion exist as to the abstract right of secession, no one denies the right of a people to *revolutionize*. The right to 'change, alter or abolish,' their form of government is a principle engrafted in the fundamental laws of the State. Your representatives have therefore steered clear of the mooted question of secession, and submitted a revolutionary document, which, if ratified by the popular vote, will sever the ties that bind Tennessee to her enemies and oppressors, and *that*, after all, is the object to be attained, by whatever name it may be called.

The military league which has been formed with the Southern Confederacy is also submitted with this address. It was a measure of safety imperiously demanded by the war that has been made upon our State. In accomplishing this object we have fallen back upon the lessons of our ancestors, and regarded the promptings of self-preservation in forming alliances when different parties are threatened with a common danger. Our State is *unarmed;* we must have weapons placed in the hands of our volunteers to defend the freedom of the South. The Confederate States can *aid us* in this all-important matter. We must have a common head to direct the armies of freedom. Those States furnish in their Chief Magistrate, a soldier who has proven his capacity to lead upon the hardest fought battle fields known to the history of American warfare. Our people must be relieved, too, from the burden of keeping up a separate and distinct military organization. By the terms of this contract, it will be seen that the expenses of the State are to be transferred to the common Confederacy that the South is forming, and will be paid from the fruitful sources of impost duties levied upon commerce when peace is established.

This league places Tennessee where she deserves to stand—in company with the old States of Virginia, North Carolina, South Carolina and Georgia, whose histories are redolent with the glories of past struggles for liberty, and whose sons are now prepared to stand upon their ancient battlefields to emulate the deeds of their ancestors. This alliance places the State, too, in close compact with the younger States of the South, with whom it is indispensably connected by a thousand ties.

It is gratifying to know the league referred to meets the approval of men entertaining heretofore all shades of opinion. Let it be remembered, that the Legislature, impelled as it was, by imperious necessity, in the formation of this alliance, is only the more confident in the correctness of its policy by the conscious belief that it has formed for the State no ignoble or degrading association. Whatever may be thought of the action of the States that have left the Union, in regard to their supposed precipitancy, all must admit that their legislative action has been marked by sound conservatism and profound statesmanship. These States have ventured upon no new or untried experiment in the formation of their Government; they have wisely refrained from making a new Constitution, but have piously adopted the one framed by the authors of independence, and under which Tennessee has always abided as a State—some alterations and changes have been made, but only such as time and experience had suggested as important improvements. It may be truthfully *averred* that the *Constitution of the United States is now* the permanent Constitution of the Confederate States; that noble instrument has no existence in any other State or Government. It has been superseded in the North by a military despotism; it no longer shields the people of Tennessee; but this admirable framework of freedom, still regarded as the ark of political safety, and strengthened in its massive proportions, has been erected upon Southern soil, and under its broad aegis generations of freemen will repose in safety.

It is painful to reflect that Tennessee has no representation in any national or confederate council; her gallant soldiers will go forth to battle for a common cause, and but for a short time, at least, her voice cannot be heard, only through the ballot box in June.

It is submitted that Tennessee has but one of two alternatives—either to attempt to maintain a distinct and separate nationality, or to unite with the other States of the South. If you decide on the former, provisions should at once be made for new departments of government. A Post Office and a Department of Foreign Affairs will be necessary, besides other arrangements peculiar to a separate nationality. We ask if the people will not be at once crushed by the burthens of taxation? The idea of a Border State Confederacy must be abandoned. The free States embraced in this plan are the first to lead off for Southern subjugation. Through their Governors they have proclaimed that there is no such thing as neutrality, and have already impudently demanded that Kentucky shall take the field against the slaveholding States. With them Tennessee can have *no Union*. It is to be hoped that a military league that has been already commenced in the South will be promptly formed with the States of Kentucky, Maryland and Missouri. They demand our sympathies and will receive our support if required. Missouri is an unarmed giant, but will respond to the calls of the South as soon as she finds that the other States are ready to come to her aid. Through the action of a treacherous Governor, Maryland has been manacled by the chains of the tyrant. The heart of the South is with her, and its sons stand ready to drive the invaders from her soil, and to give to her the rights that traitors and usurpers are seeking to destroy. Our noble and gallant neighbor, Kentucky, is an unarmed knight, confronted by the reckless assassin whose dagger is ready to be driven to his heart. The State of Tennessee, the whole South, will offer their sons to the gallant State, and who now stand ready to pour out their blood as a rich libation upon the altars of the dark and bloody ground. Let past differences, fellow-citizens, be forgotten in this hour of common danger, and let us work for a united South. Though our enemies are strong, and united in their unholy purposes, yet standing upon our own side, and defending our altars and our friends, the cause is *too sacred* to be lost. God will prosper the right; that Being who defended the fathers will not desert their children while unitedly battling for the inalienable rights of man.

When this body met, it determined to sit with closed doors. We are aware that this mode of legislation is objected to by some. It is the first time in the history of the State that the rule had been adopted, because in that history no case had occurred to call forth its exercise. The proceedings of the convention that framed the Declaration of Independence were in *secret*. The convention that framed the *Constitution of the United States*, held its secret sessions, and the Senate of the United States not unfrequently sits with closed doors. Those who have taken occasion to condemn *us*, may be purer than those who framed the Declaration of Independence, and the Constitution of the United States; but we very much doubt whether they will have a greater hold upon public confidence. But the reasons for our course are our best justification: the country was excited, and the public demands imperious. We desired to legislate uninfluenced and unretarded by the crowds that would otherwise have attended our deliberations; but still more important than this, the western portion of Tennessee 'was in an *exposed condition*, with *no* military defence whatever; the towns and counties bordering on the Mississippi river were liable to be assailed at any hour by the armed forces collected at Cairo, and we desired that no act of legislation on our part, should form the pretext for such an invasion, so long as it could be avoided. Our fellow-citizens of West Tennessee, and of Arkansas, are laboring night and day to erect batteries on the river to prevent a descent of the enemy. A duty that we owed to them and to the cause of humanity demanded that we should not make our action known till the latest possible moment. If some desired light, while we were at work, we equally desired to save the blood and the property of Tennesseans. Our doors have now been thrown open, the Journals will be published—every *vote* is recorded, and he must be a *fault-finder* indeed who will complain after hearing the reasons that prompted our actions.

We have briefly touched the principal subjects that engaged the attention of the Legislature. Tennessee has taken her position and has proudly determined to throw her banners to the breeze, and will give her strength to the sacred cause of freedom for the WHITE MAN OF THE SOUTH.

> R. G. PAYNE,
> *Chairman of Joint Select Committee.*
> EDMUND J. WOOD,
> S. S. STANTON,
> J. A. MINNIS,
> G. GANTT,
> W. W. GUY,
> ROBT. B. HURT,
> BENJ. J. LEA,
> JOSEPH G. PICKETT."

After the reading and adoption of the above address, Governor Harris transmitted to the Legislature for confirmation a list of military appointments.[279] The "top brass" specified for Majors General the

---

[279] *Senate Journal*, Second Extraordinary Session, 1861, 95–96.
House Journal, Second Extraordinary Session, 1861, 107–108.

names of Gideon J. Pillow and Samuel R. Anderson; for Brigadiers General, Felix K. Zollicoffer, Benjamin F. Cheatham, Robert C. Foster 3rd, John L. T. Sneed, and William R. Caswell.[280] Behind closed doors, the above nominations along with numerous subordinate officers were confirmed without discussion or division. At the same time, the nominations for members of the Military and Financial Board were confirmed, the same being ex-Governor Neill S. Brown, James E. Bailey, and William G. Harding. With the adoption of the address and the confirmation of the various officers recommended by Governor Harris, the Legislature on May 9 declared itself in adjournment until June 17, presumably awaiting the outcome of the voting by the people on the question of "separation" or "no separation" at the election on June 8.

Between the date of adjournment of the Legislature and the date of the election, approximately one month intervened and, theoretically at least, Tennessee was not as yet a member of the Southern Confederacy. But practically speaking, the converse was true. Under the dominant influence of Governor Harris, action by an aroused people would indicate that the June vote on "separation" had already taken place and the issue settled in favor of separation. The Governor was as busy as a beaver, among other things seeking to form an alliance with the Governor of Kentucky whereby a line of defense would be erected from Memphis to Columbus, Kentucky, thus sealing off from the enemy the Mississippi River as a line of communication and transportation. By the latter part of April, Fort Harris was being built some few miles above Memphis under the direction of an officer of the Confederate Army. Volunteer companies were being received into military service. On May 1, the Speaker of the Senate resigned the speakership "in order to meet engagements as a volunteer in the military defence of the South,"[281] though he continued to serve as a member until *sine die* adjournment. Near the end of May, some half-dozen batteries manned by ten companies of Tennesseans had been erected along the shores of the Mississippi River. General Gideon J. Pillow was in command of some fifteen thousand troops in West Tennessee, and a considerable number of volunteer troops were stationed in camps in both Middle and East Tennessee.

Such beehive activity could be only construed as a true harbinger of things to come at the June election. Two-thirds of the State were

---

[280] *Ibid.*

Author's note. The Governor's Message, containing the full list of nominations, may be found in the legislative *Journals* on the pages listed in the foregoing citation. On June 28, 1861, Governor Harris submitted a supplementary list of recommended appointments for military service as appears on pages 169–172 of the *Senate Journal* and pages 188–191 of the *House Journal*. For the reader's convenience, the complete list of names as recommended in the two above messages may be found in the Appendix of this volume.

[281] *Senate Journal*, Second Extraordinary Session, 1861, 36-37.

predominantly pro-Confederate in sentiment. Passionate speeches, fever-heat newspaper editorials, parades, and demonstrations became the order of the day. The ladies joined the processions, and waved hands and handkerchiefs hysterically. Supporters of the Union in East Tennessee, however, acted in strong contrast to the other two sections of the State. Heartened by the fact that East Tennessee had voted overwhelmingly in the February election for Unionism, herculean efforts to keep it so were put forth by strong Union leaders like Andrew Johnson, Thomas A. R. Nelson, Thomas D. Arnold, Oliver Perry Temple, and "Parson" Brownlow whose *Knoxville Whig* declared that the people of Tennessee were on the verge of being swallowed by "a military despotism more odious than any now existing in any monarchy of Europe."[282] In an effort to checkmate the Union leaders in East Tennessee, the pro-Southern board of strategy dispatched to that region "The Eagle Orator," Gustavus A. Henry, a former Whig candidate for Governor, Henry S. Foote, and the former bellwether of whiggery, John Bell. These leaders served to reinforce such East Tennessee pro-Southern Democrats as the eloquent Landon C. Haynes.

Unquestionably terrific pressure was put upon the voters. As is characteristic of most hard-fought political contests, charges and counter-charges of coercion and downright fraud were launched by partisans on each side. The lopsided vote in certain counties seems to indicate that chicanery may have been "present and voting." Shelby County, including Memphis, out of a total vote of more than seven thousand yielded only five votes for "no separation." Its nearby neighbor, Lauderdale, reported only seven votes for Unionism. Only five West Tennessee counties, Carroll, Decatur, Hardin, Henderson, and Weakley, returned majorities for the Union. West Tennessee was for separation by a ratio of more than four to one. Middle Tennessee was strongly for "separation," the ratio being seven to one. Three counties in this area reported not a solitary vote for Unionism, namely, Franklin, Lincoln, and Humphreys. In East Tennessee it was altogether a different story, for Unionism triumphed by a more than two-to-one ratio. Taking the State as a whole, the vote for alignment with the Southern Confederacy was impressive and decisive, the majority vote being in the neighborhood of fifty-five thousand.[283]

---

[282] *Knoxville Whig*, May 11, 1861.

[283] Author's note. The actual vote will likely never be known. Exhaustive research in the State Archives failed to locate the original election returns. Recourse was had to contemporary newspapers and historical works. Below are listed figures as given by the indicated sources regarding the vote on SECESSION.

Source	Separation	No Separation
Nashville Republican Banner, June 26, 1861.	104,913	47,238
Nashville Union and American, June 25, 1861.	102,172	47,238
Nashville Patriot, June 25, 1861.	102,177	47,238

As may be noted in the foregoing footnote, the newspaper tabulations ranged from a vote of 102,172 to 108,457. The differential is largely accounted for in the conflicting figures reported by the vote in military camps, varying from 2,711 to 6,241. The *Nashville Union and American* and the *Nashville Patriot* are substantially in agreement, there being a variable of only five votes. Since the two above papers, with a minor exception in one county, are in agreement on the vote, by counties, their tabulations for the respective counties are presented as a sort of "compromise" tabulation. The Governor's Proclamation and the results of the election were as follows:

"PROCLAMATION.

By ISHAM G. HARRIS, Governor of the State of Tennessee

To all whom these presents shall come, greeting:

WHEREAS—By an Act of the General Assembly of the State of Tennessee, passed 6th May, 1861, an election on the 8th day of June, 1861, was held in the several counties of the State, in accordance therewith, upon the Ordinance of Separation and Representation; and also, whereas, it appears from the official returns of said election (hereto appended) that the people of the State of Tennessee have in their sovereign will and capacity, by an overwhelming majority, cast their votes for 'Separation,' dissolving all political connection with the late United States Government, and adopted the Provisional Government of the Confederate States of America:

Now, therefore, I, Isham G. Harris, Governor of the State of Tennessee, do 'make it known and declare all connection by the State of Tennessee with the Federal Union dissolved, and that Tennessee is a free, independent government, free from all obligation to

Source	Separation	No Separation
Nashville Daily Gazette, June 26, 1861.	102,172	47,238
Memphis Daily Appeal, June 22, 1861.	108,457	48,093
Brownlow's Knoxville Whig, July 13, 1861.	102,672	47,238
Alexander: *Thomas A. R. Nelson of East Tennessee,* 83.	102,172	47,238
Miller: *Official Manual of Tennessee,* 43.	104,913	47,238
Hamer: *Tennessee-A History,* Volume II, 550.	108,511	47,238
Moore: *Tennessee—The Volunteer State,* Volume 1, 471.	104,913	47,238
Fertig: *Secession and Reconstruction of Tennessee,* 27.	104,913	47,238
Patton: *Unionism and Reconstruction in Tennessee,* 21.	108,399	47,233
Hale and Merritt: *Tennessee and Tennesseans,* Volume III, 576.	104,913	47,238
Goodspeed: *History of Tennessee,* 534.	108,511	47,338
Foster and Roberts: *Tennessee Democracy,* Volume II, 274.	104,913	47,238

or connection with the Federal Government' of the United States of America.

In testimony whereof, I have hereunto set my hand and caused the great seal of the State to be affixed at the department in Nashville, on this, the 24th day of June, A. D. 1861.

ISHAM G. HARRIS.

By the Governor.

J. E. R. RAY, Secretary of State.

Election Returns for June 8, 1861

East Tennessee	Separation	No Separation
Anderson	97	1278
Bledsoe	197	500
Blount	418	1766
Bradley	507	1382
Campbell	59	1000
Carter	86	1343
Claiborne	250	1243
Cocke	518	1185
Grainger	586	1492
Greene	744	2691
Hamilton	854	1260
Hancock	279	630
Hawkins	908	1460
Jefferson	603	1987
Johnson	111	787
Knox	1226	3196
Marion	414	600
McMinn	904	1144
Meigs	481	267
Monroe	1096	774
Morgan	50	630
Polk	738	317
Rhea	360	202
Roane	454	1568
Scott	19	521
Sequatchie	153	100
Sevier	60	1528
Sullivan	1586	627
Washington	1022	1445
Total	14,780	32,923
Middle Tennessee		
Bedford	1595	727
Cannon	1149	127
Cheatham	702	55
Coffee	1276	26
Davidson	5635	402
DeKalb	833	642

Middle Tennessee	Separation	No Separation
Dickson	1141	72
Fentress	128	651
Franklin	1652	0
Giles	2458	11
Grundy	528	9
Hickman	1400	3
Humphreys	1042	0
Jackson	1483	714
Lawrence	1124	75
Lewis	223	14
Lincoln	2912	0
Macon	447	697
Marshall	1642	101
Maury	2731	58
Montgomery	2631	33
Overton	1471	364
Robertson	3839	17
Rutherford	2392	73
Smith	1249	676
Stewart	1839	99
Sumner	6465	69
Van Buren	308	13
Warren	1419	12
Wayne	409	905
White	1370	121
Williamson	1945	28
Wilson	2329	353
Total	57,767	7,147

West Tennessee		
Benton	798	228
Carroll	967	1349
Decatur	310	550
Dyer	811	116
Fayette	1364	23
Gibson	1999	286
Hardeman	1526	29
Hardin	498	1051
Haywood	930	139
Henderson	801	1013
Henry	1746	317
Lauderdale	763	7
Madison	2754	20
McNairy	1318	586
Obion	2996	64
Perry	780	168
Shelby	7132*	5
Tipton	943	16
Weakley	1189	1201
Total	29,625	7,168

* According to the *Nashville Patriot* the Shelby County vote was 7137.

RECAPITULATION

	Separation	No Separation
East Tennessee	14,780	32,923
Middle Tennessee	57,767	7,147
West Tennessee	29,625	7,168
Totals	102,172	47,238"

The decisive vote of June 8 was, in reality, a mere ratification by the people of what had already taken place under the leadership and influence of Governor Harris. It would not be amiss to assert that Governor Harris and the Legislature, by the action of May 6, had pulled off a real *coup d' état* which, in practical results, transferred Tennessee from the Union to the Southern Confederacy. Only certain formalities remained to be consummated. On July 22, 1861, Tennessee was admitted to membership in the Confederate States of America.[284]

With the results of the election before them, the Legislature reassembled on June 17 pursuant to adjournment on May 9. Two new faces appeared in the membership of the reconvened General Assembly, Senator Washington Barrow of Davidson County replaced Senator John Trimble who had resigned and Representative Ira P. Jones of Davidson County replaced Representative Edward H. East, resigned. After notification had been transmitted to Governor Harris that the Legislature had reconvened and was ready for the transaction of public business, the Executive sent the following Message:*

"EXECUTIVE DEPARTMENT,
Nashville, June 18, 1861.

GENTLEMEN OF THE SENATE AND HOUSE OF REPRESENTATIVES:

Since your adjournment on the 9th of the last month, the people of Tennessee, acting in their sovereign capacity, and in the exercise of an inalienable right, have, in the most solemn and deliberate manner dissolved their connection with the Government of the United States, and by the adoption of the Provisional Constitution of the Confederate States of America, have made Tennessee a member of that Government.

I pause in the midst of the arduous duties which devolve upon me, to congratulate you and the country upon the near approach of unanimity, and the readiness with which the brave and patriotic people of our proud commonwealth have severed their connection

---

[284] *Journal of the Confederate Congress*, I, 272.
   * *Acts of Tennessee*, Second Extraordinary Session, 1861, 11–14.
   Senate Journal, Second Extraordinary Session, 1861, 103–106.
   House Journal, Second Extraordinary Session, 1861, 115–118.

with a Government endeared to them by so many recollections, and to which they had been so long attached, but which has been subverted by gross usurpations and converted into an engine of oppression, destructive of their rights, liberties and equality, and which in the mere wantonness of its boasted power, demands that these inalienable attributes of freemen shall be promptly—nay, basely surrendered or maintained at the point of the bayonet.

Those who have read and comprehended the patriotic devotion of our people to the eternal principles of justice, equality, and right, their native love of independence, and their chivalrous deeds in defence of those principles, as shown by the whole history of the State, could not have doubted as to the position that Tennessee would occupy upon the presentation of such an issue.

While it is to me a source of regret that entire unanimity was not attained at the ballot-box, in the decision of the vitally important and exciting questions referred to, I have entire confidence that now the deliberate and impartial judgment of the overwhelming majority of the people of the State having been recorded, the whole people, forgetting these differences of opinion, however earnestly and honestly entertained, will stand together as one man in maintaining the rights, honor and dignity of Tennessee, and in preserving the domestic tranquility of the community. The time for crimination and re-crimination has passed; threatened by a common enemy, imperiled by a common danger, bound together by ties which cannot be severed, we are identical in interest, we must be so in action.

The State of Tennessee, co-operating with her sister States of the South, has been compelled to take up arms in defence of rights she could not surrender. To this war thus forced upon us, there can be but two sides. I cannot believe that there is any portion of our people who will espouse the cause of the enemies of Tennessee, or be indifferent spectators of the contest.

Impartial history will attest that no free people, jealous of their rights, have been more observant of their constitutional duties, or more loyal to their Government. Exacting no peculiar privileges, they have at all times been ready to acknowledge and maintain the rights of others. In times of common peril they have always stood firm and contributed their full proportion of talent, both to the Cabinet and the field, and now that we have exhausted the last remedy, have made the last appeal to the reason and justice of those who would oppress us, and have been driven to the necessity of taking our rights into our own hands and defying the power that assails them, there certainly cannot be a part of our people who will not spurn the usurper and resist him to the last extremity.

In the midst of the gloom and privations necessarily incidental to a state of war, let us console ourselves with the reflection that we occupy the same relation to posterity that our fathers of the first revolution occupied to us.

They enjoyed the glorious privilege of establishing the great principle, which secured to us civil and religious liberty, and political equality; while it is our privilege and solemn duty to maintain and transmit to posterity the same great principle unimpaired.

The spirit and determination manifested by the people of the whole South, to maintain this principle against the tyranny of usurpation, gives the highest and most cheering assurance that America will still be the abiding place of self-government and free institutions; and proves the truth of the long disputed theory of our fathers, that a brave and enlightened people, educated in the doctrine of individual and State equality, are capable, and of right, ought to govern themselves. In the midst of federal revolution, perfect order has been preserved in our State Government; in the moment of dissolving our former federal fabric, another, new, and of perfect and enduring proportions, is reared, leaving us at no time without the full benefit of Government, or the security of laws.

The new relations which we have assumed, in becoming a part of the Provisional Government of the Confederate States, imposes the necessity of some additional legislation. I cheerfully submit to your consideration all questions pertaining to our federal relations, for such legislation as may be necessary to us as a part of that Government.

There has been, for many years, a statute in the State defining the crime of treason, and prescribing the punishment.

I respectfully recommend that you amend that law to the extent of striking out the words 'United States,' and insert, in lieu of them, Confederate States.

Under the provisions of the act of 1852, the principal and interest of the internal improvement bonds of the State are made payable in the city of New York. It will be impossible to pay the interest accruing, at that point, during the continuance of the war.

I recommend that you so amend the law referred to as to require the payment at the Bank of Tennessee, at Nashville, or at Charleston, or New Orleans, of all sums may become due from the State to the people of all Governments, which are on terms of peace and friendship with us, who are and were, previous to the commencement of the war, *bona fide* owners of our bonds, and that you adopt such policy towards the owners and holders of our bonds, who are citizens of States at war with us, as is recognized and justified by the law of nations regulating their intercourse, as belligerents.

The ordeal through which the country is now passing necessarily prostrates the trade and commerce of the country, and deranges the currency to a greater or less extent. Such legislation as will tend to secure a uniform currency throughout the Confederate States is of the highest importance. I therefore submit the question to your consideration for such action as in your opinion the general welfare demands.

By the . . . . . . section of the act of the 6th of May, 1861, it is made the duty of the Governor to issue bonds of the State, for the purpose of raising a fund with which to defray the expenses of the provisional army of the State. In view of the scarcity of a circulating medium, and the probable difficulty of converting any considerable amount of bonds into money in times like the present, I respectfully recommend that you so modify that act as to authorize the issuance of Treasury Notes to the extent of three-fifths of the amount authorized to be issued, in lieu of that amount of said bonds; and that the same, when issued, be made receivable by the State in payment of all taxes or government dues.

In obedience to your act of 6th May, 1861, I have caused to be organized, armed and equipped, twenty-one regiments of infantry now in the field, ten artillery companies in progress of organization, and a sufficient number of cavalry companies to compose one regiment. The organization of an engineer corps is nearly completed.

In addition to which, we have three regiments mustered into the service of the Confederate States now in Virginia, and a number of our citizens in the service of that government stationed at Pensacola. For full and accurate information as to the army organization, I refer you to the reports of the proper officers, hereafter to be laid before you, if desired. It is proper to remark, in this connection, that without even a call being made upon them, a much larger number of our patriotic citizens have tendered their services to the State than I have thought proper to accept. Should the necessities of the State at any time require a larger force, I feel assured that our brave and gallant people will rush with alacrity to the field, so as to swell the force to the point of equaling any such necessity.

I commend those brave and patriotic citizen soldiers to your most favorable consideration, and recommend the adoption of such measures as will most tend to promote their health and comfort while in the field.

It is proper that I call your attention to the fact that a few days since, Return J. Meigs, Esq., resigned the office of Librarian to the State. The office is now vacant, and the duty of filling it by election devolves upon you.

I cannot, in justice to my own feelings and sense of duty, close this communication without urging upon you, and through you upon those you represent, the importance and propriety of moderation, forbearance, and conciliation in your intercourse with each other, however widely and earnestly you may have differed in your opinions and actions upon the important and exciting questions so recently settled.

Invoking a continuation of the blessings of the Supreme Ruler of the universe upon our cause, our country, and our people, I submit the matter to your hands.

Isham G. Harris."

Bubbling over with enthusiasm at the outcome of the June 8 election, Governor Harris tendered his heart-felt congratulations to the Legislature and the citizenry of the State upon "the near approach to unanimity" with which Tennessee's affiliation with the Union had been severed. Subsequent events in East Tennessee during the military conflict proved that the Governor's measuring rod was not an accurate instrument, for that section of the State did not "stand together as one man" in defence of Tennessee's withdrawal from the Union. Quite the contrary was the case.

The Governor's Message contained rather minor recommendations. His overall objective had been set forth in his Message of April 25, and that great objective had been obtained—separation from the Union and a close and effective affiliation with the Southern Confederacy. In conformity with Tennessee's break with the Union, the Legislature followed a recommendation of the Governor by repealing all laws requiring attorneys, members of the Legislature, and other public officials to take an oath to support the Constitution of the United States.[285] Cases involving debt and money were declared suspended for a period of twelve months, the Judges of the Supreme Court and Circuit Courts as well as Chancellors being requested to observe this regulation.[286] With the exception of Kentucky, Missouri, and Maryland (slave States), no suit by any citizen "of either of the States of the late United States of America, now adhering to the Government of which A. Lincoln claims to be President" would be countenanced in the courts of law or equity in Tennessee.[287] Section 4743 of the *Code of Tennessee*, as related to offenses of a treasonable nature against the United States, was wiped from the statute book.[288] Inability of the Governor to sell all the authorized bonds led him to recommend that three-fifths of the five million dollars of bonds be converted into legal tender treasury notes,[289] a request granted by the Legislature.

The most basic piece of legislation had been that of May 6 whereby the resources of the State, both men and money, were placed in the hands of the Governor who was empowered to raise, organize, and equip a provisional army of fifty-five thousand men "fitted for the field at the earliest practicable moment."[290] None conversant with the activities of Governor Harris will deny that he spent all possible energy and effort to fulfill that duty and responsibility. Historians are all pretty well-agreed that no Southern Governor contributed more to the prosecution of the war from a Southern viewpoint than did Isham Green Harris. And what counted was that his ability and activity equalled his zeal.

With Tennessee's entering the Southern Confederacy, the State was to be transformed into a battle front and its chartered confines become a battleground where, next to Virginia, the largest number of skirmishes and major battles were to take place. To add to this sanguinary picture that, as yet, lay in the future, was the revolt of East Tennessee. Union leaders in that section foresaw a secession victory in the June election. Without adopting a "watchful waiting" attitude, strong Union leaders late in the month of May called a convention in Knoxville where two of the ablest men, Democrat United States Senator Andrew Johnson and old-line Whig Thomas A. R. Nelson, forgot political differences and fought disunion side by side. When the results of the election of June 8 became known, however, Chairman Nelson called for a second meeting at Greeneville on June 17. When the convention met, it was "a condition and not a theory" that confronted them. Should opposition

[285] *Acts of Tennessee*, Second Extraordinary Session, 1861, Chapter 21.
[286] *Ibid.*, Resolution 32, 89.
[287] *Ibid.*, Chapter 23.
[288] *Ibid.*, Chapter 8.
[289] *Ibid.*, Chapter 14.
[290] *Ibid.*, Chapter 3.

to the dominant majority, as expressed at the recent election, be continued or should obeisance to that majority prevail? That was the burning question that was debated fervidly for four days.

Chairman Nelson was the author of a set of resolutions that breathed defiance. According to an able Union member of the convention, Oliver Perry Temple, Nelson's first proposal declared that "we will not abide by the new 'Declaration of Independence' (adopted by the Legislature) or attach ourselves to the Confederate States."[291] Another proposition was that if Confederate troops from either Middle or West Tennessee or other Confederate States were stationed in East Tennessee, then aid from the Federal Government would be requested and "we will use every means in our own power for our common defense." Perhaps the most dangerous of any Nelson proposal was that in case any member of the convention or any other citizen of East Tennessee should be killed in consequence of his Union sentiments, then "we earnestly advise and recommend the most prompt and decided retaliation by our people, leaving it to them to judge . . . ." Fortunately, cooler heads substituted and adopted a toned-down set of resolutions [292] which were presented to the Legislature on June 26:

"To the General Assembly of the State of Tennessee:

The undersigned, memorialists, on behalf of the people of East Tennessee beg leave respectfully to show, that at a convention of delegates, holden at Greeneville, on the 17th, 18th, 19th and 20th days of June, instant, in which was represented every county of East Tennessee, excepting the county of Rhea, it was resolved:

1st. That we do earnestly desire the restoration of peace to our whole country, and most especially that our own section of the State of Tennessee shall not be involved in civil war.

2d. That the action of the State Legislature in passing the *so-called* 'Declaration of Independence,' and in forming the 'Military League' with the Confederate States, and in adopting other acts looking to a separation of Tennessee from the Government of the United States, is unconstitutional and illegal, and, therefore, not binding upon us as loyal citizens.

3d. And it was further resolved, that in order to avert a conflict with our brethren in other parts of the State, and desiring that every constitutional means shall be resorted to for the preservation of peace, we do, therefore, constitute and appoint O. P. Temple, of Knox, John Netherland, of Hawkins and James P. McDowell, of Greene, Commissioners, whose duty it shall be to prepare a memorial and cause the same to be presented to the General Assembly of Tennessee, now in session, asking its consent that the counties composing East Tennessee, and such other counties in Middle Tennessee as desire to co-operate with them, may form and erect a separate State.

The idea of a separate political existence is not a recent one, but it is not necessary here to restate the geographical, social, economical, and indus-

---

[291] Temple, Oliver Perry: *East Tennessee and the Civil War,* 347–348.
[292] *Senate Journal,* Second Extraordinary Session, 1861, 142–144.

trial reasons which have often been urged in support of it. The reason which operated upon the convention and seemed to them conclusive, was the action of the two sections, respectively, at the election held on the 8th inst., to determine the future national relations of the State. In that election, the people of East Tennessee, by a majority of nearly twenty thousand votes, decided to adhere to the Federal Union, established prior to the American Revolution, and to which Tennessee was admitted in the year 1796, while the rest of the State is reported to have decided by a majority approaching even more nearly to unanimity, to leave the Federal Union and to join the body politic recently formed under the name of the Confederate States of America. The same diversity of sentiment was exhibited, but less distinctly, at the election on the 9th of February last, when the people of East Tennessee decided by a heavy majority against holding a convention to discuss and determine our Federal relations, overcoming by nearly fourteen thousand the majority in the rest of the State in favor of such convention.

This hopeless and irreconcilable difference of opinion and purpose, leaves no alternative but a separation of the two sections of the State; or it is not to be presumed that either would, for a moment, think of subjugating the other, or of coercing it into a political condition repugnant alike to its interest and to its honor. Certainly the people of East Tennessee entertain no such purpose towards the rest of the State. And the avowals of their western brethren, in connection with their recent political action, have been too numerous and explicit to leave us in any doubt as to their views.

It remains, therefore, that measures be adopted to effect a separation, amicably, honorably, and magnanimously, by a settlement of boundaries, so as to divide East Tennessee, and any contiguous counties or districts which may desire to adhere to her, from the rest of the State, and by a fair, just and equitable division of the public property and the common liabilities. It has occurred to the undersigned, as the best method of accomplishing this most desirable end, that your body should take immediate action in the premises, by giving a formal assent to the proposed separation, pursuant to the provisions of section 3, article 4, of the Constitution of the United States; and by convoking a convention representing the sovereign power of the people of the respective divisions of Tennessee, with plenary authority to so amend the Constitution of the State as to carry into effect the change contemplated.

With a view to such action, or to action leading to the same result, the undersigned ask permission to confer with your body, either in general session or through a committee appointed for this purpose, so as to consider and determine the details more satisfactorily than could otherwise be done.

Awaiting a response to this memorial, the undersigned beg to add assurances of every endeavor on their part, not only to preserve the peaceful relations heretofore subsisting between the people in the two portions of the State, but to remove, as far as possible, all causes of disturbance in the future, so that each may be left free to follow its chosen path of prosperity and honor, unembarrassed by any collision with the other.

O. P. TEMPLE,
JOHN NETHERLAND,
JAS. P. McDOWELL."

If the Nelson resolutions had been adopted and lived up to, the people of East Tennessee would have found themselves embroiled in the horrors of a civil war. The resolutions were defiant, and would have constituted a basis for retaliation on the part of the State and of Confederate allies. A relentless slaughter would doubtless have ensued.

Two days before adjournment, the Legislature considered the Greeneville Resolutions, and through the Joint Select Committee the following reply was unanimously adopted:[293]

"The Committee to which was referred the memorial of O. P. Temple, John Netherland and James P. McDowell, on behalf of themselves and certain citizens of East Tennessee composing the Greeneville Convention, respectfully submit the following report:

The Committee are not satisfied that the citizens, seeking by their memorial to have East Tennessee erected into a new State, represent the sentiment of the people of East Tennessee. They are not aware that the important subject of the memorial has been canvassed in the State except in the Greeneville Convention. That convention, as they are informed, was composed of delegates to the Knoxville Convention, which met on the 30th of May last. These delegates were consequently chosen before the vote on the 8th of June, and without reference to the particular result of that vote. There is nothing whatever to show that they were selected with the view to the formation of East Tennessee into a new State, or that the wish of the counties which they assume to represent on that question was ascertained. Nor, indeed, does it appear that said delegates were chosen upon a full expression of public opinion. The grounds upon which the memorialists mainly rest the application is the vote of the 8th of June, which, as the memorial assumes, exhibits an irreconcilable diversity of sentiment between East Tennessee and Middle and West Tennessee. The vote occurred, as already stated, subsequent to the appointment of delegates who composed the Greeneville Convention, and hence could not have an element in the sentiment which appointed them.

In addition to this, as the question affects the whole State, we remark, that nothing whatever of the sentiment of West and Middle Tennessee is known on the grave question presented in the memorial. In many portions of the State it is not even yet known that memorialists desire to create a new State out of East Tennessee. The fact is communicated to the General Assembly in session, and with no opportunity whatever of comparing views with their constituents on so important a question. Besides, without a full expression of sentiment to the contrary, the Committee would be inclined to the opinion that our brethren of East Tennessee would acquiesce in the result of the vote on the 8th of June. Every presumption is in favor of acquiescence. They are our fellow-citizens, identified with us by the closest ties of kindred and interest. We have been long accustomed to regard them as brothers. In the many contests in the State, at the ballot box, the will of a majority has been uniformly acquiesced in by the minority. Many are the instances in which East Tennessee had a large majority in favor of the prevailing policy. Such was the case in February last. Whilst, in numerous instances, its favorite policy has been lost. Yet the people of the entire State have invariably acquiesced. We are not prepared to believe that a contrary result will follow now.

---

[293] *Senate Journal*, Second Extraordinary Session, 1861, 176-177.
    House Journal, Second Extraordinary Session, 1861, 192-193.

If however, there exists in the breasts of a majority of the citizens of East Tennessee a desire to form themselves into a separate State, and we are mistaken in our conclusions, we submit that the question can be better disposed of by our successors, who will assemble in a few months fresh from the people. In the meantime, over the entire State the question can be discussed, and a full expression of sentiment elicited. This will enable members to act in accordance with the known wishes of their constituents.

If the memorial did not preclude us from doing so, by asking the appointment of Commissioners to confer with Messrs. Temple, Netherland and McDowell, on the single question of erecting East Tennessee into a new State, we would recommend the appointment of Commissioners to confer with these gentlemen on the subject of the grievances complained of by the citizens composing the Greeneville Convention. The careful reading of the memorial, however, we regret to say, forbids us from so doing.

We decline to discuss the policy proposed by the memorial, as well as other questions raised by it.

We earnestly hope that all causes of irritation between citizens of the different portions of the State may soon be removed, and that we may, as heretofore, continue brethren in feeling, alike zealous to maintain the honor and promote the prosperity and general welfare of the whole State. In conclusion, under the circumstances, in our judgment, the General Assembly should at this time take no action on the subject of the memorial.

Respectfully submitted,

STOKES, Chairman Senate Committee.
GANTT, Chairman House Committee."

The commendable restraint embodied in the legislative reply to the memorial from the Greeneville Convention was in marked contrast to that exhibited by some of the Tennessee pro-Confederacy newspapers. The following blast came from a West Tennessee newspaper [294] located in an area exposed to attack along the giant artery of communication and transportation, the "Father of Waters":

"THE GREENVILLE CONVENTION.

Were it not that duty calls us to notice the treason-working conclave who composed the convention recently held at Greenville, in East Tennessee, and their attack upon the *Appeal*, in their 'Bill of Grievances,' we would be loth to pay it the tribute of a moment's attention. But as the proceeding will constitute a feature in the future records of the stirring events now transpiring, this cannot be passed by without a passing notice.

So far as the 'declaration of grievances' is concerned, candor compels us to characterize it as the most undignified document ever known to be issued under the auspices of men who imagined they were possessed of sufficient political sagacity, as to presume to organize a convention so treasonable in its interests and purposes as was the assembly held at Greenville.

In one portion of their verbose preamble the following sentence occurs: 'The Memphis *Appeal*, a prominent disunion paper, published a false statement of our proceedings, under the head of "the traitorous council," and styled us, who represent every county but two in East Tennessee, "the

---

[294] *Memphis Daily Appeal*, July 3, 1861.

little batch of affected traitors who hover around the noxious atmosphere of Andrew Johnson's home." ' We plead guilty to the count, and further, aver that such a set of political lunatics should not have been permitted to foist their silly nonsense upon the grave deliberations of our legislature. It was an outrage on public sentiment and common sense, which not even the most charitable forbearance on the part of the legislature should have tolerated.

Were we to attempt to dissect the document, or endeavor to prove the falsity of its assertions, it would be a considerable undertaking. There are several items in it, it is true, which descend to the condition of contemptible falsehoods. All that, for instance, referring to espionage on union men, and the want of freedom in voting at the last election, is so evidently false that no explanation is necessary—indeed, the charge is a slander upon the freemen of Tennessee, who are wont to vote their sentiments, and always will do so regardless of consequences.

The declaration ends with the following announcement: 'In view of these considerations, and of the fact that the people of East Tennessee have declared their fidelity to the Union by a majority of 20,000 votes, therefore we do resolve and declare' in brief, to the extent of dissolving their political association with the balance of the State, and a willingness to unite with the abolition organization of the North. This action was laid before the State legislature by the committee appointed for the performance of that duty.

We are disposed to be mild upon the traitors who composed the tory assembly, but cannot avoid expressing the impatience which is general throughout the State. We have announced that the crew of irrepressibles are few at the present time, yet with such bad men and treacherous leaders as Nelson, Maynard and their coadjutors, to head the agitation, they can consummate a deal of mischief, to prevent which it is hoped there will not occur the necessity of interposing the strong arm of the law. Yet if it comes to this pass, the little nest of traitors will find a *coercive* government in this State of which they wot not at present.

Hitherto, on all occasions of great public questions, settled by the ballot box, the minority have acquiesced to the dictate of the majority; but now we see a small proportion, not even respectable in political character or numbers, treasonably opposing the will of the people. Further, they propose to aid and assist the tyrant who seeks to destroy us. This cannot be. The great South has her most important railroad lines running through this rebellious corner of East Tennessee, and the revolt must be suppressed for our own safety. A foreign country cannot be permitted to control the great avenues which connect us with the largest member of the Government.

By reference to our news columns, the report of the joint select committee, on this memorial, will be found. It presents a plain and calm defense of the State at large, against the unwarrantable aspersions of the few dissatisfied memorialists, and by dismissing the matter in an easy and quiet way, the committee has acted judiciously. Their duty was too plain to be mistaken: It was to hold no communication with our insurgents; to hold no communication with our internal enemies, who are only worthy the name and doom of traitors."

The opposite viewpoint was exhibited by acid-tongued "Parson" Brownlow who defended one of the strong Union men participating in the Greeneville Convention, Horace Maynard. Considerable excitement had been manifested on account of a rumor that Maynard was to be assassinated on account of his strong pro-Union views as expressed in the Greeneville Convention. Brownlow incorporated in his editorial defense of Maynard the following characteristic language:[295]

". . . There are those who think they can instigate some irresponsible villain to assassinate him, and as he has no relatives in this State, and no long train of influential friends to espouse his cause, the affair will pass by without any retaliation from any quarter. Such persons are woefully mistaken! Let them, if they dare, do violence to the person of Maynard, or any other Union man of East Tennessee, because of his Union sentiments, and the consequences to them will be of the most fearful character! The *tool* who is used to assassinate a Union leader, will not be sought after, but the instigators and actors in the dread scenes will have occasion, in the bitterness and anguish of repentance, to call for the rocks and mountains to fall upon them, and hide them from the vengeance of the outraged Union men of East Tennessee! Let a respectable Union man in Knox county be slain, by a Secessionist, and we can give the names of eight or ten prominent Secessionists in the county, who will instantly bite the dust. As certain as there is a God in Heaven, they will have to die!—We speak advisedly, and reflect the purposes of a large organization in this and other counties. We speak the words of truth—not to intimidate men, but to let them know what will be the result of any such murderous assaults. Commit your acts of violence, and then fortify yourselves with Regiments of troops. We tell you that you will be met with opposing Regiments, and you shall be pursued to the very gates of Hell, but what your blood shall atone for the violence!"

Three days before legislative adjournment, Governor Harris submitted for confirmation a long list of nominations for various military posts.[296] Without delay, all nominations were confirmed, although a momentary squabble developed regarding the confirmation of Colonel Milton A. Haynes whose "habits" were being questioned by the Speaker of the House, W. C. Whitthorne.

With the refusal of the Legislature to pay much attention to the request of the memorial from the Greeneville Convention, praying for the separation of East Tennessee from the rest of the State in order to organize a separate State, the Legislature finally reached an adjournment date on July 1, 1861. Thus ended in all probability the most fateful legislative session in the history of Tennessee. Tennessee "had crossed the Rubicon." The Stars and Bars were to gleam in the wild light of battle, and the direful prophecy of Isaiah was to be fulfilled—"their land shall be soaked with blood."

Exactly one month intervened between the adjournment of the Second Extraordinary Session of the Thirty-Third General Assembly on July 1, 1861 and the August 1 election for Governor, Congressmen,

---

[295] *The Tri-Weekly Whig* (Knoxville), June 25, 1861.
[296] *Senate Journal*, Second Extraordinary Session, 1861, 169–172.
House Journal, Second Extraordinary Session, 1861, 188–191.
Author's note. See Appendix for list of military appointments made by Governor Harris on May 9, 1861 and June 28, 1861.

and members of the next General Assembly. Ordinarily, such an event called forth the energies and strategy of the political cohorts of each respective political party. Fateful events, however, had changed the entire complexion of State political contests. No longer were the screams of such abolitionists as fanatical William Lloyd Garrison mere academic ravings; their concept regarding slavery had become entwined and integrated with the trappings of religious martyrdom, running the gauntlet all the way from the Quaker schoolmistress, Prudence Crandall of Connecticut, who lost friends and home for teaching Negro girls, to old John Brown who swung from a gallows in Virginia. Like a pendulum, the emphasis for thirty years had swung back and forth between moral and legal-political sanctions regarding slavery. All facets of the slavery question had at last, however, been reduced to the realism of guns and swords, for *armed forces* had supplanted the mouthings of the pulpit, press, and politicians. War had become a stark reality, and largely but not altogether Tennessee politics had "adjourned" for the time being insofar as the above political offices were concerned.

There was one individual, however, who let it be known early in 1861 that his time and talents were available for exercising the functions of the executive chair. Flushed with the outcome of the February election, in which the question of secession went down to a crushing defeat by some sixty-seven thousand votes, the ardent not to say fanatical Unionist "Parson" Brownlow on March 23, 1861, issued one thousand circulars declaring himself "a candidate for the office of Governor of Tennessee."[297] In the long-winded document, consisting of twenty printed pages,[298] the "Parson" outlined sixteen points of what he called his *"political principles"* as constituting the planks of his platform. Undoubtedly, the least controversial item on his political agenda was his statement that

"I am frank to confess that I desire the position on account of its honor . . . but, not being rich, I would like to fill the office for two years for the sake of the THREE THOUSAND DOLLARS PER ANNUM."

But the self-anointed and self-nominated "Parson's" ambitions took a nose-dive *after* the June election in which Tennessee, reversing its former stand for the Union, went "secesh" by a decisive majority. Unionism was no longer an "open Sesame," inasmuch as two-thirds of the State had made a complete switch and the "Parson's" circular went out of circulation. A bronchial affection was the lame excuse utilized by him in fading into the temporary obscurity of the "forgotten man." The most uncompromising of Unionists knew that such an acid-tongued and vehement partisan would be anathema to the strong secession sections of the State, Middle and West Tennessee. His self-inflated

[297] Brownlow, W. G.: *Parson Brownlow's Book*, 224.
[298] *Ibid.*, 224–244.

political bubble had burst and his announcement went speedily to a status characterized as that of "where the woodbine pineth and the whangdoodle mourneth." In political parlance, the "Parson's" craft had gone up Salt River.

On May 11, 1861, at a meeting of the *Southern Rights State Convention* in Nashville, it was the sense of that body that there should not be a contested race for Governor in view of the crisis confronting the State. Governor Harris was warmly eulogized for his stand against military oppression and it was agreed that his fellow citizens should express their gratitude and admiration for such splendid services rendered by him in endeavoring to prepare the State for defense against the foe. Such commendation was tantamount to a virtual renomination for Governor.

But there was evidence that the Unionists had already had ideas opposed to abdication of their party allegiance. Something like a week prior to the meeting of the above Convention, delegates appointed by the people heretofore comprising the Union Party met in Nashville on May 2 at which time the following preamble and resolutions were adopted:[299]

"WHEREAS, The Union party of the State of Tennessee did heretofore appoint delegates from each county in the State, to meet in the city of Nashville on this day for the purpose of nominating a candidate for Governor;

AND WHEREAS, Since said appointments, the aspect of affairs, both civil and military, in the General and State Governments, has undergone a most alarming change; that now, instead of peace and harmony, the whole people of the United States (so to speak) are arrayed in hostile demonstrations of fraternal strife;

We, the delegates here assembled, representing the three grand divisions of the State, deem it proper for us to express our opinion as to who would be the best man to be made the Governor of the State of Tennessee, surrounded as we now are.

Under the difficulties which now surround us, and the perils which are plainly before us, involving all that is dear to us as a people and as a State, it is, in our estimation, a matter of the greatest moment to each and every man, woman and child in the State of Tennessee, that we have as Commander and Chief of the Army and Navy of Tennessee, a military chieftain and civilian of large experience in both departments; a man of known courage, honesty, integrity, firmness, prudence, humanity, and a well balanced and sagacious, informed mind; so that our sons, brothers and ourselves may be protected in the trials, hardships and dangers of the impending war.

Resolved, That in our opinion, not intending to disparage any one, all the above characteristics are concentrated more fully in the Hon. William B. Campbell, of Wilson County, than any other man in the State, and we do therefore most respectfully recommend him to the people of Tennessee

---

[299] *Republican Banner*, May 3, 1861.
　Daily Gazette (Nashville), May 3, 1861.

as their candidate for Governor, believing as we do that he is the very man for the occasion."

Inasmuch as the ardent Secessionists viewed the action of the Unionists as amounting to the tossing of the "apple of discord" among the rank and file of the citizenry of the State, the *Southern Rights State Convention* answered the Unionists, who had attempted to hoist the flag of former Governor William B. Campbell, in the following language:[300]

"*Resolved,* That the delegates here assembled, having been heretofore appointed to represent some of the counties of the State in the Southern Rights Convention, in view of the exigency of a war, which has been waged upon the Southern States by the President of the United States, sustained by the people of the North, deem it inexpedient to suggest a candidate for Governor at the present time, and do refer the whole subject back to those from whom we have received our authority.

Resolved, That, inasmuch as an election for Governor must take place in August next, and it is important that there be no contest, and no dictation from any quarter, we recommend that the people in their primary capacity having buried all party prejudices and erased old divisions, do hold primary meetings on Saturday, June 15th, for the purpose of harmonizing sentiment with regard to their choice for Governor.

Resolved, That we cannot adjourn this assemblage without expressing our warm and cordial concurrence in the action of the late extra session of the Legislature, in placing Tennessee in an attitude to resist an odious and tyrannical military usurpation, and to unite their fortunes with the Southern Confederacy, and that the patriotic and energetic policy of Governor Isham G. Harris, in the hour of his country's trial, entitles him to the gratitude and admiration of his countrymen.

Resolved, That we cannot too strongly or earnestly urge upon the people of Tennessee and the whole South, in consideration of the entire unanimity in the councils of our enemies who are seeking to destroy our rights, to undermine our institutions, and to lay waste our land, the absolute importance of unity and harmony in our movements, and that he is an enemy of the public safety who would promote discord on account of minor differences, or do aught to distract our fast consolidating columns."

The action of the informal Convention received strong support from a newspaper in the western section of the State in a statement that was well-expressed and one that hit the nail on the head during those harrowing times:[301]

"We are pleased to notice that the character and tenor of the resolutions passed upon the occasion were such as to effectually obliterate the last vestige of party feeling that may be harbored in the bosom of any Tennessean. Partisanship might have dictated another course—but patriotism imperatively demanded that such paltry promptings should be subdued if

[300] *Nashville Union and American,* May 12, 1861.
   Daily Gazette (Nashville), May 12, 1861.
[301] *Memphis Daily Appeal,* May 14, 1861.

not sacrificed. No nomination, or even recommendation, was consequently made, but the whole matter was referred back to the people for impartial arbitrament at their hands. It is suggested that primary meetings be held on Saturday, the 15th of June, for the purpose of harmonizing sentiment with regard to a choice for governor. This plan we think to be eminently judicious, and is tantamount to what we suggested some three or four weeks since, when striking the flag of party from the head of our columns. We care not, apart from our private and personal predilections, who may be the successful candidate for the high position sought, so far as past party ties are concerned, provided only that his fidelity to the State of Tennessee in her sovereign capacity is unquestioned. This essential prerequisite every aspirant must possess, unless he desires an overwhelming and disgraceful defeat.

The liberal and catholic spirit manifested in the proceedings of the convention, cannot fail to accomplish its intended mission of solidifying the sentiment of the State. Men of all parties—whether of Southern Rights Union or Southern Rights Secession—can compromise upon the broad platform erected on principles so self-evident and axiomatic. All that is demanded is a truce to the hostilities of the past, and a concord of feeling for the future. No step is counseled which does not look to the interest, the safety, and the honor of the Commonwealth—no sentiment avowed that is not a necessary postulate to the attainment of those objects. Everything done has an eye solely to the patriotic and foremost desire of the ancient Romans, and the 'Republic may receive no detriment.' We only assert the prevailing sentiment of our State when we reiterate the language of the resolutions—that 'he is an enemy of the public safety who would promote discord on account of minor differences, or do aught to distract our fast consolidating columns.'"

Despite the fact that two so-called Conventions had met in Nashville for "considering" nominations of candidates for Governor, neither Convention actually nominated anybody for the office. The pro-Secession body strongly commended Governor Harris for his fidelity to duty and his beaver-like activity in promoting the Secession cause, but in reality left off any nomination as such. On the other hand, the pro-Union aggregation "suggested" the name of former Governor William B. Campbell as a suitable man to take over the helm of State, but no formal nomination was made by that body. Matters rocked along for some two weeks whereupon a strong Whig and, later, a Know-Nothing newspaper acted upon its own initiative and placed at the top of its masthead the name of William H. Polk as its candidate for Governor. In presenting the name of William H. Polk, a brother of President James K. Polk, as a candidate for gubernatorial honors, the editorial indorsement was as follows:[302]

"The Gubernatorial Canvass.

The name of Hon. Wm. H. Polk, of Maury County, appears at the head of our columns this morning, as a candidate for Governor of the State

---

[302] *Republican Banner*, June 30, 1861.

of Tennessee. We run up his name in the firm belief that his candidacy will be acceptable to a large majority of the people of the State, and that, in view of the peculiar condition of the public mind, and the importance of securing harmony and unity of sentiment at such a crisis in the history of the State, the whole people will be willing to lay down personal preferences, and forget old party prejudices, and unite in his support.

The name of Governor Campbell has been prominently mentioned in connection with the candidacy, and the announcement of his name as a candidate would be hailed with pleasure throughout the State. It is generally known, however that Governor C. has uniformly and firmly resisted all solicitations to permit his name to be used in connection with the office. Colonel Polk has been indicated by men of all parties as a suitable person for the occasion. We and most of our readers have differed with him, upon the issues which divided old parties, but those differences, like the issues upon which they arose, are with the past, and we shall support Col. Polk cordially and with our best ability.

The present distinguished incumbent of the Gubernatorial Chair has been prominently spoken of as a candidate for re-election for a third time. We have heretofore expressed our views as to the impolicy of such a movement, and we have to say that those views have met the cordial approval of leading and influential men of all parties in all parts of the State. We know of no good reason why the friends of Gov. Harris should press him into the field for a third time, and we have given, as we conceive, good reason why they should not. But we do not propose to discuss this question this morning. We merely desire to place the name of Col. Polk before the people as a candidate for the office of Governor. We have done so, upon the earnest solicitation of men from the ranks of all the old parties, and with the full approbation of our judgment."

Two days later, another editorial [303] in the same newspaper announced that

"It is with this conviction of the good to be achieved, and of the importance of promoting a man fresh from the masses, that Colonel Polk yielded to solicitations from leading men of the several old political parties in Tennessee, is thus presented to the people. . . . Cannot all unite upon him in the approaching election? Surely we can—at least we feel that neither the prejudices of the past, or the fancies of personal preference now, will influence the mind of any considerable number of voters in the State. Tennessee, in choosing her Governor for the next two years, would present a spectacle truly sublime—in keeping with the devotion of her great heart to the cause of Southern Independence."

In a follow-up editorial next day, a subtle suggestion was introduced that was doubtless calculated to divert support from Governor Harris in the event of his declaring himself a candidate for a third term. A challenge was thrown at the supporters of Governor Harris in this manner:[304]

". . . We have no hesitation in predicting that Gov. Harris will be a

[303] *Ibid.*, July 2, 1861.
[304] *Ibid.*, July 3, 1861.

candidate before the next General Assembly for Senator in the Congress of the Confederate States, and most likely he will be elected—that he has no expectation of serving another two years as Governor of Tennessee—but that the people, if they should elect him, would only in fact transfer the selection of their Executive to the State Senate, whose Speaker would in that event be Governor of Tennessee for two years.

Is it necessary, then, to re-elect Governor Harris for the purpose of securing his election to the Confederate Senate, and giving the State Senate an opportunity to make John Doe Governor for two years.

We submit these considerations to the public. They are sufficient for present thought. We may have occasion to proceed with the subject."

As an antidote to the *Banner's* pronounced opposition to the re-election of Governor Harris, an ardent Democratic newspaper, *Nashville Union and American,* ran a lengthy editorial entitled "The August Election":[305]

"The old machinery of party having worn out, or been superseded by the free voice of the people, the citizens in various counties of the State, without recognizing past party distinctions, have held public meetings, and, so far as we have observed, have unanimously expressed the wish that the present distinguished incumbent of the Executive office of Tennessee, Isham G. Harris, should consent to serve them for one more term. It has not hitherto been a custom for the Governor of the State to seek or consent to a second re-election, though, by the Constitution, a citizen is eligible for three terms out of four. There has been no exception to this rule, excepting in the case of Gov. Wm. Carroll who held the office, we believe, for six years in succession.[306] It is believed, however, that this custom has arisen out of a disinclination in the incumbents to serve longer in the Executive chair, and not from any jealousy, by the people, of an abuse of power, by too long a tenure of office. It is within our personal knowledge that the present Executive is anxious to be released from the fetters of office, and that consent, on his part, to serve a third term, will involve heavy sacrifices of feeling and of interest. All who know his often reiterated expressions on the subject, to all who have approached him, will bear testimony to the sincerity and earnestness with which he deprecates a re-election. But in the present position of affairs, when Tennessee, as a member of the Confederate States, is engaged in a war of defence, for her rights, liberties, and independent existence, when her military and financial resources, which have been organized and have received direction under his hand, are familiar perhaps to no other man in the State, and when it will require some time for a new incumbent to sufficiently inform himself of their condition, the popular sentiment unmistakably demands of him to again make the sacrifice of his time and talents and to permit himself to be voted for once more for the responsible position which he has so ably, satisfactorily and worthily filled. In obedience to that sentiment, whose embodiment has found expression in the public press, in the record of all the public meetings that have been held, we this morning place the name of Gov. Harris at the head of our columns

---

[305] *Nashville Union and American,* July 4, 1861.

[306] Author's note. The editor of the *Union and American* suffered a lapse in memory. In addition to Governor William Carroll, John Sevier served a total of six terms also. Moreover, Willie Blount and Joseph McMinn served three successive terms as Governor.

as the candidate, we are sure, of an overwhelming majority of the people of Tennessee, for the Chief Executive office of the State. In doing so, we have not asked the consent of Gov. Harris. But we have felt certain, that while he is not willing to regard himself as a candidate, by his own act, he will not decline a position which, for such overwhelming reasons, it is deemed essential for him to occupy. It is proper that his countrymen should understand, in the outset, that, for obvious reasons, he cannot, in the present perilous condition of the country, abandon his post and undertake a canvass. Nor do his fellow-citizens desire any political electioneering now. There are higher and more manly duties for every patriot to perform. And especially is it desirable that those who are placed at posts of responsibility should stand at the helm and direct the movements of the vessel of State over the storm-waves that surround her.

There never was a time in our history when it was more desirable that entire unanimity should direct and animate the counsels of our countrymen. A generous confidence should inspire the hearts of the people in those who are selected to lead them. While they should not fail to point out and condemn any fatal mismanagement or misconduct in office, they should, at the same time, remove far from them hypercritical, factious and idle complaints and animadversions. Our public servants have a hard and responsible career before them. When they manifest a spirit of patriotism and evince energy, determination and capacity, they should be cheered instead of discouraged by the voice of their countrymen, in the presence of a boasting and insolent foe.

We are aware that this encouraging unanimity is not to be expected, even at a period fraught with the highest interests of the State. Many honestly and sincerely, others from factious and selfish motives, differ from a policy of the highest wisdom. But this partial discord is inevitable, where freedom unfolds its sacred banner. It is the privilege of a free citizen to think and act as inconsistently as he may choose or as wise as he can.

There were Hooks to disturb the revolutionary era. There were Gates and Conways to throw obstructions in the pathway of the Revolutionary leaders. And there were differences, honestly entertained also, to mar the unity of council in the days of '76. These must be met with resolution and with a sincere desire to make them harmless.

We know there are some who have other preferences. They have a right to entertain them. But when the voice of the people is heard, in distinct utterances, on the 1st of August, they will bow to its edict, if they be patriots. If they be factious demagogues, they will continue their occupation of agitation."

Sandwiched in between the editorials of the two above highly partisan newspapers is a refreshing view of the attitude of a non-partisan journal which carried the following editorial devoid of "party" bias: [307]

"The Coming Political Canvass in Tennessee.

In August next, the people of Tennessee decide at the ballot-box who is to be their Governor, members of the State Legislature, and Representatives in the Confederate Congress. For obvious reasons, we had indulged the hope

---

[307] *The Daily Gazette* (Nashville), July 6, 1861.

Author's note. See reference 105 containing a statement as to the non-partisan position of the *Gazette*.

. . . . [next few words illegible] . . . .
political contest, such as have hitherto characterized such elections. But this
hope, it now seems, is not to be fully realized; for it is palpably evident that
an effort is at present being made, which, if successful, will divide our people and introduce anew the old partisan strife, an event which good and
patriotic men are disposed to avert. Circumstances will not justify us in
saying that an attempt is being made to create a Lincoln party in Tennessee, nor will we even say that a *reactionary* movement is in contemplation by the parties seeking to inaugurate unnecessary political strife. In
doing so, are they discharging their duty as good, patriotic citizens? Let us
see. The people of the State have lately determined their political status and
relation. Their choice was made, as all will admit, fairly, calmly, deter-
minedly. Why seek, then, to change or revoke the verdict rendered? Why
endeavor to make the approaching canvass a season of bitter partisan feeling? Should not every man strive rather to eradicate all vestiges of old
party prejudices, and apply his shoulder manfully to the wheel, and work
diligently to place Tennessee permanently in a good and safe position. We
charge no man here with Lincolnism, but fear Mr. Lincoln himself may be
deceived into the supposition that he has sympathizers and supporters in our
midst. Those whose conduct is likely to be so far misunderstood, should
look at the effect of their movement upon the Lincoln Administration,
rather than at the view Tennesseans will take of it. No good can possibly
result from their course. After we shall have definitely established, beyond
cavil, our connection with the Confederate States, and our independence
as a nation, it will certainly be time to form new parties and spring new
political issues. He who is unwilling to bide that time is either not a patriot
or in other respects unfit to lead or advise the people. We are at this time
re-enacting the scenes of our first Revolution. We are now fighting again
the battles of Concord, Monmouth, and Brandywine, to be followed, by the
grace of God, with another Yorktown. Is it right, therefore, is it proper,
is it decent for Johnny Hooks to go through the camp yelling 'beef, beef?'
We do not think so, neither do we think any threats in connection with
the 64,000 majority of the 9th of February in very commendable taste. That
day and its events are gone forever. In view of what has occurred within
the last sixty days, how is it possible for a sensible man to believe that the
political tragedy of the 9th of February can ever be re-enacted in Tennessee. To believe so is to brand with imbecility and cowardice the sovereign people of the State.

Some gentlemen are disposed to lay great stress upon the position assumed by the Eastern Division of the State. Who has harmed her, and in
what do her wrongs consist? Who has deprived her of any right she ever
enjoyed? Have THE PEOPLE of East Tennessee really complained, or
have they sufficient cause of complaint? It may be true that Nelson, Brownlow and Johnson feel aggrieved by the vote and action of the State, but so
far no evidences whatever have been presented to show that THE PEOPLE
of East Tennessee have been in any degree damaged. Several of their prominent citizens are pursuing a course treasonable to the State. Can it be possible that these vile plotters against the public peace and welfare have
friends, sympathizers and coadjutors in our midst? Can any man hitherto
enjoying the respect of his fellow-citizens be so lost to all the influences of
patriotism as to endorse the course of the few traitors now seeking to array
East Tennessee in deadly hate against other portions of the Commonwealth?
It is especially desirable that our people, having just accomplished a

revolution in a quiet, orderly and patriotic manner, shall not be called upon to re-enact it. They are content with the present order of things, and will hold to a fearful accountability those who strive to disturb their quietude."

Analyzing the line-up of the newspapers in the gubernatorial controversy, only two of any appreciable influence were opposing the renomination of Governor Harris. These were two influential papers of former Whig persuasion, namely, the Nashville *Republican Banner* and the *Knoxville* (Brownlow) *Whig*. Among the Nashville newspapers supporting Harris for re-election were the *Union and American*, the *Patriot*, and the *Daily Gazette*. In Memphis, the *Daily Appeal* claimed the honor of being the first newspaper "to suggest the policy of the renomination of Governor Harris."[308] The *Knoxville Register*, a strong Whig journal up to 1859, switched over to the Democratic fold in that year and supported Governor Harris for re-election. The vast majority of small-town newspapers were for Harris, although two of the ablest, the *Franklin Review* and the *Maury Press* of Columbia, opposed Harris for re-election. In commenting upon its anti-Harris position, the *Review* offered this explanation:[309]

". . . We doubt not that the Governor, although he has been elected twice, would be acceptable to a respectable portion of the people of the middle and western sections of the State.

But unfortunately for us in this hour of our country's deepest peril and gloom, our brethren of East Tennessee do not meet and act with us in the spirit of yore. Her gallant sons, who have won imperishable renown, side by side with the sons of the middle and west, whose common valor and intrepid daring, on a hundred battle-fields, has cast a rich sheen of glory over her fair escutcheon and made Tennessee the warrior State of the continent, seem laggard in marching with their brethren to win undying glory in defence of Southern Rights and Southern honor. God grant that some fortunate stroke of policy may yet peaceably settle our dissensions, prevent civil war within our own borders and cause her hardy sons to pour forth from her mountain fastnesses, and shoulder to shoulder, shield locked in shield, move with us in this great struggle against tyranny and despotism, and preserve untarnished the fair renown of our glorious commonwealth.

We have been a life-long opponent of Gov. Harris, but the searcher of all hearts knows that we have laid aside all our past prejudices, and regard them as but dust in the balances, as nothing compared to the terrible realities of the present. We are not hard to please. We will support any true and tried man. But East Tennessee will not support him under any circumstances. And we know of no event which will tend more to widen the breach between her and us than his candidacy. Her people are *especially* embittered against him. No matter how weak and puerile his friends may say these opinions are, still the *solemn fact* stares us in the face.

If this spirit is not conciliated by compromise, it will settle sullenly down upon a basis of unyielding hatred and opposition to us and our cause. We must win them over by forebearance, or the scenes of Toryism will be

---

[308] *Memphis Daily Appeal*, July 26, 1861.
[309] Quoted in the Nashville *Republican Banner*, July 6, 1861.

enacted upon Tennessee's soil. Gov. Harris, if he has aspirations, should lay them aside. The present peace and unity of the State imperatively demand it. His friends, in view of these facts, should cease to urge his claims. We again repeat Gov. Harris will not do. There are other fields of labor opened to him. Let him seek them, and let us immediately cast about and *get the man for the crisis.*"

A persistent rumor had been circulated by the opponents of Governor Harris that he had given no authoritative intimation that he would accept the office of Governor if re-elected, and that his silence afforded strong indication that he was aspiring to be elected a Senator to the Confederate Congress. As was always the habit of Isham G. Harris, he never permitted half-truths or pure fabrications to go unanswered. In a letter to S. R. Cockrill of Nashville, Governor Harris spiked the rumor in an effective manner:[310]

"NASHVILLE, July 11, 1861.

STERLING R. COCKRILL, Esq.,–Dear Sir: Your note of yesterday was handed to me this morning, in answer to which I have to state that previous to the commencement of the war which is now being so unjustly waged against the South, it was my settled purpose, often repeated, both publicly and privately, not to be a candidate for re-election to the office of Governor of Tennessee. But having most cordially and earnestly co-operated with the great majority of the people of the State, in resisting the usurpations and tyranny of the federal government, and in making a formal declaration of independence of that government and uniting our fortunes and our destiny with the provisional government of the Confederate States of America, which policy has resulted in making Tennessee a party to this unholy war, inaugurated for the destruction of our rights, liberties, and our equality; and believing that the adoption of the permanent Constitution of the Confederate States and the successful prosecution of the war are measures of the greatest possible importance to the people of the State, as an earnest advocate of this policy, I have heretofore said to many friends, and now repeat to you, that there is no position, where it is believed that I can contribute materially to the success of this great cause, in which I am not willing to serve, to the fullest extent of my ability, during the continuance of this struggle—no position in which I am not willing to devote all that I am, all that I have, to a vigorous prosecution of the war until the independence of the Confederate States shall be acknowledged. And believing, from the proceedings of many public meetings throughout the State, the declarations of the public press, and the many urgent solicitations verbally and by letter, that it is the wish of a decided majority of the people that I shall be a candidate for re-election, a proper sense of duty, as well as gratitude to my fellow-citizens for the confidence reposed, and the honor they have heretofore done me, will not allow me to decline a position accepted in time of peace, the duties of which have been rendered so highly responsible, important and arduous by a state of war. You may therefore rest assured that if the people of the State see proper to assign me to the duties of this office, I shall not shrink from an honest effort to perform them fully and in good faith. In assuming the position of a candidate I regret that I

---

[310] *Memphis Daily Appeal*, July 17, 1861.

cannot meet and confer personally with my fellow citizens upon the important questions of the day; but the many responsible duties devolving upon the office, the proper discharge of which cannot be safely delayed, require my constant presence and attention at the Department. I must, therefore, content myself by referring the people of the State to my public acts of the past as the highest guarantee that I can offer for the future, feeling assured that from them my positions and opinions are known and distinctly understood by all who desire to know them.

Allow me in conclusion to tender you my thanks for the flattering manner in which you were pleased to speak of my humble efforts to discharge, with fidelity, the duties which the kindness and confidence of the people of Tennessee have heretofore devolved upon me.

I have the honor to be, very respectfully, yours, etc.

Isham G. Harris."

In the meanwhile the *Republican Banner* was pushing the case of William H. Polk who had been "nominated" by this Whig organ. As a means of furthering the Polk candidacy, the *Banner* announced that a pamphlet of sixteen pages had been prepared advocating the election of Polk and that the pamphlets were available at the rate of $1.95 per hundred [311] "on receipt of an order enclosing the money."

But the Union leaders of East Tennessee were not disposed to permit the *Banner's* solo nominee to run unopposed by ardent East Tennessee Unionists. To their way of thinking, the gubernatorial candidate must not be tinctured with Middle or West Tennessee political virus. Accordingly, "Parson" Brownlow's *Knoxville Whig* announced that Connally F. Trigg of Knox County had been agreed upon as a candidate for Governor. A Nashville newspaper [312] quoted the *Whig* as follows:

"The Union party of Tennessee have resolved to run CONNALLY F. TRIGG, of Knox, for Governor, as well as a candidate for Congress, in each of the three Districts of East Tennessee. Col. Trigg is expected to respond to the call in an Address, in our paper, at least as early as next week. Col. Trigg is a true Union man, well tried, and reliable. He is well and favorably known to the Union men of the State, and especially of East Tennessee, and will receive, as he ought to have, the full strength of the Union party of our division of the State. We shall have occasion to refer to this subject again, and we do nothing more now than announce the fact that he has been agreed upon as the Union candidate."

In their zeal for the nomination and election of an East Tennessean for Governor, the East Tennessee Unionists had overlooked a constitutional requirement regarding a seven-year residency in Tennessee as a prerequisite of eligibility for that office. Colonel Trigg, in obedience to that insurmountable requirement, had nothing to do except decline the nomination which was commented upon as follows by his partisan newspaper: [313]

[311] *Republican Banner*, July 11, 1861.
[312] *The Daily Gazette* (Nashville), July 16, 1861.
[313] Quoted in the Nashville *Union and American*, July 20, 1861.

"The Knoxville *Whig* withdraws the name of Col. Trigg, as the Union candidate for Governor, and hoists the name of Col. Wm. H. Polk, in association with those of Nelson, Maynard and Bridges, heading it 'the Union ticket.' The *Whig* gives the following reasons for its support of Polk. They will probably be perfectly satisfactory to the men in East Tennessee who are threatening to rebel against the State Government and join Lincoln. The italics are ours:

William H. Polk.

It will be seen from the card of Col. Trigg, that he is ineligible to the office of Governor—not having resided in the State as long as the Constitution requires. We regret this, as we desired to run an East Tennessee Union man. But having now only two weeks to go upon, and having to choose between Isham G. Harris and Wm. H. Polk, we don't hesitate to take the latter. Harris has shown his hostility to East Tennessee in every movement he has made; and his bitterness towards Union leaders and Union men, by the hands he has placed the Banks in. Polk is an original Union man and a Douglas Democrat; *and although he yielded to the Secession pressure, as everybody did in Middle and West Tennessee, he was among the last men to surrender, and continued to make Union speeches until his friends remonstrated, because of the danger he was exposed to.* He is kind in his feelings toward East Tennessee and East Tennessee Union men, and will do us justice, the very thing Harris and his party will never do. As a choice of evils and as a peace measure, we go for Polk, and no Union man in East Tennessee ought, for one moment, to hesitate about supporting Polk. We can give him 20,000 of a majority in this end of the State, and let us do it."

But the ardent Secessionist journal, minimizing the constitutional ineligibility of Colonel Trigg for the governorship, did not allow to pass by unnoticed the position that the ineligible aspirant had taken. After lambasting Trigg for being opposed to Tennessee's declared alliance with the Confederacy, the newspaper [314] warned its clientele against "the burrowing of Lincolnites and Tories who will be endeavoring to procure votes against the permanent constitution of the Confederate States." In support of its warning, an extract from Colonel Trigg's letter of declination was published, to-wit:

". . . But inasmuch as the *permanent* Constitution of the Confederate States is to be submitted to the people for their adoption or rejection, I must be pardoned for adding a word on that subject. The action of the people of Tennessee upon that Constitution will have a most important bearing upon their future destiny. For if the people adopt it, they plunge themselves irrevocably into the Southern Confederacy, and be the consequences what they may, they must abide them. What these consequences are likely to be, and of the utter ruin which is to attend them, we have already had a melancholy foretaste, by the brief connection we have thus far had with that Confederacy.

But if that Constitution shall be rejected by the people at the approaching election, the *status* of Tennessee will be changed, and she will then be in a condition to take such a course, in the impending crisis, as her best interests shall dictate.

---

[314] *Ibid.*

Apart from the unconstitutional 'Military League,' which was formed by her Legislature, with the Confederate States, the State of Tennessee has no other alliance with said States, than that which arises from the adoption of their *provisional* Constitution. That Constitution provides for its own *duration* by declaring that it shall 'continue one year from the inauguration of the President, or until a *Constitution* shall be put in operation.' The permanent Constitution, to be submitted to the people, *provides* that 'the ratification of the conventions of *five* States shall be sufficient for the establishment of this Constitution *between the States so ratifying the same.*'

So that by the very terms of the instrument it is apparent that any State which has adopted the Provisional Constitution, and which *refuses* to adopt the permanent one, will no longer be regarded as one of the Confederate States, for it is only to be established *between the States ratifying it.* Hence, if Tennessee shall refuse to ratify it, on the first Thursday in next month, her connection with the Confederate States will cease, except as far as she is bound by her 'Military League,' and the adoption of the Provisional Constitution. By the latter act, she can at most be held only for a year from the inauguration of the President, and not so long if *five* States shall ratify the Permanent Constitution, which will no doubt very shortly occur. And the 'Military League,' being a Legislative enactment, may be repealed and annulled by the same authority which brought it into existence."

The result of the August election for Governor was never in serious doubt. Governor Harris never made a single speech during the campaign, and Colonel Polk's speechifying was on an extremely limited scale. When the ballots were counted, it was ascertained that Governor Harris had been re-elected by a majority of more than 31,000 votes.[315] No violent editorials emanated from the press hostile to Harris. The *Republican Banner,* in a moderate tone, gave a résumé of its position and the reasons for having opposed Governor Harris:[316]

". . . We early gave expression to our opinion that the best interests of the State and of the cause of Southern Independence would not be promoted by the candidacy of Gov. Harris for a third term, and gave our reasons for that opinion at some length. Those reasons are familiar to our readers. The principal one referred to the peculiar attitude of the people of East Tennessee—the importance of conciliating them and disabusing their minds as to the real character of the revolution, and satisfying them that their interest and duty required that they should acquiesce in the will of the majority. We did not then and do not now believe that the best way to accomplish this was to re-elect the man of all others in the State the most obnoxious to the disaffected people, and as there was really no necessity for such a course, we opposed it. At that time our Legislature was in session, and the spirit of that body was in the highest degree conciliatory towards the East. We had reason to believe, from voluntary expressions, that our views of the Gubernatorial canvass met the approbation of a majority of the members of that body, including some of the warmest friends of Gov. Harris. Members from East Tennessee were particularly pleased with them, and hailed them as an indication calculated to promote harmony in the State.

---

[315] *House Journal,* 1861, 116–117.
[316] *Republican Banner,* August 2, 1861.

We had no choice as to who should be the candidate—we had no personal or old party preferences to gratify—and all who state or insinuate to the contrary state or insinuate what is without the shadow of foundation in truth.

But the policy which we regarded as important to be pursued was not adopted—the friends of Gov. Harris took the ground that he was a *sine qua non* to the success of the Southern Confederacy, and he was brought out to contest for a third term.

We supported Col. Polk because we believed the cause of Southern Independence would be as effectively promoted by him, as Governor of Tennessee, as it could be by Gov. Harris—because he occupied precisely the same position which the majority of our people occupied upon the great question of Southern nationality—because we believed his influence, as Governor, would be more potent in inducing the people of the Eastern Division of the State to acquiesce in the will of the majority.

We opposed Gov. Harris mainly because we believed and still believe that his election will be a stumbling block in the way of the reconciliation of East Tennessee, for the reason that a majority of the people there are strongly prejudiced against him, and his occupancy of the Executive chair will have a tendency to confirm their purpose to attempt the erection of an independent State. In the course of the canvass, when it was claimed that Gov. Harris was the only man fit to be Governor, we took occasion to expose his repeated violations of the State Constitution in making appointments, and also to expose the proscriptive character, as regards Union men on the 9th of February, of those appointments.

In the course of the canvass the supporters of Gov. Harris insinuated, and, in many irresponsible instances, as we have been informed, openly charged, that Col. Polk was a reconstructionist—a counter revolutionist—a Unionist—and these insinuations and charges have been made to include his supporters.—The enemies of the *Banner*—the ultraists, proscriptionists and furious fanatics, especially about this city—the men who have ever found in our paper a firm, calm and constructive advocate of law and order—have made this an occasion to seek, by operating upon individuals and by combinations—by contemptible insinuations and by gross falsehoods—to injure our business and impair our influence. These contemptible efforts have never in the least disturbed our equanimity. They are as futile to injure us—as powerless to move us from the discharge of our duty as journalists—as have been all similar efforts in this country to interfere with or restrict the freedom of the press. Their insinuations to the effect that we assume one set of opinions in the columns of our paper for the purpose of covering up another set of antagonistic opinions, could only have originated in the breasts of men themselves capable of such base hypocrisy, and of the cowardice of the malicious slanderer who stabs his victim in the dark and when his back is turned.

We shall hope for and labor for the best from the result of the election. We have our apprehensions that trouble will come which might have been honorably and easily avoided and without sacrifice. We shall, if disappointed in this, be very agreeably disappointed. The most dispassionate judgment, the wisest forethought, the most scrupulous and disinterested patriotism, will be required to steer the ship of State safely through the breakers that environ her, carelessly and recklessly as many, who claim to be the peculiar *par excellence* friends of the South, and who denounce all who disagree with their views as traitors, are disposed to regard them."

In a brief editorial "Parson" Brownlow gave expression to his sectional feeling, exhibiting remarkable restraint, for him, in that his remarks were free from his customary compound of fire and brimstone. Somewhat chastened perhaps by the triumphant election of Governor Harris, the "Parson" muttered this abbreviated requiem:[317]

"We supported Polk—not because we regard him as a Union man, but because we knew he was kind in his feelings towards East Tennessee, and we believed he would exert a great influence in restoring peace to the State, and especially to our section. We knew that the people of East Tennessee cherish towards Harris hostility, deep and lasting, and not without cause."

Along with the triumphant victory of Governor Harris a pro-Confederate Legislature was swept into office, although East Tennessee sent a delegation retaining its pro-Union sentiment. Opposition to ratification of the Confederate Constitution was reflected in the vote cast by East Tennessee, the same being 27,738 to 15,494. The vote for Governor was 27,115 for Polk and 14,887 for Harris. As a whole, however, the Legislature was overwhelmingly of the Secession persuasion. In accordance with constitutional requirements, the Legislature convened on the first Monday in October, the same being October 7, 1861. Three members of the House of Representatives were nominated for Speaker, William L. Martin of Wilson County, John Martin of Shelby County, and Edward A. Keeble of Rutherford County. After withdrawal of William A. Martin, the twelfth ballot resulted in the election of Mr. Keeble by a vote of 37 to 31.[318] There is not extant any *official* record in the fragmentary *Senate Journal*[319] concerning the election of a Speaker of the Senate, but the *House Journal*, 1861, page 18, discloses that Edward S. Cheatham was elected Speaker.

On the opening day of the Legislative session, Governor Harris was ready with his major Message* to the Legislature:

"EXECUTIVE DEPARTMENT
Nashville, October 7, 1861.

GENTLEMEN OF THE SENATE, AND THE HOUSE OF REPRESENTATIVES:
Since the adjournment of the last regular session, I have deemed it my duty to convene the Legislature, twice in extra session.

---

[317] *Brownlow's Weekly Whig*, August 10, 1861.
    Author's note. On August 3, 1861, two days after the gubernatorial election, Brownlow changed the name of the *Knoxville Whig* to *Brownlow's Weekly Whig*.
[318] *House Journal*, 1861, 10.
[319] *Senate Journal*, 1861 (manuscript).
    Author's note. The *Senate Journal* for the Thirty-Fourth legislative session has never been printed. In fact, there is only a fragment of the *Journal* extant, covering only two days of the session. The *House Journal* of this session was not printed until 1957, when the Tennessee Historical Commission sponsored its publication.
* *House Journal*, 1861, 19–30.

My Messages to, and the Legislation by those extra sessions, will furnish full information as to the action of the State in the most important period of its history, resulting in the resumption of her original sovereignty, by the almost unanimous action of her people, and a Union with the Government of the Confederate States of America.

Impelled to this action by 'a long train of abuses and usurpations, pursuing envariably the same object,' evincing a settled purpose on the part of those controlling the Federal Government to degrade the Southern States below the level of equality, depreciate and destroy their property in open violation of the plainest guarantees of the Constitution, leaving these States no alternative but humiliating submission, or manly resistance to the tyranny of Usurpation. In contemplating the present condition of the country and the exciting and important events which are now transpiring it may not be unprofitable to review, briefly, the history of the past, and follow step by step the progress of that revolution in the public sentiment of the North which has culminated in the utter repudiation of those vital principles of personal freedom, political equality and State Sovereignty upon which the Union of the States was originally established. As our country expanded into the magnificent proportions of a great empire, a majority of the Northern people were dazzled by the opening splendor of the nation as a unit. In contemplating with pride and satisfaction the development of a gigantic power, capable of contending with equal terms with any other nation of the earth, they overlooked the important truth, that this colossal government was indebted for its greatness to the aggregated power of the separate sovereign States which composed it, developed by their respective local laws and institutions.

The country being naturally divided by geographical distinctions—dissimilarity of pursuits, institutions, local laws and diversity of interests, into two great sections, upon the very instant when the equality and sovereignty of the States were denied by a majority of the members composing the confederacy, the tendency of the stronger section was to widen the breach between them, and to stimulate sectional animosities, in order that it might seize upon the exclusive control of the power and purse of the General Government.

The struggle for supremacy, therefore, was soon narrowed down to a contest between these two great sections, the South gallantly battling for the maintenance of Constitutional liberty, State sovereignty and political equality, while the North, disregarding these great cardinals, sought to obtain power and spoils upon their ruins.

In such a contest the victory at the ballot box necessarily inured to that section which was numerically the stronger. The exclusion of all the Southern States from all practical participation in control of the General Government was the immediate and unavoidable consequence.

Upon the election of President Lincoln under such auspices, the Southern people were left in a condition of dependence as hopeless as that held by their fathers when they occupied the position of provincial subjects of the British Crown.

All positions of influence and power in the Government at the disposal of the Presidential Chief, were immediately with those who were the most bitter and clamorous enemies of the South.

He who had maintained the greatest degree of virulence against the domestic institutions and well-defined constitutional rights of the Southern States and people was regarded as possessing the highest claim to Executive favor and patronage. What hope could the Southern people indulge for justice, at the hands of such rulers?

The Congress which was in session at the inauguration of the President enacted a tariff law for the undisguised purpose of transferring the earnings of the farmer and planters of the South, into the pockets of the manufacturers of the North.

The Executive, Legislative and Diplomatic functions of the Government were in the possession of a party backed by the power of a dominant section, declaring and inaugurating a policy revolutionary in its self, and destructive of the rights and liberties of the people of the Southern States, and measures were in active progress to carry out their oft-repeated threats to reorganize the Judiciary, so as to make that last and only remaining bulwark of Constitutional liberty subservient to their selfish and sectional purposes.

Having exclusive control of the Government, they refused to listen to any overtures on the part of the South for a peaceful solution of the difficulties and dangers which they had thus precipitated upon the Country.

In the blind wantoness of Sectional pride and imaginary power, they haughtily refused to entertain any terms of Compromise, or to abate in the smallest degree their arrogant pretensions.

They insultingly proclaimed that the will of a majority was the will of the Government, and hence, the will of a majority of the people of the Northern States must be regarded as the law of the Union, regardless of Constitutional restrictions, justice and equality. Having exhausted every peaceful measure which the most devoted friends of the Union could devise, in fruitless efforts to induce this sectional party to pause in its career of unjust aggressions, the people of the South, almost as one man, prepared to meet the crises as became descendants of a brave and liberty-loving ancestry.

Eleven States have resumed the power which they had delegated to the General Government, and in the exercise of their inalienable rights, have united themselves together and started out on their career under the auspices of a new Confederacy.

Our late associates, dissenting from our course, and maddened by unexpected resistance to their assumptions of authority, have hurled upon our unoffending people their legions of mercenary soldiers in order to bend the necks of the freemen of the South to the galling yoke of a military despotism.

Their President has officially announced through the medium of his message, the monstrous heresy, that the several States of the Union are indebted to the Federal Government for their existence, and the duration of their separate authority, in effect assigning to them, the same relation to the Union that counties bear to States, and foreshadowing policy of consolidating such states as submit to it into a single sovereignty, while such as have the spirit to resist, are to be subjugated and held as conquered provinces.

Let us for a moment survey the humiliating spectacle which is presented by the present condition of the people of the North, who, in their suicidal efforts to aid the despotism which has been established at Washington, have suffered themselves to be despoiled of the last vestige of that real liberty which they inherited from their fathers.

However bitterly the opponents of the Republican party may have resisted its advent to power who of its most determined enemies could have believed that within six short months after the inauguration of its chosen president the freedom of the press would have been utterly annihilated, and the circulation of all newspapers through the mails prohibited which dared to question the wisdom of his policy or his measures. Who could have believed that within so brief a period, the citizen who ventured to express his disapproval of the policy of the President, or even to utter 'words of peace and good will' would have been guilty of a crime sufficient to consign the offender to a dungeon?

Who could have imagined that the writ of habeas corpus that great bulwark of personal freedom, would have been suspended or denied, and entire States placed under martial law by the mere proclamation of a military chief?

Almost every public journal throughout the North, whether political or religious which failed or refused to give its support to the policy of the President, has been suppressed, or compelled its support to the Government.

Editors who have declined yielding obedience to their demands have been committed to prison.

Citizens against whom there was no imputation of crime have been dragged from their beds at midnight, and hurried away to distant fortresses without warrant of law, and without the poor consolation of knowing the charge upon which they were arrested.

The sanctity of the church has been invaded and their ministers driven from their pulpits. Woman, whose person has been held sacred by all civilized nations, has been taken from her home and imprisoned under the reign of this brutal despotism. And in mere wantoness of cruelty they have denied to these victims of tyranny the privilege of communication with their families and friends even in the presence of their jailors.

In whatever direction we may turn to examine the operations of the Government of the United States under the control of the party now in power, we behold the same disregard of the rights and privileges of the people.

Look, for example, at the fate of down-trodden Maryland! A ruthless soldiery lords it over every City, village and hamlet within her limits. Men, women and children are fleeing from their homes to seek an asylum amongst their friends in the South. Many of her best and noblest citizens are the tenants of dungeons and of all the free men who a few short months ago discussed without restraint, the policy and measures of the Government, there remain none who dare to speak in terms of adulation of the tyranny which has robbed them of their liberties. Not content with the degradation imposed upon the people, they have caused to be arrested and imprisoned their elected Representatives to the Legislature, who were suspected of entertaining opinions adverse to the measures of President Lincoln.

In Missouri the despotic rule of the military leaders sent there by the United States, has been even more galling and oppressive, if such were possible.

The bloody code of military laws by which that unhappy country is at present governed, is equal in enormity to any of which there is a record in the pages of history of the civilized world.

Martial law has been proclaimed and established, so far as the Federal Government has the physical power to establish it, and the civil authorities superseded by the military. A citizen charged with an offence against the law is no longer allowed the privilege of a fair and impartial trial by a jury of his peers, but is subjected to the mockery of a trial by a drum-head court martial, composed of members who may not even comprehend a word of the language in which the laws are written; and who have entered the military service of the United States as mere adventurers, or mercenary cut throats, who are willing to butcher their fellow men for hire.

As independent States, both Missouri and Maryland have ceased to exist! They have been blotted from the catalogue of sovereignties, and a foreign Master has placed his foot upon the necks of their once free and happy people.

What may be said of that once proud Kentucky, which Tennessee has always regarded as a twin Sister?

She, too, seems almost ready to fall a victim to the arms of our common enemy.

For the admiration we feel for her noble sons who are rallying by thousands to rescue her from the perils which overhang her present and future, and in memory of her glorious past, let us hope, and hope without doubting, that she will hurl the manacles from her limbs before they have been firmly rivetted, and once more stand forth amongst her Sister States of the South redeemed and disenthralled, the same as we have known her in other and better days.

Maryland, Missouri and Kentucky, may have to bear yet a little longer, the tortures of their enslavement, but the day of their deliverance will come.

Millions of their sympathising friends of the South regard their cause as their own, and if it is the wish of those States to be saved, the soldiers of the south will never lay down their arms until the last Northern Mercenary has been driven beyond their borders!

The States of the South now engaged in this momentous struggle for freedom, may behold in the present condition of Maryland and Missouri a faint picture of what their own would have been, if they had delayed their declarations of independence, and postponed the work of preparing to resist the encroachments of an unscrupulous enemy.

Had we remained a short time longer in inglorious ease, living in the enjoyment of the delusive hope that a returning sense of Justice would induce the Northern people to award to us our full measure of constitutional right, we would, like the victims encircled by the anaconda, have been crushed without the power of resistance.

The condition of Maryland and Missouri furnish us with a dim foreshadowing of what our fate would be if the fortunes of war should result even in a partial subjugation of any of the Confederate States.

We would be blind indeed, if we did not see that for us there can be no future to which annihilation would not be preferable, except in the establishment of our independence. All that we have, and all that we hope for, is dependent upon a successful issue to this conflict. Not only our estates and our rights of every description but our liberties and our lives are staked upon the result.

The South has entered into the struggle with enthusiasm and unanimity, knowing well the consequences which would surely follow defeat.

Already have our enemies parceled out in prospective the property of our people, and their deluded soldiers are revelling in imagination in the promised homesteads of the gallant defenders of our soil.

The Northern taxpayers who hesitate to encourage the prosecution of a war, which, even in the first months of its progress, is increasing the national debt at the rate of over a million of dollars per day, are silenced into acquiescence by the promise that the South shall pay the entire expense, past, present and future, so soon as she is subjugated. And visions of prospective positions of dignity and power in the government of the conquered provinces of the South, are dazzling the fancy of their ambitious military chiefs.

Never before did any people engage in a war in which they had more to gain by success, or to lose by defeat than have the people of the Confederate States in the present struggle and never yet have any people marched forward with a nobler, firmer or more united purpose, to gain or lose all.

They have known from the beginning, that there was for them no intermediate stopping place, between complete victory and entire ruin.

In the stand they have taken the present [is] the noblest spectacle of sublime devotion to liberty. Unselfish patriotism and perfect fraternity wherein the wealth of money, and the best blood of the country are all thrown into the common stock without stint or reservation, to achieve a common and glorious deliverance, or to perish by a common disaster!

In the providence of Almighty God, it was never designed that such a people should fail in achieving their independence, despite the power of superior numbers to which their invaders may lay claim. The pages of History do not furnish a single example where eight millions of united freemen have been permanently subdued by any power, however formidable, which may have been brought against them. The spirit which animates men who combat in defense of their families and homes, render them more than a match for twice their number of mere mercenary adversaries who fight for plunder and for conquest.

Witness the various engagements which have already marked the progress of the war.

Remember the seige of Sumter, the battle of Bethel, the crowning glory of Manassas, where our victorious legions drove back the 'Grand Army' in wild confusion and dismay into the very presence of the despot who sent them forth, and into the very capital from whence they had marched only a short time before, flushed with the assurance of an easy victory.

Remember the brilliant achievements at Springfield and Lexington.

The difficulties which beset us for a time, are resulting in permanent advantages. The rigid blockade which it was vainly supposed would starve us into submission has not only taught us how easily we can dispense with the luxuries to which we have been accustomed but having thrown us upon our resources, it has developed internal sources of wealth of which we had lived in comparative ignorance.

Instead of the bread which we have heretofore purchased beyond our own limits, we have furnished it ourselves in fourfold abundance from our own teeming and generous soil.

The contemplation of a possible future necessity, has taught us that we can produce within the limits of the Confederacy, every necessary article for which we have been heretofore dependent upon others.

Tennessee alone, under the stimulant of constant demand, can supply food and clothing for more than three times her population.

The very enormities which have characterized the acts of the Government of the United States, and which were designed to strike terror to the bosoms of the Southern people, have only served to steel our hearts and nerve our arms and to add another and an irresistable impulse to our determination to free ourselves now and forever from all political association with our former confederates.

Although the patriotic devotion of the entire South to the noble cause in which we have all staked 'Our lives, our fortunes, and our sacred honor', is worthy of all praise, yet I may be pardoned for referring with feelings of pride and satisfaction to the proud and patriotic stand which Tennessee has taken in this great struggle, and the liberal contributions of gallant men and munitions of war which she has made to the cause of Southern Independence. It is due to Tennessee to say, and it may be said without disparagement to other States, that our people have done more in raising, organizing, arming and equipping an army than was ever before accomplished by any State in the same length of time.

Having no military organization, and almost without arms, and destitute of authority to raise troops or procure arms, untill the passage of the act of the sixth of May last, within less than two months from the passage of this act, Thirty thousand volunteers were organized and thrown into the field.

Too much credit cannot be awarded to the patriotic people of the State, for the alacrity with which they rushed to the Standard of their country upon the first intimation of necessity.

I have been compelled to decline the services of a large number tendered in excess of the demands. Much credit is due, also, to the officers of the Provisional Army for the promptitude with which they organized and prepared so large a force for effective service in the field.

I refer you to the report of Adjutant General McHenry for full particulars in detail as to the organization of the Provisional Army of Tennessee.

This Army was, on the 31st day of July last, by my general order of that date, transferred to the service of the Confederate States of America.

In addition to the Provisional Army of the State, a number of Regiments have been raised for Confederate service, making in the aggregate, thirty-eight infantry Regiments, Seven Cavalry batallions and sixteen artillery companies which Tennessee has contributed to the common defense.

The duty of furnishing arms, munitions, and the means necessary to clothe and subsist the Provisional Army devolved upon the Military and Financial Board. Cut off from Northern markets, and Southern ports blockaded, they found it difficult, if not impossible, to procure either arms or munitions, to any considerable extent, by purchase in the market.

The Board therefore adopted all practicable means of stimulating private enterprize to produce those articles of indispensable necessity within our own limits.

They established an armory at Nashville for the manufacture of arms, and made liberal contracts with various companies for the casting of cannon, the purchase of army guns to be manufactured in Tennessee, and delivered within different times within the year, from which sources we have for some time past, been receiving about two hundred and fifty guns per week.

They have also made liberal advances to manufacturers of powder, to enable them to increase the capacity of their machinery to the highest degree of efficiency, and under the supervision of Samuel D. Morgan Esq. established a percussion cap factory, which has already yielded to the Confederate States more than twelve millions of caps, and is now producing over 225,000 per day.

(For full particulars as to the action of the Board, I refer you to their report, from which it will be seen that the expenses incurred in organizing and supporting, arming and equipping the Provisional Army are as follows, to wit:

Quartermaster General's Department	$1,657,706.65
Commissary General's Department	627,064.87
Paymaster General's Department	1,104,800.00
Medical Department	24,761.21
Ordnance Department	990,291.20
Recruiting Service	723.25
Advance to Gen'l Pillow, Missouri Service	200,000.00
Contingent Expenses	31,851.59
Total	$4,637,198.77

There are some balances of expenditures still due and unpaid, which it is believed will consume the balance of the five millions appropriated by the 6th of May 1861.)

Those expenditures will be assumed and refunded to the State by the Confederate Government. Having transferred the army to the Confederate States, it was deemed proper that the army supplies of every description should be transferred also: We have therefore transferred to that Government the cap factory, all of our contracts for arms, powder, saltpetre, and all of our army items of every description.

The Armory would have been transferred also, but the Government declined accepting it.

The services of this Board have been of incalculable advantages to the State, and the duties imposed upon it have been performed with a degree of promptitude and ability, highly creditable to the distinguished gentlemen who compose it.

To the vigilance and care of the Medical Department we are indebted for an able and skillful medical Staff, and the adoption of all measures calculated to promote the health and comfort of the Army.

For full information you are respectfully referred to the report of the Department, which will, in due time, be laid before you.

To supply and provision the immense force in actual service required for the defense and maintainance of the Government we have established, is the first and imperative duty of the public authorities, in the discharge of which, great effort and expenditure is demanded;

and it is not to be expected that the Government can at all times overcome difficulties at once, and promptly meet the wants of its soldierly.

The Congress of the Confederate States fully appreciating this arduous duty, provided by law that the States might furnish to their volunteers in the Confederate Service, clothing—and directed that the Secretary of War should pay the money value therefor.

Your attention is directed to this law approved August 30th 1861. As well as to the probable wants and necessities of your Constituents now in active service, It is believed that without relieving the General Government of its duty to make ample provision for its soldierly, you can, by proper legislation, secure the comforts of your own volunteers, and make provision against any probable privations or sufferings upon their part, by adopting the course indicated by the Congress of the Confederate Government in the law referred to: extending your aid even beyond the article of clothing. Let your volunteers feel and know that you are determined that in no event shall they be allowed to suffer, if the State, by the action of its authorities, can prevent it.

It is a beautiful episode in the history of our struggles to note the fact, that our fair country women with that heroic devotion and loyalty that characterized the women of '76, are contributing their time, their efforts and their means, to aid, to cheer, and sustain the men, who are imperilling their lives upon the battle fields of the country.

Countless in value and number are the articles which their patriotism and affection have sent to the relief and comfort of the soldiers of the South. The future historian of our country, will have a bright page to write, in recording the deeds of love, kindness and patriotism of the women of the South. I mention their name and their efforts in this connection only for the purpose of urging upon your attention the propriety of devising some means for the safe transmission and delivery of such articles as they may contribute, as well as such as are voluntarily tendered by the friends and kindred of the soldier.

I regret that it is my duty to call your attention to the tendency to monopoly and extortion which exists to a ruinous extent with a class of our citizens, who, intent upon the sordid purposes of gain, are taking advantage of the peculiar circumstances of the times, to reap exorbitant profits from the necessities of the government and the wants of the people.

Complaints have reached me from various portions of the State, of this unpatriotic and destructive tendency to extravagant speculation, placing every article, indespensable to the support of an army, as well as the ordinary necessaries of life, at prices far above those warranted by the legitimate laws of trade, and in many cases, beyond the reach of the more indigent classes of society.

The Merchant and tradesman, while restrained within proper limits, are useful and necessary members of the community and in common with every other legitimate pursuit, are entitled to the fostering care of the Government, but when forgetful of their duties as citizens, they suffer themselves tempted so far upon the sea of speculation as to become serious evils rather than conveniences to the public, it becomes your duty as guardians of that public to adopt such measures as will but tend to restrain illegitimate and improper speculation, and put down an evil which is fast becoming so prevalent and mischievous.

In ordinary times, an outraged public sentiment and the laws of trade would accomplish this end, but in times of general distress and threatened danger, when the government is involved in war, and must secure, regardless of price, whatever may be necessary to the comfort and maintainance of our patriotic and brave countrymen who have gone to the field to uphold the rights and honor of their country, and to defend the lives and property of this class, who are thus speculating upon their privations and necessities; the authorities cannot be too vigilant in their efforts to restrain the excesses of avarice and protect society against the evils to which it is exposed.

By a law of the Congress of the Confederate States of America entitled an Act 'To put into operation the Government under the Permanent Constitution of the Confederate States of America, approved May 21, 1861, it is provided, that an election shall be held in the several States of this Confederacy on the first Wednesday of November, 1861, for members of the House of Representatives in the Congress of the Confederate States under the Permanent Constitution'; and said act further provides and directs that on the same day the several States shall elect or appoint electors for President and Vice President of the Confederate States of America, according to said Constitution.

The act directs the time and manner in which said electors shall discharge their duties, and designates the time at which the first Congress under the Permanent Constitution shall assemble, being the 18th day of February, 1861. This law of Congress was approved prior to the ratification and adoption of the Permanent Constitution by the people of Tennessee, but anticipating that it would be done, the Congress of the Confederate States enacted that the State of Tennessee should be entitled to elect eleven members to the House of Representatives.

The people of Tennessee having adopted the Permanent Constitution of the Confederate States of America are therefore entitled to participate in the election of Executive and Legislative officers conformably to its provisions, and the law enacted to put the Government under it into operation.

It will therefore devolve upon you to digest and enact such laws as will secure the representation of your State in the Congress and Electoral College of the Government of the Confederate States of America. Inasmuch as the State is entitled to Eleven Representatives in the Congress of the Confederate States, and there are but ten Congressional districts as now laid off, it will become your duty to redistrict the State, which will be doubtless done by you in a spirit of fairness and equality, looking to the Geographical position of counties and their populations and as the time which intervenes between the day of your assembling and that fixed for the election is very short, it is important to the State that you discharge that duty, by defining the districts at the earliest day possible.

In this connection, it is proper I should state to you that there is on file in the office of the Secretary of State, full returns from the Marshalls of the three Grand Divisions of the State of the Census taken in the year 1860. The information contained in these reports will be valuable, if not indespensably necessary for this purpose immediately printed for the use of the General Assembly.

The universal interest felt in this important struggle, involving as it does, the destiny of a Republic, and the independence of a great people, renders the dry details of ordinary legislation distasteful to the public mind. The important duties, however, which are imposed upon the State Government by the pending conflict demands at our hands the strictest scrutiny into all of its departments in order that it may be made fully equal to such emergencies as may probably arise.

The necessities of civil government, however, demand very little legislation, except such as may be necessary to its economical administration and the development of all of our internal resources.

The reports of the Comptroller and Treasurer show the following to be the Fiscal Condition of the State:

Balance in the Treasury 1st Oct. 1859	$ 180,303.33
Receipts into the Treasury for the year ending 1st Oct. 1860	$ 790,247.38
Total	$ 970,550.71
Disbursements for same year	$ 891,944.23
Leaving balance in the Treasury 1st Oct. 1860	$ 78,606.48
Receipts into the Treasury for the year ending 1st Oct. 1861	$ 936,827.53
Total	$1,015,434.01
Disbursements for same year	$ 829,937.29
Leaving balance in the Treasury 1st Oct. 1861	$ 185,496.72

It will be seen by reference to the report of the Comptroller, that the aggregate value of taxable property in the State in 1860, was $389,011,468, and in 1861 $368,269,308, showing a depreciation in one year of $20,752,362, with the latter assessment made previous to the commencement of the war. It is confidently believed that if the assessment of the taxable property of the State should be made at this time, it would still show a further reduction, leaving the aggregate at about $200,000,000.

This depreciation in the value of taxable property demonstrates the necessity of the most rigid economy in public expenditures, or an increase of taxation to support the civil government.

I cannot too strongly urge upon your consideration the policy of retrenchment and reform in every department of the Government where it is possible, and thus husband our resources to the utmost extent for the support of our armies, and the maintenance of our independence. In this connection, it is proper that I should call your attention to the 4th section of the act of the Confederate Congress, approved 19th August, 1861, imposing a tax upon certain descriptions of property therein named, 'for the special purpose of paying the principal and interest of the public debt and supporting the Government.'

It is believed from the best estimates that can be made based upon the previous assessments of the taxable property of the State, that the amount to be collected from the people of Tennessee, under this act, will not fall very far short of $2,000,000.

The 24th Section of the act provides, that, 'If any state shall on or before the 1st day of April next, pay, in the Treasury Notes of the Confederate States, or in specie, the taxes assessed against the citizens of such State, less ten per centum thereon, it shall be the duty of the Secretary of the Treasury to notify the same to the several tax collectors in such State, and thereupon their authority and duty under this act shall cease.'

If the State should avail herself of the provisions of this Section, she will save to her people ten per cent of the amount assessed against them, in the aggregate amounting to $200,000, and the sum to be raised will be collected by the revenue officers of the State, obviating the necessity of two classes of revenue collectors, which will reduce the expenses of collection and relieve the people from the necessity of more than one revenue settlement. I therefore respectfully recommend that you provide for and pay, according to the provisions of the 24th section the amount assessed against the State; but in doing so, care should be taken that no part of the burthen is imposed upon that class of the people who are wisely exempted by the act of Congress.

BANKS

I refer you to the report of the supervisor for information as to the condition and business of the Banks of the State, from which it will be seen that their line of discounts has kept pace with the legitimate wants of the business of the country. The present condition of public affairs has diverted from former channels their business operations, some of their chief points of exchange having become centres of an enemy's country are closed against them, and they are engaged in the pioneer work of opening new channels and finding new fields for the enterprize of Southern commerce.

Therefore certain modifications which, under other circumstances might have been recommended, are not at present deemed appropriate.

Let the system remain as it exists under the present law, 'leaving the rest to the ability, prudence and good faith of those whose duty it is to direct its practical operation.'

For full and accurate details as to the present condition business and profits of the 'Bank of Tennessee', you are referred to the report of the President and Directors from which it will be seen that the net profits for the two years ending July 1st 1860, have amounted to the sum of $552,125.58.

Of this amount $407,681.81, has been paid into the Treasury, the balance being reserved by the Bank to cover bad and doubtful debts, heretofore contracted. It is due the President and Directors of the Bank of Tennessee, and indeed to all the officers of the other Banks, to state that they have extended to the Government every facility and assistance in their power to place the State in a position to repel invasion and maintain her independence, without which it would have been difficult, if not impossible to have accomplished much that has been done in that respect.

RAIL ROADS

By the act of the 6th May 1861, it is left to the discretion of the Governor to appoint receivers to take possession of the Roads, property and effects of Rail Road Companies failing to pay the semi-annual interest upon the bonds of the State, loaned to aid in the construction of their roads.

The Comptroller has reported the following Rail Road Companies as having failed to pay the interest falling due 1st July 1861, to wit,

Mobile and Ohio Rail Road Company	$33,720.00
Memphis and Little Rock Company	10,500.00
Nashville and North Western Company	43,650.00
Rogersville and Jefferson Company	4,770.00
Tennessee and Alabama Company	21,000.00
Memphis, Clarksville and Louisville Company	31,260.00
East Tennessee and Virginia Company	27,970.00
Nashville and Chattanooga Company	4,500.00

Believing as I do, that their failure to pay resulted from no want of inclination on their part, nor from bad or improper management on the part of their officers or employees, but from the fact of general prostration of trade and commerce, almost their entire business for the last six months having been the transportation of troops and munitions of war, which they have done with the utmost promptitude and upon the most accommodating terms, I have felt that neither the security of the State nor the interest of the Companies would be promoted by placing them in the hands of receivers, and I have therefore declined appointing such receivers.

The Edgefield and Kentucky and the Winchester and Alabama Rail Road Companies having failed to pay the interest due upon their bonds on the 1st January 1861, previous to the above recited act, I appointed Adna Anderson, receiver to take charge of the former, and James B. Lamb receiver of the latter.

These Roads with the property and effects of the Companies were placed in the hands of their respective receivers and have been operated by them up to this time; the operations of neither having as yet refunded to the treasury the amount of interest paid on their account.

For an accurate statement of the account of each with the treasury, I refer you to the report of the Comptroller.

By reference to the report of the agent and Inspectors of the Penitentiary, it will be seen that there has been a gradual increase in the number of convicts for the last two years, and that the business for that period has been large, resulting in a net profit to the State of $32,729.68.

By the act of the 24th March 1860, the sum of $100,000 was appropriated for the purpose of enclosing and grading the Capitol grounds, said fund to be raised by issuing that amount of coupon bonds of the State which were to be cashed by the Bank of Tennessee at par.

The work progressing under the supervision of the Capitol Commissioners on the 17th day of September 1860, I issued $25,000 of Bonds and delivered the same to the Bank of Tennessee, the Bank placing to the credit of the Commissioners that amount. By the act of the 1st Feb., 1861, the appropriation was repealed, and the Commissioners directed after paying all debts against them, to pay the balance of the fund in their hands into the treasury. It will be seen from the report of the Comptroller that after settling their accounts, they paid into the treasury $5,003.61.

Under the 3rd Section of Said act, I appointed James Plunkett receiver to take into his possession the mules, carts and tools belonging to said state and used upon the Capitol grounds, and ordered him to sell the mules and such other property as was perishable, but to receipt for and retain the tools, as they would at no distant day, be needed, and could not be sold except at a very great sacrifice. The receiver reports the net proceeds of sale of mules, corn, and hay at $725.38, which sum has also been paid into the treasury.

The other property remains in the possession of the receiver, subject to any order that you may see proper to make with regard to it.

CHARITABLE INSTITUTIONS.

I refer you to the reports of the Trustees of the Hospital for the Insane, the Blind School, and the Deaf and Dumb School, for full and accurate information as to the condition and progress of each of these institutions. I am pleased to believe that a critical examination of their reports will show each of them to be in a very satisfactory condition, contributing greatly to the relief, comfort and improvement of these unfortunate classes of our citizens.

Whatever may be the general necessity for retrenchment and economy, we must not forget that these victims of misfortune are entitled to the fostering care of the Government.

ISHAM G. HARRIS"

A representative sample [320] of pro-Secession sentiment on the part of the press, approving the tone of the Governor's bristling message, appeared two days after its transmission to the Legislature, to-wit:

"Governor's Message.

A large portion of our columns this morning is occupied by the Message of his Excellency, Governor Harris, which we earnestly commend to the readers of the Union and American as worthy of the most careful and thoughtful perusal. The analysis in it of the causes of the great revolution which has culminated in the separation of Tennessee from the sectionalized Union is one of the most forcible, succinct, and comprehensive reviews of that great question which has emanated from the pen of any statesman. So also the just tribute to the patriotism of the people of the State in the promptitude with which they responded to the call for volunteers will be interesting to every Tennessean who feels a pride in his native or adopted State. No branch of the Executive business is neglected but full information for the benefit of the Legislature is clearly given. We can only invoke a careful reading of this important State paper."

[320] *Union and American,* October 9, 1861.

On the day following the reception of the Governor's Message, legislative attention was turned to the issue that predominated throughout the entire session, namely, preparation for war. Representative Henry T. Osborne of Maury County introduced a comprehensive bill [321]

"... To amend an Act passed June 25, 1861, entitled an Act to raise and equip a provisional force. ..."

With a slight amendment proposed by the Military Committee, the Osborne bill passed third and final reading by a vote of 61 to 5.[322] On October 24, the House was advised that the Senate had also passed the above bill on third reading and that the bill was ready to be enrolled.[323] Section 1 of the law [324] provided that all white males, between the ages of eighteen and forty-five, should constitute the Reserve Military Corps, while all able-bodied white males from forty-five to fifty-five years should compose a Military Corps "for the defence of the State." Various and sundry provisions of the law specified certain details to be carried out by designated officials, among which was that the Governor was named Commander-in-Chief of the armed forces. Another important and essential provision was a three million dollar appropriation to be floated by the issuance of State bonds, the funds derived therefrom to be used in supporting war measures. Section 17 authorized the establishment of an Ordnance Bureau designed to facilitate putting the State on a war-time basis. On the whole, this law was the most important measure enacted by the Thirty-Fourth General Assembly.

Evidence of the unflagging vitality and fervor with which Governor Harris was prosecuting war measures may be seen in a glance at the official record dealing with his inauguration for his third term of office. Having been officially notified that he had been re-elected Governor, the inauguration date was fixed for Friday, November 1, 1861. The ceremonies were marked by the total absence of all hullabaloo and fanfare. Herewith is a verbatim account of the brief ceremonies:[325]

"His Excellency, Isham G. Harris the Gov. Elect attended by the Joint Committee of the two Houses was conducted to the Speaker's Chair.

After a prayer by the Rev. Dr. McFerrin the Governor Elect addressed the Convention as follows:

MR. PRESIDENT AND GENTLEMEN OF THE CONVENTION:

Having been reelected Governor of the State I am here to take the oath of Office which I am now ready to do.

The Oath of Office was then administered to him by the Hon. W. K. Turner one of the judges of the State of Tennessee.

---

[321] *House Journal*, 1861, 32.
[322] *Ibid.*, 42.
[323] *Ibid.*, 78.
[324] *Acts of Tennessee*, 1861–62, Chapter 26.
[325] *House Journal*, 1861, 136.

The ceremony was closed by a prayer from the Rev. Dr. Baldwin and the Convention adjourned."

No other gubernatorial ceremony thus far in the annals of Tennessee can compete in brevity with the induction of Governor Harris into his third term of office. His terse statement is reminiscent of Caesar's famous laconic message to the Roman Senate: *Veni, vidi, vici* (I came, I saw, I conquered).

In perfect accord with the spirit of Governor Harris' executive Message, Representative John Martin of Shelby County introduced the following Resolution:[326]

"Whereas the State of Tennessee is now being threatened by the invading armies of the Federal Government, and our forces to resist their approach to the Capitol of the State, are daily passing through this City and crowding the various thoroughfares of travel to the battle field: And Whereas the legislation of this General Assembly that is of real importance to the interests of the State can be finished at an early day, and such as is not important or pressing may be delayed until the War is over, or the invasion of the State is less imminent: And whereas the people of the State by the election of the members of this body and the other branches of the Government have confided to us and to them its interests and its honor, rendering by this civil trust higher and stronger the duty to serve her interests and to guard and protect her in every way within the scope of their ability and power both civil and military.

1st Be it resolved That the General Assembly of the State of Tennessee hasten to the completion of all legislation deemed essentially necessary, and then to form its members into a Military Company with his Excellency Isham G. Harris as Captain, Hon. Ed. S. Cheatham as first Lieutenant and the Hon. E. A. Keeble as second Lieutenant, and promptly report the Company to Gen. A. S. Johnston for such services as may be required for the protection of the State.

2. Be it further resolved that all persons or parties now in attendance in this General Assembly for Office or place, and especially all candidates for the Senate of the C.S.A. be and are hereby respectfully requested to join this Company and give the State their Military with the alacrity they exhibit in offering their civil services.

3. Resolved that this Company tender its Services to Gen. A. S. Johnston for such a period as in his judgment the exigencies of the Service shall demand in protecting the State from invasion."

A number of minor amendments were offered, chief of which read as follows:[327]

"Resolved by the House of Representatives that leave of absence be granted to the Senior Representative from Shelby, John Martin, during his pleasure, in order that said Martin may forthwith report himself at the headquarters of Gen. A. S. Johnston, that the Confederate Government may have the benefit of his eminent military talents in this the most gloomy period of our existence as a nation."

---

[326] *Ibid.*, 52–53.
[327] *Ibid.*, 69–70.

The above resolution together with sundry amendments was laid on the table where it remained from October 22, 1861, until March 19, 1862, whereupon it was passed in the House by a vote of 35 to 17.[328] This legislative action came just the day before the Legislature adjourned *sine die*. Representative Martin was present on the day of adjournment, and along with five other fellow-members entered the following protest:[329]

"We the undersigned Members of the Tennessee Legislature, would and do hereby avail ourselves of the Constitutional right of protest.

This right we desire and do hereby Exercise in regard to House Bill No. 270, known as the appropriation Bill, against the passage of Which we do enter this our Solemn and Earnest protest, and ask that the same be spread upon the Journals.

R. HILL.
JOHN MARTIN.
WM. SIMPSON.
D. W. C. SENTER.
JAMES H. RANDOLPH.
S. K. N. PATTON."

Whether or not the amendment pertaining to Representative Martin's military ability was a genuine tribute to his talents or was of a facetious nature must remain perhaps conjectural. At any rate, the official record discloses without a doubt that he remained a member of the General Assembly until the close of the session.

Imbued as he was with a fervid patriotic spirit calculated to extend every possible aid to the cause of the Confederacy, Governor Harris must have regretted to call attention to reports of speculation and graft regarding the necessities of life. It must have galled his ardent spirit to learn that the profiteer was plying his unholy trade when the life and destiny of Tennessee were at stake. With clarity and vigor he called for an end to such alleged conduct. In response to his admonition that the authorities could not be "too vigilant in their efforts to restrain the excesses of avarice and protect society against the evils to which it is exposed," Representative H. C. Lockhart of Stewart County proposed the following:[330]

"Whereas It is believed there are persons in the State of Tennessee who are so lost to patriotism as to engage in Speculation in articles necessary to the maintenance and comfort of the Army of the South, In many instances assuming the character of agents to the Military Authorities, they have it is believed purchased many articles from the honest and patriotic masses at extremely low prices which they have and will turn over to the Army at immense profit; Thus robbing the patriotic masses of their substance, the

---

[328] *Ibid.*, 474.
[329] *Ibid.*, 478.
[330] *Ibid.*, 57–58.

Soldiers of articles necessary to smooth his rugged pathway, placing the prices of necessaries of life out of the reach of his family, and increasing the cost of every thing purchased by the War department, Therefore,

Resolved by the General Assembly of the State of Tennessee, That we the representatives of the people do solemnly declare the action of Such persons as wholly unworthy of the name of Tennesseans, unpatriotic, Selfish and contemptible, and we do most earnestly advise and recommend the producing classes of Tennessee to give no countenance to Such Speculators, Sell them nothing, avoid them as they would a Leper or Judas Iscariot."

On October 21, Representative Abe Caruthers of Wilson County, Chairman of the Judiciary Committee, submitted the following report:[331]

"The Committee on the Judiciary to whom was referred so much of the Governors Message as relates to frauds, Speculations, and Monopolies respectfully Submit the following report.

The evils which have so justly aroused the indignation of the Country are divisable into two classes. First, the buying up of commodities under the false pretense of doing so for the use of the government or its Soldiers. People are thereby induced to part with articles that they would not part with at all for any other purpose, or they demand a Smaller price than they would take from any one who was purchasing for purposes of his own.

To suppress this evil the Committee Submit a bill entitled a bill to Suppress buying under false pretenses.

Secondly the buying up of Commodities without any false pretenses, but with intent to produce a Scarcity in the market and to enable the purchaser to Secure to himself exorbitant prices by reason of the monopoly he has effected.

The Committee find it very difficult to frame a law which will check this evil, without interfering with the freedom of legitimate trade. They have undertaken to accomplish the object by a bill which they Submit, to the House entitled a bill to Suppress monopolies.

The line drawn by this bill between legitimate and unlawful Speculation is this: When the intent in purchasing commodities is to produce a Scarcity in the general market and thereby enhance the price, it is denounced as unlawful.

But where a man buys commodities in the expectation that there will be a scarcity or an increased demand and consequently an increased price, but at the same time he does not buy with intent to produce the scarcity he anticipates this is legitimate trade.

The legitimate trader does not buy with the intent to produce a scarcity in the general market although that result may to Some extent result from his act.

The unlawful speculator intends to produce that result and will in general accumulate the article in his own hands, withholding it from the market until he has obtained a complete monopoly, and then extorting extravagant prices from the necessities of the government or the people.

Both these bills are expressly limited in their operation to the continuance of the War. In times of peace all Such evils will correct themselves. Competition and the laws of demand and Supply will operate as Sufficient correctives.

<hr />

[331] *Ibid.,* 64.

But the exigencies of the War should Seem to demand Some attempt at correction. And therefore the Committee respectfully Submit the accompanying bills as War measures.

Ab Caruthers, Chairman."

The bill for suppressing monopolies was suffered to linger in the legislative hopper for more than a month. Apparently somewhat irked at the delay, Representative Alfred Robb attempted to spur the Legislature to take some action by the introduction of the following resolution: [332]

"Whereas, the Legislature is informed that in certain sections of this State, breadstuffs and other necessaries of life have been raised to such extravagant prices as greatly to check and embarrass the patriotic spirit of many of the good Citizens of this State, who are nobly endeavoring to sustain themselves, and the State in the present struggle for human liberty.

And Whereas by the blessing of the ever Kind Providence to whose guidance we have and commit ourselves, our soil has yielded the most abundant supply of everything necessary to sustain human life, so that in the opinion of this Legislature, there is in our granaries and store houses full enough and 'to spare' to supply at a very moderate price the necessary wants of our whole people. And believing as we do that the excessive high prices complained of are not attributable to the ordinary laws of supply and demand, but are ascribable to the devices and Machinations of soulless, and sordid speculators and others who are alike inhuman and unpatriotic.

And believing that it is the duty of the Legislature to protect by law the patriotic citizens of the Country from oppression of the soulless money lovers who are alike deaf to the appeal of patriotism and Common humanity.

Therefore be it resolved by the General Assembly of the State of Tennessee, That a joint Select Committee be raised consisting of Six Members of this House and —— from the Senate, to whom shall be committed the subject embraced in the preamble to this resolution and whose duty it shall be, if in their opinion the same is practicable and right after a full investigation thereof to report a bill to the legislature providing a full remedy for the evil complained of and to make such other suggestions touching the Same as in their judgment may be proper and right."

In the meanwhile, however, the Judiciary Committee had come forth with the following bill which had been substituted for a previous bill on the same subject: [333]

"Section 1. *Be it enacted by the General Assembly of the State of Tennessee,* That no person shall buy any article of food or Clothing or any other property, upon the false pretense that he is employed or authorized to do so by the Confederate States of America, or any one of said States, or any Officer or agent thereof; or by any society for the aid or relief of the soldiers of the Confederate States, or any one of said States, or by any individual, society, partnership or corporation engaged in manufacturing or preparing Arms, munitions or other Warlike stores, or food, clothing or

[332] *Ibid.*, 206–207.
[333] *Ibid.*, 177–178.

other material or other Warlike stores, or food, clothing or other material for the use of the Soldiers aforesaid; or upon the false pretense that he is buying any of the articles or property aforesaid for the use or benefit of the Confederate States, or any of them, or for the use or benefit of the Soldiers thereof, whether he pretends to have authority to do so or not, and whether the person buying under the false pretense aforesaid, shall pay for the property so bought at the time of the purchase, or shall buy the same on credit, shall make no difference in his guilt nor shall it make any difference at what price he obtained it.

Section 2. *Be it enacted*, That no person shall buy up livestock, or any Commodity whatever, with intent to produce a scarcity of the same in the market, so that by reason of such scarcity he may obtain a higher price therefor.

Section 3. No person shall Combine to buy up livestock or commodities of any kind with intent to produce a scarcity thereof, in market, so that by reason of such scarcity, they may obtain a higher price therefor.

Section 4. Any violation of this Act shall be a high misdemeanor, and the offender shall be punished by both fine and imprisonment.

Section 5. Grand Juries shall have the same powers in inquiring into violations of this Act that they have in Tippling Cases.

Section 6. In indictments or Presentments under this act it shall be sufficient to State the Offence generally.

Section 7. The Judges shall give this Act in charge to the Grand Juries, and it shall be in force from the date of its passage."

For some undisclosed reason, there appears to have been timidity and hesitation on the part of the Legislature to enact any law bearing upon the topic. The bill above mentioned never received any serious consideration. After having been passed over informally, upon one or two occasions, the bill finally received a solar plexus blow by Chairman Caruthers himself who, on February 4, 1862, moved successfully that the bill "be laid on the table."[334] Certain it is that no law or resolution on the subject was enacted.

Governor Harris reminded the Legislature that Tennessee was a member of the Confederate States of America, membership having been obtained on July 22, 1861. The duty, therefore, of electing Senators to represent Tennessee devolved upon the incumbent Legislature. Because of the enactment of a law by the Confederate Congress, alloting Tennessee eleven Congressmen instead of ten, a reapportionment law [335] was enacted whereby an election for Congressmen was held in early November, 1861, with the following results:

First District	J. B. Heiskell
Second District	W. G. Swan
Third District	W. H. Tibbs
Fourth District	E. L. Gardenhire
Fifth District	Henry S. Foote

[334] *Ibid.*, 365.
[335] *Acts of Tennessee*, 1861–62, Chapter 12.

Sixth District	Meredith P. Gentry
Seventh District	George W. Jones
Eighth District	Thomas Menees
Ninth District	J. D. C. Atkins
Tenth District	John V. Wright
Eleventh District	David M. Currin

On October 24, 1861, the Legislature met in joint session for the purpose of electing "Confederate States Senators." Representative John Martin of Shelby County moved that but one Senator be elected at a time.[336] Senator R. W. Bumpass of Haywood County moved that one Senator be elected from each of the old political parties. Senator Bumpass accepted an amendment by Senator Robert Barton

"That we will now go into the Election of one Senator, and on the first ballotings we will nominate no man nor vote for any man who has not heretofore acted with the old Democratic Party."[337]

After the defeat of this motion by a vote of 54 to 36, and after another bit of maneuvering, announcement was made by the presiding officer that nominations for Senator were in order. Three nominees were offered, namely, Landon C. Haynes of Washington County, A. O. W. Totten of Madison County, and John A. Gardner of Weakley County. On the first and only ballot cast, Haynes received 58 votes, Totten received 24 votes, and Gardner received 2 votes, whereupon Haynes was declared "duly and constitutionally elected a Senator in the Congress of the Confederate States of America for the State of Tennessee."[338]

Nominations for the election of the second Senator were next on the agenda. Three names were presented, Gustavus A. Henry of Montgomery County, Edwin H. Ewing of Davidson County, and Robert L. Caruthers of Wilson County. For three days balloting ensued. On the thirty-second ballot, the results showed that Henry had received 53 votes and Ewing had 36. Thereupon Gustavus A. Henry, "The Eagle Orator," was declared elected.[339] With the eleven Congressmen heretofore indicated, plus the two elected Senators, Tennessee's Confederate Congressional representation was complete.

Military preparations superseded all civil demands, and Governor Harris placed before the Legislature the financial conditions of the State. Laying before the lawmakers the financial balance in the State Treasury, amounting to less than $200,000, Governor Harris called attention to the prerequisites of a law enacted by the Confederate Con-

---

[336] *House Journal*, 1861, 80.
[337] *Ibid.*, 80.
[338] *Ibid.*, 83.
[339] *Ibid.*, 84–108.

gress levying taxes upon certain species of property. In support of the recommendation by Governor Harris, a law [340] was enacted authorizing and directing the Governor to issue State Bonds in "a sufficient amount to pay said tax." In the event that the war tax exceeded the amount of two million dollars, additional bonds of a like nature were to be issued. For the payment of the bonds upon maturity, a tax of ten cents on each hundred dollars of taxable property was laid for the ensuing five years, a tax of ten cents of each poll, and one-fourth a cent on each dollar of merchandise whether purchased within or without the State. The law further provided that the above war tax should be paid on or before the first day of April, 1862. In addition to this war tax, an additional bond issue of three million dollars was authorized to supplement the bond issue of five million dollars authorized in the preceding month of May at a called session of the Legislature.[341]

Quite obviously, the above war tax would have entailed a heavy financial burden upon the public purse had the provisions of the law been carried into effect. But about ten days prior to the due date of payment, due on April 1, 1862, the Legislature in session at Memphis adjourned *sine die* on March 20, and the Confederate Government of Tennessee came to an end. It is doubtful whether any of the above war tax was ever collected, for the shortness of time and the almost immediate occupation of the major portion of Tennessee by Federal troops rendered tax-collecting under the circumstances a virtual impossibility. As to the issuance and disposal of the five million dollar bond issue of May, 1861, that is another story that gave rise to the most persistent political myth in the annals of Tennessee. At the proper time, a recital of the facts underlying that bond issue and the disposal of the bonds will be presented.

Governor Harris concluded his major message of October 7, 1861, with citing three or four matters of minor concern. He gave his reason for not placing in a receivership eight railroads operating in Tennessee, although the railroads had defaulted in payment of interest on the State bonds which had been loaned them in aid of construction of said roads. Work on the State Capitol grounds was suspended, and an agent was appointed to dispose of all perishable supplies amounting to $725.38, all of which was deposited with the State Treasurer. All appropriations for the Agricultural Bureau and the State Library were suspended, although the salary of the State Librarian was continued.[342] The sum of twenty-five thousand dollars was appropriated for the benefit of the Hospital for the Insane,[343] with a proviso that each Senatorial District be allowed to send six instead of four indigent patients to the institution.

---

[340] *Acts of Tennessee*, 1861–62, Chapter 54.
[341] *Ibid.*, Section 16, Chapter 26.
[342] *Acts of Tennessee*, 1861–62, Chapter 9.
[343] *Ibid.*, Chapter 17.

If any financial support was given the Blind School and the School for the Deaf and Dumb, the appropriation was omitted in the list of laws enacted. In this respect, the Legislature failed to heed the admonition of Governor Harris who reminded the Legislature that "we must not forget that these victims of misfortune are entitled to the fostering care of the Government."

Representative R. G. Ellis, recognizing that war involves alert and intelligent participation by civilian as well as military personnel, proposed the following: [344]

"*Resolved by the General Assembly of the State of Tennessee,* That having full confidence in the justice of our cause, in this time of peril to our country, we should invoke the guidance and protection of Him in whose hands are the destinies of all Nations, That in view of the momentous interests involved in the struggle now going on between the United States and the Confederate States, we believe the success of our cause to be vital to every freeman of Tennessee, That while civil war in its mildest form is a calamity to be lamented by all good men, yet we would regard that form of civil war in which neighbor is arrayed against neighbor, and members of the same community or State are brought into hostile collision as a calamity far more disastrous to our people, That the people of Tennessee regardless of geographical divisions have a common interest involved in and a common destiny dependent upon the great issue of arms now pending, and that therefore motives of patriotism and their highest interest alike demand of the people of Tennessee their firm and united efforts in support of the Confederate Government; believing as we do, that in the most perfect harmony will be found the surest guarantee for present safety and future success. And that anyone who would in this hour of danger to the Country in violation of that potential voice which has been spoken by the people of Tennessee, attempt to get up dissensions and internal strife, and thereby insidiously seek to draw any portion of the people into the clutches of the Lincoln despotism, should be regarded as a traitor, and avoided as an enemy who would sacrifice our best interests upon the Altar of his unholy ambition.

We would therefore earnestly appeal to our respective constituencies throughout the State to discard Minor differences of opinion which may have existed in reference to the Old political parties, or touching the great revolution through which we are passing, and for the future stand as one man in support of the Confederate Government, and against our Common enemy, who in violation of the sacred right of self government would, if possible, subjugate our people and desolate our homes.

Resolved further, That to make sure our defense against the invading foe, large armies on the part of our government, are indispensable, and while our ports are blockaded, we must depend upon the agricultural resources of the Confederate States for subsisting both the people and Army of the Confederacy.

In our opinion therefore it becomes equally the patriotic duty and the best interests of those who do not engage in the Military Service of the Country to use their best exertions to provide for the ensuing year more than an ordinary quantity of provisions,—and to that end we would call the

---

[344] *House Journal,* 1861, 79.

attention of our respective constituencies throughout the State, and especially those who may be engaged in agricultural pursuits, to the importance of seeding a sufficient quantity of their arable lands to provide an abundant harvest for the ensuing year to supply the wants of the Country.—And we would also call their attention to the importance of raising an increased quantity of live stock, particularly cattle, hogs and sheep, the two former of which are so essential for subsisting and the latter for comfortably clothing our gallant troops."

So far as official records disclose, the Ellis appeal for unity against "the common enemy" was adopted without discussion or opposition.[345]

In order to make available all possible resources for the prosecution of the war, Representative W. H. M. Brooks of Weakley County proposed that *The Hermitage* be tendered to the Confederate Government for the purpose of converting same into a Military Academy upon the plan of West Point.[346] The Committee on Confederate Relations, after considering the Brooks resolution, recommended the following amended resolution, to-wit:[347]

"Tendering the Hermitage grounds to the Government of the Confederate States of America for the purpose of establishing a Military School and also tendering the temporary use of the Capitol building to the same Government, on condition that the said Government is removed from Richmond to Nashville, and have unanimously instructed me to report resolutions in lieu.

The Resolutions of the Committee are in substance the same as the resolutions referred to the Committee, the difference being in the conditions.

In regard to the necessity for the establishment of a Military School by the Government of the Confederate States, there is no doubt in the opinion of the Committee.

When our independence shall have been acknowledged the government will be under the necessity of educating such a portion of our young men in the science of War as will be necessary to Officer our standing Army in the time of peace or the whole Army in time of War. If this necessity is admitted your Committee know no spot in all the Government so appropriate for such a school as the Hermitage.

The State of Tennessee purchased the Hermitage consisting of Five Hundred acres from the heirs of Gen. Jackson after making the reservation of fifty-acres provided for in the resolution, on which the tomb and mansion are situated and the one Acre for the church, there is left Four Hundred and fifty-nine acres for the use of the school. This would give ground enough for the use of the school, the location is healthy, the neighborhood is productive, making the expenses for purposes of living cheap.

But while all these considerations are more or less important, there is another, which in the opinion of your Committee should govern the Action of the Legislature upon this question, as well as that of the Confederate Congress and that is the fact that this school is to be established on the Hermitage grounds, the Home of Jackson, the Patriot, the Statesman, the Hero.

---

[345] *Ibid.*, 140 and 161.
[346] *Ibid.*, 110.
[347] *Ibid.*, 182-183.

The Knowledge of the fact, to the Military Student, that he was in the neighborhood of the tomb of Jackson, would nerve and stimulate him to exert himself in the pursuit of studies that would prepare him to imitate his glorious example, if opportunity should ever offer.

The Memories and glories of Jackson's Military and Civil life, would cluster around the school and would have a most powerful influence for good.

These and other considerations operating on your Committee determined them to recommend the passage of the Resolutions offered in lieu.

All of which is respectfully submitted.

Resolutions in lieu.

Resolved by the General Assembly of the State of Tennessee, That the Hermitage with the exception of Fifty Acres including the Tomb and Mansion House of the Hero of New Orleans, and with the further exception of the One Acre of ground upon which the church building stands and the right of way to the same, be, and the same is hereby tendered to the Government of the Confederate States of America, upon the Condition that said Government shall within two years after the termination of the existing war, establish a permanent Military school or Academy, for the instruction of the youth of the Confederate States in all knowledge appertaining to Military science and that said Government of the Confederate States of America shall have two years from the passage of this resolution to accept the ground hereby tendered for the purposes expressed with the conditions attached.

2. *Resolved,* That our Senators in the Confederate Congress be instructed and that our Representatives be requested to use their influence to have the proposition made in the foregoing resolution accepted by the Congress.

3. *Be it further Resolved,* That the use of the Capitol buildings of the State be, and the same is hereby tendered to the Government of the Confederate States of America for the use of the Congress and various departments of the Government until such time as the Government can provide suitable and necessary buildings, provided said Government shall be removed from the city of Richmond to the City of Nashville."

By a vote of 45 to 13, the above resolution was adopted by the House of Representatives, the favorable vote having been made on Thanksgiving Day.[348] But on the following Monday, the official record discloses that

"The Senate has indefinitely postponed . . . House Resolution No. 42 tendering the Hermitage and Capitol buildings to the Confederate States."[349]

Throughout the entire session of the Thirty-Fourth General Assembly, the bee-hive activity of Governor Harris was not only apparent but real. He did not overlook any detail that might contribute to a successful outcome of the military conflict. Among other important duties was that of selecting various military officials. As has already

---

[348] *Ibid.,* 206.

[349] *Ibid.,* 217–218.

Author's note. Inasmuch as the *Senate Journal,* 1861–62, has never been printed, and only a small fragment of the original seems to be extant, it is impossible to ascertain from official records the cause of the defeat of the above resolution.

been pointed out, Governor Harris had submitted his recommended appointments of high-ranking military chieftains on May 9, 1861, all of whom were promptly confirmed by the Legislature. Again, on June 28, 1861, Governor Harris submitted for confirmation a rather lengthy list of names for various military posts, all such nominations being confirmed without exception. With the war progressing rapidly and the imperative need for additional officers to take active command in the field, Governor Harris supplemented his former appointments with another list.[350]

More than two weeks elapsed before the Legislature acted upon the nominations of Governor Harris, but this delay should not be construed as indicative of any dissatisfaction with or opposition to the confirmation of the proposed officers. Several matters of concern had to be attended to, such as reporting the official vote for Governor, the inauguration of the Governor-elect, and the election of various State officials. On November 16, the Legislature met in Joint Convention for the purpose of taking action upon the nominations by Governor Harris. Representative J. N. Little from the counties of Benton and Humphreys received this entry in the official record:[351]

"On motion of Mr. Little the nominations were ratified and confirmed as a whole."

Such unanimity of mind on the part of the legislative membership was eloquent evidence of the confidence which the Legislature had in the wisdom and earnestness of Governor Harris. There was neither jockeying, bickering, nor any attempt to indulge in a bit of legislative maneuvering, much of which is frequently characteristic of deliberative bodies.

Another important measure [352] was the creation of an Ordnance Bureau whose object primarily was to provide, by purchase or manufacture, arms and munitions for the prosecution of the war. Authorization was given for an initial expenditure of $300,000. As one means of procuring firearms, each man inducted into service was commanded to bring along "any gun or guns and accoutrements he may have"; failure to comply with this law subjected the offender to a fine of not less than fifteen dollars. In addition to this recruiting of arms from inductees was a provision for the appointment of an agent in each county "to collect the arms of the citizens of this State." After the delivery of the "shooting paraphernalia," such citizens could then legally purchase or make guns "for home defense."

---

[350] *Ibid.,* 113–115.
Author's note. On October 29, 1861, Governor Harris submitted a third list of nominations for various military appointments. This list is shown on pages 113–115 of the *House Journal* of 1861–62 and may be found in the Appendix of this volume.
[351] *Ibid.,* 157.
[352] *Acts of Tennessee,* 1861-62, Chapter 55.

Section 1 of the above law provided that the personnel of the Ordnance Bureau should consist of the Governor and three other persons to be nominated by the Governor and confirmed by the Legislature. On December 6, 1861, notice was given that Governor Harris had sent a Message [353] nominating members of the Ordnance Bureau. Three days later the nominees, namely, Samuel D. Morgan, James Woods, and R. C. McNairy, "were unanimously confirmed."[354] About a week before *sine die* adjournment of the Legislature, the law creating the Ordnance Bureau was amended [355] whereby the Governor was authorized to appoint three additional members subject to confirmation by the Legislature. On March 19, 1862, the day before final adjournment, Governor Harris transmitted a Message nominating as additional members of the Ordnance Bureau the following: [356] Sam Tate and F. W. Royster of Shelby County, and Dr. Alexander Jackson of Madison County, all of whom were confirmed by unanimous vote.

On December 21, 1861, the Legislature recessed until January 20, 1862. At the end of the month's "vacation," the Legislature reconvened in Nashville at the appointed time but no quorum in the House of Representatives was present, forty-nine members being absent.[357] A future Governor of Tennessee, D. W. C. Senter, advised Mr. Speaker Keeble that an attack of typhoid fever had necessitated his absence on the day of reconvening. Difficulty was had in obtaining a quorum during the next two days, but finally the Doorkeeper was directed to round up the stragglers which he did by bringing in thirteen absentees for the afternoon session on January 23, thereby providing a quorum.

For some three weeks the Legislature dealt largely with routine matters of a rather inconsequential nature. Doubtless the membership was thrown into a state of shock on receiving notice of the death of General Felix Zollicoffer which had occurred on January 19, 1862, from wounds received in a battle near Fishing Creek, Kentucky.

---

[353] *House Journal*, 1861-62, 238.

Author's note. This Message and a number of other minor Messages were not printed in the official *Journal of the House of Representatives*. Diligent search in the State Archives failed to locate these documents, and their contents have to be ascertained as far as possible from the language of the *Journal* when such Messages were up for consideration by the Legislature.

[354] *Ibid.*, 255.

[355] *Ibid.*, 439.

Author's note. The amendment, authorizing the addition of three more members of the Bureau, does not appear in the organic act. Under the strain and stress of imminent invasion of Memphis by hostile forces, doubtless the Legislature waived the usual formalities characteristic of such legislative action.

[356] *Ibid.*, 468.

Author's note. It will be noted that all three of the new members were residents of West Tennessee, two being from Memphis. Doubtless the access afforded by the Mississippi River was a factor that led Governor Harris and the Legislature to desire that some of the members of the Ordnance Bureau be "on the spot."

[357] *Ibid.*, 318.

A legislative committee reported the following arrangements in regard to the funeral ceremonies concerning General Zollicoffer and Lieutenant Balie Peyton, Jr., to-wit:[358]

"The Senate and House of Representatives will proceed from the Capitol in a body to the L & N R.R. Depot, preceded by the Governor of the State and heads of Executive Departments, and thence attend the remains of deceased in procession to the Hall of the House of Representatives—Where they will lay in state subject to such further disposition as the military authorities in conjunction with your committee may make."

Added to the discomfort and dismay produced by reports of the advancing foe was the news of the fall of Fort Donelson, guardian of Nashville and vicinity. Successive setbacks from the Confederate viewpoint doubtless were reminiscent of Shakespeare's well-known dictum

> "One woe doth tread upon another's heel
> So fast they follow."

After a hurried round-up of the members of the Legislature, an emergency session was held informally on Sunday morning, February 16, 1862. On motion of Representative A. S. Jarnagin, a committee was appointed to confer with Governor Harris in order to ascertain his wishes. The committee reported that

"It was the intention of the Governor to convene the Genl. Assembly in the City of Memphis on the 20th instant. When on motion the House adjourned to meet upon the call of the Governor."[359]

On the same Sabbath Day, Governor Harris issued the following proclamation:[360]

"EXECUTIVE DEPARTMENT,
Nashville, Tenn., February 16th, 1862.

The Members of the General Assembly of the State of Tennessee will assemble at Memphis, Tennessee, on Thursday next, the 20th inst., for the dispatch and transaction of such business as may be submitted to them.

ISHAM G. HARRIS."

Pursuant to the above Proclamation, the General Assembly met in Memphis on Thursday, February 20, 1862. From February 20 through March 10, no quorum was present on the part of the House of Rep-

[358] *Ibid.*, 357.
[359] *Ibid.*, 422–423.
[360] *Ibid.*, 423.

resentatives.[361] On March 11, although twenty-five House members failed to answer to the roll call, Mr. Speaker Keeble announced that a quorum was present. Next followed a Message from Governor Harris, dated February 20, although not transmitted to the Legislature until March 11, due to the absence of a quorum. The Message was as follows:

Legislative Message,* February 20, 1862.

"EXECUTIVE OFFICE
Memphis, February 20, 1862.

GENTLEMEN OF THE SENATE AND HOUSE OF REPRESENTATIVES:

Under your joint resolution adopted the 10th of February inst., providing 'that the Governor and Heads of Executive Departments may at any time during the present war, by proclamation of the Governor, temporarily change the seat of Government, remove the papers and records of the Executive Departments, and the Governor by proclamation shall convene the legislature when he deems it necessary, at a place determined upon as the temporary seat of Government;' And the report of a legislative Committee from the House which called upon me on the 16th inst. to inform me that the Legislature was ready to meet at such time and place as I might designate—I deemed it my duty to remove the records of the Government to, and convene the Legislature at this City, for the following reasons:

The disaster to our arms at Fishing Creek had turned the right flank of our army, and left the country from Cumberland Gap to Nashville exposed to the advance of the Federal Army.

The fall of Fort Henry had given the enemy the free navigation of the Tennessee river, through which channel he had reached the southern boundary of Tennessee, and the fall of Fort Donelson, left the Cumberland river open to his gunboats and transports, enabling him to penetrate the heart of the State, and reach its Capitol at any time, within a few hours, when he should see proper to move upon it.

Immediately upon hearing of the fall of Fort Donelson, I called upon General Johnston to tender to him all the resources of the

---

[361] Ibid., 423–430.
* Ibid., 430–433.

State which could be made available, with my full co-operation in any and all measures of defense of our State and Capitol. General Johnston informed me that under the circumstances which surrounded him, with the small force then under his command, he regarded it as his duty to the army he commanded and the government he represented, to fall back with his Army south of Nashville, making no defense of the City, and that he would do so immediately upon the arrival of the army from Bowling Green.

The necessity for this retrograde movement, I am certain, was deeply regretted by General Johnston. None could have deplored it more Seriously than Myself.

You have for months past, witnessed the constant and earnest efforts which I have made to raise troops, collect arms, and prepare them for the field, for the defense of our long line of frontier, but it is evident that the Country has not been sufficiently aroused to a full sense of the dangers with which it was Menaced.

While it is true that Tennessee has sent large numbers of her sons to the field, who are performing their duty nobly and her people have shown a high degree of energy in developing all the resources of the State, which could aid the Government in this struggle, it is equally true that there is scarcely a locality within our limits which could not have done, and which cannot now do more.

Many weeks before this crisis in our affairs, Gen. Johnston sent a highly accomplished officer and able engineer, Major Gilmer, to Nashville, to construct fortifications for the defense of the City. Laborers were needed for their construction. I joined Major Gilmer in an urgent and earnest appeal to the people to send in their laborers for this purpose, offering full and fair compensation.

This appeal was so feebly responded to that I advised Gen. Johnston to impress the necessary labor, but owing to the difficulty in obtaining the laborers, the works were not completed; indeed some of them little more than commenced when Fort Donelson fell.

Under the act of 6th May, 1861, I raised, organized, armed, and equipped a large volunteer force, but under the Military league and the act of the General Assembly it was made my duty to transfer that army, with all of our Munitions, to the government of the Confederate States. Which I did on the 31st day of July 1861.

Since that time I have had no authority to raise, or means of subsisting a State army, being only authorized to raise, organize, and put into the field such troops as were demanded of the State by the government of the Confederate States, that government having control of the devices of the State as well as our Munitions and Means of defense.

Since the passage of the act of May, 1861, I have organized and put into the field for the Confederate service fifty nine regiments of infantry, one regiment of cavalry, eleven cavalry battalions, and over twenty independent companies, mostly artillery.

The Confederate government has armed about fifteen thousand of these troops, but to arm the remainder of this large force, I have had to draw heavily upon the sporting guns of our Citizens.

Having bent every energy to fill the requisition made by the Confederate States for troops, when Fort Donelson fell there was not a single organized and armed company in the State subject to my command, the only force under my control being an undisciplined, unarmed Militia, which, under our inefficient and sadly defective Militia system, I have had no power to discipline, drill and prepare for service in the field. Under these circumstances, when the Confederate army fell back from the Capitol, leaving it exposed to the assaults of a large army of the enemy, it would have been worse than folly on me to have attempted its defense.

There was no alternative left but for the Officers of the Government to remove the public records to a place of greater security, or to allow themselves and the records to fall into the hands of the Federal army, resulting in the Subversion of the State Government and the establishment of a Military despotism or a provisional government, under Federal authority, over the people of the State. I could not doubt or hesitate as to my duty under such circumstances.

Having assembled here at a period when a part of our territory is overrun, and other portions seriously threatened by the invader, the one great duty which devolves upon us is the immediate adoption of such Measures as will concentrate every possible energy and all the resources of the State in a determined effort to drive back the invader, redeem every inch of our soil, and maintain the independence of our State.

By a majority approximating unanimity, we have voted ourselves a free and independent people. Shall we falter now in maintaining that declaration at any cost, or at any sacrifice. The alternative presented to us is, the maintenance of our independence, however long or bloody the struggle, or subjugation, dishonor, and political slavery.

I trust there are very few Tennesseans 'who can long debate which of the two to choose.'

The apprehensions which I expressed, and the dangers of which I warned you in my special Message of the 1st inst. have been fully realized by the Country, and the necessity for prompt, energetic and decided action is even more imperative now than at that time.

I now respectfully repeat to you the recommendations of that Message, and earnestly urge that you so amend our Militia system as will not only enable the Executive to fill promptly all requisition made by the Confederate Government upon Tennessee for her just proportion of troops but also give full power to discipline and prepare for efficient service in the field the whole Military strength of the State, Classifying the Militia so that the burthens of our defense will fall upon the young and vigorous, who are best able to bear them. I also recommend that you authorize the organization of a part of the Militia into Cavalry and Artillery Corps, as well as infantry; and in all instances where it it deemed proper to call out the Militia, authorize the reception of volunteers in lieu of the Militia so far as they may present themselves; and for the present defense of the State I recommend the passage of a bill authorizing the raising, arming and equipping of a provisional army of Volunteers, appropriating ample means for this purpose.

Believing that at least one fourth of the present Militia strength of the State can be armed by collecting all the sporting guns in the Country, I have ordered that proportion to be placed in camp, immediately.

Appropriations to equip, pay, subsist and clothe this force while engaged in the public defense, will be necessary.

While there is much to regret in the past, there is much to hope in the future. Our fathers of the first revolution experienced more serious reverses and many darker hours than any we have known, yet they did not falter until their independence was achieved.

Tennessee holds her fate in her own hands; a fixed and unalterable resolve, a bold, firm and united effort to maintain our independence at any and at all hazards, gives us the means of repelling the invader at once.

The Confederate Government is sending her legions to our aid;

our Sister States of the South are rallying their gallant sons to the rescue.

Let Tennessee remember that the invader is upon her soil; that her independence and the freedom of her people from tyranny and oppression are involved in this struggle, and putting forth her whole strength, act as becomes the high Character which the gallantry of her sons has won for her on other fields.

Respectfully

ISHAM G. HARRIS."

The Message of Governor Harris is self-explanatory. Although deeply distressed at the setback sustained by the Confederate forces, the militant Governor faced the future with a dogged determination to throw every ounce of Tennessee strength into the military conflict. His fears and apprehensions had been founded upon factual conditions which, he reminded the Legislature, had been pointed out by him in a Special Message [362] transmitted on March 1.

Actual difficulty in obtaining a quorum plus flying rumors undoubtedly handicapped the Legislature during its brief session in Memphis. On February 26, a Memphis newspaper [363] reported editorially that

"We learn that it is not impossible that the Legislature will finally adjourn from Memphis to McMinnville, at which point, it is believed, there will be less difficulty in obtaining a quorum."

Two thousand copies of the Governor's Message were ordered to be printed for the use of the House. On February 13, the Senate passed a bill to amend a former law dealing with the raising and equipping of a provisional army. This action was taken in a secret session of the Senate.[364] The House likewise passed the measure on first reading in secret session at an afternoon session on the same day, and referred the bill to the Military Committee.[365] Two days later, Representative D. M. Kennedy of Montgomery County, Chairman of the Military Committee, reported the bill with sundry amendments. At this stage of the game, the fall of Fort Donelson was announced and the Legislature was directed by Governor Harris to reassemble in Memphis. As already

---

[362] *Ibid.*, 432.

Author's note. The Special Message alluded to by Governor Harris was not incorporated in the legislative *Journal*, nor located in the State Archives. Furthermore, none of the extant newspapers of that period printed the Message. The Message was considered in secret session and probably dealt with the military strength of Tennessee. To have printed the Message in the newspapers would have revealed vital military secrets to the enemy.

[363] *Memphis Daily Avalanche*, February 26, 1862.

[364] *House Journal*, 1861–62, 407.

[365] *Ibid.*, 411.

pointed out, extreme difficulty was encountered in obtaining a quorum of the House. Finally, after marking time from February 20 until March 11, a quorum was obtained and the bill was again up for consideration. There followed a flood of proposed amendments, amounting to some thirty-odd in number.[366] The bill was jockeyed back and forth from one body to the other, resulting in the appointment of a conference committee for trying to iron out the kinks. On March 15, the House was notified that the Senate "had concurred in some and non-concurred in other" of the pending amendments.[367] Later, the Senate reconsidered its action and requested the return of the bill to the Senate. Thereupon the Senate adopted the report of the conference committee and transmitted the bill to the House. Perhaps the pressure of time aided in final action by the House, inasmuch as only one day remained before *sine die* adjournment. At any rate, Representative James R. Garner of Obion County moved that the report of the conference committee be adopted. By a vote of 37 to 17, the motion was carried and thereby an exceedingly vital law was enacted.[368]

Under the provisions of the nineteen-section law,[369] the manpower of Tennessee was called into action. The white male population, between the ages of eighteen and forty-five, constituted the Reserve Military Corps, and all able-bodied white men from forty-five to fifty-five years of age were to be designated as the Reserve Corps. The latter group was not to be called into action until the former group had been inducted into actual service. Judges and Chairmen of County Courts were directed to appoint "a competent person in every civil district, ward, and town of their respective counties" to make a list of the able-bodied male citizens and report same to the Adjutant General, whereupon the Governor was authorized to cause these men to be organized into companies, battalions, and regiments. All persons embraced in the above classifications were to be subject to the rules and articles of war of the Confederate Government. The Governor was named commander-in-chief so long as the forces remained in State service, and he was directed to fill from the Reserve Corps any requisition upon Tennessee by the Confederate Government for troops. The sum of $3,000,000 was voted for the support of the armed forces, the same to be provided by a bond issue.

In addition to the above basic law, other war measures were enacted. One such law [370] authorized medical directors and surgeons at hospitals to impress "any free person of color" for nursing services. Another law [371] was designed to aid the families of indigent soldiers. To finance

---

[366] *Ibid.*, 433–442.
[367] *Ibid.*, 453.
[368] *Ibid.*, 472.
[369] *Acts of Tennessee*, 1861–62, Chapter 26.
[370] *Ibid.*, Chapter 35.
[371] *Ibid.*, Chapter 52.

this matter, all common school funds with the exception of one hundred thousand dollars annually were to be set aside for this purpose. Furthermore, the fund was to be bolstered up by levying an annual tax, for the years 1862 and 1863, of nine cents on each one hundred dollars of taxable property plus twenty-five cents on each one hundred dollars of merchandise purchased within or without the State.

During the entire session of the Thirty-Fourth General Assembly there was ever present the grim spectre of WAR. Actually, military conflict had begun a few months prior to the convening of the Legislature. For the most part, the rigid party lines of past years were all but erased from the minds of the legislators as they turned their attention to the perilous duties at hand. In the more than 500 pages of the *House Journal*, there appear only two instances of what might be termed frivolity. In considering a bill to protect the property of married women, Representative J. H. Randolph of Cocke County attempted to annex his idea of alleged humor to the bill in the following amendment [372] which was rejected:

"Be it enacted by the General Assembly of the State of Tennessee, That all women of whatever age, rank, profession or degree, whether virgins, maids or widows, that shall from and after the passage of this act, impose upon, seduce or betray into matrimony any male subject in the Confederate States of America and particularly in the State of Tennessee, by means of scents, paints, cosmetics, masks, artificial teeth, false hair, Spanish wool, iron stays, high-heeled shoes, or bolstered hips shall be guilty of a misdemeanor and upon conviction shall be fined in the Sum of One Hundred Dollars and imprisoned at the discretion of the Court trying the Cause."

In a vein, more facetious than factual, the same member just a week before final adjournment introduced the following resolution [373] which met its merited fate—silence:

"Whereas the Legislature is now convened in the City of Memphis under extraordinary circumstances, having been driven from the Capitol of the State of Tennessee, by the armies of the Confederate Government,

And Whereas from the demonstrations around us, we are liable to be driven from this City of refuge and the blockade is likely to become so effectual that it is exceedingly doubtful whether or not many of the Members can reach their homes without great trouble and expense,

And Whereas the Members of this Legislature have but few days at most to consider the bills so important and indispensable to the public interest,

Therefore Resolved, That hereafter no other new Bill or Resolution shall be introduced for further consideration of this Legislature.

Resolved further, That hereafter no Member of this Legislature, shall speak more than once on any one proposition, nor longer than ten minutes at any one time.

---

[372] *House Journal,* 1861–62, 237.
[373] *Ibid.,* 445.

Resolved further, That this Legislature adjourn sine-die on the 20th of this instant."

At an afternoon session, on March 20, 1862, the House was notified that the Senate "has transacted all the public business before it and is now ready to adjourn." Whereupon, on motion of Representative R. H. Hodsden, representing the counties of Knox and Sevier, Mr. Speaker Edwin A. Keeble declared the House adjourned *sine die.*

Confederate Government in Tennessee was at an end!

CHAPTER TWO

Interlude[1]

February, 1862–April, 1865.

With the partial occupation of Tennessee by Federal troops early
in 1862, the collapse of the Confederate Government in Tennessee occurred in March of the same year. On February 22, General Ulysses S.
Grant proclaimed martial law in West Tennessee which proclamation
forbade any courts to be held under State authority. All causes falling
within the purview of the military arm were to be held under the
auspices of authorities appointed by the Federal Government. Only
when a sufficient number of citizens announced their readiness to maintain law and order were the military regulations to be removed. General Grant's action was quickly followed up by President Lincoln who,
on March 3, 1862, appointed Andrew Johnson Military Governor of
Tennessee with the rank of brigadier general, thereby indicating that
Johnson had military status in addition to his civil station. Johnson, a
United States Senator at the time, accepted the appointment and arrived in Nashville on March 12 to undertake the difficult task of trying
to lure Tennessee back into the Union.

---

[1] Author's note. Andrew Johnson's incumbency as Military Governor of Tennessee does not fall within the title and scope of the volumes entitled *Messages of
the Governors of Tennessee*. Yet a thumb-nail sketch of his administration is essential for an understanding of the events that led to the restoration of civil government
after a stormy interlude of more than three years between the administrations of
Governors Isham G. Harris and "Parson" Brownlow. The reader is exhorted to recall the laconic statement of Vergil in his *Aeneid: longae ambages; sed summa se-
quar fastigia rerum* (The details are lengthy; but I shall touch upon the main points
of the story). For those who may desire detailed information covering the period,
the following works should be consulted: Alexander, Thomas B., *Political Reconstruction in Tennessee*; Brownlow, William G., *Sketches of the Rise, Progress, and
Decline of Secession* ("Parson Brownlow's Book"); Coulter, E. Merton, *William
G. Brownlow*; Fertig, James Walter, *The Secession and Reconstruction of Tennessee*; Hall, Clifton R., *Andrew Johnson, Military Governor of Tennessee*; Hamer,
Philip M., *Tennessee—A History*, Vol. II, Chapters XXXVI and XXXVII; Milton,
George Fort, *The Age of Hate*; Patton, James Welch, *Unionism and Reconstruc-
tion in Tennessee*; Stryker, Lloyd Paul, *Andrew Johnson*; and Temple, Oliver Perry,
Notable Men of Tennessee.

The following narrative dealing with the Interlude has been based largely upon
the above cited sources.

Within the body of Johnson's commission, appointing him Military Governor of Tennessee, the scope of his duties and responsibilities was thus defined:

"You are hereby appointed military governor of the State of Tennessee, with authority to exercise and perform, within the limits of that state, all and singular the powers, duties and functions pertaining to the office of military governor (including the power to establish all necessary offices and tribunals and suspend the writ of habeas corpus) during the pleasure of the president, or until the loyal inhabitants of that state shall organize a civil government in conformity with the Constitution of the United States."

Accompanying instructions added the following:

"It is obvious to you that the great purpose of your appointment is to re-establish the authority of the Federal government in the state of Tennessee, and provide the means of maintaining peace and security to the loyal inhabitants of that state until they shall be able to establish a civil government. Upon your wisdom and energetic action much will depend in accomplishing the result. . . ."

A critical study of Tennessee's role, as related to "the irrepressible conflict," discloses that all the elements of a Greek drama were involved. Conflict is an essential element of drama, such conflict being based upon a clash of ideas and ideals. With this in mind, the story of Tennessee's secession and reconstruction presents a drama consisting of a prologue and three acts. The prologue deals with the secession movement which was mirrored in the second and third administrations of Governor Isham G. Harris in the preceding chapter. Act I relates to the three-year regime of Andrew Johnson as Military Governor. Act II deals with Tennessee's readmission to the Union and with the control of State politics by "Parson" Brownlow and the Radicals. Act III is concerned with the restoration of the Conservatives to political power in Tennessee.

There were other factors that intensified the dramatic situation regarding Tennessee. Tennessee was the last State to secede and the first to fall under the blow of Federal force; Tennessee was the only seceded State not mentioned in Lincoln's Emancipation Proclamation, and the only State freeing her own slaves; Tennessee was the only seceded State having a considerable body of citizens who constantly sided with the Union; Tennessee was the first seceded State to regain admission to the Union; and Tennessee was the first State in the American Union in which a Military Governor was appointed to take over the reins of State Government.

Andrew Johnson's return to Tennessee as Military Governor was by no means to him a gala occasion. Unionists in East Tennessee, on the whole, received him with open arms, but in Nashville and throughout Middle and West Tennessee Confederate sympathy and sentiment predominated and Johnson was looked upon as a "traitor." Insults and threats upon his life by his enemies and opponents of the Union were of frequent occurrence. Guerillas were hopeful of capturing and punishing him for his "betrayal" of his State and the South. Plots were formed against the life of him who now had become the official instrument to rule over their subjugation.

One week after his arrival in Nashville, Johnson initiated his administration with a proclamation—later published under the title of *Appeal to the People of Tennessee*—in which he attempted to explain the nature and the circumstances of his appointment and, in fairly mild language, sought to assure the people that the restoration of Tennessee's former civil government was the great aim and purpose entertained by him. To aid him in the execution of his duties as Military Governor, Johnson appointed Edward H. East as Secretary of State; Joseph S. Fowler, Comptroller; Horace Maynard, Attorney General; and Edmund Cooper, private secretary. It goes without saying that all of these appointees were strong Union men whose views and opinions were well known.

General Buell had advised Johnson by a letter that reached him en route to Nashville that the majority of Tennesseans were "either inimical or overawed by the tyranny of opinion and power" and that Johnson would be wise to enter upon his official duties "without any display." This advice by Buell may have influenced Johnson to conclude his address by his assurance "to the people themselves the protection of the Government," and that "the erring and the misguided will be welcomed on their return." But alongside these comforting assurances there appeared the direct and stern statement that "it may become necessary, in vindicating the violated majesty of the law, to punish intelligent and conscious treason in high places. . . ." This toned-down proclamation was but faintly reminiscent of Johnson's tones in the United States Senate Chamber, while a United States Senator, that "treason must be made odious" and that traitors should be hanged.

Johnson's imperious and often despotic will soon became manifest. In less than two weeks after he assumed command as Military Governor he proposed that the Mayor and City Council of Nashville take an oath of allegiance to the United States. Upon their refusal to do so, Johnson had Mayor Richard B. Cheatham committed to prison and a new council was appointed which filled many city offices with Union men. Also, an ordinance was passed requiring all lawyers appearing before the City Court to take an oath of allegiance. A similar demand was made of the teachers and school officials, both public and private, on pain of forfeiting their positions. Another drastic step was applying a gag to the public press. Johnson ignored Article I of the Bill of Rights which forbade Congress passing any law abridging "the freedom of speech or of the press" and substituted his own ideas by suppressing

The Daily Times, The Gazette, The Patriot, and *The Republican Banner,* with the editor of the latter being thrust into prison. The printing plants of the Methodist and Baptist Churches were seized and shut down. After this display of autocratic rule, a vehement Union rabble-rouser from Kentucky by the name of S. C. Mercer was imported to start an administration journal, *The Daily Union.*

From the suppression of the press, Johnson next moved to the pulpit. When six ministers declined to take the oath of allegiance to the United States, Johnson had them committed to Camp Chase with the stern order that no visitors would be permitted to see them without express permission of the Governor. In a plea of justification of his action, Johnson stated that

"The assumed ministers of Christ have done more to poison and corrupt the female mind of this community than all others, in fact changing their entire character from that of women and ladies to fanatics and fiends. One of those very ministers, in leaving here for Louisville, told those who were collected to see him off: 'Don't forget your God, Jeff Davis and the Southern Confederacy.' "

In May, 1862, the voters of Nashville gave evidence of their refusal to be coerced into loyalty to the Union. Upon orders from Johnson, an election of a Circuit Court Judge for Davidson County was to be held. The two Union candidates were soundly defeated by Turner S. Foster, who was in sympathy with the Confederate cause. Johnson refused to commission Foster and later had him arrested and transported to a Northern prison. Such action by Johnson was substantially repeated later when another Union candidate, M. M. Brien, was defeated for Judge of the Criminal Court by a Confederate sympathizer. This time, the Military Governor gave the successful candidate his commission, but immediately had him arrested for "treason" and committed to prison. This early movement by Johnson and the Unionists for restoration of civil government even in a limited area proved a failure.

These elections were a keen disappointment to the Union supporters. That Confederate sentiment in and around Nashville was still dominant could not be discounted. A convention, supported by Johnson, was organized by a number of prominent Union leaders including such men as ex-Governor William B. Campbell, Balie Peyton, Edmund Cooper, Jordan Stokes, and others. With Campbell chosen to act as presiding officer, resolutions were adopted declaring that the welfare of Tennessee, political, social, and economic, demanded the return of the State to its former status in the Federal Union. An invitation was extended to the citizenry of Tennessee to cooperate in this undertaking. Ex-Governor Campbell made an earnest and conciliatory speech in which he declared that "We wish to welcome back cordially all our deluded fellow-citizens." Johnson himself addressed the Convention,

State of Tennessee,

EXECUTIVE DEPARTMENT.

Nashville, August 18th, 1862.

Anthony W. Johnson,
Davidson Co, Tenn.

Sir:

There are many wives and helpless children in the City of Nashville, and County of Davidson, who have been reduced to poverty and wretchedness in consequence of their husbands and fathers having been forced into the Armies of this unholy and nefarious rebellion. Their necessities have become so manifest, and their demands for the necessaries of life so urgent, that the laws of justice and humanity would be violated unless something was done to relieve their suffering and destitute condition.

You are therefore requested to contribute the sum of *Three Hundred* Dollars, which you will pay over *within the next five days* to James Whitworth, Esq., Judge of the County Court, to be by him distributed amongst these destitute families in such manner as may be prescribed.

Respectfully, &c.

ANDREW JOHNSON,
Military Governor

ATTEST:

Edward H East
Secretary of State.

A sample of Andy's hard-boiled policy.
Original in Tennessee State Archives, Nashville.

and it is highly probable that he had laid the groundwork for such a meeting and that Campbell's speech was but an outline of Johnson's official policy at the moment.

The premature movement had been prompted by the successes achieved by the Federal army. Memphis had been occupied, the Union military forces had advanced to Corinth, and the capture of Cumberland Gap gave prospects of clearing East Tennessee of Confederate occupancy. Moreover, the concentration of the Union and Confederate armies on the Tennessee River, preparatory to the bloody battle of Shiloh on April 6-7, had siphoned off considerable bodies of troops in Middle Tennessee, and relatively small garrisons remained for the Union defense of the principal towns in that area. At this stage of the game, there suddenly appeared the dashing and daring raids of General Nathan Bedford Forrest and General John H. Morgan, threatening Union control. The Confederates were bent on redeeming Tennessee. Toward the middle of July, Murfreesboro was captured and Forrest advanced within six miles of Nashville. Nashville was besieged by the Confederates for two months and was almost completely isolated from the outside world. The Confederates finally withdrew from Murfreesboro, and with the arrival of General Rosecrans in Nashville the siege was raised. But this see-saw tilting between the contending military forces rendered futile all efforts for the time being as regards the restoration of civil government in the State. No progress was possible so long as rival armies wrestled desperately on her soil, with her cities converted into military camps and with the cavalry forces of Forrest and Morgan scouring the country.

Late in 1862, a feeble but futile effort was made to increase Tennessee's representation in the United States Congress. In compliance with President Lincoln's request, Johnson ordered Congressional elections to be held, on December 29, in the Ninth and Tenth Districts in West Tennessee—an area under Federal control. There was a mixup as to the date of the election, and in addition a raid by General Forrest disrupted election procedures in the Tenth District. Alvin Hawkins claimed to have been elected in the Ninth District, but he was refused a seat in the National House of Representatives. No claimant from the Tenth District appears to have presented any credentials certifying his election.

For the ensuing six months—January to June, 1863—the armies of General Rosecrans and General Bragg lay facing each other south of Nashville, the one extending from Murfreesboro to Franklin and the other from Manchester to Lewisburg, the principal object of each being to prevent the other from engaging in the campaign around Vicksburg. Perhaps an additional reason actuated Bragg to remain in Tennessee. The biennial State election was approaching, and the presence of his army might be of aid in maintaining order. On June 17, 1863, the

Secession supporters held a convention in Winchester and nominated candidates for Governor, the State Legislature, and the Confederate Congress. A proclamation was issued from Chattanooga by Isham G. Harris, who still considered himself the Governor of Tennessee, calling for the election to be held on the first Thursday in August. Just who voted, and how many or how few, will probably never be known; official records are so scattered and meager as to be non-conclusive. In the State Archives in Nashville, returns from only thirty-two counties are found, some of which reported the vote of only one civil district. Not a single report was from West Tennessee counties, and only eight Middle Tennessee counties made returns. The gubernatorial nominee, Robert L. Caruthers, on the face of returns was declared elected, but he was never inaugurated. Confederate Congressmen were elected and took their seats in Richmond, but no Confederate State Legislature ever convened.

In the meanwhile, the Union leaders were not unaware of the importance of an August election and accordingly on June 20 issued a call for a convention to meet in Nashville on July 1. But harmony by no means pervaded the Union membership when the convention met. Sharp divisions of opinion soon developed. The Radicals, strongly supported by "Parson" Brownlow, Horace Maynard and others, desired nominees for Governor and the State Legislature only. Many others favored nominations for a Civil Governor and all other State officers to be elected at the same time as the Legislature. Some argued that political chaos would ensue if a Military Governor, not responsible to the State, were to attempt to deal with a Legislature elected by the people. Others pointed out that the convention was not properly a representative body, but only an irregular assembly of loyal citizens.

To plague the convention still further, there arose *sectional* disagreements. West Tennessee, now that the Mississippi River was open, wanted restrictions on commerce removed. Middle Tennessee preferred above all else the restoration of Civil Government. East Tennessee wanted the Military Government to continue until the State was cleared of all Confederate forces. This latter view finally prevailed, and resolutions were adopted declaring all laws and ordinances passed by the Tennessee Legislature since April 12, 1861 null and void. Appointment of a Military Governor by Lincoln was approved, and a request was made for the Military Governor to set the wheels in motion for the election of a State Legislature at the August election.

The sharp dissension in the convention, however, convinced Johnson that any attempt to hold an election for State officials would be fraught with great danger. The wrangling had clearly demonstrated that unity in purpose was conspicuous by its absence. Perhaps as disconcerting as the bickering during the convention was the action taken, a bit later, by some conservative Unionists, headed by Emerson Etheridge, a bold and outspoken Union leader. He devised a scheme for getting out a vote for governor on the day fixed by the State Constitution, whether Johnson acted or not. By electing their candidate, whoever he might be, Etheridge and his cohorts would be in position to say that their man had been elected by the people. By brushing aside all rules and regulations governing elections, some sort of a so-called election was actually held in about three counties with the Etheridge candidate, ex-Governor William B. Campbell, receiving some twenty-five hundred votes. Etheridge himself went to Washington and pleaded with Lincoln to recognize Campbell and install him as governor. It was clear to Lincoln that the whole episode was a farce, and Etheridge's project met with a decided rebuff. The fantastic scheme, however, served to disclose significant breaches in the civilian ranks of the Unionists.

What the Nashville convention of Unionists finally did was to leave in Johnson's hands the responsibility for holding elections in August. Even a superficial analysis of the discordant factions composing the Union convention brings to surface the antagonistic views prevailing among its membership. Johnson, always a keen political diagnostician, decided that the time had not yet arrived when civil government could be re-established. Accordingly, he by-passed the August elections by refraining from taking any action regarding the matter.

In the meanwhile, military operations had gained ground for the Unionists. Toward the latter part of June, 1863, after a long delay, General Rosecrans finally went on the offensive against General Bragg and forced him to fall back to Chattanooga. General Burnside invaded East Tennessee and early in September his cavalry forces entered Knoxville. Rosecrans, however, following Bragg into Georgia, was defeated at Chickamauga and narrowly escaped annihilation. Thereupon, General Ulysses S. Grant who had been placed in supreme command replaced Rosecrans with himself and General Thomas and they took command of operations against the Confederates. In a three-day battle at Chattanooga, in late November, Bragg was defeated and forced to retreat again into Georgia. About the same time (late November), upon learning of the advance of General Sherman, General Longstreet abandoned the siege of Knoxville and started toward Virginia.

With the exception of a brief invasion by General Hood's army late in 1864, Tennessee was no more the scene of major military contests. Union forces were, generally speaking, in command of the entire State with the exception of the uppermost corner of East Tennessee.

With the expulsion of the Confederates from Tennessee, the time appeared to President Lincoln to be ripe for the re-establishment of State government in Tennessee and the renewal of its former connection with the Union. Acting upon this belief, Lincoln wrote a letter to Johnson, on September 11, 1863, advising him that

"All Tennessee is now clear of armed insurrectionists. You need not to be reminded that it is the nick of time for reinaugurating a loyal State government. Not a moment should be lost."

Lincoln further advised Johnson that the new government must be loyal to the United States and that nobody, suspected of disloyalty, should be allowed to participate in the job of reconstruction. A few days later Lincoln authorized Johnson to use such power as he deemed necessary to re-establish such a republican form of government as would entitle Tennessee to the protection of the Federal Government.

In another letter to Johnson on December 8, Lincoln disclosed his plans for the reconstruction of the governments of the seceded states. The plan was incorporated in what is generally known as the "amnesty proclamation." Full pardon was offered to all who had supported the war against the United States—except those who had held offices of high rank in the Confederacy or who had left high office in the United States Government in order to support the Confederacy—provided that such persons take the following oath:

"I ————————, do solemnly swear, in presence of Almighty God, that I will henceforth faithfully support, protect, and defend the Constitution of the United States, and the union of the States thereunder; and that I will, in like manner, abide by and faithfully support all acts of Congress passed during the existing rebellion with reference to slaves so long and so far as repealed, modified, or held void by Congress, or by decision of the Supreme Court; and that I will, in like manner, abide by and faithfully support all proclamations of the President made during the existing rebellion having reference to slaves, so long and so far as not modified or declared void by decision of the Supreme Court. So help me God."

In addition to taking the above oath, there was another prerequisite that must be met. Whenever qualified voters in any state, amounting to one-tenth of the votes cast in the Presidential election of 1860, should take the amnesty oath and reorganize the state government on the basis of said oath, then and in that case such government would be recognized as the true government of said state. As a safeguard, Lincoln expressly stated that he would not guarantee Congressional representation to the reorganized state, that being the prerogative of Congress itself. As a basis for issuing his proclamation, Lincoln cited the Act of 1862 providing for the suppression of insurrection plus that clause of the Federal Constitution guaranteeing to every state a republican form of government.

The grand kick-off was provided by a meeting in Nashville of the Unionists on January 21, 1864. A resolution was passed stating that civil government would best be restored by a Constitutional Convention chosen by the loyal citizens of the State. Johnson, it was agreed, should fix the date for the Convention when in his judgment all sections of the State could be represented. A pledge was made that delegates should be elected who favored immediate and universal emancipation, thereby "freeing ourselves and our posterity from the bondage in which we have been so long enslaved by the influence of an arrogant and domineering aristocracy." Though Johnson took no part in the formal adoption of the Convention's resolutions, there can be little or no doubt but that his fine "Italian hand" played a significant part in the drafting of the resolutions. He was present at the meeting, and was called upon for a speech. For two hours, he hammered away on his ideas of what should be done in the matter of re-establishing civil government. He made the categorical statement that the State of Tennessee had never been out of the Union and was, therefore, still a State of the Union—"Its functions have only been paralyzed—its powers only inactive." During the long speech, Johnson could not—at least did not—refrain from giving rein to his vindictive attitude toward Confederate leaders. After declaring that all loyal persons should be allowed to vote, he opened the vials of his wrath upon the leaders of Secession by thundering out a denunciation that

"They ought to be hung. Treason must be made odious; traitors must be punished and impoverished. . . ."

Five days after the meeting of the Unionist Convention, Johnson ordered that an election of county officers be held throughout the State on the first Saturday in March. He proposed to reorganize the State Government by starting with the local units, a move that he doubtless believed would create local interest and thereby get out the vote. He made it clear that only "loyal" persons would be allowed to vote, and his test of "loyalty" was the application of an oath much more severe than the amnesty oath proposed by President Lincoln. The Johnson oath, which by many was called the "damnesty oath," was as follows:

"I solemnly swear that I will henceforth support the Constitution of the United States and defend it against the assaults of all its enemies; that I will henceforth be and conduct myself as a true and faithful citizen of the United States, freely and voluntarily to be subject to all the duties and obligations, and entitled to all the rights and privileges of such citizenship; that I ardently desire the suppression of the present insurrection and rebellion against the government of the United States, the success of its armies and the defeat of all those who oppose them, and that the Constitution of the United States, and all laws and proclamations made in pursuance thereof, may be speedily and permanently established and enforced over all the people, states and territories thereof; and further, that I will hereafter aid and assist all loyal people in the accomplishment of all these results. So help me God."

To understand the divided sentiment in Tennessee upon the slavery issue, it is necessary to recall that Lincoln's Emancipation Proclamation, freeing the slaves, did not apply to Tennessee. Conservative Unionists in Tennessee believed that the Union should be restored on the basis of a resolution supported by Johnson as United States Senator and adopted by Congress in 1861. The core of that resolution was that the war was being waged for the sole purpose "to defend and maintain the supremacy of the Constitution, and to preserve the Union, with all the dignity, equality, and rights of the several States unimpaired, and that as soon as these objects are accomplished the war ought to cease." If restoration to the Union could be obtained "under the Constitution as it is," then the rights of the states would be unimpaired and the institution of slavery could remain in such states as desired same. The Tennessee Radical Unionists opposing such measures referred to themselves in 1864 as "unconditional Union men" and later on under the Brownlow regime became known as Radicals. To capsule the situation, the Unconditional Unionists wanted slavery abolished and they opposed participation by Confederate sympathizers in the restoration of civil government.

In the oath Johnson required of voters in the March election, the prospective voter was required to swear in effect that he "ardently desired" the extension of Lincoln's Emancipation Proclamation to Tennessee. Only by a complete change of heart or by swearing falsely could a former supporter of the Confederacy go to the polls and have a voice in the government of his own State. Large numbers of the Conservative Unionists, but by no means all of them, had at the beginning of the war been supporters of the Confederacy. Many had taken Lincoln's amnesty oath, and were screwing up their courage in order to take Johnson's "damnesty oath." But nearly a month prior to the March election, Attorney General Horace Maynard threw a bombshell into the works. His ruling was that citizenship had been forfeited by rebellion and could only be regained by taking the amnesty oath; that the election was being held under the Constitution of Tennessee which required six months residence as a prerequisite for eligibility to vote; and that all persons guilty of a "disloyal" act could not vote until six months after being "amnestied."

The net result of all this dissension, agitation, and opposition was that the election was a complete fiasco. Few votes were cast, and such meager returns as were reported show reconstruction efforts were checkmated for the time being. Four days after the election, March 9, Johnson's own supporting newspaper, *The Nashville Daily Union*, admitted that what was called an election was nothing less than a serious farce. Johnson's enemies, increasing in number and in hatred of him, grew bolder and charged that the State Government could and would have been restored but for Johnson's unwarranted interference with Lincoln's requirements. Johnson was charged with being really opposed to the reorganization of State Government, in that such an event would have terminated his own reign and power as Military Governor. Viewed from another angle, there may have been some merit in Johnson's claim that the time was not yet ripe for the restoration of civil government. Guerillas and Confederate raiders were still making things uncomfortable and unsafe for Unionists in various portions of the State. There can be no question but that the farcical "election" episode had been intensified and aggravated by Johnson's "damnesty oath" and Maynard's ruling, although other factors entered into the critical issues at hand.

As was perfectly natural and logical, pro-slavery supporters were opposed to some of Lincoln's policies. Opposed as they were to the abolition of slavery, those who believed in States' Rights proclaimed Lincoln's Emancipation Proclamation unconstitutional. Clinging to the emancipation philosophy meant the continuance of the war until the "rebels" were crushed by military force. Furthermore, many believed that Lincoln's policy had made the restoration of the Federal Union more difficult. In harmony with this conviction, there developed a movement for the opening of negotiations for peace with the Confederate States on the basis of "the Constitution as it is and the Union as it was." On this point, they felt themselves strongly fortified by the very legality of their position, and both Democrats and Conservative Unionists in Tennessee were pretty well in agreement. Ex-Governor William B. Campbell, a former Whig, along with other prominent Tennesseans attended the Democratic National Convention in Chicago, in August, and denounced the arbitrary and military despotism of Johnson, and urged that peace negotiations be instituted on the basis of universal amnesty and the restoration to Southerners of their property and rights as existed before the war. Inasmuch as it was a foregone conclusion that Lincoln would be the Presidential candidate of those desiring to continue the war until unconditional surrender of the Confederates was accomplished, an opposition candidate had to be provided. Accordingly, General George B. McClellan was nominated by the Democrats to oppose Lincoln. In Tennessee, a convention of Conservative Unionists picked a McClellan electoral ticket in order to wage a campaign against Lincoln and Andrew Johnson, the latter having been selected as the running mate of Lincoln. The McClellan electors in Tennessee included such influential Union leaders as ex-Governor Campbell, Henry Cooper, Balie Peyton and John Lellyett. Another elector was the resourceful Emerson Etheridge of West Tennessee, who had opposed secession in 1861, but was now denouncing Lincoln as "a usurper and despot" and Johnson as "the most infamous rebel in the South." At a warm-up meeting of the Unionists in Nashville, on October 1, the eloquent Balie Peyton declared that Lincoln's re-election insured the destruction of the South while the election of McClellan, "who brandished a sword in one hand and the olive branch in the other," would bring peace and harmony to a disrupted Nation. Peyton aroused his hearers to a state of wild excitement by condemning Lincoln's ideas of "emancipation, subjugation, and extermination."

The naming of McClellan presidential electors, the fervor and influence of leading political evangelists, and the deep undercurrent of bitter feeling against Lincoln and Johnson served to warn the Unconditional Unionists in Tennessee that trouble was in store for them. Johnson, of course, did not want to be defeated in his own State in the Presidential and Vice-Presidential race, and to checkmate the possibility of any such political disaster, a cunningly prepared defense was hatched up for meeting the crisis. On August 2, 1864, the Union State Executive Committee issued a call for delegates from some forty-odd counties to meet in Nashville on September 5. The gist of the call for a convention embraced three propositions: (1) the general condition of the country; (2) plans for the restoration of civil government in Tennessee; and (3) the expediency of holding a Presidential election in Tennessee in November. Most of the "delegates" were not regularly chosen, a considerable number having been self-appointed. "Soldiers, who could be depended upon to support radical measures, were numerous among them." When the convention got down to the organizational stage, it was discovered that the "unconditional Unionists" were in control. Samuel R. Milligan, a powerful and uncompromising Radical, was elected presiding officer. All committees dealing with credentials, organization, and business were dominated by Radical majorities. The Conservative Unionists, many of whom had been lured to Nashville by the broadly-phrased language in the call of the State Committee, were rudely awakened. It soon became apparent that the primary purpose was to deliver the Tennessee electoral vote into the hands of Lincoln and Johnson. Conservative Unionists, who were denounced as copperheads and secessionists at heart, withdrew from the convention, rather than be even a minority part of such a movement as was now being brewed. The Radical majority then proceeded "to shoot the works."

Certain miscellaneous items were disposed of, such as naming electors on the Lincoln-Johnson ticket, appointment of an executive committee to fill vacancies on the ticket, approval of the action of the Baltimore Convention naming Lincoln and Johnson as candidates, indorsing Johnson's course of action as Military Governor of Tennessee, and a demand for the immediate abolition of slavery and its prohibition in the future by all suitable and proper amendments. Next came consideration of the report of the "Business Committee" which prescribed the required qualifications of a voter. It was decreed that the requirements of the State Constitution must be met, and the prospective voter must have either voluntarily borne arms in the service of the United States during the war or must be a known active friend of the government of the United States. But the acid test was the taking of the following oath,[2] concerning which numerous qualified authorities (Clifton R. Hall and Philip M. Hamer, for example) have ascribed to the authorship of Johnson himself:

"I solemnly swear that I will henceforth support the Constitution of the United States and defend it against the assaults of all its enemies; that I am an active friend of the government of the United States; that I sincerely rejoice in the triumph of its armies and navies and in the defeat and overthrow of the armies, navies, and all armed combinations in the interest of the so-called Confederate States; that I will cordially oppose all armistices or negotiations for peace with rebels in arms, until the Constitution of the United States and all laws and proclamations made in pursuance thereof shall be established over all the people of every state and territory embraced within the National Union; and that I will heartily aid and assist the loyal people in whatever measures may be adopted for the attainment of these ends; and further, that I take this oath freely and voluntarily and without mental reservation. So help me God."

It will be observed that the opening clauses of the oath unquestionably disfranchised Confederate sympathizers. Another clause of the oath was aimed directly at the supporters of McClellan by requiring the prospective voter to swear that "I will cordially oppose all armistices or negotiations for peace with rebels in arms." Peace by negotiation, it will be recalled, was one of the demands of the National Democratic Convention that had nominated McClellan. The above clause and the succeeding one, committing the voter to be bound by "whatever measures may be adopted for the attainment of these ends," constituted death blows to pro-slavery Unionists and guaranteed that every man who cast a ballot in the November Presidential election would be either an "unconditional" or a liar. Small wonder that some Conservative newspapers, as the *Nashville Daily Press*, charged that Johnson had devised this new oath in order to insure victory of the Lincoln-Johnson ticket in Tennessee. "Andy will let us vote," the editor of the above journal commented, "if we swear to vote for him—not otherwise."

The outraged feelings of the Conservative Unionists and the Democrats can be readily understood. A highly reputable deputation repre-

---

[2] Author's note. The so-called "iron-clad oath" was prescribed by an act of Congress, July 2, 1862. In taking this oath, every person elected or appointed to any Federal office of honor or profit was compelled not only to swear allegiance to the Constitution but in addition declare that he had never voluntarily borne arms against the United States or aided, recognized, or supported any jurisdiction hostile to the Constitution. This oath was the political key to the disqualifications which Radical Republicans forged and fastened upon the Confederates during the Reconstruction era. This oath applied to the Confederate States as a whole.

The Johnson oath ("damnesty oath") was more stringent than the Congressional oath (iron-clad oath) but dealt with Tennessee alone.

The oath prescribed by the Union Convention (Tennessee) of September, 1864, was even more drastic than Lincoln's amnesty oath or the Congressional oath of 1862 (iron-clad oath), or Johnson's "damnesty oath." By numerous authorities, Johnson has been declared the author of this Union Convention (Tennessee) oath.

senting the McClellan electors went to Washington and presented to President Lincoln a vehement protest against the arbitrary and high-handed proceedings of the Radicals. After listening to the objections as set forth in an able document, Lincoln coyly inquired how long it took the delegation and the New York politicians to concoct the protest. After being assured that the protest had been prepared by Tennesseans only, Lincoln brushed them off with this retort:

"I expect to let the friends of George B. McClellan manage their side of this contest in their own way, and I will manage my side of it in my way."

A few days later, however, Lincoln forwarded a formal letter in which he said he would not interfere with the matter. Former Governor William B. Campbell, Balie Peyton, and John Lellyett announced shortly thereafter the withdrawal of the McClellan electoral ticket in Tennessee.

With the Radical Unionists in complete control of the election machinery, plus the effectual bar provided by the Union Convention oath, the November election was just another farce. The total vote for the Lincoln-Johnson ticket is not ascertainable, but it was small indeed. In Nashville, the Lincoln vote was 1,317 and McClellan 25. In Shelby County, Lincoln received 1,579 votes and McClellan 24. Under the circumstances, the Lincoln-Johnson electors were successful throughout the State. When Congress later on met to count the electoral vote, the Tennessee vote was thrown out by a joint resolution on the ground that no valid election had been held. Tennessee's electoral vote was not necessary, however, inasmuch as Lincoln and Johnson had received a large majority of the electoral votes in other states and, on March 4, 1865, the rail splitter and the tailor were inaugurated as President and Vice-President of the United States.

Flushed with victory in the November election, the Radicals initiated a movement that soon ushered in the return of civil government in Tennessee. On November 12, 1864, less than a week after the Presidential election, the Union Executive Committee of East Tennessee called for the selection of delegates to attend a State Convention in Nashville, December 19. The object of the Convention was the nomination of a Union ticket for delegates to a State Constitutional Convention whose election was to be authorized by a proclamation issued by the Military Governor, Andrew Johnson. Another need accentuated the desirability of such a meeting in the near future. Andrew Johnson would be leaving Tennessee in the coming March for induction into the office of Vice-President of the United States. The date of the preliminary convention was set for December 19, 1864, but a brief delay was necessitated by General Hood's invasion of Tennessee followed by the terrific battles of Franklin and Nashville. The meeting date of the convention was postponed until January 8, 1865, in commemoration of the battle of New Orleans.

On Saturday, January 7, about one hundred and fifty East Tennesseans, headed up by "Parson" Brownlow, arrived in Nashville after a cold and dreary ride in box cars. Since January 8 fell on Sunday, the meeting did not assemble formally until the next day. In the meantime, some five hundred persons from sixty counties had poured into the city. Some of these individuals had been selected at local mass meetings, and some had been self-appointed. Many had been absent for months from the counties that they were supposedly representing. After organization had been effected by the election of Samuel R. Rodgers of Knoxville as president and three vice-presidents from the three grand divisions of the State, there arose the question of determining the actual membership of the convention.

The first day of the convention was devoted to consideration of membership in the convention. Immediately, a fierce controversy arose. The contemporary newspapers afford no consistent account of the bitter fight. After reading the varying and conflicting stories of the convention fight, one is reminded of the report of an amateur newspaper correspondent who had been sent by the editor of the Chicago *Daily News*, Melville E. Stone, to get the particulars of a catastrophe in another portion of Illinois. To Stone's earnest plea for "particulars," the amateur wired back: "All is excitement; can learn nothing."

The presiding officer announced that the objective of the convention was the nomination of delegates to a constitutional convention which would consider plans for the reorganization of the State government. Invitation was extended to Union soldiers and all others who had not voluntarily borne arms against the United States to take seats in the convention. It is apparent that the crux of this invitation hinged upon the degree of "loyalty." The next question was what should constitute the basis of voting in the convention. And here was the beginning of a bitter fight that lasted two entire days. Roderick R. Butler, a Radical Unionist of Johnson County, offered a resolution giving each county at least one vote, with an additional vote for every hundred votes cast by that county against "separation and representation" in 1861, the time that Tennessee voted on the question of secession.

The Conservative Unionists proposed to give a vote to each member of the convention. Fierce opposition to the Butler resolution came from Middle and West Tennesseans who claimed that the 1861 election had been well-nigh thwarted in their respective sections by "force and fraud," and that the returned vote did not truly represent the Union sentiment and strength in those areas. For hours a bitter debate on the Butler resolution raged. Finally, Lewis Tillman of Bedford County poured oil on the troubled waters by suggesting a bargain. He assured the East Tennessee Unionists that the loyal men of Middle Tennessee would join East Tennessee in abolishing slavery and in supporting "Parson" Brownlow for Governor of Tennessee. In order to restore harmony and prevent a serious division in the ranks of the Unionists, the Butler resolution which had been adopted was reconsidered and withdrawn. Thereupon, the "one man, one vote" technique was substituted for the Butler method which had all but disrupted the convention. Had the Butler plan of voting prevailed, East Tennessee would have had the lion's share. In the election of 1861, the thirty East Tennessee counties had cast 33,000 votes against secession; the thirty-four Middle Tennessee counties, 8,000; and the eighteen West Tennessee counties, 6,000. Under the Butler plan, East Tennessee would have had 250 votes; Middle Tennessee, 87; and West Tennessee, 58.

The next question to arise was a declaration of the purpose of the meeting. During six sessions of the convention the question was hotly and, at times, fiercely debated. The salient points brought out in the arguments seem to boil down to the following propositions: (1) slavery should be abolished; (2) civil government should be restored; (3) the actions of the "secession Legislature" of 1861 should be repudiated; and (4) "Parson" Brownlow should be elected Governor of the State.

Quite obviously, there were differences of opinion as to how these objectives could be gained. Some delegates favored adhering to the original plan by considering the present meeting a mere preliminary one whose primary duty was to make arrangements for holding a Constitutional Convention to meet later on. Other delegates desired to declare the present convention clothed with plenary powers and competent to undertake the job of amending the State Constitution. Samuel Milligan of Greene County, a close personal and political friend of Andrew Johnson, spelled out a program of action. Milligan proposed that the present body adopt and submit to the voters for ratification (1) amendments to the State Constitution to abolish slavery and (2) a schedule declaring null and void certain laws and ordinances enacted by the secession Legislature of 1861. In addition, Milligan proposed that the present group authorize the Military Governor to order the election of a Civil Governor and members of the Legislature.

Chancellor Daniel C. Trewhitt of Hamilton County, Chairman of the Business Committee, held the opposite view. He regarded the present body without power to assume the functions of a Constitutional Convention, and maintained that its duty and only power were restricted to the selection of a general ticket of delegates to constitute a Constitutional Convention which should undertake the task of amending the State Constitution. He later on asked to be released from the chairmanship. For three days the hotly contested *constitutional* point was debated. At the close of the debate, it appeared that the Conservatives held the upper hand and, had a vote been taken at that particular time, in all probability they would have won out.

But the Radicals had not played their major trump card. Andrew Johnson was appealed to and agreed to address the body. Having been a strong constitutionalist throughout his political career, always alluding to the Constitution as the bedrock upon which he stood, it appears singular to note the trimming of his sails and his setting forth on another course. The core of his argument and position was grounded upon that of *necessity*. He justified such action by referring to the Bill of Rights which guaranteed the people the right to amend, alter, or abolish their government, if they saw fit to do so. In an effective and dramatic manner, Johnson related the story of the Roman consul who had overstepped the law in attempting to quell a dangerous conspiracy. When asked, "Will you swear that you have observed the law?" the consul replied: "I swear that I have saved the Republic." Johnson had delivered a *coup de maître* (master stroke).

On the next day, what had been called in the first place as a mass-meeting converted itself into an alleged Constitutional Convention, action that was clearly and unquestionably extra-legal and unconstitutional. But there was no stopping the political juggernaut which the Radicals had thrown into high gear. This body had proposed an amendment to the Constitution whereby slavery in Tennessee would be abolished and the Legislature denied power to legalize "the right of property in man," all of which were to be submitted to the voters on a date to be set by Johnson. At this same election, a "schedule" was to be voted on. Said schedule declared (1) certain specified acts and ordinances of May 6 and 7, 1861, (secession acts) as acts of "treason and usurpation, unconstitutional, null and void"; (2) repudiated all acts of the "disunion government" since May 6, 1861; (3) ratified Johnson's appointments, both civil and military; and (4) delegated to the first General Assembly meeting under the revised Constitution the power to determine and define the qualifications of voters.

In compliance with the authority granted by the convention, Johnson issued a proclamation on January 22, 1865, calling for an election on February 22 regarding the proposed amendments. The Union Convention oath was to be invoked against all voters except those known to be unconditional Union men. No prophetic insight was required to predict the outcome, as the barricade from the polls was effective. The amendments and the schedule to the State Constitution were ratified by a vote of 26,865 to 67. As disappointingly small as was the vote, the total exceeded the ten per cent of the vote cast for President in 1860, a prerequisite in Lincoln's amnesty proclamation of December 8, 1863. In other words, the above vote more than met the provisions of Lincoln's demand. Johnson by proclamation declared the amendments duly ratified, and next authorized an election be held on March 4 for Governor and members of the Legislature.

The mechanics of the election were reduced to the following device. A general ticket or "slate" was picked by the Convention, carrying the name of Brownlow for Governor and the names of men to be elected members of the Legislature. Another provision was that voters throughout the State should cast their ballots either for or against this ticket as a whole. Furthermore, each voter was required to write his name on the back of his ballot and the ballot was to be preserved by the Clerk of the County Court. Any who dared to vote against the will and plans of the Radical Unionists could be readily identified! Qualified voters were those who were well known to the election judges as being unconditional Union men and those who would take Lincoln's amnesty oath that had been utilized in the preceding Presidential election. On this broadside ticket appeared only the name of Brownlow and the names of the future legislators, twenty-five for the Senate and eighty-five for the House. Quite obviously, there could be but one result. For this "Liberty and State Union Ticket," only 23,222 votes were cast. Thirty-five brave souls scratched Brownlow's name from the list and wrote in the names of their own choice.

On February 25, 1865, Andrew Johnson proclaimed to the people of Tennessee that the amendments to the Constitution were in effect, and he authorized the organization of civil government thereunder. He issued a final statement as Military Governor "congratulating the people of Tennessee on the happy result of the election." When the violence, turbulence, and corruption of the Brownlow regime are viewed, as will be done in the following chapter, Johnson's prophetic powers pass into total eclipse. On that same day Johnson left Nashville for Washington where, on March 4, he was inaugurated Vice-President of the United States.

In the manner briefly sketched in this chapter, the Radicals took over the running of Tennessee. In utter disregard of the provisions of the State Constitution, but aided by the suggestions and support of Andrew Johnson, a relatively small group of self-appointed Union men assumed the powers of a properly-elected Constitutional Convention. This group exercised extra-judicial and unconstitutional prerogatives by annexing amendments to the fundamental sheet anchor of the State—the Constitution—and their irregular proceedings were sanctioned by the Military Governor of Tennessee. Not the people of Tennessee, but a minority of less than twenty-five thousand put Tennessee into the hands of the Radicals for more than four years.

LOYAL UNION STATE TICKET.

FOR GOVERNOR,

Wm. G. Brownlow.

FOR SENATORS.

1st District—R. R. Butler.
2d District—Charles J. McKinney.
3d District—James H. Randolph.
4th District—D, W. C. Senter.
5th District—Samuel R. Rodgers.
6th District—George W. Keith.
7th District—Thomas B. McElwee.
8th District—A. M. Cate.
9th District—William Bosson.
10th District—John W. Bowen.
11th District—Z. W. Frazier.
12th District—William Spence.
13th District—W. H. Wisener.
14th District—R. E. Lasater.
15th District—W. Stewart.
16th District—Thomas J. Cypert.
17th District—Joshua B. Frierson.
18th District—John Trimble.
19th District—B. R. Peart.
20th District—Thomas A. Muse.
21st District—Fielding Hurst.
22d District—Almond Case.
23d District—W. K. Hall.
24th District—David Nunn.
25th District—John W. Smith.

FOR REPRESENTATIVES.

Richard H. Coward.	W. J. Smith.
James H. Donaldson.	Thomas Maxwell.
Jesse H. Gaut.	W. P. Bond.
Reuben Rodgers.	Peter Pearson.
Pleasant Williams.	Thomas Crutchfield.
J. R. Shultz.	J. N. Puckett.
Furney Jones.	A. C. Gillem.
G. H. Groye.	W. A. Garner.
James Jones.	T. A. Kirchival.
L. M. Jarvis.	W. Watterson.
W. W. Willis.	A. A. Steele.
James R. Hood.	Jerry Gilmore.
John B. Minnis.	S. L. Warren.
Joseph Wagner.	William Wines.
William Heiskell.	W. M. Woodcock.
R. S. Ralston.	F. A. Smith.
James M. Henderson.	A. E. Garrett.
G. W. Gaines.	W. Y. Elliott.
Thomas J. Mason.	William Wright.
Wilson Duggan.	John Porter.
William Mullinix.	C. Underwood.
A. A. Snodderly.	G. W. Anders.
Samuel E. Griffith.	A. W. Moss.
James A. Doughty.	W. L. Waters.
Elijah Simmerly.	W. H. Grimmet.
Samuel McCammon.	W. B. Lewis.
D. G. Thornburg.	S. J. Carter.
J. P. Walker.	J. W. Tomeny.
James M. Melton.	M. T. Ridler.
Captain Doughty.	J. F. Thomas.
W. J. Copeland.	Joseph Hudson.
Ed. Cooper.	James Mullins.
William Barton.	David McGahey.
John Norman.	Samuel L. Arnell.
John A. Fusan.	Dorsey Thomas.
William Shelton.	John Stegald.
J. G. Simmons.	W. W. Woods.
J. E. McNair.	William Scales.
Jos. R. Dillan.	C. C. Smith.
P. S. Richards.	Gilbert Brittel.
A. D. Nicks.	James Wood.
J. S. Mulloy.	Asa Falkner.
T. Hermans.	

The Radical juggernaut in high gear! As shown above, each voter required to sign his name on reverse side of ballot.

Original ballot furnished through courtesy of Mrs. Penelope J. Allen, Chattanooga.

W. G. Brownlow

Frontispiece in *Parson Brownlow's Book*, 1862.

CHAPTER THREE

William Gannaway Brownlow

William Gannaway Brownlow, the eldest of five children of Joseph A. Brownlow and Catherine Gannaway, was born in Wythe County, Virginia, on August 29, 1805. While yet a youngster, his parents moved to East Tennessee and a few years later, within a period of less than three months, both father and mother died, leaving a family of five orphaned children, William being only eleven years old. Young William returned to Virginia and lived with his mother's relatives until a short time prior to his joining the ranks of the Methodists as a minister "on trial" in 1826. According to his own statement, his education was "plain, though regular in those branches taught in common schools." This elementary education was supplemented by "pouring (sic) over books, pamphlets, and periodicals of every description, by night and day. . . ."

During his adolescent years, William worked on an uncle's farm for seven years followed by a three year stretch as a carpenter. His parents and relatives were not of the rich valley people, although both the Brownlow and Gannaway families owned a few slaves. In later life, William rather boasted of the straightened circumstances of his family and relatives, declaring in a public address in Cincinnati during the War Between the States that he "descended from one of the *second* families of Virginia." "All others," he asserted, "are descended from the F. F. V.'s which, since their numerous retreats before Rosecrans and others, signifies *Fleet-Footed Virginians!*"

For a decade, 1826 to 1836, Brownlow was a member of the Holston Conference, advancing from the status of "preacher on trial" to that of receiving "elder's orders" in 1830. Holston Conference was not confined to Tennessee, but embraced portions of Virginia, North Carolina, South Carolina, and Georgia. The first assignment of the twenty-one year old circuit rider was to a rough and tough section in North Carolina in a mountainous area. He suffered the common hardships of the frontier preacher, having to deal with rowdies, drunks, and sectarianism

391

that provoked constant irritation and warfare among the churchmen. "Parson" Brownlow, as he came to be known far and near, was of fighting stock himself.

According to his own biographical sketch in his *Life, Travels, and Circumstances Incident Thereto,* he was usually involved in some sort of dispute or bitter controversy. What seems to corroborate his self-analysis is that he was, while a minister, defendant in lawsuits for both slander and libel. Moreover, he never served any church circuit longer than one year, his tenure in one instance lasting only three months. Not only did he lash with his tongue the Baptists and Presbyterians, but he dipped his caustic pen in printer's ink and wrote newspaper articles, pamphlets, broadsides, and even books leveled at all those disagreeing with his religious or political views. He was, throughout a larger part of his life, a prolific and caustic writer. In one of his early books, *Helps to the Study of Presbyterianism,* he admitted that he did not exhibit in his looks the piety of Abraham or the meekness of Moses. As for people disliking him, he boasted that he expected to stand as a target for the vengeance of cankered hearts and the malice of envenomed tongues. He requested his enemies to have a *blot* on their optics and through the spectacles of *malice* never to speak one word in his favor. He seemed to enjoy being hated!

In 1836, the "Parson" took unto himself a wife, Eliza O'Brien. This step put the Parson out of step with the prevailing customs of the Methodist Church. No circuit rider could support a wife and family upon the meager earnings of a circuit rider, and consequently a married preacher was often forced to "locate," that is, withdraw from the active ministry and seek some other vocation that would enable him to support a family. With an already demonstrated penchant for writing, Brownlow turned to the most natural thing in the world—establishing a newspaper. In the town of Elizabethton, the first issue of the *Elizabethton Whig* appeared on May 16, 1839, displaying at its masthead the slogan, *Life, Liberty, and the Pursuit of Happiness.* A strong believer in mottoes, his pugnacity induced him to change his motto in less than two months to *Cry Aloud and Spare Not.* For more than a quarter of a century, Brownlow's beloved *Whig* appeared under the different names of the *Tennessee Whig, Jonesboro Whig and Independent Journal, Knoxville Whig,* and the *Knoxville Whig and Rebel Ventilator,* the titles indicating the various places of publication.

There is no doubt but that Brownlow's rise in political affairs can be traced chiefly to his journalistic activities. When he moved to Knoxville in 1849, his subscribers amounted to about 2,000. His picturesque language, surfeited with gripping figures of speech and coupled with his ability to employ satire, ridicule, and sarcasm in an effective though exaggerated degree, kept him and his newspaper constantly before the public. As an editorial writer, he was aggressive, alert, original, and uncompromising. He never pulled his blows, and they were steady and powerful. By the outbreak of the war, his subscription list had grown to approximately 14,000. Just prior to his arrest and imprisonment in the Knoxville jail, he maintained that his newspaper was "the only Union paper in the eleven seceded States." On December 6, 1861, the Parson was arrested upon a charge of "treasonable" editorials appearing in his paper and he was committed to jail. While confined in prison, he professed to believe that he would be hanged. In harmony with his flair for the melodramatic, he prepared a lengthy speech which he proposed to deliver from the scaffold just before he was launched into eternity. But the Parson was doomed to disappointment. The Confederate authorities did not elect to adorn him with a hemp necktie, and his fulminations and curses of the "Rebels" were restricted to his distorted imagination and his diary. The inimitable Parson was denied the sweets of martyrdom!

Released from prison and under a flag of truce, Brownlow hied himself to Nashville where, on March 15, 1862, he met his long-time enemy, Brigadier General Andrew Johnson, Military Governor of Tennessee. They buried the hatchet, temporarily, each being now on common ground—fighting for the Union and bitterly opposing Secession. There were a few days of speech-making in Nashville in which the liberated Parson uncorked his vials of wrath and reached his peroration by screaming out "Grape for the Rebel masses and hemp for their leaders." It was the belief of his hearers that such a dramatic speaker should not be confined to Southern localities. His services were needed to wake up and spur into activity certain languishing elements in the North. Invitations began to pour in from Northern cities, pleading for the Parson to heed the Macedonian call. Even President Lincoln invited him to visit Washington.

Brownlow's celebrated "Tour of the North" began at Cincinnati on April 4, where he addressed a large audience, the admission fee of fifty cents enriching the Parson by some eleven hundred dollars. Elated by his reception, the Parson began a trip that carried him to such important cities as Indianapolis, Chicago, Philadelphia, New York City, and Boston. At all these places, the Parson did not fail to lug in a "plug" for his beloved *Whig*, and Northern subscriptions poured in for his paper. During his tour, an enterprising publisher, George W. Childs, contacted Brownlow in regard to writing a book portraying his experiences with the Rebels. Ten thousand dollars was the sum offered and accepted for the manuscript, and Brownlow retired to Crosswicks, New Jersey, where he wrote his widely publicized book of 458 pages entitled *Sketches of the Rise, Progress, and Decline of Secession; with a Narrative of Personal Adventures Among the Rebels.* A bit of textual surgery was performed by the publisher whereby the long title was abbreviated to read *Parson Brownlow's Book.* Within three months after publication, a hundred thousand copies had been sold, and it was confidently predicted that a half million copies would be marketed.

With the proceeds derived from his lectures, book, and the aid of the Federal Government to the extent of $1,500 and the use of five army wagons to transport paper and other newspaper materials from Cincinnati, Brownlow after a hiatus of more than two years revived his *Whig* on November 11, 1863. The title was changed to *Knoxville Whig and Rebel Ventilator!* Once more, a "voice" had risen, phoenix-like, from the ashes and through its editorial column would funnel pent-up anger, a cry for vengeance, and a demand for the hangman's noose for the despicable "traitors" who had led the Secession movement.

Not only through journalistic enterprise did Brownlow hold sway over most of East Tennessee just prior to the close of the war. He was appointed an agent of the United States Treasury and became a dictator in commercial matters, his consent being necessary in order to buy, sell, or import commodities. In this manner, he became dictator of economic welfare in East Tennessee which had suffered immeasurably from both armies which, in turn, had occupied that region. Destitution was abroad in that section, and actual starvation was the ghastly ogre confronting the people. Brownlow was made a member of the East Tennessee Relief Association which dispatched an appeal to President Lincoln for help. Northern cities responded with more than a quarter-million of dollars with which to purchase the necessities of life. But Brownlow's sympathy for the destitute was exceeded only by his bitterness against the Rebels whom he held responsible for the disastrous conditions. East Tennessee, like Belgium in World War I, became the object of national sentiment, but Parson Brownlow's position was that only the destitute Unionists should be fed and clothed "and none others." Fortunately, wiser heads saw to it that humanitarian considerations were broadened and invoked.

Toward the latter part of 1864 two important factors were clearly discernible, the oncoming collapse of the Confederacy and the almost-sure re-election of Lincoln. With the triumph of Lincoln in November and the disastrous defeat of Hood at Nashville next month, the strategic opportunity of East Tennessee Unionism was at hand. Andrew Johnson, Military Governor of Tennessee, would be moving to Washington to take over the Vice-Presidency in March. The return of Tennessee to a *civil* government basis was an ardent desire on the part of Johnson. What was called the East Tennessee Central Committee met in Nashville, in January, 1865, and transformed itself into an all-powerful dictator as to just how Tennessee would return to its former civil status. Overleaping all legal and constitutional boundaries, the Unionist group converted itself into a so-called Constitutional Convention and proceeded immediately to free Tennessee's slaves, repudiate the secession ordinances and all Confederate debts, and provide for two elections.

The first election was to be held on Washington's birthday for the purpose of ratifying the constitutional amendments; the second election was to take place on March 4, the day that Lincoln and Johnson would be inaugurated, whereby a Governor and a Legislature would be chosen. To insure itself against any breaches developing in the Unionist plans, the above Central Committee, *alias* Constitutional Convention, did another chameleon-like change by acting as a political convention and nominated Parson Brownlow for Governor and selected the entire legislative slate. In this manner was Brownlow elevated to the office for which he had been a temporary candidate four years earlier.

Brownlow's election as Governor was, of course, an act of wartime vintage and was obtained in much the same manner as battles are won. Tennessee, torn by war and devastation, longed for an orderly return to peace-time status when military hostilities came to an end. But with a man installed as Governor, who had breathed unbridled threats of vengeance for more than five years against a majority of his fellow-citizens, a worse choice could not have been made. His program from the day he entered upon his official duties was to make use of his vast powers as a dictator, ushering in a new type of democracy whereby a small minority trampled upon the civil and political rights of the majority. From a financial standpoint, Tennessee was bankrupt; Brownlow pushed her deeper into the red by sponsoring huge financial obligations to numerous railroads, some of which were already in self-confessed bankruptcy. He encountered social chaos and disorder among Unionists and Rebels alike, but he added to the seething turmoil by placing the Negro upon the back of his former master. Throughout his gubernatorial career, he never ceased berating the Confederates, frequently branding them as monsters and undeserving of any respect or confidence. He dispatched numerous messages to the Legislature and issued proclamations by the score, utilizing the latter as propaganda with which to deter and browbeat the vast majority of citizens. Contrary to law, he appointed most of the Judges of various courts, including the Supreme Court, although the existing law called for elections of Judges by the people.

With a pliant Legislature under his command, Brownlow not only disfranchised the overwhelming majority of Tennessee's citizens, but pursued them constantly with additional hostile legislation. He was as vindictive in his gubernatorial denunciations of the opposition as he had been coarse and vulgar in his pastoral days when he hurled his personal anathemas at Presbyterians and Baptists alike. He knew he represented a party that was in the minority, and that it could remain in power only through might. MIGHT was incorporated in disfranchisement laws and the use of troops at the elections of public officials. His spirit of vengeance blinded him to the fact that secession did not disqualify the majority of Tennesseans from participating in the restoration of civil government in their own State.

As Governor, Brownlow was by no means constructive or reconstructive; he was pre-eminently destructive. For almost four years, he
ruled with an iron rod. To his way of thinking, everybody was "loyal"
who voted for and supported him and his policies. All others were
"disloyal" and not to be trusted. As a result of such conditions, his own
party became disrupted shortly after his departure from the State and
ere long Brownlowism was headed for the scrap heap.

Brownlow's grip upon the State was demonstrated shortly after his
re-election as Governor in 1867. Although no vacancy would exist in
one of Tennessee's U. S. Senatorships for something like seventeen
months, yet the wily Governor had a weather-eye upon the job. Accordingly, upon the heels of his inauguration for his second term as
Governor in October, 1867, he let it be known that he wanted to succeed the incumbent, David T. Patterson, whose term would not expire
until March 3, 1869. Although too feeble to deliver his inaugural address, his legislative constituents apparently believed him "sound in body
and mind" and gratified his desire by electing him to the exalted office.
On February 25, 1869, the stormy petrel of Tennessee politics resigned
as Governor in order to take office as United States Senator. The political fates had been kind to the Senator-elect—he would be displacing
the son-in-law of his bitter enemy, Andrew Johnson! And so, on March
4, 1869, the "Fighting Parson of the Southern Highlands" donned the
senatorial toga and witnessed the departure not only of the son-in-law
of Andrew Johnson but also Andrew Johnson himself, the latter being
succeeded by General Ulysses S. Grant. Undoubtedly the "Parson's"
cup of joy was overflowing.

Brownlow's role as United States Senator was undistinguished. His
physical condition was pitiable. He was too feeble to even stand up
when the oath of office was administered. He had to be carried back
and forth from his near-by boarding house to the Senate Chamber. Due
to the loss of his voice, he delivered few speeches during his senatorial
tenure, most of them being committed to writing and being read by the
Senate Clerk. The old warhorse had run his tempestuous course.
Though physically more dead than alive, yet the intrepid old fellow
attended the Senate sessions with reasonable regularity, although severe
illness prevented his being present at any of the Second Session of the
Forty-Third Congress.

On March 3, 1875, the public career of William Gannaway Brownlow came to an end. What must have been the innermost thoughts of
the "Parson" when he reflected that his Senatorial seat next day would
be occupied by none other than his inveterate foe, Andrew Johnson?
Perhaps the Parson solaced himself with the couplet of Dryden:

> "All human things are subject to decay.
> And, when fate summons, monarchs must obey."

Upon his return to Knoxville, Brownlow did not dream of and drift over the scenes of former battles. Two objects had been dearer to him than life itself—his wife and his *Whig*. The former he still had; the other had passed into alien hands. He drummed up a partnership with William Rule and established the *Weekly Whig and Chronicle,* though the former part of the name was sadly out of date. But the Parson had to have *Whig,* somewhere and somehow. For two years the Parson miraculously, it seems, clung to a tenuous thread of life, a helpless paralytic who could not speak above a hoarse whisper. On April 28, 1877, he was piddling around his home watching some workmen patch up a porch and fix some fences. That night another paralytic stroke occurred. On the following day in the early afternoon the long expected event was announced. Parson Brownlow was dead. As his chief biographer so aptly stated:

"He was a product of his times, but his times produced none other like him."

Legislative Messages of
Governor William G. Brownlow 1865–1869

In accordance with a schedule attached as a sort of appendix to the State Constitution by a spurious Constitutional Convention, what may properly be called the *Brownlow Legislature* [1] convened in Nashville on April 3, 1865. At the pilot wheel of the Ship of State stood the radical, acid-tongued, and vindictive "Parson" Brownlow who had been elevated to the office of Governor in the March election from which all but unconditional Unionists had been barred. Confederates (for the most part former Democrats) and Conservative Unionists were shunted aside by the required taking of an iron-clad oath which, in all good

---

[1] Author's note. The General Assembly of 1865, unlike all preceding and succeeding legislative sessions, has no number in the official *Journals* of that legislative session. Both the *Senate and House Journals* carry the statement, "First Session of the General Assembly of the State of Tennessee, 1865." Curiously enough, the published *Acts* of that session carry the legend "Acts of the State of Tennessee, passed at the First Session of the *Thirty-Fourth* General Assembly for the year 1865." See title pages of the respective *Journals* and *Acts.* If the legend carried on title page of the 1865 Acts be accepted, then the Brownlow Legislature ignored the "Secession Legislature" that convened on October 7, 1861 and adjourned *sine die* March 20, 1862, and regarded the session meeting in April, 1865, as being the *Thirty-Fourth* Session. The latter interpretation seems to be substantiated by the fact that the General Assembly, convening on October 7, 1867, is numbered as the *Thirty-Fifth* Session. The conflict regarding the *numbering* of the legislative sessions boils down to this: The "Brownlow Legislature" of 1865 ignored the legislative session of 1861 which, in reality, was the Thirty-Fourth Session. On the other hand, the Brownlow Legislature was not given a *regular number* in the series of legislative sessions. There is, however, no escaping the fact that *two legislative* sessions—that of 1861 and of 1865 —have each been labeled the *THIRTY-FOURTH* Session. Take your choice!

conscience, they could not swallow. The result of the election ushered into the gubernatorial chair and the legislative seats a considerable group of men unreservedly committed to the doctrine of "punishing the rebels." The members of the General Assembly as a whole were not, as erroneously stated by some writers, "carpetbaggers." From an on-the-spot inventory by a Nashville newspaper,[2] twenty of the twenty-five Senators were Tennessee-born, while sixty-two of the Representatives were likewise natives. One conclusion reached by numerous writers is that the Legislature was composed largely of native Republicans and/or "scalawags." In some instances, men wholly unfit to sit as legislators had been elected in order to eliminate those whose "loyalty" did not measure up to the thumb-screw prerequisites incorporated in the iron-clad oath and those who were "suspect" by election officials whose power over acceptance or rejection of prospective voters was well-nigh absolute.

As to the ability or lack of same on the part of the membership of the Legislature, a survey of the personnel leaves much to be desired. Only five of the twenty-four [3] Senators had had any previous service in a lawmaking body. Among the leaders may be numbered DeWitt Clinton Senter (later Governor), Roderick R. Butler, Samuel R. Rodgers, John Trimble, and William H. Wisener. Eleven Senators, almost one-half of the total membership, never held any other State office at any time. Before this General Assembly adjourned *sine die*, ten of the members resigned. The lack of legislative experience on the part of the House members was even more glaring than that of the Senate. Of the eighty-five members elected, only three had seen previous service as legislators. As scum rises to the top of a kettle of boiling water, so the seething cauldron of war spewed up its froth. Not more than a "baker's dozen" can be considered to have been *representative* citizens. Among the leaders were William Heiskell of Knox County; Edmund Cooper of Bedford County; Samuel M. Arnell representing the counties of Williamson, Maury, and Lewis; and Dorsey B. Thomas from the counties of Benton and Humphreys. Far from a flattering appraisal of the House members was made by a competent scholar near the turn of the century:[4]

"Fully two-thirds of these men served four years and ended their terms of service still unknown for anything they had done or said. Their duties were performed by voting yes, when asked to do so."

---

[2] *Daily Times* (Nashville), April 6, 1865.

[3] *Acts of Tennessee*, First Session, 1865, Chapter 36, 59.

Author's note. The pay schedule of members of the Senate shows that David A. Nunn from the counties of Madison, Haywood, Lauderdale, and Tipton never served a single day. Opposite his name appears this statement—"Did not take his seat."

[4] Fertig, James Walter: *The Secession and Reconstruction of Tennessee* (1898), 62. (Doctoral dissertation, University of Chicago)

On April 3, 1865, pursuant to an amendment to the State Constitution, the General Assembly met in Nashville. The Senate was called to order by Senator William H. Wisener, representing the counties of Bedford and Marshall, who nominated as Speaker *pro tempore* Senator Roderick R. Butler from the counties of Johnson, Carter, Washington, and Sullivan.[5] After the unanimous election of Senator Butler, Edward H. East,[6] who had served as Secretary of State during the term of Andrew Johnson as Military Governor, certified that he had received and examined the returns for the election held on March 4, 1865, and thereupon read out the names of the members-elect for both the Senate and the House of Representatives.[7] The oath of office was then administered to the Senators-elect by Chancellor D. C. Trewhitt. The next order of business was the election of a permanent Speaker. Senator Wisener nominated Samuel R. Rodgers from the counties of Knox and Roane who received all the votes cast, amounting to nineteen. Mr. Speaker Rodgers delivered a brief address of thanks for the honor conferred upon him, alluding to the "storm of destruction, devastation, and war" that had "uprooted the resources of wealth and demoralized the people." A final admonition was that "nothing should be done in haste, but everything should be done upon due and proper reflection."[8]

The House of Representatives, with William Heiskell of Knox County acting as temporary Speaker, listened to Secretary East's report on the election of members of the General Assembly and then took a one-hour recess preparatory to permanent organization. Eight ballots were necessary before a majority vote was procured by any candidate. Edmund Cooper of Bedford County and James R. Hood of

[5] *Senate Journal*, First Session, 1865, 3.

[6] *Ibid.*, 3.

Author's note. The official records are not clear as to who acted as Governor of Tennessee from the time of Johnson's resignation as military governor to the inauguration of Brownlow. Dr. Philip M. Hamer, Executive Director, National Historical Publications Commission, Washington, D. C., under date of January 30, 1959, made an intensive investigation among the records in Washington and advised the author as follows:

"On January 14, 1865, Lincoln telegraphed Johnson that he '. . . would be glad to have your suggestion as to supplying your place of Military Governor . . .' On January 17 Johnson telegraphed Lincoln '. . . Gov will be elected on the fourth of March . . . legislature will meet on the first of April . . . I would prefer remaining where I am until that time.' On January 24 Lincoln telegraphed Johnson that '. . . members of Cabinet with myself considered today as to time of your coming on here . . . is unsafe for you not to be here on the 4th of March . . .' On March 3 Johnson, in a letter to Stanton, resigned as Military Governor, and on the same day Stanton accepted the resignation.

On March 10 R. Johnson telegraphed A. Johnson '. . . shall I order commission . . . Col. Smith . . .'; and on March 12 A. Johnson telegraphed R. Johnson 'Mr. East, Secy State was to attend to issuing of all commissions.' "

Apparently Mr. East as Secretary of State acted somewhat in the capacity of an interim governor.

[7] *Ibid.*, 4–6.

[8] *Ibid.*, 7.

Hamilton County led on the first seven ballots, but a scattering vote for other members prevented either from receiving a majority vote. On the eighth and final ballot, Mr. Cooper withdrew his name and nominated William Heiskell of Knox County. The results of the balloting were for Heiskell, 37 votes; for Hood, 29 votes; for Cooper, 1 vote; and for Dillin, 1 vote. Thereupon, William Heiskell was declared elected Speaker of the House of Representatives.[9]

With the principal organizational business attended to, the Legislature met in joint session to count the vote for Governor. A roll call by counties disclosed the following:[10]

William G. Brownlow	23,222
William B. Campbell	25
Horace Maynard	7
J. W. Leftwich	1
———— Bullock	1
———— Merriman	1

After the official announcement of the results of the gubernatorial election, but before the inaugural ceremonies took place, the House displayed its eagerness to "get down to brass tacks." Without a single opposition vote,[11] a resolution was passed ratifying the Thirteenth Amendment to the Constitution of the United States—an amendment, when soon ratified by the required number of States, abolished slavery throughout the whole of the United States. Immediately following Brownlow's inauguration, the Senate adopted the same resolution by unanimous vote.[12]

At eleven o'clock on the morning of April 5, the inaugural ceremonies took place. The legislative *Journals* give a skimpy account of the event, the Senate's official record contenting itself with the following laconic statement:[13]

"The Senate then took a recess to participate in the inauguration ceremonies, and in a body proceeded to the Hall of the House of Representatives, at 11 o'clock, A.M.
The Inauguration being closed, the Senators returned to the Senate Chamber."

In striking contrast to the official records, the contemporary news-

[9] *House Journal*, First Session, 1865, 6–10.
[10] *Ibid.*, 15–16.
Author's note. Campbell's twenty-five votes came from the following counties: Montgomery, 21; Sumner, 2; Rutherford, 1; Shelby, 1. Shelby County cast six votes for Maynard. The *Senate Journal* did not give the vote by counties, but presented the total vote. Fifty-one counties gave Brownlow a clean sweep, not a single opposition vote against Brownlow being recorded. The "slate ticket" concocted by the bogus Constitutional Convention back in January did the trick!
[11] *Ibid.*, 18.
[12] *Senate Journal*, First Session, 1865, 15.
[13] *Ibid.*, 14–15.

papers went to considerable length in describing the inaugural fanfare. It will be recalled that more than three years had passed since the pro-Confederate Legislature had speedily adjourned and departed from the very building in which the present Union Legislature was assembled. Furthermore, on the very first day of the session, news reached Nashville that Richmond had fallen, foretelling the fateful end of the war which soon became an actuality. Unionists were wild with excitement, many of whom had fought under the Union flag. United States Flags were flying from many places, and bands were marching through the streets playing *Hail Columbia* and *Yankee Doodle*. Cannons on Capitol Hill belched forth salvos, and newsboys scurried hither and yon shouting "Extra." But to many, who had remained faithful to the idea of Southern Supremacy, the news brought sadness and sorrow.

At the appointed hour, the grim-visaged Governor-elect appeared in the Hall of the House of Representatives. Accompanying him as ushers was an array of Union "big brass" military officers including Major General George H. Thomas, Major General Rousseau, Major General Milroy, and Brigadiers General Donaldson, Towers, and Miller. The inaugural exercises were opened with a prayer by one Dr. Hottzinger, followed by the administration of the oath of office by Judge Samuel Milligan of the State Supreme Court. At the conclusion of the oath-taking part of the ceremonies, Governor Brownlow delivered his Inaugural Address:[14]

Inaugural Address

"GENTLEMEN OF THE SENATE, AND HOUSE OF REPRESENTATIVES:

The period has arrived, fixed by the Amended Constitution, for a change in the Executive affairs of this State, by the election of a civil Governor. This distinguished honor, by the generous confidence of the loyal people of Tennessee, has been conferred upon me. The oath required by the Constitution has been administered

---

[14] Author's note. Neither of the legislative *Journals* makes mention of any Inaugural Address. A printed pamphlet in the State Library, at Nashville, however, is conclusive that such an Address was delivered. The Address as herein incorporated follows verbatim the pamphlet above mentioned. The title page of the printed pamphlet bears this wording:

MESSAGE
and
INAUGURAL ADDRESS
of
GOV. WM. G. BROWNLOW,
to the
SENATE & HOUSE OF REPRESENTATIVES
of Tennessee.
Session of 1865.

to me, and I at once enter upon the high and responsible duties pertaining to the office. Without affectation, I may say, none can realize more sensibly than myself, the weight of these new responsibilities, and the ability required for the faithful and profitable execution of them. None can feel more sensibly than myself, the weight of these new responsibilities, and the ability required for the faithful and profitable execution of them. None can feel more sensibly than I do, the moderate qualifications I bring to the discharge of these duties, and that want of experience in legislation, which, in some degree, might atone for my want of ability. I have no doubt that each of us will properly appreciate the responsibilities under which we are placed, by the fact that we are here to legislate so as to promote the physical, the social, the intellectual, and the religious welfare of the State. Of one thing, gentlemen, I can assure you, and through you, those whom you have the honor to represent: I bring with me a settled determination to discharge these duties to the very best of my limited abilities—with an equally determined purpose of faithfulness, integrity, impartiality, and devotion to the State, and to the generous people who have placed me here, to the close of my period of service.

I am free to admit, that I have been promoted to this high position, by the Union people of Tennessee, without regard to old party lines, and I am justly expected by them, to administer the executive duties with a view to no partisan or selfish purposes; and thus relieved of many of the troubles and burdens which invariably connect themselves with a mere party triumph, I am left free with you, gentlemen, to follow the suggestions of patriotism and duty—and to know no man because he has been a Whig, or a Democrat, but to honor all, as they may honor the Federal Union.

The maxim is one of long standing, and of world-wide renown, that 'the pen is mightier than the sword.' 'This,' says a late writer, 'is a sort of half truth that in the midst of popular speech has obtained the stamp of authority, and henceforth has passed current without a very close examination as to its correctness.' Major-General Thomas, a true soldier and a modest gentleman, might utter this maxim, but the rebel General Hood, less modest, might question its correctness, alleging that his *experience* has taught him that the sword has made the pen powerful, and pointed its periods!

And though often used as the instrument of wrong and injustice, patriots, philanthropists, and even Christians, will not fail to remember the invaluable services of the sword, in the cause of truth and liberty; they will remember that it wrung the great *Charter of English Rights* from the hands of an obstinate King; they will remember that in the grasp of an inexorable people, the sword perpetuated their rights at the block where Charles the First lost his head! Coming down to our own day and time, the sharp logic of the sword has solved with its trenchant blows the Gordian Knot of Southern Independence! The pen did its work in the getting up of this rebellion, by instructing the Southern mind and firing the Southern heart; but Grant, Sherman, Sheridan, Thomas, Farragut and others, by the use of the sword, have brought the Southern people to consider seriously, whether or not 'the triumphs of peace are greater than the triumphs of war.'

Gentlemen, your Amended Constitution wipes out the institution of slavery, and denies to the Legislature in all time to come, the right to recognize property in man. In this sweeping act of Emancipation, you have, in due time, abated a nuisance, which, for years past, has obstructed all the avenues to agricultural, mechanical, manufacturing, and commercial development. In this emergency the duty of prompt action becomes imperative, and even the advocates of gradual emancipation— which means the gradual putting down of the Rebellion—found themselves powerless in the claims of a higher civil and State necessity, which demand the prompt abatement of the evil. The wicked authors of this rebellion were told, that *in* the Union, and under the Constitution, their slave property was safe, and that it could not be safe anywhere else. Not one year elapsed after the war commenced before the institution of slavery, in all the border States, became utterly demoralized. The owner lost all control over his slave; and the slave having *got out of the Union*, and from *under the Constitution*, has either been *itinerating* at will, or *lying around loose!*

The history of the past shows to every candid mind, that slavery has conferred no benefits upon Tennessee. It has been a stumbling block in the way of her advancement. Her people have felt the effect of its degrading influence, and her growth and prosperity have been retarded, by the exclusion from her borders, of both capital and educated labor.

One of the signs of the times is, that the natural features of the

Southern States are now everywhere expatiated upon, in order that enterprising emigrants may be led to come among us, and add to our capital and enterprise. Tennessee holds out inducements to wealthy and industrious emigrants, that no other border State offers. The soil, from Johnson to Shelby, possesses extraordinary fertility; it abounds in clear and delightful gushing streams; its mineral wealth of coal, iron, lead, zinc, copper, and other valuable products, is inexhaustible. Its climate is mild and salubrious, avoiding the extremes of both North and South, and affording remunerative markets for every thing grown upon our prolific soil. Land is cheap and by no means difficult to clear. No State is so admirably adapted for the growth of cereals, fruits, grapes, cattle, sheep, hogs, horses, and mules. The winters are short, and generally so mild that stock may run out without particular care. The summers are free from the intense heat of the Gulf States, and the entire South abounds with valuable mineral springs, many of which are handsomely improved, and before the Rebellion, were places of popular resort.

The signs of the times indicate very clearly, that the war is about drawing to a close; that the rebels are exhausted; that their Commissariat has no food, and their Treasury no money; that their army is melting away by desertions and deaths on the battle-field, and that there are no materials left with which to fill up their depleted ranks. In short, there is everything to encourage the friends of the Union, as they enter upon the Summer Campaign; but there is also everything to admonish us that we must gird ourselves for our best efforts. The hardest work, nay, the bloodiest work of the war, is, in all probability, before us, in ridding our country of guerrillas, robbers, and professional thieves, passing for Confederate soldiers.

But, gentlemen, this great conflict has had its useful lessons. We understand now, the full meaning of that abominable doctrine of 'State Sovereignty,' the Southern interpretation of which has involved us in all our troubles. For thirty years past, the iniquitous phrase of 'State Sovereignty,' has worked its way into public documents, political speeches and platforms—into every treasonable daily and weekly journal of the country, and finally into the common language of the honest people, until it was understood to mean that there was no other 'sovereignty' in America, but *State Sovereignty*—that the greatest amount of this was lodged in the Cotton States, and that whatever they resolved to do, it was marvelously proper to perform!

Even in the Pulpits of the South, the charges were rung upon the mischievous doctrine of 'State Sovereignty,' backed up by the unbounded influence of the worst class of men that have made tracks upon Southern soil—*Secession Preachers*. And thus, the treasonable doctrine of 'State Sovereignty,' has gradually been undermining the Union for more than thirty years, and in my humble way I have opposed it that long.

When applied simply to the authority of a State over her own domestic affairs, and her local institutions, the doctrine is sound, though even then, the word *sovereign* signifies too much. How ridiculous the idea is, of a sovereign member of the Federal Union, existing, without authority to declare war, or conclude a treaty of peace—to protract alliances, to levy duties and imports, or even to coin money! This is sovereignty with a vengeance, and a degree of sovereignty that is not likely to hold the nations of the earth in awe, while these several *powerless* sovereigns confederate to overthrow a truly sovereign power and achieve their boasted independence!

I hold that, under the Constitution of the United States, there can be but one SOVEREIGN AUTHORITY, and to that all State Sovereignties are subordinate. Hence, I am not one of those men who are alarmed at the powers assumed by the Federal Government at this time, regarding them as a departure from former precedents. A state of war forced upon the country, by a set of bad men in rebellion, calls for the exercise of the whole war power of the National Government. So far from finding fault with the National Administration, for the exercise of these alleged startling powers, I have felt inclined to grumble that we have not had more of the same sort. The real people have not made any factious complaints as to the liberties of the country being endangered by these encroachments on the part of the General Government, but have sustained the Administration with great unanimity.

If I am anything in politics, I come under the hated appellation of a *Federalist*, a name given to the friends of the Constitution of the United States, at its formation and adoption, and to the political party that favored the Administration of President Washington—the most pure and patriotic party that ever existed in America. I hope I may be allowed to repeat, without subjecting myself to the charge of egotism, that I have all my life long been a FEDERAL WHIG, of the WASHINGTON and HAMILTON school. I am the advocate of a *concentrated* Federal Government; or, if more acceptable to the fastidious, of a *Strong Central Government*, able to maintain its dignity, to assert its authority, and to crush out any rebellion that may be inaugurated. Such a government is what we want, and what we must have, with ample powers to sustain itself, having due regard for the constitutional rights of the States, which are clearly defined and sufficiently guarded. I have never been a *Sectional*, but at all times a *National* man, supporting men for the Presidency and Vice Presidency, without any regard to which side of Mason and Dixon's Line they were born, or resided at the time of their nomination.

I am for doing what every American citizen should feel prepared to do—willing to live and die for America, as she is and has been; but America without the Federal Union, blight, ruin, and decay come upon us, and we bid a long farewell to the last remnant of earth's beauty, and the light of civil and religious liberty!

Who among us, gentlemen, of our generation, can estimate the value of the American Union? Proud, happy, thrice-happy America! the home of the oppressed, the asylum of the emigrant, where the citizen of every clime, and the child of every creed, roam free and untrammelled as the wild winds of heaven! Baptized at the fount of Liberty in fire and blood, during our Revolutionary struggle, cold must be the heart that thrills not at the name of the American Union!

When the Old World, with 'all its pomp, and pride, and circumstance,' and the malice of its monarchies towards our Government, shall be covered with oblivion—when thrones shall have crumbled and dynasties shall have been forgotten—may this glorious Union, despite the mad schemes of Southern fire-eaters, and Northern Copper-heads, stand amid regal ruin and national desolation, towering sublime, like the last mountain in the Deluge—majestic, immutable, and magnificent!

In pursuance of this, let every loyal man who loves his country and her institutions, shake off the trammels of Southern treason, and swear upon the altar of his country, in the language of that inflexible patriot of the Hermitage: 'THE FEDERAL UNION—IT MUST AND SHALL BE PRESERVED.' Then we shall see every heart a shield, and a drawn sword in every hand, to preserve the ark of our political safety! Then we shall see reared a fabric upon our National

Constitution, which time cannot crumble, persecutions shake, fanaticism disturb, nor revolution change, but which shall stand among us like our lofty and stupendous Lookout Mountain, while the earth rocks at its feet, and the thunder peals above its head!

In conclusion, gentlemen, allow me to say, that this session of the Legislature will be one of vital importance. Grave questions will be agitated, discussed, and passed upon. But I leave for a future and official communication, the mention of measures proper for your consideration. And may the blessings of our Heavenly Father, attend your deliberations while here, and may the guidance of the Unseen Hand preserve your families in your absence; may your legislation prove salutary; and may your sobriety, morality, industry and patriotism, win for you the merited commendation of 'well done, good and faithful servants.' "

Without an acquaintance with the background of Brownlow's position on slavery, one might conclude from the above Address that he had always been a vigorous anti-slavery advocate. Quite the contrary is true. Seven years prior to his inauguration as Governor of Tennessee, he engaged in a prolonged debate with a Northern minister, Abram Pryne, on the topic—*Ought American Slavery to be Perpetuated?* In his opening speech before a large audience in Philadelphia, Brownlow laid down the following categorical thesis as setting forth his position:[15]

"Not only will I throughout this discussion openly and boldly take the ground that *Slavery as it exists in America, ought to be perpetuated*, but that slavery is an established and inevitable condition to human society. I will maintain the ground that God always intended the relation of master and slave to exist; that Christ and the early teachers of christianity, found slavery differing in no material respect from American slavery, *incorporated into every department of society.*"

Four years later, in 1862, Brownlow's unqualified statement revealed him as still being a pronounced pro-slavery man. His own words, as written by none other than himself, are direct and self-explanatory:[16]

"I am a pro-Slavery man, and so are the Union men generally of the border Slave States. I have long since made up my mind upon the Slavery question, but not without studying it thoroughly. The result of my investigation is, that there is not a single passage in the New Testament, nor a

---

[15] Brownlow, W. G. and Pryne, Abram: *Ought American Slavery to be Perpetuated?*
A DEBATE Between Rev. W. G. Brownlow and Rev. A. Pryne.
Held at Philadelphia, September, 1858, p. 18.
[16] Brownlow, W. G.: *Sketches of the Rise, Progress, and Decline of Secession* ("Parson Brownlow's Book"), 1862, 108.

single act in the records of the Church, during her early history even for centuries, containing any direct, professed, or *intended* censure of slavery."

Contrary to the negative answer implied in Jeremiah's query, "Parson" Brownlow demonstrated that the Ethiopian could change his skin and the leopard his spots! Apparently unmindful of his inconsistency on the slavery question, Brownlow attacked the institution of slavery and attributed to it the manifold hardships and sufferings to which the Nation had fallen heir.

On the day following his inauguration, the Legislature was advised by the Governor that he "is ready to communicate his message" which was as follows:*

"EXECUTIVE DEPARTMENT,
Nashville, April 6, 1865.

GENTLEMEN OF THE SENATE, AND HOUSE OF REPRESENTATIVES:

In accordance with long established custom, and in obedience to the requirements of the Constitution, it becomes my duty to communicate to the Legislature the condition of the State, and to recommend for their consideration such matters as I may deem expedient.

When we contemplate the distracted condition of the country, four dreadful years of trial through which we have passed, and the manner in which it has been preserved, our minds naturally turn to Him whose care has been over us, who has protected and preserved us through scenes of blood and carnage, unprecedented in the history of wars. For the preservation of our lives and certain remnants of our property; for the care and protection of Providence over those who have gone forth to battle, and are still risking their lives in defense of the principles upon which our happiness and property rest; for life, health, food and raiment; for our safe conduct through untold changes, by a kind Providence; for the prospect of the restoration of law and order in our distracted State; for the gleam of light, looking to peace, now breaking through the clouds that have enveloped us for the four years past; for these and numerous other blessings of which we have been the recipients, let us, in all humility and sincerity, render thanks to Almighty God, and let us earnestly implore a continuance of his favor.

Secession is an abomination that I cannot too strongly condemn,

---

* *Senate Journal*, First Session, 1865, 18–32.
  House Journal, First Session, 1865, 20–34.

and one that you cannot legislate against with too much severity.—
What has it done for our country in the space of four years? It has
plunged our country into civil war, paralyzed our commerce, destroyed our agricultural pursuits, suspended the whole trade and
business of our country, lessened the value of our property, destroyed many of the pursuits of life, and has involved the South in
irretrievable bankruptcy and ruin.

What has it done for Tennessee? It has formed odious and unconstitutional military leagues, passed military bills, and inaugurated
a system of oppressive taxation, without consulting the people, and
then, in mockery of a free election, has required them by their votes
to sanction its usurpation, at the point of the bayonet under the
penalty of imprisonment and death. It has offered a premium for
crime, in ordering the discharge of culprits from prison, on condition that they would enter the rebel army, and in recommending the
Judges to hold no courts for the trial of offenders. It has stained our
statute book with the repudiation of honest Northern debts, and
has palpably violated the Constitution, by attempting through its
unlawful extensions, to do away with the right of suffrage. It has
passed laws making it treason to say or do anything in favor of the
Government of the United States, or against the so-called Confederate States. It has prostrated and overthrown the freedom of speech
and of the press; it has involved the whole South in a war whose success is now proven to be utterly hopeless, and which, ere another
year roll round, must lead to the ruin of the common people. Its
bigoted, murderous and intolerant spirit has subjected the people
of Tennessee to many grievances. Our people have been arrested
and imprisoned; our houses have been rudely entered and shame-
fully pillaged; our families have been subjected to insults; our women
and children have been tied up and scourged, or shot by a ruffian
soldiery; our towns have been pillaged; our citizens have been
robbed of their horses, mules, grain and meat, and many of them assassinated and murdered.

Hundreds, yes, thousands of our young men, middle-aged and old
men, have been driven from our State, and compelled to enter the
Federal army, in strange regiments, and their bones now lie bleaching
upon the many battle-fields of the South and West, and all this because our people were true to the traditions of their fathers, and re-

fused to worship rebel gods. And to the honor of the people be it known, that more regiments to-day swell the number of the armies of the Union than there are living traitors in the ranks of the enemy.

In this once proud capital of the 'Volunteer State,' there have been thousands of Union refugees, men, women and children, broken-hearted, naked and starving; a great many are here still. They have fled from the wicked and murderous guerillas, after being robbed of everything they possessed. They have lived in camps or tents, by fires in the open woods, have dragged out a miserable existence for a time, and died among strangers. Hundreds have suffered from actual want of necessary food, shelter and clothing, while many residences in this *rebellious city* have been occupied by the families of those who were fighting against their country, or, being *citizen rebels* and *home traitors*, have fled within the rebel lines. These families have remained here protected, and have wielded an over-ruling social influence. Many of them are wealthy, and live in ease and comfort. They have busied themselves in giving information to the enemy, in carrying delicacies to rebel prisoners who have been confined here for their crimes and treason. And it is stated upon undoubted authority, and the fact is notorious in this capital, that the disloyal families never contributed in the slightest degree to the relief of the poor and distressed women and children, or disabled soldiers thrown upon this population by the operations of the war. I state these facts, which may have the appearance of a personal and local character, that you may know how to shape your course when personal and local legislation is called for.

I have the honor to submit to the General Assembly of the State of Tennessee, a copy of a joint resolution of Congress, passed by a vote of two-thirds of each house, entitled 'A resolution submitting to the Legislatures of the several States a proposition to amend the Constitution of the United States,' which is in the following words:

'*Resolved,* by the Senate and House of Representatives of the United States, in Congress assembled (two-thirds of both houses concurring therein), That the following article be proposed to the Legislatures of the several States as an amendment to the Constitution of the United States, which when ratified by the Legislatures of three-fourths of said States, shall be valid to all intents and purposes, as a part of said Constitution, namely:

'ARTICLE XIII.

'Section 1. Neither slavery nor involuntary servitude, except as a punishment for crime, whereof the party shall have been duly convicted, shall exist within the United States, or any place subject to their jurisdiction.

'Sec. 2. Congress shall have power to enforce this article by appropriate legislation.

'Approved, February 1, 1853.' †

The slavery question here comes up in a form hitherto not discussed in our politics. It is not a question as to the right of Congress to exclude slavery from the Territories, to legislate upon the matter themselves, nor does it involve the discussion of any doubtful powers, but is the simple proposition to amend the Constitution of the United States in the manner prescribed by that sacred instrument, so as to strike down the monster institution which has embroiled the Government for half a century, and culminated in the most wicked, uncalled for and bloody war known to the history of the civilized world.

Slavery, secured to the people of the South more permanently by the Constitution of the United States, and the laws enacted in pursuance thereof, than any species of property claimed by them—not even excepting their lands—will now perish by the war it brought about to enlarge its power and perpetuate its existence. Let us do our part in this great work by ratifying the action of Congress, and carrying out the wishes of our people. After the ratification by the people of our State of our Amended State Constitution, embracing the same proposition, and after your election to the General Assembly on this platform, and by the same people, I have not considered an elaborate argument in favor of the proposition submitted by Congress at all necessary. I may be allowed to say, however, that to prohibit slavery in a State requires a change in the State Constitution. Pregnant as we find slavery to be of all sorts of political mischief, it is not to be got rid of, under the Constitution, in any other than a constitutional manner. And, while the sooner this can be done the better, it does not appear in what part of the Constitution of the United States the power of regulating it at all, in times of peace, is to

---

† Author's note. Through error, the *House Journal* of 1865 gives the date of approval as being "February 1, 1853." By referring to the original manuscript of Governor Brownlow's message, the date is given as February 1, 1865.

be found. Fortunately for the future happiness of the country, the Constitution has provided a way in which the people can remedy the evil, without any questionable exercise of power, and that is by amending the Constitution, just as Congress has proposed.

Slavery was so far made the subject of constitutional cognizance, by the people of the United States, when they adopted the Articles of Confederation, that it found a place in the compromises of that instrument, both in fixing the ratio of representation and the apportionment of direct taxes; and also in requiring the people of a free State to surrender so much of this 'sovereignty' as not to have the right to protect the slave that sought refuge from bondage—it would seem too late in the day to question the right of the people to adopt amendments to that instrument, in regard to this or other subjects embraced in its provisions. It becomes us, therefore, to approach this subject with an enlightened statesmanship, and with a degree of moral courage that is not afraid to do right, appealing to the ultimate judgment of mankind to vindicate our action.

It is in this way, and in no other, that a uniform rule can be provided, and an end put thereby, in all time to come, to a possibility of reviving that which has been the fatal cause of all the mischief in the country. To insist upon excluding slavery from a State by amending her Constitution, before recognizing her again as within the pale of the Union, would look awkward, and fall below the dignity of political sagacity. Our State has shown her hand, and placed herself square upon the record; and I flatter myself that her representatives here assembled are ready for a measure which shall forever exclude slavery from the United States.

Some legislation is necessary for the protection, government and control of the emancipated slaves among us. When this war is over a portion of those who fought to perpetuate slavery will show the emancipated slave no quarter, and especially that class of slaves who have been rude and violent toward their former owners. What the character of this legislation should be, I leave the good-sense, prudence and reflection of the members of the General Assembly to determine.

It is certainly proper and right for the Legislature of Tennessee to determine to what extent this State shall be overrun with the emancipated slaves of other States. If their presence in any State is a blessing they should be distributed; if an evil, it is but just that we should be taxed only with our own share of them. I am, myself, the advocate of providing for them a separate and appropriate amount of territory, and settle them down permanently, as a nation of freedmen. In this case, as in most others, it will probably be well to guard against exceptive legislation. The negro has had no agency himself in bringing on our troubles, and does not merit unkind treatment at our hands.

The attention of the Legislature is earnestly called to the subject of the roving bands of guerrillas, and squads of robbers and murderers who frequent those counties and portions of counties remote from our military forces. The depredations and murders committed by them are of such frequent occurrence as to have created a general feeling of insecurity among our citizens, causing hundreds to sacrifice their property and abandon their homes and the graves of their parents and loved ones, seeking new homes, among strangers in the Northwestern States.

The criminal laws of Tennessee prior to the rebellion were equal to the demands of justice and the wants of society, but they are now inadequate in both these cases. The corruptions of the rebellion have exhibited themselves in every quarter, and the effects of the same have been to demoralize all classes of society, more or less, calling for more stringent enactments, so as to meet the numerous cases arising in our country. I advise that horse-stealing, house-breaking and highway robberies be punished with death. Let the proof in all such cases be clear and unquestionable, and then let the offenders be hung, even for the first offense. This character of a law will close out all those acts of perfidy which now render life and property insecure, more or less in all counties of the State; and when the necessary reform is had, a future Legislature can repeal or amend the statute. Such a law may look to others like a bloody act, but it can never affect injuriously an honest man or a law-abiding citizen. And you, gentlemen, should feel no concern for the opposite class of men but to punish and reform them.

The attention of the Legislature is especially directed to the militia laws of the State. The occurrences of the past four years have disclosed the fact that our militia laws, as they now are, are very imperfect, and need further amendments to make them effective.

The State arms were carried into the rebellion, through the influence of the bad men in authority four years ago, and throughout the length and breadth of the State she has not arms enough to arm a captain's company. This deficiency should be provided for at once. I have no doubt that the Federal Government, upon a fair presentation of the case, would come to our relief with a liberal hand.

If, in the wisdom of the Legislature, an efficient military force, over and above what is provided for in general terms, should be placed at the disposal of the Executive, I suggest an appropriation for military contingent expenses. In any rate, the Legislature would do well to pass an act providing for a Military Contingent Fund, of a moderate character, confiding it under the control of the Executive, and making it his duty to report to the Legislature at each session. Should there be no use for the fund, the Executive will, of course, make no drafts upon it, and it will be his pleasure to report that the money belonging to the Military Contingent Fund remains in the State Treasury unexpended.

I am aware that a proposition to increase the salaries of public officers in the State will meet with opposition—that it is not a popular measure, and that demagogues will use such a vote upon the stump against members voting for an increase. Acting alone from a sense of duty, and desiring to see justice done to those patriotic men who are serving the State, I suggest an increase in the pay of all civil officers whose compensation is fixed by law. Supreme Judges should be paid a salary of $5,000; Chancellors and Circuit Judges should be allowed $3,000, and the Treasurer, Comptroller, Secretary of State, Attorney General and other officers should be allowed a corresponding increase in their salaries. And I respectfully, but frankly suggest, that the pay of members of the General Assembly be increased, and the more so as such increase could not take effect during your term of office.

It is folly to think of a man in public office now supporting his family on the salary he received four and five years ago. Boarding, clothing, meats, vegetables—in fact, everything has increased to twice former prices. And yet the wages of the public officers are down at the old prices. If any one of the incumbents named is worthy of his office he is worthy of a support from that office. His pay should be made equal to his necessary expenses. The State cannot reasonably expect a man to devote his individual time and his whole energies and talents to an office, when the salary of such office will not defray the necessary expenses of his family. Gentlemen capable of filling such offices are capable of supporting themselves in other vocations; and it is obvious that they will be forced to turn their attention to other pursuits in order to gain a livelihood. The increase of such salaries will add something to our taxes, but the amount will be so small as scarcely to be felt by the people. I doubt not they will cheerfully contribute in this way to aid in sustaining good and competent men in important official positions. I recommend, therefore, that immediate action be taken in this matter.

The financial condition of the State demands the early and prompt attention of this General Assembly. The reports of the Comptroller and Treasurer are to the 1st of October, 1861. From that time to the restoration of the capital to the National authority, February following, and the flight of the State authorities, the information left us is imperfect and insufficient. The subsequent operations will appear from the current report of the Comptroller, whose high character for integrity and truth commend him to your confidence. The balance in the Treasury on the 1st of October, 1861, according to the Treasurer's Report, was $185,496.69. Besides, warrants for payment remain in the Treasury for $60,401.04. Warrants for payment out of the Treasury had been issued but not presented for $145,417.12. How far the figures were modified by the operations of the next four months and a half, to the middle of February, 1862, I have no information. Except the military expenses, it is presumed that the balance was not changed, judging from the uniformity apparent in the fiscal operations of the preceding four years. Since that time Middle and West Tennessee have been generally within the Federal lines, and East Tennessee since the first of September, 1863. Governor Johnson has occupied the Capitol, and exercised gubernatorial jurisdiction over those portions of the State held by Federal authority. Governor Harris, who adhered to the rebel cause, is very generally understood to have collected revenue in the counties within their military lines. The Comptroller will be found to have given in his report the financial history of Governor Johnson's administration. This report is respectfully submitted for your careful consideration, and the recommendations of that officer are approved by me. What monies were collected by Governor Harris and his subordinates, I am unable to state, nor am I prepared to say that it is important for you to inquire. It will be a matter for your consideration whether the arrearage of taxes for the past four years shall be collected in whole or in part. The principal, if not the current liabilities during that period, are the interest on the State debt. The usual payments to common schools and academies, and to several charitable institutions of the State, were not made. The consequences of the failure would not be atoned for by reaching them now. The same is substantially true of various other items of ordinary expenditures.

The State Debt, as reported by the Comptroller, in October, 1861, is said to be $6,896,606.66, and this demands your attention.— This includes $3,000,000 of eight per cent. bonds for the 'defense of the State,' which has recently been discarded by the people at the ballot-box. This unauthorized and most unjust indebtedness, repudiated, leaves the indebtedness of the State properly, $3,896,606.-06, at an annual interest of $212,388.25. The interest is presumed to have been paid on the first of January, 1861. It is not known how much has since been paid, if any. The bonds will show, either by the endorsements or the absence of the coupons. Besides this debt, the State has bonds for internal improvement purposes, and has endorsed the bonds of railroad companies to the amount of $16,211,-000.00. For these the State is ultimately liable upon the failure of the companies. These bonds it is believed the State will have to provide for, to preserve its credit, making an aggregate indebtedness of $20,005,606.66, and the annual interest $1,185,048.25. Of this debt proper, $66,666.66 matured in 1861; $61,250 in 1862; $177,750 in 1863; and $58,500 in 1864—in all, $366,166.66, at once to be provided for. The Comptroller states that the bonds maturing in 1861 were 'taken possession of and held by the State, subject to adjustment at the end of the war.' Besides these, the State held bonds, mostly her own, as follows: The Spencer T. Hunt Fund, 6; The Railroad Sinking Fund, 161; deposited by the free banks, 341; deposited by foreign insurance companies, 80; and in all 588 bonds. These bonds, held in trust, were carried away, it is believed, with the valuables of the State Treasury, by the State officers, who ingloriously fled on the approach of the National flag. Double payment can probably be avoided. Evidence must be in existence by which they can be identified. The notorious condition of our State affairs has been sufficient to put dealers upon their guard. So that if any of the bonds have been fraudulently sold, payment to the present holders may be justly stopped. Furthermore, it will be well to consider how far it is your duty as agents of the State, not only not to pay the bonds held by those who have been actively engaged in the rebellion to overthrow the Government, whether held by them or parties who may seek to conceal them for the benefit of the rebels, as they will likely do, I advise that you adopt measures to prevent their payment. The bonds can in no event compensate for the loss the disloyal holders have occasioned the State. The justice of holding them responsible in this way, it is believed, cannot be successfully controverted.

The arrearage of interest, amounting to nearly twenty-five per cent of the principal, is more than the people can easily pay at sight, with the other burdens, public and private, thrown upon them by the war. It will be necessary, therefore, to anticipate the means, so as, at the same time, to preserve the State credit by satisfying the creditors, and to preserve the people from oppressive taxation.

The recent amendment to the State Constitution abolishing slavery will require some changes in the revenue laws. The item of slaves will no longer appear in the list of taxables. The census of 1860 shows there were in the State about 275,000. The assessors' returns show that 130,425 were reported for taxation. Their average value had steadily increased from $413.72 in 1846, to $886.40. It is a significant fact that the next year, the first of the war, the average fell to $769.36, taxes being at the low rate of seven cents upon the one hundred dollars to which our State taxation was reduced in 1860, the slaves averaging a little the rise of sixty-two cents each, amounting to $80,000 in the aggregate. The slaves held no property. Being emancipated, they will now be subjected to a poll tax. Many of them will soon acquire taxable property far beyond their personal value as slaves.

As soon as this war ceases, there is every reason to expect a large accession to our population. Thousands of sensible and practical men have been here, connected with the army, and have looked with astonishment and delight at our productive soil, charming climate and great advantages of agriculture. They have seen that a farm hand in a Northern State is ordinarily worth from thirty to fifty dollars a month—that is to say, he earns that much, or say $600 per annum. In our State a good farm hand can make five bales of cotton, of five hundred pounds each, which would make the profits of his labor worth $2,000 per annum, against $600 in a Northern State—a better and more certain business than going to California or any of the gold regions. Therefore it is, the value of land with us will be proportionately increased. If the tax of seven cents on the one hundred dollars, to which our burdens had been reduced in 1860, shall be increased to a reasonable extent, it is believed sufficient revenue will be realized in the next three years over and above the ordinary expenditures, to meet the arrears of interest on the debt, to pay the sum now due, and the further sum of $1,245,000, falling due in 1868.

It is further suggested that the list of taxable property might be increased without being oppressive. By the returns of 1860, it appears that all 'other property' subject to taxation, besides land, amounted in value to but $24,362,151—less than one half the assessed value of the town lots. Before the war our financial resources were so ample, compared with the limited demands upon them, that it was necessary to tax but a few of the principal articles of property. Our affairs are now quite changed, and every interest should be made to bear its proper burdens.

The common school system will, in this connection, demand your attention. The fund appropriated for this purpose has been squandered by the bad men and dishonest functionaries, who fled on the approach of the old flag. What shall be done to replace this great loss? At no period in the history of the State has the young and rising generation appealed so affectingly for legislative aid. Practically denied all scholastic advantages during the last four years, and deprived, as thousands have been of their natural protectors, if they are not soon provided for it will be too late for them. Indeed, not a few have already passed beyond the age to attend school, hopelessly illiterate.

In this connection your attention is called to an act of Congress providing for the establishment of an Agricultural College. Most of the States are in advance of us in accepting the offer, and perhaps we might profit by examining their legislation in regard to this subject.

The currency and the Banks are nearly allied to Finances, and are in such a demoralized condition as to demand prompt action and most positive legislation. The State owes it to herself to look into the condition of the three old banks, the Bank of Tennessee, the Union and the Planters' Banks, each having its parent bank in Nashville, with affiliated branches extending over the State; also several stock banks, and the free banks. With perhaps one or two exceptions, it is believed they are all hopelessly insolvent. All have beyond doubt violated their charters, and may properly be closed up. Nay, where they have value received for their notes, and are worth it, they should be made to redeem their issues. The policy formed by these banks, even before the war, was to keep their paper at lower quotations than that of any of the surrounding States. Even at home it was at a discount, and in some of the neighboring States it was uncurrent. This imposed upon our commerce the payment of large sums of premiums upon all remittances beyond the State, which, in the end, came off the people. Such a currency could only result from unsound financial principles, for the balance of trade with most of the surrounding States, was decidedly in our favor. It is therefore recommended that all existing banks be wound up at once, and that no more State banks be chartered. The several hundred thousand in real estate owned by the State bank should be cashed without delay. The stock was owned by the State, and it held large deposits of currency and securities. As the Union army advanced to the possession and occupation of the towns where the branches were located, the officers fled with the assets beyond the limits of the State, and they are now doubtless irretrievably gone. In the outset of the rebellion, this bank was used by the guilty conspirators, and large issues were made to further their schemes of treason. It has been determined by the people that these issues shall not be paid.

There are many notes outstanding of the bank, issued after the date specified in your amended Constitution, and intended alone for the benefit of the rebellion. Shall they be redeemed by a tax imposed upon the people? I know of no legal or moral obligation to redeem those notes, even if they occupied such an attitude that such an obligation could be enforced. It is known that when bank notes become uncurrent they are sold by the small holders, who are not in a condition to hold such paper, and bought up by speculators, generally at their own figures. In this way they accumulate in the hands of a few, often at prices almost nominal. The notes of the Bank of Tennessee it is believed, are held in this way and by this class of dealers. Having lost the principal of this banking capital, and having sold these issues in small quantities, at a heavy discount, shall our people be taxed to make these issues good in the hands of speculators? I confess I can see no equity in it. Doubtless instances will occur of individual hardship, and others will be pressed upon your attention, not so much by the parties themselves as by others interested in the adoption of a general policy, based upon these existing cases. There remain to the bank large assets, uncollected debts, and the present liabilities of the faithless officers. Suits are understood to be pending against many of these officers of branches. The others should be held to their responsibilities. I content myself with these general suggestions, trusting in your wisdom, if you deem them practicable, to arrange the details.

The National Banking system is believed on many accounts to be preferable. This would give us a circulation current all over the country, and subject our banking to more correct principles of finance. Other States are adopting the National Banking System, and I recommend the same to the Legislature of Tennessee. Such an institution could be used profitably as the fiscal agent of the State, and if you can secure the means, one in each of the other grand divisions of the State would work to advantage.

The qualifications of voters, and other limitations of the elective franchise, have been entrusted to you by the people. This delicate responsibility will devolve upon you a heavy task, and merits your whole attention. That there should be some additional limitations prescribed few will deny. Many persons in the State, by every act of which they were capable have disfranchised themselves. Probably they neither expected or desired the privilege of again voting, and would not exercise it if granted them. Many others have committed acts deserving disfranchisement, who nevertheless will resist it, and strive for every civil right they enjoyed before the war, and before their treason had involved the State in so much suffering. While I would not recommend you to give way to the impulse of vengeance any more than to the appeals of sympathy and pity, I would urge you to guard the ballot box faithfully and effectually against the approach of treason, no matter in what character it may come. The loyal people of the State, who sent you here, expect you to act decisively in the matter, and have no child's play in determining the qualification of voters. The subject has been considered by several of our sister States, whose reform was not any more loudly called for than with us. It is quite probable that this action and its effects may assist you in deciding what to accept and what to avoid.

As you are aware, upon the approach of the national forces and their occupation of our country, the Government took possession of our railroads, in most of which the State is a large stockholder. The State is deeply interested in her internal improvements, as she has endorsed bonds at the rate of ten thousand dollars per mile, for nearly all the railroads in Tennessee. And as most of these bonds are held by guardians, for the benefit in many instances of minors and widows, I think it nothing more than simple justice to pay them the interest already due them.

The Nashville and Chattanooga Railroad was taken possession of by the Federal authorities on the 7th of March, 1862, and has been held and used ever since, and, regarded as a military necessity, it was proper and right. Presuming the Government to have kept the account strictly, she is now about ready to make a settlement. My information is that certain officers of the company visited Washington on two different occasions for the purpose of obtaining a settlement with the Quartermaster General. They failed in their efforts, though the President of the United States, who was present on both occasions, expressed his views verbally as favoring the payment of the Company for the use of the road. You should now call upon the proper authorities at Washington for payment to this and other companies, requiring the money received to be applied to the payment of interest on their bonds. The amount endorsed by the State for the Nashville and Chattanooga Railroad Company is $1,535,000, and the interest accrued thereon is now nearly $300,000. It is believed that upon a just settlement the Government will owe the Company largely over that amount. This road cost the Company $3,846,900, including its equipment and depots.

The other roads in the State are similarly situated, and demand your attention. Those officers of roads, and stockholders who fled South, carrying with them the rolling stock and funds, should be held to a strict accountability, and their property and stock should be made, in part, to atone for these losses to the State and country. The case of the East Tennessee and Georgia Railroad and its faithless President, requires our special attention.

It is believed the time has now come for the companies again to use their roads—for the Government, if need be, under even a Military Superintendent—thereby effecting a vast saving to the Government, asking only the same pay for freights and passengers they are now paying to the Louisville and Nashville Railroad Company. As this war is for the benefit of the whole nation, it is not believed that the General Government intends that Tennessee shall pay more than her just proportion of the war debt.

Your attention is called to the fact that the Louisville and Nashville Railroad Company is running a portion of that road in this State, say about sixty miles, with another branch from Bowling Green to Clarksville, and for all that portion of road in our State, the Government pays the Kentucky Company, as if the road were in any other loyal State. The information I have is to the effect that the Kentucky Company treats with indifference the claims of Tennessee upon that road. It is your duty to let that Company know, in decided, but respectful terms, what your rights are, and that you dare assert and maintain them.

The duty devolves upon you, at this session, of electing two Senators to the Congress of the United States, and of re-districting the State, so as, without delay, to provide for the election of eight Representatives to the next Congress. It is with profound regret that I have observed several Republican journals, and some leading politicians, of ability and influence, are opposed to the admission of Senators and Representatives from Tennessee. They take the ground that the State should be treated as a territory, and continued under military government, subject to the arbitrary orders of military rule. If their dangerous and revolutionary doctrine is adhered to by any considerable portion of Senators and Representatives in Congress, I shall, for one, dread the consequences. My confidence in the wisdom and patriotism of Senators and Representatives, leads me to believe they will discard, indignantly, any such proposition. The loyal people of Tennessee have resolved through the ballot-box to rule themselves under the Federal flag; taking the ground that the

State has never been out of the Union, and boldly denying that the unconstitutional and treasonable acts of those in rebellion ever carried them out of the Union. Besides, the inauguration of the Vice President from this State, and the withdrawal of a Military Governor, to give place to civil authority, fix the status of Tennessee in the estimation of the Federal authorities proper. And to your good sense and unyielding firmness I submit this grave question, not doubting that your action will be correct.

Your attention is called to the condition of affairs in the State Prison, full and specific details of which are given in the report of the officer who is in charge of that institution. I have every confidence that the Legislature will look into the wants of the institution, and do for it what, in the judgment of members, may seem proper. Meanwhile, I suggest the establishment of branches of the Penitentiary in the Western District, and in East Tennessee. The cost of building on a moderate scale, would be saved to the State, in fifteen or twenty years, in the single item of a cash market in each end of the State, for provisions to sustain, and raw material to keep the convicts employed in manufacturing—such as lumber, marble, iron, coal, leather, &c. The erection of buildings would furnish employment and cash wages to a number of mechanics; and, as there are several salaried officers attached to such an institution, it would distribute the patronage of the State in her three natural divisions. If this be not done, an enlargement of the State Prison will be required. The demoralized condition of both our white and colored population, will cause scores to be sent to the Penitentiary, as our courts go into operation.

The Tennessee Hospital for the Insane, one of the charitable institutions of the State, located in this vicinity, deserves your attention, and your aid. The prosperity and success of that noble State charity were all that its friends and the friends of humanity could desire at the breaking out of this wicked rebellion; but the Institution has struggled hard to keep above the waves of oblivion for four years past. It kept its deposits in the Bank of Tennessee, and my information is, that when the faithless officers of the bank fled, on the approach of the national flag, they carried with them some $30,000 belonging to the Institution. For the details in regard to its past operations and present necessities I refer you to the report of the Superintendent and Chief Surgeon, a faithful and intelligent citizen.

The Tennessee Blind School, a State institution in this city, has been utterly destroyed by the Federal forces, and the unfortunate pupils, some forty in number, are distributed among their friends and the friends of humanity. It was not a military necessity that called for the destruction of the Institution, but it was the work of recklessness, and if this General Assembly will present the subject to the Government at Washington in this light, it is believed that proper steps will be taken to restore this noble charity. The hopes of those pupils at best are blasted, and their cup of bitterness is full, when we have done all that lies in our power. We look out upon the world and we know it by its visible beauty; we know our wives by their affectionate looks, our children by their smiles and features, our neighbors by their faces and manner of address; but these, and all other earthly things, are to these blind people shrouded in darkness, and friends, children, and the world, are lost to them forever.

The Tennessee Deaf and Dumb School, located at Knoxville, merits your attention, as it is one of the charitable institutions of the State. The exciting events which are daily transpiring in the country, should not induce us to lose sight of those whose misfortunes so strongly appeal to us for aid and comfort. The buildings and grounds, erected and purchased at a heavy expense by the State are now used for hospital purposes by our army. Of the fourteen Trustees, nine of them went into the rebellion, and most of them fled South. An equal proportion of the officers and teachers of the school proved to be rebels. An early organization of the Institution upon a loyal basis is called for, and it is hoped will attract your attention.

The East Tennessee University, located at Knoxville, is a time honored Institution, and was chartered and endowed by the State, in 1807. It has been almost destroyed by the Federal Army. The library, furniture and fixtures are hopelessly destroyed. The main buildings are standing, and it is but just to the educational interests of the most loyal portion of the State, that the Government should place that Institution on as good a footing as it found it. A majority of the Board of Trustees turned out to be rebels, and their places should be filled with loyal men.

There are doubtless other Institutions in the State, which deserve the attention of this General Assembly, but I am not informed as to their situations. The members representing all the counties will be able to look after their interests, and should feel that the duty devolves upon them.

Having thus fully placed before you the information requisite to enable you to judge of the condition of the State, the evils which environ us, and the measures of legislation needed for averting them, and ridding ourselves of them, it remains for me but to invoke your attention to the consideration of those means by which, above all others we may hope to restore order and prosperity to our country. And if one be more prominent than another, it is the necessity for earnest and cordial cooperation between the State and Federal Government. To you, especially, as Senators and Representatives, do the loyal people of Tennessee look for encouragement and counsel. And to your action in the halls of legislation will all eyes be turned —not only in Tennessee, but in other States—for examples of what is befitting loyal men. I feel full confidence that you will prove yourselves equal to the emergency, and meet expectations both at home and abroad. I feel assured, that being united in a common and holy cause, you will rise above all selfish considerations, and bowing submissively to the Divine Will, you will unite with all good men in reverently invoking the blessings of our Heavenly Father upon all we say and do, while in the service of the State.

It is, perhaps, proper for me to state, that since writing this Message, important facts have come to my knowledge, and upon unquestionable authority, relating to the use of a portion of the funds of the Bank of Tennessee, that may require me to send you, at no distant day, a special message. The interests of the State, and the just rights of the people, should be sacredly and vigilantly guarded, no matter who suffers ruin and disgrace.

WILLIAM G. BROWNLOW."

In the annals of Tennessee, there is perhaps no Executive Message comparable to the strange mixture of polemics, sermonizing, and outpouring of personal revenge as set forth in the foregoing document. The traditional dignity usually exemplified in such formal communications was conspicuously absent. Outbursts of anger and expressions of burning hatred toward those who had participated in the military conflict on the part of the South saturated the harangue from beginning to end. The vials of wrath were broken and poured upon the heads of Secessionists. The "Parson's" proclivity to appeal to the Scriptures is reminiscent of Shakespeare's well-known dictum, "The Devil can cite

Scripture for his purpose." His declaration that "Secession is an abomination" which he could not condemn too strongly was followed by a statement that disclosed the attitude and desire of the Executive regarding legislation. To the Legislature, the Governor revealed what he expected of that body—restrictive, proscriptive, and severe measures directed against those who had supported Secession. That a Radical Legislature followed the suggestions of Governor Brownlow will become evident as his administration is reviewed. Toward the end of his philippic, the Governor attempted to galvanize his tirade into some degree of respectability by citing the status and needs regarding State finance, banking, railroads, the Hospital for the Insane, and the School for the Blind. But these after-thoughts were preceded by what lay nearest and dearest to the Executive's heart—drastic restrictions on the elective franchise. In this matter, the Legislature proved to be but potter's clay in the hands of the "Parson."

Towering above all other considerations by Brownlow and the Radical Legislature and of greatest concern to this minority, which had been thrust into power by the use of the iron-clad oath and the "slate ticket" already mentioned, was the elective franchise. Brownlow tipped his hand on this topic by urging the Legislature "to guard the ballot box faithfully" and not to indulge in "child's play in determining the qualification of voters."

Fifteen bills on franchise restrictions were introduced in the Legislature. At the time, the status of the franchise was governed by a provision of the 1835 State Constitution providing that all white men meeting the prerequisites as to age and residence were entitled to vote. As amended by the Union Convention of January 1865 and ratification by the voters in February of the same year, the provision was that "the qualification of voters and the limitations of the elective franchise" were matters to be determined by the first General Assembly meeting under the amended Constitution. The situation, then, was as follows: the constitutional provision of 1835 regarding suffrage could continue or it could be changed by the Legislature now (1865) in session.

In considering the fifteen bills on the franchise question, the Legislature was divided as to whether or not the recently-freed Negro should be allowed to vote. A minority of the legislative members desired to place the ballot in the hands of former slaves. Senator B. R. Peart from the counties of Robertson, Montgomery, and Stewart introduced a bill

"To aid in the burial of the Southern Confederacy."[17]

This bill proposed that Negro soldiers and all other Negroes who should be free for five years, of good character, and able to read and write should be permitted to vote. After considerable discussion, it was

---

[17] *Senate Journal*, First Session, 1865, 136.

finally decided to postpone action and attempt to settle first the question of white suffrage.

The Legislature then buckled down to the question of white suffrage. Samuel R. Rodgers, an extreme Radical and in the powerful position of Speaker of the Senate, hurled anathemas at all supporters of the Confederacy. The rebels, said he, should be put on probation until they showed a change of heart. They even had no right to expect to vote, and ought to be satisfied if the Unionists allowed them to live in Tennessee. They really ought to be hanged, continued he, but the job was too big to be undertaken.

The temper of some members of the Legislature may be guaged by examining some of the bills introduced. Take, for example, a bill introduced by James Mullins, a Representative from Rutherford and Bedford counties, who later served as Speaker of the House of Representatives and spent one term in Congress. In the person of Mullins, the Radicals had a witch-hunter *par excellence*. On April 28, 1865, in keeping with his political heresy-mania, he introduced a bill, No. 56, entitled

"To prohibit persons from wearing a rebel uniform."[18]

Upon recommendation by the Committee on Military Affairs, a substitute bill was passed by the overwhelming vote of 58 to 5.[19] The oppressive measure passed routinely first and second readings in the Senate,[20] but for some undisclosed reason never reached a third reading. Fortunately, the Senate ditched the venom-filled proposal that would have forced many Confederates into nudeness, for their battered and tattered uniforms constituted their sole wearing apparel for the time being.

Arm in arm with Mullins was another vindictive legislator by the name of Pleasant Williams from Carter County, whose given name was a misnomer. On April 7, he introduced the following bill:[21]

"An Act refusing Protection to Secession Ministers.

Section Ist Be it enacted by the General Assembly of the State of Tennessee That no Minister or Ministers of any Denomination that Volenteerly Aided or Abeted in bringing about this Rebelion against the United States Shall have the protection here tofore given Ministers of the Gospel

Sec IInd That all Ministers that aided or abeted in bringing about this Rebelion either by word or by Deed Shall here after be Subject to Pay Poll Tax work on Public Roads and be Subject to the Military Law in this State.

---

[18] *House Journal*, First Session, 1865, 94.
[19] *Ibid.*, 179.
[20] *Senate Journal*, First Session, 1865, 178.
[21] Ms. bill in State Archives, Nashville.

Sec IIIrd   That no Minister that aided or Abeted in bringing about this
             Rebelion Shall here after have the rite to Solemnize the Rites of
             Matrimony in this State
Sec IVth   That this Act Shall take effect from and after its Passage."

Two weeks later, Representative Pleasant Williams became the
recipient of some unpleasant news, for his own fellow Representatives
rejected his bill, the same never being transmitted to the Senate.[22]

On April 29, Representative D. G. Thornburgh representing a tier
of upper East Tennessee counties incorporated his ideas of retribution
in the following bill:[23]

"An Act to disfranchise Certain persons

Be it enacted by the General Assembly of the State of Tennessee, that
all persons, who have been guilty of Treason against the United States, or
the State of Tennessee, or persons who have given aid and comfort, to those
in Rebellion against the United States, or who have freely & voluntarily
taken up arms or induced others to take up arms against the United States,
or who have freely and voluntarily entered into any conspiracy with those
in rebellion, against the United States, for the purpose of establishing a
Southern Confederacy, or Who Shall have recruited, or persuaded, others
to enter the Army, of the So Called Confederate States, Shall be and they
are hereby precuded [precluded] from and forbidden the privilege of Casting their votes, in the elections for State or County officers, and the election
for Members to the Congress of the United States, for the next Five years
and until this law Shall be repealed.

Sec. 2nd. Be it further enacted, that the persons named in the first Section of this Act, are disallowed the privilege, of holding any office of Trust
or Honor, in the State of Tennessee, Provided that all such persons, who
have taken the amnesty oath under the proclamation of the President of the
United States, dated 8th Decr 1863, in good faith and who can Show affirma-
tively by Loyal Witnesses that they have lived up to the Spirit and intent
of said oath, doing every thing in their power to sustain the United States
Government, against her enemies by their Conduct and Conversation, in all
such cases such person or persons Shall and may be allowed the privilege of
Casting their votes but not hold office in this State.

Sec (3d) Be it further enacted that this Act take effect from and after
its passage."

The bill was referred to the Judiciary Committee from which it
never emerged; perhaps more influential and ambitious members in the
House of Representatives did not propose to be denied the authorship
of a franchise bill even more drastic and restrictive in its provisions.

After a month's haggling over various and sundry franchise bills,
none of which seemed to be quite satisfactory to a majority of the legislators, Senator D. W. C. Senter (later Governor) offered a resolution
to this effect:[24]

---

[22] *House Journal*, First Session, 1865, 65.
[23] Ms. bill in State Archives, Nashville.
[24] *Senate Journal*, First Session, 1865, 102.

"Whereas, This General Assembly was convened under extraordinary circumstances, and that the passage of certain bills of a general nature demand immediate action; therefore be it

Resolved by the General Assembly of the State of Tennessee, That we will take up and perfect the following named bills, in the same order as they are named in this resolution, to-wit:

A bill to authorize the Governor to call out the militia of the State.
A bill to raise revenue.
A bill to re-district the State, and
A bill to fix the qualification of voters."

Although the Senter resolution was never formally adopted, yet its provisions were all enacted into laws with the exception of the one authorizing the Governor to call out the State militia. Instead, a call was made upon the President of the United States to provide troops for the protection of the "loyal citizens."[25]

The most important and far-reaching law enacted by this Legislature was that of limiting the elective franchise. The franchise bill was the master key that "fit" the whole program of political domination envisioned by Brownlow and other Radicals.

A veritable hodgepodge of franchise bills was dumped into the legislative hoppers, amounting in all to fifteen proposed measures. The captions frequently bore evidence of the vindictive attitude of the authors. For example, Representative Thomas Kercheval of Lincoln County proposed a bill

"To prohibit rebels from holding office in the State of Tennessee."[26]

Representative W. H. Grimmett of Wilson County wanted

"To disfranchise rebel soldiers and citizens."[27]

Representative Wilson Duggan of Sevier County yearned

"To disqualify rebels and traitors from holding office, civil or military."[28]

Senator James H. Randolph, representing four East Tennessee counties, offered a bill carrying the innocent and euphonious title

"To preserve the purity of the ballot box."[29]

In a benevolent spirit, Senator Joshua B. Frierson, representing the four Middle Tennessee counties of Maury, Lewis, Hickman, and Dickson, wanted a law which would

"Determine the qualification of voters."[30]

[25] *Acts of Tennessee*, 1865, Resolution XXXIX, 151-152.
[26] *House Journal*, First Session, 1865, 70.
[27] *Ibid.*, 189.
[28] *Ibid.*, 192.
[29] *Senate Journal*, First Session, 1865, 60.
[30] *Ibid.*, 121.

Senator B. R. Peart from the counties of Robertson, Montgomery, and Stewart authored the following resolution: [31]

"Be it Resolved by the General Assembly of the State of Tennessee, That all persons who voted willingly on the 8th day June, 1861, for Separation and Representation are now, and will ever be looked upon as infamous by all loyal men in this State; that it fixes a stain upon them which is indelible and must remain upon them forever."

Senator Z. W. Frazer from the counties of Wilson and DeKalb wanted the Peart resolution to be a bit more specific. Accordingly, he suggested the following amendment: [32]

"Who are now, or may hereafter utter words of justification of or sympathy with Jefferson Davis or Robert E. Lee, who held the youths of our State in the rebel army eighteen months after they had lost all hopes of success, and thereby murdered thousands of the citizens of the United States."

The multiplicity of the franchise bills was convincing evidence of the diversity of opinion as to what would constitute a "clincher." Inasmuch as none of the bills seemed to be satisfactory, it was decided to have the Judiciary Committee review the various franchise bills and draft one which would embody the salient points desired by the Radical majority. The Judiciary Committee, which had been appointed during the first week of the session, was composed of the following members: [33] Edmund Cooper of Bedford; Wilson Duggan of Sevier; Jesse H. Gaut of Bradley; Abner A. Steele of Marshall; Samuel M. Arnell representing the counties of Williamson, Maury, and Lewis; Thomas A. Kerchival of Lincoln; W. J. Smith of Hardeman; S. L. Warren of McNairy; and A. E. Garrett of Overton.

All along the Senate was dominated by such extreme Radicals that practically any sort of severe franchise bill would pass that body. The House, while maintaining a Radical majority, was far more lenient in its demands respecting a franchise measure. As a result of these differences of opinion, the Judiciary Committee was unable to agree upon a franchise bill. On May 22, Edmund Cooper, Chairman of the Judiciary Committee, reported that a minority of the Committee favored a bill at variance with the views of the majority. According to Chairman Cooper, the majority opinion was that

"The great difficulty with the committee has been when, where, and how will we fix the line of disfranchisement? Upon this point many views were expressed, and much diversity of opinion existed. The majority of your committee, however, believe that pure political wisdom and sound policy suggested when, where, and how the line should be drawn, and that

---

[31] *Ibid.,* 216.
[32] *Ibid.,* 216.
[33] *House Journal,* First Session, 1865, 36.

the amnesty proclamations of Abraham Lincoln, as President of the United States, and proclamations of Andrew Johnson, as Military Governor of the State of Tennessee, and the actions of the Union Convention in the Fall of 1864 and the month of January, 1865, furnished the broad foundation upon which all could stand. . . . It only excludes from the elective franchise such persons as were exempted from the amnesty proclamation of the President, on the 8th day of December, 1863, and such conscious and intelligent traitors in the State of Tennessee as ought not, because of their conduct at present, be admitted to all the privileges of the elective franchise. . . ."[34]

On the following day, May 23, Samuel Arnell, a rabid Radical, submitted a minority report [35] in which it was proposed

". . . to admit to the privileges of the elective franchise all known and true friends of the Government, and in no case to exclude any such person; but they do most unhesitatingly and boldly propose to exclude any rebel opposed to its authority, and who have failed to give evidence of friendship thereto by some specific act, both in spirit and letter, most in harmony with the amnesty proclamation, and the proclamations of Governor Johnson, and is absolutely necessary both to the safety of the State and of the Republic."

This minority report was signed by only three members of the nine-member committee, namely, Arnell, Duggan, and Smith of Hardeman. This meant that two-thirds of the Judiciary Committee favored a franchise bill more lenient than that proposed by the minority.

Inasmuch as there was considerable Conservative Unionist sentiment in the House of Representatives, the Radical Unionists in both branches of the Legislature realized that any extreme franchise bill would encounter stiff opposition in the Lower House. Brownlow scented trouble and, in his perplexity, beseeched President Andrew Johnson to "put forth something" to influence a stubborn minority in the House.[36] After the bitter battle over the franchise bill had ended, Brownlow's post-diagnosis was that there had been a "troublesome minority in the House, some of whom have acted worse than Rebels would have done." He branded William Heiskell, Speaker of the House, as having shifted "clear over on the Copperhead side."[37]

The substance of the Minority Report of the Judiciary Committee was whipped into a bill sponsored by the Radical element under the leadership of Arnell, the rampant Radical. From May 23 to June 2, the Arnell bill was up for consideration by the House. Efforts by Representative J. S. Mulloy of Robertson County to postpone further action until the October session failed by a vote of 37 to 25.[38] Representative

[34] Ibid., 191–192.
[35] Ibid., 196.
[36] Letter of May 19, 1865: W. G. Brownlow to Andrew Johnson. In Johnson Papers, Division of Manuscripts, Library of Congress.
[37] Letter of June 8, 1865: Brownlow to Johnson. In Johnson Papers, Division of Manuscripts, Library of Congress.
[38] House Journal, First Session, 1865, 218.

Abner A. Steele of Marshall County wanted to exempt each person disfranchised by the pending bill from the payment of taxes, working on the public road, and doing military service. His proposal was defeated by a vote of 42 to 22.[39] At a later date, Representative Steele proposed that the franchise bill be submitted to the people for reaction, but an adverse vote of 40 to 22 doomed his effort.[40] All attempts to amend or postpone action having failed, the bill was called up on third and final reading, and was passed by a vote of 42 to 21.[41] In order that posterity may learn how the several Representatives voted on this highly discriminatory bill, their names and counties represented were as follows:[42]

AYE

Name of Representative	County or Counties Represented
Arnell, Samuel M.	Williamson, Maury, and Lewis
Coward, Richard	Anderson
Donaldson, J. H.	Blount
Doughty, J. A.	Anderson and Campbell
Duggan, Wilson	Sevier
Elliott, W. Y.	Rutherford
Fuson, John A.	DeKalb
Garner, W. A.	Lawrence
Griffith, Samuel E.	Washington
Grimmett, W. H.	Wilson
Grove, G. H.	Grainger
Heermans, Theodore	Smith, Sumner, and Macon
Hudson, Joseph	Davidson, Robertson, Montgomery, and Cheatham
Inman, Charles	Knox and Sevier
Jones, Furney	Claiborne
Jones, James	Greene
Kerchival, Thomas A.	Lincoln
Maxwell, Thomas	Hardin
McNair, J. E.	Gibson
Melton, James M.	Fentress, Morgan, Scott, and Cumberland
Minnis, J. B.	Jefferson
Moss, A. W.	Williamson
Mullins, James	Rutherford and Bedford
Norman, John	Carroll

[39] Ibid., 220.
[40] Ibid., 228.
[41] Ibid., 228–229.
[42] Ibid., 228–229.

Name of Representative	County or Counties Represented
Porter, John	Wayne
Puckett, J. N.	Hickman
Raulston, R. S.	Marion
Rogers, Reuben	Campbell
Ryder, M. T.	Shelby
Shultz, J. R.	Cocke
Smith, W. J.	Hardeman
Smith, F. A.	Obion
Snodderley, A. A.	Union
Thornburgh, D. G.	Greene, Hawkins, Hancock, and Jefferson
Wagner, Joseph H.	Johnson
Walker, J. P.	Rhea, Hamilton, and Sequatchie
Warren, S. L.	McNairy
Waters, Wallace	Madison
Waters W. L.	Wilson
Williams, Pleasant	Carter
Wines, William	Montgomery
Woodcock, W. M.	Macon

NO

Anderson, G. W.	White
Barton, William	Cannon
Brittle, Gilbert	Smith
Cooper, Edmund	Bedford
Copeland, W. J.	Polk, McMinn, and Meigs
Faulkner, Asa	Warren
Gaines, G. W.	Monroe
Garrett, A. E.	Overton
Gaut, Jesse H.	Bradley
Heiskell, William	Knox
Henderson, J. M.	McMinn
Hood, James R.	Hamilton
Jarvis, L. M.	Hancock
Mason, Thomas G.	Roane
Nicks, A. D.	Dickson
Simmons, William	Franklin
Stegald, Jerry	Perry and Decatur
Steele, Abner A.	Marshall
Thomas, Dorsey B.	Benton and Humphreys
Willis, W. W.	Hawkins
Wright, William	Sumner

NOT VOTING

Name of Representative	County or Counties Represented
Carter, S. J.	Davidson
Dillin, Joseph R.	Giles
Dowdy, Rufus	Fentress, Morgan, Scott, and Cumberland
Gillem, A. C.	Jackson
Gilmer, Jeremiah	Maury
Hill, Anderson	Knox
Lewis, W. B.	Davidson
Mullenix, William	Sullivan
Mulloy, J. S.	Robertson
Richards, P. S.	Tipton, Shelby, and Fayette
Scales, William	Dyer and Lauderdale
Simmerley, Elijah	Carter and Johnson
Thomas, J. F.	Grundy, Coffee, and Van Buren
Underwood, C.	Weakley
Woods, James, Jr.	Stewart

If space did not prohibit, it would be interesting to incorporate some of the speeches made in behalf of and in opposition to the pending bills. There were, at the time, two major bills on the franchise topic, one by the Conservative Unionist, Edmund Cooper, and the other by the militant Radical, Samuel Arnell. In a brilliant argument, Cooper pointed out that the Arnell bill would exclude from the privilege of the franchise "all except those publicly known to have entertained uncondi-tional sentiments from the outbreak of the rebellion to the present time." Attacking the minority position which maintained that the "schedule" approved by the Union Convention in January, 1865, was a part of the amended Constitution, Cooper contended that the schedule was merely a suggestion or directive designed for either a judicial or legislative body to determine. The legalistic argument of Cooper, able and judicious, was swamped by the razzle-dazzle and "waving the bloody shirt" type of denunciation by the eloquent Arnell. In a frenzied, not to say frenetic vein, Arnell painted a dismal picture of desolation and despair, all brought on by the Secessionists. Said he, in part:[43]

"The barn is empty; the flocks and herds have been hunted down and killed; the fields are unfenced and unfurrowed; the old homestead stands out on the common and dismally rattles its broken blinds; the 'old folks' talk to you in a low hushed tone about their boys in the grave; and it needs no spoken voice to tell you that their wealth has taken to itself wings and disappeared. In the refugee's hut the widow crouches on her low stool and hushes her child to sleep, but with no promise of the father's coming—he

---

[43] *Nashville Daily Union*, June 4, 1865.

died in Georgia or Virginia. Blank despair, gaunt famine are staring her in the face. In vain she tries to hide their spectres with the manly form that stood by her side at the marriage morning, but the recollection of now and then, the sense of loss overcomes her, she breaks down, her eyes swim, and she prays in her agony to the only friend left—the widow's God. Droves of homeless children flock over our streets daily asking you openly for charity —asking you silently, by the dear love of brotherhood and the love of God, for home and education. Our public calamities are even greater than our private misfortunes. . . ."

In a peroration, charged and surcharged with venom and vindictiveness, he shrieked to his fellow-members:

"I represent on the floor no rebel. God helping me, never shall I stoop so low. I represent Union men alone—men who have walked forty miles on foot from guerilla infested country. I want protection for them. . . ."[44]

The House-approved bill encountered no difficulty whatsoever in the Radical-controlled Senate, no effort being made to amend or postpone action on the bill. Twenty Senators voted in the affirmative, with only Senator Z. W. Frazer from Wilson and DeKalb counties voting in the negative. The names of the other Senators and counties represented were as follows:[45]

Name of Senator	*County or Counties Represented*
Bosson, William	White, Jackson, and Macon
Bowen, J .W.	Smith and Sumner
Butler, R. R.	Johnson, Carter, Washington, and Sullivan
Case, A.	Henry, Weakley, and Obion
Cate, A. M.	Rhea, Bledsoe, Bradley, Hamilton, and Sequatchie
Cypert, T. J.	Giles, Lawrence, and Wayne
Frierson, Joshua B.	Maury, Lewis, Hickman, and Dickson
Hall, W. K.	Gibson, Carroll, and Dyer
Hurst, Fielding	Hardin, McNairy, and Hardeman
Keith, G. W.	Morgan, Scott, Fentress, and Overton
Lasater, R. E.	Warren, Cannon, Coffee, Grundy, and Van Buren
McElwee, Thomas B.	Meigs, McMinn, Polk, and Monroe
McKinney, Charles J.	Hawkins, Hancock, and Jefferson

[44] *Ibid.*
[45] *Senate Journal,* First Session, 1865, 195–196.

Name of Senator	County or Counties Represented
Muse, Thomas A.	Benton, Humphreys, Perry, Decatur, and Henderson
Peart, B. R.	Robertson, Montgomery, and Stewart
Randolph, James H.	Greene, Cocke, Sevier, and Blount
Rodgers, Samuel R.	Knox and Roane
Senter, D. W. C.	Claiborne, Grainger, Anderson, and Campbell
Smith, J. W.	Fayette and Shelby
Trimble, John	Davidson

NOT VOTING

Spence, William	Rutherford and Williamson
Stewart, William	Franklin and Lincoln
Wisener, William H.	Bedford and Marshall

Now that the Arnell bill had been enacted into law, what were the provisions of that law? Sections one, two, and three contained the real franchise features of the law. Section one outlined the conditions and qualifications whereby the privilege of voting was allowed. That section was as follows: [46]

"Section 1. *Be it enacted by the General Assembly of the State of Tennessee,* That the following persons, to-wit:
1. Every white man twenty-one years of age, a citizen of the United States, and a citizen of the County wherein he may offer his vote six months next preceding the day of election, and publicly known to have entertained unconditional Union sentiments from the outbreak of the rebellion until the present time. And
2. Every white man, a citizen of the United States, and a citizen of the County wherein he may offer his vote six months next preceding the day of election, having arrived at the age of twenty-one years since March 4th, 1865: *Provided,* that he has not been engaged in armed rebellion against the authority of the United States voluntarily. And
3. Every white man of lawful age, coming from another State, and being a citizen of the United States, on proof of loyalty to the United States, and being a citizen of the County wherein he may offer his vote six months next preceding the day of election; and
4. Every white man, a citizen of the United States, and a citizen of this State, who has served as a soldier in the army of the United States, and has been or may be hereafter honorably discharged therefrom. And
5. Every white man of lawful age, a citizen of the United States, and a citizen of the County wherein he may offer his vote six months next preceding the day of election, who was conscripted by force into the so-called Confederate army, and was known to be a Union man, on proof of loyalty

---

[46] *Acts of Tennessee,* First Session, 1865, Chapter 16, Section 1.

to the United States, established by the testimony of two voters under the previous clauses of this section. And

6. Every white man who voted in this State at the Presidential election in November, 1864, or voted on the 22d of February, 1865, or voted on the 4th of March, 1865, in this State, and all others who had taken the 'oath of allegiance' to the United States, and may be known by the Judges of election to have been true friends to the Government of the United States, and would have voted in said previously mentioned elections if the same had been holden within their reach, shall be entitled to the privilege of the elective franchise."

It will be observed that the first section of the law disfranchised all Tennesseans who had not been "publicly known to have entertained unconditional Union sentiments from the outbreak of the rebellion until the present time." This retroactive provision, reaching back to the beginning of the war, amounted in effect to the passage of an *ex post facto* law which is forbidden by both the Constitution of the United States and the Constitution of Tennessee.[47] The heresy-hunting Radicals, in their zeal to punish former Confederates, did not hesitate to violate one of the most fundamental and constitutional rights guaranteed to American citizens.

Sections two and three of the law were the "excluding" clauses:[48]

"Sec. 2. *Be it further enacted*, That all persons who are or shall have been civil or diplomatic officers or agents of the so-called Confederate States of America, or who have left judicial stations under the United States or the State of Tennessee, to aid in any way, the existing or recent rebellion against the authority of the United States, or who are or shall have been military or naval officers of the so-called Confederate States, above the rank of Captain in the army, or Lieutenant in the navy; or who have left seats in the United States Congress, or seats in the Legislature of the State of Tennessee to aid said rebellion, or have resigned commissions in the army or navy of the United States, and afterwards have voluntarily given aid to said rebellion; or persons who have engaged in treating otherwise than lawfully as prisoners of war, persons found in the United States service as officers, soldiers, seamen, or in any other capacities; or persons who have been or are absentees from the United States for the purpose of aiding the rebellion; or persons who held pretended offices under the Government of States in insurrection against the United States, or persons who left their homes within the jurisdiction and protection of the United States, or fled before the approach of the national forces and passed beyond the Federal military lines into the so-called Confederate States, for the purpose of aiding the rebellion, shall be denied and refused the privilege of the elective franchise in this State for the term of fifteen years from and after the passage of this Act.

Sec. 3. *Be it further enacted*, That all other persons, except those mentioned in section 1 of this Act, are hereby and henceforth excluded and denied the exercise of the privilege of the elective franchise in this State for the term of five years from and after the passage of this Act."

[47] Constitution of the United States, Article I, Section 9.
Constitution of Tennessee, Article I, Section 11.
[48] *Acts of Tennessee*, First Session, 1865, Chapter 16, Section 2.

It will be noted that those who had achieved leadership in civil, diplomatic, or military positions were regarded as the more heinous criminals, and were to be disfranchised for a period of fifteen years. All others—and this included the great mass of ex-Confederates—were denied the privilege of suffrage for five years. In pressing relentlessly for the passage of this law, Brownlow went far beyond President Johnson's program as set forth in his Amnesty Proclamation of May 29, 1865. Johnson's reconstruction program permitted all Confederates to vote with the exception of a small class—the leaders. Brownlow, in his so-called reconstruction program for Tennessee, disfranchised virtually all Confederates, both high and low.

Sections six and seven dealt with the mechanics of registration. A meticulous screening process was provided whereby every voter, except those of "known Union sentiments," was to be subjected to a searching inquiry reminiscent of the Spanish Inquisition. It is a safe assumption that few ex-Confederates could qualify under the provisions of this law and the prescribed oath without committing perjury. In the event that the present law should be found to contain a loophole through which former Confederates might escape any of the thumb-screw prerequisites, a safeguard was fabricated whereby the Legislature reserved the power to alter, amend, or change the provisions of the Act. This franchise Act may justly be characterized as devilish in design, iniquitous in intent, and effective in disfranchising the vast majority of Tennessee citizens. With such a law on the statute books, the Tennessee majority was, like the ancient victims of Roman conquest, forced to pass *sub jugum* (under the yoke).

The passage of this severe franchise law was not the result of any conflicts and opposition that had developed during the legislative session. Deep-seated hatred and a fanatical determination "to punish the rebels" was evident in the early part of the session. Approximately three weeks after the convening of the Legislature, Senator Roderick R. Butler offered a Senate Joint Resolution [49]

"Declaratory of the treason of Isham G. Harris, ex-Governor of the State of Tennessee."

A motion to refer the resolution to a Select Committee was rejected, whereupon the resolution was adopted by the Senate without a record vote. When the resolution came up for consideration in the House of Representatives, Abner A. Steele of Marshall County proposed to strike out "five thousand dollars" and insert "*one cent.*"[50] Representative Wallace Waters of Madison County countered with a motion to strike out "five thousand dollars" and insert "ten thousand." Both motions were

[49] *Senate Journal*, First Session, 1865, 75.
[50] *House Journal*, First Session, 1865, 103.

withdrawn, and the original resolution was concurred in by a vote of 53 to 7.[51]

The Resolution [52] was couched in the following language:

"NUMBER XXXIV.

Joint Resolution offering a Reward of Five Thousand Dollars for the apprehension of Isham G. Harris.

WHEREAS, Treason is the highest crime known to the laws of the land, and no one is presumed to understand the true meaning of the term better than Governors of States, and certainly no one should be held to a more strict account for their treason. And

WHEREAS, The State of Tennessee, before the rebellion enjoyed a high social, moral, and political position, and had the well-earned reputation of the Volunteer State. And

WHEREAS, By the treason of one Isham G. Harris, Ex-Governor of Tennessee, the State has lost millions of dollars; and thousands of the young men of the State have been killed in battle and died of disease, and thousands of the middle-aged and old men have been murdered and imprisoned, and defenceless women and children driven from the State, heart-broken and pennyless. And

WHEREAS, The voters of Tennessee did, in the month of February, 1861, by a majority of sixty thousand, repudiate treason and rebellion, but the aforesaid Isham G. Harris, well knowing the true sentiments of the State upon treason and rebellion, and wholly disregarding the overwhelming expression of popular sentiment, did use his position as Governor as aforesaid, to put the State in rebellion and hostility to the Government of the United States, and is guilty of treason, perjury, and theft, and is responsible to a great extent for the war, misery, and death of thousands of the citizens of the State and for the desolation of the same from East to West and from North to South. The cries of the wounded and dying, the wail of the widow, the weeping of the orphan, come to us upon every breeze, imploring us to punish the instigators of the rebellion. Therefore, for the reasons aforesaid, be it

Resolved by the General Assembly of the State of Tennessee, That the Governor of the State is hereby authorized and instructed to offer a reward of five thousand dollars for the apprehension and delivery to the civil authorities of the State, the aforesaid Isham G. Harris; and he shall fully describe said fugitive from justice, and shall make publication for three months, or longer, if he may think proper, in one newspaper in each of the grand divisions of the State, and a paper published in Richmond, Virginia; Raleigh, North Carolina; Savannah, Georgia; Little Rock, Arkansas; New Orleans, Louisiana; and shall publish the preamble with his proclamation.

WILLIAM HEISKELL,   SAMUEL R. RODGERS,
Speaker of the House of Representatives.   Speaker of the Senate."

In compliance with a requirement of the resolution, "Parson" Brownlow dipped his trenchant pen in gall and wormwood and proceeded to indict a gubernatorial predecessor in language that was as ribald as it was unjust. One needs not strain his imagination to envision in his mind's eye the palsied hand and the Mephistophelian mien of the

---

[51] Ibid.
[52] Acts of Tennessee, First Session, 1865, Resolution XXXIV, 147–148.

"Parson" whose eyes danced in a sort of fiendish glee as he scathingly denounced the alleged "refugee from justice." The diatribe was as follows:[53]

"The aforesaid refugee from Justice, without the authority of law, and in violation of all law human and Divine, was the Chief instrument in thrusting upon Tennessee this terrible Rebellion, and its innumerable evils; a Rebellion which has stormed every citadel of order, every defense of virtue, every sanctuary of right, and every abode of decency, When those villainous but frantic efforts were astonishing mankind with their success, as much as appalling them with their atrocity; when the fairest portion of this great Commonwealth had been made hideous by the triumphs of this Arch-traitor and his corrupt and treasonable associates, and their prelusive orgies had profaned our Churches, like dastards they ingloriously fled, upon the approach of the National flag of beauty and Glory, carrying with them to the heart of treason the funds and other valuables of the State.

From that period until now, the said Isham G. Harris has been roving through the South, swept along by the unparelleled hurricane of licentiousness and furious tempest of anarchy, never before equaled upon earth, Said Harris has been periodically visiting the border counties of this State, issuing bogus proclamations, and collecting revenue, falsely pretending to be the Governor of Tennessee.

This culprit Harris, is about five feet ten inches high, weighs about One hundred and forty-five pounds and is about fifty-five Years of Age. His complexion is sallow—his eyes are dark and penetrating—a perfect index to the heart of a traitor—with the scowl and frown of a demon resting upon his brow. The study of mischief, and the practice of crime, have brought upon him premature baldness and a grey beard. With brazen-faced impudence, he talks loudly and boastingly about the over throw of the Yankee Army, and entertains no doubt but the South will achieve her independence.

He chews tobacco rapidly, and is inordinately fond of liquor. In his moral structure he is an unscrupulous man—steeped to the chin in personal and political profligacy—now about lost to all sense of honor and shame—with a heart reckless of social duty, and fatally bent upon mischief.

If captured, he will be found lurking in the Rebel Strongholds of Mississippi, Alabama, or Georgia, and in female society, alleging with the sheep-faced modesty of a virtuous man, that it is not a wholesome state of public sentiment, or of taste, that forbids an indiscriminate mixing together of married men and woman. If captured, the fugitive must be delivered to me alive, to the end that Justice may be done him here, Upon the theatre of his former villainous deeds; The city papers of Nashville and Memphis, as well as the Chattanooga Gazette and Knoxville Whig will each insert three times in addition to the other papers suggested by the Legislature.

In testimony whereof, I have hereunto set my hand and affixed the

(SEAL)

seal of the State, At the City of Nashville, this 3rd of May, 1865.

WILLIAM G. BROWNLOW."

By the Governor:

ANDREW J. FLETCHER,
    Secretary of State.

_____

[53] In Ms. [Brownlow] *Proclamation Book*, 1865, 2–4.

He chews tobacco rapidly, and is inordinately fond of liquor. In his moral structure, he is an unscrupulous man — steeped to the nose and chin in personal and political profligacy — near about lost to all sense of honor and shame — and blind to all the beauties of patriotism — with a heart reckless of social duty, and fatally bent upon mischief. If captured, he will be found lurking in the rebel strong holds of Mississippi, Alabama, or Georgia, and in female society, alleging with the sheep-faced modesty of a virtuous man, that it is not a wholesome state of public sentiment, or of taste, that forbids an indiscriminate mixing together of married men and women! If captured, the fugitive must be delivered to me alive, to the end that justice may be done him here, upon the theatre of his former villainous deeds.

The city papers of Nashville, and Memphis, as well as the Chattanooga Gazette and Knoxville Whig, will each insert three times in addition to the other papers suggested by the Legislature. In testimony whereof, I have hereunto set my hand and affixed the seal of the State, at the city of Nashville, this 3d of May, 1865.

By the Governor.   William G. Brownlow.

Andrew J. Fletcher, Secretary of State.

Concluding page of Brownlow's description of Governor Harris.
Original in Tennessee Historical Society, Nashville.

With the enactment of the franchise law which handcuffed the ex-Confederates, only two other important matters came before the Legislature, the election of United States Senators, and a Congressional redistricting of the State. In compliance with a Joint Resolution, the Legislature proceeded on May 4 to the election of two Senators to succeed Andrew Johnson and A. O. P. Nicholson whose terms had expired. Four nominations to succeed Johnson were placed before the Convention, Horace Maynard of Knox, A. A. Kyle of Hawkins, Nathaniel G. Taylor of Carter, and David T. Patterson of Greene, all being East Tennesseans. On the fifth ballot, the vote was: For Patterson, 52; for Maynard, 38; for Taylor, 1.[54] Thereupon, the Speaker of the Senate declared Patterson elected to succeed his father-in-law, President Andrew Johnson. Next, there followed nominations for the successor of A. O. P. Nicholson. Eight nominations were placed before the Convention: Joseph S. Fowler of Davidson, John Trimble of Davidson, Return J. Meigs of Davidson, Francis B. Fogg of Davidson, William H. Wisener of Bedford, J. R. Hawkins of Carroll, J. R. Rodgers of Van Buren, and William B. Stokes of DeKalb. On the fourth ballot, Joseph S. Fowler was declared to have received a majority of the votes cast. After some of the candidates had been withdrawn, the final ballot [55] was: For Fowler, 49; for Wisener, 28; for Meigs, 12; for Rodgers, 2.

One more necessary step had to be taken in order that Tennessee might be properly represented in Congress when the State was restored to its former status. A redistricting law [56] was passed setting up eight Congressional Districts, thus providing for proper representation in the Lower House of Congress.

The Radical Legislature, whose chief concern centered on political matters, adjourned on June 12, 1865, and in view of a Joint Resolution was due to reconvene on the first Monday in October. Its chief objective had been attained—fastening minority rule upon the majority. The franchise law did just that.

The condition of various State activities was presented during the legislative session. For the most part, the reports are fragmentary and, therefore, inadequate. Some light is thrown upon the condition of the State Treasury, Judiciary, State Library, State Capitol, School Fund, Banks, Railroads, Penitentiary, Hospital for the Insane, and the School for the Blind.[57]

---

[54] *Senate Journal*, First Session, 1865, 93.
  House Journal, First Session, 1865, 116.
[55] *Senate Journal*, First Session, 1865, 96.
  House Journal, First Session, 1865, 121.
  Author's note. These two Senators proved to be of untold value to President Andrew Johnson in his Impeachment Trial in 1868. Each Senator voted for Johnson's acquittal.
[56] *Acts of Tennessee*, First Session, 1865, Chapter 34.
[57] Author's note. Inasmuch as incomplete reports render accurate and dependable

A tyrant never feels safe; his only certainty is uncertainty. In less than a month after the adjournment of the Radical Legislature, Brownlow was made aware of mutterings of deep discontent. The franchise law was being subjected to direct attack, not only by practically all ex-Confederates but also by numerous Conservative Unionists among whom were prominent and influential leaders in the State. For example, ex-Governor William B. Campbell, who had opposed secession and who had reached high military rank in the Union Army, denounced the "new amendments" to the Constitution as illegal and invalid. He likewise opposed the franchise law. Parson Brownlow's "prophetic soul" began to foresee trouble. In pressing for the franchise law, he should have known that *might* rarely triumphs over *right* in the long run. And now, that bold and outspoken opposition was developing throughout two-thirds of the State, the "Parson's" mind may have reflected upon the alarm expressed by Hamlet:

> "..................... Present fears
> Are less than horrible imaginings."

There arose clamors for ignoring the present government, it being considered by many as illegal and unconstitutional. With the approach of August, at which time Congressmen were to be elected, demands were being made that a Governor and Legislature also be elected by those qualified to vote under the Constitution of 1835—that is, by *all white* men who were twenty-one years of age and who possessed the residential qualifications. The "Parson's" fears mounted to the sky, resulting in his initiating a device that he maintained throughout his gubernatorial career—flooding the State with PROCLAMATIONS. Knowing that the franchise law would be put to acid test in the August election of Congressmen, Brownlow sent forth the following Proclamation [58] some three weeks prior to the date of the election:

"PROCLAMATION.

STATE OF TENNESSEE,
EXECUTIVE DEPARTMENT,
Nashville, July 10, 1865.

WHEREAS, It has been made known to me that in many parts of Middle and Western Tennessee, those who have been lately in

---

conclusions impossible, the author prefers to refer any person interested in the above items to the *Appendix* in each legislative *Journal* (First Session, 1865), for such information as may be available.

[58] *Appendix* to *Senate Journal*, First Session, 1865-66, 155-156.

rebellion against the United States, with their friends and sympathizers—and with hands yet red with the blood of our loyal people—are either openly defying, or indirectly setting at naught, an important law of the land;

AND, WHEREAS, It is made the duty of the Governor, by the Constitution and his oath of office, 'to take care that the laws be faithfully executed;'

Therefore, I, WILLIAM G. BROWNLOW, Governor of the State of Tennessee, do proclaim, that the act of the General Assembly, passed on the 5th day of June, 1865, entitled 'An Act to limit the Elective Franchise,' having been deliberately passed under an express authority delegated to said General Assembly by the Convention of the 9th of January last; which delegation of power was solemnly ratified by the people at the ballot box, and proclaimed by the Military Governor, on behalf of the United States, as the organic law—IS THE SUPREME LAW OF THE LAND, and will be *rigidly enforced;* and all who shall band themselves together for the purpose of defeating the execution of said law will be declared in rebellion against the State of Tennessee, and dealt with as rebels.

And I do proclaim that no person is entitled to vote at any election by the people of this State, unless he shall first actually prove by testimony *under oath* that he comes within the provisions of the first section of said law; and shall obtain a certificate of Registration as prescribed in said law, upon such proof in *fact made;* and that the votes of all persons and all counties contrary to the strict provisions of this law, will be thrown out, and will not be taken into account in the office of the Secretary of State.

And I do further proclaim, that said law requires that every candidate for office shall take the oath prescribed by the Seventh Section of said act; and no person is or can be a candidate until he shall have properly taken and subscribed said oath; and I do declare that any person pretending to be a candidate for Congress, or other office, who shall fail to take and subscribe said oath, and file the same in the office of the Secretary of State, on or before the third day of August next, will not be treated as a candidate, and all votes for such person will not be taken into account.

And I call upon the civil authorities throughout the State to arrest and bring to justice all persons who, under pretence of being candidates for Congress, or other office, are travelling over the State denouncing and nullifying the Constitution and laws of the land, and spreading sedition and a spirit of rebellion.

I, also, command all the clerks of the County Courts, and judges of elections, faithfully and strictly to perform, *and not evade*, the responsible trust confided to them by said law; and I solemnly warn them that they will be held to a strict account for any failure in this respect.

In testimony whereof, I have hereunto subscribed my [SEAL] name and caused the great seal of the State to be affixed, at the Department in Nashville, this 10th day of July, A. D., 1865.

WILLIAM G. BROWNLOW.

By the Governor:

A. J. FLETCHER, Secretary of State."

Apparently the "Parson" was not entirely happy with his Proclamation, for two days later he attempted to dignify his threats with the title of an *Address to the People of Tennessee.*[59]

"Address to the People of Tennessee

Fellow Citizens:—Called to the Chief Magistracy of the State without my own seeing [seeking], by the unanimous nomination of a great Convention, and almost unanimous election by the loyal people; entering upon the discharge of my duties nearly simultaneously with the fall of the rebellion, I fondly hoped that the whole people, wearied with war, desolation and anarchy, would hail with delight and support with alacrity the coming of civil government and the inauguration of law and order—that a patriotic people would leave me, like my predecessors of other days, with little to do but to witness and encourage the cultivation of the soil, the pursuits of Commerce and the arts, and the redress of grievances by the Courts. But I am pained to announce my serious apprehensions that a different order of things is soon to be encountered. The harangues of aspiring politicians denouncing the termination of Slavery, the establishment of a free State Constitution, and the very existence of the Government over which I am called to preside, as unconstitutional,

---

[59] In Ms. [Brownlow] *Proclamation Book*, 1865, 18–23.

Author's note. During his incumbency as Governor, Brownlow issued ninety-seven proclamations. Small wonder that he acquired the nickname of "Old Proc."

spurious and a usurpation—the conduct of numerous County Officers in evading or failing to perform their duties, the holding of numerous local elections in defiance of the law and the instalment into Office of disfranchised rebels, proclaim too plainly to be misunderstood, that the spirit of Rebellion and nullification still exists and must be defeated.

In order that all who desire may understand the basis and true foundation of the present Constitution and Government of Tennessee, I propose, in a few plain words, to show its validity and Constitutionality.

The Constitution of the United States declares that, 'the United States shall guarantee to every State in the Union a Republican form of Government.' The Government of Tennessee was usurped by a Military despotism, resulting in anarchy and a reign of terror. Our noble and glorious National Government determined, at the cost of many thousand lives and many millions of money, to perform its duty by guarteeing [guaranteeing] to us a free Government. Both Military and Civic measures had to be brought into requisition. The Military performed its duty in blood on the field of battle. But it appointed a Civilian in the person of the present honored Chief Magistrate of the Nation, to carry out such civil policy as was found necessary to execute in good faith its guaranty to the people. After over three years of patient toil his labors resulted in the establishment of the Government now in power, which is so fearcely denounced. It is his workmanship—the fruit of his mind, acting under National Authority, and proudly proclaimed by him 'the Supreme law of the State of Tennessee,' and from his heart he congratulated the people on the happy result. Does any suppose he will not stand by it and maintain it with the force of the Nation? Strange to say there are those who, not understanding the man or his duty, declare that he will not sustain it, but will set it aside and not allow its Legislature to meet again. It may be some relief to the friends of the new Government to be assured that most of those who so claim to represent the President, are men in whose honesty he never had any confidence. The President will sustain his model scheme of reconstructing the Government of the rebellious States, and that with just so much force, applied in just such manner as may be necessary.

When the Nation entered upon its task of furnishing the People of Tennessee with a republican form of Government, it had a right to present just such particular form of free Government as was most adapted to the condition of the People; and to choose the means of setting the Government on foot. If it had chosen the Constitution of Kentucky or of Maine it is difficult to see what objection could have been made on Constitutional grounds. But in deference to the tastes and habits of our people it chose our own Constitution, divested only of the feature which had caused all our sufferings, and proceeded to present us with our own abandoned ship of State, clothed in its ancient rigging. It is not for us to say there were irregularities in the mode or time of setting the State Government in motion. It was for the National power in performing its guarantee to choose for itself the manner and the time of discharging its duty. It chose to revive the State Government through the loyal People of the State, those who had not proved themselves unworthy of free Government. It prescribed through its agent its own plan of operations, and had a right to do so.

The State Government is thus the gift of the Nation, and is certainly a compliance with the obligation in the Constitution to guarantee to us a Republican form of Government.

With this general statement I might conclude, but I feel called upon to meet specifically, the complaints of those who affect to be aggrieved. It is said the Convention of January last was self-constituted and irresponsible, and assumed to amend the Constitution. The Convention was the initiatory means chosen by the National Administration, through its civil agent. The people of Tennessee had no right to prescribe to the General Government what should be its first step toward a republican form of Government for the State. The Convention consisted of over five hundred delegates; if it had been but five, or one, or if Governor Johnson himself had sat down in his Office and drawn up a form of Government, and by authority of the Nation had proclaimed it to the people it would have been all the same—a national act.

It is said the amendment and schedule were submitted to only a part of the people, and was therefore partial and unfair.

It may well be questioned whether the National authority was under any Constitutional obligation to submit it to a vote at all, its business being to place over us a Republican form of Government, choosing itself the means and the channel of transmitting it to us. It was submitted to a vote of the loyal people, and why submit it to the disloyal who were in arms and in the field fighting to destroy the Nation itself. But this, too, was a national act in which we were strictly entitled to take no part. Again, it is said that the State Government was forced upon the people. Certainly it was forced upon the rebellious majority of the State. So was the authority of the United States forced upon them, and at the point of the bayonet; and Just so the nation had a right to force upon them a republican form of Government, for nothing but force was recognized by them. The next cause of complaint, and that which is now endangering the peace of the State, is that the Legislature has passed, and the Governor is trying to enforce, 'An act to limit the Elective Franchise.' Serious and alarming as the question is, there are just two classes of persons who object to it: viz: Rebels and those who want rebel votes. Loyal men are never heard to complain of it.

It is said this law is unconstitutional. This is impossible, as the law is part of the Constitution itself. The Federal Government, by its agent, Governor Johnson, though [through] the Convention, and the ratification of the people, conferred upon the first General Assembly that should convene the power to limit the qualification of voters. The qualification of voters is prescribed by the Constitution. The convention proposed that the Legislature might amend the Constitution in this particular, and the people ratified the proposition. Thus the true power of amendment was delegated to the Legislature, which because, while acting upon this subject, to all intents and purposes a Constitutional Convention, The power of the Convention to delegate this authority was legitimate and beyond question, by being the chosen instrument of the Federal Government, whose authority was supreme. Finally, it is said the Law is harsh and wanting in magnanimity. By Law the crime of the disfranchised is treason, and the punishment death and confiscation of property. All this is waived and it is said to be cruel to refuse them the privilege of voting for a few years. Magnanimity requires that they should go to the ballot box and with bloody hands deposit their ballots, and by force of numbers seize the reigns of the Government they have tried to destroy—elevate their baffled leaders to power—renew their persecutions of Union Men, and at last have the victory in the State. East Tennessee, with her thousand martyrs to remember is again to come under the rule of such men as Harris or Cheatham, or Bates, or Pillow, as mere appendage to a rebel State; a province to a rebel

Government; And yet this will be the early result of the repeal or failure of the 'Act to limit the Elective Franchise.'

Having said this much by way of friendly explanation, I come to the principal object of this address: And that is that this important law is already set at naught in many localities by the evasion of those whose official duty it is to execute it, and to announce that it will be enforced on the day of election as far as the Civil and Military authorities can enforce it. And all elections effected by illegal votes will be annulled, and if necessary, the officers elected will be arrested. The civil and military authorities understand each other and will act in harmony.

The commander of the military division of Tennessee will aid the civil authorities in all instances where the powers of the latter are inadequate. To protect the ballot box from fraudulent voting, or to remove the county Officers in one half of the State when elected, Judicial proceedings will be utterly impracticable and the civil remedy wholly inadequate. The military will assist in this particular. This step, so likely to become necessary, is much to be regretted, and the Clerks and Judges of election yet have time to correct much they have done, and the hope is expressed that many of them will do so, and save their respective Counties from military intervention.

It is my sincere desire that the entire State be represented in the next Congress. If the Election in Middle and West Tennessee proves a failure, it will not be my fault. I have issued two proclamations, and now this address, warning the people against an illegal election. If they persist in it, they must go without representation in the councils of the Nation.

With a sincere hope that the present cloud may pass away, and that quiet and contentment may yet come to our suffering People,

I remain Your Servant

W. G. BROWNLOW.

Knoxville, July 12, 1865."

Brownlow knew beyond the peradventure of a doubt that the franchise law would be given a stern test at the Congressional election in August. In an attempt to boost the law into general acceptance, he went into a lengthy explanation as to the legitimacy of the Act. He sketched the background of the establishment of military government in Tennessee under Andrew Johnson, and then explained how the present government had succeeded the former. His overall objective was to point out that the existing government had been the work of one man—President Andrew Johnson—and that that man would unquestionably support the existing government in Tennessee. And then, in an expression that Brownlow hoped would serve as an "alarm bell," he indulged in a bit of prophecy that "The President will sustain his model scheme of reconstructing the government of the rebellious States, and that with just so much force, applied in just such manner as may be necessary." With this assertion, Brownlow was hoping to instill into the public mind the fear of Federal troops and military domination.

Next, Brownlow let it be known that he would not hesitate to call into action the State military power "to protect the ballot box from fraudulent voting." And then, in a succinct but dynamite-laden sentence, he stated that "The civil and military authorities understand each other and will act in harmony." Here was a sly reference to an innocent-looking law [60] enacted just a week before adjournment of the Legislature, authorizing all sheriffs to raise a posse of men not to exceed twenty-five in number "to aid them in enforcing civil law and order." The soothing-syrup caption of the law, "An Act for the protection of Sheriffs and other Civil Officers of the State," was now unmasked, revealing its political potentialities for "protecting the purity" of the ballot box!

It would not be amiss to assert that the election of Congressmen was a sort of incidental matter. The overwhelming issue was a test at the polls of the Arnell franchise law. A heated battle was waged between the Radical Unionists who upheld the legality of the franchise law and the Conservative Unionists who denounced the above law as being unconstitutional. In the meanwhile, the disfranchised ex-Confederates had to stand aside, although they represented a majority of the citizenry of the State. Brownlow, of course, defended the Arnell franchise law with all the powers of his invective and political bias. In reply to the suggestion that a Governor and a Legislature should also be elected at the August election, Brownlow let his indignation burst beyond control by asserting that such a movement would be tantamount to a declaration of war and would be treated as *rebellion*.

On August 3, the Congressional election took place, but no massive opposition appears to have materialized—a remarkable tribute to the patience and forbearance of a people accustomed to law observance. A comparison of the vote cast in 1861 and that in this August election, 1865, will demonstrate how effectually the Brownlow regime restricted

---

[60] *Acts of Tennessee*, First Session, 1865, Chapter 24.

the vote through its proscriptive provisions. The vote in the two elections by Districts was as follows:[61]

District	June 1861	August 1865
I.	21,678	11,345
II.	20,625	12,786
III.	18,813	7,848
IV.	16,138	7,918
V.	22,043	8,098
VI.	17,150	5,156
VII.	16,851	5,131
VIII.	16,787	3,486
	150,085	61,768

As one travels from East to West, the loss of votes is made manifest. The greatly diminished number of votes in Middle and West Tennessee, the two strong Secession sections of the State, can be attributed to the provisions of the Arnell franchise law.

The "Parson" was quite unhappy over the results of the Congressional election. On the face of the returns the Conservatives had elected five of the eight Congressmen: Nathaniel G. Taylor (father of Bob and Alf) in the First District; Edmund Cooper in the Fourth District; William B. Campbell in the Fifth District; Dorsey B. Thomas in the Sixth District; and John W. Leftwich in the Eighth District. The Radicals elected Horace Maynard in the Second District; W. B. Stokes in the Third District; and Isaac R. Hawkins in the Seventh District. Two facts disturbed Brownlow exceedingly. More than half of the Congressmen were moderately Conservative Unionists who did not subscribe to Brownlow's imperious and radical commands and were, therefore, classed by him as opponents. The other fact related to the 61,768 votes which, to Brownlow, seemed to be too many in view of the fact that he had received for Governor in the preceding March election only 23,222 votes.

Immediately, Brownlow called upon the sheriffs and county clerks for a report as to the methods of registration used in the recent election. After perusing the replies to his Proclamation [62] of August 11, incorporating certain queries to the above officials, he tossed into the discard the votes of twenty-nine counties amounting to a total of 22,274 votes. The rejected votes were scattered throughout the State, but Brownlow's "revisions" made a significant change in one Congressional District, namely, the Sixth. It so happened that the two candidates in that District were members of the House of Representatives, Dorsey

[61] Fertig, James Walter: *The Secession and Reconstruction of Tennessee*, 70.
[62] *Appendix* to *Senate Journal*, First Session, 1865, 156–157.

B. Thomas, Conservative, and Samuel Arnell, Radical and the author of the franchise law. Inasmuch as Thomas on the face of returns had defeated the Parson's legislative henchman, the said Thomas was selected as the victim of the Parson's chopping block. The reported vote was 2,805 for Thomas, and 2,350 for Arnell. The "revised" vote of Brownlow took 2,284 votes from Thomas and 804 from Arnell, thereby giving Arnell a majority.

In throwing out approximately one-third of the total votes cast in the August Congressional election, Brownlow had exercised a power based not upon *right* but upon *might*. In a high-handed manner, he had acted not only as judge and jury, but he added the roles of prosecutor and persecutor. Blinded as he was by a maniacal hatred of all Secessionists, still he knew that his following constituted a minority party and that its continuance in power would call for some type of chicanery. Some six months after his "revising" procedure in the Congressional election, he confessed that "there were twice as many Rebels in Tennessee as there were Unionists."[63] Something must be radically wrong with a law that permitted 22,274 Tennesseans to vote, he opined, and that loophole must be eliminated by a more stringent franchise law. To that consideration he mustered all his strength and artifice when the Legislature reconvened. For the time being, however, the Brownlow regime aided by Federal troops and sheriffs' posses of twenty-five men had leaped the first hurdle in a desperation move to subject to a small but militant minority the great majority of Tennesseans who represented the wealth, culture, and real leadership of the State.

In compliance with a Joint Resolution, passed June 10, 1865, the Legislature met in its first adjourned session on October 2, 1865.[64] Inasmuch as Speaker of the Senate, Samuel R. Rodgers, had resigned, it became necessary to elect another Speaker. Three names were placed in nomination, namely, Senators John W. Smith of Shelby, DeWitt C. Senter of Grainger, and Joshua B. Frierson of Maury. After the second ballot, Senators Smith and Senter withdrew and Senator Frierson was unanimously elected Speaker.[65] The House met pursuant to adjournment with Mr. Speaker Heiskell in the chair, but adjourned until next day for lack of a quorum.[66]

When advised by the Legislature that it had reconvened and was ready for any communication which he desired to transmit, the Parson demonstrated that he had not been idle during the legislative recess. Forthwith came the following Message*:

[63] *Knoxville Whig and Rebel Ventilator,* January 31, 1866.
[64] *Senate Journal,* First Adjourned Session, 1865, 3.
[65] *Ibid.,* 3–4.
[66] *House Journal,* First Adjourned Session, 1865, 3.
* *Senate Journal,* First Adjourned Session, 1865, 4–26.
  House Journal, First Adjourned Session, 1865, 5–26.

"EXECUTIVE DEPARTMENT,
Nashville, October 3, 1865.

GENTLEMEN OF THE SENATE AND HOUSE OF REPRESENTATIVES:

Re-assembling at the Capitol of the State, after visiting your homes and mingling with the people so as to learn their wishes, it is your duty, as the Legislative Department of the State Government, to repeal, amend, and enact laws so as to protect the rights of your constituents, and to support and encourage the General Government in exercising its large and legitimate powers to preserve the interests of the whole country, so recently and fearfully endangered by the wicked and protracted resistance to its authority. It is truly a proud epoch in our lives to have been privileged to witness the termination of the rebellion, and the signal triumph of our country's honor and independence. Seen in the light of a gigantic struggle of four years' duration, Tennessee and her heroic soldiers and unfaltering loyal citizens stand transfigured before an admiring world, and we realize at once the grandeur of the part they played, and the vastness of the influence which their courage and patriotism must exert upon our future history. The wave of war first rolled through Tennessee four and a half years ago, and swept on from West to Middle and East Tennessee, and from State to State, traversing Missouri and Kentucky, encircling traitorous North Carolina, and desolated Virginia, bearing high upon its brazen crest the infamous banner of the so-called Southern Confederacy. Under the gallant THOMAS the stars and stripes were thrown to the breeze, the army of traitors was met upon the plains, and soon our banner floated over the blackened and shattered ramparts of a retreating foe; emblematic of the fortunes of a routed army of rebels, whose death-rattles were heard in every direction as they fled South.

I never doubted the final success of the Government in putting this most infamous rebellion under its feet, though I, with you knew not how long we might be fated to suffer, bleed, fight, and die, either on fields of carnage or in the loathsome prisons of the South. The assurance was always with me that, sooner or later, as our cause was just, we must and should triumph. For four dreadful years the Divine Face seemed hidden from us, or shrouded in impenetrable obscurity, and our State, above all others, seemed furrowed with graves; yet Divine Providence, in whose hands are the issues of life and death, came out from among the clouds which had surrounded Him, and led our armies to victory. And while our gratitude to the Father of us all should be boundless, we should hold in everlasting remembrance the services of our unconquerable armies and navy, rejoicing and exulting in their achievements.

With profound gratitude let us recognize the goodness of GOD in giving us this last overwhelming evidence of the devotion of the people to Constitutional Liberty and National Unity, as well as fresh proof of the strength and stability of the best form of government on earth. After four years of great domestic violence, we are now cheered with the prospect of restoring public tranquility, of staying the effusion of fraternal blood, and of exhibiting to the admirers of free institutions everywhere, as well as to the monarchies and despotisms of the Old World, a great Republic rescued from destruction in an hour of imminent peril, by the united action of a great people, under the guidance of Divine Providence. In these events we have grounds for boundless rejoicing and exultation. But our exultation should be in no unhallowed or unmerciful spirit. Before the world we should rejoice with joy unspeakable—joying and rejoicing that the great rebellion, with all its crimes and attendant evils, is at length ended, and the bow of peace again spans the sky! I cannot, therefore, neglect to call upon you, again and again, to bow your heads in adoring thankfulness before 'Him who rides upon the storm and calms the roaring seas,' that He still rules the armies of earth and heaven, and that the American people are still the people of His special care. From every house of prayer in all the land, from every loyal church, and from every devout heart should go up to God a continual prayer, asking that the fruits of this prolonged and sanguinary conflict may not be lost upon our generation, and that we may cherish, with our latest breath, the memory of our martyred thousands, who so nobly died that Constitutional Liberty might live.

You, gentlemen, are now called upon to legislate upon some subjects not agitated at your session in the Spring, and to meet demands that were not then developed as fully as they are now. To your good sense and patriotism are these new and delicate subjects confided; not doubting that, after mingling with your constituents as you have, you are prepared to reflect their wishes. And allow me to say, *the honest people are always right*, and therefore safe counsellors. It should not be your concern how many, but how few, new laws you shall enact and meet the pressing demands of the hour; nor should you study to protract, but to shorten your session, making its expenses as light as possible.

Under the workings of a most excellent and necessary law, passed at your spring session, known as the 'Franchise Act,' we have held Congressional elections in the eight districts of the State, and have elected eight Representatives to the next Congress of the United States. As a general thing, the election passed off quietly, with here and there exceptions, and was characterized by much better behavior than was anticipated. Most of the districts were thoroughly canvassed, and a large vote, considering all the circumstances, was polled. As many as 60,000 votes have been reported to the Secretary of State's office as cast, which, in view of the registration required, and the restrictions so properly thrown around the ballot-box, as well as the short time allowed to prepare for the election, was all that could have reasonably been expected. The clerks in some counties are reported to have neglected their duty, and to have granted certificates of registration to many who were disfranchised by law. I think that law can be improved by amendments and additions, but I must be allowed to say that I am by no means an advocate of its repeal. Nor do the loyal people of this State desire its repeal, if I understand their sentiments.

The authority of the Constitution and laws of the United States and of the State of Tennessee has now extended over almost every county in the State; the machinery of civil government is working well, except in a few instances, and it affords me great pleasure to say that our people are rapidly recovering from the effects of insurrection, while prosperity is promised in every section. Our people are farming successfully, and the indications are that in two or three more years, under present legislation, our State will be herself again.

The closing of the war and disbanding of the rebel armies returns thousands of men to civil life, and distributes them among the various counties of the State. How are these men to be treated? Are they to make good citizens, or discontented subjects? Are the wounds made by the war ever to be healed? These are weighty questions, taking the place of those that engrossed our attention during the war. It is not our policy or interest to treat oppressively the thousands who fought bravely in a bad cause, provided they act as becomes their circumstances. As for the masses—the young and deluded masses—who blindly followed the standard of revolt, let them have a full and free pardon, if you will, on their sincere return to loyalty; but as many of them are guilty rebels, they should cheerfully submit to five or ten years of disfranchisement, so as to give them time to wash the blood of loyal men from their hands. As for the original conspirators and leaders, who, through long years of speaking, writing, and agitating got up this rebellion; who, without provocation, or even the pretense of wrong to themselves, traitorously set the rebellion on foot; bad men and men of talent who pressed it forward with all the malignity of fiends and the cruelty of savages; 'good Southern men,' who, through rapine, arson, perjury and butchery, have filled the land with mourning; they are entitled to neither mercy nor forbearance. Let us not give a new growth and respectability to TREASON in the South, or in the border States, by sending these unwhipped malefactors forth with new schemes for a second rebellion.

True, the national honor has been vindicated. The insult offered to the country by rebellion has punished itself most bitterly in the ruin it has brought upon rebel communities, and the sorrow and mourning it has carried to hearts that only advocated treason. The Government of the United States has demonstrated the hopeless nature of all future attempts at destroying the Union. But no thanks to these original conspirators for all this exhibition of strength on the part of the Government. No thanks to them, either, for their failure in their grand experiment at insurrection. It is our duty to teach these leaders a lesson that they will never forget, and one that will profit generations yet to come; teach them that leniency, without a distinction between loyalty and treason, is more certain to subvert the Government than is rebellion itself; teach them that clemency at the sacrifice of justice, is the criminal abandonment of government; teach them that treason is a crime against law and liberty, and that they who are guilty of it have forfeited all claims to protection and all rights of citizenship.

The opposers of the Franchise Act of this General Assembly are suddenly enamored of the virtue of *Repentance;* and no parable ever written has such attractions for them as the parable of the Prodigal Son. They never weary of quoting this parable of unequalled beauty and pathos. It is interesting to note the difference between the Prodigal Son and these returning rebels. First, the Prodigal Son did not secede; he went with his father's consent, and the Scriptures indicate with his blessing. Next, he *went;* he did not stay and vilify the old man in his own house; he asked for something to start him in the world; did not point a pistol and demand the old man's greenbacks; he received the portion his father gave him; he did not *steal* it, and, receiving it, he started out to 'seek his fortune.' He did not go to the *south* side of the farm and join a band of robbers who were plundering the old man, but quietly took his journey into a far country. Finally he repented of his folly, not because the old man *whipped* him into repentance, but because he 'came to himself,' and saw that he had wasted his substance in riotous living. He went back home, not with murder in his heart, threatening what he would do, but bowed down in honest contrition, and asking all sorts of pardon. He did not go back saying 'I have fought you four years and until I was overpowered,' but he went back crying, 'Father, I have sinned against heaven and before thee, and am no more worthy to be called thy son.' He went back because, through all his riotous living, *his heart was there.* He did not return demanding his 'lost rights,' but said, 'make me as one of thy hired servants.' He did not ask instant forgiveness, upon an oath of amnesty, but proposed to demonstrate his repentance *by his works.*

The story is one of sincere, deep, heartfelt, voluntary repentance. Do rebels, coming home, come repenting of their unparalleled crimes? As long as rebellion promised success, did they show any signs of repentance? Are they coming back because they love the Union, or their property? Are they not coming back because they are whipped, and 'perish with hunger?' All who return peaceably to their homes, cultivating friendly relations, abstaining from hostile acts, and discountenancing every attempt at disorder, should be met in the same spirit and treated with leniency.

We want a population in Tennessee that shall be thoroughly loyal. In order to secure this the Legislature should adopt a fostering policy, which will encourage immigration and hasten the return of prosperity. The vast importance of a large emigration to Tennessee from our North-Western States, and from Germany and Switzerland, whence the tide has hitherto set the strongest, to the interests and future prosperity of the State, cannot be too strongly insisted upon, or over-estimated. The inauguration of a policy looking to this end cannot be too vehemently urged upon our property-holders generally, and especially upon large land-holders at this peculiar and most interesting juncture in our affairs. While I would abstain from making any invidious distinctions among emigrants, candor requires me to say that the Germans have shown themselves more loyal than any other class of our foreign population. As farmers, as mechanics, and as loyal voters they are a most desirable class of emigrants to bring among us, and I should like to see our unoccupied and unculti- vated lands dotted over with thrifty Germans.

We are now at the close of a period of unexampled depression and paralysis throughout all departments of industry. By an immu- table law the reaction and the rebound will come soon. There is a tide in the affairs of States, as well as of men, which taken at the flood leads on to fortune. Tennessee is now at the ebb of this tide, and we may look with certainty for its returning flood. Shall we ride upon it into the haven of a magnificent future, of a splendid agricultural and commercial prosperity, population, wealth, education, refinement, position and power, or shall we drift inertly to ruin, without an effort to save ourselves? The proper answer to these anxious enquir- ies will be found in the wisdom of your legislation and its adaptation to the present emergencies. Shall we let the propitious moment pass away unimproved, and thus miss the golden opportunity of placing Tennessee upon the high road to the magnificent destiny which is within her reach? I am not speaking at random when I say that Ten- nessee is now in the very crisis of her career, and that as her legisla- tors shall act with a determined and enlightened liberality in develop- ing her vast resources and calling to their aid the means and facilities within their control to promote her prosperity and enlarge her borders, so will that career be onward and upward, and Tennessee will become the Empire State of the South—a great mart for manu- facturers, trade and commerce and the great field of agricultural in- dustry and prosperity. Skilled and educated labor will come here for the asking. Into the *free* State of Tennessee emigrants—mechan- ics, artisans, tillers of the ground and others—from the over-crowded States and towns of the North and from Europe will pour in a con- tinuous stream, if we adopt a course of legislation that shall en- courage them and afford remunerative occupation. Our genial cli- mate invites them, our navigable streams, our fertile soil, and moun- tains rich in their inexhaustless mineral resources, our numerous railroads, making access easy to all portions of the State, and convenient outlets to all products that seek distant markets, all these offer inducements which, presented in proper shape by fitting legislation, will attract all the labor we need, of every description, as fast as there is a demand for it.

The statistics of emigration from Europe during the present year show a very large increase compared with the past year, and it appears from statements made in the foreign journals that there is not sufficient transportation to be had for those who are waiting to embark for this country. Both the Liverpool and London journals allege that the seaports of Europe are crowded with emigrants, provided with the means of coming and only detained by a want of vessels. It is estimated that before the close of 1865 we will have received two hundred thousand emigrants from all the ports of Europe. It is a moderate calculation to say that they bring, on an average, $50 each, in gold. This brings to our shores ten million of dollars. What a vast addition to our specie circulation! What a vast addition to our force of able-bodied laborers! With proper legislation a majority of these men will be drawn to the Southern States. Not a few will find their way to Tennessee. Shall we not have a State Commissioner at the East to give them the necessary information? Other Southern States have established agencies at New York for this purpose, and if we would compete successfully with them we must resort to similar means.

In connection with this subject of emigration, I beg leave to say that it is a far more safe and rational process of regenerating the South than any sudden and compulsory admission of the blacks to the ballot-box. It involves no controverted question of State rights. It occasions no necessity for arbitrary military rule. It does not exasperate our native-born citizens and make them life-long enemies of the Government. If carried out as indicated, it will accomplish the end we all have in view; while, on the other hand, the indiscriminate grant of the right of suffrage to the colored population would increase the evils that keep the South depressed, and exasperate those who, under other circumstances, would become devoted friends of the Government and accept the emancipation of the slaves as an event not at all offensive. With proper legislation on the part of the Southern States, but little time would be necessary to secure a flood of immigration to the South and all the beneficial results before referred to. In view of the immense interests at stake, affecting the future prosperity of the State so vitally, it is expected this subject will receive your special attention.

Actuated by a sense of duty, and desiring to see justice done to a class of patriotic men who are serving the State as Judges and Attorneys General I again urge upon the Legislature an increase in the pay of those officers, from the highest to the lowest. Several Judges have resigned their offices, who were entirely acceptable to the people and useful to the State, on the ground that the compensation allowed them by law was wholly inadequate. Supreme Judges should be paid a salary of four or five thousand dollars, Chancellors and Circuit Judges should be allowed at least twenty-five hundred or three thousand dollars per annum, and Attorneys General should be allowed a corresponding increase in their pay. Their salaries can be increased at the expense of the parties to the suit without making the peaceable tax-payers feel the burden. If something of this kind is not done I am assured that many Attorneys for the State will resign. Indeed, it has been with difficulty that many useful officers have been induced to hold on to their positions. The people are willing to see competent men in these important positions properly remunerated. They know it is idle to talk of a public officer supporting his family on the salary of five years ago. The honest people feel that if any one of the incumbents alluded to is worthy of his office, he is worthy of a support from that office. The State cannot reasonably expect a good lawyer to devote his time, talents and energies to the interests of the Commonwealth, when the salary of his office falls below the necessary expenses of his family. Gentlemen capable of filling such positions are capable of making money in the practice of their profession, and it is obvious that our Judges and Attorneys will have to turn their attention to the practice of the law in order to gain a livelihood. Good lawyers cannot afford to serve the State without a fair and reasonable compensation. The consequence is that indifferent lawyers, who cannot live by their practice, will accept our present inadequate salaries, and the public interests will suffer.

I may seem to be importunate on this subject, but if I am it is because of the interests involved. When the salaries of these officers were fixed some years since, the amount of business was less than one-fourth what it now is. Our Judges and Attorneys are now absent from their homes three-fourths of the year. During that time they live at hotels at an expense of from three to five dollars per day, to say nothing of the expense of travel by rail or otherwise. With the present salary of two thousand dollars for a Chancellor or Circuit Judge, after paying his necessary expenses of board and travel and clothing himself, he has *less than eight hundred dollars* left for the support of his family. I repeat, these inadequate salaries will drive competent men from the Bench, and the important causes pending in every Court will be tried and adjudicated by incompetent men, and the rights of citizens will be sacrificed, instead of being secured as the Constitution and laws of the State contemplate.

Who shall vote in Tennessee in future elections? Will you authorize emancipated slaves to vote? Will you invest them with all the rights incident to citizenship? Have you the power to do it under the Constitution of the United States? These are weighty questions which will be before the country for an answer; and a contest will shortly arise in Congress upon the presentation of the credentials of two Senators and eight Representatives from Tennessee who are asking admission to seats in Congress, while the people sending them have denied the emancipated slave the right of suffrage. I am free to admit that, for the present, we have done enough for the negro, and, although negro voting cannot suit my natural prejudices of caste, there is a class of them I would be willing to see vote at once. A large class, ignorant, docile, easily led by designing men, and not safely trusted with political power, I am not willing to see at the ballot-box; but as even these have been faithful among the faithless, if rebels are to be restored to the right of the elective franchise, I would say let us no longer deny these political rights to the slaves. In my judgment a loyal negro is more eminently entitled to suffrage than a disloyal white man.

Whatever may be the result of the contest anticipated in Congress upon this subject, I take occasion to say, in advance, that Congress has no right to fix the qualification of a voter within a State. The subject of negro voting in any State claiming her rights under the Constitution, is one for the exclusive decision of the State. In a revolted State it is a question of policy and military government until such State is fully restored. Some of the Southern States should be left longer under military rule, until they can offer more security for the future. Tennessee is an exception to this rule, as she is not now in insurrection and has her civil machinery in successful operation.

Congress cannot fix the qualification of a voter within a State. The Constitution, as I understand it, provides for but three elections —that of President, and those of Senators and Representatives. The President is chosen by Electors appointed in such manner as the legislators of the State may elect. Senators are chosen by the Legislatures of the respective States and Representatives are chosen by the people of the several States, just as we have recently chosen two Senators and eight Representatives. The Electors of each State are required to possess the qualifications requisite for the most numerous branch of the State Legislature. Therefore, if any point be settled, it is clear that the framers of the Constitution intended that each State should prescribe who should vote, and who should not. The only limitation upon this power is the duty of the National Government to maintain in each state a 'republican form of government.' The question may arise and doubtless will, in the next Congress, are not all these rights and guarantees changed in a State where the voters have voluntarily renounced their allegiance and gone into the work of rebellion? Can a State renounce its allegiance, engage in the treasonable work of rebellion, and yet come forward and insist upon its rights in this respect? It will be admitted on all hands that the United States has the right to punish traitors, by depriving them of their lives, their property, or their franchise. It will be urged that it is absurd to kill traitors and confiscate their property, and yet deny that we have the power to prevent their voting. And if we may determine who shall not vote, why not say who shall vote? This may apply to South Carolina, Alabama, Mississippi, Florida, Texas and other States that led off in the work of treason. My arguments are in vindication of the rights of Tennessee. I am no Southern advocate of the wild doctrine of State SOVEREIGNTY, as held by the Secessionists of this, our day. Article 1, Section 1, of the Constitution, the 9th and 10th Articles of the Amendments say: 'The people shall not be disparaged, and the powers not delegated to the United States by the Constitution are reserved to the people'—that is to say, to the States. Again, this authority is made obvious by Article 1st, Section 4th, which read as follows, viz: 'The time, place and manner of holding elections for Senators and Representatives shall be prescribed in each State by the Legislature thereof. *But* the Congress *may*, at *any time*, *by law*, make or alter such Regulations, except as to the place of choosing Senators.' The Constitution of the United States and laws in pursuance thereof say: 'A person charged with treason, felony, or other crimes, who shall flee from justice and be found in another State, shall be delivered up to be removed to the State having jurisdiction of the crime.'

I think that negro suffrage is bound to follow as one of the great results of the rebellion; that the time will come when it will be proper and right; but that the time has not yet come when the ballot-box should be turned over to the emancipated slaves of this State, and the thousands who would rush into Tennessee from the Cotton States on this account. To the silly objection that negro suffrage implies social equality, I beg leave to respond that negroes, at one time or another, have voted in most of the Southern States, and yet they were in no way advanced to social equality with the whites. My recollection is that in every Southern State, except South Carolina, the right of suffrage was originally exercised by free blacks. The original Constitutions of Delaware, Maryland, Virginia, North Carolina and Georgia, members of the Old Thirteen, make no mention of color in defining the qualifications of voters. Up to the time of the adoption of the Amended Constitution, in 1835, negroes voted* in Tennessee, and the leading politicians of the State importuned them for their votes. In Maryland they voted until 1833, and in North Carolina they voted as late as 1835. All this failed to advance the negroes in the scale of equality, so foolishly talked of now and so offensively deprecated; and *amalgamation* was not so common in those days as it has become since!

In Pennsylvania negroes voted until 1838. Yet in that great, free State a negro had not the privileges that he enjoyed in Tennessee before the rebellion. In Ohio they are allowed to vote upon proving that they have more white than African blood in their veins! In Connecticut negroes voted until 1817, and, strange to say, they did not attain for themselves an equality sufficient to preserve the privilege of continuing to vote. There is even a constitutional provision in the State of Massachusetts, excluding all men from the ballot-box who cannot read the Constitution and write their own names. This provi-

---

* Author's note. Under the Constitution of 1796, the privilege of suffrage was extended to that class of Negroes who were generally called Free Persons of Color. This, of course, referred to that limited class of Negroes who had either been emancipated by their owners or who had purchased their freedom from their masters. This privilege of suffrage, however, was denied to the Negroes by the Constitution of 1835.

sion, of course, excludes the colored people of that State who cannot read and write, and would exclude our entire colored population, with but few exceptions—assuming that they are not competent to judge of the administration of public affairs. If a man who cannot read and write in Massachusetts is unable to judge intelligently of questions of public policy, how can the uneducated blacks of the South do so? I understand those politicians of the North who urge the claims of the Southern negroes to the right of suffrage, place it upon the ground that they are in favor of the Government, admitting that they are not competent to judge of questions of public policy.

Even in New York, the great Empire State of the Union, the negro has not advanced one step in the scale of equality, so insultingly and offensively paraded before us in this day by the pro-slavery men of the country. In that State the negro may vote now if he have the requisite property qualification. Although this odious property qualification was removed as to the white voters of New York in 1826, it still applies to the colored electors, as I understand! What then shall we say of the equality in the stronghold of 'freedom and equal rights,' so officiously talked of by rebels and rebel sympathizers who are so pertinaciously insulting the common sense of decent people when the right of a negro to vote is urged who has shouldered his gun in defence of our common country! All this outcry against a negro voting in any contingency, comes from a lingering sentiment of disloyalty in the South, added to ancient prejudices, and to the savage instincts inspired by this institution in connection with the rebellion.

We are entering upon a state of quiet consequent upon the overthrow of the military power of the rebellion, and when this quiet is secured, the obligation will press upon us not only to strike the last fetter from the limbs of the bondman, but also to see that all this ignorance and poverty, social and political disfranchisement to which they have been heretofore subjected are removed. Upon the solution of this momentous question of suffrage the emancipated slaves can well afford to wait, and it is their duty to wait, lest, by precipitation, false steps should be taken which could never be retrieved. And if the Legislature shall feel itself called upon to act in this matter, there should be the utmost patience and circumspection, but no haste. Certain it is that the majority in Congress has no right to expect the Southern States, recently in rebellion, to do that for the colored population of the South which the people of the North have refused to do for a better educated class of free colored men in their own midst. And, being satisfied that the immediate and indiscriminate extension of the franchise to the negroes will not prove as beneficial as many suppose, I cannot recommend the measure for your adoption. I think it would be bad policy, as well as wrong in principle, to open the ballot-box to the uninformed and exceedingly stupid slaves of the Southern cotton, rice and sugar fields. If allowed to vote, the great majority of them could be influenced by leading secessionists to vote against the Government, as they would be largely under the influence of this class of men for years to come, having to reside on and cultivate their lands. When the people of Tennessee become satisfied that the negro is worthy of suffrage they will extend it, and not before; and I repeat that this question must be regulated by the State authorities, and by the loyal voters of the State, not by the General Government. The Northern States regulate this question, and exclude negroes from the ballot-box, and it would be unjust in them not to allow us to manage this thing for ourselves, as they do, under the same national Constitution. A majority of the American people have not determined to establish negro suffrage unconditionally; but the time may come when they will do so, and if the active leading men of the South desire to prevent it, they would do well to cease their hostility to the Government, for that will hasten its establishment. I am free to confess that if it become necessary to enfranchise the blacks, in order to keep the control of the country out of the hands of the rebels and traitors, I am for the measure. And when the nation finds that all its liberality and offers of pardon to rebels are in vain, it will take steps to give suffrage to the blacks, and I shall cordially approve the act. As I stated in January to the Convention which nominated me for the office which I now hold, I desired that the natural rights of the colored people should be guaranteed to them. I was not ready to confer upon them a privilege which was purely conventional, at least, till convinced they were qualified to exercise it intelligently and discreetly. I repeat, that we cannot hear of any excessive anxiety on the part of the earnest men of Ohio, Illinois, Indiana, Pennsylvania and New York, to change the constitutions of their respective States so as to admit colored men to suffrage. They are distressed because the ballot is not at once thrust into the hands of the ignorant blacks of the cotton States, but they are proposing nothing of the sort for the thousands of free blacks among themselves. A decent respect for consistency, and the colored people they have in their own midst, should lead them, first of all, to confer upon them a right which they insist the freedmen of the South are entitled to. It being a matter over which the States themselves have paramount control, our friends at the North should begin by setting a good example to less enlightened and patriotic States of the South. As they have a beam in their own eye, they should pluck it out before taking the mote out of the eye of their Southern neighbors.

While upon the subject of the colored race, I may be permitted to say that some definite legislation is necessary for the protection, disposition, government and control of the emancipated slaves among us. What the character of that legislation should be, it is not my province to say; but I leave it to the good sense, experience and reflection of the members of the General Assembly to determine. Heretofore the legislation of the State has been against the slave population. When the Federal forces are withdrawn from Tennessee, many of those who fought to perpetuate slavery will show the emancipated slaves no quarter; and especially that class who are now rude and insolent toward their former owners and the whites generally. A long and intimate acquaintance with affairs in the South has convinced me that the white and colored people cannot live together, politically or socially, as equals, and therefore all our legislation should look to a peaceable separation of the two races on Southern soil—the blacks in their separate condition to enjoy full political rights—if you please, the right of suffrage and representation. In this way I would settle the most difficult question that has grown out of a terrible war of four years' duration. It is certainly right and expedient for the Legislature of Tennessee to say to what extent the State shall be overrun by the emancipated slaves of other States. Illinois, at the breaking out of the rebellion, enacted stringent laws, forbidding negroes from other States to settle there. Other free States enacted similar laws. I would say, guard against excessive legislation upon this subject, but, by all means, see that Tennessee is not burdened with any but her own slaves. I am, myself, the advocate of appropriating a separate and suitable amount of territory, within such degrees of latitude as are adapted to their nature, and there settling them as a nation of freedmen. Texas, affording the requisite amount of territory and a suitable climate, and Texas having declared that slavery never should be abolished, it seems to me that Government should confiscate the rebel lands, pay the loyal men for theirs, and turn the State over to the freedmen of the South. If this scheme should not strike the National Government as plausible, then let Mexico be cleaned out and turned over to the emancipated slaves of the South. The advent of Maximilian into Mexico was a part of the rebellion. It was the effort of France to flank the American Government. Our work in crushing out the rebellion will not be complete until we drive the usurper out of Mexico, and give to that unfortunate sister republic a permanent government. Aware that this is not the legitimate work of the Legislature, I suggest that an expression of opinion, bearing upon this momentous question, if made with absolute unanimity, would have its effect.

I do not advocate the removal of the colored race to a country of their own because of any prejudice I entertain, but I am their friend, deeply impressed with the troubles I see ahead, growing out of the antagonism of the races. But if the colored man, after looking over the whole ground, shall still ask to stay in the land of his birth, to till the soil and labor in the workshop, and to fill positions of usefulness under the bright skies that smiled on his infancy, I say, in all conscience, let him remain.

I recommend that you examine our entire code, so far as it is shaped by the institution of slavery, and adapt it to the requirements of a free State. I call your attention especially to the propriety and necessity of conferring upon the freedman the privilege of testifying in courts of justice. His *status* and his relation to the white race are entirely changed. He was *property;* he is now a *person.* For the first time he has a right to enter into contracts, and to enforce them in the courts; to sue and be sued, and to prosecute those who may injure him in person or property. These rights will avail him but little if any evil-disposed white person may deprive him of them with impunity. As our law now stands, a freedman may be deprived of his life in the presence of a hundred colored witnesses, whose lips are sealed in the courts. This state of our law has brought among us the 'Freedman's Bureau,' a tribunal established by the Federal Government from necessity, but foreign to our Constitution and domestic laws; necessarily arbitrary, and which must be presided over by military men without judicial experience, without juries. This institution will become permanent unless we remove the necessity which called it into existence.

I am of opinion that much of our repugnance to what is called 'negro testimony' is the result of education and habit. It is required of the white witness that he shall be disinterested, and shall have sufficient intelligence to 'understand the obligation of an oath.' Let the same be required of the negro. He is now subject to the same penalties for perjury that the white man is, and as he is religiously inclined, he will no doubt take the proper view of the penalty in the world to come. Again, it must be remembered that our juries are the exclusive judges of the weight of evidence, and they will not fail to take into consideration the degree of intelligence and the character for honor and veracity of the witnesses, whether white or black.

In short, let us ask and demand for this long oppressed race the protection and enjoyment of his liberty. And let us shape our own legislation in this direction, and by our acts show to the world that there is virtue, patriotism and religion in at least one seceded State; and as the rising sun of prosperity drives away the darkness of the past, it will be seen standing out upon the foreground amid the wreck of civil war, fresher and brighter than ever before.

In my former message, I called your attention to the Bank of the State, as allied to its finances, and represented them as being in a demoralized condition, demanding prompt action and prompt legislation. This is the most important subject I have to bring before you, and the State owes it to herself to look carefully into the condition of the Bank of Tennessee, having its parent bank in Nashville, and a number of affiliated branches in different parts of the State.

A careful examination of the assets captured in Georgia has been made by a committee of competent men, and a report of the result is herewith submitted. It will be seen that the great body of the assets was found in the shape of Confederate notes and bonds. These, not worth the paper on which they are printed, were not considered worth the labor of counting, but will amount to six or eight millions of dollars. Only the sum of $446,719.70, in gold and silver, was found among the assets, being $280,346.24 less than was shown by the last report of the Bank, in 1861. This amount was doubtless embezzled during the war, or sunk in cotton speculations by the faithless officers of the institution. The foregoing sum of $446,719.70 in coin has been sold under a resolution of your honorable body for $618,250, in 7-30s United States Bonds, which, I am pleased to say, are yielding the State an annual interest of $45,132.25.

It will be seen that this great banking institution is but a mere wreck, and that its ruins only are in possession of the State. Still, there are large sums due to the Bank and its various branches in notes discounted before the rebellion, which many of the debtors are anxious to pay. There are also owned by the Bank and its branches large amounts in real estate, banking houses, dwellings and farms, in a dilapidated condition, and every day depreciating in value. I advise that these debts be collected, and this property be disposed of at once for cash or approved securities. A number of suits are pending against the Bank, and some have lately been instituted against those having control of the assets by depositors whose deposits were wholly or in part Confederate currency. In other and similar cases the Executive has been sued alone, on the ground that the assets captured in Georgia were placed in his hands. I advise prompt and positive legislation in all these cases, to prevent this annoyance, and defeat the attempted collection of fraudulent and treasonable claims, as many of them are known to be. I advise that the Bank and its branches be at once placed in process of liquidation. The courts are now open in all parts of the State. Bank attorneys can be appointed for each branch in each banking district, and the rights of all parties may soon be settled.

I advise that out of the proceeds of what is left of the Bank, the Common School Fund shall be, as far as possible, replaced. This large fund emanated mainly from the General Government, and was held by the State in sacred trust. The declaration of this trust may be found in the act of Congress which created it, and is 'for the instruction of children forever.' And by the Constitution it is declared to be 'a PERMANENT FUND,' 'never to be diminished by legislative appropriation,' nor the interest 'devoted to any other use than the support and encouragement of common schools.' Perhaps a more perfidious act than the appropriation of this fund to treasonable purposes was not committed during the late perfidious rebellion.

I hold, and I think the courts will sustain the opinion, that the State, by virtue of her sovereignty, has priority over all other creditors of the Bank. The State, as Trustee, represents the School Fund as against the Bank; and that the School Fund, by virtue of the peculiar constitutional trust with which it was clothed, has priority over all other creditors of the State. Certainly, this fund has priority over the common depositors or note-holders of the Bank. I therefore advise you to lay your hands upon every dollar you can constitutionally seize, to replace this fund. Let the State keep her faith with the destitute and long neglected school children, no matter who else may suffer, and then settle with other creditors as best she may.

Since the adjournment of your honorable body, much embarrassment has been caused for the want of some person legally authorized to represent the Bank in important transactions. Suits pending in Nashville were about to come to trial, and an important, and, as I believe, an unjust suit was commenced at Knoxville. In the former case I employed H. H. Harrison, Esq., and in the latter Messrs. Temple & Rogers, to act as attorneys for the Bank. I ask the Legislature to approve my action in this respect.

The assets of the Branch Bank at Athens were not captured, and no coin belonging to that branch was found. But the cashier, Thos. A. Cleage, reported to me at the Capitol, and represented himself as having at his command about $60,000 in gold and sterling exchange. He promised to produce the money in a few days, failed to do so, and made his escape into Illinois. While taking steps for his arrest Thomas H. Calloway, a responsible and honorable gentleman, proposed to pay $50,000 of this defalcation, and to use his efforts to secure the remainder. Believing the interests of the State would be best subserved by accepting Mr. Calloway's proposition, I did so, received his check for $50,000, and receipted him for that amount paid on Cleage's liability. When this check is paid, as it will be in a few days, I ask you to approve the transaction.

The financial condition of the State demands the early and prompt attention of the General Assembly. While I have every confidence in the ability of the great State of Tennessee to meet her liabilities, and of the disposition of her people to have them met, action on your part—prompt and intelligent action—is called for. The condition of our finances will appear from the reports of the Comptroller and Treasurer, which give the details. The State debt now due and to be provided for at once, as reported by the Comptroller, is $1,213,719.66. This amount of money must be raised and the credit of the State sustained. How this sum is to be raised, I leave it to your wisdom to determine.

The Comptroller's Report will further disclose to you that there is now due on the Railroad Bonds loaned to the different Railroad Companies in the State, $3,769,509. This is the interest now due upon the Bonds endorsed by the State for the Railroad Companies, amounting to $16,211,000. For this debt the State is ultimately liable upon the failure of the Companies. But these Companies are able to pay their interest debts, and should be required to do so at once. They can as well extend their credit to meet their pressing liabilities as for the State to do so for their benefit, with her already heavy obligations weighing upon her.

Most of the Railroads in the State, having been turned over to the Companies respectively owning them, are being repaired and run by said Companies. They have been turned over by the Government on terms liberal and advantageous. The Road from this city to Chattanooga, and from that city to the Virginia line, a distance of four hundred miles, owned by three Companies, is, as a general thing, in splendid order; much of the track has been re-laid, the embankments well dressed, and the cuts well ditched and drained. The best bridge near the Virginia line is nearly finished and the connection with the East complete. Upon the Roads in Middle and West Tennessee repairs are progressing rapidly, and the indications are that the Companies have a profitable business before them, as there is a large amount of travel and a large demand for freights as the country becomes quiet and business is resumed. As a general thing I may say these Companies have reorganized upon a loyal basis and are controlled by Union men. Especially is this true of East Tennessee. The Edgefield and Kentucky, and the Louisville, Clarksville and Memphis Roads have been placed in the hands of Receivers as the law directs. They are in the hands of reliable and energetic men, and I have all confidence that they will be managed to advantage.

I feel it my duty to lay before you the condition of the Hermitage Property, now owned by the State. This property was purchased by one of my predecessors, under the act of 1856, chapter 96, for the sum of forty-eight thousand ($48,000) dollars, for which amount the Bonds of the State were issued to the occupant on his mortgage. The act provided that Mr. A. Jackson, the proprietor, should retain possession for two years thereafter, unless the General Government should apply for it for a branch of the Military Academy at West Point, for which purpose the State Government was to tender it.

In the event the General Government did not accept the offer within two years, it was made the duty of the Governor of the State to have fifty acres laid off, including the mansion, spring and tomb of the illustrious Hero of New Orleans, and expose the balance to public sale for cash, and report the sale to the Legislature of 1859-60.

By the act of March 24th, 1860, the Governor and Secretary of State are required to make such repairs and improvements as in their judgment are deemed necessary, and to employ laborers to keep the mansion, garden, tomb and surroundings in a good state of repair. This act recites by way of preamble, that the property was at that date in a 'dilapidated condition.' It seems that nothing was ever done under this act in the way of repairs. And as the property was in a 'dilapidated condition' in 1860, you can readily imagine its condition now, after four years of a great civil war.

At the request of Major Wm. B. Lewis and myself, Major General THOMAS, of the United States Army, has ordered a preliminary survey of the Hermitage Property, and the report and plot are in my possession for your inspection. Impelled by a spirit of reverence for the illustrious dead, Gen. Thomas has generously had the tomb repaired and otherwise materially benefitted the property, for which he has the thanks of all good men. The flooring of the tomb has been raised and properly re-laid, and new cornices made, but the roof, which is of copper, leaks badly, and if not soon repaired will destroy the ceiling, flooring, &c. The mansion is much damaged from leaks in the roof and deficiency in the guttering. The ceiling and plastering are badly cracked, and in many places the plastering is falling off. Some of the joists have rotted from the same cause—the foundation has been undermined, and the brick walls cracked open in consequence. Should this condition of things continue another year, it will become necessary to partially tear down and rebuild the mansion.

The liability of the State on account of the Hermitage Property, principal and interest, now amounts to about seventy thousand ($70,000) dollars. I propose to the Legislature to lay off one hundred acres, including the tomb and mansion, and tender it to the Federal Government, or use it as a State institution for a 'Hotel des Invalides,' or asylum for invalid soldiers, similar to the one founded in Paris by the Emperor Napoleon. Let the remaining four hundred acres be sold, the debt against the State be discharged, and the surplus go towards the purchase of a mansion for the Governor of the State. I am informed that the large and convenient brick building in front of the Capitol is for sale, and I recommend its immediate purchase for that purpose. The great State of Tennessee should, by all means, provide a Governor's residence. The present incumbent of the Executive office would derive no advantage from such a purchase, but asks that it be made for the honor of the State and the accommodation of his successors in office, whoever they may be.

Your attention is especially called to the condition of affairs in the State Penitentiary, details of which will be given by the new Board of Inspectors, appointed to act with the newly appointed officer in charge of the Institution. A portion of the prison has been occupied by the United States military authorities for the past three years. I suggest the appointment of a joint special committee of your two houses, consisting of business men, who shall make a thorough investigation of affairs and report at once for your action. Meanwhile, in view of the fact that convicts are rapidly increasing since the Courts are being generally held, and no more ground can be had in the vicinity of the present Penitentiary for its enlargement, I revive the proposition, made in my former message, to establish branches at Knoxville and Memphis. The cost of building on a moderate scale would be saved to the State in fifteen years in the several items of transporting convicts, in the reduction of the cash market in each end of the State for provisions to subsist, and raw materials to keep the convicts employed in manufacturing—such as lumber, marble, iron, leather, &c. East Tennessee affords all these materials in abundance, while Memphis has the advantages of steamboat navigation, putting her in direct and speedy communication with the great North-West. Starting out on a moderate scale, the erection of buildings would furnish employment and cash wages to a large number of laborers and mechanics; and as there are several salaried officers attached to such institutions, it would distribute a large patronage in the three natural divisions of the State. In a short time the enlargement of these prisons could be carried on by the labor of the convicts, and the whole made self-sustaining, for it cannot be disguised that the demoralized condition of both our white and colored population will crowd the Penitentiary with convicts as the Courts go into operation.

I invite the early attention of the Legislature to the condition of the different Land Offices of the State. Of the five Registers elected at your late session, not one has qualified by taking the prescribed oath and executing the necessary bond. The reason is to be found in the fact that the fees are wholly inadequate to command the services of capable men. The consequence is that the records of the titles of all the lands granted by the State are in the possession of those into whose hands they accidentally fell during the war, who are under the obligations of neither oath nor bond. The interests endangered are immense, so much so that the law requires a bond of fifty thousand ($50,000) dollars from each Register. I recommend the consolidation of the several offices into one, and the concentration of all the records in the Capitol. If the fees of the office should still be deemed insufficient, as they probably will be, the office may be consolidated with that of Secretary of State, in which event the salary of that officer would have to be increased or a clerk furnished him.

Among the archives of the State captured in Georgia, I found the receipt of Brown, Bros. & Co., Bankers of New York, showing that, in November, 1861, G. W. Burton deposited forty-one thousand ($41,000) dollars in State Bonds to be forwarded to Brown, Shipley & Co., Bankers in Liverpool. In February following Burton assigned these Bonds to the Governor, Comptroller, and Treasurer of Tennessee. I wrote to this Liverpool house in July, making enquiries as to the state of these funds. They replied that the funds were in their hands, but they had recently received orders from Burton, forbidding them to pay over said funds to any one unless by his direction. This amount consists of forty-one Tennessee State Bonds of one thousand ($1,000) dollars each, which were given in satisfaction to the State of a defalcation on the part of Burton's brother, a former Secretary of State. I wrote at once to Hon. Thomas H. Dudley, the American Consul at Liverpool, sending all the necessary papers and directing him to demand the funds as belonging to the State of Tennessee. Payment was refused, and under my instructions Mr. Dudley brought suit. If justice be done Tennessee will recover these bonds, and if she fail it will be her duty to repudiate their payment. There will be no difficulty in identifying them as they are all numbered and their numbers are recorded in the Comptroller's office, as well as in the aforesaid receipt of Brown, Bros. & Co. The correspondence is at your disposal. I ask that you approve my action in this matter, and place at my disposal the means of carrying on this suit.

Your attention is called to the embarrassed condition of our people in most of the counties of the State, and prompt and positive legislation is recommended for their relief. In many of the counties they are not able to pay their taxes. In some counties they are overwhelmed with debts, created in part before the war, and partly during the war. I advise the passage of a law requiring that when real estate is sold for debt it shall bring two-thirds, or, if you please, three-fourths of its assessed value, or otherwise the sale shall be null and void. And I advise that further time shall be given for the redemption of lands sold for debt. If some such law is not enacted the lands in several counties will fall into the hands of a monied aristocracy—the most hateful as well as the most oppressive aristocracy in the world. I am not particular as to the measures of relief desired, but urge upon you appropriate legislation for the relief of our people, just emerging from the horrors of a four years' civil war. Most of you are of the people, and fresh from the people, and know what the wants of your constituents are. I, therefore, content myself with these general suggestions, trusting in your wisdom to arrange the details, if you deem them practicable.

Under the 7th section of the schedule to the Amended Constitution and your resolutions of May 20, 1865, I have filled a large number of vacancies in the County and District offices by appointment. The necessity for this action was imperative, as many of the counties were without a single officer. While I do not doubt the validity of these appointments myself, I am informed that others do. As these doubts may lead to litigation I recommend that the Legislature, out of abundant caution, declare the official acts of these officers valid, and thus cure any irregularities in the time and manner of their qualification.

In all parts of the country the friends of law and order are realizing the giant strides king Alcohol has made within the four years covering this rebellion, and the consequent demoralization directly attributable to the alarming increase of intemperance is now attracting the attention of the best members of society, and of the most profound statesmen of the country.

Good men and patriots can but hail every movement against this monster vice of the age as a pleasing augury of the times, and they must heartily approve every enterprise, and every act of legislation, designed to break the back of this monster whose victims multiply with such frightful rapidity, and whose power increases daily and nightly. Intemperance did its work in the army, and now that peace has been declared it is transferring its baneful influence to the walks of civil life, demoralizing the young and rising generation and sending to premature graves many of our best and most useful citizens. Throughout the length and breadth of Tennessee distilleries, wholesale and retail liquor dealers are multiplying with frightful rapidity, and the increasing evils arising therefrom, call upon the friends of humanity and of religion to educate the public mind in opposition to this vice, and, if possible, to stay the tide that now bids fair to overwhelm and degrade society. I suggest to the members of the General Assembly the imposition of such a tax upon the manufacture and sale of ardent spirits as will amount to prohibition of the traffic. Such a recommendation by the Executive, and such legislation by you, will be any thing but acceptable to those who are wedded to their cups and who are living by the traffic. So far as I am concerned I choose, nay, I *dare*, do what I think is right, looking to the good of my race and to the welfare of my country, leaving an enlightened and Christian people to pass upon the recommendation. Intemperance is blowing up steam-boats, upsetting stage-coaches, and, through the carelessness of drunken engineers or switch-tenders, it is bringing trains in collision or running them off the track. All this appalling loss of life and limb, resulting from the wickedness, carelessness and contempt for human life of the owners, directors, superintendents, agents and employees on the various lines of travel, is attributable, in a great degree, to the vice of intemperance. With the recklessness following upon the heels of a devastating war, we may look for corresponding slaughters in Tennessee. A general revision of our State laws in reference to railroads and steamboats, is believed to be needed. The least that can be done by the Legislature—and this ought to be satisfactory to the friends of morality and religion—is to authorize the prohibition of the traffic through the ballot-box once in two years, either by counties or civil districts. This would enable those who desire to rid themselves of the numerous and alarming evils of intemperance to do so legitimately, while it would enable those counties or civil districts who are 'joined to their idols' to cling to them, and suffer the consequences.

The Tennessee Hospital for the Insane, the most noble of the charitable institutions of the State, located in this vicinity, deserves your attention and still further aid. That noble State charity is an honor to Tennessee, erected after an inspection of most of the similar institutions in other States, at a cost of several hundred thousand dollars. In company with the Secretary of State, I have visited the institution, spent the day there, and by its efficient officers we were shown through all its in-door and out-door departments. In its condition and management we found it to be all that its friends and the friends of humanity could desire. I was astonished to learn that patients were coming in at an average of one for every thirty-six hours! But the ruinous effects of this wicked rebellion will be to fill all the Insane Asylums of the South with patients. For the details in regard to past operations and present necessities of this institution, I refer you to the report of the Superintendent and Chief Surgeon, an intelligent citizen, and a faithful and able officer.

I am unwilling to close this message without calling the attention of the Legislature to the measures proposed by President JOHNSON for the organization of the States recently in rebellion. The President stands up nobly for the Constitution and the Union of these United States, uninfluenced by any geographical considerations of North, South, East or West, and is therefore entitled to the sympathy and support of this General Assembly. So far as his purposes have been developed, I understand him to adhere to his principles and pledges made while Military Governor, both in regard to treason and traitors. His position from the beginning has been that loyal men must govern the revolted States; that conscious and intelligent traitors must be punished, and thus treason made odious. There is a moral sublimity in this position, and the loyal masses, North and South, will not fail to appreciate it, and will warmly and unswervingly sustain him against the assaults of extreme men. The hope of the country is suspended upon carrying out these measures of the President. His failure will involve horrors and evil consequences which all true patriots will shudder to contemplate. It is not to be denied, however, that many good and loyal men do not find themselves able to agree with the President in his policy, as indicated, toward the seceded States. But this difference may be wholly owing to a difference of information. The President stands at the focus of all political information disseminated from the South; and though there may be many influences surrounding his position calculated to distract and bias a mind less strong than his, yet, making all proper allowances, it still remains that his opportunities for forming a correct judgment upon the state of affairs in the South are vastly better than that of the great majority of men at the North, who are finding fault with and complaining of his position. Great weight, therefore, should be given to his opinions, which, so far as they have been expressed, are consolatory and refreshing to all loyal minds in the seceded States.

The Government will act wisely in guarding against precipitate action in the organization of the rebel States; and I even concede to the Government the right to demand guarantees and conditions for their future loyalty, as well as for the protection of Union men and the emancipated slaves. These demands are necessary to guard us against a new rebellion. This much is necessary to retain harmony in the ranks of the great Union party, without which there is no safety or security for the future. With these guarantees and conditions, the great North ought to be satisfied, as she does not thirst for vengeance. In other words, what we want, in this trying crisis, is perfect frankness and mutual forbearance among the great minds North and South, to whom the people look for light and leadership. The loyal States of the North have an interest of 300,000 graves in the rebel States, and an expenditure of untold millions of money in putting down a wicked and unauthorized rebellion, and they are entitled to a voice in arranging the terms upon which these States shall be restored.

Having thus placed before you, somewhat in detail, the information requisite to enable you to judge of the condition of the State, the evils which environ us, and the measures of legislation which I deem necessary for averting them and ridding ourselves of them, it remains for me but to invoke your attention to the consideration of those means by which, above all others, we may hope to restore order and prosperity to our country. And if one be more prominent than another, it is the necessity for earnest and cordial co-operation between the State and Federal Governments. To you especially, as Legislators, do the loyal people of Tennessee look for encouragement and counsel. Fresh from the people, you are presumed to know their wishes; and to your action in the halls of legislation will all eyes be turned, not only in Tennessee and the loyal States North, but in the late seceded States, for examples of what is befitting loyal men, and a great State redeemed, disenthralled and regenerated. I have, gentlemen, full confidence that you will prove yourselves equal to the emergency, and meet the anxious expectations of the public, both at home and abroad. Having embarked in a glorious and holy cause, I feel assured that you will rise above all selfish and personal considerations.

In conclusion, gentlemen, I again congratulate you upon the restoration of peace to our distracted country, and upon the favorable circumstances under which you have again assembled in the Capitol. On the issue of the struggle now closed were staked, as I honestly believe, the fruits of the battles for free government in all ages of the world, and in all climes; and this great country of ours, with its unequalled soil and climate, its beautiful rivers and lakes, and its wonderful mountain ranges, so admirably adapted for a Temporal Paradise for man, may be proudly pointed to by the nations of the earth as proof of the capacity of our race for self-government. We are now able to look England and France in the face without a blush, because our starry banner, undimmed and untorn, floats on every breeze, from Maine to the Gulf of Mexico, and from the Atlantic to the golden shores of the Pacific; inviting the oppressed of every clime to a Republic redeemed from the wild heresy of secession, from the machinations of its despotic conspirators; regenerated and purified by the struggle through which it has passed, now entering upon a career of prosperity, of freedom, of national greatness, so vast, so grand, that the splendor of its glory throws far into the shade all the pretensions of all the governments on earth! May ours remain an undivided nation; may our prosperity be increased; may our peace be uninterrupted, and may our liberties be eternal!

W. G. Brownlow."

The Legislature which convened in its First Adjourned Session on October 2, 1865 had been stripped of some influential leaders by means of resignations. There remained in the Senate only three members who had ever had previous experience in a Legislature, namely, DeWitt Clinton Senter, John Trimble, and Z. W. Frazier. There was stronger leadership in the House in both Radical and Conservative ranks, with the Conservatives having probably more members possessing both experience and ability. It was to this somewhat amateurish body that Governor Brownlow addressed his Message.

As will be observed, the Message was a cross between a political harangue and a Thanksgiving sermon. Inasmuch as the Parson was at present a politician and formerly a Methodist minister, possibly he possessed some qualifications in each field. Two of the recommendations set forth in the introductory part of the Message were totally disregarded by the Legislature, namely, the passage of few laws and a short session. Actually, two hundred and nineteen laws were passed, one hundred and nine resolutions adopted, and the session dragged along over a period of two hundred and thirty-nine days, the longest and stormiest in the annals of Tennessee history. Only sixty of the laws were classified as Public Laws, the remainder dealing largely with private affairs such as incorporating private concerns of which one hundred and five were mining companies. Space limitations forbid analysis, interpretation, or comment upon the trifling and even ridiculous measures that comprise by far the bulk of the legislation enacted.

As soon as the Parson in his Message had exhausted his vocabulary of gratitude to Providence and the Union soldiers, he turned to the issue that towered above all others in his estimation—tightening up the franchise law. The opposition strength that had been demonstrated in the recent Congressional election had chilled the marrow in his bones. Unless some sort of stop-gap could be fabricated, it was not only possible but highly probable that his regime would be terminated shortly. With this fearful idea staring him in the face, he opened the vials of his wrath upon the "conspirators and leaders" of the Confederacy and suggested that they deserved five or ten years of disfranchisement in order "to give them time to wash the blood of loyal men from their hands." He sounded the tocsin of legislative warfare that he proposed to launch against all those who did not bow to his imperious will and fanatical desires. By no means should the existing franchise law be repealed, he exclaimed; rather it "can be improved by amendments and additions."

Before the Legislature launched into any proposed revisions of the franchise law, a feeling of the pulse of legislative members appeared desirable. On account of numerous resignations, no real opportunity had been presented as to how newly elected members stood upon administration measures. Moreover, from time to time, no quorum was present. Uncertainty seems to have prevailed to such an extent that the Legislature recessed from December 16, 1865 to January 8, 1866. For the ensuing three days after reconvening, no quorum was present. So critical had this "no quorum" business become that House Speaker Heiskell ruled that it was proper to qualify new members without a quorum.[67] To add to the confusion and the "dragging of the feet" procedure, numerous contests arose as to the eligibility of newly elected members. So disorganized and disrupted had the Legislature become

---

[67] *House Journal*, First Adjourned Session, 1865–66, 249.

that practically no legislation, except on extremely minor matters, was enacted during the first three months of the session.

Despite continued interruptions, the consideration of various and sundry minor matters, the absence of a quorum, and the reception of several interim Messages from Governor Brownlow from time to time, an effort will now be made to trace the course of the touchy franchise question through the Legislature. The path is long, tedious, and devious.

One week after the convening of the Legislature, Representative William B. Lewis of Davidson County introduced a bill

"To repeal an act to limit the Elective Franchise."[68]

Major Lewis, an able Conservative who had sounded out public sentiment on the franchise question, incorporated in his bill provisions for repealing certain objectionable features and admitting to the privilege of suffrage all who subscribed to the oath prescribed in the Amnesty Proclamation of President Lincoln or President Johnson.[69] Consternation seized a number of the Radical members of the Lower House. Such a law would do away with the iron-clad oath as prescribed in the franchise act of June 5, said oath requiring former Confederates to swear that they took such oath "freely, voluntarily, and without mental reservation." No true Confederate could have taken this oath without committing perjury. Samuel Arnell, who had been the sponsor and driving force behind the existing franchise law, sprang up immediately and moved that the Lewis bill go to the table. From a parliamentary standpoint, the only member entitled to speak on the motion to table was the author of the original bill, Major Lewis. But Arnell, probably surmising that Lewis might swing some sledge-hammer blows in his argument that might "brain-wash" some of the recently-elected members whose sentiments were still unknown, immediately withdrew his motion to table the bill. After this parliamentary maneuver had succeeded, the bill was allowed to pass first reading and then was referred to the Committee on Judiciary where the bill was hermetically sealed up and salted away. This skirmishing occurred on October 9, 1865.

No further significant action on the franchise bill appears to have taken place in the House until January 24, 1866. On that date, Samuel Arnell, Chairman of the Select Committee on Franchise, submitted the report of the committee, to-wit:[70]

"The Select Committee on Franchise have directed me to report House Bill No. 436 to alter and amend an Act entitled an Act to limit the elective franchise, passed June 5th, 1865. The Committee have given to this subject the most careful and serious consideration, and have been impelled alone by

[68] *Ibid.*, 38.
[69] Ms. bill in State Archives, Nashville.
[70] *House Journal*, First Adjourned Session, 1865–66, 291.

a desire for the good of the State and country, and are of opinion, considering the unsettled condition of the State, that true friendship and loyalty to the Government of the United States is the proper basis for suffrage; they have no desire or wish to exclude any truly loyal man from the ballot-box."

Three hundred copies of the bill were ordered to be printed, and the bill was then set for special order a week later. Action on the bill was postponed again, but a day or so later six franchise bills were ordered to be read. Once more, a postponement was ordered by the close vote of 39 to 33.[71] On February 13 a lot of legislative jockeying took place. Various amendments to the major bill were proposed, whereupon a polite filibuster was attempted by successive motions to adjourn, such motions numbering eighteen. During all this melee, it was discovered that a number of members were "absent with authority," disclosing the fact that a quorum was not present.[72] However, adjournment was finally effected.

While House Bill No. 436 was quite drastic, even so it was apparently too lenient in the eyes of the Radicals toward ex-Confederates and Conservative Unionists. Consequently, the franchise thumbscrews were tightened down by the substitution of House Bill No. 505. The latter bill transferred more power into the hands of the Governor who by the existing law was already virtually a dictator in election matters. By a vote of 46 to 27, the substitute bill was passed on second reading.[73] When the bill came up for third reading on the following day, five members were in their seats but refused to vote. These five plus sixteen absent members broke the quorum. For several days this situation prevailed. On the afternoon of February 22, Representative L. M. Blackman of Monroe County decided to reprimand the absentees by offering the following resolution:[74]

"*Whereas*, the following named persons, to-wit:—J. R. Hood, of the County of Hamilton; A. E. Garrett, of Overton; A. R. Wynne, of Sumner; and Wm. Simmons, of Franklin, have, on divers occasions, shown the most utter contempt and disrespect, to this House, and to the State of Tennessee, by absenting themselves without leave, for the purpose of defeating an important measure, now before this body; and
Whereas, Such conduct is seditious and revolutionary in its character, and dangerous to free government, and is in contempt of this House, and disrespectful to the State of Tennessee; therefore,
Be It Resolved, That the aforesaid persons are hereby declared expelled from this Body, and their seats vacant; and that the Governor be requested to issue writs of election to fill said vacancies."

Before any formal action was taken on the Blackman resolution, resignations began to pour in to the Speaker. The initial exodus con-

---

[71] *Ibid.*, 320.
[72] *Ibid.*, 362–365.
[73] *Ibid.*, 371.
[74] *Ibid.*, 392.

sisted of five members, the most influential being William B. Lewis of Davidson County.[75] Major Lewis was "fed up" with the tactics and objectives of the Radical majority, and assigned the following reason for his resignation:[76]

"I have attended with a sincere purpose to facilitate a divided people, and to legislate for the best interest of the country. Recent events have reluctantly forced me to the conclusion that I can no longer be of service in this capacity. I am too old to be a party to the strife and discord now prevailing, and can not, in justice to my convictions of duty, participate in legislation which seems to meet the approval of a majority of this Body. . . ."

Shortly thereafter, there was "more of the same" in the nature of additional resignations. Headed by Representative A. A. Freeman of Haywood County, nine other Representatives tendered their resignations "to take effect *instanter*."[77] Without a quorum present, the House was stymied and could do nothing but mark time. At this juncture Speaker Heiskell, a Conservative Unionist, was granted a leave of absence for the ensuing six weeks. For Speaker *pro tem*, the Radical majority elevated to that post the Radical running mate of Arnell, namely, sixty-five year old James Mullins representing Bedford and Rutherford Counties.

With twenty-one resignations plus several "absences with leave," the House was without a quorum and could not, legally or constitutionally, transact any business. Despite the patent fact that the House did not have a quorum, yet the militant and persistent Radical, Samuel Arnell, moved that the House "recognize as a legal quorum two-thirds of the members occupying seats in this Body; provided that said two-thirds include a majority of the whole number entitled to seats in this Body. . . ."[78] Undoubtedly advised by competent legal counsel that such action would be held unconstitutional, Arnell later on withdrew his motion. He further displayed his intense partisanship by moving that the Franchise Bill be transmitted to the Senate,[79] although he must have known that such action by the House, without a quorum, would not stand up when legally contested.

By the resignation of the twenty-one members, the House had reached an *impasse*. Actually, the House was without a quorum from February 23 until April 12. In their desperation, growing out of the resignation strategy employed by the Conservatives, the Radicals reported the situation to Governor Brownlow who issued the following Proclamation:*

"It is my painful duty to announce that civil Government is again imperiled in the State of Tennessee. The events of the last

---

[75] *Ibid.*, 395–396.
[76] *Ibid.*, 396.
[77] *Ibid.*, 402–403.
[78] *Ibid.*, 403–404.
[79] *Ibid.*, 408.
* In [Brownlow's] *Proclamation Book*, 45–50.

three weeks give rise to serious apprehensions that a large portion of our people have not sufficiently recovered from the demoralizing effects of the late rebellion to enable them to appreciate the blessings of peace that their passions have not sufficiently cooled to enable them to avoid a relapse into anarchy or military rule.

A small majority of twenty-one members of the House of Representatives, by factious and Revolutionary proceedings, have succeeded in breaking up the Legislature and paralyzing the State Government. I characterise this conduct as revolutionary, because it was violative of the spirit of the Constitution and laws, and arrested the machinery of the State Government as effectually as if the same had been done by force of arms.

They have been able, under the construction of parliamentary law which prevailed in the House, to reduce it below what was held to be a quorum for the transaction of business, and the great body of the members of both Houses have gone to their homes, and legislation has entirely ceased.

When an important measure of State policy was proposed—a measure referred to, and a duty imposed upon, this Legislature by the amended Constitution—they either withdrew from their seats or remained and refused to answer to their names when called, the Speaker holding that a member in his seat, refusing to answer, was not present so as to be counted as part of the quorum.

After worrying the majority in this way for several weeks, and after the consultations of the Convention of the 22nd February, they have publicly announced their secession from the Legislature, through the Newspapers, in a document that will not fail to remind its readers of the address of the Legislature of 1861, who transferred the State to the Southern Confederacy. The pretext for this Legislative rebellion was a proposition to discharge the duty imposed upon the Legislature by the ninth section of the schedule to the amended Constitution, which provides for 'the limitation of the elective franchise' by this Legislature. There was nothing new or startling in this measure. From the earliest inception of the idea of reorganising a State Government, upon the ruins of the rebellion, the policy of disfranchising those who had lately destroyed the State Government, and attempted to destroy the National Government was deemed a necessity, and was adopted and rigidly executed. In the election held on the 22nd February, 1865, upon the adoption of the amended Constitution, rebels were all disfranchised by an oath which required every voter to swear that he was an enemy of the so-called Confederate States. The same course was pursued in the election for Governor and members of the General Assembly in March, 1865. The Millitary Governor naturally believed that those who had wantonly destroyed the Government were not the proper persons to rebuild it, or to administer it when re-established. This policy and principle of disfranchisement was a feature of the amended Constitution approved by the qualified voters of the State. No subject has been more thoroughly discussed and understood by all classes for the last year, than this subject of disfranchising the disloyal. Several of the seceding members were also members of the Convention which adopted it into the schedule, and sustained it before the people, and accepted Office under it, and are therefore estopped from denying its binding force. All of them had been elected under a law or proclamation disfranchising rebels. The pretense that the measure was sprung upon them suddenly, is therefore most manifestly a subterfuge to cover up the attempt at disorganization.

The resigning members appeal to their Constituents to sustain them, and most of them are announced as candidates for re-election to the places they have just made vacant under a pledge, of course, again to withdraw from their seats, and again to break up the Legislature. This discloses the whole plan of the conspiracy. They ask their constituents to approve their act, and to send them back to repeat it. This will place their constituents in the attitude of disorganizers—commit them to a rebellion against the State Government, and render futile any attempt to fill the vacancies by writs of election, as the same routine would be repeated. The danger to the State is therefore imminent. Should the civil Government fail, the Millitary authorities will take control of the State, And it is not likely that the General Government will, at an early day, permit a people who will have displayed such incapacity for self-Government to attempt another State organization. Nor is it likely, if the effort should be permitted, that the different divisions of the State will agree upon a new Constitution, and discord and a separation may follow. If the plan of the seceding members, now so manifested, is successful, many of the important laws already passed, including those conferring important civil rights upon freedmen can never go into effect. No appropriation bill can be passed; the Penitentiary, Lunatic

Asylum and other State institutions must be broken up and abandoned; and the interest accruing on the debts of the State and all other expenses requiring an appropriation must remain unpaid. The credit of the State will be destroyed, and the bonds of the State already appropriated must be depreciated, so as to fail of the objects of their issuance. Emigrants will shun a State in such confusion and discredit, and capital will seek investment in more promising localities, and thus the brightest hopes of the State will be blighted. Even if the conspirators should fail of success, incalculable mischief has already been done to the State. Eight millions of her bonds are soon to be thrown upon the market.

The ruinous depreciation of her credit consequent upon a disorganized condition of the State, inflicts a deep injury, not only upon the bondholders, but upon our works of internal improvement, dependent now upon a sale of our bonds to enable them to revive their operations.

Our political prospects, too are severely injured. By the acts of a rebelious population we have lost our representation in the Council of the Nation. Our Senators and Representatives are in Washington asking admission to seats in Congress. That body is watching all our movements with a view of determining whether we have an established government or not, and whether those Senators have been sent there by a Government capable of maintaining its existence and authority. They may now conclude that our people are not in a temper for self government. Certainly the opponents of our representation will be furnished by our present condition with an argument against our admission. Nor is the moral effect upon the reputation of our State and people less to be deplored. A large portion of our people, Just out of rebellion, are proffessing reconstructed loyalty, while a portion of their representatives display not only a rebellious spirit but a disregard for the solemn obligations of legislators and are unmindful of that dignity and sense of honor which should always characterize the Statesman.

But aside from the injury to the moral, political and financial character of the State and the danger of dissolution, the actual loss to the State Treasury, is immense. Nearly a month has already been lost by the Legislature from business. Another month must transpire before the vacant seats can be filled by election, and then some days must elapse before the members can appear in their seats. Estimating the expense to the Legislature of $650 per day, and a loss of seventy days from business, and a total loss of $45,500 is the result even if the conspirators should succeed no further in their designs. The loyal people of the State will not fail to hold the guilty parties and their advisers responsible for this worse than useless expenditure.

It may be that the constituents of the resigning members may re-elect them or others pledged to a like course, and thereby render this proclamation useless, but the responsibility shall be upon them.

The Constitution requires that 'When vacancies happen in either House, the Governor, for the time being, shall issue writs of election to fill said vacancies.' Therefore, The following representatives having in a public printed address announced their withdrawal from the General Assembly, thereby leaving their seats vacant, viz.: W. B. Lewis, Rep. from Davidson; Samuel P. Walker, Rep. from Shelby; A. E. Garrett, Rep. from Overton; Asa Faulkner, Rep. from Warren; A. A. Freeman, Rep. from Haywood; J. T. Thomas, Rep. from Coffee, Grundy and Van Buren; Abner A. Steele, Rep. from Marshall; Wm. B. Scales, Rep. from Dyer, and Lauderdale; A. R. Wynne, Rep. from Sumner; Thomas H. Bledsoe, Rep. from Lincoln; Wm. Barton, Rep. from Cannon; P. Williams, Rep. from Carter; C. N. Ordway, Rep. from Giles; N. Brandon, Rep. from Stewart; W. K. Poston, Rep. from Shelby; M. E. W. Dunnaway, Rep. from Bedford; W. W. Willis, Rep. from Hawkins; A. D. Nicks, Rep. from Dickson; James R. Hood, Rep. from Hamilton; Wm. Simmons, Rep. from Franklin.

Whereas, Also, a vacancy has occurred in the said House of Representatives by the resignation of the Hon. Jos. H. Travis, Representative from Henry County; and,

Whereas, Also, a vacancy has occurred in said House of Representatives by the resolution of the said House that the seat of the Hon. A. C. Gillum, Representative from the County of Jackson was vacant; and

Whereas, also, a vacancy has occurred in the said House of Representatives by the death of the Hon. Wallace Waters, Representative from the County of Madison; and

Whereas, Also, a vacancy has occurred in the Senatorial branch of said General Assembly by the death of the Hon. B. R. Peart, Senator from the Counties of Robertson, Montgomery and Stewart; And,

Whereas, Also, a vacancy has occurred in the Senate aforesaid, by the resignation of John W. Bowen, Senator from the Counties of Smith and Sumner;

Now therefore, I, William G. Brownlow, Governor of the State of Tennessee, do hereby command the Sheriffs, Coroners, or other Officers authorized by law to open and hold elections, at all the places of voting in the respective Counties of Davidson, Shelby, Overton, Warren, Haywood, Coffee, Grundy, Van Buren, Marshall, Dyer, Lauderdale, Sumner, Lincoln, Cannon, Franklin, Carter, Giles, Stewart, Bedford, Hawkins, Dickson, Hamilton, Robertson, Montgomery and Smith, on Saturday, the 31st day of March, 1866, for the purpose of filling the vacancies from said Counties respectively, as hereinbefore set forth. Said Sheriffs shall make returns of said elections according to law.

In testimony Whereof, I have hereunto subscribed my (SEAL) name, and caused the great seal of the State to be attached, at the Department in the City of Nashville, This 3rd day of March 1866.

By the Governor, W. G. BROWNLOW.
A. J. FLETCHER, Secretary of State."

The extraordinary event—deadlocking legislation by breaking a quorum through resignations—put the issue strictly up to Governor Brownlow to step into the breach. This he did with promptness and firmness as exemplified by the language and tenor of the above Message. He charged the "seceders" with a desire to paralyze the State government and to block the return of Tennessee to the Federal Union. He mentioned certain disasters that would result unless the Legislature acted upon such imperative matters as maintaining the credit of the State and providing legislative appropriations for various State institutions. Included in his Message was a warning that military power would take over unless civil government could and would demonstrate its readiness and ability to uphold the due processes of law through constitutional agencies, one of which was the Legislature. Denouncing the resignation strategy as a sort of "second rebellion," he called for special elections in the various counties to elect legislative members to fill the vacant seats. This "by-election," incidentally, provided an opportunity for a test of the strength of Radical and Conservative sentiments of the voters.

What Brownlow failed to perceive was the swelling tide of opposition to his extreme policies regarding the privilege of voting. Not only

Confederates, but Conservative Unionists were propounding the query that Cassius put to Brutus regarding Caesar:

> "Why, man, he doth bestride the narrow world,
> Like a Colossus; and we petty men
> Walk under his huge legs, and peep about
> To find ourselves dishonorable graves.
> ....
> Upon what meat doth this our Caesar feed,
> That he is grown so great?"

Brownlow's threat of military occupation, in the event men were elected or re-elected whose main motives would be "to break up the Legislature," fell upon stony ground. His strategy to purge the Legislature of militant opposition to his franchise bill in the "by-election" went to naught, because only four Radicals were elected. Twelve of the members who had resigned were returned with rather significant majorities. All told, there were twenty-four seats in the House of Representatives to be filled, but twenty-one of the Representatives-elect were denied seats. But even so, with the election of four Radicals and the exclusion of all returned Conservatives, the House finally mustered up enough members to constitute a quorum by seating three of the Radicals, W. H. Shephard of Hawkins County, Hiram Morris of Cannon County, and D. A. Nunn of Haywood County.[80]

According to the *official* record,[81] Governor Brownlow submitted at least one superfluous Message to the Legislature. Greatly disturbed by the results of the special elections to fill vacancies in the Legislature, he rushed the following Message* to the Legislature under date of April 13:

"STATE OF TENNESSEE,
EXECUTIVE DEPARTMENT,
Nashville, April 13, 1866.

GENTLEMEN OF THE SENATE AND HOUSE OF REPRESENTATIVES:

The extraordinary circumstances under which you resume your seats after the untoward events of the past six weeks, make it my duty, as I conceive, to send you this communication, giving such information as I possess concerning the state of the government.

---

[80] *House Journal*, First Adjourned Session, 1865–66, 424.

[81] *Ibid.*, 428.

Author's note. Under date of "Friday Morning, April 13, 1866," the *House Journal* carries the following item: "A Message from the Governor was received and read." On the preceding afternoon, April 12, the same official record discloses that "House Bill 505 passed third reading; Ayes, 41; Noes, 15." Whether or not the "Parson" was a day late with his admonition depends upon the accuracy or inaccuracy of the "timing" as set forth in the above *House Journal*. House Bill 505, of course, was the Franchise Bill.

* *Senate Journal*, First Adjourned Session, 1865–66, 423–426.

Two elections have occurred since your deliberations were broken up by the action of a portion of the House; the one a general election of county officers on the 3d of March, the other a special election of twenty-four Representatives and two Senators, in different parts of the State. The result of these elections, carefully studied, will furnish you much instruction in the discharge of your present duties. It will appear that the public safety absolutely requires a thorough revision of the present suffrage laws. While it is true that in many counties in West Tennessee a very creditable, and in some instances, a successful effort was made to execute the act of the 5th of June last, in some counties of that section, and in the greater portion of Middle Tennessee, the law was totally disregarded. In the county of Davidson, for instance, where there has been so much clamor against the law, charging that three-fourths of the people were disfranchised by it, the aggregate vote exceeded, by over a thousand, the average vote in county elections before the passage of the law. Candidates in many localities openly and publicly based their claims to election upon wounds received and losses incurred in the cause of rebellion, and were often successful.

In the special election nearly all of those who had by revolutionary conduct broken up the Legislature and paralyzed the government were candidates for re-election, under pledges to repeat their performances unless the majority will yield to them the control of your proceedings. With two exceptions in West Tennessee, one in Middle Tennessee, and two in East Tennessee, they have been returned by large majorities. This result may well excite the apprehensions of the friends of civil government. It shows that not only the revolting representatives, but their constituents, are ready to destroy the State government. The fear expressed in my proclamation of the 3d of March, that 'our people have not sufficiently recovered from the demoralizing effects of the late rebellion to appreciate the blessings of peace,' is thus painfully realized.

As the legality and propriety of my proclamation of the 3d of March in ordering some of the elections have been questioned, and may come incidentally before you in determining the qualifications of the new members, I will present briefly the grounds of my action.

The Constitution provides that 'where vacancies *happen* in either House, the Governor for the time being shall issue writs of election to fill such vacancies.' No particular form of vacating a seat is prescribed. It is sufficient if the seat is not occupied, and no legitimate excuse or reason given for its remaining so. If a member wilfully and persistently refuses to occupy his seat and perform any of the duties of his place, the seat is in fact and in law, vacant. It may be the duty of the House to notify the Executive when a vacancy happens, but when the House is disorganized or not in session, it becomes his duty to know when to act. Upon this construction of the Constitution and this view of my official duty, I issued writs of election to fill the seats of those who had absented themselves from the House for the declared purpose of disorganizing it, and who had publicly proclaimed that they had withdrawn from your deliberations. This much I deem proper to say in justification of my action. You are the exclusive judges of the qualification and election of your members, and I only announce my own action and the reason which governed it, and refrain from any recommendation as to the rights of the newly elected members. The extreme peril of the crisis in which we find ourselves will, however, justify me in calling your attention to the fact that a number of members are asking seats in your body under a pledge, endorsed by their constituents, to disorganize the Legislature by revolutionary conduct. I therefore invite your serious attention to the grave question it presents.

The objections to a stringent suffrage law are plausible, and made under the guise of equal rights and republican liberty, but experience will show that those who, but a few months since, were engaged in the work of destroying all government, and who succeeded in destroying our State government, and only failed to destroy the national government by being overpowered by force of arms, are not yet safe depositories of the elective franchise. It is not a question as to who shall be *dis*franchised, but as to who shall be *en*franchised. Those who committed treason disfranchised themselves. To restore them at once to the right of suffrage is simply to hand over to them that government which was organized in spite of them upon the ruins of the one they had destroyed. This is now what they demand. The red-handed marauder who has inflicted the most frightful wounds upon the body politic, claims that he, of all others, is the proper surgeon to heal them. They claim the exclusive right to destroy and build up—to kill and to restore to life. You alone, gentlemen, can dispose of this question. In a crisis like this, we should adopt no timid course. Let us fearlessly perform our part, and leave the result to God. I invoke your prompt attention to this vital subject. We can have no hope that capital or loyal emigrants will come within our borders until they are assured of protection against rebel rule. I am assured that the tide of emigration now flowing into Missouri, is owing to the ample protection given to them in that State by the disfranchisement of the destroyers of law and order.

I have been compelled, by a sense of humanity, to direct the Comptroller to issue his warrant upon the Treasury for a considerable sum, without any act of appropriation, to supply the convicts of the Penitentiary with the necessaries of life. I am informed that they are again in danger of suffering. The agent of the institution is procuring supplies on credit, relying upon you to meet the payment. The Hospital for the Insane is in like necessitous circumstances, and the salaries of the officers of both institutions are unpaid. Your early action in relief of both is an absolute necessity.

I apprehend that sufficient provision has not yet been made to meet the July interest on the State debt proper, and upon the bonds loaned to such railroads as may fail to pay their coupons then falling due. I recommend the temporary appropriation of the funds realized by the sale of the specie captured with the remains of the Bank of Tennessee for that purpose, without permanently withdrawing it from the school fund.

After mature deliberation, I have determined to recommend to your favorable consideration the remuneration of loyal citizens of this State for losses sustained by the occupation of the country by the national armies. The passage of the so-called ordinance of secession, and the assumed transfer of the State to the so-called Southern Confederacy, placed Tennessee in the attitude of rebellion, and her people in the position of enemies to the national government. The consequence was that upon the occupancy of the State by the national forces, our people were treated as enemies, with but little discrimination between the loyal and disloyal. Their lands and houses were occupied, their property impressed or destroyed, and their provisions consumed. In East Tennessee this was done from necessity, by an unsupplied army, to an extent that reduced the people to absolute suffering. Thus far the Federal government, classing Tennessee with the rebel States, and unwilling to assume the losses incurred in the whole South, has not regarded the applications of our loyal people for remuneration. I understand that similar losses by the citizens of Indiana, Pennsylvania and Ohio have been promptly assumed, and yet the nation knows, and the world knows, that a more loyal people than those in Tennessee who remained steadfast to the national cause, through so long and terrible an ordeal, are not to be found in the Union. But I cannot and will not lose confidence, in the justice and magnanimity of the American people. I believe they will yet cheerfully repay the loyal sufferers among our people, many of whom were deprived of their property by the national forces, while they were themselves absent fighting for the national cause. But you, gentlemen, can afford present relief, relying upon the General Government hereafter to assume and pay these just and meritorious claims.

I recommend that proper officers be appointed to ascertain and audit those claims, and that the bonds of the State of denominations from $50 to $100 be issued in payment. I am aware that this proposition will meet with fierce opposition from those who would give preference to the millions of debt contracted by the usurped State Government, or by Rebel Quartermasters. I am also aware that objection will come from a better class upon the ground of so considerable an increase of the State debt; but if the American people are just, they will assume the amount long before it falls due, and, upon principle, treat the suffering loyalists of Tennessee, as they have treated the loyalists of other States.

In view of the protracted length of your session, caused, in part by difficulties attending a reorganization of the State Government, but chiefly by the refractory and rebellious conduct of a minority, you will pardon me for expressing the hope that you will proceed promptly and vigorously with the necessary legislation, not only as a matter of economy to the Treasury, but to give quiet and repose to the people by the final and permanent establishment of a State policy which shall give security to the loyal, and restrain the disloyal.

WM. G. BROWNLOW."

In all probability little attention was paid to the above "rush" Message, inasmuch as the real crisis had been reached and passed on the day preceding receipt of the Parson's admonition. There can be little or no doubt, however, but that its contents were already known to the Radical leaders and the Message was simply recorded in the official proceedings as a matter of course. Now, that the "Rubicon had been crossed," namely, the passage of the franchise bill by the stubborn House of Representatives, the tension became markedly relaxed. All along the Senate had been predominantly Radical, and no fears were entertained as to the passage of the franchise bill by that body. Actually, the Senate dispensed for the time being with the reading of the Governor's Message.[82]

From March 5 to April 16, the Senate was without a quorum [83] and consequently had not been able to transact any business. Upon April 17 a roll call showed seventeen Senators present, this number constituting a quorum.[84] During the "by-election" in March, two new Senators had been elected, Cave Johnson and A. E. Garrett, neither of whom was permitted to be seated. Political animosity and deep-seated prejudice prevailed, especially in the case of Johnson. He had been elected without opposition in his district. His certificate of election was accompanied by proof that he had taken the amnesty oath and had received a pardon by President Lincoln. Despite these uncontested and uncontradicted facts, his case was promptly referred to the Senate Committee on Elections. An extract from the Committee Report will disclose just how the Radicals disposed of any "inconvenient item":[85]

". . . The claimant has been for more than a quarter of a century a prominent, distinguished citizen of Tennessee and, for many years in succession, a member of Congress of the United States, a member at one time of a cabinet of a President of the United States and, therefore, a citizen of great weight and influence throughout the State; that his weight of character and influence was given in behalf of the rebellion, involving also, necessarily the overthrow and destruction of the Government and Constitution of the State, therefore,
A majority of the Committee, in view of the facts herein stated, and in the present situation of the State of Tennessee, are of opinion that the claimant is disqualified to sit in the Senate of Tennessee. . . ."

It is questionable whether there can be found in the annals of Tennessee history an instance of a more pronounced case of political malignancy.

On April 18, the second day after a Senate quorum had been obtained, the Franchise Bill which had been passed by the House was received by the Senate. The bill passed routinely first reading and was referred to the Committee on the Franchise.[86] At this juncture, the Senate resumed consideration of a franchise bill of its own brew that had been introduced by the Committee on the Franchise on February

[82] *Senate Journal*, First Adjourned Session, 1865–66, 428.
[83] *Ibid.*, 406–417.
[84] *Ibid.*, 418.
[85] *Ibid.*, 453–454.
[86] *Ibid.*, 430–431.

9.[87] Two unsuccessful efforts were made to amend the bill, one amendment providing that "Free Men of Color" be debarred from voting for ten years, while the other amendment provided that the pending Senate bill "be in lieu of all other bills now pending before this Legislature on this question." Thereupon the Senate bill was put on third reading and defeated by a vote of 16 to 5.[88]

Inasmuch as the Radical-controlled Senate had been unable to agree upon its own franchise measure, recourse was then had to the House-approved bill. Senator John G. Carrigan from the counties of Franklin and Lincoln attempted to soften up the stringent oath appearing in the House bill by requiring the prospective voter to swear that he would support the Constitution of the United States and the Constitution of Tennessee; that he would oppose any effort looking toward State secession from the Union; and that he would aid in the restoration of civil government in the State.[89] The acceptance of Senator Carrigan's proposal would have permitted former Confederates to exercise their voting privilege; consequently, Senator Carrigan saw his amendment defeated by the Radicals by a vote of 14 to 4.[90] After two other ineffectual efforts to amend the bill, third and final reading was called and the bill was passed by a vote of 13 to 6.[91]

What was apparent to most of the legislators was that the bitterly contested measure was loaded with political dynamite. As one means of attempting to "square" themselves against future attacks regarding their votes on this particular bill, a number of legislators resorted to filing protests and explanations. Typical of such devices was that of Senator W. R. Hall from the counties of Gibson, Carroll, and Dyer. His position was set forth in positive language, even though his assigned reasons were couched in phraseology devoid of any basic knowledge of such elementary things as spelling, capitalization, punctuation, or sentence structure. Here is a verbatim copy of his effusion:[92]

"Mr. Speaker
and Gentlemen of the Senate—
in recording my vote on this very important Bill—I most respectfully ask leave to give some of the reasons why I shall vote most unhesitatingly as I do.
It is well Known to you Sir—as well as many members of this honorable body—That There is Some clauses in this Bill that I donot fully concur in—and should have been pleased to have had them modified to Some Extent

[87] Ibid., 328 and 473.
[88] Ibid., 473.
[89] Ibid., 479.
[90] Ibid., 479.
[91] Ibid., 483.
[92] Ms. document in State Archives, Nashville.
Author's note. Senator Hall's explanation, after textual surgery by somebody who had at least a fifth grade education, was incorporated in the *Senate Journal*, First Adjourned Session, 1865-66, 483-485.

But when I look around and See the isue So distinctly made by the Two Parties in this State—
it is Easy for me to deside—
I behold on the one Side—anarchests Confusionest and Extremest—
Men Banded together—that has drenched our beloved Country in Blood—
And filled our Land with Widows and Orphans—
On the other I find the great Union or Republican Party—that has carried the Flag of our Country Successfully and Triumphantly threw the reasant mity Rebellion.

This is My Party—whare I shall be found—Now as Ever in harmony with its Majority—
Altho the Bill under consideration may not fill my wishes to the letter I am willing to pass it—and take my chances for a Subsequent Bill covering the points I may think necessary to purfect this one—Believing as I do—That the National reputation of this State—now depend upon the action of this Legislature in the disfranchisement of all dis-Loyal and the infranchisement of all Loyal Citizens Either Black or White—and believing further that None but Loyal Men that has stood firmly to the Union—and the Flag of our Country in her hour of Trial Shold vote or hold office—under any circumstances untill the government that they have used Every Effort in thair power to distroy Shall have ben fuly restored to its former grandeur—by its Friends—I Shall Therefore vote—*Yea*—

Hall"

A viewpoint diametrically opposed to the preceding explanation was a protest filed by Senator B. Frazier representing the counties of Knox and Roane. His reasons for voting against the franchise bill were as follows:[93]

"Mr. Speaker—I respectfully ask leave to enter upon the Journal of the Senate some of the most prominent reasons that impelled me to vote against the Bill No. 505, known as the House Franchise Bill.

First.—The bill, in my opinion, in effect operates as a punishment upon a large class of citizens, for offenses committed long before the passage of the act, and is therefore *ex post facto*, and, if so, is expressly forbidden by the Constitution.

Second.—The bill proposes to lessen, abridge and take away from a large majority of the people of the State, a cherished privilege, without trial or conviction of any offense, in direct contravention of that section of the Constitution which declares that no man shall be disseized of his liberties or privileges, but by the judgment of his peers, and the law of the land.

Third.—The legal effect of the bill will be to invest a minority of the people of the State with exclusive power and authority to make laws, levy taxes and impose burdens, exactions and requirements upon a very large majority of the citizens, without their consent, thus establishing an irresponsible aristocracy in direct conflict with a republican form of government, and subversive of the Constitution of both the State of Tennessee and the United States.

Fourth.—The bill, in my judgment, is in direct contravention *of* and conflict *with* the spirit and intention of the several proclamations of amnesty and pardon, issued by the President of the United States, and, in its execu-

---

[93] *Senate Journal*, First Adjourned Session, 1865–66, 493–495.

tion, will violate the plighted faith of the government towards a large portion of the citizens affected by the bill.

Fifth.—The bill proposes to grant powers to the Executive of the State that are, in my opinion, dangerous, and subversive of liberty.

Sixth.—The bill proposes to place in the hands of the Executive the power to establish tribunals in every county in the State to determine from time to time, the extent of the elective franchise in each county, and to adjudicate and determine the right of each citizen to exercise that privilege, from whose decision there is no appeal—a tribunal utterly unwarranted by the Constitution, and in conflict with the laws and usages of the State.

Seventh.—The seventh section of the bill appears to me to have been drawn indefinite and uncertain, and liable to be construed to admit all the colored soldiers from Tennessee to the ballot-box, and this must be the construction intended to be put upon it by the friends of the bill from their persistent refusal to permit it to be altered or amended in this particular; and, if such construction is to be put upon this section, it will admit to the ballot-box a class of persons heretofore excluded by the Constitution and in direct opposition to the will of the majority of the present qualified voters of the State, and is making a distinction between the white and the colored man, inconsistent with the provisions of the late act of Congress, known as the Civil Rights Bill.

Eighth.—The main provisions of the bill appear to me to be in direct conflict with that part of the oath required to be taken by every member of this Legislature, in which they swear 'that they will not vote for any bill injurious to the people or consent to any act or thing whatever that will have a tendency to lessen or abridge their rights and privileges.'

Last.—The bill, as a whole, is cumberous, expensive and unnecessary, as the object aimed at could have been attained without any violent departure from the Constitution, by adopting a different policy altogether.

For these reasons, and others not mentioned, I was compelled to vote against the bill, and I hereby enter my protest against its passage, believing as I do, that it is a dangerous departure from the fundamental principles of Republican Government, and a direct violation of the Constitution of the State of Tennessee.

B. FRAZIER."

Before any analysis is made of the highly controversial law that had been enacted, a bit of legislative "local color" will demonstrate how tempers flared and difficulties arose while the bill was pending in the House. "Parson" Brownlow's *Knoxville Whig* [94] reproduced an article from a Radical newspaper, the *Nashville Press and Times*, which discloses a bit of the brawling that took place on the floor of the House of Representatives:

"THE REBEL SPIRIT DISPLAYED

We copy a calm and temperate account of the late disgraceful conduct in the Tennessee House of Representatives, from the Nashville Press and Times, and call attention to it, and to the votes of certain East Tennessee members who are misrepresenting the sentiments of the people of their counties. Several members acted worse in going out of the House and

---

[94] *Knoxville Whig*, February 28, 1866.

refusing to vote, than those who remained and voted with the revolutionists. The conduct of the minority was the more disgraceful as they had had the whole week for discussion—They continued their fillibustering on the next day, walking about the Hall, with their hats on, and cursing and swearing, evincing the true rebel spirit.

The case has been stated to us by parties who were in the House and witnessed all that passed, and they make it stronger than the Nashville paper does. While the members were refusing to vote and walking out, talking and swearing, Col. Mullins, of Bedford, an old gray-haired man, and a staunch loyalist, obtained the floor and said: 'There are members in the House who refuse to answer to their names, and there are others walking out to avoid voting. I believe it to be the result of a previous agreement, perhaps a caucus arrangement.'

To this Mr. Speaker Heiskell took offence, when, it was thought, he had no just cause for it, and in a most excited and angry tone, enquired: 'Does the member from Bedford intend to insinuate that the Chair was privy to any such arrangement.'

Col. Mullins replied in a spirited manner: 'I do, and would as soon suspect the Speaker as any one else.'

The Speaker sprang from the chair, and pronounced the member from Bedford 'A G-d d--d old liar and a d--d thief,' at the same time throwing his hammer with violence at Mullins, and missing the head of John Caldwell, of East Tennessee, about two feet.

Col. Mullins retorted with emphasis, in a hard tone of voice: 'You are a G-d d--d liar, a d--d old scoundrel, a partial presiding officer, and one of the conspirators.' Mullins started towards the Speaker, with his hand in his pocket, and a personal collision was alone prevented by a rush of the members between the parties.

The foregoing is the version given by members of the House and by citizens. We make no comments but give the facts to the public as they have been reported by eye-witnesses to the scene."

On the day following the enactment of the franchise law, the Conservative *Republican Banner* of Nashville issued an incisive but highly prophetic statement as to what such a law would bring forth in the future. The thirteen "Black Knights" were singled out for severe denunciation, while the mere half-dozen Senators who resisted the passage of the measure were duly applauded. Here is the bill of indictment:[95]

"At fifteen minutes before eleven o'clock, on yesterday morning—mark the day, the hour and the minute with a black stone—the Senate of Tennessee completed the deep damnation of legislative infamy, begun in the House of Representatives, by the passage of the Franchise Bill.

It is a measure which, if carried into successful effect, places the entire State Government in the hands of the few bad men who now possess it, and who use it for their own profit, as they would use a horse or an ox.

---

[95] *Republican Banner*, May 4, 1866.

Author's note. The names and counties represented by the various Senators and Representatives who cast votes on the franchise bill may be found by consulting the *Appendix* containing the list of legislative members of the "Brownlow" legislature, 1865–1866.

The process is simple. No one is to be permitted to vote except such as are chosen by commissioners selected by the Governor. We print the bill in full elsewhere. Its wantonness is borne upon its face. You may not recognize a harlot upon the street more easily than the lust which inspired it, the depravity which perfected it, and the viciousness which pervades it. It needs no argument to set forth to the unbiased mind the crime of those who voted for it. We give the disgusting list in full. It reads as follows:

Aldridge, Bosson, Cate, Case, Cypert, Hall, Keith, McElwee, Nelson, Powell, Senter, Trimble and Mr. Speaker Frierson.

Each one of these persons forfeits the right to be considered a citizen of Tennessee or an honest man. No honest man would cast such a vote; and no honest man can respect those who have cast it.

We implore an outraged people to bear this fresh indignity with fortitude. If the individuals whose names are recorded above, dare to go home, let them go in peace. We would not harm a hair of their head. Their own infamy, and the scorn of their fellowmen, will be sufficient punishment.

And now, a word for the true men, who stood by the right, and did all they could to avert the degradation to which we have been subjected.

There they are—

Carrigan, McFarland, Frazier of Knox, Muse, McKinney and Smith.

Blessed are the peace makers; and great shall be the reward of the faithful Steward! Messrs. McKinney, Smith, and Muse have been hithertofore acting with the Radicals; but in this record at least they have written themselves in lines of gold. We thank them in the name of the people.

And we thank all of them—though they be only six—and the time will come when the other thirteen will wish from the bottom of their hearts that they had done likewise; when they will cry to the mountains for concealment and shelter."

What were the provisions of the amended franchise law which had precipitated and prolonged one of the bitterest fights ever waged upon the floor of the General Assembly of Tennessee? Why was it thought by the Radicals that the year-old franchise law needed amending? To answer the second query first, it needs only to be recalled that the county elections held in March, 1866,—while the Legislature was still in session—threw a bombshell into the Brownlow camp and his camp-followers. The Conservatives had made a clean sweep of practically every such office in Middle and West Tennessee. Most of these county officials had been previously appointed by either Andrew Johnson (while Military Governor) or Brownlow and were, as a matter of course, men of Union sentiment. Now, that they had been swept out of office and replaced largely by ex-Confederates or Conservative Unionists, it was conclusive to Brownlow that the existing franchise law needed drastic amendment. In a word, too many anti-Brownlow men were voting! Under the existing law, the County Court Clerk acted as registrar and the County Sheriff held the election. These two local officials held the key positions in election contests and, as a result of the March election, these highly strategic positions would henceforth be in the hands of ex-Confederates and Conservative Unionists.

Moreover, Brownlow himself knew that he was heading a minority party, for his own organ [96] had stated that the "Union Party" in Tennessee numbered about 40,000 voters while the ex-Confederates and their sympathizers numbered about double that number. Like Belshazzar of old, Brownlow "saw the handwriting on the wall—thou art weighed in the balances and found wanting." Something had to be done to keep the opposition away from the ballot-box!

Some sort of political juggernaut had to be fabricated and put in operation if the Radicals were to remain in control. Control of the election machinery, therefore, throughout the State was a *sine qua non*, and that must be done *NOW!* To that end, Brownlow and his adherents turned all their efforts which, after a terrific battle, terminated in their favor through a tightening up of the law governing voting privileges.

With a tongue of flame, Governor Brownlow castigated, condemned, and damned the "disloyal traitors" who, of course, were those who opposed his tyrannical regime. With the zeal of a crusader, he called for such revision of the franchise law as would bar "those with bloody hands from depositing their ballots." Comparable to a bunch of trained seals, the ultra-Radical members of the Legislature rallied to the Parson's Macedonian call and whipped into shape a revision of the franchise law that closed the ballot-box to an estimated nineteen-twentieths of the voting population of the State.[97]

The new franchise law [98] turned over to Brownlow lock, stock, and barrel all voting privileges by means of a transparent device. Under the former law, County Court Clerks registered the voters and attended to other routine duties concerned with local election machinery. Those county officials, of course, were elected locally and Brownlow's disappointment at recent election returns led him to suspect that too much conservatism had prevailed, and that dyed-in-the-wool UNIONISM had not been strictly regarded as the "Open Sesame" to the ballot-box. To close this gap in the old law, the new law simply placed the appointment and dismissal of "Commissioners of Registration" for each county in the hands of Governor Brownlow. These commissioners would all be Brownlow henchmen and under oath were to follow certain restrictions set forth in the law. Each prospective voter had to follow through a prescribed regime in order to qualify for a certificate entitling him to vote. He was required to swear that he had never borne arms against the Government of the United States; that he had not voluntarily given "aid, comfort, countenance, counsel, or encouragement to any rebellion against the authority of the United States Government"; and that he had neither sought nor voluntarily accepted any civil or military office

[96] *Knoxville Whig*, January 31, 1866.
[97] *Republican Banner*, May 8, 1866.
[98] *Acts of Tennessee*, 1865–66, Chapter 33.

under "the pretended authority of the so-called Confederate States." As if this iron-clad procedure might let some former qualified voters slip through its meshes, all former election certificates were declared null and void. Statecraft had been turned into political witchcraft, and Brownlow was the Grand Wizard! The strict enforcement of the new franchise law, it was estimated, would reduce the number of qualified voters to approximately 50,000 of whom three-fourths were East Tennesseans—the Radical section of the State. Inasmuch as members of the Legislature were apportioned according to the number of *qualified* voters,[99] the practical effect of Brownlow's new franchise law was to hand over to East Tennessee three-fourths of the votes in the next legislative session. There were none so naive as not to know that Brownlow and the Radicals were fully aware that their party was a minority one, and that drastic measures had to be invoked if they were to survive politically in the forthcoming elections. That their prognostications were based upon practical aspects of the situation will be fully revealed in the gubernatorial and legislative races a year hence, August, 1867.

Three days after the passage of the franchise law, a Conservative newspaper gave a resume of a huddle by the Radical leaders regarding the enforcement of the new law. Governor Brownlow's physical condition was poor, and he seems to have turned over to his Secretary of State the job of getting the Radicals "told," as evidenced by the following report [100] of the Radical meeting:

---

[99] 1835 Constitution of Tennessee, Article II, Sections 5 and 6.

[100] *Republican Banner*, May 6, 1866.

Author's note. Colonel John Baxter of Knoxville favored the public with a cameo-like sketch of Andrew Jackson Fletcher, Secretary of State, and a former resident of Greeneville, Tennessee. The following excerpts are taken from an address of Colonel Baxter of Knoxville that appeared in the Nashville *Republican Banner*, September 4, 1866:

". . . In the early part of the rebellion, Mr. Fletcher was doubtless a Union man, but it is also true that as the contest waxed warm, and dangers began to accumulate, either from honest convictions, influence of friends, excitement, fear or some other reason, he began to falter in the good cause.

About the fall of 1861, he took and subscribed a solemn oath of allegiance to the Confederate Government. Soon afterwards he applied to the Confederate authorities for permission to raise and organize a Confederate regiment. This he has recently admitted in a published address, to the State. But it is due to him to say that he also stated in mitigation, that at the time of his application he was very much scared, and for the purpose of averting these apprehended dangers, and playing what he is pleased to term a 'trick' upon the Confederate Government, and with the view of recruiting the Union conscripts and marching them into the Federal lines, he held himself out as a friend, and applied for a commission in the Confederate army. He thereby manifested his readiness to take a solemn oath of fidelity to the Confederate cause, to have his contemplated regiment of loyal East Tennesseans also sworn to bear true allegiance, and honestly and faithfully serve the Confederate States—to pledge their lives, their fortunes and their sacred honor for the maintenance of the Confederate authority—in order that he might betray the cause to which he had thus bound them and himself with the most imposing sanctions known to honorable men, by marching his regiment into the Federal lines. How far this statement may comport with the truth no one can possibly know, but Mr. Fletcher himself . . .

"THE FRANCHISE INIQUITY
Conclave of Brownlow and His Parasites.

EAST TENNESSEE TASK MASTERS TO BE IMPORTED

The Whole Infamous Programme.

In accordance with the invitation of the Governor, a meeting of radical members of the Legislature and others, convened at the Capitol at 8 o'clock, last night to discuss the appointment of registry officers in the various counties, under the Franchise law.

Gov. Brownlow called the meeting to order, and he stated that his object was to consult with those present as to the proper men to be appointed as registers by votes [of voters]. He told them that he would hear all their suggestions, but would not promise to select the men suggested in all cases. He said he hoped no man would be nominated, unless he had the nerve to carry out the law. No man must be selected who could be corrupted or driven. In either Nashville or Memphis, a corruption fund of $50,000 or $100,000 could be raised at any time, to defeat the Franchise law. This must be guarded against.

Secretary Fletcher was called out. He said, 'All that the Governor wants, and all that I want, is that the law shall be executed in letter and spirit.' He then said that in Middle and West Tennessee difficulty was apprehended; but this would not be the case in East Tennessee. He hoped no one would be appointed Register in the Middle or Western division, who was a candidate for office himself; in East Tennessee this was not so important.

The Middle and West must be guarded against rebel bribes and rebel power; no rebel must be allowed to approach the ballot box or hold office. He wanted men appointed who could read the law, and who could understand the law.

The fate of the State, he continued, was dependent upon the selection of registers, and he said:

We intend to look with close scrutiny, with regard to every candidate for that position. If we can't get good men in Middle and West Tennessee, we will send them from East Tennessee. The intention is to execute the law,

* * * * *

Fletcher then fled to the mountains of Hepsidam for safety, and, 'lingering in the rear,' waited for the gallantry of others to open up the way and make easy his return to his family. Finally the long-promised relief came. Burnside with his army occupied Knoxville and held all central East Tennessee, and the people began to settle down in the conviction that the evils of war had passed over them. About this time Mr. Fletcher returned. Then, as now, he was effervescing with loyalty; overflowing with loyalty; saturated with loyalty; furious with loyalty; almost bursting with loyalty; and threatening with words of direful import, unsparing retaliation and vengeance upon the rebel miscreants who had dared to raise their impious hands against the 'Government of our Fathers.' But how unreliable are the calculations of the most sagacious men. In a few weeks, Longstreet advanced on Knoxville, and Fletcher again 'struck for tall timber,' and landed in Paducah. He had not been there long, however, as Col. Baxter tells us, before Forrest came along and sent an ugly, whizzing, screaming shell into the town, and the faithful and irrepressible legs of Fletcher carried his indignant and courageous body up to Evansville, Indiana, and there he reposed until the close of the war . . ."

and keep rebels from the ballot-box, and out of office. I wish this distinctly understood.

The dirtiest part of the whole work was then commenced—each mis-representative of the people writing the name of some still more villainous tool on a piece of paper, and handing it to that fat incubus on the body politic, yclept the Governor's private secretary. We couldn't stand it any longer."

Brownlow had succeeded in riveting the franchise manacles upon all former Confederates in Tennessee. But the hymn of hate nurtured by the Radicals found expression in the passage of a resolution [101] whose objectives reached far beyond the chartered limits of Tennessee:

"RESOLUTION NUMBER CII

Joint Preamble and Resolution Declaring that death, the extreme penalty of the law, should be inflicted upon the leaders of the rebellion.

WHEREAS, The Constitution of the United States established a Na-tional Government, the chief and highest allegiance of all citizens was due that government; the Constitution and laws passed under it, were the su-preme law of the land. Rebellion against it was the greatest of crimes; it in-cludes all crimes; and,

WHEREAS, Jefferson Davis and James M. Mason, R. M. T. Hunter, Robert Toombs, Howell Cobb, Judah P. Benjamin, John Slidell, Robert E. Lee and John C. Breckinridge were citizens of that government, in high offices under it, and under oaths to protect and defend it; instigated by pride, lust of power and ambition, they did deliberately conspire together, and with others of less eminence, to overthrow and destroy it; they were the master spirits, and instigators of the late wicked rebellion; through their influence, the Treasury of the nation was plundered; its arms were taken and distributed among their followers; its Post Offices, Mints, Arsenals, Magazines, and Forts were seized and held; its small army was betrayed; its navy dispersed over distant seas; its flag at the head of its vessel, on a mis-sion of mercy, was fired at; its guns were turned on its forts, and blood was sprinkled on the face of the people. Bodies of conspirators, under the names of conventions, were suddenly called together, to give color of law to their wicked proceedings, and to deceive and betray the people, and were made to act in haste and with precipitation, spreading terror among the people and disorganizing society. A so-called Confederate States Government was made. It purported to be a Confederacy of Sovereign States. It was an organ-ized military despotism; Jefferson Davis was the despot at its head. The liberties of the people were utterly crushed under its iron rule. A gigantic military force was raised. Plain men and innocent youths were alike either seduced or deceived or pressed into it, and a wicked war was waged against their government. The substance of the country was consumed; industry was paralyzed; towns and cities burned; lands and farms laid waste; and by fire, famine and slaughter, thousands of people perished. Our own Ten-nessee, the home of him who declared, 'The Federal Union, it must and shall be preserved,' had ever been faithful to that great sentiment; the ac-cursed doctrine of 'secession' never stuck root in its soil. It was never so eloquently denounced as in the proclamation of her own heroic Jackson. After the madness of adjoining sister States, by a majority of sixty-four

[101] *Acts of Tennessee*, 1865-66, Resolution 102, 450–451.

thousand, her people declared their fidelity and adherence to the Union. A convention, when proposed, was voted down, because it was secession. It was through the base treachery of Isham G. Harris, her then Executive, and the moral cowardice of the majority of her Legislature, and the diabolical agency of Jefferson Davis, then styled President of the Confederate States, that Tennessee, against her deliberate will, was dragged into rebellion; and,

WHEREAS, The aforesaid Jefferson Davis, and his aforesaid accomplices, are recommended as fit subjects of pardon and amnesty; therefore,

Resolved by this General Assembly of the State of Tennessee, That for their bad, inimical and great crimes against their fellow citizens and the United States, it is the deliberate sense of this General Assembly, that said Jefferson Davis and his said accomplices have justly forfeited their lives, and that in expiation of their great crime, and as an example for all time, they deserve and ought to suffer the extreme penalty of the law, and be held as infamous forever.

WILLIAM HEISKELL,
Speaker of the House of Representatives.
JOSHUA B. FRIERSON,
Speaker of the Senate."

Adopted May 12, 1866.

There is official documentary evidence that the foregoing outburst of the vindictive and revengeful attitude of the Radicals was NOT the result of a spontaneous impulse, but rather of a cool and calculated purpose. As early as November 14, 1865, Senator John Trimble of Davidson County authored and offered the foregoing resolution of *ultra vires* nature, that is to say, *exceeding the jurisdiction of the State.*[102] So impressed were the Senators with the content and objectives of the resolution that one thousand copies were ordered to be printed "for the use of the Senate." But with the all-important franchise business confronting the Legislature, on which the political salvation of the Radicals depended, the hate-saturated resolution by Trimble remained for six months in a state of animated suspension. But a week after the thumbscrews had been inserted in the new franchise law, the dormant resolution was resurrected and approved [103] on May 12, 1866.

One more measure remained to be placed on the statute books before the Legislature adjourned. Post-Civil War conditions had reached a crisis in Memphis by the infiltration of large numbers of freedmen who were being indoctrinated and somewhat emotionally "hypnotized" by the teaching and preaching of Northerners sent there by the Freedman's Bureau. Imbued with the idea of becoming the "equals" of white people, some of the recently-freed Negroes became insolent and overbearing. In addition, large groups of idle Negroes spent their time in loafing, drinking "mean whiskey," and raising the dickens generally.

---

[102] *Senate Journal,* First Adjourned Session, 1865–66, 131–132.
[103] *Ibid.,* 519.

Adding to the social ferment were clashes between Radical and Conservative whites, a situation greatly intensified by opposite reactions to Brownlow and the franchise law. Spirited fights between Negroes and Irish policemen were frequent and head-smashing. Furthermore, since 1863, Memphis had been designated as a collection depot for all drafted Negroes in the West, and near-by Fort Pickering was the base of several Negro regiments. When "on leave," many of the Negro troops would invade the city and a free-for-all ruckus generally ensued. Law and order were lost in the general melee. A minor incident on April 30, 1866, lighted the fuse. For three days and nights, a massive riot ensued during which time a kill-crazy mob of riff-raff whites seized upon the opportunity of attacking, shooting, and killing at random. In all, more than forty persons were killed, hundreds of others wounded, and over a hundred buildings burned including Negro huts and freedmen's schools.[104]

At the close of the war, the recently-freed Negroes tended to flock into towns and cities where the widespread belief among them was that freedom meant freedom from work. A Memphis census by midsummer of 1865 disclosed that between 20,000 and 25,000 Negroes were in that city. The "forty acres and a mule" phantom restrained many from attempting to do any sort of work. Other urban centers suffered from the same influx of idle Negroes, and racial hatred sprang up as a natural consequence. So widespread was the friction between the races that legislative action was begun prior to the outbreak of the race riot in Memphis, decidedly the worst in Tennessee during the Reconstruction Era. Almost three months before the Memphis riot, Representative W. J. Smith of Hardeman County introduced a bill [105]

"To establish a Metropolitan District and provide for the government thereof."

The bill was shuttled back and forth from one committee to another, and seemed destined to a lingering legislative death. But a queer coincidence seems to have taken place. On the very first day of the initial fracas (April 30) that culminated in the Memphis Riot, Representative Smith's measure was passed in the House by a vote of 39 to 17.[106] A week later, after numerous amendments had been added by including Chattanooga and Nashville the bill was passed in the Senate.

The law [107] creating the Metropolitan Police District, embracing forty-three sections, virtually abolished local self-government in the three municipalities with respect to maintenance of law and order. The

[104] *Tennessee Historical Quarterly*, Volume XVII, 1958, 195–221.
A well-documented article on the Memphis Race Riot, 1866, by Jack D. L. Holmes.
[105] *House Journal*, First Adjourned Session, 1865–66, 354.
[106] *Ibid.*, 494.
[107] *Acts of Tennessee*, 1865–66, Chapter 35.

local police system was abolished and replaced by commissioners nominated by the Governor and confirmed by the Senate, thus depriving the local citizens of exercising any choice in the selection of these officials. Staggered terms of office were provided, covering from four to eight years. All the members of the police force were appointed by this Board of Commissioners. The law required the local County Court to levy and collect taxes sufficient to bear all the expenses of running the department. This law enabled the Radical regime to place top-control of all police administration and protection in the hands of Governor Brownlow.

Numerous contemporary newspapers are crowded with news items and editorials highly critical of the transfer of local self-government to a central agency. Within a year this alleged police protection was extended to political proscription. For example, in the Nashville mayoralty election in 1867, large flocks of Negroes were herded together and voted in bunches. Troops were stationed at all the polling places, seeing to it that the Conservatives were held in check and most of them forbidden to vote. The result was what might have been expected, the Radical candidate receiving 2,423 votes to his opponent's 258.[108] Under the baleful shadow of Brownlow's influence and Radical legislation, it appears that Nashville had to bear the brunt of the brazen effrontery of Radical rule. The "Ring" had so entrenched itself in political domination that it was estimated that more than three-fourths of a million dollars in checks were issued without any legal basis [109] before the harpies could be driven from the city. The Capitol City, along with others, was getting a real taste of Brownlowism!

In an attempt to halt the operation of the franchise law, which was at the bottom of all the trouble, resort was had to court action. Lieutenant-General Bromfield L. Ridley of Murfreesboro on August 1, 1866, applied to Freeman Sherbrook, the registration commissioner of Rutherford County, for a certificate of registration. In Ridley's application, it was stated that the applicant was fifty years of age, a white man, a citizen of Rutherford County for more than twenty years, and that he had been accustomed to exercise the privilege of voting. His application furthermore pointed out that he had served in the Confederate Army, but had received a pardon from President Andrew Johnson on July 26, 1865, and that he had committed no crime subsequent to that date. Inasmuch as the applicant could not qualify under the provisions of the franchise law, enacted May 3, 1866, the certificate was refused. Thereupon, General Ridley applied to Judge Henry Cooper of the Circuit Court for a writ of mandamus requiring Sherbrook to issue the certificate.[110]

[108] *Nashville Union and Dispatch*, September 29, 1867.
[109] *Nashville Union and American*, June 2, 1869.
[110] *Tennessee Reports*, 3 Coldwell, 460–463.

The facts in the case were admitted, and the trial was based upon the question of the constitutionality of the franchise act. Judge Cooper, in an able and searching opinion, declared the law unconstitutional upon the ground that the law had been enacted at a time when several members of the Legislature had been wrongfully denied seats in the Legislature. An appeal from Judge Cooper's decision was made to the Supreme Court composed of three Radicals, Sam Milligan, Alvin Hawkins, and J. O. Shackelford. This Court reviewed rather elaborately the background of Tennessee's secession from the Union, the state of war that ensued, and the conditions obtaining at the close of the war, when

". . . A dismal anarchy overspread the land. Roving bands of banditti plundered the citizens with impunity. They were without protection of law, and there was no security for life or property. Fear had seized upon the hearts of the people. The land was drenched in blood and anarchy reigned supreme. . . ."

A rehash was then made of the actions of the unauthorized group that assembled in Nashville, in January, 1865, when it decided to call itself a Constitutional Convention. Under that guise, slavery was abolished and a schedule attached to the alleged amended Constitution providing for the election of a Governor and a Legislature. One provision of the schedule was the delegation to the Legislature of power to fix the status of the elective franchise. Next, the Supreme Court attempted to differentiate between *civil* rights which were declared to be "inalienable" and *political* rights which stood "upon a very different principle." It was then admitted by the court that Ridley's pardon by President Johnson restored him to his right to vote "under the Constitution of 1834" [date should be 1835], but that the franchise act of 1866 was now in force and compliance with its provisions was a prerequisite for qualification as a voter. Since this statute could not be complied with by Ridley, he having been a Confederate soldier, the court dismissed his appeal, his petition being declared "Wholly untenable." With this decision in the bag, there is but one inescapable conclusion to be drawn—the Radicals were in control of all three branches of the State Government, Executive, Legislative, and Judicial. While shouting for joy at the moment of their temporary triumph, the Radicals overlooked Sir Thomas Browne's maxim—"Revenge only feathers the arrow of the enemy." If history has taught one lesson, it is that revenge is injustice, and that eventually it hurts most those who indulge in it. Some three years later, this assertion was verified in the rout of the Radicals in the gubernatorial race of 1869 between Senter and Stokes.

Before concluding with the record of the Legislature that embraced a period of two hundred and thirty-nine days, October 2, 1865 to May 28, 1866, there remains one more hassle to be mentioned. The stubborn resistance to the passage of the franchise bill had alarmed the Radical Unionists, for failure to disfranchise the Confederates and their sympathizers boded ill for the future political control of the State by the Radicals. While the franchise battle was being waged in the Legislature, with the outcome hanging in the balance, a group of East Tennessee Radicals called a convention to meet in Knoxville on May 3 and 4 for the purpose of reviving former abortive efforts to erect East Tennessee into a separate State. The Convention went on record by presenting to the Legislature a memorial requesting that an election be held in the East Tennessee counties in order to ascertain the wishes of the people in regard to "seceding" from the State and erecting the State of East Tennessee.[111] Brownlow's organ, the *Knoxville Whig*, pointed out that the proposed "new State" would embrace thirty-one counties with an area eleven times as large as the State of Rhode Island.[112] A further reason for this new State, so the memorialists must have argued to themselves, was that the now-Radical Congress of the United States would admit the "new State" because of the undoubted "loyalty" of its citizens.

Whether the movement was based upon actual sincerity or was utilized as a political club to whip the hesitant Unionists of Middle and West Tennessee into support of Brownlow's franchise measure must, perhaps, remain conjectural. One fact seems to support the thesis that it was a political maneuver, despite the support of such leaders as Thomas A. R. Nelson and Oliver Perry Temple. Just as soon as the franchise bill was passed, the "new State" movement died a-borning. The final action on the matter was embraced in a report submitted by a special committee appointed to consider the memorial:[113]

"Mr. Speaker—A majority of the Special Committee on the memorial of certain citizens of the State of Tennessee, residing in that portion of the State known as East Tennessee, asking the General Assembly to consent to the separation of that part of the State and its erection into a new State, having given to the matter of the memorial a full and deliberate consideration, are decidedly of opinion, that the request of the memorialists cannot and ought not to be granted. The Constitution of the State of Tennessee forbids it. The limits and boundaries of the State are defined in Article 1, Section 31, of the Declaration of Rights, which is declared by Article 11, Section 12, to be part of the Constitution, and 'shall never be violated on any pretence whatever.' As a part of the Constitution can be changed or amended only as provided for and prescribed in Article 11, Section 3, or by a Constitutional Convention, it follows that the General Assembly has no power to grant the request of the memorialists; in fact, is restrained from giving any consent to a change of the limits and boundaries of the State.

The Committee are also of opinion that the welfare of the people of Tennessee will be best promoted under one State Government; that for that

---

[111] *Senate Journal*, First Adjourned Session, 1865-66, 517-518.
[112] *Knoxville Whig*, April 4, 1866.
[113] *Senate Journal*, First Adjourned Session, 1865-66, 546.

State Government the citizens of the State, without regard to the division of the State in which they may reside, should habitually and virtually cultivate love and reverence, second only to that for the National Government; that the name of Tennessee should be second only to the highest and dearest of names and titles—'American.'

> JOHN TRIMBLE.
> ALMON CASE.
> THOS. C. MUSE.
> W. SPENCE."

As every beginning must have an end, so the fussing, feuding, and fighting "Brownlow" Legislature brought its long and proscriptive session to a close on May 28, 1866. Throughout the session, its deliberations consisted largely of storms and strife. Its course was aptly described by the majestic Milton:

> "The lazy, leaden-stepping Hours,
> Whose speed is but the heavy plummet's pace."

With one notable exception—the legislative session of 1867—the 1865–66 session dealt with in the preceding pages was the most prejudiced and pernicious in the annals of Tennessee history. Equity and simple justice were never on its agenda. The following example is typical of a Legislature whose vision was comparable to that of a ground mole. At the specific request of the Legislature, ministers were requested to be present and open the day's session with prayer. On the final day of the session, a resolution was introduced to authorize the Secretary of State

"To divide between the several Ministers of the Gospel who have officiated during this Session of the General Assembly, by opening the same with prayer, the amount [$200] to be divided *pro rata* among the Ministers according to the service performed by each."[114]

Witness the niggardly action on this meager proposition: "The resolution was laid over until the November Session."

The Legislature, on May 28, 1866, adjourned to meet again on the first Monday in November, 1866. It will be noted that the adjournment was not of a *sine die* nature, but in reality was a recess from May 28 to November 5, 1866. Doubtless the legislators thought they would be free to pursue their several vocations during the ensuing five months. But instead of the contemplated vacation of five months, they were called into an extraordinary session within five weeks. Before the deliberations of that extra session are considered, it is desirable to take a glance at the National picture which rendered the extra session expedient in the opinion of Governor Brownlow.

The war had been over for more than a year, and yet no Congressmen from the Southern States had been allowed to take their seats in

---

[114] *Ibid.*, 616.

"The parting of the way."
Harper's Weekly, Volume X, 1866, p. 232.

that body. When Congress met in December, 1865, signs of discord between Congress and President Andrew Johnson were evident. Johnson's Reconstruction plans were objectionable to certain Radical leaders in the North, particularly Thad Stevens and Charles Sumner, who possessed powerful influence and who soon became embittered and relentless foes of the President. In February, 1866, the open break came on Johnson's veto of the Freedmen's Bureau. This action on the part of Johnson also displeased Brownlow who said that the veto constituted the greatest Rebel victory since the battle of Bull Run.[115] It was not difficult for Brownlow to find fault with Johnson and his official action, because the two had been long-time enemies. If exception be made to their harmonious relations in support of the Union against Secession—a comparatively brief period—they were in each other's hair politically throughout their lifetime. Moreover, Brownlow nursed personal animosities against Johnson if the statement of a distinguished East Tennessean be given credence. Judge Oliver Perry Temple, who knew personally both Johnson and Brownlow over a long period of years, throws considerable light on their political feud. Said Judge Temple, quoting Brownlow:[116]

". . . But Andrew Johnson, as President, determined to interfere in the administration of the Government of the State [Tennessee]. . . . I was nominated and elected by the loyal people of the State, and in defiance of the known opposition of Andrew Johnson. . . . Johnson opposed me because he desired to hold at the same time the offices of Vice-President and Governor of Tennessee. . . ."

The concluding sentence in the above assertion of Brownlow, like thousands of other wild accusations by him against those who opposed him, is too ridiculous to merit any comment. Moreover, Brownlow had been considerably nettled by formidable opposition to his extreme demands regarding the franchise bill in the preceding Legislature. Brownlow also professed to believe that Johnson had helped stir up the "little rebellion" against the passage of the franchise act, alleging that Johnson had repaid the debt by appointing six of the "bolters" to Federal jobs.[117] Neither did Brownlow appreciate the Legislature's calling upon him to explain why he had thrown out the window so many votes in the August, 1865, election in which a Conservative Unionist had defeated an arch-Radical, Samuel Arnell who was a Brownlow hatchet-man.

Early in 1866, Congress passed under Radical control. Thad Stevens, whose chief regret seems to have been that his skin was not ebony-hued and who requested that he be buried in a Negro graveyard, opened the floodgates of his wrath toward President Johnson. A persistent insist-

---

[115] Coulter, E. Merton: *William G. Brownlow, Fighting Parson of the Southern Highlands*, 309; *Knoxville Whig*, April 4, 1866.
[116] Temple, Oliver Perry: *Notable Men of Tennessee*, 344.
[117] *Knoxville Whig*, June 27, 1866.

ence that the Negro be enfranchised was the "consummation devoutly to be wished," the acquirement of which was believed would aid the Republican Party to remain in control of National politics. With this objective in mind, the Fourteenth Amendment to the Constitution of the United States was formulated and tossed to the various States for ratification.

Brownlow, who at heart detested the Negro, was hard pressed by this proposition. Two factors entered into his deliberations regarding this proposed amendment which would give the ballot to the Negro: (1) currying favor with the Radical Congress, and (2) the hope and probability that the ratification of the amendment would win Negro votes for himself in any subsequent political contest. In all probability, a third consideration was also in his mind; his inveterate political enemy, President Johnson, was in "hot water" with the Congressional Radicals.

The five-section amendment, it was made clear, would have to be ratified by any seceded State before such State would be fully re-instated in the Union. On June 16, 1866, Governor Brownlow received a copy of the proposed amendment and three days later issued a call* for an extraordinary session of the Legislature to meet on July 4, to consider said amendment:

"STATE OF TENNESSEE,
Executive Department,
Nashville, Tenn., June 19, 1866.

To the Members of the General Assembly of the State of Tennessee:

Gentlemen:—For more than five years the State of Tennessee has been deprived of her privileges in the Union of our fathers. By the treason of our people we have fallen from our high estate as a member of the great American Confederacy. For more than a year past the loyal people of the State have been trying to place her in a position, and to prove her worthy to be recognized and readmitted to all her forfeited rights. Our Senators and Representatives have lingered for many months at the threshold of the Government, asking to be re-seated in the National Councils.

In view of the rebellious conduct of so many of our people, and the treachery of those who controlled her action, Congress has deemed it necessary to require of us certain conditions, precedent, as guarantees for our future loyalty. To this end it has been deemed

---

* *Senate Journal*, Extra Session, 1866, 3–4.
   House Journal, Extra Session, 1866, 3–4.

necessary to the future security of the whole country that the State Legislature should ratify certain amendments to the Constitution of the United States, which may be briefly stated, as follows:

1. Equal protection of all citizens in the enjoyment of life, liberty and property.

2. That classes who are disfranchised without crime shall not be taken into account in fixing the basis of Federal representation.

3. That certain persons who have proved themselves dangerous to the peace of the country shall not be eligible to office.

4. The validity of the National debt shall not be questioned, while all debts incurred in aid of the rebellion are illegal and void.

As to the disloyal portion of our people, these terms are mild in the extreme; and it is hoped that there is nothing in them repugnant to the sentiments of the loyal, or if there be, that all objections will be yielded upon the altar of our common country.

Therefore, I, William G. Brownlow, Governor of the State of Tennessee, in consideration of the premises, and viewing the present as an 'extraordinary occasion,' do issue my proclamation, convening the General Assembly in extraordinary session, to consider of said amendments to the Federal Constitution, and do call upon the members thereof to assemble in the State Capitol, on Wednesday, July 4, 1866, when and where 'the purposes for which they will have been convened' will be more fully stated to them.

> *In testimony whereof*, I have hereunto subscribed my name and caused the Great Seal of the State to be affixed, (SEAL) at the Department in the city of Nashville, the 19th day of June, 1866.

By the Governor, W. G. BROWNLOW.

A. J. FLETCHER, Sec'y. of State."

In pursuance of Governor Brownlow's Proclamation, a certain number of the members of both branches of the Legislature met on July 4. The *Senate Journal* discloses that a quorum was not present in that body on the opening day. On motion of Senator Trimble, the Senate adjourned to meet at ten o'clock the next day.[118]

On the following day, July 5, a quorum was present and a resolution was introduced whereby a committee was appointed to inform the Governor that

---

[118] *Senate Journal*, Extra Session, 1866, 4.

". . . The Senate is organized and ready to receive and consider any communication from him."[119]

On the third day of the session, the following resolution [120] was introduced by Senator P. P. C. Nelson from the counties of Carter, Washington, and Sullivan:

"*Resolved,* That the Principal Clerk of the Senate be directed to communicate to the House of Representatives, by message, that the Senate is now organized and ready to proceed with the transaction of public business."

At this juncture, a tip-off was given that some shenanigans would be expedient, indeed necessary in view of existing circumstances. The Senate knew there was no quorum in the House and that that body had not been organized. In order to short-circuit matters, Senator DeWitt C. Senter (later Governor of Tennessee) from the counties of Claiborne, Grainger, Anderson, and Campbell moved into action by submitting the following resolution [121] in lieu of Senator Nelson's resolution:

"*Resolved,* That the Clerk of the Senate inform the House that the Senate is organized and ready to proceed to business;

Resolved further, That a Joint Committee of five, to consist of two on the part of the Senate and three on the part of the House, be appointed to wait upon his Excellency, the Governor, and inform him that both branches of the Legislature are organized and ready to receive any communication he may deem necessary to make them."

Senator Senter's resolution was adopted. Trickery was involved in the second paragraph of Senter's resolution. Senator Senter, as well as the Senate as a whole, knew that the House was NOT ORGANIZED, because no quorum was obtained until July 19, and it is highly questionable whether a constitutional quorum was present on the latter date.

In view of the importance of the matter to come before the Legislature—the ratification of the Fourteenth Amendment—it may be advisable to summarize the *attendance* of the House members from the opening day, July 4, till July 19, when an alleged quorum was present *for the first time.* The House of Representatives in 1866 consisted of 85 members. According to the Constitution, Article II, Section 11, "two-thirds of each House shall constitute a quorum to do business." According to the Constitutional requirement, it took 56 members to make a quorum. The following summary, day by day, is taken directly from the official record, the *House Journal:*

[119] *Ibid.,* 5.
[120] *Ibid.,* 6.
[121] *Ibid.,* 6.

July 4	The House met informally and adjourned so as "to permit all the members present [number not indicated] who desire to do so, to participate in the celebration of the day."		Page	4
July 5	Members present	43	Page	5
July 6	" "	51	"	6
July 7	" "	51	"	8
July 9	" "	55	"	8
July 10	" "	51	"	9
July 11	" "	52	"	10
July 12	" "	52	"	11
July 13	" "	53	"	12
July 14	" "	51	"	13
July 16	" "	50	"	14
July 17	" "	50	"	16
July 18	" "	35	"	21
July 19	" "	54?	"	22-23

A bit later, close scrutiny will be made of the *attendance* on July 19, the date on which the Fourteenth Amendment was declared to have been approved by the House of Representatives. In the meanwhile, let's see what was going on in the Senate.

On July 6, two Senators appointed on a committee to notify the Governor that the Legislature was organized and ready for business reported back to the Senate that the duty had been performed and that "the Governor will at once communicate with the Senate."[122] It should be noted that notification to Governor Brownlow was made by the Senate alone; the House was not represented, no quorum having been obtained. Despite the fact that the *Legislature was not organized*, Governor Brownlow proceeded without delay to lay his Message* before the Senate, although the Message was addressed to both Houses:

"STATE OF TENNESSEE,
EXECUTIVE DEPARTMENT,
Nashville, Tenn., July 6, 1866.

GENTLEMEN OF THE SENATE AND HOUSE OF REPRESENTATIVES:

Having convened you in extraordinary session, it is made my duty by the Constitution to state to you the purposes for which you have been convened. The main purpose, and that which constitutes the present an extraordinary occasion, is briefly, but directly stated

---

[122] *Ibid.*, 7.
* *Senate Journal*, Extra Session, 1866, 7–10.
   House Journal, Extra Session, 1866, 26–28.

in my proclamation of the 19th of June, calling you together. To that paper I respectfully refer you.

Under the fifth article of the Constitution of the United States, Congress has proposed, as an amendment to that instrument, a fourteenth article, which has been duly certified and communicated to this Department, by the Secretary of State, of the United States. Copies of said proposed amendment, with the authenticating certificate, and letter of enclosure of the Secretary of State, are herewith transmitted for your consideration, and I invoke your action as promptly as is consistent with the gravity and importance of the subject.

I beg you to bear in mind, in your deliberations, that while the most of you have been at all times, personally and individually, loyal to the United States, as a whole you represent a State, the most of whose people went into rebellion, raised one hundred and fifty-four regiments, and sent them into the field to fight against the National Government; levied war against the United States for four years, and were finally conquered and reduced to the condition of inhabitants of a subjugated province, wholly at the mercy of the conqueror. By the laws of nations and the laws of war, the General Government has an undoubted right to prescribe terms of settlement to the State of Tennessee. These terms have been prescribed, and are now presented for your acceptance or rejection. I have every assurance that when they are accepted, your Senators and Representatives will be admitted to their seats in Congress, and the State at once re-clad with her long lost rights. Are these terms reasonable? For my own part, they seem to me to be but the decree of political justice and equity, made necessary by the result of the rebellion.

By the first section, equal protection in the enjoyment of life, liberty and property, is guaranteed to all citizens. Practically, this affects mainly the negro, who having been emancipated by the rebellion, and having lost that protection which the interest of the master gave him, became by the very laws of nature, entitled to the civil rights of the citizen, and to the means of enforcing those rights.

To deny this to him, would be to place his life, property and labor in the power of every unfriendly local authority, or evil disposed person, and would be an instance of barbarism unworthy of the age. It will also prevent unjust and oppressive discrimination by one State against the citizens of other States.

By the second section, classes who are disfranchised without crime, are not to be counted in ascertaining the basis of Federal representation. This, too, may be regarded as one of the results of the rebellion; a change made necessary by our changed condition. We have now among us a class of freemen, to whom we deny the ballot and all other political rights. Have we a right to count them against the enfranchised citizens of other States? If so, then will three of our citizens, (rebels though they be,) equal in the political balance four citizens of any Northern State, however patriotic; and one citizen of South Carolina or Mississippi will balance two citizens or Union soldiers who may reside North of the Ohio. Certainly the South is not in a condition to claim so great a political advantage in the national adjustment now proposed, unless, indeed, there be merit in rebellion.

The third section is intended to prevent that class of rebel leaders from holding office, who, by violating their official oaths, added one great offense to another. It is meant as a safeguard against another rebellion, by keeping out of power those who brought on and are mainly responsible for that through which we have just passed. These men, in law and justice, forfeited their lives and property, but a benign and merciful Government inflicts no other punishment or disability upon them than such as is necessary to prevent them from repeating their crime. No loyal citizen will object to this section.

The fourth section declares the validity of our national debt, and that debts incurred or losses sustained in aid of rebellion, are void. This is simply a declaration of the honorable intentions of the Nation, and will be endorsed by every American citizen who is worthy of the title. It also refuses compensation for slaves lost or emancipated by the war. As our slaves were lost by the rebellious conduct of our own people, we should not expect to tax the nation to pay for them.

This brief analysis of the proposed amendment, exhibits a magnanimity on the part of the American people, through their Representatives in Congress, which challenges our admiration. Viewed as terms of final adjustment, between the conqueror and the conquered, their mildness and freedom from all penalty is without a parallel in the history of nations.

I congratulate you on your good fortune, in having the opportunity of being the honored agents of restoring the ship of State to her ancient moorings, soon again to set sail upon her voyage of prosperity and glory. But little over a year ago, you assembled in the Capitol, and took charge of the State. She was prostrate, bleeding and helpless. The courts were nowhere held with safety, and justice was administered only within a few fortified posts. County governments were broken up, and peace officers made no efforts to perform their duties, and anarchy, with all its horrors, reigned supreme. Without a treasury or revenue laws, the credit of the State was destroyed, and our grand system of railroads was in ruins, while guerrillas prowled without restraint over the State. You have placed our great State upon its feet. Under your judicious legislation, the treasury has been able to meet the heaviest demands. The credit of the State is rapidly rising to its former maximum height. Your railroads are nearly all in running order, paying the interest on their loans, while all your courts are open, and justice is administered in every part of the State. It is now your proud privilege to restore the noble old Commonwealth to her ancient position in the Union of our fathers. As you have performed your duty heretofore, in defiance of the abuse and denunciation of traitors, so I am confident you will do so in the future, heedless of threats or dictation from any source.

I regret that duty requires me to bring to your notice any other subject than the weighty question I have already submitted. But I am constrained to call your attention, to the necessity of amending an Act, passed at your last Session, entitled, 'An Act to establish a Metropolitan Police District, and to provide for the government thereof.' Having appointed Commissioners for the cities of Memphis and Chattanooga, the force in each case was promptly organized, and the prospect for relief to the peaceable citizens was quite promising. But the law in its practical workings, is found to be quite defective. Chief among these defects, may be mentioned the want of an adequate remedy in case of the refusal of the County Courts to levy and collect the necessary revenue to defray the expenses of the police, and the power of evil disposed persons in combination, to arrest the operations of the Commissioners, by injudicious and wanton litigation. Other defects will present themselves, and it is believed will be easily corrected. A thorough perfection of the law is recommended.

WILLIAM G. BROWNLOW."

Accompanying Governor Brownlow's Message were properly attested copies of the proposed Fourteenth Amendment and letters of transmittal from U. S. Secretary of State, William H. Seward and A. J. Fletcher, Secretary of State for Tennessee.[123] Ten thousand copies of Governor Brownlow's Message were ordered printed, with two thousand additional copies to be printed in German.[124] Upon completion of the reading of the Governor's Message, Senator John Trimble of Davidson County moved to suspend the rules for the adoption of a resolution approving the Fourteenth Amendment. In an effort to check the now-apparent speed which the Radical-dominated Senate was demonstrating, Senator John G. Carrigan from the counties of Lincoln and Franklin proposed a resolution [125] in lieu of Senator Trimble's, to-wit:

"*Whereas,* The Legislature of the State of Tennessee has been called together under extraordinary circumstances, by proclamation of the Governor, for the solemn purpose of ratifying certain amendments proposed to the States composing this Union, by the Congress of the United States, and,

Whereas, The amendments are questions upon which the greatest wisdom and statesmanship should be exercised, and its importance fully comprehended by the most sagacious judgments among them, and,

Whereas, About one-third of the State is not represented in this Body, nor indeed can it be, until writs of election are issued to fill the vacancies that now exist, and,

Whereas, The Constitution of the United States requires that amendments thereto shall be ratified by three-fourths of the Legislatures of the States, and,

Whereas, It is right and proper that all the people should be fully, faithfully and legitimately represented in said Legislature, and feeling it to be our duty before entering upon the discharge of the responsible duties entrusted to us by the people of the State, to have them as fully represented as possible by law, and feeling a deep and anxious solicitude for the speedy and complete resumption of our relations with the Federal Government, and desiring the establishment of harmony and good feeling among the people of our State, and the permanent restoration of impartial justice to all classes whatsoever; therefore,

Be it resolved by the General Assembly of the State of Tennessee, That we believe it unwise and impolitic, just at this time, in view of the fact aforesaid, to entertain or adopt the Constitutional amendment by the Congress of the United States.

Be it further resolved, That the present extra session adjourn *sine die.*"

By a vote of 13 to 6, Senator Carrigan's resolution went down to a speedy defeat.[126] The Conservatives next attempted to delay the vote on

---

[123] *Senate Journal,* Extra Session, 1866, 12–13.

[124] *Ibid.,* 13.

Author's note. A number of the Governor's Messages carried a supplementary number printed in German. All along, Brownlow and the Radical leaders were playing for the support of the Germans. In fact, the Sergeant-at-Arms for the House of Representatives was a German by the name of William Heydt.

[125] *Ibid.,* 15.

[126] *Ibid.,* 16.

ratification by submitting the following resolution [127] by Senator James P. Thompson from the counties of Cannon, Coffee, Grundy, Van Buren, and Warren:

"Resolved by the Senate of the State of Tennessee, (the House concurring,) That the proposed amendment to the Constitution of the United States, submitted by the Governor to the Legislature, be submitted to the legally qualified voters of the State, the first Thursday in October next, for their ratification or rejection, and that the Sheriffs of the several counties in the State be authorized and required to advertise, open and hold an election in the several civil districts in each county, on the day aforesaid, and that each voter who shall be in favor of the ratification of the proposed amendment, shall have written upon his ticket 'Ratification,' and those opposed to said amendment shall have written upon their tickets the word 'Rejection,' and that the said several sheriffs shall make due and separate returns of the result of said election by the 8th day of November next, to the respective Speakers of both Houses of the General Assembly. All of which is respectfully submitted for your consideration."

Senator Thompson's resolution was defeated by the narrow margin of one vote, 10 to 9.[128]

On July 11, apparently a strategic movement was initiated by Senator B. Frazier of Knox County. Aware of the strong anti-Negro sentiment in East Tennessee, Senator Frazier proposed to place a suffrage restriction [129] in the Fourteenth Amendment which would eliminate the Negro from voting privileges, to-wit:

"Provided, That the foregoing proposed amendments to the Constitution of the United States shall not be so construed as to confer the right of suffrage upon a negro, or person of color, or to confer upon such negro or person of color the right to hold office, sit upon juries, or to intermarry with white persons; nor shall said proposed amendments be so construed as to prohibit any State from enacting and enforcing such laws as will secure these ends, not inconsistent with the present Constitution of the United States, nor shall said proposed amendments be so construed as to abridge the reserved rights of the States in the election and qualification of their own officers, and the management of their domestic concerns, as provided and secured by the present Constitution of the United States."

But Frazier's strategy backfired, for his proposal was defeated by a vote of 13 to 5.[130] There can be no question had Senator Frazier's amendment been adopted, Tennessee would have experienced further delay in being received back into the Union. Thad Stevens and Charles Sumner would have attended to that detail!

These delaying tactics were growing monotonous and somewhat alarming to the red-hot Radicals. The Senate, although heavily loaded

[127] *Ibid.*, 18.
[128] *Ibid.*, 19.
[129] *Ibid.*, 23.
[130] *Ibid.*, 23.

in favor of the Radicals, had just witnessed the narrow defeat of the Thompson resolution by an eyelash majority of one vote. Unable, perhaps, to surmise the next move by the Conservatives, the Radical leadership under the tutelage of Senator Trimble decided to put the steam-roller into immediate operation. Accordingly, Senator Trimble called for the previous question which, if sustained, would put an end to all discussion and any further amendments being offered. His call was upheld by a vote of 11 to 7.[131] Thereupon, he immediately moved for the adoption of the Fourteenth Amendment which passed by a vote of 14 to 6. The next move was up to the House of Representatives.

The situation in the lower branch of the Legislature was reminiscent of Alexander Pope's expressive line,

"Chaos of thought and passion, all confused."

As previously pointed out, from July 4 through July 18, the House had not had a quorum. It had never been constitutionally organized; it had notified neither the Senate nor the Governor that it was "ready for business." So irksome and fearsome had the situation become to some of the Radical bigwigs that on July 14 the Radical bellwether, Samuel Arnell, proposed to violate the State Constitution by means of the following resolution:[132]

"*Resolved,* That the House recognize as a legal quorum, two-thirds of the members holding seats in this body;

Provided, That said two-thirds include a majority of the whole number entitled to seats in this body, and that we proceed to transact business with said quorum."

So desperate had the Radicals become that the House of Representatives was little more than a madhouse—a mass meeting of political maniacs. On the following day, however, when the above resolution came up for discussion, Representative J. A. Doughty from the counties of Anderson and Campbell had gumption enough to move for adjournment. Nothing further was heard of this rough-sledding effort to win at all costs and by any means, however unlawful or unconstitutional.

There is no doubt whatsoever but that a number of Conservatives were determined to prevent ratification of the proposed Fourteenth Amendment by breaking a quorum. On the second day of the session, Representative M. E. W. Dunnaway of Bedford County submitted his resignation to Governor Brownlow who replied as follows:[133]

"SIR: As it is evident the design of your resignation is to reduce the House below a quorum, and to break up the Legislature, the same is not accepted."

---

[131] *Ibid.,* 24.
[132] *House Journal,* Extra Session, 1866, 13-14.
[133] *Ibid.,* 6-7.

Next to the last day of adjournment, long after the Fourteenth Amendment had been jammed through the House under exceedingly dubious circumstances, the House reversed the "Parson's" decision by accepting Dunnaway's resignation "to take effect from its date."[134] It was just as well, for Dunnaway never attended the session a single day. It began to look as though the disorder which characterized the passage of the franchise law was to be re-enacted, and that for a second time a "little rebellion" was in the making. With a few vacancies in the House unfilled and with some seven or eight members still absent, no quorum could be assembled. A roll call on July 11 disclosed that only 52 members answered, still lacking four members to make a quorum. At this state of affairs, the Speaker of the House was directed to issue warrants of arrest for some seven or eight "refractory" members who were to be brought in and made to answer "for their disorderly conduct and contempt of this House."[135]

On the following day, July 12, the Sergeant-at-Arms, one William Heydt, reported that two of the absentees, A. J. Martin of Jackson County and Pleasant Williams of Carter County, had departed for their respective homes. Four others had also gone home, while two others were still in Nashville, dodging about from one boarding house to another and were still at large. In the meanwhile, various members of the House would dart in and out, keeping a sharp lookout as to whether or not a quorum was present. More than a year later, a member of the House of Representatives described the situation under oath in a famous impeachment trial that grew out of the quorum-breaking episode. Thus testified, in part, William Y. Elliott of Rutherford County:

"... whenever we approached a quorum, that either one or another member would absent himself so as to reduce the House below a quorum. It was so marked that I remember that I made some remark more jocular than otherwise in relation to it ... that we would run in and close the doors on them ... and catch them unapprised in the House of Representatives, and thereby constitute a quorum. ..."[136]

On July 16, Sergeant Heydt reported that he had dispatched two of his deputies to Carter County in search of Representative Pleasant Williams who had absented himself from the legislative session. The

---

[134] *Ibid.*, 56.
[135] *Ibid.*, 10.
Author's note. Regardless of how reprehensible or otherwise the conduct of the "refractory" members may have been by absenting themselves from the legislative session, it is incontrovertible that the House could not, CONSTITUTIONALLY, order the arrest of the absentees. The *House Journal* for July 11, 1866, shows 52 members present, four less than the constitutional quorum. With less than a quorum, all the body can do CONSTITUTIONALLY is "to adjourn." 1835 *Constitution of Tennessee*, Article II, Section 11. Likewise, the appointment of a Sergeant-at-Arms to bring in the "bolters" was, for the same reason, null and void from a *constitutional* viewpoint.
[136] *The Frazier Impeachment Trial*, 57.

deputies, one an ex-convict by the name of Thomas Frames and the other a Negro named Landson, went by train to Carter Station, and then negotiated the remaining fourteen miles "partly on mules and partly on foot," reaching Mr. Williams' residence near midnight. Representative Williams was placed under arrest and brought to Nashville where he was placed under guard in Room 3, State Capitol.[137] Representative A. J. Martin of Jackson County was also apprehended by Heydt's deputies and likewise deposited in the same room in the State Capitol occupied by Mr. Williams.

On the following day, July 17, the Radical hotspur, Samuel Arnell, introduced a resolution whose conclusion [138] stated that

"Capt. Heydt be directed to continue under arrest all members detained by him . . . until otherwise ordered by this House."

On the next day, only thirty-five members answered the roll call. This number was so far from a constitutional quorum that an adjournment was all that was done. But the following day, an entirely different picture was presented. Fifty-four members—just two short of a quorum —answered to the roll call. Representative Mullins, an ardent Radical, moved that

"Messrs. Williams and Martin be invited and required to take their seats within the bar of the House."[139]

By a vote of 50 to 4, the Mullins motion was carried. The climax had now been reached. Let the pertinent portions of the verbatim record [140] of the official *Journal* now be invoked:

"The roll of the House was then again called, and fifty-four members answered to their names; Messrs. Williams and Martin being present within the Committee room, but refused to answer when their names were called.
. . . .

There being a quorum present, Senate Joint Resolution No. 2, ratifying the Constitutional Amendment was taken up.

Mr. Mullins moved the previous question.

Mr. Jarvis claimed the floor, having been previously recognized by the Speaker.

The Speaker then ruled that he, Mr. Jarvis, had yielded the floor, and the motion of Mr. Mullins was in order.

Mr. Jarvis appealed to the House from the decision of the chair, whereupon the decision of the chair was sustained.

Ayes 37
Noes 16

[137] *House Journal*, Extra Session, 1866, 15.
[138] *Ibid.*, 20.
[139] *Ibid.*, 22.
[140] *Ibid.*, 23–25.

Mr. Speaker Heiskell and two members, Messrs. Williams and Martin, present not voting.

. . . .

The Speaker then ruled that there was no quorum present, only fifty-three members having voted.
Mr. Arnell appealed to the House from the ruling of the chair.
The vote to sustain the ruling of the chair was then taken and Lost.

> Ayes 11
> Noes 42

Mr. Speaker Heiskell and two members, (Messrs. Williams and Martin,) present, not voting.

. . . .

The vote was then taken on the adoption of the Resolution, Senate Joint Resolution No. 2, with the following result:

> Ayes, 43; Noes, 11.

The Speaker ruled that there was no quorum present.
Mr. Arnell appealed from the ruling of the Speaker.
The vote to sustain the ruling of the Speaker was then taken and Lost.

> Ayes 11
> Noes 42

The Speaker and two members, Messrs. Williams and Martin, present not voting.
The appeal of Mr. Arnell being sustained, the Speaker announced the adoption of the Resolution, Senate Joint Resolution No. 2, ratifying the amendment to the Constitution of the United States."

According to the official record, these were the circumstances under which the General Assembly of Tennessee allegedly ratified the Fourteenth Amendment.

As is frequently the case, when a highly controversial measure is put to vote, there follow protests and explanations on the part of various members. This was true in the above instance. Moreover, motions are sometimes made to "correct the *Journal*." Four days after the climax of the legislative battle, Representative S. K. N. Patton of Washington County successfully moved

> "That the Journal of Thursday, July 19th, be amended so as to show that Mr. Martin when his name was called, answered from the Committee Room door, 'Not present.' "[141]

Next followed Mr. Speaker Heiskell who asked that the following statement be spread upon the *Journal*, to-wit:[142]

> "The Speaker objects and disapproves so much of the Journal of Thursday, July 19, as states that, 'Messrs. Williams, Representative from Carter

[141] *Ibid.*, 36.
[142] *Ibid.*, 36–37.

County, and Martin, Representative from Jackson County, were present when the vote upon the previous question, by ayes and noes'; and upon the resolution, by ayes and noes, adopting the Constitutional Amendment, as proposed by the Congress of the United States, because the said Williams and Martin were under arrest, in Committee room No. 3, though they were invited several times, by direction of the House, to appear in the House as Representatives, which they refused to do. The door of said Committee room No. 3, was open, and the said Williams and Martin were within hearing of the proceedings of the House of Representatives, and when called upon to vote on the two propositions aforesaid, refused to, and did not vote when their names were called to vote upon the said two questions aforesaid."

A half-dozen Representatives desired to place themselves on record as being opposed to the method whereby the Fourteenth Amendment was declared to have been adopted by the House. These Representatives were critical of Speaker Heiskell's action in allowing an appeal of his decision that there was "no quorum" present when the final vote was taken. Here was their protest: [143]

"The undersigned solemnly protest against the action of the House of Representatives on the 19th inst., upon the Senate Resolution adopting the proposed amendment to the Constitution of the United States, for the following reasons, to-wit:

First. Being called upon as one of the States of the Union to ratify the proposed amendment, preparatory to the admission of our members to the National Congress, and the said Congress having failed as yet to recognize the State of Tennessee as a State in the Union, by admitting our Senators and Representatives, is, in our opinion, an admission of the right of a State to secede from the Federal compact, because the 5th Article of the Constitution of the United States says, 'no State shall be deprived of its suffrage in the Senate.' This clearly places the State in a probationary or territorial condition, and as such, the action of this Legislature in regard to the amendment, would not be legitimate.

Second. Because the amendment mostly affects the States now without representation, and the States thus had no voice in proposing it; and because a measure of such great importance to the people of Tennessee should not be thrust upon them without their sanction, and without full and free discussion, and without reference to any appropriate committee.

Third. Because there was not a quorum in the House voting when the resolution was said to be passed. The House being composed of eighty-four members, it was determined in the early organization of the House to establish a quorum, as provided by the Constitution, of two-thirds of its members—being fifty-six members; and upon the vote being taken upon the resolution, only fifty-four members answered to their names, and the Speaker, who is the sole judge upon a question of a quorum, announced there was no quorum present, and from whose judgment, or decision, the Speaker had no right to entertain a motion for an appeal or to occupy his chair as a Speaker until a quorum should appear. Nevertheless, contrary to our opinion of the law and the parliamentary usage, the Speaker did occupy his chair and did entertain a motion for an appeal from his decision, and

[143] *Ibid.*, 37-38.

the House, by a majority of the members present, reversed the decision of the chair, on the ground that two members were under arrest in an adjoining room, and which two members under arrest, did not vote, and were counted to contribute a quorum.

Fourth. Because the House had not at the time, or previous thereto, had read to it the Governor's message announcing the purposes for which they were called together.

Fifth. Because the amendment transfers certain State rights to the Congress of the United States, and authorizes Congress to fix the elective franchise of the States, and obliterates all distinctions in regard to races, except Indians not taxed; and fixes the basis of representation so the former three-fifths basis upon the colored population will be lost until Congress may see fit, by this amendment, to give them the elective franchise; and, because upon the great principle of equality, if the State has a basis of representation upon the disfranchised white voters, it would be equally just to have it upon the freedmen not yet allowed the elective franchise. The amendment also transfers to Congress the right to prescribe the qualifications of State officers; and repudiates the just claims of loyal men, who had the assurance by the United States, should be paid; and because the power will be vested in Congress to enforce it by appropriate legislation.

> L. M. JARVIS,
> JNO. R. SHULTZ,
> S. L. WARREN,
> G. H. GROVE,
> J. C. CLINGAN,
> J. J. STEGALD."

There were, of course, violent repercussions throughout the State and from far-away places regarding the methods used in forcing through a so-called ratification of the amendment. Space limitations will permit only a few typical samplings. On the day following the vote on ratification in the House, the Conservative *Republican Banner* delivered the following blast:[144]

". . . Certainly no such burlesque on legislation was ever known. Beyond all question, there was no quorum. The whole thing was a mere nullity, and no decent man would pretend for a moment that it was valid.

If less than a quorum had been authorized by law to compel the attendance of absent members, or if they had any such right by implication, and the two members under arrest had been brought into the House by force even, there would at least have been something in saying if they were physically present that this made a quorum; but under our Constitution and laws, the arrest of a member by order or resolution of less than a quorum is illegal, and is void *ab initio,* and a writ of Habeas Corpus may be sued out. The authorities are full, that he may be discharged by motion or by writ of *Habeas Corpus,* or by writ out of Chancery, when this writ is obtained.

Before a quorum is had, the physical presence is nothing if it is by force. Under our Constitution and laws, there can be no quorum until two-thirds consent to make a quorum. This is most surely so, as less than a quorum, by a wise provision of the Constitution, can not compel the attendance of absent members. The Legislature under our Constitution, both

---

[144] *Republican Banner* (Nashville), July 20, 1866.

Houses acting, might have passed a law authorizing less than a quorum to compel the attendance of absent members. But the Legislature, doubtless for good reasons, declined to make such a law. This is clear, too clear for debate; and a few of the members, doubtless, know it. Unfortunately, most of the members of the present Legislature don't pretend to think for themselves, and if they did, they haven't sense enough to think. It would be a piece of folly for most of them to try to think. Many of them really do not know but what they have acted according to law, and could not be convicted of perjury.

But was ever such a spectacle witnessed among enlightened people? Here is a measure that degrades the whole State . . . . if finally adopted, all hope of restoring the country, of having a free government. A measure the most odious to our people of all classes, for the Union men in the State are more bitter against it than the ex-rebels, of any measure that was ever agitated. And yet the very fact that the whole people are so bitterly opposed to the measure is the principal reason why these Radicals wanted to pass it.

Without a quorum, in defiance of all precedent, in utter contempt of the Constitution which they had in blasphemy sworn to support, with a shamelessness never before witnessed in a mob even, they voted on the amendment, and say they passed it."

Five days later, the same newspaper reprinted an article that had been carried in a distant newspaper, scoring unmercifully "Parson" Brownlow:[145]

"Parson Brownlow and Official Ruffianism.

Up to a recent date, Parson Brownlow, of Tennessee, had the reputation of being the foulest mouthed man that spoke the English language, which is equal to saying the foulest-mouthed man on earth, for the English language has capacities of vulgar foulness equalled by no other form of mortal speech with which we are acquainted. His ribaldry and blasphemy as a preacher, shocked even the rude ruffians of the Southwest, while his scurrility as a politician and editor, gave him a position which no decent man, and few innocent men, could approach.

After having done as much as any other individual of his capacities in the South to stimulate the fell spirit of Slavery to war and treason, he saw fit for selfish ends, and to the disgust of every loyal man in the country, to take sides with the Unionists of East Tennessee. Neither they nor we had any more respect for his selfish loyalty than for his ribald piety; but the course and force of circumstances kept him from open treachery by making it dangerous; and the generous attention and help he obtained from the courageous and unflinching leader of the Tennessee Unionists, who is now President of the United States, induced him to endure till the rebellion was protracted by our armies. Even the foulness of his tongue seemed to suffer an abatement for a short while, and it appeared as if time might cause him finally to be tolerated by reputable people.

*   *   *   *   *   *   *

His office as Governor gave him no more self-respect now than his vocation as preacher had given him Christian character, while the fact that Mr.

[145] *Republican Banner* (Nashville), July 25, 1866.
Article was quoted from the *New York Times.*

Johnson held the office of President seemed to add zest to the rancor of his assaults. He swore and raved more furiously than he had ever done before, and used language which would put to blush even that of the malignant madmen of Congress. He vented his personal malice 'in season and out of season,' in speech, public documents, and in his newspaper; and let no act or word of the President's pass without finding in it new opportunity of revenge for his grievances. . . ."

A small-town newspaper, removed somewhat from the tension and turbulent scenes characterizing the manipulations going on in the House of Representatives, commented as follows: [146]

". . . It was determined to force this measure through, by fair or foul means, and if the Senate resolution ratifying the proposed amendments had not been concurred in through the disgraceful disregard of law and precedent in which it was, we feel safe in asserting that it would have been soon after, on the basis of Mr. Arnell's resolution, offered a few days before, declaring that two-thirds of the members holding seats in either house constituted a quorum competent to do business. The order had come from the Star Chamber at Washington that the proposed amendment must be ratified within a specified time, and such an order is equal to the command of an officer to a squad of soldiers detailed to shoot a condemned criminal. . . . Brownlow was mad. He had applied to the military for aid to 'manage' the Legislature, and the authorities at the federal capital, in response to a telegram from General Thomas, conveying the request, *peremptorily refused.*"

Governor Brownlow was so elated at the action of the House that he rushed off a telegram the very same day (July 19, 1866) to J. W. Forney, Secretary of the United States Senate. That telegram was as follows: [147]

"We have fought the battle and won it. We have ratified the constitutional amendment in the House—forty-three (43) voted for it, eleven (11)

---

[146] *Fayetteville Observer*, July 26, 1866.

Author's note. The *Observer's* statement that Brownlow had applied to the Federal military authorities for troops is supported by the sworn testimony of Major-General George H. Thomas in the Frazier Impeachment Trial which took place a year later.

"*Testimony of Major-General George H. Thomas.*
Q. Were you in command of a Division as Major-General in July, 1866?
A. I was.

*   *   *   *   *   *   *   *

Q. Did Governor Brownlow, whilst the Legislature was in session, apply to you for aid in any way to execute the law?
A. He applied to me for aid to enforce the attendance of members."
See the *Frazier Impeachment Trial*, 45–48.

Copies of the official correspondence between General Thomas, Lieutenant-General U. S. Grant, and Edwin M. Stanton, Secretary of War, were introduced in the Frazier Trial, page 50.

[147] *Daily Morning Chronicle* (Washington), July 20, 1866.

Author's note. Diligent research, both at Nashville and Washington, failed to locate the original telegram. Through the courtesy of Dr. Philip M. Hamer, Executive Director, National Historical Publications Commission, Washington, verbatim extracts from the Washington newspaper, containing Brownlow's telegram, were against it; two (2) of Andrew Johnson's tools not voting. Give my respects to the dead dog of the White House.

W. G. BROWNLOW."

On the same day on which Brownlow's telegram reached Washington, a former Republican candidate for Governor of Connecticut in 1856, now Secretary of the Navy, recorded in his faithful diary his opinion of Brownlow and his Radical Legislature: [148]

"A telegram from the coarse, vulgar creature who is Governor of Tennessee says that there is a quorum of the legislature and that they have ratified the Constitutional Amendment. This legislature was chosen when war existed and under circumstances and animosities which would not be justified or excusable in peace. It is, of course, no exponent of popular sentiment in that State. But under the urgent appeals of the Radical Members of Congress, Brownlow, the Governor, convened a special session of this dead body on the 4th of July, to ratify the changes in the Constitution of the United States. But he was unable to get a quorum together. Fifty-six were necessary for a quorum; only fifty-four would be assembled, and two were arrested and brought to Nashville as prisoners. These made the requisite fifty-six, and forty-three of these bogus members voted for the Constitutional changes. This is an exhibition of Radical regard for honest principle, for popular opinion, and for changes in the organic law. The change is to be imposed upon the people by fraud, not adopted of choice."

About one week after the news of the ratification of the amendment by the Tennessee Legislature, another out-of-State newspaper penned the following scorching editorial: [149]

". . . Parson Brownlow telegraphed a lie, which has been the only ground of argument for the validity of its pretended passage in the House. Brownlow did not state that a quorum was present and voting. He said that 43 yeas were present, 11 nays; and 2 mutes, making a 'present' quorum of 56, if not the 'present and voting' quorum required by law.

But Parson Brownlow falsified. There were not 56 voting, nor 56 present either. The House has never had a quorum. The two members whom Brownlow stated to be present, but not voting, were *not present*. They were in the committee room, under guard, all the while. They were not in the House actually, constructively, or anyhow else. Therefore there never was a quorum of the Tennessee Legislature, and the Constitutional Amendment was never passed by that State.

The Speaker of the House refused to sign the resolution affirming the

---

forwarded to the writer of this volume. On the day following receipt of Brownlow's telegram, the telegram was read to the Senate by Senator Edgar Cowan of Pennsylvania, who
". . . asked if anything could be baser or lower than this. The signer of this claimed to be a man of God, whose mission was peace. This language was an insult to this Senate, an insult to the whole American people . . ."
[148] *Diary of Gideon Welles*, July 19, 1866, Volume II, 577.
[149] *Republican Banner* (Nashville), July 28, 1866, quoting from the *New York World.*

passage of the amendment, and the contest between him and the members of the House has been on the point whereon he insists that the journal shall show what they desire to conceal—that the two unlawfully arrested and imprisoned members were not in the hall of the House at the time of the vote on the ratification proposition, but were under arrest in the adjoining committee room.

Everywhere, and always, these Radical Republicans are a law-breaking, law-spurning, lawless set, but never more than when they have been put into the seats of law-makers. . . ."

Whether or not the circumstances under which the Fourteenth Amendment was declared ratified by the Tennessee Legislature were legal and constitutional will, probably, remain a mooted point. Perhaps the conclusion reached by a competent Tennessee historian sums up the situation correctly:[150]

"Thus, in a most extraordinary and, from the point of view of legality, in a most questionable manner was the amendment ratified by Tennessee."

Congress immediately passed a joint resolution admitting the Tennessee Congressional delegation which had been cooling its heels for approximately one year seeking admission. President Johnson reluctantly signed the resolution which he in reality opposed and regarded as unconstitutional. To have done otherwise, however, would have delayed Tennessee's readmission to the Union and would have thus postponed Johnson's fondest wish—to see his own State again restored to all her former rights and privileges. Tennessee, the last State to secede from the Union, was now the first to be readmitted. She escaped the iron hand of a Radical Congress later on exhibited in the military reconstruction of the other States of the Confederacy, but fell a victim to her own Radicals who displayed a vindictive and revengeful spirit not exceeded by the Congressional Radicals.

The Legislature which ratified in an exceedingly doubtful manner the Fourteenth Amendment was a Radical body under the domination of Brownlow. Force, threats, and intimidation were everywhere in evidence, and eventually crushed the efforts of the Conservatives who had been reduced to a party of mere protests. With their triumph, sweeter to the Radicals than "honey or the honeycomb," the Extraordinary Session came to an end on July 25, 1866, by passage of the following resolution:[151]

"Resolved, That at the close of this session of the General Assembly, (12 o'clock, M.), the national airs of Hail Columbia, the Star Spangled Banner, and Yankee Doodle be played in the Halls of the Capitol, on a full band."

[150] Hamer, Philip M.: Tennessee—A History, Volume II, 616.
[151] Senate Journal, Extra Session, 1866, 49.

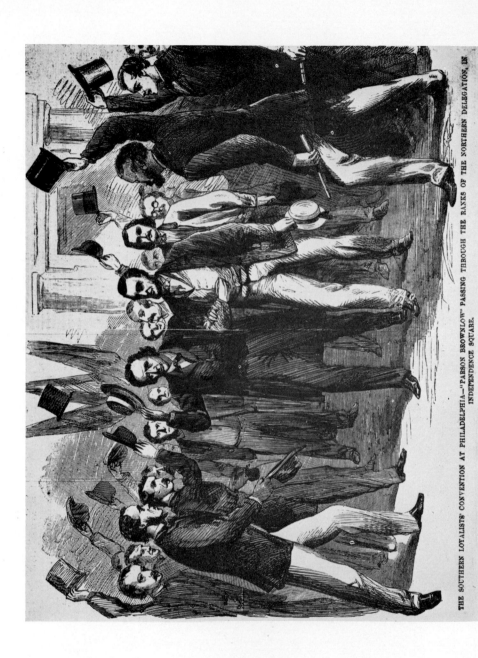

THE SOUTHERN LOYALISTS' CONVENTION AT PHILADELPHIA—"PARSON BROWNLOW" PASSING THROUGH THE RANKS OF THE NORTHERN DELEGATION, IN INDEPENDENCE SQUARE.

The year 1866 proved to be a critical year for President Andrew Johnson and his plan for Reconstruction. The ultimate outcome was dependent upon the by-elections of Congressmen that summer. Two major questions faced Johnson: (1) whether enough Conservative Congressmen would be elected and thereby enable Johnson to control Congress; or (2) whether enough Conservative Congressmen would be elected to prevent the Radical Congress from overriding a presidential veto. Those were two paramount issues before the people.

Despite the fact that Tennessee Congressmen would not be up for election until 1867, yet Tennessee Conservatives participated in the movement to give Johnson moral support and thereby help persuade Northern voters to elect Conservative Congressmen. As one means of corralling support for Johnson and his Reconstruction Plan, a National Union Convention was called to meet in Philadelphia in August. Conservative Unionists and many ex-Confederates in Tennessee met in Nashville on July 4, with the Speaker of the House, William Heiskell, as Chairman, for the purpose of perfecting a State-wide organization in support of Johnson. At Memphis, a similar meeting was held at which such notable ex-Confederate leaders as General Nathan Bedford Forrest, Gustavus A. Henry, the "Eagle Orator," and the silver-tongued Landon C. Haynes spoke in behalf of Johnson and his Reconstruction policies. In Knoxville, Thomas A. R. Nelson denounced the Radical Legislature of Tennessee and eulogized the administration and policies of Andrew Johnson.

As an antidote to the Southern expressions of approval of Johnson, a convention of "Southern Loyalists" met in Philadelphia in early September. Three Tennessee king-pin Radicals, Governor Brownlow, Horace Maynard, and William B. Stokes attended. Brownlow held the spotlight, and was reported to have said:[152]

"That he had never held a doubtful position on any question; that he had no hesitation in saying that he was for negro suffrage; that he would rather be elected to an office by loyal negroes than disloyal whites; that he would rather be buried in a negro graveyard than any rebel graveyard, and if he had to go to hell or heaven after death he would rather go with negroes than with white rebels . . . that the Tennessee Legislature had disfranchised the rebels, and at its next session it would arm the loyal masses to enforce the franchise law and either keep the rebels from the ballot box or have a fight! . . . We have one more act to pass, and that is a law en-, franchising the negro, and we will do it next winter. . . . It is necessary to have 60,000 to 70,000 votes to kick the beam, to weigh down the balance against rebelism. . . ."

A group of Southern Radicals, with Brownlow as the hatchet man, toured the North launching vitriolic attacks upon President Johnson. The Parson kept the columns of his newspaper crammed with vehement

[152] Hamer: *Tennessee–A History*, Volume II, 617–618.

attacks upon the President, and nobody doubted what he had in mind when he said [153]

"That we are to have another conflict of arms, we have no sort of doubt. . . . When it shall break out, a million loyal men will surround the Capitol and White House and soon be disposing of the heads of leading traitors after the most approved style of the age, in which the King of England lost his head."

He even paraphrased some of Thad Stevens' diabolic anathemas by declaring that the Rebel population should be exterminated and their property sold to pay off the war debt.[154] So impressed with Brownlow's zeal and fire-breathing speeches were Northern Radicals that there were random suggestions that he would be an excellent President! There can be no doubt but that Brownlow and his fellow Radicals delivered telling blows, and results of their tirades were registered in the Congressional elections when the Radicals won a two-thirds majority in Congress and swept the Tennessee Congressional delegation wholly into the Radical ranks. The President had been licked to a frazzle in the Nation, and Parson Brownlow had trimmed him to a queen's taste in Tennessee. No longer did the Parson fear Johnson, for the Brownlow strategy had temporarily paid off and he was now in high favor with the Congressional Radicals headed by Stevens and Sumner.

And now with the National political picture presented in minature, let us return to Tennessee. In September and October, 1866, special elections were held for filling such vacancies in the Legislature as had occurred by death or resignation. In three counties, Davidson, Shelby, and Franklin, the Conservatives won. Nevertheless, the Radicals won elsewhere in numbers sufficient to give them power to prevent any quorum-breaking tactics that had been employed upon former occasions by the Conservatives. Brownlow had emerged victorious and now held in the hollow of his palsied palms a Legislature thoroughly saturated with nth degree Radicalism. These were the political conditions under which the General Assembly convened in its Second Adjourned Session on November 5, 1866. Ten days later, Governor Brownlow transmitted his Message to that body:

Legislative Message,* November 15, 1866.

GENTLEMEN OF THE SENATE AND HOUSE OF REPRESENTATIVES:

If public affairs, both State and National, were not unsettled and disturbed, I might not, upon your re-assembling under your own

---

[153] *Knoxville Whig*, August 1, 1866.
[154] *Ibid.*, August 22, 1866.
* *Senate Journal*, Second Adjourned Session, 1866-67, 10–22.
House Journal, Second Adjourned Session, 1866-67, 14–27.

resolution, deem it my duty formally to address you any communication. But the rapid succession of important events, constantly affecting the public interest, demand, in my judgment, that I should recommend to your consideration such measures as I judge expedient.

The year now rapidly drawing to a close, may be said to be in the main, a year of peace and plenty. For, while a few evil disposed and turbulent politicians have sought to disturb the repose of the people, and a few riots and crimes have disgraced certain localities, the great body of the people have quietly pursued their peaceful avocations.

Abundant crops have rewarded the labor of the husbandman, and the general business of the country has greatly improved—so much so that our people appear to be rapidly approaching that degree of prosperity which blessed them in former years.

For these blessings, already realized and in prospect, we should return thanks to an overruling Providence.

At your extra session in July last, in the face of the direct opposition of the Federal administration, and in defiance of its power and patronage, you ratified the pending amendment to the Federal Constitution. The loyal people of the nation have approved the wisdom and applauded the fearlessness of your course; and the Congress of the United States signified their approbation by at once admitting to their seats your chosen representatives, thus restoring to our State all the rights and relations that had been lost or disturbed by the rebellion of our people. True, you have been abused and denounced by the President and his present followers, while those who endeavored by revolutionary acts to destroy your organization, have been honored and rewarded; yet you have enjoyed the approbation of your own consciences, and received the plaudits of the patriotic of the nation, and may well go on in the even tenor of your way, guided alone by a sense of duty.

Having in this distinguished manner affixed the seal of your approbation to this amendment, it is proper that you should mould your legislation to its spirit and design.

While it is true that this amendment leaves with the States, as heretofore, the regulation of the elective franchise, it is equally true that it encourages the enfranchisement of all loyal male citizens of whatever color. Our own State, for instance, under the operations of the amendment, without the enfranchisement of the colored citizens, will have but six representatives, while, with impartial loyal suffrage, it is estimated that she would have nine, thus increasing her power in the councils of the nation fifty per cent.

In my message addressed to you in October, 1865, the subject of colored suffrage is discussed in all of its bearings. Upon a careful review of that paper, I still approve the sentiments therein expressed, and respectfully refer you to them.

An eventful year, however, has passed since it was written; and while unforeseen events have happened, contingencies therein contemplated have also occurred.

The colored race have shown a greater aptitude for learning and intelligence than was expected, and by their good conduct and steadfast loyalty, have rapidly won upon the good opinion and respect of the white race; while the late rebels, under the encouragement of the President, have shown less disposition to return to true loyalty than was hoped for.

These manifestations have occasioned a rapid advancement of the national sentiment in favor of impartial suffrage.

In the message to which I have alluded, while candidly admitting that 'negro voting cannot suit my natural prejudices of caste,' it is yet stated that 'there is a class of them I would be willing to see vote at once.' The opinion is also expressed 'that negro suffrage is bound to follow as one of the great results of the rebellion; and that the time would come when it would be proper and right,' but that the time had not then come, the great objection being to 'the immediate and indiscriminate enfranchisement of the negroes;' but it is directly insisted in the message to which I refer, that 'if rebels are to be restored to the rights of the elective franchise, let us no longer deny those political rights to the late slaves who have been faithful among the faithless.' I still adhere to the opinion that 'all this great outcry against a negro voting in any contingency, comes from a lingering sentiment of disloyalty in the South.'

In all the States lately in rebellion, except Tennessee, the rebels have been fully 'restored to the rights of the elective franchise;' and even in our own State, under a somewhat stringent suffrage law, a large number of disloyal persons are unavoidably allowed to vote.

Whether the time has come when it is 'proper and right' to confer the ballot upon the colored man, or whether that time is approaching at which that sacred right shall accrue to him, are questions demanding your earnest consideration and final decision.

The admirers and followers of the President cannot, with any show of consistency, oppose the enfranchisement of the negro.

In an authorized and approved statement of his opinions, made public by his direction, long since his accession to the Presidency, he declares that if he were 'in Tennessee he would endeavor to introduce negro suffrage.' He declares that he would *begin* with three classes of negroes to be admitted to vote at once, 'Those who had served in the army; those who could read and write; and those having a property qualification of $200 or $250.'

Thus, by a system not very gradual, he desired to extend the privilege to the entire race.

If what is termed the Radical party in the Legislature shall agree with the President and his followers, on the question of negro suffrage, it would seem that an excellent opportunity for agreement and conciliation on a vexed question will be presented, and that the negro may be enfranchised with unanimity.

As for myself, while I have confessed to those prejudices of caste, resulting from education and life-long habits, I am free to say, that I desire to act in harmony with the great body of the loyal people of the Union.

I think we should not, without great and controlling reasons, sever ourselves from that great national party, whose wisdom and courage saved the life of the nation, and rescued the loyal people of Tennessee from the hands of the oppressor.

The Franchise Law, passed on the 3d of May last, is not yet fully in operation. Registers have been appointed in all of the counties of the State, but many of them have not completed their labors and made their reports.

As fast as they have done so, I have ordered elections in compliance with the law.

I am happy to state, that the Registers have been generally faithful and firm in the discharge of their important duty.

Except in the city of Nashville, the late special elections seem to have been held substantially in accordance with the law.

In this city, I am informed, that but few of the Judges and Clerks of the Municipal Election, or but few of the successful candidates for the principal offices, complied with the law by taking the important oath set forth in the 3d section. It will be your duty to provide a remedy for similar violations of the law in the future.

You are fresh from your constituents, and have had better opportunities than I have had to observe the operations of the law. As your session progresses, you will learn still more of its workings. As no future Legislature can act upon this vital subject, it will be your duty to perfect the law with the utmost care.

This law was not passed from vindictive or malevolent motives, but to protect the loyal people from oppression and the State from misrule.

The spirit and genius of republican institutions, demand that every citizen should be allowed to vote, who may do so consistently with the safety of the government. If there be classes disfranchised by the present law, who are worthy of the privilege, you should restore them; and if there be classes who are unworthy, you should restrict them. If you are satisfied that in process of time, the disfranchised class will become good citizens by learning to respect loyalty, you may fix a limit to the operations of the law, by naming some day in the future when its restriction shall wholly or partially cease. At all events, you should, before your final adjournment, see, if possible, that the law is such as to need no further amendments.

THE THREATENED STATE REVOLUTION.

I have already alluded, with pleasure, to the general disposition of the masses of our people, to pursue their peaceful avocations, and but for the sad experience of 1861, I should feel no apprehensions that they could be again betrayed into revolutionary movements. But as what has happened once, may, from similar influences, occur again, it is my duty to call your attention to the fact that disloyal newspapers, together with unprincipled and designing stump speakers, have been untiring in their efforts to set on foot a scheme of State revolution. These speakers and writers urge and predict the overthrow of the State Government, and some of them have fixed a limit, in days or weeks, to its existence, declaring that 'the work shall be done.' Many of the delegates, returning from the great political conspiracy, which assembled at Philadelphia on the 14th of August last, declared publicly, and at secret meetings of their cliques, that they had seen and conversed with the President, and agreed with him upon a programme for the overthrow of the State Government. At Knoxville, these agitators were, for a time, outspoken, and apparently determined. At Nashville, similar characters called a convention to meet there, for the avowed purpose of initiating a revolution. Either because the people of the State did not sympathize with the movement, or because they feared the displeasure of the nation, they postponed their meeting from time to time, and finally gave it the appearance of a common political gathering. It is true these men are not the fighting men of the late rebellion. They are, for the most part, those, who, after encouraging the strife, shirked all danger in order to look after their pecuniary interests. And such would doubtless be their course again, if they could succeed in involving the people in war. The present cherished design of these men is, by force, to prevent the enforcement of the existing Franchise Law, so as to secure for themselves the control of the State Government at the ensuing August elections. As they declare that they are sustained in their designs by the Acting President of the United States, and as I have reason to apprehend that this latter declaration is true, I call upon you to provide for any emergency that may arise. So far as my duties may be involved, I do not intend to tamely surrender to an illegitimate State government, no matter by whose encouragement it may be set on foot. But as the arms of the State disappeared from the Capitol during the rebellion, and there is no military organization anywhere in the State, and no funds provided by express enactment for the defense of the lawful authorities, I call your attention to this state of affairs, and to the present Militia laws, and invoke your prompt and fearless action. I recommend that you authorize the enlistment of a few regiments of loyal militia, to be armed and held as minute men, subject to the call of the Executive, to suppress insurrection or protect the ballot-box. If sufficient provision be made, the Executive pledges himself to see that the law is sustained, be the consequences what they may.

THE JUDICIARY.

At the risk of being considered importunate, I again call your attention to the absolute necessity of increasing the salaries of our Judges. An enlightened and impartial judiciary constitutes the bulwark of civil liberty, and there never has been a time in the history of the State, when such a judiciary was of such vital importance. It is a pleasing, but shallow view of the subject, to say that eminent lawyers should accept judicial positions and perform laborious and expensive duties, for honor alone, or even from patriotism. Those halcyon days, if they ever existed, are past. It is true that in our first efforts to restore law and order, many of the best jurists in the State did tender their services and accept positions on the bench. They were actuated by patriotic and self-sacrificing motives, and by the reasonable hope that their salaries would be increased, at least in proportion to their personal expenses. Disappointed in this, and having done what they considered their share of the public burdens, many of them have resigned, and others have only been prevailed upon to continue in office by the members of the bar and their clients. In the exercise of the appointing power, I have experienced the utmost difficulty in finding suitable persons to fill the vacancies, as they have occurred; nor will I say that I have always succeeded. Gentlemen of the bar, while they admit that they owe something to the public service, conceive that their families have a still higher and stronger claim upon them. Nearly all of our Judges have long journeys and fatiguing labor to perform, attended with heavy expense and privations, and for a salary that is barely sufficient to defray their actual outlays, much less to compensate them for losses of time and business. As it is possible that most of these offices will soon be filled by election, and as under the Constitution, their salaries cannot be increased during the time for which they may be elected, I once more, finally and earnestly, invite your attention to this subject, involving as it does, the vital rights and interests of every citizen of the State.

THE HERMITAGE.

I refer you to my former message and my official report concerning that fine estate, which is now the property of the State, known as the 'Hermitage Farm.' The Legislature of 1855-6, purchased this estate out of respect to the memory of its former illustrious owner, at the cost of $48,000, and incurred a debt of that amount by the issuance of its bonds, which debt now amounts to about $80,000. Since the purchase, the interest of the State in the property has been wholly neglected. The present occupants have enjoyed it without being called on for a single dollar either for rent or repairs; nor have they volunteered to repair the dwelling, fences, or even the tomb itself. It would seem that the use of such a magnificent estate by private individuals, would compensate them for keeping it at least in some sort of repair. But the entire property presents a dreary aspect of dilapidation and neglect. As I do not understand it to have been the object of the purchase to establish a State charity, I recommend the sale of the property as a measure due to the State, and satisfactory to the tax-payers, and to meet in part the debt incurred in the purchase.

HOSPITAL FOR THE INSANE.

I refer you to the report of the Superintendent of the Tennessee Hospital for the Insane. Under the efficient management of its present able officers, this noble institution of charity proves to be an honor to the State and a blessing to its unfortunate inmates. It is proper that I should call your attention to the fact, that there are at the Institution a number of pay patients from the Southern States, whose bills have not been met for four or five years. The accounts of the parties who placed these patients in the hospital, have been regularly made out and forwarded to them repeatedly. Some have replied that they were unable to meet them, while others have treated these calls with silent contempt. The outstanding debt due to this Institution, in items of this character, now amounts to nearly $40,000. Many of these patients were sent here through pride, and a desire to have them far removed from their homes and families.

It is not just that our people should be taxed to support the unfortunate of other States, especially when the presumption is that their relatives are able to defray their expenses. Such a course would be a departure from the rule that our charities should begin at home. I recommend that the relatives of these unfortunates be once more notified, and if no settlement is made within a reasonable time, the patients be conveyed to their homes at the expense of the State, and be turned over to their families.

THE PENITENTIARY.

The condition and workings of our Penitentiary system will command your attention. Recently the number of convicts has been rapidly increasing, and will soon probably exceed all former calculations. This was to be expected, as resulting from the demoralization of the war, and the remission of the colored race to the penalties of our criminal code instead of the summary treatment applied to them when slaves. But I apprehend that these penalties have not been impartially administered. The violent prejudices and high passions engendered by the war, have not so far subsided as to secure from juries, in many cases, that most sacred right—an impartial verdict. From information derived from numerous and reliable sources and actual investigation, it appears that in some localities, discharged Federal soldiers and colored defendants have a poor showing, when once arraigned before those against whom they lately fought, or by whom they were claimed as property. These classes, and others equally obnoxious, are convicted with alacrity, and generally sentenced to the maximum punishment allowed by law. I feel that I am warranted in the estimate, that twenty-five per cent. of the convicts now in the State Prison, are there on account of the color of their skin, or their antecedents as soldiers or active Unionists, or at least who would not have been there if they had had different antecedents or a different color. I am pained to make this statement, seeing no adequate remedy. The courts can and should do much to prevent such wrongs, and the Executive may occasionally afford partial relief by the exercise of the pardoning power. But the trial by jury is a sacred constitutional right—with all its faults, is probably the best form of trial that can be desired. Whether additional safeguards can be thrown around this great institution, and whether it may not be well to enlarge the power of the courts and to prescribe the duties of the Attorney Generals, in relation to the doubtful verdicts or excessive punishments, are questions submitted to your gravest consideration. To relieve the State Treasury of the immense burden of the costs of petty prosecutions, I recommend that some of the milder classes of petit larceny, and other milder felonies, be reduced to misdemeanors, and triable under what is termed the 'small offense law,' as is now done by the ordinances of some of our cities.

Resulting from the condition of things I have mentioned, there are pending now in the Executive Department about seventy applications for pardon. The greater part of the applicants are discharged Federal soldiers or negroes, and there is great uniformity in their complaints. I have caused a number of cases to be investigated, and though averse to the exercise of the pardoning power, a few have been set at liberty, some of whom were proved to be entirely innocent. But it is impossible for the Executive to investigate all these cases, in person or through others. Most of the petitioners have no relatives, efficient friends or counsel, and the result is that the merits of the cases are unascertained. I recommend that a committee of your own body, or of enlightened citizens, be appointed to take charge of the whole subject, investigate every case, and make reports for the guidance of the Executive. If the Legislature shall adopt this suggestion, prompt action is respectfully invited, as he will feel it his duty to order such investigations, however laborious and unsatisfactory they may be.

HOSPITAL.

In 1829, an appropriation was made for the establishment of a State Hospital at Memphis, and Trustees were appointed, valuable grounds purchased and buildings erected. Appropriations have since been made from time to time, for its support. The grounds are beautiful, and by the appreciation of real estate, have become of immense value. During the war the property fell first into the hands of the one belligerent and then the other. Its restoration to the State has been recently proposed by the military authorities, but for the want of an appropriation for its support, no action has been taken upon the proposition. I recommend an inquiry into the rights of the State in this Institution, and for such action as its condition may require.

In this connection, I invite your attention to the fact, that certain humane and enterprising citizens of Knoxville, have undertaken by private donations, to establish a Medical Hospital in that city. Three valuable acres of land, well watered, and in a desirable locality, within the corporate limits of the city, have been donated by deed, and as much as thirty-five hundred dollars ($3,500) in money has been contributed. The parties are not able to complete their noble enterprise in a style worthy of its design.

The interests of the State, as well as humanity, demand that it should not fail. As the subject is worthy of your consideration, and as that division of the State has received comparatively but little from the State, in aid of public charities, I recommend the appropriation of a sufficient sum—say five or ten thousand dollars—either in money or bonds, to the establishment of the institution contemplated.

BANK OF TENNESSEE.

It may be necessary for you to look into the management of the assets of the Bank of Tennessee, now in process of liquidation. Complaints as to this management have reached me, but whether they are well founded or not, I have no means to determine. But I will mention one fact, that I hear of no suits being brought against those who so thoroughly plundered the Bank during the war, though the plunderers and their sureties appear to be accessible by writs.

The act passed in February last, 'to wind up and settle the business of the Bank,' intrusts the work of liquidation to six directors, nominated by the Governor and confirmed by the Senate.

The act further provides for an assignment of the assets, with a view to protect the collection and distribution from vexatious suits and costs.

The assignment having been made, defects in the working of the law are manifested.

It is left uncertain whether the Directors have any further control over the assets after the assignment, or whether by the assignment their powers and duties are not transferred to the Assignee. As clauses in the old charter of the Bank of Tennessee, remaining unrepealed, prohibit the compensation, in any form, of the Directors for services rendered, doubts are entertained as to whether the present Board can be paid, as the law stands, for time and labor bestowed on the assets. They are really not Directors, though so termed in the act, but commissioners or agents, not for ordinary banking, but for collection and settlement.

The law should be amended so as to prescribe the duties and powers of the Assignee and the Directors, and so as to allow compensation for such services as have been or may hereafter be rendered by the Directors.

EAST TENNESSEE RAILROADS.

When the military authorities turned over the railroads of the State to their owners, the different railroad companies were compelled to purchase largely of the rolling stock and supplies belonging to the Government—their own having been captured during the war. Large debts were thus incurred, some of which are already pressing upon the companies for payment. Most of these roads had large claims against the United States, which they had a reasonable hope would be credited to them. But in this they have been disappointed. As to the East Tennessee and Virginia and the East Tennessee and Georgia Railroads, the Government seems inclined to extend no indulgence whatever. The President of the former company has been notified from Washington, that the Government would take possession of his road about the present time, and similar notice is expected as to the latter. Such a step will be a great misfortune to the companies and to the interests of the State. It will disable them from meeting the interest on their share of the State debt, which will have to be paid by taxation on the people, or the creditors of the State be postponed, which every Tennessean will deplore. The commendable spirit with which you have come to the rescue of the railroads of the State, and the ability with which you have restored and sustained the State credit, emboldens me to ask of you still further exertions in behalf of the same great interests. I recommend the appointment of commissioners to urge a settlement of accounts with the General Government, and if need be, the extension of further State aid to said roads. The State has already invested in the two roads I have mentioned, over four millions (4,000,000) of dollars. They are main trunk roads, and will ultimately repay every dollar the State may loan them, so that the path of both interest and duty, is plain. I further advise that the four per cent. of a sinking fund, required on all roads of the State, be reduced to two per cent, as this will be ample.

COMPENSATION TO LOYAL CITIZENS.

I must again call your attention to the subject of remunerating loyal men for the losses they sustained by the Federal Army. We have able and efficient representation in Congress, and I propose that you lay the subject before our Representatives and Senators, and urge their immediate action in behalf of these just and pressing claims.

EMIGRATION.

It was our fond hope that, upon the restoration of peace, the termination of slavery, and the establishment of civil government, a tide of emigration would set into this State from the Northern States and from Europe; that men of capital and enterprise, attracted by our mild and healthy climate, fertile soil, magnificent scenery, pure and abundant water, would come among us and aid in the rapid development of our vast resources. Our disappointment is attributable to the intolerant and proscriptive spirit of a large portion of those lately in rebellion. With them every Union man is an 'abolitionist,' and every 'abolitionist' an enemy, to be proscribed, despised and driven from the country. I attribute the violence of these pestilential disloyalists, to the insane policy of the President, who constantly holds out to them the prospect of being restored to power at an early day. The treatment of the few who have brought their families and means among us, has been such as to engender a feeling of insecurity of life and property, a sense of social isolation, and a consciousness that they are liable at any time to be expelled from the country. Some good citizens, men of enterprise and capital, have actually returned to the Northern States, in consequence of ill treatment.

It is to be hoped, however, that these passions and prejudices will wear away, and common sense resume its sway; that as the power and influence of the President, now so rapidly waning, shall cease to stimulate their vain and foolish hopes for supremacy in the country, they will see the great advantage of not only treating immigrants with common respect, but of encouraging them to settle among us. It is to be hoped that they will soon learn that their former contracted and sectional ideas can never again prevail, and they will soon fall into the great radical idea of equal rights to all men in all sections of our great country. Hoping and believing that a better spirit will soon prevail, without going into details, I recommend that you extend every encouragement within your constitutional power to immigration. Agencies may be established and paid; companies to facilitate immigration may be incorporated with liberal charters, and material aid may be extended to the foreigner to enable him to journey to our borders. One company has already been incorporated and organized, at the head of which is the illustrious hero of Tennessee. The company is composed of public spirited citizens who, also, make it a business enterprise. They have a capital of one million dollars paid in, and have already purchased......acres of land, and design to sell to immigrants in small farms, and on reasonable terms, both as to price, and time of payment. I recommend this company to your care and encouragement, if they ask for additional privilege.

BOLTERS AND REBEL SUITS.

Stimulated by the spirit of rebellion, and encouraged by the Administration at Washington, a revolutionary faction in the Representative branch in your body, have twice succeeded in reducing the House below a quorum, by withdrawing from their seats or by refusing to attend its sessions, thus endangering the existence of the Government itself. Such conduct shows that the official oath of such members is not a sufficient guarantee for their good conduct, when under the influence of Presidential intrigues.

At the instance of disloyal men—enemies of the State and National Governments—malicious suits have been brought against the Sergeant-at-Arms and a portion of the members, for attempting to enforce a plain provision of the Constitution. While I do not doubt the power of less than a quorum of either House, to compel the attendance of members, I recommend that the constitutional provision on this subject, be amplified by enactment prescribing the mode and means of exercising that necessary power. While it is your peculiar province to punish those who insult the dignity of the Legislature of Tennessee, and obstruct its lawful action, I may be permitted to recommend, as a duty to yourselves, to your country and posterity, that you protect the faithful men, who so persistently upheld the Government against all such wicked and malicious suits, and that you summarily punish the guilty agents concerned in these indignities. The very existence of the law-making power is involved in this affair, and should not be treated lightly.

Prompted by a similar spirit of rebellion and nullification, writs of mandamus have been sworn out, to harrass and annoy the Commissioners of Registration, and to defeat the operation of the 'Franchise Law.'

Bills of injunction have been filed against those intrusted with the duties imposed by the Metropolitan Police Law, intended to preserve order and prevent crime, in certain large cities of the State; while County Courts, in defiance of the laws, have refused to levy the necessary tax to carry out its provisions.

All of these proceedings are but the outcropping of that rebellious disposition which for four years set all law at defiance.

You have the power, and it is your duty to meet these movements by such legislation as cannot be misunderstood or misconstrued by designing men.

RELIANCE UPON CONGRESS.

I am happy to announce to you, officially, that since your last adjournment, when the President had not only abandoned us, but as I have every reason to believe, was contemplating the overthrow of the State Government, the Congress of the United States, by Joint Resolution, have solemnly recognized it, and declared it to be the lawful government of the State of Tennessee, and have admitted our Representatives and Senators to their seats, and our noble State has resumed its relations to the American Union.

In the struggle which yet awaits us, we can look alone to the great body of the loyal American people to sustain and protect us. In this connection, I congratulate you and the country on the recent triumphs at the ballot-box, in the loyal States, of sound national principles as represented by Congress, over the insane policy of the President. The victory was obtained by the Union people over a party, consisting of a combination of rebels at the South and traitors at the North, sustained by the power and patronage of the President. As it was decided in the field, in the great military struggles, that this nation shall live, so it has been decided at the ballot-box that loyal men alone, shall govern it. The great heart of the loyal people is in sympathy with us; and they will require their representatives to sustain us against the assaults of rebels at home, or the usurpation of an unscrupulous President.

The loyal people, in advance of their leaders, have declared that the Government shall not pass into the hands of its enemies, and that the people of the rebellious States, who labored for four years to destroy the Government, shall not be restored to fellowship in the Union, without proper guarantees for the future safety of the country.

It has been, moreover, determined at the ballot-box in the loyal States, that the loyal men, North and South, shall be protected; that the basis of representation throughout the Union shall be equal; that leading and malignant traitors shall not hold office; that the doors of Congress shall not be opened to blood-stained rebels, merely because the President so orders; and also, that the President has no right to set up a policy in opposition to the policy inaugurated by the representatives of the people—in short, that 'traitors shall take back seats,' and 'treason shall be made odious.'

Thus the sky brightens to the loyal men of the Nation, so recently cast down by the afflictions of war. During the dark days of the rebellion, their enemies laughed at their calamities. Since peace came, a faithless Executive sought to betray them into the hands of these same enemies.

But the right has triumphed. Those great trials and afflictions which have endured for four years, have worked out for the Republic 'a far more exceeding and eternal weight of glory.' The late great struggle exhibited her immense power and vast resources, and placed her where she will stand throughout recorded time, in the front rank of the naval and military powers of the earth.

WILLIAM G. BROWNLOW."

There can be no serious doubt but that Brownlow bestowed a great deal of thought in the preparation of the above Message to the Legislature. He was fully aware that his former intense hatred of the Negro race could conceivably alienate him from the Northern Radicals, such as Stevens and Sumner. His *private* opinion of the Negro had been in 1858 *publicly* expressed in a spirited joint debate with a Northern minister in Philadelphia. Brownlow knew that his opinions as expressed in that debate might lead to trouble. He had declared in that debate [155]

"That the curse of slavery was imposed upon the descendants of Ham. ... The descendants of Ham were *black when born* ... [Ham's] wife was a *negro wench*, inheriting Cain's *mark*, and that mark was a *black skin*. ... That the African, in maturity, exhibits the imperfect brain of a Caucasian *foetus* two months before birth. ..."

When reduced to plain English, could not Brownlow's opponents cite his above expression as meaning that a full-grown African had about as much sense as a white baby, two months before its birth? Those hasty and ill-conceived taunts, might they not now rise up like Banquo's ghost and haunt him? He had broken completely with President Andrew Johnson by forcing through the Tennessee Legislature approval of the Fourteenth Amendment. But the Fourteenth Amendment did not confer the right of suffrage upon the Negro, as the question of suffrage was left optional with the States of the Union. And NOW Parson Brownlow had to face that problem! To advocate or not to advocate Negro suffrage was the question! And the Northern Radicals would demand that he take a position!

And so, with quite a bit of pussy-footing, Brownlow finally blurted out in his Message that he "desired to act in harmony with the great body of the loyal people of the Union" and that he had noted "a greater aptitude for learning and intelligence than was expected" on the part of the Negro race.

Although the Legislature was in control of the Radicals, yet there were delay and procrastination regarding the question of granting

---

[155] Brownlow and Pryne, *Ought American Slavery to be Perpetuated?* 204; 213–14.

suffrage to the Negro. East Tennessee, the stronghold of the Radicals, had never liked the Negro, and most assuredly the Conservative Unionists and ex-Confederates of Middle and West Tennessee did not desire to see the former slave placed on an equal footing with the former master and landlord. And so, nearly three months of the legislative session had rolled by with nothing done regarding Negro suffrage. Brownlow's tepid admonition that the conferring of the ballot upon the colored man was a question that demanded the earnest consideration and final decision of the Legislature had not spurred the Radical leadership to take any significant steps to consummate that objective. The legislative lagging eventually "smoked out" Brownlow from the "easy" position which he had assumed in his first Message. On January 23, 1867, he was forced "to break his silence" and come forth with a more definite proposal. Here was his Message* in part:

"GENTLEMEN OF THE SENATE AND HOUSE OF REPRESENTATIVES:

*   *   *   *   *   *   *   *

THE FRANCHISE QUESTION.

I deem this a proper occasion on which to call your attention to other matters of vital importance.

I must, therefore, be permitted to express the hope that this General Assembly will not close its present session without the passage of a Bill granting suffrage to all loyal males, properly qualified by age and citizenship. Onward, is the watchword which thrills and inspires two Continents! And now is the time for Tennessee to show to the world, that she belongs to the advance guard on the great question of equal suffrage. With the loyal men of the State allowed to vote, the Government thereof will remain in loyal hands—without their votes, the State will pass into disloyal hands, and a reign of terror, not so easily described as realized, will be the result.

THE TENNESSEE PACIFIC RAILROAD.

I advise that additional State aid be granted to the Tennessee Pacific Railroad. This is not a local, but a general enterprise, in which the three grand divisions of the State are alike interested. Nay, it is

---

* *Senate Journal*, Second Adjourned Session, 1866–67, 167–172.
    House Journal, Second Adjourned Session, 1866–67, 171–176.
    Author's note. The first portion of this Message dealt with an exchange of letters between Governor Brownlow and the State Treasurer regarding the transfer of State funds. The funds were deposited in a private bank which quickly "folded up," and censure by the Legislature led to the resignation of State Treasurer, R. L. Stanford, who shortly thereafter committed suicide.

a great National measure, in which the whole country is interested, and no State more than Tennessee, as it will tend to develop her great mineral and other resources.

To offer an argument in favor of the great enterprise, I would be offering an insult to the intelligence and patriotism of the General Assembly.

DEFEAT OF THE SCHOOL BILL.

It is with the deepest regret, I have witnessed the bad effect upon the best interests of our State, in other sections, of the defeat of the 'School Bill.'

The cry comes up from every quarter, that men of enterprise and capital will not settle where they cannot educate their children. The failure to pass the School Bill, is construed into opposition to the cause of Education, and if this impression is not removed by the passage of a sound and liberal School Law, the State will languish for want of immigration and capital.

CRIMINAL COURTS.

Criminal prosecutions have so multiplied in our Circuit Courts, since the war, that parties having important civil suits, have been prevented from a hearing, to their great injury, and, in many instances, to their ruin. I propose to remedy this evil by providing a Criminal Judge for every Chancery District where there is not now a Criminal Judge. But if the Legislature, in its wisdom, should not agree with me in this recommendation, I respectfully urge that body to provide some other remedy against this great and growing evil. The State owes relief to her citizens, who have important civil suits in the Courts of the Country.

LIQUOR SELLING NEAR COLLEGES.

Frequent applications are being made to the Legislature by petitions and otherwise, for special Acts prohibiting the sale of ardent spirits within certain distances in the vicinity of certain institutions of learning. I advise that a general law be enacted, affording this character of protection to every college and academy in the State. We owe it to the cause of Christian morality, to the cause of popular education, and to the young and rising generation, to separate liquor shops from our institutions of learning. Should we neglect this work, not only will all the terrible evils of intemperance increase and multiply, till they sweep away every vestige of propriety, peace, good order and liberty from the State, and bring down upon us, as a State, Sodom's guilt and Sodom's doom.

ACCOUNTS BETWEEN THE STATE AND THE RAILROADS.

The entire account of the State with the Railroad Companies— and especially that portion relating to the Sinking Fund, has been so badly kept, during the war, and before, that the books are very unsatisfactory. I advise the appointment of a committee of your body, to sit, after your adjournment, and make new settlements with all the roads, that the books may be made to show all settlements satisfactory, both to the State and Companies. The expense of such settlement will be more than compensated for by rescuing the accounts from ruinous oblivion.

INTEREST ON THE STATE BONDS.

The letters and dispatches sent to my address from New York, show that the interest upon our State Bonds has not been met as promptly as the honor and credit of the State require. The fault is ours, and the failure could have been prevented, had more vigilance and efficiency been displayed at home. I hope the like will not occur on the first of July, and I earnestly invoke the Legislature to provide against a similar disaster, by prompt action. For Tennessee to fail to meet the interest upon her bonds, and to have her credit suffer from home, is alike disgraceful to the officers of the State Government, and to the General Assembly.

I will gladly co-operate with you in the adoption of any measures that may be deemed wise, or calculated to promote the public welfare; and I earnestly invoke the blessing of the Great Ruler of nations, upon all your deliberations.

WILLIAM G. BROWNLOW."

Having spoken with such pronounced emphasis on granting the franchise "to all loyal males," which by implication included the Negro, Brownlow had the satisfaction of seeing the Legislature move into high. On the same day of the reception of the Message, Representative W. A. Garner of Lawrence County introduced a bill [156]

[156] House Journal, Second Adjourned Session, 1866–67, 179.

"To amend an Act to limit the Elective Franchise, passed May 3, 1866."

After three or four postponements, a substitute bill was introduced and adopted by a vote of 41 to 23.[157] An amendment to the substitute bill was then adopted whereby the Negro was prohibited from holding office or sitting on juries.[158] Conservative Representative John Lellyett of Davidson County offered an amendment [159] that would have enfranchised ex-Confederates as well as Negroes, but his proposal was defeated by a vote of 42 to 20. On February 6, 1867, the amended bill was passed on third and final reading by a vote of 38 to 25,[160] with seven East Tennessee Representatives voting in the negative. On February 18, the bill was passed in the Senate by a vote of 14 to 7, with two Senators from East Tennessee voting against passage.[161] The passage of this bill put the "Negro in politics" in Tennessee. True enough, Free Persons of Color had been privileged to vote in Tennessee under the 1796 Constitution, but numerically the vote was extremely limited. Even so, the Constitution of 1835 denied suffrage to the above limited class of Negroes. But now, with the passage of the "Brownlow law" of 1867, the former slave was placed on an equal footing with his former master insofar as exercising the privilege of voting was concerned.

When Brownlow hinted at Negro suffrage in his Message in the fall of 1866 but came up with a strong recommendation in a supplementary Message in early 1867, this was the first time in the history of Tennessee that any such proposal had been placed before the General Assembly by the Chief Executive. There can be no reasonable doubt but that the exigencies of the political situation drove Brownlow to this extreme. He had witnessed the gradually melting away of the Brownlow group, and his only hope to remain in political control was to buttress his support by the addition of Negro votes. And so, with his usual cry of "wolf, wolf," he pointed out that the State government was in imminent danger of passing into other hands; and that "without their votes [NEGRO VOTES, that is to say] the State will pass into disloyal hands, and a reign of terror not so easily described as realized will be the result."

Although the law [162] did not mention Negro *per se* regarding suffrage privileges, nevertheless by clear implication the Negro was embraced within its provisions. Section I declared that

"Every male inhabitant of this State, of the age of twenty-one years, a citizen of the United States, and a resident of the county wherein he may

---

[157] *Ibid.*, 235.
[158] *Ibid.*, 235.
[159] *Ibid.*, 234.
[160] *Ibid.*, 243.
[161] *Senate Journal*, Second Adjourned Session, 1866–67, 306.
[162] *Acts of Tennessee*, Second Adjourned Session, 1866–67, Chapter 26.

offer his vote, six months preceding the day of election, shall be entitled to the privilege of the elective franchise. . . ."

Inasmuch as the Fourteenth Amendment recognized the emancipated slaves as being "citizens of the United States," there could be no doubt as to their political status. With the enactment of the above law, the Tennessee Negro was advanced to the ballot-box where he was now privileged to cast his ballot. While the law clearly defined the position of the Negro regarding voting privileges, the same law also excluded a large number of white citizens from exercising the same privilege. Among those who were denied the right to vote were: (1) those who had borne arms against the Government of the United States; (2) those who had voluntarily given aid, comfort, counsel, or encouragement to any rebellion against the authority of the United States Government; (3) those who had accepted any civil or military office under the authority of the Confederate States of America; and (4) those who had contributed either money or property in support of any "pretended government hostile or inimical to the authority of the United States." In a nutshell, the above law enfranchised the Negro and disfranchised the ex-Confederate. The only restriction applied to the Negro was that he was not permitted "to hold office or sit on juries."[163] Political necessity alone drove Brownlow to espouse Negro suffrage, and when that conclusion was reached by him he was ready to "cross the Rubicon." With the enactment of the Negro suffrage law, Tennessee was the only State in the South at the time (1867) that permitted the Negro to vote. Tennessee Conservatives did not have to be reminded that their own *native* Radicals, spurred on by Parson Brownlow, had forced upon the citizenry of Tennessee a law more drastic and more extreme than any imposed up to that time by the Northern Radicals. Truly, the overwhelming majority of the citizenry of the State were to taste the bitter dregs of Brownlowism and Radicalism now run riot.

The Conservative press denounced the Negro suffrage law in fierce attacks. One of the most drastic condemnations was by a newspaper [164] in a city under Brownlow's Metropolitan Police statute:

"It would be better for the whole black breed to be swept away by a pestilence. . . . The right to vote might just as safely be given to so many South American monkeys as to the plantation negroes of Mississippi and Louisiana. . . ."

With an estimated four-fifths of the Tennesseans who constituted the landed and monied interests in the State now disfranchised by the recent law, the Radicals realized that this large group would not tamely submit to the proscriptive penalty on the whites imposed by the Negro

---

[163] *Ibid.*, Section 16.
[164] *Memphis Appeal*, February 26, 1867.

franchise act. Here and there, isolated instances of "lawless" opposition to Radical rule flared up. One episode that greatly incensed the Radicals was the murder of Senator Almon Case of Obion County. Senator Case, a native of Ohio, had moved to Tennessee and was a strong Union man. At the time of his tragic death, January 14, 1867, he was a member of the State Senate and had voted all along with the Radicals. His assailant was a man by the name of Frank Farris who was called "A rebel guerilla ruffian" by *Harper's Weekly* [165] which carried Senator Case's picture and an artist's conception of the murder. This unwarranted incident stirred the Radical Legislature to white heat and doubtless had some effect upon some extreme measures that were rapidly enacted into law. A strong resolution was adopted in which condemnation of "that spirit of hatred, malice, and uncharitableness—the legitimate fruits of treason" was voiced, and the Governor was requested to offer a reward of two thousand dollars for the apprehension of the assassin. [166]

A month after the assassination of Senator Case, Senator A. M. Cate of Hamilton County presented Senate Bill No. 537 entitled [167]

"An Act to organize a State Guard."

Within a week, the bill passed both branches of the Legislature without difficulty, and something "new under the sun" was placed upon the statute books of Tennessee.

What might properly be termed a "new army law" was embodied in the brief three-section law [168] captioned "An Act to Organize and Equip a State Guard, and for other purposes." This was a law authorizing and empowering the Governor to call into service one or more regiments from each Congressional District "when in his opinion the safety of life, property, liberty, or the faithful execution of law require it." As a safeguard against any mutiny or "soldiering on the job," only "*loyal men*" were to be enrolled. With Negroes enfranchised, all ex-Confederates and many Conservative Unionists disfranchised, and with all the election machinery rigged and in the hands of Brownlow, what earthly power could prevent the Radical regime from running rough shod over any opposition that might arise? And yet, despite such tyrant-like power, Brownlow knew that he was skating upon thin ice, politically; he realized that drastic action was imperative if Radical rule were to be maintained in the State. Consequently, he recommended in his November Message authorization for

". . . the enlistment of a few regiments of loyal militia, to be armed and

[165] *Harper's Weekly*, Volume XI, 100.
[166] *Senate Journal*, Second Adjourned Session, 1866-67, 184-185.
[167] *Ibid.*, 280.
[168] *Acts of Tennessee*, Second Adjourned Session, 1866-67, Chapter 24.

held as minute men, subject to the call of the Executive, to suppress insurrection or protect the ballot-box."

It should be noted that the Governor's phraseology, "protect the
ballot-box," was toned down by substituting in the statute a more
euphemistic expression, "faithful execution of law"! If space permitted,
countless examples could be cited showing that in the approaching
August election (1867), when a Governor and legislative members were
up for election, bayonets and muskets in the hands of Radicals and
Negroes provided potent "persuaders" at many voting precincts
throughout the State.[169]

With complete control of all election machinery in his hands and
henceforth reinforced by armed troops subject to his command, once
more the Parson displayed a Dr. Jekyll and Mr. Hyde right-about-face.
Shortly after his highhanded and ruthless manner of forcing through
the Legislature approval of the Fourteenth Amendment, Brownlow felt
the impact of an outraged public's condemnation. Perhaps the editorial
thunderbolts from numerous newspapers, both at home and abroad, led
him to take a self-inventory of his political status. At any rate, in the
summer of 1866, he addressed an effusion [170] to the "*loyal*" people of
Tennessee wherein he declared that

"It is proper for me to state that my term of office will expire in October, 1867, and that I shall not be a candidate for reelection to the office I
now hold, or to any other office within the gift of the people."

Some eight months later when the Radicals, who now styled themselves the Republican Union Party, met in convention at Nashville on
February 22, 1867, for nomination of a candidate for Governor, the
Parson transmitted to that body an unctuous epistle citing his poor
state of health. But the chronic itinerant invalid hastily added that he
would not feel free to decline the nomination should it be offered him!
The tiger cub had lapped its first blood and wanted more! Like
Homer's giant quaffing from the golden goblet of Ulysses, Brownlow
also was crying out, "Give, Oh give me more, it is divine!" And the
Radical enthusiasts shouted, "So mote it be!" The well-greased election
machinery plus the power to summon clanking swords and rattling
militia musketry blotted from the Parson's memory all traces of his

---

[169] Author's note. In Chapter X, "High Tide of Radicalism," in *Political Reconstruction in Tennessee* by Thomas B. Alexander, a detailed and well-documented
treatise is presented wherein "the use of the state guard constituted one of the
most distressing aspects of the entire campaign from the Conservative point of
view . . . twenty-one companies were organized and scattered over the state under
the command of Brigadier General Joseph A. Cooper." Dr. Alexander's analysis
and interpretation of the role played by Brownlow's armed guards constitute the
most critical and accurate account that has thus far been written.

[170] *Republican Banner*, August 25, 1866.

former declaration not to seek again "any office within the gift of the people."

With Negroes privileged to vote and with an armed guard at his command, Brownlow now felt that he was ready for any eventuality. There was no ground for any doubt as to the "loyalty" of the State Guard personnel, inasmuch as each member was required to pass a test of "loyalty" which included the taking of the franchise oath. The State Guard composed of rampant Radicals and enfranchised Negroes was a modern version of Oliver Cromwell's zealous Puritans, the "Ironsides." Two uses of the State Guard were available to Brownlow—first, as a club to back up his threats and, secondly, actual service in carrying out a "faithful execution of the law" by being stationed around and about the ballot-box if deemed expedient by Brownlow.

In less than a week after the enactment of the State Guard law, Brownlow under the war-like title of *Commander-in-Chief* issued a proclamation to the "Loyal Militia" wherein he cited certain "outrages" being committed by "disloyal men" who were alleged to have been fomenting strife and damaging the prestige of the State in general. Here was his proclamation [171] in which he quoted verbatim the recently-enacted law:

"A PROCLAMATION TO THE LOYAL MILITIA.

Whereas,

It has been made known to me, the Governor of the State of Tennessee, that certain atrocious murders and numerous outrages have been committed in certain counties in this State, by violent and disloyal men, upon the persons and property of Union men, whose only offense has been their unswerving devotion to the National Flag, and their uniform support of the State Government; and whereas, these bad men are banding themselves together in some localities, and notifying loyal men to leave within a given time. Now, therefore, I, WILLIAM G. BROWNLOW, Governor as aforesaid, by virtue of the authority and power in me vested, do hereby solemnly proclaim, that I intend to put a stop to all such outrages, by at once calling into actual service a sufficient number of Loyal volunteers, under the following recent act, which is now the law of Tennessee:

An Act to organize and equip a State Guard, and for other purposes.

Be it enacted by the General Assembly of the State of Tennessee,

[171] Ms. [Brownlow's] *Proclamation Book*, 74–75.

That the Governor is hereby authorized and empowered to organize, equip and call into active service a volunteer force to be composed of one or more regiments from each Congressional District of the State; Provided always, that the Tennessee State Guard shall be composed of loyal men, who shall take and subscribe the oath prescribed in the Franchise Act.

Sec. 2. Be it further enacted, That the Governor shall be Commander in Chief, and any member of said force shall be subject to his order, when in his opinion the safety of life, property, liberty, or the faithful execution of law require it; to be organized, armed, equipped, regulated and governed by the rules and articles of war and the revised army regulations of the United States, so far as applicable, and shall receive pay and allowances according to grade of rank, as provided for the United States army while in active service, to be paid out of any money in the State Treasury not otherwise appropriated; Provided, that the force provided for by this Act shall not be armed and equipped until called into active service by the Governor.

Sec. 3. Be it further enacted, That this act shall take effect from and after its passage.

Standing, as I do, on the broad principles of the Constitution, and sworn to enforce the laws, I have no concessions to make to traitors, no compromises to offer to assassins and robbers; and if, in the sweep of coming events, retributive Justice shall overtake the lawless and violent, their own temerity will have called it forth. The outrages enumerated *must* and *shall* cease. Having reached the foregoing conclusion, I feel justified in expressing the opinion that the present State Government in Tennessee—so generally acquiesced in by loyal and law abiding people—will be sustained and preserved, despite all the efforts of disappointed traitors and disloyal Newspapers. The interests of trade, of agricultural pursuits, of commercial intercourse between this State and others—of the development of our vast resources, of emigration, as well as justice to loyal sufferers—all require that these outrages at once cease in every County in the State.

Disloyal men are giving forth their vile utterances in railroad cars, in public hotels, on the streets, and through the newspapers, damaging the material interests of the State, those of commerce, those of mechanic arts, of religion and education, as well as bringing reproach upon the Commonwealth. I cannot, however, close this brief proclamation without endeavoring to impress upon my fellow Citizens of all parties, the importance—the absolute necessity—of remaining quiet, of preserving good order, and a quiet submission to, and a rigid enforcement of the laws every where within the limits of our State. Outrages upon loyal Citizens, whether white or black, and the setting aside of the franchise law, are all the work of bad men, who desire to foment strife, and will not be tolerated. Prudent and experienced men will be placed in charge of the 'State Guard' in every County where they are placed, who will be required to protect all good citizens, irrespective of political parties, and to punish murderers, robbers, and all violaters of law, and the number of troops called into active service will be increased or diminished as the good or bad conduct of the people shall be developed.

Hoping this proclamation will strengthen the hands and inspire the hearts of the loyal people of the State, as to the future, and deter the disloyal from further act of violence, I respectfully submit it, with a repetition of the assurance that I mean what I say, and that the General Assembly was in earnest in the passage of this military law.

In testimony whereof I have hereunto set my hand, and (SEAL) caused the great seal of the State to be affixed at the Executive Department in Nashville, on the 25th day of Feb. 1867.

WILLIAM G. BROWNLOW
Commander in Chief, Vc."

Whether the expressed "fears" of Governor Brownlow were real or feigned must perhaps remain a mooted point. Certain expressions in his proclamation, such as "I mean what I say," smack a bit of braggadocio and bluff. At any rate, on March 6, some two weeks after the creation of the State Guard, under his new monicker of Commander-in-Chief Order No. 1 was issued calling for volunteers for three years service unless sooner terminated.[172] Captains were appointed to raise companies of one hundred men, twenty-five of whom were to be mounted to act as scouts. A week prior to this call for volunteer troops, the Legislature had called upon the Federal Government "for a sufficient force of United States soldiers to keep the peace, and restore order and quiet in our State."[173] General Thomas, through whom the request was made, replied that the rebellion in Tennessee was at an end and that Federal

[172] Hamer: *Tennessee—A History*, Volume II, 620.
[173] *Acts of Tennessee*, Second Adjourned Session, 1866-67, Resolution XCI.

troops had no right to interfere in the administration of civil government. Undaunted by this adverse reply, Brownlow proceeded to implement his State Guard. These troops were stationed in various places, especially in Middle and West Tennessee, and remained there during the heated gubernatorial and legislative campaign in August, 1867.

Violent reaction and indignant protests were voiced by the disfranchised majority against Brownlow's iron-glove regime. The movement was characterized as an overthrow of civil government, and predictions were made that strife, disorder, plunder, and revenge would be the logical results of such an unwarranted disregard of law and order.

With the enfranchising of the Negro and with a State Guard to enforce the provisions of the franchise law, the chief objectives of the "Brownlow Legislature" had been attained. All other matters were of minor consideration. The Legislature, however, complied with Governor Brownlow's request for an increase in the salaries of the Judiciary. Salaries of Supreme Court Judges were raised to $3,500 per year, and all other Judges except County Judges were rewarded by an increase in salary to $2,500 per year.[174]

By recalling Shakespeare's famous encomium upon the uses of adversity

> "Which, like a toad, ugly and venomous,
> Wears yet a precious jewel in his head,"

an optimist can locate two "jewels" in the actions of the 1866–67 Legislature which held forth one hundred and twenty-seven days. One "jewel" was displayed on March 11, 1867, that being the day of *sine die* ADJOURNMENT! But, as Cervantes said in his *Don Quixote*, it is meet

> "To give the devil his due."

The above Legislature along with Governor Brownlow had one other "jewel" to chalk up on the credit side of the ledger. That praiseworthy action dealt with public education. Governor Brownlow was so saturated with the idea of a "Threatened State Revolution" that he overlooked altogether the subject of education in his November Message. The Legislature, upon its own initiative, had in the previous year formulated a comprehensive educational bill which was passed in the Senate [175] by a vote of 10 to 8, but encountered a postponement in the lower House.[176] It was to this adverse action that Governor Brownlow referred in his January (1867) Message expressing his deep regret at the "Defeat of the School Bill."

---

[174] *Ibid.*, Chapter 20.
[175] *Senate Journal*, First Adjourned Session, 1865–66, 347.
[176] *House Journal*, First Adjourned Session, 1865–66, 619.

Despite the Governor's omission of any reference to education in his November Message, Representative James Mullins from the counties of Bedford and Rutherford entered a motion on November 14, 1866, that

"Two hundred and fifty copies of Senate Bill No. 170—the School Bill—be printed."[177]

Since the present Legislature was meeting in its Second Adjourned Session, it was sound parliamentary procedure to pick up the bill that had been postponed at the First Adjourned Session and place it on the current calendar. This educational bill, comprehensive in its nature and by far the most progressive educational bill ever thus far presented to a Legislature, was passed in the lower House on February 28, 1867, by a vote of 38 to 29.[178] On March 5, the bill with a number of House amendments was called up in the Senate and upon motion by Senator John W. Smith of Shelby County, calling for the ayes and nays, the bill squeaked through by a vote of 11 to 10.[179]

An analysis of the law [180] passed by the "Brownlow Legislature" shows that the provisions of the law comprehended the establishment of a centralized supervisory agency which power was vested in a State official called the Superintendent of the Common Schools. It was also provided that the boards of education of the civil districts in the several counties of the State should elect a County Superintendent whose term of office was to be for a period of three years. For purposes of administration, each civil district in each county was coterminous with the school district, while the several school districts, then in existence, or to be thereafter established in the organized civil districts, were to be regarded as sub-districts. Each sub-district was to have three school directors, one of whom was to be designated as Clerk of the sub-district board. The various clerks of the sub-districts constituted the Civil District Board of Education. The teachers were required to prepare and submit to the Civil District Board of Education a full report concerning the school taught, said report to contain detailed information as indicated in the law. It was made unlawful for the local school officials to pay the teacher for services rendered if the teacher had not filed a certified report as above directed. The County Superintendent was required to submit to the State Superintendent of Common Schools an annual report covering all the educational activities of the county. The chief school official for the State was to be elected every two years

---

[177] House Journal, Second Adjourned Session, 1866–67, 13.
[178] Ibid., 339.
[179] Senate Journal, Second Adjourned Session, 1866–67, 407.
[180] Acts of Tennessee, 1866–67, Chapter 27.
Author's note. See Robt. H. White, Development of the Tennessee State Educational Organization, 1796–1929, for an extended analysis of all educational legislation during the Brownlow administration as set forth in Chapter IV.

by the qualified voters of the State, and was required to submit to the Governor an annual report on the status of educational conditions within the State. The Governor, in turn, was directed to place before the next legislature a copy of said report.

The Free Common Schools to be established under the provisions of this act were to be supported by the proceeds arising from any school funds then in existence and by the money raised from an annual levy and assessment of two mills on each dollar of taxable property in the State and, in addition, from a tax of 25 cents on each male citizen over twenty-one years of age and under fifty years of age. Furthermore, after June 30, 1867, every chartered railroad in the State was required to collect and pay over to the Treasury of the State every three months one-fourth of one cent per mile upon each paying passenger transported by said companies on their respective roads. The funds made available under these provisions were to be apportioned by the State Comptroller among the several counties of the State upon a basis of scholastic population. The Common School System thus established made provision for the education of colored children, specifying that they should be taught in separate schools.

On March 11, 1867, after the customary complimentary tributes were paid to the Speakers of each legislative branch, the much discussed and bitterly "cussed" General Assembly adjourned *sine die*. Of the forty-eight public laws enacted, the above educational law and the merited increase in the salaries of the Judiciary appear to have been the only measures of any significant merit that ran the gauntlet of a highly prejudiced and bitterly partisan Legislature. For repressive, depressive, and oppressive legislation, this "Brownlow Legislature" stands without parallel in the sweeping annals of Tennessee for its unenviable record.

"Men's evil manners live in brass."

The Brownlow forces had geared all election machinery and assembled all other "working parts" preparatory to the August election in which were to be elected a Governor, a General Assembly, and members of Congress. In all probability, the gubernatorial race of 1867 was the most bitterly contested of any in the political history of Tennessee. A State Convention of the Radicals, who now called themselves the Republican Union Party, met in Nashville on February 22, 1867. Fiery speeches, condemning the "rebels" and praising the "loyal people," consumed a large portion of the Convention's time. "Parson" Brownlow's letter, heretofore mentioned, was read to the Convention and wild applause rent the air. His "bodily suffering" was deplored while his "healthy mind conscious to itself of rectitude" was highly extolled. There was no other political "Moses" to lead the loyal people, so it was proclaimed, and Brownlow was declared the unanimous choice of the loyal people as their candidate for re-election to the governorship of Tennessee. Something of the spirit that dominated the group may be ascertained by reading their pronouncement,[181] to-wit:

"Resolutions Adopted at the Union Convention in Nashville, February 22, 1867.

We, the representatives of the loyal people of Tennessee, in convention assembled, are thankful to Almighty God for the success of the arms of the United States over the army of traitors, who sought to destroy the best government ever known to man, thereby saving us and our posterity the blessings and privileges of our republican institutions, and a solution of the heretofore doubtful problem that man is capable of self-government.

'We hold these truths to be self-evident':

1. 'That all men are created equal, endowed with certain inalienable rights,' and therefore the law should afford equal protection to all in the exercise of these rights, and, so far as it can, insure perfect equality under the law.

2. That a State or a nation should be governed, controlled and directed by those who have saved it in times of peril, and who seek to preserve it with friendly hands from foes and dangers, external and internal.

3. That a wise care for the public safety sometimes renders it necessary that those who have sought resolutely to overthrow a government should not hastily be restored to the privileges of which they have deprived themselves, by their crime of treason; certainly not until they have shown evidence of sincere repentance, and a disposition as energetically to support as they have, in times past, sought to destroy.

4. That rebellion is disfranchisement, and armed attempts to overthrow our common government, treasonable expatriation; and the present franchise organic law, is but the declaration of the handiwork of secession and rebellion. Those who have sought our country's ruin cannot be entrusted with its safety.

5. That lawless violence, reckless disregard of the rights of person and property, murder, assassination, arson and kindred crimes, must be put down by the strong arm of power, and be made to feel that law is indeed a terror to evil doers.

6. Therefore, in accordance with the above principles, we fully indorse the policy and action of the General Assembly of the State of Tennessee, in restricting the elective franchise to those who are not hostile to the government, in extending it to those who proved their loyalty by imperiling their lives, and who need this privilege for their own protection, and in establishing a military organization which shall give necessary physical support to the moral power of the State Government becoming a salutary terror to evil doers, and a cheerful hope to those who do well.

7. That the 'privileges and immunities' guaranteed under the constitution of our Union to the loyal from other States, and the pledge of freedom and equality in the declaration of American independence, shall be *living truths* and *practical maxims* in Tennessee, for the protection of 'life, liberty and the pursuit of happiness.'

8. That we have entire confidence in the integrity, wisdom, and ability of the Republican Union majority of Congress, and deem it signally fortu-

[181] *Daily Press and Times* (Nashville), March 11, 1867.

nate that they, in whom alone the power resides to restore, preserve and govern the country, have shown themselves so eminently fitted for these high duties, that no State should be admitted to representation in Congress without adopting the constitutional amendment.

9. That the Republican Union party of Tennessee are in favor of free speech and free discussion, and to this end we invite our friends from other States to come among us, and discuss the great issues now before the people, and we pledge the Republican Union party of Tennessee to tolerate all legitimate discussion, and at the same time claiming equal privileges on our part, and that any interference to prevent this will be regarded as an unwarranted act, and resisted to the last extremity.

10. That we honor the firmness, courage, and wisdom which has characterized the administration of our Chief Magistrate, the Hon. Wm. G. Brownlow, and while we sympathise with him in his bodily suffering, we admire the healthy mind, conscious to itself of rectitude, which bears with like equanimity, the throes of pain and the perilous cares of State; and that we declare him the unanimous choice of the loyal people of Tennessee for our next Governor.

11. That we cover our faces with shame when we contemplate the disgrace brought upon our beloved State by the defection and degeneracy of her unprincipled adopted son, who, by the bullet of an assassin has ascended to the Chief Magistracy of the nation; and we shall cordially endorse any action of Congress which shall legitimately deprive him of continued power to disturb the peace of the country."

The gist of the above Radical platform can be reduced to a single proposition—the "loyal" people and only the loyal could be trusted to run the State Government. In a bid for the votes of the recently enfranchised Negroes, Brownlow shouted that he preferred to be elected by dark-skin loyalists rather than by the suffrage of fair-skin traitors. To add color to the scene, on the walls of the House of Representatives where the meeting was being held were suspended pictures of Lincoln and Johnson. To avoid any possibility of doubt as to the attitude of the delegates, the picture of the martyred President was surrounded by flags while Johnson's was left as bare as Mother Hubbard's cupboard. An over-zealous delegate wanted thirty-six men to hold the United States flag in front of Johnson's picture so as "to keep his Accidency quiet during the session of the convention." Another fellow-traveler proposed that the President be stood upon his head! A final verbal blast was hurled at President Johnson signifying hearty approval of the now rapidly-developing plans of the Congressional Radicals to impeach the President.

Although ex-Confederates and Conservative Unionists had been debarred from voting privileges by the recent law, yet they were called to action by a statement issued by twenty-four Conservative members of the Legislature. The call [182] for a meeting of Conservative Union men was scheduled for April 16, and was released on the day of adjournment of the Legislature:

[182] *Ibid.*, March 15, 1867.

"Nashville, March 11, 1867.

The undersigned, Conservative members of the General Assembly of the State of Tennessee, deeply impressed with the dangers which imperil our beloved country, from the reckless disregard upon the part of the majorities in Congress and the Legislature of our own State, of the sage counsels of the founders of our government, and the fundamental principles of our constitution, respectfully propose that there be held in the city of Nashville, on the 16th of April next, a Convention of the true Conservative Union people of the State of all who wish, in the language of the Father of his country, that our Union and brotherly affection may be perpetuated; that our free constitution may be sacredly maintained; that its administration in every department may be stamped with wisdom and virtue; that the happiness of the people of the States, under the auspices of liberty, may be made complete by the careful preservation and prudent use of this blessing— in short, a Convention of all who oppose the tendencies and ruinous policy and practices of the dominant party, for the purposes of taking counsel for the common good of all the people of the State, and to select a standard bearer, in the approaching canvass for Governor, who shall be a true loyal Union man, a firm and determined defender of the constitution and laws of the land, and around whom may rally all the people of the State who desire the full and complete restoration of peace, prosperity and happiness in our beloved State.

J. D. Johnson,	John S. Brien,
J. P. Thompson,	Jas. Jones,
W. J. McFarland,	Wm. W. Coleman,
Harvey Brown,	J. F. Moore,
L. M. Tharp,	Dan Able,
S. L. Warren,	Petree Pearson,
J. T. Street,	L. M. Jarvis,
F. A. Loughmiller,	E. Simmerly,
Henry Biggs,	Wm. Wright,
John R. Shultz,	G. W. Overstreet
R. L. V. Schmittou,	James Lellyett,
R. E. Lasater,	James Parks."

According to the Conservative press, the Conservative Convention was a grand success. A strong Conservative newspaper [183] gave a bird's-eye sketch of the personnel gathered together for the purpose of nominating a candidate for Governor in opposition to Brownlow:

"The hall of the legislature was packed closely, every inch of standing and sitting room being occupied. The right-hand gallery was packed full with white spectators, with a black speck here and there. The left-hand gallery was full of colored people, and likewise a white person scattered here and there. . . ."

Elijah Walker was unanimously chosen chairman and "took the chair amid the deafening cheers of the jubilant assembly." Chairman Walker stated that the purpose of the Convention was "to nominate a candidate for Governor and to inaugurate a new policy, and if they

---

[183] *Memphis Daily Appeal,* April 17, 1867.

succeed they will confer a blessing upon the present generation and generations to come." By unanimous vote, the colored delegates were requested to furnish a list of all colored delegates from each county. A committee of fourteen, one from each Congressional District, and a committee of six representing the State at large had had delegated to them the job of preparing resolutions to be submitted to the Convention. While the above committees were consulting in a private room, the Convention was regaled with rousing speeches by Edmund Cooper, Emerson Etheridge, and Colonel Charles S. Cameron, of Memphis. A Negro, Joe Williams, also addressed the Convention while a colored band from Memphis livened up the meeting with music.

Next, it was announced that the Resolutions Committee was ready to submit its recommendations [184] which were as follows:

"1. We pledge ourselves to the support of the union, the constitution and the maintainance of the laws of the land.

2. That we are the friends of peace and of civil law, and that this great object can be best promoted by a legislature recognizing equal and exact justice to all, exclusive privilege to none.

3. That we are in favor of an immediate restoration of our disfranchised fellow-citizens to the rights, privileges and immunities of a full and a complete citizenship.

4. Our colored fellow-citizens, being now citizens of the United States and citizens of the state of Tennessee, voters of this state, they are entitled to all the rights and privileges of citizens under the laws of the United States and of the state of Tennessee.

5. We are opposed to the repudiation of the national debt; we are in favor of equal taxation as the proper method of paying the same.

6. That the establishment of a standing army in our state in times of peace, is a flagrant and dangerous encroachment on the rights and liberties of the state, violent and oppressive to the taxpayers, and evidently designed to over-awe the voters at the ballot-box.

7. We cordially approve of the patriotic efforts of Andrew Johnson, president of the United States, in defending the constitution, and in preserving and maintaining the supremacy of the law."

With unanimous approval of the resolutions as submitted, the Convention proceeded to nominate a candidate for Governor. Various names were suggested, among them being those of former Whig Governor William B. Campbell, Thomas A. R. Nelson, John Netherland, and Edmund Cooper. Without too much ado, Emerson Etheridge, of Dresden, was nominated as the man to tackle Brownlow and his Radicals. The Convention had nominated a seasoned veteran in political campaigns. He had served in the State Legislature, had been a three-term Congressman, and had served as Clerk of the United States House of Representatives. Furthermore, he was a fluent and powerful speaker, having been declared by a fellow-Congressman as a man possessed "of

---

[184] *Ibid.*

the most original flow of wit and humor."[185] On the other hand, a Radical pro-Brownlow journal [186] denounced Etheridge as

". . . The *blasé* party scullion, the Thersites of the stump, the trafficker of the most foul, vulgar and filthy slang ever spewed up by an obscene mind upon the hustings . . . a politician, who prior to his banishment to private life was a dead weight to his party [but with] 'A gift of gab' on the stump. . . ."

Shortly prior to the actual beginning of the political campaign, a rather amusing incident occurred. The Nashville *Christian Advocate* had carried a "mourning edition" of the death of Bishop Joshua Soule. Some prankster hit upon the idea of announcing the death of Governor Brownlow who was in feeble health, as usual. The editor of the militant pro-Brownlow paper [187] denounced two Nashville anti-Brownlow papers for their comments upon the ill-founded rumor:

"The Gazette of yesterday published the following characteristic paragraph respecting the rumor:
'BROWNLOW DEAD. The city was disturbed muchly yesterday by rumors of Brownlow's serious illness. 'Twas even said on the streets that he had died. Our private opinion is that Brownlow has been dead for the past twelve months, and that the personage at the Capitol is no other than Old Nick himself, who has assumed temporarily the shape and features of the ex-Parson.'

The Banner said: 'It was reported currently yesterday that Governor Brownlow was dead, as if that much accommodation was left in his royal highness.' "

It was a foregone conclusion reached by each contending party that the recently-enfranchised Negro would hold the balance of power in the forthcoming August election. The number of such prospective voters was estimated to be in the neighborhood of 35,000. Consequently, each party sought to snare the Negro vote into its particular fold. While the ultimate results would likely have been unchanged, yet it appears that the Conservatives might have selected a less vulnerable man as gubernatorial candidate in view of Etheridge's pronounced opposition to the Negro. Etheridge had been a former slave-holder and had denounced in bitter terms the Emancipation Proclamation. Just three days before his nomination by the Conservative Party at its Nashville Convention, Etheridge was alleged to have turned loose in a speech at Trenton a blast [188] that was repeated by Radical newspapers throughout the campaign:

"The negroes are no more free than they were forty years ago, and if any one goes about the country telling them that they are free shoot him;

---

[185] Cox, S. S. ("Sunshine Cox"): *Why We Laugh*, 148.
[186] *Daily Press and Times* (Nashville), April 17, 1867.
[187] *Ibid.*, March 15, 1867.
[188] *Daily Press and Times* (Nashville), April 19, 1867.

and these negro troops, commanded by low and degraded white men, going through the country ought to be shot down."

Etheridge denied having uttered any such statement, but the Radical press continued to play it up.

As an antidote to this political poison, the Conservatives dug up the Parson's diatribe against the Negro in his debate with a Northern preacher in the latter part of 1858, the subject of the debate being *Ought American Slavery to be Perpetuated?* From this book which had been prepared and supervised by Brownlow, the Conservative *Central Committee for Middle Tennessee* published a pamphlet [189] of sixteen pages in which Brownlow's hostility toward the Negro was shown by quoting his exact language. Numerous extracts from Brownlow's debate were inserted, the exact page being cited in each instance. For example, Brownlow was revealed as having declared that

> "American slavery is not only not sinful, but especially commanded by God through Moses, and approved through the Apostles by Christ. And I might conclude its defence by asserting what God ordains, and Christ sanctifies, should command the respect and toleration of even Northern Abolitionists."

When Brownlow was confronted by his resurrected and damaging statements regarding the Negro, the Parson with the adroitness of a sleight-of-hand trickster excused himself by saying "that he had been *on the wrong side of the subject*" in his debate with Abram Pryne![190]

The campaign was a rough and tough contest with vituperation, sarcasm, invective, and personal attacks predominating. Contrary to the pre-war custom, there was no joint debate between Brownlow and Etheridge, the Parson's poor health and loss of voice rendering him *hors de combat* (out of the scrap). But what was lacking in his voice was more than made up through the columns of his *Knoxville Whig* which bristled with his tirades and invectives throughout the campaign.

Etheridge opened his campaign in Union City on May 11, and proceeded from town to town in the West Tennessee counties which constituted heavy Conservative territory. Furthermore, heavy Negro populations in that area made it particularly important that every political device be employed to procure their votes. When he reached Nashville in the latter part of May, he spoke to a large audience of which about one-third were Negroes. Here he gave convincing evidence that he could swap verbal blows with Brownlow, by utilizing keen sarcasm, biting invective, and scathing denunciation in his description of the Tennessee Radicals as the party which paid no taxes, wore dirty shirts, and were strangers to the cleansing properties of soap. In his Nashville

---

[189] *Brownlow's Opinion of Colored People* (pamphlet), 11.
[190] *Knoxville Whig*, May 8, 1867.

BROWNLOW'S OPINION

OF

COLORED PEOPLE.

HOW HE LOVES AND ADMIRES THEM:

THEIR ORIGIN:

What He Thinks they are Fit for, etc.

Published by Authority of the Central Committee for Middle Tennessee.

NASHVILLE, TENN.:
PRINTED AT THE UNION AND DISPATCH OFFICE.

1867.

Original pamphlet in private library of Robert H. White, Nashville.

3

speech [191] Etheridge convinced his hearers that no mistake had been made in selecting him to combat Brownlow and the Radical party. In the Capitol City, before a throng of surging thousands both white and black, Etheridge and William B. Stokes, a strong Radical, locked horns in joint debate which lasted for some four hours. General Stokes, Horace Maynard, and other Radicals had to "pinch hit" for Governor Brownlow throughout the campaign. Space permits only a brief sample of Etheridge's speech:

". . . You know that in times of civil war the air is always foul, and loathsome insects are not more naturally hatched in a putrid carcass than ar engendered in the atmosphere of civil war—those loathsome creeping things which cannot exist a day in times of prosperous industry and peace. Is it any wonder, fellow citizens, that this scum, which on such occasions rises to the surface should have rallied its forces for one more grand foray on the public liberties? But they will appear for but a brief hour on the public stage, and their names will soon be forgotten. We all prefer, when goaded by tyrants, the splendid monster of massive brain and manly parts; but to be spurred by driveling imbecility; to have legislative edicts and imperial decrees promulgated in bad English; to endure the meanest of all insolence—that which hides behind bayonets and skulks within entrenched camps, and to be thankful for all this is perhaps a little more than Northern Radicals have asked of us, or any human being in the world, unless it be that which conceals the foul stomach of a Tennessee or Missouri Radical. . . . I propose to ask you now to take out your disinfectants and go with me through what is generally known in Tennessee as Brownlowism. I know it is a nauseous job, and you will be as much astonished as a young student of medicine when he enters a hospital where the wounded and the dying have lain for twenty days without attendance. [Toward the end of his speech, Etheridge said:]

Now, I have reduced my charges against Brownlow to writing. I will read them in the presence of these colored people, and I now defy any man to say that either of these is untrue. They are as follows:

1st. That throughout his whole life he has persistently pursued and persecuted the free negro and the slave, and all who evinced a disposition to elevate their condition.

2d. He has declared that he 'never entertained a doubt that God intended the Africans to serve their superiors as bondsmen and bondwomen.'

3d. He has stigmatized all propositions to free the slave as impious in the sight of heaven.

4th. He has asserted, upon the honor of a Christian minister, that our free negroes were the most 'indolent, immoral and dishonest class of persons to be found in the State.' He has compared the negro to brutes, fit for 'murder and rapine,' and associated the free negroes with Northern prostitutes who were 'skulking about our large towns and cities.'

5th. That by freeing the slaves, 'in nine cases out of ten, their condition has been made worse.'

6th. He declared it to be the Christian's duty to 'whip well.'

7th. He proclaimed as the chosen minister of Heaven, that slavery had

---

[191] *Union and Dispatch* (Nashville), May 26, 1867.

risen and spread over the world, 'by and with the consent and approval of Almighty God.'

8th. He offered to demonstrate to the world 'that slavery as it exists [existed] *in America, ought to be perpetuated*,' * * * 'as an established and *inevitable* condition of human society.'

9th. That preachers who were opposed to slavery ought to be forced 'to leave the South in hot haste.'

10th. That when the Devil went into New England two hundred years ago, he appeared in the person of a black man—that when he revived his work in Tennessee he came in the person of a 'nigger' again.

11th. He denounced the Jews who crucified our Saviour as '*anti-slavery gamblers*.'

12th. He has denounced those who advocated the freedom of the slaves as unfit for Heaven and deserving Hell.

13th. That slavery would and *ought* to exist until the end of time—that it would never cease 'until the angel Gabriel sounds the last trump of God, and calls the nations of earth to judgment'—*then and not before*, will slavery be abolished south of Mason and Dixon's line."

Throughout the campaign, Etheridge hammered away at the Radicals, declaring that they had debauched the public offices and that their chief objective was to punish those who had aided the Confederacy, though the latter group constituted largely the tax-paying citizens who had been deprived of the privilege of having any voice in the State Government. A constant appeal was made to the Negroes who were told that the Radicals were merely exploiting them for selfish purposes—that of holding on to public offices. Repeatedly Etheridge pointed out that the Radicals, in the passing of the franchise law, had denied to the Negroes the privilege of holding any sort of public office. "Again, again, and again," Etheridge stressed Brownlow's hatred of the Negro race by citing his utterances in the Brownlow-Pryne debate. Etheridge referred to his Congressional record on questions affecting the Negro race, pointing out that he was the only Southern Congressman to vote for the admission of Kansas as a free State, and that he had proposed a resolution in Congress denouncing the slave trade.

The Republicans, which was the name the Radicals had now assumed, denounced the "rebels" in lurid language. The Conservatives, so it was thundered through the columns of the Radical press, had fought to keep the Negroes in slavery; had attempted to break up the Legislature when Brownlow and the Brownlow leaders were trying to pass a law that would permit the Negroes to vote; and that every helpful measure in behalf of the Negro had been supported by the Republicans and opposed by the Conservatives. And so, the major objective of each party was to procure control of the Negro vote which was the "weight" that would likely tilt the political balance in favor of the party obtaining that vote. Some thirty-five or forty thousand votes far exceeded any sort of booby prize.

Transcending all the flaming newspaper editorials and honeyed words of the seasoned campaigners was the organization of the so-called Union Leagues. Though founded in the North as early as 1862 as an unconditional Union club, the movement reinforced by Federal troops spread into the upper South, with Tennessee Unionists joining in and forming local chapters long before the war had ended. With Conservative Unionists gradually departing from the original Radical Unionists, the logical and actual result was that the Union League passed into the hands and control of the Radicals who were in position to transform the League into an effective political gadget to serve the political interests of the Radical Republican Party. Now, that a critical election was in the offing, the strategic thing to do was to see to it that the Union League leaders become alert and active and organize additional clubs throughout the State. A note of alarm [192] was sounded by a Conservative journal as early as February, 1867:

"We are informed that the Radicals are now busy in the work of initiating our colored fellow-citizens into radical leagues. They are, we learn, required to take an oath upon admission, the exact purport of which has not been disclosed; but the object of it is understood to be the support of the radical ticket at the ballot-box and the revolutionary authority in general. The proceedings are held in secret, and the political ritual is particularly confined to the 'loyal tycoons who manipulate the party wires.' "

Quite obviously, the Negro was flattered by being inducted into an organization which whetted his natural inclination to crave the mystic and the bizarre. The secret initiation and the charm of mysticism operated as a magic lodestone that drew him into the folds of the League. What he did not know was that he was being made a mere tool by the white Radicals who instructed him to vote for the Radical ticket and oppose the Conservative candidates. Initiation ceremonies, including pass words, hand grips, and a series of oaths that became more strict as the initiate received advanced degrees, were conducted in a manner that appealed to the recently-freed slave. His craving for the mysterious was being satiated to an extent never before experienced by him, and naturally he was impressed by the attention now being bestowed upon him by the white man.

The contemporary newspapers were loaded with editorials, communications, articles, and reports of political meetings being held in various parts of the State. Bias, prejudice, and downright falsehood constituted the principal ingredients in many of these articles. Somewhere between the extremes, perhaps a modicum of truth may be ascertained. The campaign was a crusade of calumny and is mournful evidence of the decadence of real manhood at that particular era. Undoubtedly much political skullduggery was invoked, with neither party being innocent. There was an occasional newspaper editorial that seems

---

[192] *Ibid.*, February 15, 1867.

to represent the honest views of an honest editor, but these were the rarest of all the products of the pen. Space forbids and the pen falters at any attempt to present any extended account of the true status of the political conditions that permeated the State at the time. Sanity was absent and reason had been dethroned by the bitter hatreds engendered by the struggle for political supremacy.

As the gubernatorial contest neared the end, disturbances occurred in numerous places throughout the State. Enmity between Union and ex-Confederates became intensified and some serious clashes took place, notably in Franklin. From time to time, the Negroes became involved in broils with each other, inasmuch as small groups of Negroes had refused to join the Loyal League. All this hubbub alarmed the Radicals, and the "Parson" decided to step into the melee. This he did on July 1, 1867, when he launched the following unusual proclamation:[193]

"EXECUTIVE DEPARTMENT
Nashville, Tennessee, July 1st, 1867.

Whereas, An incendiary document has been issued at Nashville, by the partisan Chairman of a political Committee, in the following words, to-wit:

To the County Courts of the State. Do not fail to appoint Judges in all the precincts at your July term. This is required to be done by the County Courts of each County, at the session next preceding the election day, which is the first day of August next. Code, Sec. 821. The law is not changed on that subject. If this be neglected, as the law is amended in the last franchise Act, Sec. 10, page 31, the power devolves upon the Commissioner of Registration. Some have erroneously supposed that the power has been taken from the County Court by that Act. It will be seen the Commissioner is authorized to appoint, in cases when the Sheriff by the existing law could do so, and that was only in case the County Court failed to attend to that duty, or the persons they appointed failed to act. See Code, Sec. 842. Whatever may have been intended, the Act of the 25th of February, 1867, construed with said sections of the Code, admits of no other construction—it is certainly plain—too plain for controversy.

By order of the Central Committee.

John C. Gaut, Chairman.

Whereas, This seditious circular recommends the nullification

---

[193] Ms. [Brownlow] *Proclamation Book*, 81–82.

of the franchise law, which is now a part of the Constitution of Tennessee, and has been approved by the Supreme Court; and,

Whereas, a false and rebellious construction has been given to the law above named, by the audacious authors of the aforesaid treasonable circular, evidently for wicked and revolutionary purposes; and, whereas, the Judges and Clerks of all elections in the State are to be appointed by the Commissioner of Registration in each County, as the tenth section of the franchise law provides, in the following clear and explicit words to-wit:

Section 10. *Be it further enacted*, That in case any County Court shall fail or refuse to induct into office any of the officers elected under this act, it shall be lawful for the Commissioner of Registration, upon orders from the Governor to perform that duty, and to administer all necessary oaths, and to take and approve all necessary official bonds, and the same shall be good and valid in law. The Judges and Clerks of all elections shall hereafter be selected and appointed by the Commissioner of Registration in each County in the same manner and governed by the same rules and laws heretofore provided by law, conferring the said selection and appointments by the Sheriffs.

Now, therefore, I, William G. Brownlow, Governor of the State of Tennessee, by virtue of the authority conferred upon me, and in discharge of the duties imposed upon me by law, do hereby give notice that the franchise law was clearly and unquestionably framed so as to take the appointment of Judges and Clerks of election from the County Courts and Sheriffs, giving the same to the Commissioner of Registration; therefore, the election returns made by said Commissioner will alone be recognized at the State Department.

I warn all County Courts in the State not to act upon the advice of this Committee of seditionists, as they will lay themselves liable to be punished; and I warn all Judges and Clerks of elections whom they may appoint, not to attempt to serve, as they would come in conflict with the lawfully constituted Judges and Clerks of elections. And if it be the purpose to provoke sedition and violence in a wicked attempt to overthrow the State Government, upon their heads shall rest the consequences. General Joseph A. Cooper, in command of the State Guards, is hereby instructed so to dispose of the troops in the rebellious localities, as to enable him to enforce the franchise law in its letter and spirit, without regard to the threats of the seditionists.

Order must be maintained, and the law executed, if it require that I shall call into the field the whole available force at my command to do so.

    In testimony whereof, I have hereunto subscribed my (SEAL) name, and caused the Great Seal of the State to be affixed, at the Department in Nashville, this 1st day of July A. D. 1867.

        By the Governor, W. G. BROWNLOW

         A. J. FLETCHER, Secy. of State."

  The announcement by the Central Committee, which was a Conservative body, was the basis of Brownlow's proclamation. Had the County Courts appointed election officials, as urged by the Central Committee, control of election precincts would have been wrested from Brownlow's Commissioner of Registration. From Brownlow's point of view, such action would have been a "wicked and revolutionary" act. To squelch such a movement, Brownlow issued his order and, as a matter of fact, twenty-one companies of soldiers were organized and scattered throughout the State. The arrival of armed troops, most of whom were Negroes, put a damper on the efforts of the Conservatives, and numerous candidates of that party withdrew from further activity.

  No soothsayer was required to predict the outcome of the farcical election. The Radicals, in control of election machinery and buttressed by the presence of armed troops, swept everything before them. Brownlow was re-elected over Etheridge by a ratio of three to one. In addition, the Radicals (now called Republicans) won all eight Congressional seats, every seat in the State Senate, and all but three in the House of Representatives of the State Legislature.

  Tennesseans now had the prospect of two more years of Brownlowism! The desperate effort on the part of the Conservatives to win the Negro vote had proved to be a flash in the pan.

  On October 7, 1867, the first session of the Thirty-Fifth General Assembly convened in Nashville. On the thirteenth ballot, Senator Dewitt Clinton Senter representing the counties of Claiborne, Grainger, Anderson, and Campbell, was elected Speaker of the Senate.[194] On the second ballot, Representative F. S. Richards representing the counties of Shelby, Fayette, and Tipton was elected Speaker of the House of Representatives.[195] The Legislature differed from those of other Southern States of that period in that it contained no Negroes and only a few white members of Northern birth. By no means can the Thirty-

---

[194] *Senate Journal*, 1867, 10.
[195] *House Journal*, 1867, 7.

Fifth General Assembly be classified as a "carpet-bag" group, since fifty-five had been born in Tennessee. Eleven members were of other Southern States, nine of Northern birth, and three of foreign countries. Forty of the members were farmers, twelve were lawyers, seven were physicians, and six were merchants.

As a result of the August election in 1867, the Republicans were in complete control in State governmental affairs for the ensuing two years. The Conservatives were helpless, although they actually constituted a majority of the citizens. For the ensuing biennium, 1867–68, it would be impossible for the Conservatives to delay or block any legislation sponsored by the Radicals by resorting to the breaking of a legislative quorum by absenteeism or resignations. Despite the fact that a majority of the people were in bitter opposition to the Brownlow regime, yet the minority were in the saddle and would handle the reins of government as suited their fancy and whims. The Republican victory was an impressive one, demonstrating beyond the peradventure of a doubt that the recently enfranchised Negroes had given almost unanimous support to the candidates of the Radical (now Republican) party.

On the third day of the legislative session, the Legislature met in joint session for the purpose of counting the vote for Governor in the August election. The official vote for Brownlow was 74,034, and for Etheridge 22,550.[196] At an afternoon session on the same day, October 9, 1867, Governor Brownlow was ready with his Message:

Legislative Message,* October 9, 1867.

"GENTLEMEN OF THE SENATE AND THE HOUSE OF REPRESENTATIVES:

Having assembled in this Capitol to perform the grave and responsible duties of legislating for the public welfare, it is proper that we should, with united voice and heart, invoke the blessing of the Great Source of all good and knowledge, and ask His direction in all our deliberations. In communication with you, by Message, as required by the Constitution, the condition of the State, and in recommending such measures as may be deemed expedient, I acknowledge, with feelings of profound gratitude, the blessings vouchsafed to us by the Great Ruler of the Universe, in the auspicious condition of our State and country, and the measure of health and prosperity which has marked the year now rapidly closing out.

No people have greater reason to be thankful to an over-ruling

---

[196] *Ibid.*, 25.
* *Senate Journal*, 1867–68, 22–37.
   House Journal, 1867–68, 27–42.

Providence for the blessings of the year drawing to a close, than the people of our own State. While pestilence has been abroad in the land, we have enjoyed health in an unusual degree; the earth has yielded a plentiful harvest; the signs of the devastations of war are fast disappearing before the renewed energy and enterprise of our people; business is prospering, of every kind; indications of improvement and progress are to be seen in every section of the State; our Bonds are advancing in value; our credit is steadily improving; and men of enterprise, skill and means, are preparing to come to our State, and cast their lots with us—encouraged to do so by our having settled our political strife. I repeat, the condition of the State, as a whole, is very gratifying to the friends of law and order; and it is hoped that the disturbances in a few localities will cease at an early day.

You have met under circumstances far more favorable than those that surrounded the meeting of your predecessors. The war that then raged, gave way before the arms of the nation. The August Power that has made Himself known to man as the arbiter of battles, interfered between the government and its attempted overthrow. The desolation that followed in the track of hostile armies has been, in a good degree, repaired. An unusual display of industry among all classes of people, attended by commendable thrift and economy, and rewarded by two bountiful harvests, has restored many of the comforts of life enjoyed before the rebellion. And above all, the general health that has prevailed throughout the State, especially during the past season, has crowned our blessings and given us cause for gratitude to God for what we enjoy, and has done much to obliterate the memory of what we have suffered.

Our State Government, then in the first stage of its restoration, has become firmly established by the three-fold influences of time, Congressional recognition and popular ratification. Time has been its constant ally in demonstrating the falsehood and the dishonesty, as well as the wicked designs of its enemies. Unrecognized by Congress, it would have lacked the sanction of law, and been at the most, a Government in fact. The recognition, by Joint Resolution of Congress, approved the 24th of July, 1866, operated by relation, to give it and its acts legal validity from the beginning. But for the most effective action in its behalf, was the decision by the people at the election in August last. During the canvass which preceded, it was subject to the severest possible strain. In addition to the most search-ing criticism upon all its measures, and the harshest animadversions upon all connected with either the Legislative, Executive or the Judiciary Departments, there was the same element of hostility which, in 1861, broke out into flagrant rebellion—less open and pro-nounced, indeed, but none the less bitter and determined. The same men—stung to madness by the utter defeat of their cause, reinforced by others who had more recently, from time to time, joined them under the stimulus of a disappointed or an awakened ambition, moved by sympathy with rebel kindred and friends, or angry by reason of slaves emancipated and enfranchised as citizens—have never, for a moment, relaxed their efforts to effect a revolutionary subversion of the Government. In this work of mischief they were supported by the rebel press, the same for the most part, and con-ducted by the same counsels, that, in 1861, precipitated the State into civil war, and which the benignity of the nation has not only shielded from punishment, but has permitted to resume its machinations of treason. And I am compelled to add, that this support was not limited to the press of this State. The rebel and so-called Conservative pa-pers, and the entire Democratic press of the country, waged relent-less war upon the State Government. A large corps of newspaper correspondents traversed the land and studiously misrepresented every occurrence of the canvass, as well as the general questions in-volved in the struggle. We lacked neither unscrupulous enemies to concoct falsehoods, nor candid friends to lend them credence and to deplore our lack of discretion. Yet, against these adverse influ-ences, after a most thorough and exhaustive discussion before the people, they have sustained the Government by majorities approach-ing to unanimity. I recall your attention to these facts, not for parti-san purposes, nor in a spirit of exultation, but as a basis for our fu-ture action in executing the popular will.

Your predecessors took the Government as an experiment, you find it an establishment. They adopted measures to set in motion, your measures will look to a wise and beneficient administration. It was theirs to build the machinery, it is yours to keep it in good run-ning order.

FEDERAL RELATIONS.

Our external relations are mainly and for present inquiry, en-tirely with the Federal Government, and I am happy to inform you that they continue most amicable and harmonious. From the beginning, we have been sustained by the military authorities of the nation in keeping the peace and executing the laws in localities where the war, after subsiding, had left elements of disturbance. Your predecessors thought proper to provide a small militia force, to be used in aid of the civil law and as a part of it, when the civil law, unaided, might prove incapable of dealing with its violators. Application was made to Congress for arms and equipments, which were cheerfully granted by that body; and I take pleasure in bearing testimony to the promptitude with which their action was carried into effect by the then Secretary of War. Much anxiety was felt in anticipation of disorders on the day of election. Major General George H. Thomas, in command of the Department, co-operated with General Joseph A. Cooper, in command of the militia, so effectually, that, with a few marked exceptions, the peace was preserved and the best of order maintained all over the State. With these exceptions, there has never been so quiet an election in the State, or one that evinced more forbearance and self-control on the part of our citizens.

ELECTION OF UNITED STATES SENATOR.

By the Act of Congress of the 25th of July, 1866, it was made your duty, on the second Tuesday of your meeting and organization, to elect a Senator of the United States to succeed Mr. Patterson, whose term will expire on the 3d of March, 1869.

ELECTION OF REPRESENTATIVES TO CONGRESS.

Recent legislation by Congress seems to make desirable a change in the time of electing Representatives. The official term of a member of Congress begins on the 4th of March, and continues two years, and no longer. If a successor has not been elected, the seat is then vacant. Our practice in this State has been, to elect on the first Thursday of August succeeding the close of the preceding term. The consequence has been, that, between the 4th of March and the first Thursday of August, we had no Representative. The Constitution of the United States requires Congress to 'assemble at least once every year, and such meeting shall be on the first Monday of December, unless they shall, by law, appoint a different day.' So long as this provision remained unaltered, we experienced no inconvenience, for, except in the rare instance of an extraordinary session, Congress never assembled until the first Monday of December succeeding our August election. By a recent Act, the 22d of January, 1867, each Congress is required to meet on the 4th of March, the first day of its official existence. Under this law, the 40th Congress assembled and organized on the 4th of March last, and held two sessions prior to our election in August, at which this State was unrepresented. The importance of having members present, to assist in the organization of a legislative body, and to take their appropriate places upon the different committees, is one that you are not likely to over-estimate.

In view, therefore, of this state of facts, I recommend that you change the time of holding the Congressional elections, so as to bring them on before the close of the preceding term. Perhaps, either the month of October or November, previous, would be found the most convenient, and would correspond with the usage of most of the other States.

THE JUDICIARY.

Possibly no feature of the Government was more harshly criticised, during the late canvass, than the tenure of the Judiciary. The Schedule to the Amended Constitution, provides that 'all civil * * officers who * * may hereafter be appointed by the acting Governor of the State, * * * * * shall continue to exercise the functions of their respective offices until their successors shall be elected or appointed and qualified.' The section, taken as a whole, embraces military as well as civil officers, and previous as well as subsequent appointments. The object evidently was, in the condition of the State at that time, to confer upon the Executive large discretionary powers, in providing the people with judicial and ministerial officers. This was the view of your predecessors, who, by joint resolution of the 20th of May, 1865, after reciting that, during the greater part of the war, all civil tribunals had been closed, and most of the officers holding office, had willfully abandoned the same, requested the Governor, as soon as in his opinion he deemed it advisable, to issue his proclamation, ordering elections to be held in the respective counties of the State, where such vacancies have occurred, advising the people of the State to fill such vacancies in pursuance of the laws of the State; and, in the meantime, until such elections are held, that he proceed and fill the vacancies by the appointment of suitable and proper persons, until their succesors shall be elected and qualified.

Though well aware that such action of the Legislature, could confer no additional powers, I, nevertheless, accepted it as their opinion of what powers belonged to the Executive in the premises. As such, and in the absence of judicial decisions, I regarded it entitled to great weight, and have acted upon it. Most of the officers have been elected, except the Judges of the Supreme and Chancery Courts, and most of the Judges of the Circuit Courts, the Attorney-General and Reporter, and most of the Circuit Attorneys-General.

These have been appointed and commissioned for their respective official terms. This action was brought prominently in view before the people, by the press and upon the stump, and they have passed upon it. Sustained by their approval, I shall continue the same course; and as vacancies occur from time to time, shall order elections, when, in my opinion, it is advisable—otherwise, fill them by appointment.

LITERATURE AND SCIENCE.

By section 10 of 11th Article of the Constitution of the State, it is declared to 'be the duty of the General Assembly, in all future periods of this Government, to cherish literature and science.' The last Legislature nobly responded to this imperative duty, so far as common schools are concerned. Great benefits may justly be anticipated from this enlightened legislation. But I respectfully suggest whether the Legislature has performed its full duty under the Constitution, and whether the wants of our people and the character of our State, demand that our two State Universities shall be placed on a higher and firmer ground of usefulness. They have long insisted that the State is equitably indebted to them a considerable sum of money; and in view of the noble purpose for which this money is demanded, I recommend that this claim of the two State Universities, be investigated by your honorable body. But, independent of this claim, I hold that it is the duty of the Legislature, if the means of the State will justify it, to provide for the higher branches of learning as well as the lower. Common Schools and Universities of the highest grade, go hand in hand. One cannot flourish in a State without the other. The Universities ought to furnish teachers for the common schools, and common schools prepare our young men for entrance to the higher walks of learning in the Universities. Such is the relation between the two in those States where education has become universal. Our party justly claims to be a party of progress, and to be based on knowledge and education. Let us show the world that in this State we are alive to the spirit of the new era, and that we are equal to our pretensions.

If you should deem it your duty to aid our two State Universities, you might require a given number of worthy poor young men to be educated, from time to time, free of expense, or for a nominal sum, on condition that they would teach a given number of years in our common schools. In this way, many young men might each year be turned out of our Universities, and sent over the State, to diffuse, through our common schools, the knowledge they had acquired. Our Common School System would thus become efficient to accomplish the noble purpose designed for it. Without some plan be devised for the education of teachers, that system must, for several years at least, be imperfect and a partial failure.

ACCOUNTS BETWEEN THE STATE AND THE RAILROADS.

The entire account of the State with the Railroad Companies, and especially that portion relating to the Sinking Fund, has been so badly kept, during the war, and before, that the books are very unsatisfactory. I advise the appointment of Commissioners by your body, to sit during your session, and make new settlements with all the roads, that the books may be made to show all settlements satisfactory, both to the State and Companies. The expense of such settlement will be more than compensated for by rescuing the accounts from ruinous oblivion.

I further advise, that said Commissioners be instructed to look into the disposition made of the Bonds granted to the various Commissioners in the State, and that they be clothed with power to send for persons and papers. I have reason to believe that, in some instances, the Bonds of the State have not been disposed of according to law, while in others, the confidence of the State has been abused, and her credit sought to be injured, even by the recipients of her favors. And in all future appropriations to railroad companies, let us know the characters of the men into whose hands State Bonds go, both as to integrity and loyalty. Meanwhile, let us guard against any future increase of the State debt by the issuance of Bonds to railroads, unless it be in cases where the interests of the State would suffer for the want of further aid.

In the discharge of my duty, I have appointed Receivers on as many as seven roads; and if the interest on their indebtedness to the State is not promptly met, I shall provide guardians for others. It is an outrage that nearly a million of dollars is due the State from these defaulting Companies.

TURNPIKE ROADS.

But while I deem it of the first importance to preserve the credit of the State, and believe our present railroads, when completed, will be ample for the wants of our people, I suggest, for your consideration, the necessity and justice of the adoption of a system of Mac-Adamized or Turnpike roads for such sections of the State as are without them, and especially for such counties as are remote from railroads and navigable streams. The people of all the counties are entitled to equal facilities in reaching a market, and yet they do not possess such facilities. For example, the Counties of Sevier, Union and Hancock, have no railroads, either completed or contemplated, while they bear their equal share of the taxation necessary to aid in building or sustaining roads in other more favored counties. It is but an act of simple justice to aid such counties, in some form, in finding a cheap means of reaching a market.

On general principles, the policy of improving our county or local roads by the judicious use of the credit of the State, can easily be maintained. We need now not main lines, but good local roads, leading from county to county, and reaching the remoter parts of the country, not penetrated by railroads. These would act as feeders and supporters of the railroads, add to the prosperity of the people, greatly enhance the value of real estate, increase the revenue of the State, and largely increase the flow of immigration. Labor being the great source of wealth, we must do all we can to attract population. This we can do alone by affording labor the same facilities for reaping its just rewards, that is afforded by other States. We cannot expect the people of other States, when they have good MacAdamized roads leading from every county town, to settle among us, with our local roads impassable nearly one half the year. For these reasons, I earnestly invite your attention to the consideration of this subject.

LIQUOR SELLING NEAR COLLEGES.

Frequent applications are being made to the Legislature, by petitions and otherwise, for special acts prohibiting the sale of ardent spirits within certain distances in the vicinity of certain institutions of learning. I advise that a general law be enacted, affording this character of protection to every College and Academy in the State. We owe it to the cause of Christian morality, to the cause of popular education, and to the young and rising generation, to separate liquor shops from our institutions of learning. Should we neglect this work, not only will the terrible evils of intemperance increase and multiply, till they sweep away every vestige of propriety, peace, good order, and liberty from the State, but bring down upon us, as a State, Sodom's guilt and Sodom's doom.

In all parts of the country, the friends of law and order are realizing the giant strides king Alcohol has made within the five years covering this rebellion, and the consequent demoralization directly attributable to the alarming increase of intemperance, is now attracting the attention of the best members of society, and of the most profound statesmen of the country. Good men and patriots can but hail every movement against this monster vice of the age, as a pleasing augury of the times; and they must heartily approve every enterprise, and every act of legislation, designed to break the back of this monster, whose victims multiply with such frightful rapidity, and whose power increases daily and nightly. Intemperance did its work in the army, and now that peace has been declared, it is transferring its baneful influence to the walks of civil life, demoralizing the young and rising generation, and sending to premature graves many of our best and most useful citizens. Throughout the length and breadth of Tennessee, distilleries and wholesale and retail liquor dealers are multiplying with frightful rapidity, and the increasing evils arising therefrom, call upon the friends of humanity and of religion to educate the public mind in opposition to this vice, and, if possible, to stay the tide that now bids fair to overwhelm and degrade society.

Intemperance is blowing up steamboats, upsetting stage-coaches, and, through the carelessness of drunken engineers or switch-tenders, it is bringing trains in collision or running them off the track. All this appalling loss of life and limb, resulting from wickedness, carelessness, and contempt for human life, of the owners, directors, superintendents, agents, and employees on the various lines of travel, is attributable, in a great degree, to the vice of intemperance.

The least that can be done by the Legislature, (and this ought to be satisfactory to the friends of morality and religion,) is to authorize the prohibition of the traffic through the ballot-box, once in two years, either by counties or civil districts. This would enable those who desire to rid themselves of the numerous and alarming evils of intemperance, to do so legitimately, while it would enable those counties or civil districts who are 'joined to their idols,' to cling to them, and suffer the consequences.

THE SCHOOL FUND.

When the assets of the Bank of Tennessee and the archives of the State, were captured and brought to Nashville, the Legislature then in session, by joint resolution, adopted May 29, 1865, *directed* the Governor, Secretary of State, and Comptroller, to take charge of the assets of the Bank, etc., and receipt for the same. This was promptly done, and a constant military guard kept over them until, by Act of Assembly, passed June the 9th, 1865, the Governor, Secretary of State, and Comptroller, were ordered to invest the funds (then in coin) 'in United States or Tennessee Bonds;' and also to investigate into and schedule the assets, and ascertain the value thereof. This order of the Legislature was also promptly obeyed. The amount of coin, upon actual count, was ascertained to be $446,-719.70, which was sold to Jay Cooke & Co., for 7-30 U. S. Bonds, at a premium of nearly 40 per cent. On the 9th of October of the same year, the Governor, and his two associates, had the pleasure of reporting to the Legislature, that they had realized the sum of $518,250, in 7-30 U. S. Bonds, which, they announced, was then 'in the Comptroller's safe.' This sum remained unpacked and undisturbed until the General Assembly saw proper to pass a law, requiring the fund 'to be placed in the hands of the Treasurer of the State of Tennessee.'

By turning to the 5th section of 'the Act to wind up and settle the business of the Bank of Tennessee,' it will be ascertained how this fund got into the hands of the Treasurer. Until this time, that officer had nothing to do with the fund; but this Act of Assembly made him the lawful custodian of it. On the 5th day of June, 1866, he demanded possession of these packages of 7-30 Bonds, then 'in the Comptroller's safe.' As every other order of the Legislature had been obeyed, this was also obeyed. The fund was counted by the

Comptroller, placed in the hands of the Treasurer, and his receipt taken therefor, and the Governor and associates, at once ceased to be responsible for it; and no one was more startled than they were, to discover, six months after, that the fund was on deposit in the Tennessee National Bank of Memphis, upon a simple certificate of deposit. When this discovery was made, the Governor promptly called attention to it, and the Legislature as promptly took action in the matter. A committee of vigilant and experienced men were sent by the Governor to Memphis, who succeeded in recovering about one-half. I have appointed Thos. B. McElwee, Special Agent, to look after the remainder; and being a sensible, prudent, business man, he may be able to secure a portion of the funds in the custody of that faithless institution.

CRIMINAL COURTS.

Criminal prosecutions have so multiplied in our Circuit Courts, since the war, that parties having important civil suits, have been prevented from a hearing, to their great injury, and, in many instances, to their ruin. I propose to remedy this evil by providing a Criminal Judge for every Chancery District where there is not now a Criminal Judge. But if the Legislature, in its wisdom, should not agree with me in this recommendation, I respectfully urge that body to provide some other remedy against this great and growing evil. The State owes relief to her citizens, who have important civil suits in the courts of the country.

IMMIGRATION.

It was our fond hope that, upon the restoration of peace, the termination of slavery, and the establishment of civil government, a tide of immigration would set in to this State, from the Northern States and from Europe; that men of capital and enterprise, attracted by our mild and healthy climate, fertile soil, magnificent scenery, and pure and abundant water, would come among us, and aid in the rapid development of our vast resources. Our disappointment is attributable to the intolerant and proscriptive spirit of a large portion of those lately in rebellion. With them every Union man is an 'abolitionist,' and every 'abolitionist' an enemy, to be proscribed, despised, and driven from the country. I attribute the violence of these pestilential disloyalists to the insane policy of the President, who constantly holds out to them the prospect of being restored to power at an early day. The treatment of the few who have brought their families and means among us, has been such as to engender a feeling of insecurity of life and property, a sense of social isolation, and a consciousness that they are liable at any time, to be expelled from the country. Some good citizens, men of enterprise and capital, have actually returned to the Northern States, in consequence of ill-treatment.

It is to be hoped, however, that these passions and prejudices will wear away, and common sense resume its sway; that as the power and influence of the President, now so rapidly waning, shall cease to stimulate their vain and foolish hopes for supremacy in the country, they will see the great advantage of not only treating immigrants with common respect, but of encouraging them to settle among us. It is to be hoped that they will soon learn that their former contracted and sectional ideas, can never again prevail, and they will soon fall into the great Radical idea of equal rights to all men, in all sections of our great country. Hoping and believing that a better spirit will soon prevail, growing out of our recent elections, without going into details, I recommend that you extend every encouragement within your constitutional power, to immigration.

HOSPITAL FOR THE INSANE.

I refer you to the Report of the Superintendent of the Tennessee Hospital for the Insane. Under the efficient management of its present able officers, this noble institution of charity proves to be an honor to the State and a blessing to its unfortunate inmates. It is proper that I should call your attention to the fact, that there have been at the institution a number of pay patients from the Southern States, whose bills have not been met for years. The accounts of the parties who placed these patients in the hospital, have been regularly made out and forwarded to them repeatedly. Some have replied that they were unable to meet them, while others have treated these calls with a silent contempt. The outstanding debt due this institution, in items of this character, now amounts to nearly $40,000. Many of these patients were sent here through pride, and a desire to have them far removed from their homes and families.

It is not just that our people should be taxed to support the unfortunate of other States, especially when the presumption is, that their relatives are able to defray their expenses. Such a course would be a departure from the rule, that our charities should begin at home. Consequently, a portion of these patients have been conveyed to their homes at the expense of the State, and turned over to their families and friends.

One of the many bad effects of the late rebellion, has been, and still is, to crowd this institution with patients, so that there is a demand for more rooms. I propose to meet this demand by the erection of a hospital, of respectable size, at a suitable point in East Tennessee. The cheapness of labor, of building materials, and the salubrity of air, purity of the water, and grandeur of the scenery, all point to that section as suited for such an institution.

COMPENSATING LOYAL MEN FOR LOSSES.

After mature deliberation, I have determined to recommend to your favorable consideration, the remuneration of loyal citizens of this State, for losses sustained by the occupation of the country by the National armies. The passage of the so-called ordinance of secession, and the assumed transfer of the State to the so-called Southern Confederacy, placed Tennessee in the attitude of rebellion, and her people in the position of enemies to the National Government. The consequence was, that upon the occupation of the State by the National forces, our people were treated as enemies, with but little discrimination between the loyal and the disloyal. Their lands and houses were occupied, their property impressed or destroyed, and their provisions consumed. In East Tennessee this was done from necessity, by an unsupplied army, to an extent that reduced the people to absolute suffering. Thus far, the Federal Government, classing Tennessee with the rebel States, and unwilling to assume the losses incurred in the whole South, has not regarded the applications of our loyal people for remuneration. I understand that similar losses, by the citizens of Indiana, Pennsylvania and Ohio, have been promptly assumed; and the Nation knows, and the world knows, that a more loyal people than those in Tennessee, who remained steadfast to the National cause, through so long and terrible an ordeal, are not to be found in the Union. But I cannot and will not lose confidence in the justice and magnanimity of the American people. I believe they will yet cheerfully repay the loyal sufferers among our people, many of whom were deprived of their property by the National forces, while they were themselves absent fighting for the National cause. But you, gentlemen, can afford present relief, relying upon the General Government, hereafter to assume and pay these just and meritorious claims.

I recommend that proper officers be appointed to ascertain and audit those claims, and that the bonds of the State, of denominations from $50 to $100, be issued in payment. I am aware that this proposition will meet with fierce opposition from those who would give preference to the millions of debt contracted by the usurped State Government, or by Rebel Quartermasters. I am also aware that objections will come from a better class, upon the ground of so considerable an increase of the State debt; but, if the American people, are just, they will assume the amount long before it falls due, and, upon principle, treat the suffering loyalists of Tennessee, as they have treated the loyalists of other States.

Let such a law be well guarded in every respect, and if Congress does not at once assume the liability, and promptly meet the same, then we have elected eight able and loyal men to Congress, to look after our interests, to very, very little purpose.

THE COLORED POPULATION.

Our colored fellow-citizens have shown a greater aptitude for learning and the acquisition of knowledge, than was expected; and by their good conduct and steadfast loyalty, have rapidly won upon the good opinions and respect of the loyal portion of the white race; while their rebel opponents, under the encouragement afforded them by the pro-rebel policy of the President, have shown less disposition to return to true loyalty, than was fully expected. The exercise of the elective franchise by the colored race in this State, has shown them to be capable of exercising that right, and of selecting candidates to represent them.

Some legislation is necessary to protect the colored race in their rights as renters and laborers. In many instances they have been turned out of employ and otherwise proscribed, not to say defrauded, for opinion's sake. Coming here from every county in the State, you are familiar with the facts; and your sense of justice will prompt you to apply the remedy for this great and growing evil.

The odious Sixteenth Section of the Franchise Law is now claimed as a part of the Constitution, and it is for you to say whether it shall remain in force, or be obliterated by amending the Constitution in the only regular way.

CONDITION OF THE PENITENTIARY.

Your attention is called to the condition of affairs in the State Prison, full and specific details of which will be given in the report of the Commissioners in charge of that institution. I have every confidence that the Legislature will look into the wants of that institution, and do for it, what, in the judgment of members, may seem proper. Many complaints have been made to me, *pro* and *con*, with regard to its management, and complaints of a character which require a thorough investigating. As you are aware, one wing of the institution has been destroyed by fire. This has been re-built at a cost of several thousand dollars. This loss to the State, and the matter of these repairs, should be looked into with strict and impartial fidelity. Meanwhile, I again suggest the establishment of branches of the Penitentiary in the Western District, and in East Tennessee. The cost of building on a moderate scale, would be saved to the State, in fifteen or twenty years, in the item of a cash market in each end of the State, for provisions to sustain, and raw material to keep the convicts employed in manufacturing—such as lumber, marble, iron, coal, leather, etc. There would be a saving of thousands in the item of transporting prisoners. The erection of buildings would furnish employment and cash wages to a number of mechanics; and, as there are several salaried officers attached to such institutions, it would distribute the patronage of the State in her three natural divisions. If this be not done, an enlargement of the State Prison will be required. The demoralized condition of both our white and colored population, is causing scores to be sent to the Penitentiary, as our courts have gone into operation.

East of Knoxville, one mile and a half, the State owns one hundred acres of land, five or ten acres of which can be appropriated for a branch of the Penitentiary, and in a most suitable locality. Close to the railroad on the one side, and close to the river on the other side, I know of no more suitable locality in that end of the State. The State also owns property in Memphis, which, if not in a suitable locality, could be exchanged advantageously for other property.

THE STATE GUARDS.

The State Militia, which has been represented by a venal press, and by designing politicians, as swarming in every highway like the locusts of Egypt, and every where overawing the quiet people, and committing innumerable acts of violence, numbered, all told, seventeen hundred men—half of whom were mustered into the service but a few weeks before the election. This force, represented by the enemies of the State Government to have cost millions of money, has only cost the State a little the rise of the tenth part of one million. Clothing, rations, etc., were purchased on the most favorable terms, and strict economy was observed throughout. As soon as the election was over, and the country quieted, I directed Gen. Joseph A. Cooper, chief in command, and a prudent, firm and experienced officer, to pay off and muster out of the service, all but five companies. Most of these companies were ordered to the Western Division of the State, in several counties of which, the conduct of disloyal men is bad, and calls for correction. The small force now in service, is under the command of Major Robinson, a prudent, brave and reliable officer. I am anxious to rid the State of this item of expense, and will do so as soon as the rebellious portions of Middle and West Tennessee will permit me to disband these troops. I will not close my remarks upon the subject, without assuring your body, that the records of this, and all other branches of the service, are open to inspection, and free and full investigation is invited.

A GOVERNOR'S MANSION.

There are, in the County of Davidson, belonging to the State, three or four pieces of real estate, said to be worth not less than $200,000. This valuable and saleable property, is not only bringing the State no revenue, but is an expense. I propose to sell off this property at once, and, with the proceeds, to purchase and furnish a suitable and convenient mansion for the Governor of the State. The great State of Tennessee should, by all means, provide a Governor's residence. The present incumbent of the Executive office would derive no advantage from such a purchase, but asks that it be made for the honor of the State, and the accommodation of his successors in office. A poor man, with a family, and having to keep house, cannot afford to be Governor of Tennessee. The Executive of the State is, therefore, compelled to be absent from the Capitol frequently, when he should be here, or he must be separated from his family, and forced, by his inadequate salary, to look out a cheap boarding house, or fit up a room in this building for his individual accommodation.

THE SCHOOL BILL.

The late patriotic General Assembly enacted a wise and desirable School Law, and at a time when the want of such a system was damaging the interests of the State, both at home and abroad. The want of a sound and liberal school system, in any State, is well calculated to drive men of capital, enterprise, and intelligence, from our midst, as well as to deter others from coming among us, as it must be construed into opposition to the cause of education. The law, as it now stands, is a liberal one, and reflects much credit on your illustrious predecesors. But this law is defective in several important particulars, and should be improved by you at once. Time and discussion during the late canvass, have pointed out these defects, and, I doubt not, you are prepared to supply the remedy.

BILL OF COSTS.

The 'Bill of Costs,' coming up from the different counties in the State, are drawing from the Treasury $200,000 per annum. There is a feeling of indifference in too many instances, on the part of the officers who approve these bills of costs, as the State has them to foot. The offenses out of which these bills of costs grew should be graded, and the smaller classes left with the counties to settle, either in your work-houses or from the county revenue. I call your earnest attention to this great and growing evil, as requiring a remedy, and that without delay.

THE CASE OF ISHAM G. HARRIS.

I advise the immediate repeal of the offer of a reward of $5,000 for the arrest and return of ex-Governor Harris. My opinion with regard to active, original secessionists, and the punishment due to them has undergone no change. But no man has been punished for treason yet, from Jefferson Davis down; and the pro-rebel policy of the President warrants the conclusion that none will be punished. Besides, in Tennessee, during the late canvass, there were worse men upon the stump than Harris ever was, openly proclaiming treason and sedition, and inspiring the people with sectional malice. I advise the repeal of this offer for two other considerations—first, that of humanity towards the family of Harris; and next, but not least, that of economy on the part of the State. The State is liable to be called upon at any day, for this reward, and in return, she would have nothing to show for the outlay.

GOVERNOR'S STAFF.

The number of gentlemen on the Governor's Staff, and the salaries paid them, have been subjects of misrepresentation for two years past. I have, at no time, had more than four staff officers on duty at the same time, and the amount paid them, was the amount allowed by law. The State Guards being for the most part, disbanded, it is my purpose, in the future, to employ only two staff officers—an Adjutant-General and a Quartermaster-General. With these, and the one clerk allowed by law, I intend to transact the heavy business of my branch of the public service.

CONCLUSION.

Confiding in the intelligence and patriotism which induced your constituents to send you here, as law-makers, I assure you of my earnest desire to co-operate with you in all measures you may inaugurate for the common good. Coming here with the heavy majorities you are honored with, your action may mark your session as the epoch in our history when genuine progress asserted its sway in Tennessee. Honored in her past history, and her present claims fully responded to, we shall wipe out the foul stain of rebellion, and we may look forward to Tennessee with the utmost confidence. It will be our highest honor to have jealously guarded the fame of our State—advance her prosperity, and develop her vast resources. Destiny and events, God and history, have assigned to Tennessee an important position in the great work of restoring the Union. Let us act well our part, and, under Providence, perform the great but agreeable work of fraternity and love, and loyalty, towards the race of man.

W. G. Brownlow."

Upon the conclusion of the reading of Governor Brownlow's Message, Senator Joshua B. Frierson representing the counties of Maury, Lewis, Hickman, and Dickson moved successfully that five thousand copies of the Message be printed in English and three thousand copies in German.[197] A slightly reduced number of printed copies of the Message was ordered by the House, amounting to four thousand copies in English and one thousand copies in German.[198] Nine thousand copies in English and four thousand in German apparently were considered ample for the "use of the House and the Senate," as the official records expressed it. Inasmuch as each member of the Legislature had been voted ten dollars "to procure postage stamps," there can be little or no doubt but that the Message found much wider distribution than among the members of the General Assembly.[199] Political propaganda spread at the expense of the taxpayers was not an item that disturbed the slap-happy boys!

On the day following his Message, the Governor-elect appeared for the inaugural ceremonies on October 10, 1867. The pale, emaciated, and tottering man was assisted to the rostrum by a Senator and a Representative. The oath of office was administered by Judge Leonidas Campbell Houck. Due to the Governor's enfeebled physical condition and loss of voice, the Inaugural Address was read by his Secretary, H. H. Thomas. The brief but partisan polemic was as follows:[200]

"GOVERNOR BROWNLOW'S INAUGURAL ADDRESS

GENTLEMEN OF THE SENATE AND HOUSE OF REPRESENTATIVES:

What is dignified or undignified, appropriate or ill-timed, in the matter of an Inaugural Address, the manner of its delivery, or its length or brevity, are all mere matters of taste on the part of those who hear and criticise documents of this kind, and are usually passed upon in accordance with the likes or dislikes of the confirmed partizan. Therefore, in the brief Address which I propose to deliver on this occasion, I intend to be governed by my own convictions of what is proper, and by the feeble condition of my health. In a document of a different character, which has already been laid before you, I shall confine myself to a brief review of the principal interests of the State, and direct your attention to such recommendations as their needs have suggested.

Copperhead Vituperation.

Grateful to the people of Tennessee for the honor of a second election to the office of Chief Magistrate of the State, I assume the

[197] Senate Journal, 1867–68, 37.
[198] House Journal, 1867–68, 42.
[199] Acts of Tennessee, 1867–68, Chapter 86, Section 7.
[200] Appendix to Senate Journal, 1867–68, 22–24; also Daily Press and Times, October 11, 1867.

trust, deeply impressed with the grave responsibilities which it imposes upon me. I am the more grateful for having obtained a larger majority than has been given to any man in the State since its organization, and in one of the most bitter and unrelenting conflicts we have ever had, in which the opposition were led by unscrupulous traitors on the stump, backed by a venal press, and both acting upon the assumption that 'a lie well stuck to is as good as the truth!' My election by so great a majority and over the head of such opposition, I do not regard as a compliment alone to me, but as an endorsement of the principles represented by my nomination.

Our Party.

And here I will take occasion to say, that the only party organization in the Union, guided and controlled by men up with the advanced ideas of the times, and the paramount obligations of all patriots to the Union, is the Great Republican Party. Its wisdom, patriotism, patience and forbearance, all stand out in bold relief, in the noble legislation of the American Congress during the past five years of our history; and in the equally noble legislation of Tennessee during the past two years, in the face of opposition both fierce and formidable. In a word, the Republicans propose no monopoly—they advocate no titled aristocracy—no distinction on account of race or color—no privileged Phariseeism—they withhold no just rights— only forfeited rights—protecting alike every class, guarding, with a jealous eye, the preservation of the Union.

Tennessee the Harbinger of the New South.

Tennessee is the only stronghold Republicanism has in the South; her Executive, Legislative and Judiciary Departments being loyal, have contributed in their turn to the great work recently accomplished. And well they might, for the conflict involved the safety of the noble Union men who stood firm in the hour of danger—the safety of the colored race—the chances of a civilization for the South—and the future prosperity of our gallant old State, as well as the influence of her vote in the next Presidential election. The Tennessee elections, just over, mark a new dispensation in the political affairs of the South. The Rebel-Democratic Party goes to pieces; the Republican-Union Party looms up in bold relief as the party entitled to the confidence and regard of the whole country. This Conservative Party has, during its career, advocated no more men and no more money to carry on an 'abolition war'—a universal amnesty for traitors—secession and foreign interference—now openly advocates the repudiation of the National debt—and it only remains for it to advocate Polygamy, in order to have sounded every known depth of political infamy!

No Proscription.

I have witnessed with regret, in different localities in this State, a disposition to proscribe Northern men, and to drive them from the country. I do not enter into this spirit, nor will I administer the Executive branch of the State Government upon any such principle. If men are good enough to come to Tennessee and encounter the cold and heat and mud and rains of our climate, and face rebel bullets in putting down the rebellion, they are good enough, when qualified, to fill offices of honor and trust. We want Northern capital—Northern enterprise—and to get all this, I, for one, am willing to take a fair proportion of Northern politicians. But I yield to no man in my contempt for that class of Northern men who come among us, and for the sake of position and patronage, abandon their honest sentiments, and become rebel sympathizers.

Gentlemen, in the feeble state of my health, I shall expect your kind indulgence and generous co-operation—whilst I ask that as few burdens be imposed upon me as the public interests may allow. Mutually seeking the public good, let us accept every responsibility which our respective positions impose.

Imploring for your guidance the favor of a merciful God, which is never withheld from law-makers whose course is shaped solely by the conceptions He gives them of right and duty, I conclude with a sentiment which I trust may inspire all our actions—The Union of the Republican party for the sake of the Union!

W. G. BROWNLOW.

Nashville, October 8th, 1867."

Parson Brownlow's feeble state of health had been a matter of concern to even extreme Radical leaders during the gubernatorial contest. Time and again reports were current that his enfeebled condition had reached a critical stage. To offset this charge, Brownlow now reversed his usual rôle of chronic invalid and declared that he had never felt better than during the past twelve months. Like Hamlet, there was "method in his madness." Just a week after the convening of the Legislature, the basis of his alleged improved health became known. He let it be understood that he desired to be elected to the United States Senate, an office then filled by legislative action. In this position "of the highest honor which a State can confer upon a citizen," he declared that he believed he could render a valuable service to Tennessee citizens by obtaining payment of Civil War claims which the Federal Government had been "so tardy in bestowing." On October 15, 1867, the Parson announced openly his ambition. The fact that the Parson wanted something was sufficient to snuff out similar ambitions on the part of a number of Radicals. They interred without ceremony their ambitions, all except one of the most extreme of all Radicals. This was General William B. Stokes who professed to believe Brownlow too feeble for the job. It would be, argued Stokes, a patriotic service to the State to oppose the Parson's election.

On the same day of the Parson's announcement for the United States Senatorship, the senatorial ball was tossed into the legislative hopper. Senator William H. Wisener, Sr., from the counties of Bedford and Marshall offered Senate Joint Resolution No. 14 carrying the legend, "With respect to the Senatorial Election."[201] The Resolution was concurred in by the House and on October 22 Representative William Bosson of Rutherford County moved that the election of United States Senator be set for 11 o'clock that same day.[202] Nominations for Senator were called for with the following results: William G. Brownlow of Knox County; Horace Maynard of Knox County; William B. Stokes of DeKalb County; A. J. Fletcher of Greene County; Elijah Walker of Hardin County; and Joseph A. Cooper of Knox County.[203]

On first ballot, the vote in the Senate was as follows:

Stokes	10
Brownlow	6
Maynard	6
Fletcher	2
Cooper	1

The House vote was:

Brownlow	34
Stokes	15
Maynard	13
Fletcher	7
Cooper	5
Walker	4

No candidate having received a majority vote, there was no election. A motion to adjourn the Convention was defeated, and a second ballot was had with these results:

[201] *Senate Journal*, 1867-68, 46.
[202] *House Journal*, 1867-68, 82.
[203] *Ibid.*, 84.

In the Senate:

Stokes	10
Brownlow	7
Maynard	5
Fletcher	2
Cooper	1

In the House: (Cooper's name was withdrawn)

Brownlow	37
Stokes	18
Maynard	11
Fletcher	8
Walker	4

Since there was no election, the third ballot followed:

In the Senate:

Stokes	10
Brownlow	8
Maynard	4
Fletcher	2
Cooper	1

According to the official record, a rather unusual incident occurred. The House did not cast a vote on the third ballot at this time.[204] Furthermore, "The House adjourned until 10 o'clock tomorrow." On the following day, October 23, the Senate and House met again in Joint Convention for the purpose of getting the contest settled. After the reading of the *Journals* of each branch, the Speaker of the Senate, DeWitt Clinton Senter, announced that no candidate had received a majority and, therefore, there had been no election. He further announced that nominations were now in order. Apparently some real gum-shoe politics had been going on during the night, for only two candidates were nominated, Brownlow and Stokes.

The Speaker of the Senate ordered the Convention to proceed with the balloting, with the following results:

In the Senate:[205]

Brownlow	12
Stokes	12

In the House:[206]

Brownlow	51
Stokes	27
Walker	1

---

[204] *Ibid.*, 86.
[205] *Senate Journal*, 1867–68, 64.
Author's note. Senator A. M. Cate was not recorded as voting.
[206] *House Journal*, 1867–68, 91.
Author's note. Although Mr. Walker was not formally nominated on the third ballot, nevertheless Representative John Woodard of Robertson County voted for him.

The aggregate vote then stood:

Brownlow	63
Stokes	39
Walker	1

When the total vote had been tallied up, the Speaker of the Senate declared [207]

"Mr. Brownlow having received a majority of all the votes cast [is] duly and constitutionally elected United States Senator, to succeed Hon. D. T. Patterson, term commencing March 4th, 1869."

Thereupon, the Convention declared the vote for Governor W. G. Brownlow unanimous. Although the Senatorial post would not become vacant for some sixteen months, yet the Parson had seized time by the forelock and proceeded to "get while the getting was good." Never a statesman but always a consummate politician, seemingly Brownlow possessed a hypnotic power that was predominate. His hold on the Tennessee Radicals was well-nigh invincible. Most of the Radicals shouted for joy, although it has been stated that Stokes "sulked secretly and never forgot the 'dog-in-the-manger' characteristic which the Parson had so forcefully exhibited."[208] Another authority has maintained that there was an agreement reached between the friends of Brownlow and those of Senter whereby Brownlow was to be elected to the United States Senate and Senter would thereby be elevated to the gubernatorial post, by being elected Speaker of the Senate.[209] At any rate, that's what happened. There can be no doubt but that the Parson's cup was overflowing with joy. If he lived—and he did—the Parson would enter the chambers of the United States Senate on the very day that his hated rival, President Andrew Johnson, would be vacating the Presidential chair. Another sweet morsel was that Brownlow would be succeeding Johnson's son-in-law, Senator David T. Patterson. With the Parson taken care of for the ensuing six years, the Legislature on second thought decided to pay a bit of attention to the Parson's Message.

Governor Brownlow's Message embraced the following subjects:

1. Federal Relations
2. Election of a United States Senator
3. Election of Representatives to Congress
4. The Judiciary
5. Literature and Science
6. Accounts between the State and Railroads
7. Turnpike Roads
8. Criminal Courts

[207] *Ibid.*, 1867–68, 91.
[208] Coulter, E. Merton: *William G. Brownlow*, 347.
[209] Hamer, Philip M.: *Tennessee—A History*, Volume II, 645–646.

9. Immigration
10. Hospital for the Insane
11. Compensating Loyal Men for Losses
12. The Colored Population
13. Condition of the Penitentiary
14. The State Guards
15. A Governor's Mansion
16. The School Bill
17. Bill of Costs

In regard to Federal Relations, Governor Brownlow with smug satisfaction merely advised the Legislature that all was well in that respect, in that Federal troops had assisted in "effectually preserving the peace" on election day to such an extent that it was a quiet affair "evincing forbearance and self-control on the part of our citizens." What the Governor neglected to point out was that large bodies of Negro troops with bayonets and muskets had contributed greatly to that alleged "peace."

Inasmuch as the Senatorial election has already been discussed, attention will be given to the Governor's recommendation for a change in the time of election of Congressmen. Without difficulty, a law [210] was passed whereby the Congressional election was changed from August to November.

No significant legislation was enacted that affected the judiciary. Certain judicial circuits were changed, provisions were made for the election of County Judges in certain counties, no disqualification for jury service on account of race or color was approved,[211] and the Judges of the Supreme Court were empowered to correct any erroneous statements due to the transcription of the opinions by the Clerks of the Supreme Court.[212]

If the Conservative contemporary newspapers can be relied upon, there was dire need of correcting the abuses of Governor Brownlow who was charged with merely "appointing" Judges of the Supreme Court instead of complying with legal requirements by calling for an election within sixty days in case of a vacancy on the Supreme Court. Sections 312 and 313 of the *Code of Tennessee* were as follows:

"312. Whenever a vacancy occurs in any office herein named, the Governor shall order an election by issuing proper writs of election to fill the vacancy, giving notice thereof.

313. If the election is of a Supreme Judge, the notice must be for two months by publication in a newspaper in each of the grand divisions of the State, and the writs shall issue to each sheriff in the State."

---

[210] *Acts of Tennessee*, 1867–68, Chapter 53.
[211] *Ibid.*, Chapter 31.
[212] *Ibid.*, Chapter 61.

The *Union and American*, in a caustic editorial,[213] lambasted Governor Brownlow for ignoring the plain law in regard to his handling vacancies occurring on the Supreme Court. An extract from the editorial was as follows:

". . . The law which his oath of office requires him to see faithfully executed, provides, whenever a vacancy occurs, that he 'shall order an election' to fill such vacancy. He has never ordered an election to fill a vacancy on the Supreme bench, notwithstanding every Judge of that court has resigned during his administration. In the ukase he promulgated a few weeks ago, announcing that he had appointed Mr. Horace Maynard 'to assist in holding the court' at Knoxville for two months, Governor Brownlow made the following impudent avowal:

'The Rebel papers are manifesting quite deep concern for the holding of the courts by qualified men. When we can no longer find men of integrity and ability in our own ranks to appoint to these high judicial positions, we will call upon the Rebels to furnish us substitutes. Judges of the Supreme Court should be able, impartial and patriotic men, rising above mere party politics in their decisions, but they should be men who will stand by the State government and sustain the late important decision of their predecessors. And when we appoint a man to a seat on the Supreme Bench we must understand him to fill this bill.'

Here is an explanation of the action of Gov. Brownlow in disregarding the law and continuing to appoint Judges. He unblushingly avows his purpose to place men upon the Supreme Bench who will have no opinion of their own, but 'will stand by the State government and sustain the late important decisions of their predecessors' whether they be right or wrong. What lawyer of independence and regard for his professional reputation, would accept an appointment under such conditions? It is by such an outrageous perversion of authority that Gov. Brownlow seeks to sustain his usurpations; by the appointment of men who will declare any law of the Legislature or any act of the Governor legal. In other words, whoever now accepts an appointment of Judge from him, must perjure himself when he takes an oath, as he is required to do, 'to administer justice, without respect to persons, and impartially to discharge all the duties incumbent upon him as a Judge, to the best of his skill and ability;' for the Governor requires him, as he has publicly announced, 'to stand by the State government,' by which he means the Brownlow administration, and declare its despotic acts to be legal and in accordance with 'the laws and the amended Constitution.' The Governor has notified such men as he may appoint Judges in advance, that they must abandon their judicial independence, their right to interpret laws in the light of the Constitution, and sustain the decisions of their predecessors which were made in the interest and for the exclusive benefit of the political party which sustains Gov. Brownlow. When he finds men who he believes will 'fill the bill,' he will appoint, but he has not the remotest notion of giving the people of this State such a Supreme Court as is provided for in the Constitution. As long as litigants, and especially the bar,

[213] *Union and American* (Nashville), September 22, 1868.
Author's note. It will be noted that this criticism was leveled at Governor Brownlow almost a year after the delivery of his Message on October 9, 1867. It will also be noted that in that Message he rather brazenly declared that he would "continue the same course" and would fill Supreme Court vacancies "by appointment"!

submit to these usurpations, we shall have no Supreme Court, but a trio of men representing that body, who supinely 'resign their right to reason,' and decide important cases for the benefit of the Radical party."

The Legislature paid scant attention to Governor Brownlow's panegyric upon *Literature and Science*. The former school law was brought up for revision, but only petty amendments were adopted.[214] One of these amendments delegated to the Superintendent of Public Instruction the responsibility of handling any escheated lands that fell to the State, of which there were practically none at the time. At the August election in 1867, General John H. Eaton, a General in the Union Army and afterwards in charge of the Freedman's Bureau in Tennessee, had been elected Superintendent of Public Instruction. By a revision of the former school law, his salary was increased from one hundred dollars per month to two hundred dollars. On the whole, the revamping of the school law contributed practically nothing to the establishment and maintenance of any worthwhile public school system.

With reference to Governor Brownlow's recommendation concerning *Accounts Between the State and the Railroads*, in which he expressed great concern as to the "characters of the men into whose hands State bonds go, both as to integrity and loyalty," let the official records speak a bit later in this chapter.

The Governor's recommendation regarding turnpikes seems to have fallen on deaf ears. Outside of granting fifty-eight private companies articles of incorporation, absolutely nothing was done in regard to encouraging or aiding this particular type of project. As will presently appear, the Chief Executive and the General Assembly had their eyes and ears attuned to some real "folding money" pertaining to the issuance of State bonds for railroads.

The Governor's lecture on temperance, injected into his Message, was completely ignored by the Legislature insofar as the enactment of any prohibitive legislation. All that was done was to repeal all State laws requiring the inspection of spirituous or alcoholic liquors, leaving that job to agents of Uncle Sam.[215]

No recommendation was embodied in the historical treatise dealing with the *School Fund*, and no legislation on that particular phase of education was enacted by the Legislature.

The only legislative "wink" at the Governor's recommendation concerning the encouragement of immigration was the purchase of 2,000 copies of a book by Reverend Herman Bokum, entitled the *Resources of Tennessee*. The purchase price was $1,000.[216]

The *Report of the Superintendent of the Hospital for the Insane* was referred to in Governor Brownlow's Message. The institution had

[214] *Acts of Tennessee*, 1867-68, Chapter 83.
[215] *Ibid.*, Chapter 56.
[216] *Ibid.*, Chapter 86, Section 36.

been greatly damaged during the war and stood in need of rehabilitation. The sum of $45,000 was appropriated [217] for current obligations and $5,000 for repairs. The Governor's recommendation for the erection of a similar building "at a suitable point in East Tennessee" was not carried into effect.

Although the Negro vote went almost solidly for Brownlow in the August, 1867, election for Governor, yet his innate hostility toward the Negro impelled him to submit a rather tepid comment in regard to the Negro's being made eligible to do jury service. On this ticklish point, which had been batted to and fro in the gubernatorial race, Brownlow submitted the question to the Legislature for solution. The sixteenth section of the Franchise Law was the *bête noir*, and was mentioned by the Negroes as being the "ojus" [odious] part of the law so highly objectionable to them. That disability was removed, thus giving to the Negro the legal right to sit on juries.[218]

In regard to the penitentiary, an appropriation of $36,000 was made for replacements due to a destructive fire,[219] and another appropriation in the amount of $55,000 was made for current expenses.[220] Nothing was done in regard to erecting two branches of the penitentiary as recommended by the Governor.

A revamping of the law regarding State Guards was enacted,[221] differing from the original law in minor administrative details. There was still retained in the revised law the provision that the Governor was empowered to organize, equip, and call into active service one or more regiments of "loyal" men from each Congressional District. The purpose for which such troops were to be utilized was not revealed in the statute.

The Governor's request for a mansion for the Chief Executive was honored to the extent that a resolution on the subject was introduced by Representative T. McKinley of Sumner County, to-wit: [222]

"*Resolved by the General Assembly of the State of Tennessee*, That a Committee of——on the part of the Senate and three on the part of the House be appointed to take into consideration that part of the Governor's Message relating to the Governor's Mansion, and report by Bill or otherwise."

The resolution was adopted by the House immediately, and was concurred in by the Senate.[223] The legislative *Journals* fail to show any further action on the matter.

---

[217] *Ibid.*, Chapter 86, Section 40.
[218] *Ibid.*, Chapter 31.
[219] *Ibid.*, Chapter 9.
[220] *Ibid.*, Chapter 86, Section 38.
[221] *Ibid.*, Chapter 70.
[222] *House Journal*, 1867–68, 96.
[223] *Senate Journal*, 1867–68, 83.

Final comment on Governor Brownlow's Message will relate to his recommendation for repeal of the $5,000 reward ordered by the Legislature in 1865, for the capture and return of former Governor Isham G. Harris. It will be recalled that Harris had led Tennessee into secession, and that he was perhaps the most militant "secesh" Governor in any of the Southern States. But the passage of a few years had wrought some significant changes. For example, President Andrew Johnson had softened in his attitude toward secession participants, a position decidedly displeasing to Parson Brownlow. Governor Brownlow pointed out that during the recent gubernatorial campaign "there were worse men upon the stump than Harris ever was." Harris and Johnson had become bitter enemies over the question of secession, and never became reconciled. To show mercy toward Harris would likely rile up Johnson. The Parson's hatred of Johnson may have been a real factor in his softened-up attitude toward Harris. Furthermore, ex-Governor Harris had been an exile in Mexico and later in England, and his family was in dire circumstances. Had Brownlow based his proposed pardon of Harris upon this one proposition, his magnanimity would have been enhanced. But he could not, at least he did not, refrain from taking a nasty "dig" at the former Governor by saying that his capture would entail a financial expenditure on the part of the State for which the State "would have nothing to show for the outlay." In the Parson's eyes, ex-Governor Harris was worthless! In repealing the Joint Resolution offering the reward, the Legislature exhibited a vindictive and even vicious spirit by branding Harris "traitor."[224]

Let our steps be retraced a bit, whereby a drama will be presented in which Governor Brownlow appeared in two distinct roles, both amazing and contradictory. This drama might well be called the "Colossal Railroad Swindle." The Tennessee railroads, at the close of the war, were in desperate condition. Retreating Confederates had torn up many miles of railroads so as to disrupt communication. The then current funds, rolling stock, and records were carried away by fleeing officials. By the end of the war, enormous arrears of interest had piled up. What to do with a large group of bankrupt railroads was a herculean task facing both the railroads and the State which had acquired tremendous financial responsibility through the issuance of State bonds in aid of railroads. During the decade previous to the War Between the States, Tennessee had in the form of State bonds granted aid to the railroads in the amount of slightly more than fourteen million dollars. In less than three years of the Brownlow regime, almost an identical amount of State bonds was issued and turned over to the railroads. Confronted by this predicament, two arguments were put forth. One argument was that additional State aid would prevent the railroads from falling into the

---

[224] *Acts of Tennessee*, 1867–68, Chapter 6.

hands of "furriners." The other argument was that the railroads, without State aid, could not pay the interest already due on former bonds issued by the State. The latter argument led to such a ridiculous extreme that $4,847,000 in State bonds was loaned to insolvent railroads of East Tennessee for the alleged purpose of protecting the taxpayers from having to pay the interest on a mere $471,000 of State bonds handed over to these companies previously!

Governor Brownlow appears to have been "persuaded" by such specious argument. Buoyed up by such fantastic sophistry, Governor Brownlow in his major Message to the Legislature on November 6, 1866, praised

"The commendable spirit with which you have come to the rescue of the railroads of the State, and the ability with which you have restored and sustained the State credit, emboldens me to ask of you still further exertions in behalf of the same great interests."

But a year later, the Parson's indignation burst beyond all restraints as he hurled the following anathema at the railroads in his Message of October 8, 1867:

"In all future appropriations to railroad companies, let us know the characters of the men into whose hands State bonds go, both as to integrity and loyalty. . . ."
"It is an outrage that nearly a million dollars is due the State from these defaulting companies. . . ."

In less than two months, witness the chameleon-like change in the Parson's attitude toward railroads as set forth in his Special Message:*

"STATE OF TENNESSEE, EXECUTIVE DEPARTMENT,

Nashville, Nov. 21, 1867.

GENTLEMEN OF THE SENATE AND HOUSE OF REPRESENTATIVES:

I deem it my duty to call the attention of the Legislature to the necessity of yielding a prudent but liberal aid to the railroads of the State, to place them in a condition to be productive, and enable them to meet, hereafter, the interest on the loans made by the State to the roads. The State owns a substantial and valuable interest in the railroads, and that interest is one of the main bases of the credit of the State. Unless timely aid is extended to the railroads, the important interest the State has in them will depreciate, and this great property depreciate by decay, and by reason of the inability to use

* Senate Journal, 1867–68, 144–145.
  House Journal, 1867–68, 214–216.

them profitably. A comparatively small aid now promptly extended to them, will preserve and save the interest of the State. If such aid is not given, the State will lose much more by depreciation of the property, and their inability to operate profitably, than the whole amount required, by judicious expenditure, to place the roads in a condition of productiveness.

The whole amount of aid the State may now extend to the roads, to render them useful and profitable, if honestly and faithfully applied, will become and remain a security for the loan. Without such aid to the roads, the State may lose many times in value, the amount of the loans asked for by the roads.

The indebtedness of the State will justify the extension of aid to the roads. The income from the roads and from taxation, will enable the State to meet all the liabilities. The railroad indebtedness is the principal liability of the State. The revenue from the roads and from taxation, by judicious economy, will defray all the expenses of the State, and discharge all her liabilities, if the revenue is not collected in the issues of the Bank of Tennessee, and will, doubtless, when the State is in a more prosperous condition, be redeemed; and, so far as the property and assets of the bank can be made available, they will be applied in that way.

But important legal questions, involving the rights and interests of the State, are pending in the highest courts of the country; and, until a final decision in the case, the revenues will be collected as heretofore. Persons holding the issues of the Bank of Tennessee, desire the State should liquidate whatever may be the liability of the State for them, by funding the amount of the issues of the bank. This would be unjust and inexpedient. Unjust, because the holders of the notes of the bank bought or received them with the implied understanding, that the assets of the bank were to be applied to their redemption; and they should postpone the demand for redemption, until the assets can be converted and made available for their redemption, or, at least, for such reasonable time as will enable the State to realize from the assets the most she can. Inexpedient, because the funding of the amount of the issues of the bank, will render the State less able to give such aid to the railroads, as her best interests require.

The notes of the bank are held by a few banks, brokers and speculators, and were bought up at low rates, and few persons will suffer by delaying their redemption until the questions of law are settled by the courts, and the assets of the bank, as far as possible, realized and used in cancelling the notes. The people of the State desire to see their railroads fostered and preserved and rendered valuable, and but few persons are urging the funding of the indebtedness of the bank. No one will materially suffer by delaying the settlement of the affairs of the Bank of Tennessee, until the matters involved in litigation are settled by the courts, and the assets of this bank collected and applied to the liquidation of its liabilities.

The great interest of the State is her railroads, and these we should aid, sustain, and render valuable and profitable.

I have submitted these views in no spirit of dictation, but from a sense of duty, desiring to place myself upon the record in respect to our railroads, and the issues of the Bank of Tennessee.

W. G. BROWNLOW."

A hasty recapitulation of the issuance of State bonds for railroads during three years of Parson Brownlow's reign of terror discloses that approximately $14,000,000 were tossed into the greedy maws of certain railroad magnates. The most infamous of all these transactions related to the passage of the "Omnibus Bill" on December 7, 1867. This bill appropriated to fifteen railroads, the majority of which were in self-confessed bankruptcy, the tidy sum of $3,700,000.[225] In the above Message, Governor Brownlow specifically urged the passage of the outrageous and fraudulent "Omnibus Bill" then pending before the Legislature. Spurred to frantic action by railroad lobbyists and the urging of the Governor, the "robber bandits" otherwise called the General Assembly passed the "Omnibus Bill" in the House, on December 7 at a Saturday afternoon session, by a vote of 49 to 27.[226] The bill was then hustled across to the Senate within minutes, and was passed *instanter* by a vote of 17 to 5.[227]

Ten years rolled by before the skullduggery, bribery, and other devilish devices were unearthed in which an exposé was made by a legislative investigating committee as to just how the detestable "Omnibus Bill" was passed. An official document exposed the most putrid mess perhaps to be found in the annals of Tennessee history.[228] Two or three

[225] *Acts of Tennessee*, 1867-68, Chapter 17.
[226] *House Journal*, 1867–68, 285.
[227] *Senate Journal*, 1867–68, 186.
[228] *Appendix to House Journal of the Forty-First General Assembly*, 1879.
    Author's note. This volume contains twenty reports by various legislative committees. The report on the *State Debt*, consisting of 211 pages, will be found toward the latter part of the volume.

brief extracts from a gubernatorial message and a legislative committee report on the *State Debt* will be sufficient to give a "tip" on one of the basest betrayals of public welfare ever perpetrated upon the citizens of Tennessee.

On January 17, 1879, Governor Albert S. Marks submitted to the Legislature a formal Message in which he made the following observations [229] regarding the passage of the "Omnibus Bill" and the issue of additional State bonds to insolvent railroads:

"There were honest men in the Legislative bodies which authorized this fraud, but their efforts to protect the State were unavailing. But their manly protests exhibit the shameful methods employed in the perpetration of this vast fraud. The facts subsequently officially developed, in connection with the Journals of the two Houses, show that appropriations were refused unless the members were paid to make them. It appears that bonds were sold at a large discount to raise money to pay members to vote for further appropriations. It appears that with the proceeds of bonds so sold, a minister of the Gospel was employed to manipulate members of the Legislature, and that when he reached the Capitol, a bill authorizing the issuance of bonds, had been rejected by a decided majority. In the morning he opened the proceedings with prayer; before night the vote was reconsidered, and the next day the bill passed with but two dissenting votes. This bill appropriated $3,000,000 to the insolvent roads.

It appears that relatives of high officials were paid money, the proceeds of bonds, to induce favorable action in the further issuance of bonds.... It appears that the Governor, who was clothed with the power to decide when the law was complied with, delegated his power to issue bonds, and that many of them were signed and issued by one of his subordinates in the City of New York...."

An excerpt [230] from the Majority Report of the legislative committee, appointed to investigate the *State Debt*, dealt with the passage of the nefarious "Omnibus Bill":

"It presents a carnival of revelry and corruption. Previous investigations have discovered much corruption; the laws themselves evidence much. This committee have discovered some not known before to its members, and still the field is unexhausted.

In 1866, a majority of the people were allowed no voice in the government of the State. The act of that year was passed; $4,941,000 were unjustly and illegally added to the debt. 1867 came. The larger portion of the people were still debarred the exercise of political rights. Many corporate presidents, agents, and representatives came to Nashville to attend the sitting of the Legislature. All known influences were used upon the supposed representatives of the people. From the pulpit to the bagnio recruits were gathered for the assault on the Treasury of the State. Fine brandy by the barrel was on hand to fire thirst and muddle the brain, and first-class suits of

---

[229] *Senate Journal*, 1879, 143–144.
[230] *Appendix to House Journal*, 1879, 15–16.

Author's note. The Governor's Message is also placed among the twenty reports, and will be found beyond the middle of the volume.

clothing to capture the vanity or avarice of the gay or needy. Money, the proceeds of bonds issued by the State for specific purposes to these men, was here in abundance, and it was used. The omnibus railroad bill of that year was passed, and nearly $5,000,000 more were corruptly and wickedly added to the burdens of the people."

Posterity is indebted to the members of the legislative investigating committee which dug into this mess. That committee followed the Scriptural admonition to "Cry aloud, and spare not." Their names were S. F. Wilson, R. H. Smith, John M. Driver, D. L. Snodgrass, Thomas E. Haynes, and N. Gregg.

On February 15, 1879, the kingpin of the railroad lobbyists was subjected to a rigid examination by the above committee.[231] Having been served with a subpoena to appear before the committee, General Joseph A. Mabry of Knoxville, a former railroad president, was called upon to tell whether he and others had "at any time paid or made a present of $5,000 or any other sum to a distinguished Governor of the State, to his wife, or family?"

"ANSWER: . . . Myself and the four other gentlemen named in your question made a present of 5 one thousand dollar bills to Governor Brownlow. I tendered the money to him and he told me to hand it to his wife. . . . His wife received the money.
QUESTION: What induced this present?
ANSWER: Myself and the other gentlemen named were in New York, and engaged in bond speculations. Some of us had sold 'bonds short' and desired to depress 'their price,' and suits were instituted by some parties in New York and Nashville on some matured bonds. Some of us consulted a celebrated New York Spiritualist, Madame Mansfield, and she told us that bonds would go down and that there would be trouble in Tennessee and not to go to Nashville that we would be arrested, but we could control 'old scratch,' meaning Governor Brownlow, with money. We seen that the Legislature had been called. We came to Knoxville. We had speculated in bonds on account of Governor Brownlow, and had made nearly $5,000. We then determined to make the Governor a present of the $5,000, furnishing out of our own private means what we had failed of the $5,000 in our speculating for his benefit. I notified him the day before that we would, Callaway and myself went up to present it, he was lying on a lounge and told us to give it to his wife and we did so, as before stated."

General Mabry testified further under protest that Governor Brownlow did not have any knowledge of the manipulations described above in his testimony. In reply to another question by the committee, Mabry said that the $5,000 was in his opinion "received purely as a present." In reply to the query as to whether or not the present was made for the purpose of enabling them to control Brownlow, General Mabry's reply was:

"We were advised by the spiritualist that we could control him and we took this way of doing it and we entered into the speculations to make some money for him. We wanted to quiet him and took this way of doing it."

---
[231] *Ibid.*, 167–179.

Whether or not the financial "soothing syrup" was administered and *quieted* the Parson, "deponeth sayeth not!"

The First Session of the Thirty-Fifth General Assembly finally decided to wind up its session, having exhausted its vengeance against former Confederates and their sympathizers consisting of many former Unionists. One searches in vain for any significant constructive legislation enacted by this body for the public welfare. From beginning to end, punitive and proscriptive laws rated high on the legislative agenda of this most Radical and most corrupt of all legislative assemblies in the entire history of Tennessee. This body was not, as is sometimes erroneously stated, a "carpetbag" Legislature. A majority of its membership were native-born Tennesseans. It was a "scalawag" aggregation,[232] on the whole. During its 162 days of deliberations, ninety public acts and the same number of private acts were passed. In addition, 142 resolutions were passed, among which were: No. 75 requesting the Tennessee Congressional delegation to use its influence in procuring a reduction of the tax on liquor;[233] No. 78 requesting the Federal Government to pay expenses of the Tennessee State Guard called into action by Governor Brownlow;[234] and No. 96 recommending the impeachment of President Andrew Johnson.[235]

At long last, on March 16, 1868, legislative adjournment was declared until November 9, 1868, when the Second Session was scheduled to begin.

Social, economic, and political conditions in Tennessee had become well-nigh intolerable under the iron-handed regime of Brownlow and his Radical supporters. The times were assuredly, as Hamlet exclaimed, "out of joint." Ex-Confederates, constituting the majority of white citizens, had been denied the privilege of having any voice in their State government. Recently-freed Negroes were invested with the ballot, and had been herded by the Radicals and voted in droves in the August (1867) gubernatorial election enabling the Parson to remain in the Executive Chair. A complete breakdown of the normal social order had resulted, and Chaos had been politically enthroned. Doubtless thousands upon thousands of tax-paying citizens felt impelled to subscribe to Tennyson's pathetic refrain:

"And Time, a maniac scattering dust,
And Life, a Fury slinging flame."

---

[232] Author's note. Dictionary definitions usually define a carpetbagger as a Northern man who came to the South at the close of the War Between the States for purposes of speculation and plunder. On the other hand, a scalawag is generally defined as a native Southern white Republican who sided with the Northern Radicals. Frequently, the scalawag was called a "home-made Yankee."

[233] *Acts of Tennessee*, 1867-68, 333-334.

[234] *Ibid.*, 335-336.

[235] *Ibid.*, 346-347.

The crushing defeat of the Conservative party in the August, 1867, election brought dismay and fearful forebodings. Manacled by the proscriptions of the Franchise Act which deprived the Conservatives of any voice in the making of any laws for operation of the State Government, the Conservatives were reduced politically to ZERO status.

Two organizations, the Freedmen's Bureau and the Loyal League, each under complete control of the Radicals, served to accentuate rather than to reduce the tension between the Radicals and the Conservatives in Tennessee. By an act of Congress, March 3, 1865, there was created in the War Department "a bureau of refugees, freedmen, and abandoned lands" which agency soon came to be known as the Freedmen's Bureau. In the early stages of the Bureau's existence, Brigadier General Clinton B. Fisk was assigned to the district that embraced Kentucky and Tennessee. Later, General John H. Eaton who had served in the Union Army supervised the Bureau's work in Tennessee. In addition to ministering to the physical needs of the freedmen, schools were established for the Negroes. It is highly probable that the type of teaching done in these Freedmen's schools contributed in no small degree to the nerve-breaking tension between the two races. A particularly reprehensible class of Northern ministers and teachers, many of whom were attached to the educational division of the Bureau, were stationed in the Freedmen's schools in the South and encouraged the Negroes to aspire to social equality. One result of this movement was that the Negroes assumed a defiant and surly attitude toward the whites. Ill-feeling and serious outbreaks occurred in numerous places, resulting at times in physical combat and even the loss of life. These ill-advised "missionaries" were graphically described by a Virginia editor:[236]

"White cravatted gentlemen from Andover, with a nasal twang, and pretty Yankee girls, with the smallest of hands and feet, have flocked to the South as missionary ground, and are communicating a healthy moral tone to the 'colored folks,' besides instructing them in chemistry, botany, and natural philosophy, teaching them to speak French, sing Italian, and walk Spanish, so that in time we are bound to have intelligent, and, probably, intellectual labor."

From the very beginning, the Bureau was subjected to violent criticism. Democrats in Congress charged that the Bureau was an unconstitutional and an unnecessary agency. It was constantly accused of engaging in partisan politics in the interests of the Republican party. Official records disclose that the Bureau's financial affairs were poorly managed at times and some of its agents misappropriated funds. In the South, the Bureau was charged with fomenting race hatred and trying to advance the Negro to the detriment of the rights of white people.

---

[236] Richmond *Times,* January 16, 1866, quoted by William T. Alderson in "The Freedmen's Bureau and Negro Education in Virginia," in *North Carolina Historical Review,* XXIX (1952), 70.

The other organization contributing to disquiet and unrest was the Loyal League. Its purpose and activity, already sketched, were purely political. Its slogan in reality was—lure the Negroes into the League and command them to vote the Radical ticket from top to bottom.

One potent answer of the ex-Confederates in Tennessee to their miserable political plight was KuKluxism. Its object, especially in Tennessee where it first originated, was to checkmate Radical Reconstruction as imposed by Governor Brownlow and his subservient Legislature. The Ku Klux Klan was an antidote to the Loyal League and Freedmen's Bureau. A lot of wild speculation and weird theories have been advanced as to the origin of the name of the Ku Klux organization.[237] The surmises run all the way from the suggestion that Ku Klux Klan is a Hebrew term down to a fantastic assertion that it dated back to Chinese merchants engaged in opium smuggling! Fortunately, the sensible explanation of the name is that it is logically and etymologically associated with a Greek word, KUKLOS, meaning circle. By modernizing the Greek word into two words, KU KLUX, and adding another alliterative word, KLAN, we have a sensible explanation as to the origin and adoption of a name for the organization that waged an effective species of psychological warfare against political tyranny in Tennessee. Clad in a grotesque garb and riding horses with muffled hoofs, issuing posters and circulars couched in weird and mysterious warnings, the Klan became a terror by day and a nightmare by night to thousands and thousands of ignorant and superstitious Negroes.

The press played an important part in the Ku Klux movement by publicizing its real or alleged activities. Anti-Brownlow newspapers chortled over the fears and intimidations of superstitious Negroes, while pro-Brownlow journals condemned unsparingly the machinations of

---

[237] Horn, Stanley F.: *K K K Invisible Empire*, 7–9.

Author's note. By all odds, the most exhaustive and scholarly treatise on the Ku Klux Klan is by Stanley F. Horn, Nashville, Tennessee. The book is based upon extensive and intensive research, and the wonder is that so much documentary evidence could be unearthed regarding an order that was *secret*.

Lester, J. C., and D. L. Wilson: *Ku Klux Klan: Its Origin, Growth and Disbandment, 1884.*

This little book of 117 pages, 3½ x 6 inches and set in comparatively large type, was written something like twenty years after the Klan's birth. Without any appreciable documentation and based largely upon memory, the book smacks largely of "chimney-corner" history, and should be read in that light. Nevertheless, its contents preserve some interesting tales and anecdotes.

Alexander, Thomas B.: *Political Reconstruction in Tennessee*. Chapter XII deals with Kukluxism in Tennessee.

Patton, James Welch: *Unionism and Reconstruction in Tennessee*. Chapter VIII sketches Kuklux activities in Tennessee.

Hamer, Philip M.: *Tennessee—A History*, Vol. II, Chapter 40. A good overall sketch of the Kuklux movement in Tennessee.

House of Representatives Miscellaneous Documents, 41st Congress, 2nd Session, No. 53. Contested Election Case, Sheafe vs. Tillman. Scattered testimony in a Tennessee Congressional election.

"rebels" hell-bent on destroying the Brownlow government. With race relations strained beyond endurance and political hostilities seething at the boiling point, inevitably deeds of violence and fearful outrages sometimes occurred. Whether actually committed by members of the Klan or not, the Klan's enemies attributed all such bedevilment to the Klan. To his suspicious mind and vindictive nature, this was all Brownlow needed to nettle him into executive action. Another incentive was that the Parson had convincing evidence throughout the State that his Rebel-hating administration was far from being acceptable to the vast majority of Tennessee citizens; even some of his former stalwart Union supporters became gorged and sickened by his odious political persecution.

The fuse that seems to have lighted the Parson's political tinderbox was receipt of a brief dispatch from Samuel M. Arnell of Columbia, Tennessee, dated June 14, 1868:

"To Gov. W. G. Brownlow:

The Kuklux searched the train for me last night, pistols and rope in hand. Empower me to call upon the military here, if necessary, in your name, to suppress all armed and masked parties in this vicinity. I propose to fight it out.

S. M. ARNELL."[238]

It will be recalled that Arnell was Brownlow's floor leader and hatchet man during the legislative session that disfranchised the Confederates and enfranchised the Negroes. Furthermore, on the face of returns Arnell had later been defeated for Congress by a Conservative Unionist, Dorsey B. Thomas, and thereupon Brownlow threw out enough Thomas votes to enable Arnell to be catapulted into Congress with the stench of ballot-stealing clinging to his official garments as he entered the Congressional Hall. In the ungrammatical but emphatic language of a tyro, Brownlow must have muttered to himself, "Gentlemen, something must be did!"

And something was done! Less than three weeks later, Governor Brownlow issued the following Proclamation:*

"WHEREAS, On page 108 of the Code of Tennessee, the following constitutional provision is found:

'The Governor may, on extraordinary occasions, convene the General Assembly by proclamation, and shall state to them when assembled, the purposes for which they shall have been convened; but they shall enter on no legislative business except that for which they were specially called together.'

---

[238] *Senate Journal*, Extra Session, 1868, 5.
    House Journal, Extra Session, 1868, 9.
* *Ibid.*, 3.

NOW, THEREFORE, I, William G. Brownlow, Governor of Tennessee, issue this, my call for an extraordinary session of the General Assembly of Tennessee, to take place on Monday, 27th of July, 1868, at the Capitol, in Nashville. Senators and Representatives are required to be there at 12 o'clock, the day and date above named, when I will make known to them the purposes for which they have been called together.

The papers selected to do the legal advertising of the State, are directed to insert this proclamation, each, three times.

In testimony whereof, etc., etc., I sign and publish the same this 6th of July, 1868.

WILLIAM G. BROWNLOW."

In compliance with Governor Brownlow's Proclamation, the members of the General Assembly convened in Nashville on the appointed day. On the following day, the Governor's Message was transmitted to the Legislature:

Legislative Message,* July 28, 1868.

GENTLEMEN OF THE SENATE AND HOUSE OF REPRESENTATIVES:

The Constitutional provision, authorizing me to convene you in extraordinary session, makes it my duty to state to you the purposes for which you have been convened, and at the same time limits you in your acts of legislation to the business for which you have been called together.

At your session of last winter, by large majorities in both Houses, you repealed what was known as the militia law. I accordingly paid off the militia and disbanded them, so that, for the last ten months, there have been no State troops at my disposal. As members of the Legislature, you were assured by leading Conservatives in their respective counties, and doubly assured by the leading rebel journals of the State, there would be no necessity for any troops whatever, and that law and order would be strictly observed. It turns out that the rebellious elements of the State were at that time secretly arming themselves and perfecting a military organization known as the Ku Klux Klan, composed of ex-rebel soldiers and those who were in

* Acts of Tennessee, Extra Session, 1868, 5–13.
Senate Journal, Extra Session, 1868, 4–11.
House Journal, Extra Session, 1868, 8–15.

sympathy with them; thus violating their paroles at the time of their surrender, and violating the laws of the State, and plotting and planning mischief in every respect. These men have been arming and organizing for a year past, with an eye to the overthrow of the State Government, and, ultimately, to carrying the State in the Presidential election. They have known, as well as the political leaders and bad men who have prompted their action, that the President of the United States was bitterly hostile to the men and measures of the present State Government, and would readily favor a movement that would overthrow both. They have been confident, and have so expressed themselves, that the President would give them, as revolutionists, such aid by the disposition of troops, and changes in this military department, as would insure them an easy victory; and some of them have been so indiscreet as openly to boast of this. Their schemes have involved the overthrow of the existing State Government, the abolition of colored suffrage, the immediate enfranchisement, under the revolutionary constitution, of every rebel who fought to destroy the Government, and a wiping from the statute books of all the wholesome and patriotic laws enacted since April, 1865.

So violent and murderous have been the conduct of these armed outlaws in different counties of Middle and West Tennessee, that, acting under the authority of a resolution you adopted last Spring, I have called upon the brave and patriotic commander of this department at Louisville, to furnish me regular troops for these counties. The following correspondence will show you with what result:

EXECUTIVE OFFICE,
Knoxville, Tenn., June 15th, 1868.
Major-General Geo. H. Thomas, Commanding, &c.:
The following is a copy of a dispatch from the Hon. Mr. Arnell:

COLUMBIA, Tenn., June 14, 1868.
To Gov. W. G. Brownlow:
The Kuklux searched the train for me last night, pistols and rope in hand. Empower me to call upon the military here, if necessary, in your name, to suppress all armed and masked parties in this vicinity. I propose to fight it out.

S. M. ARNELL.

This is but in keeping with what is going on in other counties of Middle and West Tennessee, as I am advised by reliable men.

I therefore call upon you to furnish a company of troops for the counties of Lincoln and Marshall, jointly. One for the county of Obion, one for the county of Dyer, and one for the county of Gibson. Without troops in these counties the civil laws cannot be enforced, or loyal men allowed to exercise their rights and liberties. If you have the troops, I also desire that a company be sent to Fayette county.

I have the honor to be, etc.,

W. G. BROWNLOW,
Governor of Tennessee.

H'DQ'RS DEPT. OF THE CUMBERLAND,
Louisville, Ky., June 18, 1868.

His Excellency, W. G. Brownlow, Governor of Tennessee,
Knoxville, Tenn.:

SIR: I have the honor to acknowledge the receipt of your letter of the 15th inst., containing a copy of a dispatch from the Hon. S. M. Arnell, to you, and your request for troops to be sent to certain counties in Tennessee. You say that without troops in these counties the civil laws cannot be enforced, or loyal men allowed to exercise their rights and liberties. I have the honor to say in reply, that the military can only be used to aid and sustain the civil authorities in the discharge of their duties. The State of Tennessee, being in the full exercise of all the civil functions of a State, the military authority of the United States cannot legally interfere except in aid and support of the civil authority. For these purposes troops have been sent to various localities at your request. These details, together with the present demand for troops to assist the U. S. officers in collecting the revenue, has so exhausted the force at my command as to prevent the complying with your request to send companies to the counties named.

Very respectfully, your ob't sv't,
GEO. H. THOMAS,
Maj.-Gen. U. S. A., Commanding.

H'DQ'RS DEPT. OF THE CUMBERLAND,

Louisville, Ky., June 24, 1868.

To His Excellency W. G. Brownlow, Governor of Tennessee, Knoxville, Tenn.:

SIR: Referring to my letter of the 18th inst., to you, I have the honor to inform you, that since writing I have procured a copy of the Acts of the Thirty-Fifth General Assembly of Tennessee, for the years 1867-8.

I have carefully examined the Acts providing for the protection of Sheriffs, etc., and relating to the State Guard, and respectfully submit to you, as my opinion, that under these laws, if vigorously enforced, the difficulties in Tennessee, could be suppressed.

The 7th, and subsequent sections of the 'Act for the protection of Sheriffs,' etc., passed February 1st, 1868, appears to be especially available and practicable for good effect, and could be more readily and quickly enforced than the Act to 'organize and equip a State Guard,' etc., passed March 13, 1868, though, if found necessary, this would be the more powerful organization, notwithstanding its deficiencies as to a staff corps for its administration.

I take the liberty of giving an opinion on this subject, because of the probability of the necessity, in the end, for your calling on the United States for aid under the provisions of the Constitution; and as you have been informed, the force at my command is so exhausted by calls for other duties, that it is not likely that sufficient troops for the purpose could be furnished.

I have the honor to be, very respectfully, your obedient servant,

GEO. H. THOMAS,
Major-General, U. S. A.

STATE OF TENNESSEE,

Executive Department,

Knoxville, June 29th, 1868.

Major-General Geo. H. Thomas:

Your favor of the 24th inst., is now before me, and your suggestions have been duly considered. I thank you for the same, and fully appreciate your motives. The principle difficulty we have to encounter, has, perhaps, not occurred to your mind. The Sheriffs in the rebellious counties, for the most part, are strangely silent, and as strangely reluctant to comply with the provisions of the law. This reluctance arises from one of two considerations: either the fear of violence in attempting to organize a police force, or after said force shall have been disbanded. In some instances, the Sheriffs are in sympathy with the rebellious element of their respective counties.

Upon the whole, I think it likely I shall have to convene the Legislature in extraordinary session.

I have the honor to be, &c.,

W. G. BROWNLOW,
Governor of Tennessee.

This dangerous organization of ex-rebels now ramifies almost every part of the eleven States that once constituted the Southern Confederacy, and has already grown into a political engine of oppression so powerful and aggressive as to call forth in opposition, several notable military orders. Organized upon the same basis, and having the same dark designs in view, that found a fit culmination in Booth's assassination of Abraham Lincoln, it works in secret, mid signs, symbols and pass-words, hatching plots to scatter anarchy and permanent disorder wherever it may have an existence. The influential portion of the rebel press in the South hail its advent as a propitious circumstance. Of its purposes I need only extract from the constitution of one of the clubs of its order, captured by the police at Memphis, the following declaration:

'The object of this organization is for the purpose of protecting the people of the South from the band of murderers and robbers now preying upon them, even to the last resort—assassination—and we pledge ourselves one to the other, that nothing shall be allowed to deviate us from this noble object.'

Here we have assassination declared as a legitimate object of this lawless clan. That it is equal to its purposes is exemplified in the assassinations already committed in our own State and other Southern States. I recommend, most emphatically, that these organized bands of assassins and robbers be declared outlaws by special legislation, and punished with death wherever found.

I call upon members to speak and vote in the halls of legislation as they themselves and their constituents have spoken to me in private letters and petitions, calling for the militia to protect them in their person and property. True, it will take money to furnish a military force, but loyal men residing in rebellious counties, are entitled to protection, without any regard to what it may cost in dollars and cents. If I am expected to protect them, I must be allowed a sufficient clerical force to execute my orders promptly, and funds to meet the necessary demands in carrying out these orders. Gentlemen are here from the counties partially in rebellion, and it is for them to say whether a military force is necessary to afford protection and quiet among their constituents. You will also pardon me for my plainness of speech, as I have been complained of as rather tardy in my movements to protect loyal men. Therefore, it is that if our people are butchered in cold blood, and the colored population are intimidated and driven from their homes and the ballot box, I intend the responsibility shall rest with the Legislative, and not the Executive Department of the State Government. If I am regarded as extravagant and violent, I shall be gratified to have the Legislature designate some other person to take the entire control of this branch of the public service.

I again repeat, gentlemen, that you are fresh from the people, familiar with all the recent outrages complained of, and it is for you to apply the remedy for existing evils. Should you conclude to order out the militia, or a portion of them, it will be your duty to protect them by law for all proper acts done under orders, or in the line of duty. Otherwise, they will be annoyed by malicious prosecutions after they are mustered out of service.

STATE FINANCES.

I propose next, to call your attention to the subject of our State Finances. Near the close of the late session, you created a Financial Board, consisting of five members, viz: The Governor, Secretary of State, Comptroller, Treasurer, and the President of the Bank of Tennessee. I regret to say that from the time of the organization of the Board until the present, there has been great want of harmony in its councils and action. Very soon after the Board organized, the Secretary of State and the Comptroller sent in their resignations as members of the Board, as did also the Secretary of the Board. The remaining three members immediately convened at Knoxville and re-organized, electing S. Watson Chairman of the Board, and Hon.

W. Bosson, permanent Secretary. I offered a resolution, which was adopted, to the effect that we had no authority to accept the resignations of the persons before named, and alleging that their resignations should be tendered to the Legislature, the power by which they were constituted members of the Board, as the only body competent to receive their resignations. At the same meeting, we effected all the preliminary arrangements deemed necessary to provide for meeting the July interest, and the Chairman of the Board was constituted an agent to go to New York and carry out our plans. What these plans were, the report of the Board will show. Closely following the action recited, some members of the Board who had tendered their resignations, opened a most unprovoked and needless newspaper war upon the newly elected Chairman; and the policy we had adopted. The effect of this controversy was to distract our councils at home and injure our credit abroad. One member of the Board went so far as to say to another member, that he was in favor of making a publication, setting forth that the State was unable to meet the interest upon her bonds.

For the honor and credit of the State, I trust no member of either House of the Legislature will give countenance to such an idea. Pride of character, the dictates of patriotism, and a decent regard for the opinions of mankind, should lead us to frown indignantly upon anything looking toward the repudiation of our honestly contracted obligations. Of the thirty-two million dollars constituting our State debt, fully three-fourths were incurred by the State loaning her credit and issuing her bonds to the different Railroad Companies of the State. To secure the payment of these bonds, the State has a first mortgage upon all Railroads so aided, making her security fully adequate. Capitalists and dealers in stocks, well understanding these facts, have no lack of confidence in the ultimate redemption of Tennessee Bonds; indeed, our Bonds have gone up to seventy-eight cents on the dollar, at the time of the recent difficulty in New York. Here I will take occasion to say, that after arrangements were completed to meet the July interest, and everything was deemed secure, a most foul conspiracy was entered into somewhere, culminating at New York, evidently designed to injure the credit of our State and depreciate the price of her bonds, for the purposes of speculation. The result of which has been to delay the payment of the cate the guilty parties in these nefarious transactions. The New York

July interest, and also to greatly depreciate the value of the State Bonds. To meet this extraordinary emergency is, in part, the design of convening the General Assembly at this time. I am unable to indipress, as well as sundry letter writers, implicate Tennessee railroad men and members of the Financial Board. Others charge it upon New York parties, bond-holders and stock speculators. What I propose, is this: that you appoint a Joint Select Committee of your best and ablest men, with full powers to send for persons and papers, so as to sift this matter to the bottom, and ferret out the guilty parties, whoever they may be; and, if found guilty, you should proceed to sue them for damages, in the name of the State. Such summary and exemplary treatment of so flagrant offenders may serve to protect the State from like disaster in the future, and to maintain the standard value of her bonds.

Some of the railroad companies committed the great error of not making their payments in advance of the first of July. The Comptroller will inform you who they are. In the discharge of my duty, I served the following notice upon them all:

'EXECUTIVE OFFICE,
Nashville, Tenn., May 24, 1868.

To the Railroads of the State of Tennessee:

It is made your duty by the law of 1852, and also by the Act entitled "An Act to liquidate the debt of the State falling due in 1868 and 1869," passed March 13, 1868, to pay the interest on the Bonds loaned you, at least fifteen days before said Bonds become due. The penalty for the violation of this duty, is, that I am to appoint a suitable person, at your expense, to take charge of your road.

I therefore warn you, that the interest due from you on the first of July next, must be paid to the Comptroller of the State at least fifteen days before that date.

W. G. BROWNLOW,
Governor of Tennessee.'

PENITENTIARY.

Your attention is also called to the still partial confusion, indebtedness, and crowded condition of the Penitentiary. A full settlement with the lessees is desirable, if, indeed, it is not absolutely necessary. I do not advise the erection of additional buildings at this time, at Nashville; but I suggest, as I have done on former occasions, the commencement of a Branch Penitentiary in the Eastern Division of the State. The Penitentiary at Nashville ought to be self-sustaining; but, instead of this, large appropriations of money are annually required. The whole matter is with you, and to you I submit it, without entering into detail.

COLONEL A. E. BOONE,

Whom you designated by special enactment to settle with, provide for, and pay off the officers and soldiers of the late State Militia, has performed the work assigned him, and is ready for a settlement with such committee as you may designate.

POLITICAL DISABILITIES.

I have been appealed to by prominent men of both political parties, to urge upon you the propriety of removing political disabilities formerly imposed upon a large class of rebels. The conduct of that class of people has been, and it still is, such that I do not feel justified in making this recommendation. They have a military organization in this State, whose avowed object is to trample the laws under foot and force the party in power to enfranchise themselves and their sympathizers. I cannot stultify myself by yielding to this request, accompanied with threats of violence. If members of the General Assembly are alarmed for their personal safety, and feel disposed to sue for peace upon the terms proposed by an armed mob, they will, of course, take a different view of the subject. Any recommendation of this kind, if made at all, should be at a regular and not at a called session of your body. And whether such recommendation, and corresponding action thereupon, shall be deemed wise at your adjourned meeting in November next, can be then more safely determined, by strictly observing the conduct of these unreconstructed Ku Klux rebels and their sympathizing supporters, between this time and that.

Trusting that your session may be brief and useful, may the hand of a kind Providence guard your families in your absence.

W. G. Brownlow."

Five specific points were outlined in the above Message: (1) authorization for reviving the Tennessee State Guard under the Governor's command; (2) investigation of State finances; (3) elimination of the "confusion" regarding the management of the State penitentiary; (4) enactment of a law carrying the death penalty upon members of the Ku Klux Klan; and (5) refusal to recommend removal of the political disabilities imposed upon ex-Confederates.

Only four laws were enacted by the Legislature at this extraordinary session. Committees were appointed to investigate the charges that a conspiracy had been formed for the purpose of depressing State bonds whereby speculators could buy "low" and sell "high." A long drawn-out hassle arose among various State officials handling the financial matters of the State. Various officials resigned from the State Finance Board authorized to handle the sale of State bonds. The net result of all the wrangling was the passage of a law [239] which authorized the State Comptroller to borrow enough money to pay a portion of State indebtedness soon to fall due, with the issuance of additional State bonds to be used as collateral. No legislation was passed regarding the "confusion" in the running of the penitentiary, as this was an item deeply submerged beneath other matters of more concern to the Governor and the legislators.

Saturated with the idea that another "rebellion" was imminent, Governor Brownlow got down to brass tacks by levelling his official remarks at the Ku Klux Klan which he alleged was composed of "ex-rebels" who had been organized into "bands of assassins and robbers." He declared himself in favor of a law that would carry the death penalty. He called expressly for a revival of the Tennessee State Guard which had been allowed to drop into disbandment.

There was intense excitement aroused as a result of the recommendations submitted by the Governor. Real danger of civil war existed, particularly in Middle and West Tennessee where the bulk of the white citizens were disfranchised but who were now clamoring for the restoration of the right to vote. Scores and scores of petitions and memorials were forwarded to the Legislature calling for the repeal of the Franchise Law. One such petition,[240] signed by 4,000 citizens of Davidson County, urged Brownlow to call a Constitutional Convention "for the purpose of reinstating that large portion of the citizens of the State of Tennessee now suffering under disfranchisement. . . ." On August 1, 1868, thirteen ex-Confederate Generals submitted the following temperate request: [241]

"To the Honorable, the Legislature of Tennessee,
now in Extraordinary Session:
The right of petition and remonstrance being conceded by all classes in this country, and, feeling as we do, a deep solicitude for the peace and quiet

---

[239] *Acts of Tennessee*, Extra Session, 1868, Chapter 1.
[240] *House Journal*, Extra Session, 1868, 43–44.
[241] *Ibid.*, 42–43.

of our great and glorious State, and, belonging to that class in Tennessee who are regarded by some of the authorities as hostile to the present organization, we yield to a sense of duty, and respectfully invite your honorable body to a consideration of our view of the means that may avert the precipitation of the crisis which is acknowledged to be imminent. Being regarded as identified with that large class supposed to be hostile to the State Government, we beg to respectfully say that his Excellency, the Governor, wholly misapprehends our feelings and intentions, in declaring, in his late message, that we seek the overthrow of the State Government, or to do any other act by revolutionary or lawless means. Neither we, nor those with whom, in past days, we have been associated, contemplate any such rashness or folly; nor do we believe there is, in Tennessee, any organization, either public or secret, which has such a purpose; and if there be, we have neither sympathy or affiliation therewith. We believe the peace of the State does not require the organization of a military force by your honorable body, and respectfully submit that such a measure might more strongly tend to bring about and promote collision than to conserve the harmony and good order of the country. And, inasmuch as the supposed danger to the peace of the State is apprehended from that class of the community with which we are considered identified, as inducement and reason to your honorable body not to organize such military force, we pledge ourselves to maintain the order and peace of the State with whatever influence we possess; to uphold and support the laws, and aid in their execution, trusting that a reciprocation of these sentiments, by your honorable body, will produce the enactment of such laws as will remove all irritating causes now disturbing society. For when it is remembered that the large mass of white men in Tennessee are denied the right to vote or hold office, it is not wonderful or unnatural there should exist more or less dissatisfaction among them. And we beg leave to respectfully submit for your consideration, that prompt and efficient action on the part of the proper authorities, for a removal of the political disabilities, resting upon so many of our people, would heal all the wounds of our State, and make us once more a prosperous, contented and united people.

Respectfully, your obedient servants,

B. F. CHEATHAM,   W. B. BATE,
THOMAS B. SMITH,   WILLIAM A. QUARLES,
JOSEPH W. PALMER,   GEORGE W. GORDON,
N. B. FORREST,   JOHN C. BROWN,
S. R. ANDERSON,   G. G. DIBRELL,
BUSHROD R. JOHNSON,   GEORGE MANEY,
GIDEON J. PILLOW."

Deep anxiety was written upon the brows of thousands of upright citizens of Tennessee on account of Brownlow's rash vows as set forth in his initial Message. One of the clearest and most forceful analyses of the *causes* of the social and political conditions existing in the State was presented to Governor Brownlow by one of the ablest and most patriotic citizens of Tennessee. Judge John M. Lea of Nashville, a man who opposed secession as a means of trying to settle the vexing question of slavery, a man whose integrity and intelligence were beyond even the whisper of suspicion, a man who measured up to the Scriptural definition of "gold tried in the fire," pleaded with the Parson to listen to the voice of reason. In addition to his analysis of the factors that had led the State into chaos and confusion, bordering upon a violent insurrection, Judge Lea accompanied his letter with a plan for restoring peace and quiet to a people driven frantic by political persecution. Here is Judge Lea's letter:[242]

"Nashville, July 29, 1868.

His Excellency, W. G. Brownlow:

Dear Sir—I had intended to go to Knoxville to see you, but so many people have called on you that your strength as well as patience, must be nigh exhausted.

You began the work of reconstruction. I want you to end it, *and you are the only man who can do it.* The present is a most favorable time for the consummation of the work; and the very troubles that we have had in a few counties have produced a great desire in the minds of the people for a settled Government.

'There is a tide in the affairs of men,
Which, taken at the flood, leads on to fortune.'

The same remark is applicable to States.

I speak the truth, and whether you agree with me or not, I know you will give respectful attention to what I may say.

The great body of the people, excluding a few revolutionary agitators, are content with the results of the war—soon will be glad, I believe, that the Confederacy was a failure—and their exclusion from the polls is the chief and only ground of complaint. There is nothing surer under the sun than that these people, sooner or later, will be allowed to vote. An American citizen has no idea of liberty unless it is coupled with the right to vote. The public opinion of the world—certainly of the Anglo-Saxon race—is tending toward universal suffrage, and the speedy rehabilitation of all political offenders is, also, another marked feature of modern civilization. It was wise and right for the loyal people to organize the State Government—it is unwise and wrong to discriminate in favor of or against any class one moment longer than the safety of the State requires such invidious interposition. To that proposition you, and all good men, I know, will assent. Has the necessity for discrimination ceased? I do, in fact, think that it has.

I am ignorant of the contents of your message; some say it is mild, and others say it is harsh and vindictive in its tone and temper. Whatever may be the recommendations that you have made to the General Assembly, recent happy circumstances have given an entirely new phase to the entire subject. Petitions are in circulation, which will be signed, I sincerely trust and believe, by the best men in the country, pledging fidelity to the Government. The citizens who sign these petitions are in earnest, and mean what they say; they feel the responsibility of their position. Lawless bands and associations perpetrate unwarrantable outrages, and private crimes of a heinous nature are daily committed. These evils are the indications of a disordered state of society, and *all the wrong* is chargeable neither to one nor the other of the two political parties.

Let all good men unite to calm these angry passions. The petitioners ask a reinvestiture of the elective franchise, and, in my judgment, the Radi-

[242] *Ibid.,* 45–47.

cal party will place itself entirely in the wrong unless it favorably responds to the advances which have been, and will hereafter be made. I care nothing for the election of either Seymour or Grant, compared with the solicitude which I feel for a quiet, orderly, just Government in my native State. When a member of my own family lies dangerously sick, my philanthropy is not large enough to take an immediate interest in the health of the people in a distant country.

Had I my own way, every man might, from this moment, vote in all elections, but from all that I can learn, and also from my knowledge of human nature, it is not to be supposed that the desirable change can be looked for till sometime after the next Presidential election. Threats seldom obtain rights, nor does injustice long hold power. Well, the present fixed right of future enjoyment of the franchise, or an assurance of it by those in power, will, I think, give satisfaction to the people. True, they would prefer to vote at the approaching Presidential election, but the deprivation of that privilege—knowing that ever afterward they would enjoy that right—would hardly cause in their minds a feeling of regret, certainly not a spirit of discontent.

With much diffidence I take the liberty to inclose *a plan of settlement*, which, if adopted by the General Assembly, will effect the desired result in a legal, constitutional manner, without moving or dislocating a cog in the wheels of the machinery of Government. This plan requires no election of officers, and the change will only be felt in the blessings which it will bring. I trust that the direction of your mind to the subject may suggest a more feasible mode of reaching the end, and that upon consideration of the petitions aforesaid—the peace-offerings of an entire community—you may find ample warrant for making another communication to the General Assembly.

Now, what will be the effect if some such settlement is adopted? Here, *at home*, I verily believe, that peace would reign throughout the State—a general forgiveness ensue—a feeling of gratitude engendered toward those in power—*Ku Klux* organizations would be compelled to disband—Loyal Leagues would cease to exist—the people would look to the law for protection and not count on any help from secret associations; and our Presidential canvass, conducted, it might be, with warmth, would be the most quiet and peaceable that ever took place in the country. Every man, both white and black, would have more respect for himself, and, also, more respect for his neighbor, and his neighbor's rights. *Abroad*, the character of the State would be elevated. Our bonds would rise in value. The resources of the State are ample to meet our engagements.

Extraordinary taxation, the inevitable result of all wars, being the penalty that we pay out of our pockets for the exercise of unchristian passions, is a slight evil, and will be cheerfully borne by the people. Good government cannot be dear at any price. The holders of our bonds, if allowed to vote, would favor my proposition, and its success would be a confutation of the charge that reconstruction was a failure in Tennessee. In a political or party aspect—I really look beyond all such questions—it may be taken as a fact, that power will be kept out of the hands of any *malcontents* who would oppress and injure the loyal people. The excuse for vindictiveness would have ceased, and justice and moderation would guide in all our counsels. There would be no danger; indeed there would not.

If those public servants, who have, in this critical emergency, been clothed with the authority, will only advocate, and pass, some such measure as the inclosed plan, blessings will follow them through life, and their memory will be embalmed in the grateful recollections of succeeding generations. Henry IV, of France, said he would be the happiest of all Monarchs if he could put a fowl into the pot of every peasant in his kingdom. That sentiment of homely benevolence was worth all the splendid sayings that are recorded of kings. But he wished for more than he could obtain, and the goodness of the man exceeded the power of the king. How much more glorious the privilege to put a ballot, the badge of a freeman, into the hands of every citizen of Tennessee. We are more fortunate than the illustrious monarch, for happily our power is commensurate with our good intentions. That ballot could never be used—it would be an imputation on human nature to think that it could ever be used—to the injury of the men who granted it. Before God and the American people, I do not see that, since these petitions have been presented, there can be any justification for not taking a decided step toward a settlement of this question, the longer continuance of which impairs the dignity, menaces the peace, diminishes the prosperity, and impeaches the justice of the State. My faith tells me that you, and all good men, of both political parties, will join hands in striving for so great a good to our suffering country. 'Let us lay the first stone of the Temple of Peace.'

Excuse this long letter. You have known me many years, and will do me the justice to believe that I am actuated by a desire to help my country out of its difficulties.

Very truly,

JOHN M. LEA."

Judge Lea's "plan of settlement," alluded to in his letter and accompanying same, was in brief a request that the General Assembly by a vote of the people be vested with the right and power to recommend the adoption of an amendment to the Constitution whereby

"Every free man, white and colored, of the age of twenty-one years, being a citizen of the United States, and a citizen of the county wherein he may offer his vote six months preceding the day of election, shall be entitled to vote for members of the General Assembly and other civil officers for the district and county in which he may reside; *Provided*, that laws may be passed excluding from the right of suffrage persons convicted of infamous crimes."

Inasmuch as the Brownlow Supreme Court had held that the Franchise Law was *a part of the Constitution of Tennessee,* Judge Lea's sensible plan was to amend the Constitution in that particular. The proposed plan, eminently just and proper, was transmitted to Brownlow who did not have sufficient gall to ignore it completely. He did not, however, indorse Judge Lea's plan, merely submitting it to the "calm and deliberate consideration" of his scalawag Legislature which laid it away in the legislative pigeon-hole from which it emerged, "quoth the Raven, 'Nevermore'."

While the Legislature was fiddling and piddling around with State Finance and Penitentiary problems, the legislative Military Committee had been busy collecting evidence of the activities and atrocities alleged to have been perpetrated by the Kukluxers. More than a month had

rolled by and nothing had been done by the Legislature insofar as enacting any laws against the Ku Klux Klan. Brownlow was getting disturbed by the procrastination, induced perhaps by the petitions, memorials, and pleas of thousands of people and buttressed by the
forthright pledges of scores of the most prominent men in the State.
However, on September 2, the Joint Military Committee unbundled a
sheaf of "testimonials" filling thirty-eight printed pages in the official
Journals.[243] According to the official report, the above thirty-eight
pages contained only "a synopsis of the evidence taken before your
committee." Numerous counties in Middle and West Tennessee were
visited by the Military Committee, these counties embracing the largest
proportion of ex-Confederates and Conservative Unionists. By far and
large, the witnesses called before the Military Committee were former
Union soldiers, teachers in Freedmen's schools, and Negroes. Quite
obviously, such persons were Radicals and by any fair appraisal could
not be construed as being without bias or prejudice in the premises.

Apparently, the above "evidence" provided the Legislature with "a
shot in the arm." In a week, two bills heavily tinctured with Brownlowism were enacted into laws. One law, labelled "An Act to Preserve
Peace," provided a heavy penalty on any person who united with,
associated with, or who promoted or encouraged "any secret organization which prowled through country or town, disguised or otherwise,"
for the purpose of disturbing the peace.[244] The *minimum* penalty was a
fine of $500 and five years in the penitentiary. *All persons* were author-
ized to arrest "any person defendant" under the provisions of the law
without having to go through usual processes of law for making arrests.
Informers or "spys" were authorized to receive one-half of the amount
of damages assessed against any convicted defendant, the "standard of
damages" running from ten thousand to twenty thousand dollars. This
species of rewards was to apply in cases of "injuries to individuals."
This was the essence of the Anti-Ku Klux Law.

The other law [245] was entitled "An Act to Enforce the Laws of the
State." In a nutshell, this law revived in full force Brownlow's original
Tennessee State Guard statute. The Governor at his own discretion
was empowered to raise and equip one or more regiments from each
Congressional District, said regiments to be composed of "loyal" men
only. Upon the sworn application of "ten unconditional Union men"
or three Justices of the Peace in any county that the law-abiding citizens
were unable to protect themselves without military aid, the Governor
was thereupon authorized to saddle the necessary troops upon that area
in order "to protect the citizens from violence." No commentary is

---

[243] *Senate Journal*, Extra Session, 1868, 131–168.
   House Journal, Extra Session, 1868, 185–222.
[244] *Acts of Tennessee*, Extra Session, 1868, Chapter 2.
[245] *Ibid.*, Chapter 3.

necessary to show what an engine of prosecution and persecution had been placed in the hands of the irritated, irrational, and irreconcilable official occupying the gubernatorial office.

Having vented their abundant spleen, the Extra Session of the Legislature adjourned on September 14, 1868.

In compliance with a Joint Resolution, the Thirty-Fifth General Assembly convened for its Second Session on November 9, 1868.[246] On the next day, Governor Brownlow transmitted his Message.

Legislative Message, November 10, 1868.*

"Gentlemen of the Senate and House of Representatives:

I congratulate you and the whole country upon the gratifying result of the late Presidential election, which has terminated in the elevation of Gen. Grant and Hon. Schuyler Colfax to the highest official stations in the gift of the American people.

The result is especially satisfactory in view of the circumstances attending, and the principles involved in the canvass now so happily closed. The issues were clearly defined; they were fairly and strongly brought before the American people, and they were pronounced upon with a degree of unanimity seldom, if ever before, witnessed in our national history.

It is unnecessary to repeat them in this connection, further than to say that they show a just appreciation of the invaluable services rendered to the country by the highly distinguished General now elected the Chief Magistrate of the Republic; they also display a confidence in his integrity and ability, which I cannot, for a moment, allow myself to believe misplaced. They declare, moreover, most unmistakably, that the American people will sustain at the polls by the ballot—as they vindicated triumphantly in the field— the principles of loyalty and the men who adhere to them. In other words, that only thoroughly loyal men shall administer the government of the United States, and that, in such administration, as well as among those of unofficial station, loyal men, white and black, North and South, East and West, shall be protected.

The late election is the most emphatically pronounced judgment of the American people ever given, of the fundamental principles

[246] *Senate Journal*, First Session, 1867–68, 505.
     House Journal, First Session, 1867–68, 760.
  * *Senate Appendix*, 1868–69, 3–10.

underlying our whole political fabric, and contained in the immortal Declaration of 1776. As such, also, it fully vindicates the policy of the State administration of Tennessee during the last four years.

Perhaps never before, in the entire existence of the national government—now nearly one hundred years—has there been displayed an equal measure of vituperation, unscrupulous falsehood, and reckless allegations, as have been levelled against the successful candidates; a most melancholy proof, this, of the utter degeneracy and corruption of that party, which, after instigating rebellion, and aiding and abetting it during its progress, after its utter defeat gathered up its scattered fragments and adherents, and sought to invest itself with the full sanctions and powers of the government it had vainly sought to destroy. Fortunately for our future as a people, and creditably for our record in history, the utter and overwhelming and dishonorable defeat and overthrow of that party are accomplished by the intelligent energy, the incorruptible virtue, and free, unswayed, unpurchased suffrage of American citizens.

Another special occasion for congratulation, is found in the abundant favors with which a beneficent Providence has crowned the year. Goodly harvests have requited the husbandman. Sickness and wasting and mildew have been turned aside. God has graciously exempted us from 'the pestilence that walketh in darkness and the destruction that wasteth at noonday.' Plentiful rewards have compensated honest industry, and general thrift and prosperity have attended our fellow-citizens.

THE RAILROAD QUESTION.

The six railroads in the hands of Receivers, are indebted to the State, on interest account, due July 1, 1868, one million one hundred and twenty thousand nine hundred and ninety-six dollars and eighty-six cents. The interest of these roads, as well as that of the State, require that they should be sold and the proceeds thereof be applied to the reduction of the State debt.

I would have seized the two other roads for failure to pay the July interest, and placed them in the hands of Receivers, but that I had learned by experience, that to do so would only entail increased burdens upon the State Treasury.

I recommend that no more appropriations be made to railroads, except in those cases where the State has large interest in said roads, and would suffer heavy loss on account of the lack of such appropriations. Of this class are the roads running out, North and South, from Knoxville, and the one extending South from Morristown; and, also, the road of which Hon. Senator Parker is President. These roads, in order to become profitable and productive to the State, will require enough additional appropriations to enable them to complete their lines, so as to connect with other roads now in process of construction. I propose, however, to meet these demands in a way not to increase the liabilities of the State. The plan is this:

Leading gentlemen, connected with important railroads largely indebted to the State, are asking for authority to issue second mortgage bonds, with a view of exchanging them for State bonds. Thus purchasing State bonds by the avails of these second mortgage bonds, the debt now due by the State would, in like amount, be transferred to these railroad companies, and so the State would be relieved of a burden of several million of dollars of debt now resting upon it.

I regard this proposition with approval, and advise its adoption by the Assembly. The payment of large debts now due from the roads alluded to, and the sale of the roads already in the hands of Receivers, would reduce the State liabilities at least one-third.

This plan, it is seen, would enable the General Assembly not only to reduce materially the State's liabilities, but also to render such necessary additional aid to the roads whose completion is demanded by considerations of public economy.

Several of the railroad companies have unsettled accounts with the sinking fund. The State being indebted to them and they being indebted to the State, it is important that an early settlement of these accounts be had. I recommend, therefore, that the proper action be had by your respective Houses, to procure the desired settlement with the said railroads.

Since the adjournment of your Extraordinary Session, the Comptroller has visited New York and made satisfactory arrangements for the payment of the July interest. This fact, together with the result of the late State and Presidential elections, has induced an appreciation of our State bonds, and a material depreciation in the price of gold.

The occasion serves to allude to the gratifying fact, that, financially and otherwise, Tennessee occupies a far more desirable position than any of the States recently in rebellion. Thus the policy of reconstruction maintained by the Union Republican Party of Tennessee, finds ample and triumphant vindication by its achievements among us; and thus, also, the path of our future growing prosperity is traced for us by the history of the last four years. We have only to follow up with steady nerve and unfaltering step, the policy thus far so successful, to assure to this great Commonwealth that degree of thrift, wealth and power, to which our natural position, our boundless resources and our enterprising population so eminently entitle us.

THE BANK OF TENNESSEE.

This institution has been in the hands of officers appointed by authority of the General Assembly for three years past, with a view to having its affairs wound up, and its effects made available to the resources of the State. I am unable to state the condition of its affairs, or what progress has been made in the direction proposed. I have seen from time to time, as you also have, the report of its President. I have no other complaints to make against its officers than to express my regrets at the slowness of its movements towards the conclusion desired, and I recommend that measures be adopted to wind it up forthwith.

THE FRANCHISE.

Strenuous efforts were made at your recent Extraordinary Session to induce you to extend the franchise, and include within it, those who, by the law and Constitution of the State, are deprived thereof. Not unlikely the attempt will be renewed and enforced during your present meeting.

There should be a discrimination exercised concerning those who were in rebellion. They are not all alike culpable for the past, nor untrustworthy for the future. For those who were involuntarily drawn into the service of rebellion, and who, since its utter failure, have given evidence that they accept the results in good faith; that they are good citizens, quiet and law-abiding; that they have strictly observed their parole; that they will not use political power to proscribe and degrade those whom the war has emancipated and invested with the rights of citizens; for disfranchised persons of this description the franchise might safely, and, therefore, wisely, be extended. The extension should, however, be applied with suitable guards and checks, that advantage could not be taken of its liberality to the danger and harm of the State.

As to the other class of rebels, who entered into it voluntarily and continued in it from choice until their arms were wrenched out of their hands, and who, since the surrender, and in moral violation of their parole, have continued to work for the lost cause; who are restless agitators, who have fomented violence and lawlessness, who have incited to public disquiet and restiveness, the question of their restoration to full civil rights, it is very different. If the time should ever come when they should be thus restored, I submit that it would probably be when the last dollar of the national debt incurred in suppressing the rebellion has been paid, and when these unrepentant, unreconstructed rebels, had restored to the ballot-box the half million loyal voters who now sleep in premature graves.

These suggestions are made in no vindictive, implacable hostility to these persons, as men. They spring from considerations affecting the public welfare, the peace, stability and honor of the State and Nation. Withholding the franchise from persons who have proved, by four years of bloody resistance against the Government, and by four years of uncured hatred against it and its defenders, that they cannot be safely intrusted with it, is to be regarded not so much a punishment as it is a wise and necessary precaution for the safety and welfare of our civil institutions.

THE INSANE HOSPITAL.

The noble public charity known as the Hospital for the Insane, located in this vicinity, has done much for the relief of the unfortunate. It has deservedly received large assistance from the State.

There are now over three hundred patients under treatment, rendering the institution quite too much crowded for the comfort and improvement of the inmates. This is true of both the male and female wards, and also of the department for the colored insane, who are as really insane, requiring proper care and treatment, as an equal number of white lunatics. Should the Ezell farm, lying contiguous to the Hospital, be purchased, which I advise, the chronic colored insane of the male department might be taken to the farm house on that tract, which, with a slight expense, could be made to accommodate twenty-five or thirty of them.

Better provision is needed to enforce payment from those who enter their friends as pay-patients, and who give the required bond, but from poverty, or some other cause, fail to pay more than the amount of the bond, and pay that only after long delay and vexing and costly suits. The Superintendent should have authority, by law, to return such patients to their friends, or to require new and larger bonds.

The friends of many of the patients here from surrounding Southern States during the war, are using their utmost endeavors to evade payment of their liabilities. Such patients were thrown unavoidably upon the institution when care and medicines were very high. Many have served bankrupt notices on the institution, and collection is, in various ways, delayed and resisted. The amount thus due the institution is in the neighborhood of forty thousand dollars. It is quite unfair that the citizens of Tennessee should be taxed to support the indigent insane of other States.

I, therefore, advise that an appeal be made to the Governors of the respective States concerned, to pay for the care and maintenance of said patients; and, in the event that payment is declined, that the Superintendent be instructed and authorized to return the patients to the localities whence they came.

West Virginia, subsequent to the war, paid the State of Ohio— the institution at Columbus—five dollars per week for the care of her insane during the war. Nothing, it seems to me, can be more just than that our neighboring States should pay for the care of their poor insane in our Hospital.

The crowded condition of this Hospital requires that an additional building, upon a smaller and less costly scale, be at once erected. Questions of economy, public convenience and humanity, indicate that it should be built in one of the other grand divisions of the State. This will have to be done, and soon. From its greater populousness and facilities for building, as well as salubrity, East Tennessee would seem to be the better entitled to its location there. I, therefore, recommend that it be established in East Tennessee.

THE PENITENTIARY.

The Penitentiary, like the Insane Hospital, is quite over-crowded, to the injury of the discipline, and also of the health, of the institution.

Since your late adjournment, the Commissioners met, removed the Warden, and elected another in his stead. Application has been made to me to set aside their action and reinstate the Warden. This I declined to do, upon the ground that it would have been an unwarrantable assumption of power, and also in view of the fact that the General Assembly would soon again be in session. I advise that the whole subject be thoroughly investigated. Such an investigation is alike due to the State and to the parties who have been in dispute.

SALARIES OF CERTAIN OFFICERS.

I have found considerable difficulty in filling the Supreme Court bench, and the inferior courts, with qualified and suitable men, owing to the insufficiency of the salaries allowed to Judges of the Supreme, Chancery and Circuit Courts. No class of State officers do as much work for as little pay as the Judges. No offices in the State require more ability, attention and hard work, or deserve equal remuneration. I must, therefore, urge the General Assembly to fix the salaries of these officers at a sum that will better remunerate them, and thus secure an order of talent and a degree of industry which shall be creditable to the State and useful to all parties.

I make a similar recommendation concerning the salary of the Governor. The present sum allowed him is entirely too low to sustain him in a style and manner appropriate to a large and wealthy State like Tennessee; and it is less than equal services in other offices require and receive. The present salary was fixed when prices of all goods were much below the present rates.

In making this recommendation, I cannot be deemed selfish, as it cannot personally benefit me. I shall soon exchange the office which I hold at present for one to which your votes have called me. Besides this consideration, I would be estopped from receiving such increased pay by the State Constitution.

IMMIGRATION.

I have repeatedly called your attention to the importance of promoting and inducing immigration to our State. On this subject my convictions have undergone no change, except that they have become stronger. A great and pressing want of Tennessee is an increased producing population. This alone, will develop our wonderful resources, and enhance our material wealth to a degree that surpasses imagination. In its absence, our people will suffer a painful want, depressing business, retarding progress, dwarfing and paralyzing all industries.

Thus far, the great tide of foreign immigration has swept past us and poured itself out upon our vast national domain in the West and North-west; but an inconsiderable part of it has been diverted to our borders. Yet no other State offers equal inducements to those of Tennessee. Our mountains are rich in various minerals, our rivers are affluent in power to propel machinery, our State is gridironed with railroads, our forests abound with the finest of timber, our soil is capable of enriching production, climate is genial and our scenery grand and beautiful. Added to all these advantages, with a good system of common schools, and a hardy, industrious, loyal, and liberty-loving population, a central position among the States, and easy of access to market in all directions, Tennessee is certainly one of the most attractive States to those who would improve their condition by emigration, whether from foreign countries or from sister States.

Still, notwithstanding all these inducements, immigration in this State languishes. Something more effective must be done to counteract the efforts made by other States, and by other lines of travel than ours, to direct emigration Westward, so as to bring a larger proportion of it into our midst.

Other States have incorporated societies, and appropriated considerable sums of money to further this object. They keep Commissioners of Immigration at the principal American and European ports. If we successfully compete with them we must adopt their tactics and emulate their zeal. Money and effort thus expended will come back with manifold increase.

I recommend that the General Assembly grant a liberal charter to responsible and energetic men as a State Immigration Society, and appropriate an adequate annual sum to enable such society to prosecute the work of immigration to Tennessee with more vigor and upon a larger and more systematic scale than it has hitherto been done.

The present is an eminently auspicious moment for a movement of this kind. The election of Grant and Colfax means peace; it means that carpet-baggers are not to be molested in Tennessee; that capital, coming to us from abroad, whether of brains or hands or money, is not to be spurned, proscribed, persecuted, because it comes from North of a given line; that here, as elsewhere, we are to have peace, protection and security.

In pursuance of this thought, and to aid in inducing the influx of capital and labor among us, I recommend the General Assembly to pass a law exempting from taxation, for five years, all foreign capital invested in machinery within our State.

THE CATTLE PLAGUE.

My attention has been called to the ravages of the disease known as the cattle plague or the Texas fever among cattle, and also to the inadequacy of the laws enacted by the several States for the repression of this and other kindred diseases, and the conflicting provisions of these laws, which have been disclosed since the prevalence of the disease.

There should be a concert of laws in all the States to arrest the spread of a disease which threatens to destroy all our flocks and herds, and to deprive us of meat altogether, or furnish us a diseased article of food which will scatter disease among the people. To effect this uniformity and efficiency of laws in all the States, it has been believed that the best method would be the assembling of a convention of the several States interested in the subject, who would present all the information necessary for a full elucidation of the subject, and whose duty it should be to prepare a draft of a law which would insure a most perfect protection to all parties, to be recommended to the several Legislatures for adoption.

The Cattle Commissioners of New York, having been requested by the Commissioners of several of the States, and of the Dominion of Canada, to take the initiative in calling such convention, have recommended that a convention be held in the city of Springfield, in the State of Illinois, on Tuesday, December 1, 1868, at 12 o'clock, at noon, of said day. The object of such convention is, to consider the pathology, symptomatology and history of the Texas cattle fever, and other infectious and contagious diseases to which cattle and other stock are subject, and the best method of preventing the spread of such diseases, with reference to the interests of the producer and consumer; and also, to consider the sanitary requirements of the community, with reference to the feeding and resting of the animals in transit, and to the best methods of slaughtering and preparing them for market. The convention will also prepare a draft of a law, which shall provide for the accomplishment of these objects, to be submitted to the Legislatures of the States represented there, for adoption. Each State and province to be represented by three commissioners.

It seems to me these precautionary measures are wise and important, and I recommend you to take such early action as shall represent Tennessee in the proposed convention.

THE CAPITOL GROUNDS.

Your attention is called to the unfinished and unadorned condition of the grounds surrounding the State Capitol.

A building of such magnificent and beautiful proportions certainly deserves to be surrounded with grounds that would enhance, rather than detract from, its general beauty. Yet, all can see that these grounds are in a condition rather to excite disgust than to enlist admiration.

I submit that it would be a wise economy that would appropriate a few thousand dollars to the proper improvement and ornamentation of the grounds immediately around the Capitol, now so rude and unsightly. It would furnish employment to those who need it; it would raise the character of our State abroad, and so induce immigration, and would gratify the just pride of every good citizen who is interested in the growth and improvement of the State.

THE STATE GUARD.

The militia has not been mustered into service, and consequently no expense to the State has been incurred.

I have relied solely upon Major-General George H. Thomas, who has fully met my expectations. Soon after the Legislative Committee returned from Washington, General Thomas communicated with me, seeking to learn into what counties and localities I desired him to send troops, and the probable extent of resistance or opposition which might be expected. I accordingly gave him the names of twenty-two counties in all, to which he promptly sent troops in sufficient numbers to preserve the peace and maintain the laws. The result is known to you as members of the General Assembly, and I need add nothing more.

THE STATE TREASURER.

Some ten days ago, the Treasurer, John R. Henry, Esq., on account of ill health, resigned his office into my hands; said resignation to take effect as soon as he could adjust a settlement with the Comptroller of the State. I accordingly tendered the office to William H. Stillwell, Esq., of West Tennessee.

The duty will, therefore, devolve upon you to elect a Treasurer to fill out the unexpired term of Mr. Henry.

Having thus called your attention to the more material subjects deserving your official action, I close by invoking upon your labors, and upon the great Commonwealth represented by you, the blessings of Divine Providence.

Allow me to express the hope that you will go to work industriously, and complete your work in a short session.

W. G. BROWNLOW.

Nashville, November 10, 1868."

In his Message, Governor Brownlow did not refrain from exuding his satisfaction at the result of the recent Presidential election in which General Ulysses S. Grant and Schuyler Colfax had been elected President and Vice-President, respectively. Tennessee's vote had been cast for the successful candidates, the vote being 56,628 for Grant and 26,129 for his opponent, Horatio Seymour.[247] But the Parson's jubilation received a stunning shock a bit later when it became known that two Tennessee Radical candidates for Congress had been defeated by two Conservatives. To the Parson, this was inconceivable! Was not all the election machinery in his own hands? Had not the threat and even presence of military guardians around the ballot-boxes been sufficient to see that no Democratic termites be allowed to undermine the foundations of Radical supremacy in Tennessee? On the face of the belated election returns, C. A. Sheafe, the Conservative candidate in the Fourth Congressional District, had defeated the Radical candidate, Lewis Tillman, by a vote of 4,591 to 3,855. Over in the Eighth Congressional District, a three-cornered race had resulted in pitting two Radicals against one Conservative candidate enabling the latter to emerge from the battle a victor. Now, what could the Governor do under such embarrassing circumstances? Having been an ordained minister prior to his getting into politics, perhaps the Parson recalled a verse of Scripture from *Ecclesiastes*—"The race is not to the swift, nor the battle to the strong." Let the master magician, the figure-wizard deluxe tell us just

---

[247] Miller, C. A.: *Official and Political Manual of Tennessee*, 167.

how he handled the delicate situation confronting him. In the election contest case between Sheafe and Tillman, the Parson's Proclamation had appeared in his own newspaper, the *Knoxville Whig*. The Proclamation was introduced before the Congressional Committee, and the pertinent portion was as follows:[248]

". . . Now, therefore, I, William G. Brownlow, governor of Tennessee, do submit the following statements, and the conclusions at which I have arrived, after considering all the facts in the case:

From the returns in the office of the secretary of state, it seems that, in the fourth district, Sheafe received 666 votes more than Tillman. But, correcting the returns by the law governing in such cases, by throwing out the vote of Lincoln County, as the election was held by order of the county court, and the returns were made by the coroner—the law requiring elections to be held and returns made by the commissioner of registration; and by throwing out the vote in the civil districts of the counties of Coffee and Marshall, in which it appears that the judges of election had not taken the necessary oath, the vote for that district would stand as follows: For Sheafe 3,363, and for Tillman 3,795; leaving Tillman's majority 432. I therefore award the certificate to Lewis Tillman.

The returns from the eighth district show that John W. Leftwich received 6,532 votes, W. J. Smith 5,543 votes, and David A. Nunn 4,026 votes, giving Leftwich 989 majority over Smith.

I utterly repudiate the vote of Tipton County, as an exhibition of the most stupendous fraud perpetrated in the State during the late election. I also cast out the vote of Fayette County, as held in open violation of the franchise law. Besides these, a supplemental return by the commissioner of registration for Shelby County gives, for that county alone, an addition of about 700 votes in favor of W. J. Smith over Leftwich, all of which gives Smith a clear majority of over a thousand over Leftwich. I therefore award the certificate of election to W. J. Smith. . . ."

Once more the Radical juggernaut had prevailed. A Radical Governor had "elected" two Radical candidates for Congress, and a Radical Congress placed its stamp of approval upon the action of the despot.

Tossing out ballots and "counting in" the unsuccessful candidate was not a new activity with the Parson. Had not the same situation arisen in the case of Samuel M. Arnell, Brownlow's main stooge who piloted through the Legislature the Franchise Act barring ex-Confederates from the privilege of voting? Arnell was later defeated for Congress by a Conservative, Dorsey B. Thomas. Sitting in his ivory tower, the Parson decided that Thomas had been elected by fraudulent votes. Forthwith the vote was changed by Brownlow, and Arnell was awarded the Congressional plum. In Arnell's case, perhaps the Parson recalled the last words of Socrates—"I owe a cock to Asclepius; will you remember to pay the debt?" Or did the Governor, possessed of

---

[248] House of Representatives, 41st Congress, Second Session, *Miscellaneous Documents*, No. 53, 121.

unlimited power over elections, resort to the formula followed by European Nations struggling for possessions in the New World:

> ". . . Settled on this simple plan—
> Let him keep, who has the power,
> And let him get, who can."

The Parson had the power and he paid off!

The Message of November 10, 1868, was the last major communication of Governor Brownlow to a Tennessee Legislature. In keeping with most of his former Messages, it included a political harangue saturated with bitterness and hatred toward supporters of the Confederacy. At one point in the Message, there was a faint glimmer of conciliation wherein he hinted that the franchise might be extended to those who were "involuntarily drawn into the service of rebellion." But this slight indication of political justice was wiped out in the next paragraph of his Message, when his insatiable wrath was heaped upon the heads of the vast majority of the men who had served under the Stars and Bars. For them, the infuriated Governor proposed the extension of the franchise when the debt incurred by the war had been paid off and the accomplishment of the impossible—"when these unrepentant, unreconstructed rebels, had restored to the ballot-box the half million loyal voters who now sleep in premature graves."

As will be noted, Governor Brownlow submitted several recommendations to the Legislature for consideration. Aside from rather modest appropriations of $25,000 per annum for maintaining the Hospital for the Insane and $50,000 for discharging the indebtedness against the Penitentiary, no other significant appropriations were made.[249] In compliance with the Governor's recommendation, salaries of Supreme Court Judges and the Governor were raised to $4,000 per annum.[250] The Governor's roseate picture of the State's financial condition was largely erased when the Report of the State Comptroller was submitted, showing the State Debt to be $34,498,806, of which State Bonds loaned to railroads accounted for $25,747,000.[251] No specific legislation was enacted that dealt with the Bank of Tennessee, although Samuel Watson, who had been appointed Trustee to wind up the business of the Bank, submitted a lengthy report as to the status of the Bank. Reported as unpaid were "domestic bills" and "discounted notes" in the amount of $1,468,490. Of those items, so Trustee Watson reported, "$352,554 will be settled in bankruptcy . . . and a large amount will be settled by insolvency."[252] The subjects of Immigration, Cattle Plague, and the Capitol Grounds, all of which were mentioned by the Gov-

---

[249] *Acts of Tennessee*, Second Session, 1868–69, Chapter 46.
[250] *Ibid.*, Chapter 28.
[251] *Appendix*, 1868–69, 54.
[252] *Ibid.*, 59–65.

ernor, received no legislative action. On the whole, the legislative session of 113 days amounted to naught. Its deliberations were largely "sounding brass and tinkling cymbals." Its *sine die* adjournment on March 1, 1869, constituted perhaps its chief contribution to the public welfare.

What were some of the basic reasons for the relative inactivity and feet-dragging proclivities of the Second Session of the Thirty-Fifth General Assembly? First of all, the corruption, bribery, and legalized robbery characteristic of the First Session had left a stench that pervaded the State from border to border. The "odor of sanctity" was conspicuous by its absence, and numerous legislators were under deep suspicion in view of recent voting records on gigantic railroad swindles. For almost four long and weary years, the intelligent white majority in the State had been subjected to the thumb-screw tactics of a destructive Governor, for Brownlow was neither constructive nor reconstructive. His record of political persecution of all who had enlisted in the Confederacy was at last catching up with him. His disfranchisement of the intelligent, tax-paying citizens who constituted a sizeable majority and investing forty thousand former slaves with the ballot was such an undeniable record of fanatical persecution that even many staunch Unionists could no longer travel with him. So exacting was he of his idea of "loyalty" that a Congressional Committee made this diagnosis of his political philosophy: [253]

"Everybody was loyal who voted for and maintained Brownlow and his friends, and everyone was disloyal who dared to oppose them."

Brownlow either inherited or acquired early in life a cantankerous spirit that displayed itself even while he was a licensed minister of the Methodist Church. He seems to have been on the lookout for some excuse for starting a rukus. He was constantly "fighting" the Presbyterians and the Baptists. As early as 1828, while serving the Washington Circuit in East Tennessee, he had a suit for slander filed against him. Three years later, while "riding the circuit" in western North Carolina, a lawsuit for libel was instituted against him, resulting in a fine of five dollars plus costs of the suit. A deputy sheriff seized Brownlow's "elegant dun mare, saddle, bridle, saddle-bags, and umbrella, all of which he disposed of in short order" in settlement of the court costs.

Not disposed to confine himself to argumentation on *doctrinal* points of the various religious denominations, Brownlow would attack the sermonizing of various sects. For example, he declared that the Cumberland Presbyterian preachers had convinced him of "the superior advantages of *short* sermons, because too many ministers . . . tell all they know in one sermon, and some of them tell that all *twice* in the

---

[253] *Ku Klux Conspiracy,* I, 454, in the Minority Report.

same discourse." "He was annoyed," he declared, "by those people called *Baptists*." The preachers of this order

". . . Were continually haranguing the people on the subject of baptism, or rather of *immersion*. By day and by night, their cry was *water!* water!! water!!! as if heaven were an *island*, situated somewhere in the British sea, and we all had to *swim* to get there."[254]

A Baptist minister of Nashville, who was editor of the *Tennessee Baptist*, wrote and published *The Great Iron Wheel, or Republicanism Backwards and Christianity Reversed*, the seventeenth edition appearing in 1856. The book of 570 pages consisted of a series of forty letters addressed to Joshua Soule, Senior Bishop of the Methodist Episcopal Church, South. Bishop Soule incidentally "never perused one of these forty epistles." Author Graves "offered no apology for writing these letters upon the policy and doctrines of Methodism."[255]

Since the above book was of a highly controversial nature, Parson Brownlow who represented himself as "Editor of *Brownlow's Knoxville Whig*" and also "A Local Preacher of the Methodist Episcopal Church, South" felt "called to perform the painful task of refuting a series of the most scurrilous falsehoods, and a collection of the lowest abuse of the age."[256] A book of 331 pages was the result. The opening sentence of Chapter 1 foreshadows what may be expected, to-wit:

"Who has not heard the name, and read more or less about the discussions, abuse, and bigoted intolerance of the notorious and self-conceited J. R. Graves, editor of the 'Tennessee Baptist'!"

Though space forbids any analysis of the contents of Brownlow's reply to Elder Graves, yet one representative sample of Brownlow's billingsgate may suffice to indicate the *tone* of the *Great Iron Wheel Examined*. In criticizing the critics of John Wesley, Brownlow had this to say:[257]

"He [Wesley] is still the object of the most malignant, wicked, and ungentlemanly abuse from sectarian bigots of all Churches, and especially the *pig-pen orators* and *whisky-shop saints* of the Baptist denomination. Go on, ye insignificant revilers! Spit your venom at his fair name, spew your slime upon the escutcheon of his character, empty your polluted stomachs of all the pent-up spleen that is in you, for you cannot harm the illustrious dead."

When Brownlow turned from religious discussion to political controversy, his abuse, scurrility, and demagogism knew no limits. Searing

---

[254] Brownlow, William G.: *Helps to the Study of Presbyterianism, Or An Unsophisticated Exposition of Calvinism, with Hopkinsian Modifications and Policy, with a View to a More Easy Interpretation of the Same*, 249, 254, and 269–272.
[255] Graves, J. R.: *The Great Iron Wheel*, Preface V.
[256] Brownlow, William G.: *The Great Iron Wheel Examined, Or Its False Spokes Extracted, and An Exhibition of Elder Graves, Its Builder*, Dedication, III.
[257] *Ibid.*, 69–70.

similes and mixed metaphors were his stock in trade, and the editorial columns of his *Knoxville Whig* were laden year after year with his tirades and insults against any who opposed his narrow and prejudiced viewpoints. In 1856 when he embraced Know-Nothingism in a book of 208 pages, he leveled his poisoned pen at

"The hypocritical and profligate portion of the Methodist, Presbyterian, Baptist, and Episcopalian membership in this country, [who] are not so much misled by Popery, as they are influenced by *party politics*, and are in love with the *loose moral code* of Romanism."[258]

These *innate* traits of Brownlow, rather artfully concealed by pious expressions and copious Scriptural citations in his legislative Messages, slowly became manifest to a long-awakening public. His right-about-face on State aid to railroads in the First Session of the Thirty-Fifth Legislature, plus the open and notorious conduct of lobbyists and legislators which could not have been unknown to the Governor, all of this and more had begun to trickle into the public's mind and conscience. And so, when the Legislature convened in its Second Session in November, 1868, Brownlow stock had gone down considerably. The angel's feet were discovered to be made of clay. The political dykes of Radicalism had sprung leaks. A ground-swell of anti-Brownlowism was slowly but surely coming into being. No longer was the needle of the political compass pointing to the former lodestar, Parson Brownlow; a deviation and dip were not only apparent but real.

Before the legislative session, beginning November 9, 1868, was four days old, there was evidence of internal dissension within the Radical ranks. DeWitt Clinton Senter, it will be recalled, had been elected Speaker of the Senate on the thirteenth ballot at the First Session of the Thirty-Fifth General Assembly. Senator A. M. Cate of Hamilton County, a personal enemy of Senter, had nevertheless supported Senter for the speakership out of political expediency. Shortly after Senter's election as Speaker, Governor Brownlow was elected to the United States Senate and would take over the office some sixteen months later, March 4, 1869. When this happened, Senter would succeed to the governorship. This was wormwood and gall to Senator Cate. In an effort to block Senter's advancement to the Chief Executive's chair, Cate offered Senate Resolution No. 15 on November 12, 1868, that being the third day of the session. By a vote of 18 to 1, the Senate rejected Cate's resolution,[259] not permitting it to be entered on the *Journal*, thereby endeavoring to "hush up" the bitter fight. The gist of Cate's resolution was that Senter was disqualified by the Fourteenth Amendment of the U. S. Constitution from holding office be-

---

[258] Brownlow, William G.: *Americanism Contrasted with Foreignism, Romanism, and Bogus Democracy, 6.*
[259] *Senate Journal*, Second Session, 1868–69, 9.

cause, as a member of the Tennessee Legislature in 1861-62, he had taken an oath to support the Constitution of the Confederacy. Some five weeks after Cate's introduction of his resolution, Congress removed Senter's disability on December 22, 1868.

Regardless of the fact that his resolution was no longer valid, yet Cate insisted on putting his position on record. The day after Senter's inauguration as Governor, Senator Cate presented a "Communication"[260] to the Senate which was then placed upon the *Senate Journal:*

"*Mr. Speaker, and Gentlemen of the Senate:*

By the 27th Section of the 2d Article of the Constitution of the State, I am guaranteed the right to dissent from any act of this body, which I may think injurious to the public or any individual; and believing the action of the Senate, upon Senate Resolution No. 15, introduced by me, the 12th of November, 1868, in violation of the letter and intention of that part of the Constitution of the United States, therein recited, destructive to the fundamental principals of American liberty, obstructing the medium of information through which the people are alone enabled to scrutinize and correct the evils and errors of their representatives, a due respect to the honor of my constituents, and a just personal pride, unite in making it my duty to protest against said proceeding, as disrespectful and proscriptive in character; and compels me to exercise my constitutional privilege, in appealing to the wisdom and reason of public sentiment, in justification of my course. I therefore, submit a copy of the Preamble and Resolutions as containing just grounds, and the principal reason of my objections in the words and figures following, to-wit:

Whereas, Section 3, of the 14th Article of the Constitution of the United States provides, that 'No person shall be a Senator or Representative in Congress, or Elector of President and Vice-President, or hold any office, Civil or Military, under the United States, or any State, who having previously taken an oath as a member of Congress, or as an officer of the United States, or as a member of any State Legislature, or as an Executive or Judicial officer of any State, to support the Constitution of the United States, shall have engaged in insurrection or rebellion against the same, or given aid to the enemies thereof; and,

Whereas, The records now on file in the office of the Secretary of State, show that D. W. C. Senter, our present acting Speaker, was a member of the Rebel Legislature of 1861-2, and did take the oath to support the Constitution of the Confederate States of America, on the ―――― day of ――――――――, 1861, and exercised the functions of office in said Legislature, at the Capitol of the State, until about the time of the capture of Fort Donelson, by the United States forces, in February, 1862. Upon Sunday, the 16th of February, the Legislature held a session, and agreed to adjourn to such time and place as Isham G. Harris, then acting Governor of the State, might designate by proclamation; and,

Whereas, Said Legislature did subsequently meet, in compliance with said proclamation, at Memphis, Tennessee, and did then and there assume to exercise the duties and responsibilities of legislating in the interest of the rebellion; and,

Whereas, Said records show that upon the 15th of February, 1862, Mr.

―――――――――――――――
[260] *Ibid.,* 318-322.

Senter voted to authorize the removal of the State Bank of Tennessee to such place as its officers might think secure from capture by the Federal army, then approaching the Capitol of our State, from Fort Donelson; and on or about the 12th of March following, he did vote to give a bounty of one hundred dollars to married men, or heads of families, who would enlist in the service of the Confederate States, for and during the war, and fifty dollars to all young men who would do likewise; and,

Whereas, Said records show that on the 18th of March, Mr. Senter offered the following amendment to House Bill No. 185, then pending, to pay for cavalry horses, in certain cases:

'*Be it further enacted,* That all horses impressed from citizens, loyal to this State and the Confederate States, into the service, shall be entitled to all the benefits of this Act, upon their making proof such horses were so taken, and also their value.'

A motion was made to table the Bill and amendment, and agreed to by a vote of 36 to 18, Mr. Senter voting in the negative; and,

Whereas, Said records further show, that Mr. Senter was a member of said Rebel Legislature, from about the time of its organization, in the Capitol, at Nashville, in 1861, until the adjournment at Memphis, about the 20th of March, 1862, voting for and supporting similar measures to those above alluded to, many of which are equally, if not more, obnoxious to the public welfare and spirit of our government, and furnish abundant evidence that he was engaged in rebellion, plotting treason, and the overthrow of our government, in a manner so mischievous in character, that the public were sometimes excluded from their dark councils, while thousands of the patriotic sons of our State and nation shouldered the musket, and offered to sacrifice their lives upon the altar of liberty, for the privileges of freedom we now enjoy; and,

Whereas, The records of our State show that Mr. Senter was a member of the House of Representatives during the session of 1859-60, and did take the oath required by the Constitution; and,

Whereas, Said acts disqualify Mr. Senter from holding any office specified in said 3d sec. of the 14th article of the Constitution of the United States, and renders all of his official acts void, from and after the issuance of the proclamation of the Secretary of State of the United States, upon the 20th of July, 1868, announcing the ratification of the 14th article of the Constitution of the United States, by the States; therefore,

Resolved, That the Senate now proceed to the election of a Speaker.

I cannot conceive that it was wise to admit the statements in the preamble to be true, and, at the same time, deny their application in debate, and by the act of an indefinite postponement. If the 14th article had become operative, it was, and is, as applicable to Tennessee, as any State in the Union, she having accepted and adopted it as a part of that compact which gives and secures her national existence, and which every one of her citizens are bound to respect, observe and support, in good faith. By the act of an indefinite postponement, you virtually declare the disabilities do not exist, that the accused is not guilty, and that all of his official acts are valid and unquestionable, and the resolution merits no more consideration than your full measure of contempt, whilst the records of his own deliberate acts are indelibly written in the archives of the State, in volumes of guilt, and will be transmitted with your action to the people and posterity, to be criticised and scrutinized by public justice. But the absolute refusal to second my motion to spread the preamble and resolution, or their purport, upon the Journal of the Senate, which was denied unanimously, is conclusive that, in your own opinion, your action could not be vindicated before your constituents, and the country, and therefore should not go upon the record and become part of the history of our Legislature. The subject was presented as the result of much thought and deliberation, under the conviction that the disabilities actually existed, and would vitiate every act to which his official signature might be attached, and involve the people of our State in interminable strife and litigation, while our acts could only be regarded as a Legislative burlesque, a mockery upon the Statute Books, and degrading to the pride of our State; and until the evil was corrected, we would be guilty of enacting worthless laws, and taking the people's money from the treasury of the State, without due authority of law, or a corresponding consideration, and of encouraging corruption, and a disregard for that sacred instrument, upon which Americans rely for protection of right, interest, person and property, nor has my opinion undergone any change. The provisions seem to be imperative and absolute, that no person shall hold office in violation of said 3d sec., whether it be a present or prospective officer, a Justice of the Peace, a Judge, or Governor, civil or military. The various speculations as to my object in presenting the subject, should have nothing to do with investigation; if it possessed merit, it was entitled to your most careful and judicious consideration; and your attempt to cover it from the light with the veil of infamy, can be justly characterized as an extraordinary proceeding, that, in my opinion, is without precedent in the legislation of the last four years.

According to the holding of the United States District Court of Virginia, every Act passed between the 20th of July, 1868, and the 22d of December, thereafter, is void in consequence of the signature of the Speaker of the Senate. The renowned jurist, Judge Underwood, of said Court, fully sustains the principle set forth in the preamble, in his able decisions in the cases of Cesar P. Griffin, Sally Anderson, and others, charged with murder, etc., where he held that a Justice of the Peace, holding office in violation of said 14th article, would vitiate his official authority, and destroy his power to administer law, and even render a Clerk of the Court, incompetent to act, thus disqualified. In the case of Cesar P. Griffin, he uses the following significant language: 'By a well settled rule of construction when by one theory a statute is rendered unconstitutional, useless and absurd, and by another theory the same statute becomes constitutional and benificient, courts must take the course to give the statutory or constitutional provision useful effect;' and adds, 'the Act of Congress, and the 14th article is so plain and distinct in their terms, as to preclude all doubt of their intended application,' etc.

So far as I have observed throughout the nation, the question has been fully sustained by the courts, throughout the press, and in Congress, except three State papers, (one of which expired soon thereafter,) and in the Senate of Tennessee, where it was regarded as a stain upon your Journal, and too insignificant and absurd to entitle it to a respectful consideration. A report published a few days since, shows that it is the opinion of the Reconstruction Committee of Congress, that any man who would hold office in violation of said 14th article, should be punished by imprisonment for two years at hard labor, and be subject to indictment for eighteen years.

But, as I understand, at Mr. Senter's request, the question involved, has been fully settled by the following Act:

[Private, No. 3.]

'An Act to relieve certain persons of all political disabilities imposed by the 14th Article of the amendments of the Constitution of the United States:

Be it enacted by the Senate and House of Representatives of the United States of America, in Congress Assembled, (two-thirds of each House concurring therein), That all political disabilities imposed by the 14th Article of the amendments of the Constitution of the United States, upon the following citizens of South Carolina, (giving the names, etc.,) and DeWitt C. Senter, of Grainger County, Tennessee, on account of participation in the recent rebellion, be, and the same hereby are, removed.

Approved December 22d, 1868.'

And by virtue of which Mr. Senter's official acts are rendered valid from and after the date last above named.

Thus, it will be seen, that the principle is settled. The preamble sustained, the guilt acknowledged, and your acts of disrespect and injustice recoils upon your own heads. Therefore, I protest against your action, which has only been delayed for the high state of excitement resulting from the introduction of said Resolution to subside, and respectfully ask that it be spread upon the Journal of the Senate as the Constitution provides. The subject was introduced as a question of duty, and no one more sincerely regrets the feelings engendered, than myself. I did not seek them, and shall not cultivate them. Yielding to my sense of honor, duty and justice, uninfluenced, as I trust, by improper motives, I feel that it is due to me, that you could expect no less.

Respectfully, &c.,
A. M. CATE."

Further evidence that all was not well in the Brownlow circle may be ascertained by looking into the official record of this last Legislature with which Governor Brownlow had any official relation. Heretofore Governor Brownlow's recommendations of officials for various State jobs usually were accepted *instanter*. But the tide had turned. Two of his recommendations for Directors of the Penitentiary were turned down by the Senate,[261] thus indicating that his Excellency's word was no longer supreme. Another fly in the ointment may be discovered by noting the number of various State officials under fire. During this legislative session, charges were lodged against six State officials, including the Speaker of the House, the State Superintendent of Public Instruction, a former member of the Legislature but at the time a Congressman, and Colonel John B. Brownlow, son of Governor Brownlow. Some of the charges alleged that there had been a tampering with the School Fund, but the defendants were exonerated, at the time, by various legislative investigating committees. But there seemed to be a rather general opinion that "where there is so much smoke there must be a bit of fire." Ten years later, fraud, bribery, and nauseating details of the legislative debauchery were unearthed and exposed.

Even within Governor Brownlow's inner circle, internal dissension had developed. His Secretary of State, Andrew Jackson Fletcher, who had been Brownlow's good man Friday, broke with the Governor early

---

[261] *Ibid.,* 102 and 214.

in January, 1869. For more than three years, Fletcher had defended the Brownlow administration in season and out of season. An eminent jurist, who knew both Brownlow and Fletcher personally, attributed to Fletcher "the best defense of Brownlow's administration ever made, and the only one needed."[262] The same authority credited Fletcher with having originated the expression "carpetbagger." Fletcher broke with Brownlow on account of the unforgiving spirit of the latter toward the ex-Confederates. He saw that Brownlow's program of revenge and bitter hate had inflicted upon Tennessee incalculable damage, for said Fletcher

"The man who is disfranchised in a republic is not apt to feel that it is his government, or take any pride or interest in it, nor apt to make a useful or even law-abiding citizen of it.

These people are greatly impoverished by the war. They suffered defeat, wounds, and captivity. We have emancipated their slaves; we have disfranchised the master, and disabled him from holding office or sitting on juries; we have enfranchised the slave, and given him the right to hold office and sit upon juries, and thus in many localities reversing the relation of master and servant."[263]

Another indication of Brownlow's waning influence was the effectiveness with which a second Omnibus Bill for railroad aid was defeated. Again, the railroad lobbyists were swarming about the Capitol and doubtless felt that another raid on the State Treasury could be effected. Spurred on by their initial rape of the State Treasury, they planned another. Using the Governor's statement that no more State aid should be voted except "where the State has large interests," the raiders launched a second assault on the Treasury by the introduction of a

"Bill for the Relief of unfinished Railroads."[264]

The sponsor of the above bill was Senator R. P. Eaton from the counties of Knox and Roane. Relying upon the ancient maxim that "The early bird catches the worm," Senator Eaton dumped his bill into the legislative hopper on the eighth day of the session. The bill sailed merrily along and squeezed through the Senate by a vote of 10 to 8.[265] The bill was then sent to the House and routinely referred to the Committee on Internal Improvements. On November 27, Representative J. W. Brown of Franklin County, Chairman of the above Committee, reported favorably upon the passage of the bill.[266]

At this juncture, another actor entered upon the scene. G. W. Black-

---

[262] Temple, Oliver Perry: *Notable Men of Tennessee,* 126.
[263] *Knoxville Whig,* January 20, 1869.
[264] *Senate Journal,* Second Session, 1868–69, 19.
[265] *Ibid.,* 29.
[266] *House Journal,* Second Session, 1868–69, 76–77.

burn, State Comptroller and President of the State Board of Finance, had disagreed with Governor Brownlow in regard to the manner of handling financial matters involving the Bank of Tennessee. Having received notice of Governor Brownlow's position, Comptroller Blackburn exclaimed: [267]

"I was perfectly astonished. My heart grew sick, and I felt that these were truly 'evil days.' The crisis had again arrived, and the 'tug of war' had truly come."

On May 18, 1868, Mr. Blackburn resigned from the Board of Finance, declaring that

". . . Being fully satisfied that I can not advance or protect the interests of the State through the Board, . . . and being unwilling to be connected with measures—even by implication—which I do most conscientiously believe will redound to the financial injury and disgrace of the State, I hereby tender to the Board my resignation. . . ."

Since Comptroller Blackburn had disagreed with the Governor, Blackburn was thereafter *non persona grata* to his Excellency.

Comptroller Blackburn became alarmed at the direful prospects of a second railroad Omnibus Bill being pushed through the Legislature, thereby saddling more millions of dollars upon the tax-paying public. Bear in mind that this second bill had already passed the Senate, and had been recommended for passage by the House Committee on Internal Improvements, the latter indulging in a bit of stump oratory, to-wit: [268]

". . . The Iron Horse, unimpeded, moves with the rapidity of lightning, over 1800 miles of road in this State, at an estimated value of $52,000,000, and although the State has passed through the trying ordeals incident to an internal war—having lost the Treasury, and in fact everything valuable— she has recuperated. . . . This bill proposes to grant aid only to those roads that are unable to complete their lines. And knowing that the interest of the State will be materially injured by withholding the aid proposed in said Bill; and believing that it is essential and necessary to protect the interest of the State by granting the aid proposed by said Bill, the Committee have unanimously instructed me to return the same, and recommend its passage. . . ."

This was the status of this second grab bill that proposed to siphon off some three millions of dollars from the State Treasury. Comptroller Blackburn was in close touch with the money market in the East. As the financial agent of the State, he had gone to New York to discuss Tennessee's financial condition, and he informed his auditors that he

". . . gave unqualified assurances from his Excellency the Governor, and

[267] *Senate Journal*, Extra Session, 1868, 99–100.
[268] *House Journal*, Second Session, 1868–69, 76–77.

the State Legislature, that the public debt would not be increased, but lessened. . . .

The condition of our credit in New York *now*, must be inferred from the following, which I give as it is: Since the introduction of the Bill, proposing to increase the State debt nearly three millions of dollars, I have received many dispatches and letters . . . while some of the best friends the State has in New York, and those who have done us great service since July, 1866, write me *positively* that New York will carry our State no longer, if we increase our liabilities now, by issuing more Bonds to railroads. . . ."

On December 11, 1868, Comptroller Blackburn transmitted to the House of Representatives, where the bill was pending third and final reading, a letter containing the above statement of facts.[269] The receipt of this letter threw the House of Representatives into a conniption fit. On the following day, Representative J. A. Taylor of Carter County broke his vials of wrath over the head of Comptroller Blackburn, to-wit:[270]

"WHEREAS, The Comptroller of the State, G. W. Blackburn, has transmitted to this House, without authority, a message of instruction, an act unwarranted by precedence; *And whereas*, The following assertion is made in said Communication: 'I went to New York, and, as Comptroller of the State, gave unqualified assurance from His Excellency, the Governor, and the State Legislature, that the public debt would not be increased, but lessened;' which assertion, not only attacks the honor and veracity of His Excellency, the Governor, but the members of the Legislature, also; *And Whereas*, said Communication will endanger the credit of the State, if not corrected, and work to the advantage of bond speculators; Therefore,

Resolved by the General Assembly of the State of Tennessee, That the action of the Comptroller writing said Communication is an insult to this body, and deserves its condemnation.

Resolved, further, That the State of Tennessee will meet her liabilities, it matters not what may be the amount, so long as there is a dollar in the Treasury, or property in the State, subject to taxation."

The Blackburn communication seems to have produced a sort of temporary paralysis, for three days passed without any action on the Omnibus Bill which very properly could have been called the "ominous bill." On December 15, Representative W. T. Poston from the counties of Dyer and Lauderdale offered a resolution calling upon railroads to report whether or not they had paid the interest on the State bonds issued to them.[271] Inasmuch as such information might have proved embarrassing to some of the railroads "now asking for more bonds under the provisions of the present Omnibus Bill," the Poston resolution was killed by the eye-lash vote of 32 to 31! Later in the day, the Omnibus Bill on special order was called up. A rash of amendments

[269] *Appendix*, 1868–69, 75–76.
[270] *House Journal*, Second Session, 1868–69, 159.
[271] *Ibid.*, 167.

poured in, some proposing to reduce and others to increase appropriations to this and that railroad. Finally, Representative E. J. Hodges of McNairy County moved that the bill go to the table, his motion being sustained by a vote of 40 to 34.[272] An effort by Representative W. L. Waters of Wilson County to reconsider the above vote to table was defeated by a vote of 39 to 34, and that doomed the "big steal." The Blackburn letter unquestionably defeated the reckless policy of continuing to pour State funds into railroads, some of which were in hopeless bankruptcy, some of which were outright frauds, and one of which was never even built!

The Parson's troubles were multiplying with the rapidity of the plagues of ancient Egypt. Defeat of the Omnibus Bill, refusal of the Senate to confirm some of his recommendations for State jobs, the break with Comptroller Blackburn, and the lashings being laid upon him by outstanding leaders of former Union sentiment—all these and more must have reminded the Parson of a couplet in Young's *Night Thoughts:*

> "Woes cluster; rare are solitary woes;
> They love a train—they tread each other's heels."

But "the most unkindest cut of all," à là Shakespeare, came on January 9, 1869, when the Parson must have felt himself an inhabitant of that region described by Christopher Marlowe:

> "... For where we are is Hell,
> And where Hell is, there must we ever be."

Mr. Speaker of the House, F. S. Richards, representing a tier of West Tennessee counties, Fayette, Shelby, and Tipton, unleashed a severe attack upon the Brownlow policy of disfranchisement of Confederates. This Unionist, who had been Brownlow's Fidus Achates, in a lengthy speech in the House of Representatives advocated the calling of a Constitutional Convention immediately for removing all restrictions on the franchise and re-establishing an equitable method of manhood suffrage. Pertinent extracts from the Richards speech are:[273]

"... I exceedingly regret that I cannot, without painfully violating my own sense of propriety, give my approval fully to any one of the bills which have been heretofore introduced by various other members of this House, intended to minister a remedy to our present sufferings. I am not willing to delay effectual action on this subject for another long and sorrowful twelve months, as some seem to desire, or to adopt a still more tardy and circuitous course of relief, as others recommend. Any measure of relief which we may adopt, should be, in my judgment, prompt, convenient, efficacious and all embracing. The disease now festering in the body politic

[272] *Ibid.,* 173.
[273] *Daily Press and Times* (Nashville), January 11, 1869.

needs the immediate application of remedies of a most searching and drastic character. Mere emollients or *bread pills*, if I may so speak, will by no means answer the purpose.

We are suffering greatly at this moment from local dissensions, from social discord, from party rancor, and from widespread distrust among our citizens. It is high time that all these fearful evils should be removed. It is evident to my mind that there is only one safe road out of our troubles. Let us at once provide for the calling of a convention for the purpose of re-enfranchising all who are now in a state of civic disability under the franchise regulations. The beneficial effect of our doing so will at once be felt in every part of the State, among all classes of our people, and in connection with all the great material interests of the commonwealth.

*   *   *   *   *   *   *   *

... I have supposed that good effects would result from the removal of all present civil disabilities by the action of those very persons by whose hands they were imposed. It seems to me, indeed, but just and right that an opportunity should be opened to them of showing to the world that in yielding heretofore to a *temporary* necessity, it was never their intention to practice wanton oppression or to exercise a cruel and crushing tyranny, and I have thought that it would be expedient thus to enable them, by an act of present justice and generosity, to lay a solid foundation for future friendship and concord between themselves and those with whom they were formerly at issue. I am, for reasons already stated, altogether opposed to any further postponement of this much needed measure of relief. . . ."

There is internal evidence in the official records of the Second Session of the Thirty-Fifth General Assembly that Brownlow's unrelenting opposition to allowing ex-Confederates and Conservative Unionists to exercise the privilege of voting had become odious to various members of the General Assembly. For example, Senator James R. McCall representing four West Tennessee counties introduced on December 17, 1868,

"A bill to repeal An Act known as the Act to limit the Elective Franchise."[274]

On January 12, 1869, three days after Speaker Richards' speech before the House of Representatives, Guy W. Wines of Montgomery County offered the following resolution,[275] the first legislative effort regarding Woman Suffrage in Tennessee:

"Whereas, We have admitted to the ballot-box in this State, many who were scarcely qualified to exercise the right of suffrage by past education, and

Whereas, We have reason to believe that the extension of the Franchise to the women of Tennessee, is only a question of time, it would be most right and proper at this time, having a tendency to elevate the politics of the State, and raising them to a higher standard, and

Whereas, We have constituted a Constitutional Committee to take into

---

[274] *Senate Journal*, Second Session, 1868–69, 105.
[275] *House Journal*, Second Session, 1868–69, 210–211.

consideration the propriety of proposing certain amendments to the Constitution at this time; Therefore,

Be it resolved by the General Assembly of the State of Tennessee, That the Committee on the Constitution be requested to report to this House upon the propriety of striking out the word 'male,' wherever it occurs in the Constitution of this State."

A week later, a report from the Judiciary Committee chilled the hopes of the advocates of extended suffrage. Reference was made to the provisions of the bogus Constitutional Convention of January, 1865, at which time it was decreed that

"the Legislature elected in March, 1865, did determine the qualification of voters and limit the Elective Franchise, and that these Acts became parts of the Constitution. . . ."[216] This being so, the present Legislature has no power over the subject, and cannot extend the Elective Franchise to those who do not now possess it. Nor can it withhold it from those who now are entitled to vote. . . ."

The revealed opposition to a continuation of Brownlow's reign of bitterness and hostility toward the disfranchised majority of Tennessee citizens appears to have made little or no impression upon the Governor whose administration was drawing rapidly to a close. He appeared to have been blind and deaf, neither seeing nor hearing the uprising manifestations of opposition to his proscriptive program. Apparently he brushed aside the convincing evidence that his former official supporters, like Blackburn, Fletcher, Mr. Speaker Richards and others, were completely fed up with his rule or ruin policies of political punishment and civil injustice. Utterly ignoring "the handwriting on the wall," Brownlow decided to spread alarm and terror once more before he vacated the gubernatorial chair for the post of U. S. Senator on March 4, 1869, an office to which he had been elected some sixteen months earlier. Accordingly and characteristically, on January 20 he issued another embittered Proclamation, declaring that there existed in Middle and West Tennessee utter defiance of all law and order. He alluded to those "masked villains called Kuklux" whom he charged with committing practically every crime in the decalogue. It will be recalled that these two sections of the State had partially overthrown Brownlow's nefarious election machinery by electing two Conservative candidates to Congress, necessitating the application of Brownlow's "counting out and counting in" technique. Instead of leaving a parting gesture of friendship to all Tennesseans, he breathed forth dire threats of imminent military rule and warned that he was "not to be cajoled or terrified." Instead of registering his Proclamation in the official record book and having it bear the signature of the Secretary of State and the official State Seal, as correct procedure required, he followed

[216] *Senate Journal,* Second Session, 1868–69, 149–150.

his now year-old method of unleashing through the newspaper columns [277] his proposed military attack.

"PROCLAMATION

Whereas, There exists in Middle and West Tennessee, lawless bands who set at defiance civil law, and, in certain localities render it impossible for the civil officers to enforce the laws of the State; and whereas, these masked villains called Kuklux, are taking prisoners from jails and hanging them without trial, and are abducting passengers from railroad trains, and notifying conductors of Northern birth to leave the State, they having driven four conductors from one road, and whereas, certain ambitious men have made incendiary speeches, advising the overthrow of the State government, thereby encouraging these bands; and whereas, certain rebel newspapers have encouraged these men by denying the existence of the Kuklux, by ridiculing their acts, and failing to condemn them; and whereas, the Legislature has amended the Militia Law, and given me authority to meet such outrages;

Now, therefore, I, William G. Brownlow, Governor of Tennessee, do call upon all good and loyal citizens to enter the ranks of the State Guard, to be mustered into service, and aid in suppressing this lawlessness.

Those enrolling in East Tennessee will be transported to Nashville and armed, and placed under command of General Joseph A. Cooper.

Another proclamation will be duly issued designating the counties in which I shall declare martial law, the effect of which will be to set aside civil law and turn over the offenders to the military to be tried and punished summarily.

These outrages have been long borne, but the executive is not to be cajoled or terrified. All citizens are warned against harboring any Kuklux. The Governor will make the guards numerous and effective enough to make Middle and West Tennessee as orderly and quiet as East Tennessee is to-day.

In testimony whereof I have signed the foregoing, and affixed the great seal of the State, this 20th day of January, 1869.   WM. G. BROWNLOW."

---

[277] *Daily Press and Times* (Nashville), January 21, 1869.

Brownlow's call upon the "good and loyal citizens" to enter the State Guard resulted in some eighteen hundred men, most of whom were from East Tennessee, enrolling and mobilizing at Nashville under command of General Joseph A. Cooper. With the Brownlow "army" now readied and poised for "duty," Brownlow issued a Proclamation on February 20 that established martial law in the following nine counties: Overton, Jackson, Maury, Giles, Marshall, Lawrence, Gibson, Madison, and Haywood. And so it was, *four years after the War Between the States had ended*, nine counties in Tennessee were thrust under military law! Despite all of Brownlow's expressed fears of Kukluxism, the fact remains that not a man in Tennessee was ever indicted or convicted as being a Kukluxer! At the time, courts and law-enforcement agencies were practically all pro-Brownlow.

Brownlow's inability to discriminate in a political sense between fact and fiction had for more than three years embroiled Tennessee in partisan strife that became intolerable. Too eager to listen to thousand-tongued rumor, he failed to recognize the basic fact that a stable government could not be established upon a peace based upon terror and despotism. People are quiet and moderate when free; they become disquieted and unruly only when their government seeks to debase and despise them. In a nutshell, this was the fundamental trouble with Brownlowism.

Kukluxism was organized at first to frighten superstitious Negroes, and arose out of some frivolities on the part of a half-dozen young men at Pulaski. Terrifying tales were hatched up for the purpose of checking idle Negroes from roaming about and pilfering. Their visits to homes of Negroes and their "mummicking" about their deaths at Manassas and Shiloh; their carrying concealed rubber buckets which they filled with a mammoth gush of water brought by terrified Negroes; their display of counterfeit flesh bags in shape of the human heart and their yelling for "fried nigger meat"—all of these and scores of kindred pranks paralyzed with terror the credulous blacks.

All history discloses that similar secret societies are usually the result of tyranny. Wise statesmanship will avoid furnishing proximate or even remote causes for the existence of such organizations. The South had accepted the results of war and desired to rebuild its devastated region and re-establish its broken homes. The teachings of all history would have been reversed if the social and political revolution, resulting from war, had gone into operation smoothly and harmoniously, especially with a Radical Congress imposing harsh and vindictive measures upon the conquered States. The transition involved such a factor as the domination of the white race over the colored race—a situation that had existed unquestioned for centuries. In Tennessee, Brownlow's franchise law had deprived the most prominent men in the State from either voting or holding office, while the Negroes were enfranchised and provided the balance of political power. Resistance to this state of things gave rise to some form of organized opposition, the Kuklux Klan being the largest and most influential of such movements. The Kuklux Klan was transformed from a fun-making frolic into a political organization as an offset to the Loyal League into which Negroes were inducted by white Radical leaders. In this important respect, the Klan became an organization designed for self-protection.

On February 10, 1869, Governor Brownlow transmitted his final Message* to a Tennessee Legislature:

"RESIGNATION OF THE GOVERNOR

STATE OF TENNESSEE,
EXECUTIVE DEPARTMENT,
Knoxville, February 10, 1869.

To the Members of the General Assembly of Tennessee:

GENTLEMEN:—I herewith tender my resignation as Governor of Tennessee, to you, as the Representatives of the loyal people of the State; the resignation to take effect on Thursday, the 25th inst.

The occasion serves to express my profound sense of obligation to the officers and members of your respective Houses, for your faithful and generous co-operation with me, in the endeavor to administer the State Government for the protection of the loyal people thereof, and for the quiet and welfare of all the citizens; and also to say, that if there have been any lack of complete realization of these objects, the fault has not been from want of purpose and effort on my part, nor of co-operation on yours.

It has been my study and labor to bring Tennessee up from the ruin in which she was left by the war, to that degree of moral and material prosperity and progress to which she is so eminently entitled; to develop her ample resources; render efficient all her charitable and educational enterprises, and maintain her financial integrity—in a word, to place upon her the crown of honor she so well deserves to wear.

There can be no doubt, our success, in all these respects, would have been far greater but for the fierce hostility with which the Ad-

* Senate Appendix, 1868–69, 237–238.

ministration has been fought, from the beginning and at all points, by the rebel element. Probably no man ever filled the office who encountered equal opposition to that through which it has been my lot to pass.

How far we have succeeded in our honest purpose and earnest effort, even under these disadvantages, the present condition of the State, with her industries active; her financial credit sustained; her old lines of commerce in full operation, with new ones opening; her school system in fair working, and eleemosynary institutions all crowded and sustained, and her future smiling with so much of promise, will sufficiently attest.

Feeling, as I do, a lively and abiding interest in the future welfare of the State, and of the Union Republican Party of Tennessee, my regrets, on retiring, would be greater were it not that the gentleman who will succeed me for the remainder of my official term—the Honorable Speaker of the Senate, Mr. DeWitt C. Senter—is a loyal man, capable, tried and trusty, who is sound in his principles, and who will steadfastly adhere to them upon the platform of the Union Republican Party of Tennessee.

It will be my honor, as well as pleasure, in the new official position to which you have called me—to represent, in part, our State, in the Senate of the United States—to watch over and subserve her interest with as much of ability and fidelity as I may. If at present, owing to my physical feebleness, it shall be impossible to make my voice heard in the Senate Chamber, my constituents may be assured I shall be found voting, in all cases, in favor of the principles we in common so earnestly cherish.

Thanking you, gentlemen, for your generous official confidence and courtesy, I invoke upon you, and the great State you represent, the blessings of an all-watchful and benignant Providence.

W. G. Brownlow."

Even Brownlow's farewell salvo to the General Assembly evidenced his intense partisan spirit which had dominated his official acts throughout his gubernatorial terms. He could not resist praising the "loyal people" any more than he could refrain from taking a parting shot at "the rebel element." In the Brownlow vocabulary, there were no such words as reconciliation or reason. Perhaps this should be no surprise to anyone who has scrutinized his public career and evaluated his political reactions. In his makeup and personality, it appears that the ingredients were about equally divided between fanatic and politician. For the most part, he may be said to have been the embodiment of the evils of each, without possessing much of their virtues—if any. An amazing character he was! His chief biographer captioned the closing chapter in his book with an appropriate title, *The Like Shall Not Be Seen Again.*[278]

A review of his two administrations will disclose Brownlow's inability to deal with social, economic, and political matters with any appreciable degree of efficiency. What a travesty on truth and justice for him to assert in his final Message that he had *"endeavored* to administer the State Government . . . for the quiet and welfare of all the citizens!"* Abuse, slander, vituperation, recrimination, chicanery, and political punishment constituted his stock in trade while Governor. Instead of placing upon Tennessee "the crown of honor" as he blatantly boasted of having "labored" to do, he left Tennessee's "honor rooted in dishonor," burdened with a bonded indebtedness of sixteen and one-half millions of dollars, more than half of which had been incurred unjustly, illegally, and corruptly by the machinations of swindlers and itchy-palm legislators. Sane economy was unknown, the actual running expenses of the two Brownlow legislative bodies approximating three-fourths of a million dollars. For all their law-making during the 784 days in which these two General Assemblies were in session, only one constructive law out of 286 public acts had any appreciable significance, that being the educational statute that recognized the value and importance of educating the youth of the State.

For nearly four years, Brownlow held the threat of military rule over the heads of a people who, he exclaimed, had injured him and the Unionists. As Governor, with a pliant Radical Legislature, he bullied, browbeat, and berated a majority of the most intelligent and worth-while citizens in the State by disfranchising them and reducing them politically to the status of serfs. When he passed from the gubernatorial chair to a seat in the United States Senate, there was at least a feeling of relief at his absence from the State. The political atmosphere was purified by his departure, even though the bitter outrages perpetrated by him were not soon forgotten. Small wonder that his full-length portrait in the State Capitol bears grim testimony to the bitter hatred he had incurred; from the waist down, copious squirts of ambeer from tobacco-chewing legislators in the post-Brownlow years found the target with unerring accuracy and left a brownish veneer. For purposes of sure identification, the wrinkled and mummy-like face of the Parson was not "touched up" by the salivary marksmen!

What sort of man was this fellow, Brownlow, who seems to have been a sort of gadfly to his contemporaries and an enigma to future generations? The elements were so mixed in him that one is inclined to

[278] Coulter, E. Merton: *Parson Brownlow,* 373.

"After the deluge."
Original painting in Tennessee State Library, Nashville.

think that Mark Twain's famous epigram is quite apropos—"Sired by a hurricane, and dam'd by an earthquake." His private life was diametrically opposite to what he exhibited in public life. Nothing has been unearthed to refute the Parson's self-diagnosis:[279]

"I have never been arraigned in the Church for any immorality. I never played a card. I never was a profane swearer. I never drank a dram of liquor, until within a few years—when it was taken as a medicine. I never had a cigar or chew of tobacco in my mouth. I never was in attendance at a theatre. I never attended a horse-race, and never witnessed their running, save on the fair-grounds of my own county. I never courted but one woman; and her I married.

I may be allowed to say that I have ever been, as I still am, quite a politician. . . ."

Brownlow came nearest to admitting in a narrative sketch [280] of his career that he was not "the perfect man":

"I have my *faults*, no doubt, as well as all other men. I am not *infallible*, because I am not immortal. There are *spots* in the sun—there are *specks* in me."

As to the charge that he was always engaged in quarreling, bickering, and raising a rukus wherever he went, the Parson had a ready reply:[281]

"Then let it be urged, that I am, and always have been 'a mover of seditions'—the pest of general society, and the fruitful source of domestic broils; or a being whose heart is full of rancor and animosities, jarring affections, and discordant and malevolent feelings! Yes, ring my death knell from steep to steep—let its swelling sounds be heard in startling echoes, mingling with the rush of the mountain's torrent, and the mighty cataract's earthquake voice! Spread the unfurled banner of calumny upon every breeze—let it float in the atmosphere till my name becomes a mockery and a byword. Like the Phoenix, in newness of beauty and majesty, amid fires of opposition, I hope to rise to victory and triumph. What can be more noble than to brave the censure of disappointed ambition—to bear with the arrogance, pride, and infirmities of a priest-ridden community and blind bigots, for the good of mankind! To suffer all this, I am perfectly aware, must require a considerable degree of moral courage; and I think I possess the courage that can endure it all, and even death itself. I pretend not to be a candidate for the honors of martyrdom, yet I should feel that I had gone down to my grave disgraced, did I not incur the censure and abuse of bloated bigotry, and priestly corruption."

Gifted with an amazing ability to coin gripping figures of speech in which simile, metaphor, hyperbole, antithesis, and sarcasm each played a significant rôle, Brownlow riveted attention upon his florid phraseology and became a name to conjure with politically. In all his

---

[279] Brownlow, William G.: *Parson Brownlow's Book*, 19.
[280] ————— *Helps to the Study of Presbyterianism*, 290.
[281] *Ibid.*, 293.

writings and utterances, perhaps no better example of his word-dexterity can be exhibited than his famous reply [282] to one Jordan Clark of Arkansas:

"Multum in Parvo.

Camden, Ark., June 30, 1860.

W. G. Brownlow:—I have learned with pleasure, upon which I consider reliable authority, that you have made up your mind to join the Democratic party, and in future to act with us for the benefit of the country. When will you come out and announce it? It will have a good effect in the present election, if you will make it known over your own signature. Hoping to hear from you, I am, very truly,

JORDAN CLARK."

"Knoxville, August 6, 1860.

Mr. Jordan Clark:—I have your letter of the 30th ult., and hasten to let you know the *precise time* when I expect to come out and formally announce that I have joined the Democratic party. When the sun shines at midnight and the moon at midday; when man forgets to be selfish, or Democrats lose their inclination to steal; when nature stops her onward march to rest, or all the water-courses in America flow up stream; when flowers lose their odor, and trees shed no leaves; when birds talk, and beasts of burden laugh; when damned spirits swap hell for heaven with the angels of light, and pay them the boot in mean whiskey; when impossibilities are in fashion, and no proposition is too absurd to be believed,—you may credit the report that I have joined the Democrats!

I join the Democrats! Never, so long as there are sects in churches, weeds in gardens, fleas in hog-pens, dirt in victuals, disputes in families, wars with nations, water in the ocean, bad men in America, or base women in France! No, Jordan Clark, you may hope, you may congratulate, you may reason, you may sneer, but that cannot be. The thrones of the Old World, the courts of the universe, the governments of the world, may all fall and crumble into ruin,—the New World may commit the national suicide of dissolving this Union,—but all this, and more, must occur before I join the Democracy!

I join the Democracy! Jordan Clark, you know not what you say. When I join Democracy, the Pope of Rome will join the Methodist Church. When Jordan Clark, of Arkansas, is President of the Republic of Great Britain by the universal suffrage of a contented people; when Queen Victoria consents to be divorced from Prince Albert by a county court in Kansas; when Congress obliges, by law, James Buchanan to marry a European princess; when the Pope leases the Capitol at Washington for his city residence; When Alexander of Russia and Napoleon of France are elected Senators in Congress from New Mexico; when good men cease to go to heaven, or bad men to hell; when this world is turned upside down; when proof is afforded, both clear and unquestionable, that there is no God; when men turn to ants, and ants to elephants,—I will change my political faith and come out on the side of Democracy!

Supposing that this full and frank letter will enable you to fix upon *the*

---

[282] _____ *Parson Brownlow's Book,* 62–64.

period when I will come out a full-grown Democrat, and to communicate the same to all whom it may concern in Arkansas,

I have the honor to be, &c.,

W. G. BROWNLOW."

Brownlow's political foresight was so obscured by his intense partisanship that he did not anticipate the downfall of Radicalism in Tennessee which followed swiftly his departure from the gubernatorial chair. So sanguine was he of its continuance that he in effect congratulated the people of Tennessee that his successor, DeWitt Clinton Senter, was a "loyal" man who would stick to the platform and principles of the Union Republican Party in Tennessee. In this prediction, Brownlow was grievously mistaken. Senter broke quickly with the Radicals, largely upon the subject of suffrage, and was elected to succeed himself. Radicalism was now doomed, and Tennessee returned to Conservatism. Most of Brownlow's radical measures were soon relegated to the dump heap. He made one contribution, however, which still remains virtually intact. By his rash, ill-conceived, and vindictive policy against all supporters of the Confederacy, the majority of old-line Whigs were driven into the Democratic Party. When this increment was added to the Democratic Party, the balance of political power was tilted in that direction. With few exceptions, Tennessee became and has remained since Brownlow's reign a Democratic State. The Republican Party in Tennessee has "Parson" Brownlow to thank for that *unintentional* contribution, for to him more than to any other man the shift in political domination became fact.

What verdict has history rendered in regard to Brownlow's public career? The testimony of the following ought to help supply the answer:

I. Historical Works

"William Gannaway Brownlow, who thus became Governor of Tennessee in one of the most critical periods in its life, was a man of marked influence upon the history of this State. No study of political, economic, social, or religious history of Tennessee for four decades can fail to take note of him. Born in Wythe County, Virginia, August 29, 1805, he was left an orphan at the age of eleven. He received a common school education and at eighteen years of age he was apprenticed to a carpenter. For ten years he was a circuit-riding Methodist minister in Virginia, North and South Carolina, and Tennessee. In 1839 he brought from the press in Elizabethton, Tennessee, the first issue of a newspaper, the 'Tennessee Whig,' and thus embarked upon an editorial career that lasted much of the remainder of his life. In the following year he transferred himself and his paper to Jonesboro and in 1849 moved to Knoxville. His paper was influential and widely circulated. In his sermons, in his editorials, and in his public speeches Brownlow's chief characteristic was his willingness and his ability to castigate his enemies in the most picturesque and vituperative language. His reliance was not upon reason but upon denunciation. Because of the unre-

strained character of his attacks upon his enemies, he was frequently involved in personal difficulties and in slander suits. Whatever his faults, however, undoubtedly he possessed a large measure of moral and physical
courage. . . .
. . . In politics he was successively a Whig, a Know-Nothing, a Constitutional Unionist, and a Republican. He was unmerciful in his denunciation
and his misrepresentation of his political, as well as his denominational,
enemies. He was an advocate of temperance and of the building of railroads. For years before the Civil War he was a champion of the institution
of slavery and in 1858 he publicly defended slavery in a five-day debate in
Philadelphia with Rev. Abraham Pryne. His opposition to disunion and his
championing of the Union during the Civil War have already been mentioned. As a result of his experiences during the war, Brownlow, in 1865,
was filled with a bitter hatred of the Confederates. At a time when a for-
giving spirit and a willingness to promote the reconciliation of recent
enemies was needed, he was promoted to high office by men, who, like him,
sought vengeance and power."
——Hamer, Philip M.: *Tennessee—A History*, Vol. II, 600-601.

"The new Governor [Brownlow] was an extraordinary character. Born
in Virginia in 1805, he became a circuit rider of the Methodist Church at
the age of twenty-one, thereby earning the name of 'Parson' which never
left him. In 1838 he began the publication of the Knoxville *Whig*. Five years
later he ran for Congress, to be defeated by Andrew Johnson. In his family
and private life he was gentle enough. In his editorials and speeches, caustic,
bitter and vituperative, he was anti-secession but not anti-slavery. Only two
years before the outbreak of war he had upheld the 'institution' in public
debate with a Northern minister at Philadelphia.
With the coming of war, and with East Tennessee forcibly held by Confederate troops, the Parson found it necessary to escape to the North. There
he remained in exile, picturesquely lecturing to huge and profitable audi-
ences on the persecution of Unionists in East Tennessee by the 'hell-born
and hell-bound rebels.' In the spring of 1864, with the state cleared of Confederate forces, he returned to Tennessee and now, largely by grace of his
ancient enemy, Andrew Johnson, he was at the head of the government of
the state.
It was Tennessee's misfortune that the new Governor, like so many of
the more single-minded Reconstructionists, felt that he was called to preach
and to execute the righteous judgments of a wrathful God. These judgments which aforetime had been directed at Baptists, Presbyterians, Democrats and Abolitionists, were now concentrated on 'rebels,' by which the
Parson meant not only those who had actively or passively aided the Confederacy but also those who did not now support his own regime."
——Henry, Robert Selph: *The Story of Reconstruction*, 43-44.

"It was a strange and dangerous act to set a person of Brownlow's record
to rule over a million people. In peaceful times it would have been perilous;
in the confusion incident to the closing of a civil war, it might well seem
preposterous. Unless the wild threats of his terrible vengeance upon the
majority of his fellow-citizens, made constantly for the previous five years,
were merely deep acting upon a broad stage, Tennessee might look forward
to conditions worse than war. For the promoting of the orderly progress of
peace, it would have been impossible to make a worse choice; for carrying
out a war of vengeance of a minority against a majority, Brownlow was

incomparably the best selection that could have been made throughout the land. As a master in whipping up hate and revenge, he had no peer.

It therefore became Brownlow's program from the beginning to use his power as dictator of Tennessee to punish those against whom he had a grudge, public or private, and to introduce to Tennessee that new variety of democracy which made it possible for a small minority to dominate completely the civil and political existence of the vast majority. . . ."
———Coulter, E. Merton: *William G. Brownlow, Fighting Parson of the Southern Highlands*, 262-263.

"Vindictiveness was a deliberate policy. He [Brownlow] did not practice it as a necessary evil to be apologized for, but as a virtue in itself. To him secession was a capital crime, and its leaders were guilty of murder for every death that the war had occasioned. That they were spared their lives he considered a show of unwarranted mercy; that they should expect more was almost inconceivable. The concept that men could honestly differ and defend their beliefs with their lives was a shape of things which his mind could not receive. All was good or evil. Since he apparently never doubted his own identification with the right, he was as well satisfied that opposition was evil in itself. . . ."
———Alexander, Thomas B.: *Political Reconstruction in Tennessee*, 164.

"This was the man who became the chief executive of Tennessee in 1865. Austere in his habits and almost fanatical in his love and devotion for the Union, he was determined to restore the state to the control of the truly loyal citizens and to bend his efforts toward punishing and impoverishing those who had aided and participated in the rebellion. Although sympathetic and kind to these persons as individuals, he regarded the former Confederates, as a group, as degenerate, dishonest, and corrupt, and was willing to countenance any scheme of his advisers and supporters that would serve to embarrass and humiliate them. Keenly aware of the distress and hardship that the war had caused in East Tennessee, and always out of contact with the ideals and institutions of the other sections of the state, he naturally filled offices with and conferred favors upon the citizens of his own region. With certain notable exceptions, Tennessee suffered little from 'carpet-bag' rule in comparison with the other Southern states, but it did suffer from Brownlow rule, which was the domination of East Tennessee Republicanism."
———Patton, James Welch: *Unionism and Reconstruction in Tennessee*, 83.

". . . The scalawags, such as Brownlow of Tennessee, Smith of Alabama, and Holden of North Carolina, were usually honest but narrow, vindictive men, filled with fear and hate of the conservative whites. . . ."
———Fleming, Walter Lynwood: *The Sequel of Appomattox*, 224.

"Governor Brownlow was possessed of no real knowledge of state affairs and no real ability save his ability to say hard things about his enemies. He was too obstinate and vindictive for a politician and too much of a partisan for a statesman even if he had possessed the ability and the experience. He was, therefore, wholly unfit for the position to which he had been elected. His only redeeming trait was his uncompromising Unionism, and his election shows how the Union men were willing to put the Union before all else."
———Fertig, James Walter: *Secession and Reconstruction of Tennessee*, 62.

"... And now began four years of misrule more trying upon the brave men and women of Tennessee than the four years of terrible war. It was a condition from which they sought deliverance for years in vain. . . ."

"... [Brownlow] was especially known for his bitter vituperation and vindictive spirit. On account of his unpopularity he was compelled to suspend his paper on Oct. 24, 1861. He was an advocate of slavery, but violently opposed to secession. His value to the Union lay only in his radical, vindictive partisanship; otherwise he was wholly unfit for high office, and conspicuously without ability."

———The South in the Building of the Nation, Vol. II, 526, article by Carey A. Folk, entitled "Tennessee Since the War of 1865-1909."

"... Brownlow was, perhaps, the most strikingly original personality in the state at that time, not even excepting Johnson himself. But he seems to have possessed few qualifications for the office of governor except the one qualification which was of paramount importance in the view of the administration, namely, intense, unswerving, self-sacrificing devotion to the Union. Being bitter, narrow-minded, and extravagant in action and expression, he was not considered by the conservative element in the state as a suitable man, as governor, to allay strife and bring about a peaceful coordination of the divergent and suspicious elements in Tennessee which would make for the best interests of all."

———Moore, John Trotwood, and Austin P. Foster: Tennessee The Volunteer State, Vol I. 526.

"Brownlow was a man of passion—what Bishop Haven pronounced him to be, 'a good hater'—and while his political education and associations naturally led him to espouse the cause of the Union, his course was in part attributable to the zeal of partisanship and his powerful resentments. . . ."

———Price, R. N.: Holston Methodism, From Its Origin to the Present Time, Vol. III, 322-323.

II. Contemporary Newspaper Editorials:*

"Brownlow himself is the real source of trouble in Tennessee. If that state was less quiet than the others of the Southern states, it is because Brownlow has made it so. . . . Tennessee is the only state that is in the hands of a born swaggerer and bully—a man who has no conception and no care that the surest way to cultivate disturbance is to be always defying it, to be always oppressively irritating those from whom it may come, and to desire nothing so much as to crowd pride into the last possible corner. . . . It is a pity that the quiet of the country should be threatened by the prominence of such a character in public life; that the country should hear the murmur of war, even though faintly simply because an irritable, ill-natured, narrow minded, and pugnacious man happens to be governor of Tennessee."

———Knoxville Daily Free Press and Herald, September 25, 1868.

"... It is pretty extensively believed in Nashville that Brownlow is insane. We don't believe it. Insanity has been defined to be 'the entanglement of thought,' but he hasn't thoughts enough to make a tangle.

---

* Scores of editorials were read, and almost without exception exhibited bias and prejudice. For that reason, only two "samples" are cited—R.H.W.

'Tis a pity for him that he isn't insane, for it would be the only excuse, utter mental imbecility excepted, for the disgrace he is inflicting upon the State in which he dwells. He calls himself a man of God. He professes to be a messenger of 'peace and good will to men.' He holds himself up or out as a saint ordained and annointed to establish the spirit of Christianity among mankind. But he has ever promoted strifes, and fights and bloodshed in neighborhoods.

He has been a pest, an itch, a leprosy, a yellow plague in every community. He has distilled venom like a human *bohun upas*. His tongue has ever been 'set on fire of hell,' his heart being the hell to kindle the wagging member. Beelzebub's tail is forever coiled like a snake around the old miscreants neck. There has never been any more religion or decency in his sermons or his prayers or his exhortations or his talk at death beds, than in the yellings of hyenas, the cursings of pirates, or the objurgations of harlots.

He has desecrated the house of God as much by his blasphemies as if he had stolen the sacramental vessels or used them in treating his congregation to applejack. It is a wonder that in his pulpit he has never been transfixed by the forked arrows of God's vengeance. He professes to guide men to heaven, and curses them to hell. He would go for universal damnation, provided he could be exempted himself. In his black robes and white cravat, he might remind one of a black snake with a white streak around his neck.

What an infinitely miserable old man this must be. He never did a generous or kind thing in his life. He was ever meditating the gratification of his malice. He has ever been seeking to steal upon his unsuspecting neighbors like a hungry cat upon a bird. Every man has a deadly antipathy to him. They say there are people who have such an antipathy to black cats that they instinctively know if one is within a hundred yards of them in the darkest night, and we are sure that decent people would recognize his proximity at twice that distance.

He can have no healthful slumber—only convulsions. The whole of the beautiful world—sky, earth and sea—must be as black as Erebus to his eyes. Every sound must be to his ears like a wail or shriek of the damned. Every drop of rain must hiss upon his burning head. Every breeze must seem to him a blasting sirocco—every morsel of food a dose of internal brimstone. The poor old wretch must feel terrible remorse.

He must feel as if his ribs were red-hot gridirons, broiling his entrails. If every malignant and accursed lie he has told were a coal of fire upon his body, he would writhe and twist under a taller mountain of flame than ever the old Titans did. His heart is as black as ten thousand devils. He sees behind him only the mounds over the graves of buried victims and before—only the Dead Sea of Despair.

Heaven,   and even hell abhor him—though the latter will somehow manage to gulp him down. His very face looks like that of a dead man, who, mistaking a boy's tooting horn for Gabriel's trumpet, has got up for judgment before his time. His evil passions have killed every semblance of human nature in his features, if there ever was such a semblance there.

People of Tennessee! to your Governor!

'With one hand clenched to batter noses
While 'tother scrawls 'bout Paul and Moses.' "

——*Louisville Journal*, May 14, 1868. Editor, George D. Prentice. Extract from an editorial, *Compliments of the Season from the Editor of the Louisville Journal to the Governor of Tennessee.*

III. Appraisal by a Contemporary Friend

"Perhaps no individual could be named in this country whose home character was so unlike that which he had among strangers. Seldom has any man lived who so constantly and so persistently presented to the world a false and distorted picture of himself, while the genuine picture was seen only by those who were near him. He seemed to delight in creating on the minds of strangers at a distance the most unfavorable impressions; in presenting a false and exaggerated, not to say a revolting, idea of himself. Those who did not know him, and judged him from his writings and speeches, would have supposed his heart was a boiling cauldron full of all evil passions —envy, hate, revenge, unforgiveness, and murderous intents. They could not have believed that the sunshine of peace and good will ever rested on his rugged and tempestuous brow, but that it was always covered with storms and dark clouds. When he wrote he dipped his pen in gall. He seemed to delight in a pandemonium of strife and storm and raging passion.

Yet, nothing could be more unlike than his apparent and his real nature. As a matter of fact, he was far from bitter and malignant. But few men had so much good will, such kindliness, such sympathy, such deep and universal charity. True, at a real or a fancied offense, he flared up in a tempest of wrathful indignation. He poured forth a flood of angry and terrible words. But that was the last of the matter unless the offense was repeated. He would laugh heartily, not in a mocking spirit, but in the utmost good nature over what he had said. By that time all anger had passed away and he was ready for peace. The offer of reconciliation was never declined by him. On accepting peace he neither asked nor granted terms. The quarrel was treated as a thing that had never existed; the reconciliation was sincere and complete; there was no looking backward. There was never a time in his life, in my opinion, when he would not have met the friendly approaches of his bitterest enemies half way; indeed, more than half way. His pride and haughty spirit would have kept him from taking the first step, but when taken by his enemy he would have met the offer in the most sincere and generous manner. . . ."

——Temple, Oliver Perry: *Notable Men of Tennessee,* 277-278.

In doing the research preparatory to writing this volume, all the pages of the legislative *Journals,* the Session Laws, and the legislative Resolutions were scrutinized. In addition, original manuscript documents in the State Archives were examined, contemporary newspapers were "worked," and scores of secondary sources were consulted. The writer of this volume desires to leave on record his appraisal of Brownlow. From the "testimony" of the above "witnesses," and from the official record itself, the evidence is preponderate and the presumption very great that "Parson" Brownlow was

THE WRONG MAN IN THE WRONG PLACE AT THE WRONG TIME!

INAUGURAL CEREMONIES OF TENNESSEE GOVERNORS, 1857–1869

Name	Date of Inauguration	Place	Oath of Office Administered By:	Term Ended
ISHAM GREEN HARRIS	Nov. 3, 1857 Nov. 3, 1859 Nov. 1, 1861	Nashville Nashville Nashville	S. D. Frierson, Chancellor Nathaniel Baxter, Circuit Court Judge W. K. Turner, Criminal Court Judge	Nov. 3, 1859 Nov. 1, 1861 Mar. 20, 1862*
ANDREW JOHNSON (Military Governor) Took office on March 12, 1862, and resigned on March 3, 1865.				
WILLIAM GANNAWAY BROWNLOW	Apr. 5, 1865 Oct. 10, 1867	Nashville Nashville	Samuel Milligan, Supreme Court Judge Leonidas Campbell Houck, Circuit Court Judge	Oct. 10, 1867 Feb. 25, 1869

* Extreme difficulty is encountered in trying to determine when the third term of Governor Isham G. Harris ended. He was in Memphis performing the functions of his office when the Legislature adjourned on March 20, 1862. In the meanwhile, Andrew Johnson was appointed Military Governor by President Lincoln and took up his official duties on March 12, 1862 upon his arrival in Nashville. There is no escaping the fact that from March 12 to March 20, 1862, inclusive, Isham G. Harris was civil governor of Tennessee and Andrew Johnson was military governor of Tennessee. Upon the adjournment of the Legislature on March 20, 1862, Governor Harris went immediately south and joined up with the Confederate army in which he remained until the close of the war. There is official evidence that Governor Harris considered himself the civil governor of Tennessee until February 1, 1865. In a legislative committee report[1] in 1869, said committee having been appointed to investigate the status of the Bank of Tennessee, the following statement appeared, to wit: ". . . that Isham G. Harris received of Joel A. Battle, Treasurer of Tennessee, $750.00 in gold coin which is in full of my salary as Governor of Tennessee for the quarter ending the first of February, 1865." Upon the fall of Fort Donelson, early in 1862, the Bank of Tennessee was removed to Chattanooga and later to different points in Georgia. The assets of the bank were seized at Augusta, Georgia and returned to Nashville in 1865, the actual amount of gold coin being $446,719.70. From the above committee report, it is quite clear that Governor Harris and other State officials drew their salaries from 1862 to February, 1865.

[1] *Senate Appendix*, 1870–71, 291–326.

APPENDIX

VOLUME V

📖

CONSTITUTION of the STATE OF TENNESSEE, 1835[1]

"WHEREAS, THE PEOPLE of the territory of the United States, south of the river Ohio, *having the right of admission into the General Government as a Member State thereof, consistent with the Constitution of the United States, and the act of cession of the State of North Carolina, recognizing the ordinance for the government of the territory of the United States, north west of the river Ohio, by their Delegates and Representatives in Convention assembled, did, on the sixth day of February, in the year of our Lord one thousand seven hundred and ninety-six,* ordain and establish a constitution or form of government; *and mutually agreed with each other to form themselves into a free and independent state, by the name of* 'THE STATE OF TENNESSEE'; *and whereas the General Assembly of said* State of Tennessee, *(pursuant to the third section of the tenth article of the Constitution) by an act passed on the twenty-seventh day of November, in the year of our Lord one thousand eight hundred and thirty-three, entitled* 'An act to provide for the calling of a Convention,' *did authorize and provide for the election, by the People, of Delegates and Representatives, to meet at Nashville, in Davidson county, on the third Monday in May, in the year of our Lord one thousand eight hundred and thirty-four,* 'for the purpose of revising, and amending *(or changing)* the Constitution':

WE, *therefore,* the Delegates and Representatives of the People of the State of Tennessee, *elected and in Convention assembled, in pursuance of the said Act of Assembly,* have ordained and established *the following* amended Constitution and form of Government for this State, *which we recommend to the* People of Tennessee *for their ratification; that is to say:*

---

[1] *Journal of the Constitutional Convention,* 1834, 389–411.

ARTICLE I.

DECLARATION OF RIGHTS.

Sec. I. That all power is inherent in the people, and all free governments are founded on their authority, and instituted for their peace, safety and happiness; for the advancement of those ends, they have, at all times, an unalienable and indefeasible right to alter, reform or abolish the government in such manner as they may think proper.

II. That government being instituted for the common benefit, the doctrine of non-resistance against arbitrary power and oppression, is absurd, slavish and destructive to the good and happiness of mankind.

III. That all men have a natural and indefeasible right to worship Almighty God according to the dictates of their own conscience; that no man can, of right, be compelled to attend, erect or support any place of worship, or to maintain any Minister against his consent; that no human authority can, in any case whatever, control or interfere with the rights of conscience; and that no preference shall ever be given, by law, to any religious establishment or mode of worship.

IV. That no religious test shall ever be required as a qualification to any office or public trust under this State.

V. That elections shall be free and equal.

VI. That the right of trial by jury shall remain inviolate.

VII. That the people shall be secure in their persons, houses, papers and possessions, from unreasonable searches and seizures; and that general warrants, whereby an officer may be commanded to search suspected places, without evidence of the fact committed, or to seize any person or persons not named, whose offences are not particularly described and supported by evidence, are dangerous to liberty and ought not to be granted.

VIII. That no free man shall be taken or imprisoned, or disseized of his freehold, liberties or privileges, or outlawed, or exiled, or in any manner destroyed or deprived of his life, liberty or property, but by the judgment of his peers, or the law of the land.

IX. That in all criminal prosecutions, the accused hath a right to be heard by himself and his counsel; to demand the nature and cause of the accusation against him, and to have a copy thereof; to meet the witnesses face to face; to have compulsory process for obtaining witnesses in his favor; and in prosecutions by indictment or presentment, a speedy public trial, by an impartial jury of the county or district in which the crime shall have been committed; and shall not be compelled to give evidence against himself.

X. That no person shall, for the same offence, be twice put in jeopardy of life or limb.

XI. That laws made for the punishment of facts committed previous to the existence of such laws, and by them only declared criminal, are contrary to the principles of a free government; wherefore no *ex post facto* law shall be made.

XII. That no conviction shall work corruption of blood or forfeiture of estate. The estate of such persons as shall destroy their own lives, shall descend or vest as in case of natural death. If any person be killed by casualty, there shall be no forfeiture in consequence thereof.

XIII. That no person arrested or confined in jail, shall be treated with unnecessary rigor.

XIV. That no free man shall be put to answer any criminal charge but by presentment, indictment or impeachment.

XV. That all prisoners shall be bailable by sufficient sureties unless for capital offences when the proof is evident or the presumption great. And the privilege of the writ of *habeas corpus* shall not be suspended, unless when in case of rebellion or invasion the public safety may require it.

XVI. That excessive bail shall not be required, nor excessive fines imposed, nor cruel and unusual punishments inflicted.

XVII. That all courts shall be open; and every man, for an injury done him in his lands, goods, person, or reputation, shall have remedy by due course of law, and right and justice administered without sale, denial, or delay. Suits may be brought against the State in such manner, and in such courts, as the Legislature may by law direct.

XVIII. That the person of a debtor, where there is not strong presumption of fraud, shall not be continued in prison after delivering up his estate for the benefit of his creditor or creditors, in such manner as shall be prescribed by law.

XIX. That the printing presses shall be free to every person who undertakes to examine the proceedings of the Legislature, or of any branch or officer of Government; and no law shall ever be made to restrain the right thereof. The free communication of thoughts and opinions is one of the invaluable rights of man, and every citizen may freely speak, write and print on any subject, being responsible for the abuse of that liberty. But in prosecutions for the publication of papers investigating the official conduct of officers or men in public capacity, the truth thereof may be given in evidence; and in all indictments for libels, the jury shall have a right to determine the law and the facts, under the direction of the Court, as in other criminal cases.

XX. That no retrospective law, or law impairing the obligations of contracts, shall be made.

XXI. That no man's particular services shall be demanded, or property taken, or applied to public use, without the consent of his representatives, or without just compensation being made therefor.

XXII. That perpetuities and monopolies are contrary to the genius of a free State, and shall not be allowed.

XXIII. That the citizens have a right, in a peaceable manner, to assemble together, for their common good, to instruct their representatives, and to apply to those invested with the powers of government for redress of grievances or other proper purposes, by address or remonstrance.

XXIV. That the sure and certain defence of a free people, is a well regulated militia: and, as standing armies in time of peace are dangerous to freedom, they ought to be avoided, as far as the circumstances and safety of the community will admit; and that in all cases the military shall be kept in strict subordination to the civil authority.

XXV. That no citizen of this State, except such as are employed in the army of the United States, or militia in actual service, shall be subjected to corporeal punishment under the martial law.

XXVI. That the free white men of this State have a right to keep and to bear arms for their common defence.

XXVII. That no soldier shall, in time of peace, be quartered in any house without the consent of the owner; nor in time of war, but in a manner prescribed by law.

XXVIII. That no citizen of this State shall be compelled to bear arms, provided he will pay an equivalent, to be ascertained by law.

XXIX. That an equal participation of the free navigation of the Mississippi, is one of the inherent rights of the citizens of this State: it cannot, therefore, be conceded to any prince, potentate, power, person or persons whatever.

XXX. That no hereditary emoluments, privileges, or honors, shall ever be granted or conferred in this State.

XXXI. That the limits and boundaries of this State be ascertained, it is declared they are as hereafter mentioned, that is to say: Beginning on the extreme height of the Stone mountain, at the place where the line of Virginia intersects it, in latitude thirty-six degrees and thirty minutes north; running thence along the extreme height of the said mountain to the place where Watauga river breaks through it; thence a direct course to the top of the Yellow mountain, where Bright's road crosses the same; thence along the ridge of said mountain between the waters of Doe river and the waters of Rock creek, to the place where the road crosses the Iron mountain; from thence along the extreme height of said mountain, to the place where Nolichucky river runs through the same; thence to the top of Bald mountain; thence along the extreme height of said mountain, to the Painted Rock, on French Broad river; thence along the highest ridge of said mountain, to the place where it is called the Great Iron or Smoky mountain; thence along the extreme height of said mountain, to the place where it is called Unicoi or Unaka mountain, between the Indian towns of Cowee and Old Chota; thence along the main ridge of the said mountain, to the southern boundary of this State, as described in the act of cession of North Carolina to the United States of America: and that all the territory, lands and waters lying west of the said line, as before mentioned, and contained within the chartered limits of the State of North Carolina, are within the boundaries and limits of this State, over which the people have the right of exercising sovereignty and the right of soil, so far as is consistent with the constitution of the United States, recognizing the articles of confederation, the bill of rights, and constitution of North Carolina, the cession act of the said State, and the ordinance of Congress for the government of the territory north west of the Ohio: *provided*, nothing herein contained shall extend to affect the claim or claims of individuals, to any part of the soil which is recognized to them by the aforesaid cession act: *and provided also*, that the limits and jurisdiction of this State shall extend to any other land and territory now acquired, or that may hereafter be acquired by compact or agreement with other States or otherwise, although such land and territory are not included within the boundaries herein before designated.

XXXII. The people residing south of French Broad and Holston between the rivers Tennessee and Big Pigeon, are entitled to the right of pre-emption and occupancy of that tract.

ARTICLE II.

I. The powers of the Government shall be divided into three distinct departments; the Legislative, Executive and Judicial.

II. No person or persons belonging to one of these departments, shall exercise any of the powers properly belonging to either of the others, except in the cases herein directed or permitted.

III. The Legislative authority of this State shall be vested in a General Assembly, which shall consist of a Senate and House of Representatives, both dependent on the people.

IV. An enumeration of the qualified voters and an apportionment of the Representatives in the General Assembly, shall be made in the year one thousand eight hundred and forty-one, and within every subsequent term of ten years.

V. The number of Representatives shall, at the several periods of making the enumeration, be apportioned among the several counties or districts according to the number of qualified voters in each; and shall not exceed seventy-five, until the population of the State shall be one million and a half; and shall never thereafter exceed ninety-nine; *provided,* that any county having two-thirds of the ratio, shall be entitled to one member.

VI. The number of Senators shall, at the several periods of making the enumeration, be apportioned among the several counties or districts, according to the number of qualified electors in each, and shall not exceed one-third the number of Representatives. In apportioning the Senators among the different counties, the fraction that may be lost by any county or counties, in the apportionment of Members to the House of Representatives, shall be made up to such county or counties in the Senate as near as may be practicable. When a district is composed of two or more counties, they shall be adjoining; and no county shall be divided in forming a district.

VII. The first election for Senators and Representatives shall be held on the first Thursday in August, one thousand eight hundred and thirty-five; and forever thereafter, elections for Members of the General Assembly shall be held once in two years, on the first Thursday in August; said elections shall terminate the same day.

VIII. The first session of the General Assembly shall commence on the first Monday in October, one thousand eight hundred and thirty-five; and forever thereafter, the General Assembly shall meet on the first Monday in October, next ensuing the election.

IX. No person shall be a Representative, unless he shall be a citizen of the United States of the age of twenty-one years, and shall have been a citizen of this State for three years, and a resident in the county he represents one year immediately preceding the election.

X. No person shall be a Senator unless he shall be a citizen of the United States, of the age of thirty years, and shall have resided thee [three] years in this State, and one year in the county or district, immediately preceding the election. No Senator or Representative shall, during the time for which he was elected, be eligible to any office or place of trust, the appointment to which is vested in the Executive or the General Assembly, except to the office of Trustee of a literary institution.

XI. The Senate and House of Representatives, when assembled, shall each choose a Speaker and its other officers, be judges of the qualifications and election of its members, and sit upon its own adjournments from day to day. Two-thirds of each House shall constitute a quorum to do business; but a smaller number may adjourn from day to day, and may be authorized by law to compel the attendance of absent members.

XII. Each House may determine the rules of its proceedings, punish its members for disorderly behaviour, and, with the concurrence of two-thirds, expel a member, but not a second time for the same offence; and shall have all other powers necessary for a branch of the Legislature of a free State.

XIII. Senators and Representatives shall in all cases, except treason, felony or breach of the peace, be privileged from arrest during the session of the General Assembly, and in going to and returning from the same; and, for any speech or debate in either House, they shall not be questioned in any other place.

XIV. Each House may punish by imprisonment, during its session, any person not a Member, who shall be guilty of disrespect to the House, by any disorderly or contemptuous behaviour in its presence.

XV. When vacancies happen in either House, the Governor for the time being, shall issue writs of election to fill such vacancies.

XVI. Neither House shall, during its session, adjourn without consent of the other for more than three days, nor to any other place than that in which the two Houses shall be sitting.

XVII. Bills may originate in either house, but may be amended, altered or rejected, by the other.

XVIII. Every bill shall be read once on three different days, and be passed each time in the House where it originated, before transmission to the other. No bill shall become a law, until it shall be read and passed on three different days in each House, and be signed by the respective Speakers.

XIX. After a bill has been rejected, no bill containing the same substance shall be passed into a law during the same session.

XX. The style of the laws of this State shall be, *'Be it enacted by the General Assembly of the State of Tennessee.'*

XXI. Each House shall keep a journal of its proceedings, and publish it, except such parts as the welfare of the State may require to be kept secret; the ayes and noes shall be taken in each House upon the final passage of every bill of a general character, and bills making appropriations of public moneys; and the ayes and noes of the members on any question shall, at the request of any two of them, be entered on the journal.

XXII. The doors of each House and of Committees of the Whole, shall be kept open, unless when the business shall be such as ought to be kept secret.

XXIII. The sum of four dollars per day, and four dollars for every twenty-five miles travelling to and from the Seat of Government, shall be allowed to the Members of the first General Assembly, as a compensation for their services. The compensation of the Members of the succeeding Legislatures, shall be ascertained by law; but no law increasing the compensation of the Members shall take effect until the commencement of the next regular session after such law shall have been enacted.

XXIV. No money shall be drawn from the treasury, but in consequence of appropriations made by law: and an accurate statement of the receipts and expenditures of the public money, shall be attached to and published with the laws at the rise of each stated session of the General Assembly.

XXV. No person, who heretofore hath been, or may hereafter be, a collector or holder of public moneys, shall have a seat in either House of the General Assembly, until such person shall have accounted for and paid into the treasury, all sums for which he may be accountable or liable.

XXVI. No Judge of any court of law or equity, Secretary of State, Attorney General, Register, Clerk of any court of record, or person holding any office under the authority of the United States, shall have a seat in the General Assembly; nor shall any person in this State hold more than one lucrative office at the same time: *Provided,* that no appointment in the militia, or to the office of Justice of the Peace, shall be considered a lucrative office, or operate as a disqualification to a seat in either House of the General Assembly.

XXVII. Any member of either House of the General Assembly shall have liberty to dissent from, and protest against, any act or resolve which he may think injurious to the public or to any individual, and to have the reasons for his dissent entered on the journals.

XXVIII. All lands liable to taxation, held by deed, grant, or entry, town lots, bank stock, slaves between the ages of twelve and fifty years, and such other property as the Legislature may from time to time deem expedient, shall be taxable. All property shall be taxed according to its value; that value to be ascertained in such manner as the Legislature shall direct, so that the same shall be equal and uniform throughout the State. No one species of property from which a tax may be collected, shall be taxed higher than any other species of property of equal value. But the Legislature shall have power to tax merchants, pedlars, and privileges, in such manner as they may, from time to time, direct. A tax on white polls shall be laid, in such manner and of such an amount, as may be prescribed by law.

XXIX. The General Assembly shall have power to authorize the several Counties and Incorporated Towns in this State, to impose taxes for county and corporation purposes respectively, in such manner as shall be prescribed by law; and all property shall be taxed according to its value, upon the principles established in regard to State taxation.

XXX. No article manufactured of the produce of this State, shall be taxed otherwise than to pay inspection fees.

XXXI. The General Assembly shall have no power to pass laws for the emancipation of Slaves, without the consent of their owner or owners.

ARTICLE III.

I. The Supreme Executive power of this State, shall be vested in a Governor.

II. The Governor shall be chosen by the electors of the Members of the General Assembly, at the times and places where they shall respectively vote for the members thereof. The returns of every election for Governor shall be sealed up, and transmitted to the seat of government, by the returning officers, directed to the Speaker of the Senate, who shall open and publish them in the presence of a majority of the members of each House of the General Assembly. The person having the highest number of votes, shall be Governor; but if two or more shall be equal, and highest in votes, one of them shall be chosen Governor by joint vote of both Houses of the General Assembly. Contested elections for Governor, shall be determined by both Houses of the General Assembly, in such manner as shall be prescribed by law.

III. He shall be at least thirty years of age, shall be a citizen of the United States, and shall have been a citizen of this State seven years next before his election.

IV. The Governor shall hold his office for two years, and until his successor shall be elected and qualified. He shall not be eligible more than six years in any term of eight.

V. He shall be commander-in-chief of the army and navy of this State, and of the militia, except when they shall be called into the service of the United States.

VI. He shall have power to grant reprieves and pardons, after conviction, except in cases of impeachment.

VII. He shall, at stated times, receive a compensation for his services, which shall not be increased or diminished during the period for which he shall have been elected.

VIII. He may require information in writing, from the officers in the executive department, upon any subject relating to the duties of their respective offices.

IX. He may, on extraordinary occasions, convene the General Assembly, by proclamation; and shall state to them, when assembled, the purposes for which they shall have been convened; but they shall enter on no legislative business, except that for which they were specially called together.

X. He shall take care that the laws be faithfully executed.

XI. He shall, from time to time, give to the General Assembly, information of the state of the government, and recommend to their consideration such measures as he shall judge expedient.

XII. In case of the removal of the Governor from office, or of his death, or resignation, the powers and duties of the office shall devolve on the Speaker of the Senate; and in case of the death, removal from office, or resignation of the Speaker of the Senate, the powers and duties of the office shall devolve on the Speaker of the House of Representatives.

XIII. No member of Congress, or person holding any office under the United States, or this State, shall execute the office of Governor.

XIV. When any officer, the right of whose appointment is by this Constitution vested in the General Assembly, shall, during the recess, die, or the office, by the expiration of the term, or by other means, become vacant, the Governor shall have the power to fill such vacancy, by granting a temporary commission, which shall expire at the end of the next session of the Legislature.

XV. There shall be a Seal of this State, which shall be kept by the Governor, and used by him officially, and shall be called the *Great Seal of the State of Tennessee.*

XVI. All grants and commissions shall be in the name and by the authority of the State of Tennessee, be sealed with the State Seal, and signed by the Governor.

XVII. A secretary of State shall be appointed by joint vote of the General Assembly, and commissioned during the term of four years: he shall keep a fair register of all the official acts and proceedings of the Governor; and shall, when required, lay the same, and all papers, minutes and vouchers relative thereto, before the General Assembly: and shall perform such other duties as shall be enjoined by law.

ARTICLE IV.

I. Every free white man of the age of twenty-one years, being a citizen of the United States, and a citizen of the County wherein he may offer his vote, six months next preceding the day of election, shall be entitled to vote for Members of the General Assembly, and other civil officers, for the County or District in which he resides: *provided,* that no person shall be disqualified from voting in any election on account of color, who is now by the laws of this State, a competent witness in a court of justice against a white man. All free men of color, shall be exempt from military duty in time of peace, and also from paying a free poll tax.

II. Laws may be passed excluding from the right of suffrage, persons who may be convicted of infamous crimes.

III. Electors shall in all cases, except treason, felony or breach of the peace, be privileged from arrest or summons, during their attendance at elections, and in going to and returning from them.

IV. In all elections to be made by the General Assembly, the Members thereof shall vote *viva voce;* and their votes shall be entered on the journal. All other elections shall be by ballot.

ARTICLE V.

I. The House of Representatives shall have the sole power of impeachment.

II. All impeachments shall be tried by the Senate; when sitting for that purpose, the Senators shall be upon oath or affirmation. No person shall be convicted without the concurrence of two-thirds of the Senators sworn to try the officer impeached.

III. The House of Representatives shall elect, from their own body, three Members, whose duty it shall be to prosecute impeachments. No impeachment shall be tried until the Legislature shall have adjourned *sine die,* when the Senate shall proceed to try such impeachment.

IV. The Governor, Judges of the Supreme Court, Judges of Inferior Courts, Chancellors, Attorneys for the State, and Secretary of State, shall be liable to impeachment, whenever they may, in the opinion of the House of Representatives, commit any crime in their official capacity, which may require disqualification; but judgment shall only extend to removal from office, and disqualification to fill any office thereafter. The party shall, nevertheless, be liable to indictment, trial, judgment and punishment, according to law.

V. Justices of the Peace, and other civil officers, not hereinbefore mentioned, for crimes or misdemeanors in office, shall be liable to indictment in such courts as the Legislature may direct; and upon conviction, shall be removed from office, by said court, as if found guilty on impeachment; and shall be subject to such other punishment as may be prescribed by law.

ARTICLE VI.

I. The Judicial power of this State, shall be vested in one Supreme Court, in such Inferior Courts as the Legislature shall from time to time ordain and establish, and the Judges thereof and in Justices of the Peace: The Legislature may also vest such jurisdiction as may be deemed necessary in Corporation Courts.

II. The Supreme Court shall be composed of three Judges, one of whom shall reside in each of the grand divisions of the State; the concurrence of two of said Judges, shall in every case be necessary to a decision. The jurisdiction of this Court shall be appellate only, under such restrictions and regulations as may from time to time be prescribed by law; but it may possess such other jurisdiction as is now conferred by law on the present Supreme Court. Said Courts shall be held at one place, and at one place only, in each of the three grand divisions in the State.

III. The General Assembly shall, by joint vote of both Houses, appoint Judges of the several Courts of law and equity; but courts may be established to be holden by Justices of the Peace. Judges of the Supreme Court shall be thirty-five years of age, and shall be elected for the term of twelve years.

IV. The Judges of such Inferior Courts as the Legislature may establish, shall be thirty years of age, and shall be elected for the term of twelve years.

V. The Legislature shall elect Attorneys for the State, by joint vote of both Houses, of the General Assembly, who shall hold their offices for the term of six years. In all cases where an Attorney for any district fails or refuses to attend, and prosecute according to law, the court shall have power to appoint an attorney *pro tempore*.

VI. Judges and Attorneys for the State, may be removed from office by a concurrent vote of both Houses of the General Assembly, each House voting separately; but two-thirds of all the Members elected to each House must concur in such vote: the vote shall be determined by ayes and noes, and the names of the Members voting for or against the Judge or Attorney for the State, together with the cause or causes of removal, shall be entered on the journals of each House respectively. The Judge or Attorney for the State, against whom the Legislature may be about to proceed, shall receive notice thereof, accompanied with a copy of the causes alleged for his removal, at least ten days before the day on which either House of the General Assembly shall act thereupon.

VII. The Judges of the Supreme and Inferior Courts, shall, at stated times, receive a compensation for their services, to be ascertained by law, which shall not be increased or diminished, during the time for which they are elected. They shall not be allowed any fees or perquisites of office, nor hold any other office of trust or profit under this State or the United States.

VIII. The jurisdiction of such Inferior Courts, as the Legislature may from time to time establish, shall be regulated by law.

IX. Judges shall not charge Juries with respect to matters of fact, but may state the testimony and declare the law.

X. The Judges or Justices of such Inferior Courts of law as the Legislature may establish, shall have power, in all civil cases, to issue writs of *certiorari* to remove any cause or transcript thereof, from any inferior jurisdiction, into said court on sufficient cause supported by oath or affirmation.

XI. No Judge of the Supreme or Inferior Courts, shall preside on the trial of any cause, in the event of which he may be interested or where either of the parties shall be connected with him by affinity or consanguinity, within such degrees as may be prescribed by law, or in which he may have been of counsel, or in which he may have presided in any Inferior Court, except by consent of all the parties. In case all or any of the Judges of the Supreme Court, shall be thus disqualified from presiding on the trial of any cause or causes, the Court, or the Judges thereof, shall certify the same to the Governor of the State, and he shall forthwith specially commission the requisite number of men of law knowledge, for the trial and determination thereof. In case of sickness of any of the Judges of the Supreme or Inferior Courts, so that they or any of them are unable to attend, the Legislature shall be authorized to make provision by general laws, that special Judges may be appointed to attend said Courts.

XII. All writs and other process shall run in the name of the State of Tennessee; and bear test and be signed by the respective clerks. Indictments shall conclude, *'against the peace and dignity of the State.'*

XIII. Judges of the Supreme Court shall appoint their Clerks, who shall hold their offices for the period of six years. Chancellor (if Courts of Chancery shall be established) shall appoint their Clerks and Masters, who shall hold their offices for the period of six years. Clerks of such Inferior Courts as may be hereafter established, which shall be required to be holden in the respective counties of this State, shall be elected by the qualified voters thereof, for the term of four years; they shall be removed from office for malfeasance, incompetency or neglect of duty, in such manner as may be prescribed by law.

XIV. No fine shall be laid on any citizen of this State, that shall exceed fifty dollars; unless it shall be assessed by a jury of his peers, who shall assess the fine at the time they find the fact, if they think the fine should be more than fifty dollars.

XV. The different counties in this State shall be laid off as the General Assembly may direct, into districts of convenient size, so that the whole number in each County shall not be more than twenty-five, or four for every one hundred square miles. There shall be two Justices of the Peace and one Constable elected in each district, by the qualified voters therein, except districts including county towns, which shall elect three Justices and two Constables. The jurisdiction of said officers shall be co-extensive with the County. Justices of the Peace shall be elected for the term of six, and Constables for the term of two years. Upon the removal of either of said officers from the district in which he was elected, his office shall become vacant from the time of such removal. Justices of the Peace shall be commissioned by the Governor. The Legislature shall have power to provide for the appointment of an additional number of Justices of the Peace in incorporated towns.

ARTICLE VII.

I. There shall be elected in each County, by the qualified voters therein, one Sheriff, one Trustee, and one Register; the Sheriff and Trustee for two years, and the Register for four years; *provided*, that no person shall be eligible to the office of Sheriff more than six years in any term of eight years. There shall be elected for each County, by the Justices of the Peace, one Coroner and one Ranger, who shall hold their offices for two years. Said officers shall be removed for malfeasance, or neglect of duty, in such manner as may be prescribed by law.

II. Should a vacancy occur, subsequent to an election, in the office of sheriff, trustee, or register, it shall be filled by the justices; if in that of the clerks to be elected by the people, it shall be filled by the courts; and the person so appointed, shall continue in office until his successor shall be elected and qualified; and such office shall be filled by the qualified voters at the first election for any of the county officers.

III. There shall be a Treasurer or Treasurers appointed for the State, by the joint vote of both Houses of the General Assembly, who shall hold his or their offices for two years.

IV. The election of all officers, and the filling of all vacancies that may happen, by death, resignation, or removal, not otherwise directed or provided for by this Constitution, shall be made in such manner as the Legislature shall direct.

V. The Legislature shall provide, that the election of the county and other officers by the people, shall not take place at the time that the general elections are held for Members of Congress, Members of the Legislature, and Governor. The elections shall commence and terminate on the same day.

ARTICLE VIII.

I. All Militia officers shall be elected by persons subject to military duty, within the bounds of their several companies, battalions, regiments, brigades and divisions, under such rules and regulations as the Legislature may, from time to time, direct and establish.

II. The Governor shall appoint the Adjutant General and his other Staff Officers; the Majors General, Brigadiers General and commanding officers or regiments, shall respectively appoint their Staff Officers.

III. The Legislature shall pass laws, exempting citizens belonging to any sect or denomination of religion, the tenets of which are known to be opposed to the bearing of arms, from attending private and general musters.

ARTICLE IX.

I. Whereas, Ministers of the Gospel are, by their profession, dedicated to God and the care of souls, and ought not to be diverted from the great duties of their functions; therefore, no Minister of the Gospel or Priest of any denomination whatever, shall be eligible to a seat in either House of the Legislature.

II. No person who denies the being of a God, or a future state of rewards and punishments, shall hold any office in the civil department of this State.

III. Any person who shall, after the adoption of this Constitution, fight a duel, or knowingly be the bearer of a challenge to fight a duel, or send or accept a challenge for that purpose, or be an aider or abettor in fighting a duel, shall be deprived of the right to hold any office of honor or profit in this State, and shall be punished otherwise, in such manner as the Legislature may prescribe.

ARTICLE X.

I. Every person who shall be chosen or appointed to any office of trust or profit, under this Constitution, or any law made in pursuance thereof, shall, before entering on the duties thereof, take an oath to support the Constitution of this State, and of the United States, and an oath of office.

II. Each Member of the Senate and House of Representatives, shall before they proceed to business, take an oath or affirmation, to support the Constitution of this State, and of the United States, and also the following oath: 'I, ..., do solemnly swear (or affirm,) that, as a Member of this General Assembly, I will, in all appointments, vote without favor, affection, partiality, or prejudice; and that I will not propose or assent to any bill, vote or resolution, which shall appear to me injurious to the people, or consent to any act or thing whatever, that shall have a tendency to lessen or abridge their rights and privileges, as declared by the Constitution of this State.

III. Any elector who shall receive any gift or reward for his vote, in meat, drink, money, or otherwise, shall suffer such punishment as the laws shall direct. And any person who shall directly or indirectly give, promise or bestow, any such reward to be elected, shall thereby be rendered incapable for six years, to serve in the office for which he was elected, and be subject to such further punishment, as the Legislature shall direct.

IV. New Counties may be established by the Legislature, to consist of not less than three hundred and fifty square miles, and which shall contain a population of four hundred and fifty qualified voters. No line of such county shall approach the court house of any old County from which it may be taken, nearer than twelve miles. No part of a county shall be taken to form a new County or a part thereof, without the consent of a majority of the qualified voters in such part taken off. And in all cases where an old County may be reduced for the purpose of forming a new one, the seat of justice in said old county shall not be removed without the concurrence of two-thirds of both branches of the Legislature, nor shall said old county be reduced to less than six hundred and twenty-five square miles: *provided,* however that the county of Bedford may be reduced to four hundred and seventy-five square miles; and there shall not be laid off more than one new county on the West, and one on the East, adjoining the county of Bedford, and no new county line shall run nearer than eleven and a half miles of the seat of justice of said county. The line of a new county may run within eleven miles of the seat of justice of Franklin county; *provided,* it does not reduce said county to less contents than six hundred and twenty-five square miles. The counties of Carter, Rhea, Tipton, Dyer and Sullivan are excepted out of the provisions of this section: the county of Humphreys may be divided, at such time as may be prescribed by the Legislature, making the Tennessee river the dividing line; a majority of the qualified voters of said county voting in favor of said division: the counties of Carter, Rhea and Humphreys, shall not be divided into more than two counties each; nor shall more than one new county be taken out of the territory now comprising the counties of Tipton and Dyer; nor shall the seats of justice in the counties of Rhea, Carter, Tipton and Dyer, be removed, without the concurrence of two-thirds of both branches of the Legislature. The county of Sullivan may be reduced below the contents of six hundred and twenty-five square miles, but the line of any new county which may hereafter be laid off shall not approach the county seat of said county nearer than ten miles. The counties of Marion and Bledsoe shall not be reduced below one thousand qualified voters each, in forming a new county or counties.

V. The citizens who may be included in any new county, shall vote with the county or counties from which they may have been stricken off, for members of Congress, for Governor and for members of the General Assembly, until the next apportionment of members to the General Assembly after the establishment of such new county.

ARTICLE XI.

I. All laws and ordinances now in force and use in this State, not inconsistent with this Constitution, shall continue in force and use, until they shall expire, be altered or repealed by the Legislature.

II. Nothing contained in this Constitution, shall impair the validity of any debts or contracts, or effect any rights of property, or any suits, actions, rights of action, or other proceedings in courts of justice.

III. Any amendment or amendments to this Constitution may be proposed in the Senate or House of Representatives; and if the same shall be agreed to by a majority of all the members elected to each of the two Houses, such proposed amendment or amendments shall be entered on their journals, with the yeas and nays thereon, and referred to the General Assembly then next to be chosen: and shall be published for six months previous to the time of making such choice. And if in the General Assembly next chosen as aforesaid, such proposed amendment or amendments shall be agreed to by two-thirds of all the members elected to each House, then it shall be the duty of the General Assembly to submit such proposed amendment or amendments to the people, in such manner, and at such time, as the General Assembly shall prescribe. And if the people shall approve and ratify such amendment or amendments, by a majority of all the citizens of the State, voting for Representatives, voting in their favor, such amendment or amendments shall become part of this Constitution. When any amendment or amendments to the Constitution shall be proposed in pursuance of the foregoing provisions, the same shall at each of the said sessions be read three times on three several days in each House. The Legislature shall not propose amendments to the Constitution, oftener than once in six years.

IV. The Legislature shall have no power to grant divorces, but may authorize the courts of justice to grant them for such causes as may be specified by law: *provided*, that such laws be general and uniform in their operation throughout the State.

V. The Legislature shall have no power to authorize lotteries for any purpose, and shall pass laws to prohibit the sale of lottery tickets in this State.

VI. The Legislature shall fix the rate of interest—and the rate so established shall be equal and uniform throughout the State.

VII. The Legislature shall have no power to suspend any general law for the benefit of any particular individual, nor to pass any law for the benefits of individuals inconsistent with the general laws of the land; nor to pass any law granting to any individual or individuals, rights, privileges, immunities, or exemptions, other than such as may be, by the same law, extended to any member of the community, who may be able to bring himself within the provisions of such law: *provided* always, the Legislature shall have power to grant such charters of corporation as they may deem expedient for the public good.

VIII. The Legislature shall have the right to vest such powers in the courts of justice, with regard to private and local affairs, as may be deemed expedient.

IX. A well regulated system of internal improvement is calculated to develop the resources of the State, and promote the happiness and prosperity of her citizens; therefore it ought to be encouraged by the General Assembly.

X. Knowledge, learning, and virtue, being essential to the preservation of republican institutions, and the diffusion of the opportunities and advantages of education throughout the different portions of the State, being highly conducive to the promotion of this end; it shall be the duty of the General Assembly in all future periods of this government, to cherish literature and science. And the fund called the *common school fund,* and all the lands and proceeds thereof, dividends, stocks, and other property of every description whatever, heretofore by law appropriated by the General Assembly of this State for the use of common schools, and all such as shall hereafter be appropriated, shall remain a *perpetual fund,* the principal of which shall never be diminished by legislative appropriation, and the interest thereof shall be inviolably appropriated to the support and encouragement of common schools throughout the State, and for the equal benefit of all the people thereof; and no law shall be made authorizing said fund, or any part thereof, to be diverted to any other use than the support and encouragement of common schools; and it shall be the duty of the General Assembly, to appoint a Board of Commissioners, for such term of time as they may think proper, who shall have the general superintendence of said funds, and who shall make a report of the condition of the same, from time to time, under such rules, regulations and restrictions as may be required by law; *provided,* that if at any time hereafter a division of the public lands of the United States, or of the money arising from the sales of such lands, shall be made among the individual States, the part of such lands, or money, coming to this State, shall be devoted to the purposes of education and internal improvements; and shall never be applied to any other purpose.

XI. The above provisions shall not be construed to prevent the Legislature from carrying into effect any laws that have been passed in favor of the colleges, universities or academies, or from authorizing heirs or distributees to receive and enjoy escheated property, under such rules and regulations as from time to time may be prescribed by law.

XII. The Declaration of Rights hereto prefixed, is declared to be a part of the Constitution of this State, and shall never be violated on any pretence whatever. And to guard against transgression of the high powers we have delegated, we declare every thing in the Bill of Rights contained, is excepted out of the general powers of government, and shall forever remain inviolate.

Schedule.

I. That no inconvenience may arise from a change of the Constitution, it is declared, that all officers, civil and military, shall continue to hold their offices; and all the functions appertaining to the same shall be exercised and performed according to the existing laws and Constitution, until the end of the first session of the General Assembly, which shall sit under this Constitution, and until the government can be re-organized and put into operation under this Constitution, in such manner as the first General Assembly under this Constitution shall be held in Nashville.

II. The General Assembly which shall sit after the first apportionment of representation under the new Constitution, to wit, in the year one thousand eight hundred and forty-three, shall, within the first week after the commencement of the session, designate and fix the seat of government; and when so fixed; it shall not be removed except by the consent of two-thirds of the members of both Houses of the General Assembly. The first and second sessions of the General Assembly under this Constitution shall be held at Nashville.

III. Until a land office shall be opened, so as to enable the citizens south and west of the congressional reservation line, to obtain titles upon their claims of occupancy, those who hold lands by virtue of such claims, shall be eligible to serve in all capacities where a freehold is, by the laws of the State, made a requisite qualification.

Done in Convention at Nashville, this thirtieth day of August, one thousand eight hundred and thirty-four, and of the Independence of the United States of America the fifty-ninth. In testimony whereof, we have hereunto subscribed our names.

WILLIAM B. CARTER, *President.*

ROBERT ALLEN,
HUGH C. ARMSTRONG,
ADAM R. ALEXANDER,
RICHARD BRADSHAW,
ROBERT M. BURTON,
WILLIE BLOUNT,
MACLIN CROSS,
JAMES GRAY,
NEWTON CANNON,
WILLIAM G. CHILDRESS,
TERRY H. CAHAL,
ROBERT L. COBBS,
RICHARD CHEATHAM,
BURCHETT DOUGLASS,
FRANCIS B. FOGG,
GRAY GARRETT,
JAMES GILLESPY,
BOLLING GORDON,
CALLAWAY HODGES,
ISAAC HILL,
ADAM HUNTSMAN,
WEST H. HUMPHREYS,
NELSON I. HESS,
JOHN KELLY,
ANDREW A. KINCANNON,
JOSEPH KINCAID,
PETER KENDALL,
BRADLEY KIMBROUGH,

WILLIAM LEDBETTER,
WILLIAM H. LOVING,
ABRAHAM MCCLELLAN,
ROBERT J. MCKINNEY,
JOSEPH A. MABRY,
JOHN MCGAUGHEY,
JOHN MONTGOMERY,
GEORGE W. L. MARR,
JOHN NEIL,
RICHARD NELSON,
THOMAS C. PORTER,
JOHN PURDY,
WILLIAM C. ROADMAN,
GEORGE W. RICHARDSON,
HENRY RIDLEY,
JULIUS C. N. ROBERTSON,
MATTHEW STEPHENSON,
WILLIAM T. SENTER,
JAMES W. SMITH,
WILLIAM C. SMARTT,
HENRY SHARP,
JAMES SCOTT,
ESSIE URY,
JOHN WHITSON,
ISAAC WALTON,
JOHN J. WHITE,
JONATHAN WEBSTER,
ROBERT WEAKLEY.

WILLIAM K. HILL, *Secretary.*"

MEMBERS OF THE GENERAL ASSEMBLY OF TENNESSEE

THIRTY-SECOND GENERAL ASSEMBLY

Held at Nashville, October 5, 1857–March 22, 1858.

SENATORS—J. E. T. Harris, Johnson, Carter, Washington, and Sullivan; J. B. Heiskell, Hawkins, Hancock and Jefferson; Lloyd Bullen, Greene, Cocke, Sevier, and Blount; F. H. Bratcher, Claiborne, Grainger, Anderson, and Campbell; H. J. Welcker, Knox and Roane; J. D. Goodpasture, Morgan, Scott, Fentress, and Overton; J. J. Wright, Meigs, McMinn, Polk, and Monroe; J. C. Burch, Rhea, Bledsoe, Bradley, Hamilton, and Marion; Holland Denton, White, Jackson, and Macon; W. S. Munday, Smith and Sumner; J. F. Goodner, Wilson and DeKalb; W. L. McConnico, Rutherford and Williamson; W. P. Davis, Bedford and Marshall; B. J. Hill, Warren, Cannon, Coffee, Grundy, and Van Buren; Joel J. Jones, Franklin and Lincoln; Thomas J. Brown, Giles, Lawrence, and Wayne; W. C. Whitthorne, Maury, Lewis, Hickman, and Dickson; A. F. Goff, Davidson; Thomas Menees, Robertson, Montgomery, and Stewart; S. L. Ross, Benton, Humphreys, Perry, Decatur, and Henderson; A. G. McDougal, Hardin, McNairy, and Hardeman; W. E. Travis, Henry, Weakley, and Obion; Isaac J. Roach, Gibson, Carroll, and Dyer; J. Knox Walker, Fayette and Shelby; A. R. Reid, Madison, Haywood, Lauderdale, and Tipton.

REPRESENTATIVES—A. L. Gammon, Sullivan; W. M. Bayless, Washington; David R. Johnson, Greene; Jacob Hamilton, Hawkins; J. H. Randolph, Cocke; William Brazelton, Jr., Jefferson; D. C. Senter, Grainger; W. A. L. Blackburn, Claiborne; Moses White, Knox; S. T. Bicknell, Blount; Elisha E. Griffith, Monroe; S. T. Turner, Roane; A. J. Dodson, McMinn; George W. Rowles, Bradley; J. W. White, Hamilton; R. S. Raulston, Marion; Tazewell W. Newman, Franklin; H. J. St. John, Cannon; G. M. Smartt, Warren; William Renshaw, White; James R. Copeland, Overton; S. S. Stanton, Jackson; R. C. Saunders, Smith; A. M. Savage, DeKalb; D. S. Donelson, Sumner; J. W. Richardson, Rutherford; Henry Cooper, Bedford; James Fulton, Lincoln; E. A. Wilson, Marshall; E. E. Harney, Giles; C. W. Beale, Williamson; S. H. Benton, Robertson; M. D. Davie, Montgomery; T. B. Summers, Stewart; F. F. V. Schmittou, Dickson; J. J. Williams, Hickman; W. H. Polk, Maury; L. M. Bentley, Lawrence; W. P. Kendrick, Wayne; J. M. Carter, Hardin; A. G. Shrewsbury, Henderson; J. B. Algee, Carroll; J. J. Lamb, Henry; W. P. Caldwell, Weakley; B. L. Stovall, Obion; B. E. Holmes, Gibson; T. H. Newbern, Madison; J. W. Estes, McNairy; T. B. Low, Hardeman; William Maris, Fayette; Hiram S. Bradford, Haywood; Joseph L. Ewing, Michael

Vaughn, Davidson; E. J. Golladay, Z. W. Frazer, Wilson; W. C. Dunlap, E. W. M. King, Shelby; James T. Carter, Carter and Johnson; J. G. Rose, Greene, Hawkins, Hancock, and Jefferson; C. D. Anderson, Knox and Sevier; J. L. Keeney, Anderson and Campbell; Jesse Wood, Scott, Morgan, and Fentress; J. H. Dobson, Polk, McMinn, and Meigs; R. P. Loyd, Rhea, Bledsoe, and Hamilton; R. B. Roberts, Grundy, Coffee, and Van Buren; J. J. Turner, Smith, Sumner, and Macon; Henry Maney, Davidson, Robertson, and Montgomery; T. B. Ivie, Rutherford and Bedford; James M. Davidson, Lincoln, Marshall, and Giles; W. V. Thompson, Williamson, Maury, and Lewis; J. E. Mickley, Benton and Humphreys; Micajah Bullock, Carroll, Gibson, Madison, and Henry; James A. Lackey, Dyer and Lauderdale; T. C. Taylor, Perry and Decatur; H. R. Bate, Fayette, Tipton, and Shelby.

Note: R. Cantrell replaced Abram M. Savage who died in office.

THIRTY-THIRD GENERAL ASSEMBLY

Held at Nashville, October 3, 1859–March 26, 1860.

SENATORS—George R. McClellan, Johnson, Carter, Washington, and Sullivan; W. M. Bradford, Hawkins, Hancock and Jefferson; D. V. Stokely, Greene, Cocke, Sevier, and Blount; M. V. Nash, Claiborne, Grainger, Anderson, and Campbell; James S. Boyd, Knox and Roane; R. T. Hildreth, Morgan, Scott, Fentress, and Overton; James T. Lane, Meigs, McMinn, Polk and Monroe; J. A. Minnis, Rhea, Bledsoe, Bradley, Hamilton and Marion; S. S. Stanton, White, Jackson and Macon; J. L. Thompson, Smith and Sumner; Jordan Stokes, Wilson and DeKalb; John W. Richardson, Rutherford and Williamson; James M. Johnson, Bedford and Marshall; Ed. J. Wood, Warren, Cannon, Coffee, Grundy, and Van Buren; Tazewell W. Newman, Franklin and Lincoln; H. W. Hunter, Giles, Lawrence and Wayne; Thomas McNeilly, Maury, Lewis, Hickman, and Dickson; John Trimble, Davidson; Judson Horn, Robertson, Montgomery, and Stewart; J. E. Mickley, Benton, Humphreys, Perry, Decatur, and Henderson; George B. Peters, Hardin, McNairy and Hardeman; R. W. Bumpass, Madison, Haywood, Lauderdale, and Tipton; B. L. Stovall, Henry, Weakley, and Obion; V. S. Allen, Gibson, Carroll, and Dyer; R. G. Payne, Fayette and Shelby.

REPRESENTATIVES—J. F. Trevitt, Sullivan; William M. Bayless, Washington; James Britton, Greene; Philip Critz, Hawkins; T. S. Gorman, Cocke; William Brazelton, Jr., Jefferson; D. C. Senter, Grainger; John W. Kincaid, Claiborne; John Williams, Knox; S. T. Bicknell, Blount; A. J. Vaughn, Monroe; A. L. Green, Roane; Alfred Caldwell, McMinn; Richard R. Harris, Bradley; Daniel C. Trewhitt, Hamilton; James S. Havron, Marion; Madison Williams, Franklin; J. G. McCabe, Cannon; John Smith, Warren; W. M. Russell, White; W. E. B. Jones, Overton; W. R. Kenner, Jackson; Joseph G. Pickett, Smith; J. J. Ford, DeKalb; R. A. Bennett, Sumner; John Woods, Rutherford; George V. Hebb, Lincoln; H. N. Cowden, Marshall; J. J. Beaty, Giles; William Ewing, Williamson; John Woodard, Robertson; John J. Williams, Hickman; N. B. Dudley, Montgomery; H. C. Lockhart, Stewart; William L. White, Dickson; George Gantt, Maury; Joseph M. Sowell, Lawrence; Jonathan Morris, Wayne; D. A. Roberts, Hardin; A. G. Shrewsbury, Henderson; John Norman, Carroll; C. Frazier, Henry; Samuel Baker, Weakley; Robert C.

Nall, Obion; J. L. Williamson, Gibson; R. B. Hurt, Madison; J. S. Morphis, McNairy; W. W. Guy, Hardeman; R. M. Ingram, Fayette; B. J. Lea, Haywood; E. H. East, J. B. White, Davidson; John R. Davis, William L. Martin, Wilson; John Pat Farrelly, W. T. Farley, Shelby; R. R. Butler, Carter and Johnson; Robert Johnson, Greene, Hawkins, Hancock, and Jefferson; R. H. Armstrong, Knox and Sevier; Alvis Kincaid, Anderson and Campbell; R. H. Bledsoe, Scott, Morgan, and Fentress; P. B. Mayfield, Polk, McMinn, and Meigs; James W. Gillespie, Rhea, Bledsoe, and Hamilton; J. M. Sheid, Grundy, Coffee, and Van Buren; R. B. Cheatham, Davidson, Robertson, and Montgomery; William R. Doak, Rutherford and Bedford; T. J. Kennedy, Lincoln, Marshall, and Giles; W. C. Whitthorne, Williamson, Maury, and Lewis; J. W. Davidson, Benton and Humphreys; J. D. Porter, Jr., Carroll, Gibson, Madison, and Henry; Stith Richardson, Dyer and Lauderdale; W. N. Baker, Perry and Decatur; C. H. Whitmore, Fayette, Tipton and Shelby; William H. Barksdale, Smith, Sumner, and Macon; W. H. Wisener, Bedford.

THIRTY-THIRD GENERAL ASSEMBLY—*First Extra Session*

Held at Nashville, January 7, 1861–February 4, 1861.

Membership of this first extra session of the Thirty-Third General Assembly was the same as the original session which met October 3, 1859–March 26, 1860.

THIRTY-THIRD GENERAL ASSEMBLY—*Second Extra Session*

Held at Nashville, April 25, 1861–July 1, 1861.

SENATORS—Membership of the Senate for this second extra session of the Thirty-Third General Assembly was the same as the original session which met October 3, 1859–March 26, 1860, with the following exception: Washington Barrow succeeded John Trimble who resigned during the session.

REPRESENTATIVES—Membership of the House of Representatives for this second extra session of the Thirty-Third General Assembly was the same as the original session of October 3, 1859–March 26, 1860, with the following exceptions: Ira P. Jones succeeded E. H. East who resigned; J. J. Beaty of Giles, Daniel C. Trewhitt of Hamilton, and William L. White of Dickson did not serve during this session.

THIRTY-FOURTH GENERAL ASSEMBLY

Convened at Nashville, October 7, 1861–Adjourned in Memphis, March 20, 1862.

SENATORS—Paulding Anderson, Wilson and DeKalb; Washington Barrow, Davidson; Robert Barton, Hawkins, Hancock, and Jefferson; R. W. Bumpass, Madison, Haywood, Lauderdale, and Tipton; M. D. Cardwell, Henry, Weakley, and Obion; Edward S. Cheatham, Robertson, Montgomery, and Stewart; W. C. Dunlap, Fayette and Shelby; James S. Havron, Marion; Reece T. Hildreth, Morgan, Scott, Fentress and Overton; W. H. S. Hill, Rutherford and Williamson; Allen Hurst, Claiborne,

Grainger, Anderson, and Campbell; Joel J. Jones, Franklin and Lincoln; James T. Lane, Meigs, McMinn, Polk, and Monroe; W. H. Maxwell, Johnson, Carter, Washington, and Sullivan; J. A. McDearmon, Gibson, Carroll, and Dyer; Thomas McNeilly, Maury, Lewis, Hickman, and Dickson; William P. Morris, Benton, Humphreys, Perry, Decatur, and Henderson; Samuel Pickens, Greene, Cocke, Sevier, and Blount; Joseph L. Rosson, Hardin, McNairy, and Hardeman; J. L. Spurlock, Warren, Cannon, Coffee, Grundy, and Van Buren; James J. Turner, Smith and Sumner; Samuel Turney, White, Jackson, and Macon; John W. Wester [Webster], Knox and Roane; D. F. Wilson, Giles, Lawrence, and Wayne; Ewing A. Wilson, Bedford and Marshall.

REPRESENTATIVES—Alvin M. Millard, Sullivan; S. K. N. Patton, Washington; James P. McDowell, Greene; William Simpson, Hawkins; J. H. Randolph, Cocke; J. Monroe Meek, Jefferson; D. C. Senter, Grainger; J. J. Bunch, Claiborne; John M. Fleming, Knox; Stephen J. Matthews, Blount; Joseph Walker, Monroe; B. F. Martin, McMinn; R. M. Edwards, Bradley; William R. Rankin, Marion; H. T. Carr, Franklin; Stephen H Woods, Cannon; Daniel Parker, Bedford; John J. Lowery, Warren; William Donaldson, Overton; R. P. Brooks, Jackson; Wilson Y. Martin, Smith; James M. Head, Sumner; E. A. Keeble, Rutherford; William Tolley, Lincoln; W. L. McClelland, Marshall; Samuel S. House, Williamson; John E. Garner, Robertson; A. L. Demoss and Ira P. Jones, Davidson; J. D. Easley, Hickman; D. N. Kennedy, Montgomery; H. C. Lockhart, Stewart; J. Eubank, Dickson; H. T. Osborne, Maury; Thomas H. Paine, Lawrence; James M. Carter, Hardin; William Clark Tucker, Henderson; J. C. Hawkins, Carroll; H. F. Cummings, Henry; W. H. M. Brooks, Weakley; James R. Gardner, Obion; J. T. Carthel, Gibson; A. S. Rogers, Madison; W. D. Jopling, McNairy; Austin Miller, Hardeman; F. B. Ragland, Fayette; Richard Hill, Haywood; Abe Caruthers and W. L. Martin, Wilson; John Martin and B. M. Estes, Shelby; R. R. Butler, Carter and Johnson; James Britton, Jr., Greene, Hawkins, Hancock, and Jefferson; R. H. Hodsden, Knox and Sevier; William Wallace, Anderson and Campbell; Nathan Ward, Smith, Sumner, and Macon; A. S. Jarnagin, Polk, McMinn, and Meigs; James C. Warner, Rhea, Bledsoe, Sequatchie, and Hamilton; Isaac C. Garrettson, Grundy, Coffee, and Van Buren; Alfred Robb, Davidson, Robertson, Montgomery, and Cheatham; Thomas G. Moseley, Rutherford and Bedford; John Laws, Lincoln, Giles, and Marshall; R. G. Ellis, Williamson, Maury, and Sevier [Lewis]; J. N. Little, Benton and Humphreys; William A. Dunlap, Carroll, Gibson, Madison, and Henry; S. D. Whitten, Dyer and Lauderdale; M. J. Fisher, Perry and Decatur; R. B. Somervell, Fayette, Tipton, and Shelby; S. V. Bowden, Morgan, Scott, and Fentress; William Floyd, DeKalb; Henry S. Hill, Hamilton; James W. Lea, Roane; James McCallum, Giles; W. H. Ross, Wayne; G. G. Dibrell, White.

THE "BROWNLOW" LEGISLATURE

Held at Nashville, April 3, 1865–June 12, 1865.

SENATORS—R. R. Butler, Johnson, Carter, Washington, and Sullivan; Charles J. McKinney, Hawkins, Hancock, and Jefferson; James H. Randolph, Greene, Cocke, Sevier, and Blount; DeWitt C. Senter, Claiborne, Grainger, Anderson, and Campbell; Samuel R. Rodgers, Knox and Roane; George W. Keith, Morgan, Scott, Fentress, and Overton;

Thomas B. McElwee, Meigs, McMinn, Polk, and Monroe; A. M. Cate, Rhea, Bledsoe, Bradley, Hamilton, and Sequatchie; William Bosson, White, Jackson, and Macon; John W. Bowen, Smith and Sumner; Z. W. Frazer, Wilson and DeKalb; William Spence, Rutherford and Williamson; William H. Wisener, Bedford and Marshall; Robert E. Lasater, Warren, Cannon, Coffee, Grundy, and Van Buren; William Stewart, Franklin and Lincoln; Thomas J. Cypert, Giles, Lawrence, and Wayne; Joshua B. Frierson, Maury, Lewis, Hickman, and Dickson; John Trimble, Davidson; B. R. Peart, Robertson, Montgomery, and Stewart; Thomas A. Muse, Benton, Humphreys, Perry, Decatur, and Henderson; Fielding Hurst, Hardin, McNairy, and Hardeman; Almon Case, Henry, Weakley, and Obion; W. K. Hall, Gibson, Carroll, and Dyer; John W. Smith, Fayette and Shelby.

REPRESENTATIVES—Richard H. Coward, Anderson; Edward Cooper, Bedford; J. H. Donaldson, Blount; Jesse H. Gaut, Bradley; William Barton, Cannon; Pleasant Williams, Carter; John Norman, Carroll; Furney Jones, Claiborne; Reuben Rogers, Campbell; J. R. Shultz, Cocke; John A. Fuson, DeKalb; A. D. Nicks, Dickson; William Simmons, Franklin; J. E. McNair, Gibson; Joseph R. Dillin, Giles; G. H. Grove, Grainger; James Jones, Greene; James R. Hood, Hamilton; W. J. Smith, Hardeman; Thomas Maxwell, Hardin; W. W. Willis, Hawkins; J. N. Puckett, Hickman; L. M. Jarvis, Hancock; Joseph Wagner, Johnson; A. C. Gillem, Jackson; William Heiskell, Knox; J. B. Minnis, Jefferson; W. A. Garner, Lawrence; Thomas A. Kercheval, Lincoln; Wallace Waters, Madison; R. S. Raulston, Marion; Abner A. Steele, Marshall; Jeremiah Gilmer, Maury; S. L. Warren, McNairy; J. M. Henderson, McMinn; G. W. Gaines, Monroe; William Wines, Montgomery; F. A. Smith, Obion; A. E. Garrett, Overton; Thomas G. Mason, Roane; J. S. Mulloy, Robertson; W. Y. Elliott, Rutherford; William Mullenix, Sullivan; William Wright, Sumner; Gilbert Brittle, Smith; Wilson Duggan, Sevier; A. A. Snodderly, Union; Samuel E. Griffith, Washington; Asa Faulkner, Warren; John Porter, Wayne; C. Underwood, Weakley; G. W. Anderson, White; A. W. Moss, Williamson; W. M. Woodcock, Macon; W. L. Waters and W. H. Grimmett, Wilson; W. B. Lewis and S. J. Carter, Davidson; M. T. Ryder, Shelby; Samuel M. Arnell, Williamson, Maury, and Lewis; W. J. Copeland, Polk, McMinn, and Meigs; J. A. Doughty, Anderson and Campbell; Rufus Dowdy and James M. Melton, Fentress, Morgan, Scott, and Cumberland; Theodore Hermans, Smith, Sumner, and Macon; Joseph Hudson, Davidson, Robertson, Montgomery, and Cheatham; James Mullins, Rutherford and Bedford; P. S. Richards, Tipton, Shelby, and Fayette; William Scales, Dyer and Lauderdale; Elijah Simmerley, Carter and Johnson; Jerry Stegald, Perry and Decatur; Dorsey B. Thomas, Benton and Humphreys; J. F. Thomas, Grundy, Coffee and Van Buren; D. G. Thornburgh, Greene, Hawkins, Hancock, and Jefferson; J. P. Walker, Rhea, Hamilton, and Sequatchie; Charles Inman, Knox and Sevier.

Note: The following eight members of the House did not serve during this session of the Legislature:
William Shelton, Fayette; W. P. Bond, Haywood; Peter Pearson, Henderson; Thomas Crutchfield, Henry; James Woods, Jr., Stewart; J. M. Tomeny, Shelby; Samuel Tighe, Shelby; and W. W. Woods, Carroll, Gibson, Madison, and Henry.

THE "BROWNLOW" LEGISLATURE—*First Adjourned Session*

Held at Nashville, October 2, 1865–May 28, 1866.

SENATORS—John Aldridge, Hardin, McNairy, and Hardeman; William Bosson, White, Jackson, and Macon; John W. Bowen, Smith and Sumner; A. M. Cate, Rhea, Bledsoe, Bradley, Hamilton, and Sequatchie; Thomas J. Cypert, Giles, Lawrence, and Wayne; Almon Case, Henry, Weakley, and Obion; John G. Carrigan, Franklin and Lincoln; Joshua B. Frierson, Maury, Lewis, Hickman, and Dickson; Z. W. Frazier, Wilson and De-Kalb; B. Frazier, Knox and Roane; W. K. Hall, Gibson, Carroll, and Dyer; J. D. Johnson, Bedford and Marshall; G. W. Keith, Morgan, Scott, Fentress, and Overton; R. E. Lasater, Warren, Cannon, Coffee, Grundy, and Van Buren; Thomas A. Muse, Benton, Humphreys, Perry, Decatur, and Henderson; Charles J. McKinney, Hawkins, Hancock, and Jefferson; Thomas B. McElwee, Meigs, McMinn, Polk, and Monroe; W. J. McFarland, Madison, Haywood, Lauderdale, and Tipton; Thomas H. Newbern, Madison, Haywood, Lauderdale and Tipton; P. P. C. Nelson, Carter, Washington, and Sullivan; B. R. Peart, Robertson, Montgomery, and Stewart; Joseph Powell, Greene, Cocke, Sevier, and Blount; John W. Smith, Fayette and Shelby; DeWitt C. Senter, Claiborne, Grainger, Anderson, and Campbell; William Spence, Rutherford and Williamson; John Trimble, Davidson; James P. Thompson, Warren, Cannon, Coffee, Grundy, and Van Buren.

Note: James P. Thompson succeeded R. E. Lasater who resigned.

REPRESENTATIVES—G. W. Anderson, White; Samuel M. Arnell, Williamson, Maury, and Lewis; Nathan Brandon, Stewart; James Baker, McMinn; Thomas H. Bledsoe, Lincoln, Marshall, and Giles; L. M. Blackman, Monroe; Gilbert Brittle, Smith; Hervey Brown, Madison; Henry Biggs, Fayette; Charles S. Cameron, Shelby; Samuel J. Carter, Davidson; P. H. Coward, Anderson; J. K. Clingan, Bradley; M. E. W. Dunnaway, Bedford; Wilson Duggan, Sevier; J. A. Doughty, Anderson and Campbell; Rufus Dowdy, Fentress, Morgan, Scott, and Cumberland; James Donaldson, Blount; W. Y. Elliott, Rutherford; H. A. Freeman, Haywood; John A. Fuson, DeKalb; Asa Faulkner, Warren; George D. Foster, Hamilton; G. H. Grove, Grainger; W. A. Garner, Lawrence; A. E. Garrett, Overton; Jesse H. Gaut, Bradley; W. H. Grimmett, Wilson; Jeremiah Gilmer, Maury; James R. Hood, Hamilton; William Heiskell, Knox; Joseph Hudson, Davidson, Robertson, Montgomery, and Cheatham; James Hale, Jefferson; Charles Inman, Knox and Sevier; L. M. Jarvis, Hancock; James Jones, Greene; Thomas A. Kercheval, Lincoln; W. B. Lewis, Davidson; J. S. Mulloy, Robertson; James Mullins, Bedford and Rutherford; James M. Melton, Fentress, Morgan, Scott, and Cumberland; W. A. Moss, Williamson; H. P. Murphy, Johnson; Thomas G. Mason, Roane; J. E. McNair, Gibson; Thomas Maxwell, Hardin; H. H. Marable, Benton and Humphreys; Hiram Morris, Cannon; A. J. Martin, Jackson; John Norman, Carroll; A. D. Nicks, Dickson; D. A. Nunn, Haywood; C. N. Ordway, Giles; G. W. Overstreet, Overton; P. P. Pearson, Henderson; S. K. N. Patton, Washington; William K. Poston, Shelby; James Parks, Polk, McMinn, and Meigs; John Porter, Wayne; Nathaniel Porter, Henry; F. S. Richards, Tipton, Shelby, and Fayette; R. S. Raulston, Marion; Reuben Rogers, Campbell; Abner A. Steele, Marshall; Jerry Stegald, Perry and Decatur; William Simmons, Franklin; Elijah Simmerly, Carter and Johnson; A. A. Snodderly, Union; W. P. Scales, Dyer and Lauderdale; J. R. Shultz, Cocke; W. J. Smith, Hardeman; F. A. Smith, Obion; W. H. Shepherd, Hawkins; J. F. Sinclair, Dyer and Lauderdale; Joseph H. Travis, Henry; D. G. Thornburgh, Greene, Hawkins, Hancock, and Jefferson; D. B. Thomas, Benton and Humphreys; John F. Thomas, Grundy, Coffee, and Van Buren; C. Underwood, Weakley; William Wines, Montgomery; W. M. Woodcock, Macon; William R. Wright, Sumner; John Welsh, Sullivan; W. L. Waters, Wilson; W. W. Woods, Carroll, Madison, Gibson, and Henry; Wallace Waters, Madison; S. L. Warren, McNairy; J. P. Walker, Rhea, Hamilton, and Sequatchie; Pleasant Williams, Carter; W. W. Willis, Hawkins; Samuel P. Walker, Shelby; A. R. Wynne, Sumner; William Barton, Cannon; Theodore Hermans, Smith, Sumner, and Macon; Furney Jones, Claiborne; J. N. Puckett, Hickman.

Note: With reference to the number of representatives, there are discrepancies between the number of names listed in the *Journal* and in the law providing for their per diem compensation. While 85 members constituted the total membership of the House, there appear 96 names in the official records. The variation is due to deaths or resignations. In some instances the vacancies were filled by a new election, while in other cases the post vacated by death or resignation remained unfilled.

THE "BROWNLOW" LEGISLATURE—*Special Session*

Held at Nashville, July 4, 1866–July 25, 1866.

SENATORS—John Aldridge, Hardin, McNairy, and Hardeman; William Bosson, White, Jackson, and Macon; A. M. Cate, Rhea, Bledsoe, Bradley, Hamilton, and Sequatchie; Thomas J. Cypert, Giles, Lawrence, and Wayne; Almon Case, Henry, Weakley, and Obion; Joseph G. Carrigan, Franklin and Lincoln; Joshua B. Frierson, Maury, Lewis, Hickman, and Dickson; Z. W. Frazier, Wilson and DeKalb; B. Frazier, Knox and Roane; W. K. Hall, Gibson, Carroll, and Dyer; J. D. Johnson, Bedford and Marshall; George W. Keith, Morgan, Scott, Fentress, and Overton; C. J. McKinney, Hawkins, Hancock, and Jefferson; Thomas B. McElwee, Meigs, McMinn, Polk, and Monroe; W. J. McFarland, Madison, Haywood, Lauderdale, and Tipton; P. P. C. Nelson, Carter, Washington, and Sullivan; Joseph Powell, Greene, Cocke, Sevier, and Blount; John D. Smith, Fayette and Shelby; D. C. Senter, Claiborne, Grainger, Anderson, and Campbell; William Spence, Rutherford and Williamson; John Trimble, Davidson; James P. Thompson, Warren, Cannon, Coffee, Grundy, and Van Buren.

Note: Although the total membership of the Senate amounted to 25, only 22 Senators appeared during the session. The absentees were Senators John W. Bowen, Thomas H. Newbern, and Thomas A. Muse.

REPRESENTATIVES—G. W. Anderson, White; Samuel M. Arnell, Williamson, Maury, and Lewis; James Baker, McMinn; L. M. Blackman, Monroe; Gilbert Brittle, Smith; Hervey Brown, Madison; Henry Biggs, Fayette; Samuel J. Carter, Davidson; R. H. Coward, Anderson; J. K. Clingan, Bradley; M. E. W. Dunnaway, Bedford; Wilson Duggan, Sevier; James A. Doughty, Anderson and Campbell; Rufus Dowdy, Fentress, Morgan, Scott, and Cumberland; James Donaldson, Blount; W. Y. Elliott, Rutherford; John A. Fuson, DeKalb; George D. Foster, Hamilton; G. H.

Grove, Grainger; W. A. Garner, Lawrence; W. H. Grimmett, Wilson; Jeremiah Gilmer, Maury; William Heiskell, Knox; Joseph Hudson, Davidson, Robertson, Montgomery, and Cheatham; James Hale, Jefferson; Charles Inman, Knox and Sevier; L. M. Jarvis, Hancock; James Jones, Greene; Furney Jones, Claiborne; Thomas A. Kerchival, Lincoln; William B. Lewis, Davidson; J. S. Mulloy, Robertson; James Mullins, Bedford and Rutherford; James M. Melton, Fentress, Morgan, Scott, and Cumberland; A. W. Moss, Williamson; H. P. Murphy, Johnson; Thomas G. Mason, Roane; James E. McNair, Gibson; Thomas Maxwell, Hardin; H. H. Marable, Benton and Humphreys; Hiram Morris, Cannon; A. J. Martin, Jackson; John Norman, Carroll; David A. Nunn, Haywood; George W. Overstreet, Overton; P. P. Pearson, Henderson; S. K. N. Patton, Washington; James Parks, Polk, McMinn, and Meigs; John Porter, Wayne; N. Porter, Henry; J. N. Puckett, Hickman; F. S. Richards, Fayette, Tipton and Shelby; R. S. Raulston, Marion; Reuben Rogers, Campbell; Jerry Stegald, Perry and Decatur; Elijah Simmerly, Carter and Johnson; A. A. Snodderly, Union; J. R. Shultz, Cocke; W. J. Smith, Hardeman; F. A. Smith, Obion; W. H. Shepherd, Hawkins; J. F. Sinclair, Dyer and Lauderdale; D. G. Thornburgh, Greene, Hawkins, Hancock, and Johnson; C. Underwood, Weakley; William Wines, Montgomery; W. M. Woodcock, Macon; John Welsh, Sullivan; W. L. Waters, Wilson; W. W. Woods, Carroll, Madison, Gibson, and Henry; S. L. Warren, McNairy; J. P. Walker, Hamilton, Rhea, and Sequatchie; Pleasant Williams, Carter.

Note: Of the 85 members constituting total membership in the House only 72 names appear in the *Journal*. The following nine names appearing in the *Journal* are not listed in the law providing for per diem compensation:

Hervey Brown, Samuel J. Carter, M. E. W. Dunnaway, George D. Foster, W. B. Lewis, H. H. Marable, P. P. Pearson, N. Porter, and Elijah Simmerly. The deficiency was due to resignations, purposeful absenteeism or denial of their seats.

THE "BROWNLOW" LEGISLATURE—*Second Adjourned Session*

Held at Nashville, November 5, 1866–March 11, 1867.

SENATORS—John Aldridge, Hardin, McNairy, and Hardeman; William Bosson, White, Jackson, and Macon; A. M. Cate, Rhea, Bledsoe, Bradley, Hamilton, and Sequatchie; Almon Case, Henry, Weakley, and Obion; Thomas J. Cypert, Giles, Lawrence, and Wayne; Joseph G. Carrigan, Franklin and Lincoln; B. Frazier, Knox and Roane; Joshua B. Frierson, Maury, Lewis, Hickman, and Dickson; W. K. Hall, Gibson, Carroll, and Dyer; J. D. Johnson, Bedford and Marshall; G. W. Keith, Morgan, Scott, Fentress, and Overton; Thomas C. Muse, Benton, Humphreys, Perry, Decatur, and Henderson; C. J. McKinney, Hawkins, Hancock, and Jefferson; Thomas B. McElwee, Meigs, McMinn, Polk, and Monroe; W. J. McFarland, Madison, Haywood, Lauderdale, and Tipton; P. P. C. Nelson, Carter, Washington, and Sullivan; Joseph Powell, Greene, Cocke, Sevier, and Blount; H. S. Patterson, Smith and Sumner; W. T. Robinson, Wilson and DeKalb; John W. Smith, Fayette and Shelby; D. C. Senter, Claiborne, Grainger, Anderson, and Campbell; William Spence, Rutherford and Williamson; James P. Thompson, Warren, Cannon, Coffee, Grundy, and Van Buren; John Trimble, Davidson.

REPRESENTATIVES—Dan Able, Shelby; G. W. Anderson, White; John Anderson, Hamilton; James Baker, McMinn; Hervey Brown, Madison; L. M. Blackman, Monroe; Henry Biggs, Fayette; John S. Brien, Davidson; David Brewer, Benton and Humphreys; J. K. Clingan, Bradley; R. H. Coward, Anderson; W. W. Coleman, Shelby; A. J. Clements, Smith, Macon, and Sumner; W. J. Cleveland, Smith; S. L. Colville, Warren; Rufus Dowdy, Fentress, Morgan, Scott, and Cumberland; J. A. Doughty, Anderson and Campbell; Wilson Duggan, Sevier; James H. Donaldson, Blount; William Davidson, Jackson; W. Y. Elliott, Rutherford; J. A. Fuson, DeKalb; W. H. Grimmett, Wilson; Jeremiah Gilmer, Maury; G. H. Grove, Grainger; W. A. Garner, Lawrence; William Heiskell, Knox; Joseph Hudson, Davidson, Robertson, Cheatham, and Montgomery; James Hale, Jefferson; Charles Inman, Knox and Sevier; L. M. Jarvis, Hancock; James Jones, Greene; Furney Jones, Claiborne; Thomas A. Kercheval, Lincoln; R. E. Lasater, Coffee, Grundy, and Van Buren; F. A. Loughmiller, Franklin; John Lellyett, Davidson; R. P. Ledbetter, Williamson, Maury, and Lewis; Thomas G. Mason, Roane; Thomas Maxwell, Hardin; James M. Melton, Fentress, Morgan, Scott, and Cumberland; W. A. Moss, Williamson; James E. McNair, Gibson; Hiram Morris, Cannon; James Mullins, Bedford and Rutherford; J. S. Mulloy, Robertson; H. P. Murphy, Johnson; W. R. Moore, Shelby; J. F. Moore, Lincoln, Giles, and Marshall; John Norman, Carroll; D. A. Nunn, Haywood; G. W. Overstreet, Overton; P. P. Pearson, Henderson; John Porter, Wayne; James Parks, Polk, McMinn, and Meigs; S. K. N. Patton, Washington; J. N. Puckett, Hickman; F. S. Richards, Fayette, Shelby, and Tipton; R. S. Raulston, Marion; Reuben Rogers, Campbell; Jerry Stegald, Perry and Decatur; Elijah Simmerly, Carter and Johnson; A. A. Snodderly, Union; John R. Shultz, Cocke; W. J. Smith, Hardeman; J. T. Street, Marshall; F. A. Smith, Obion; R. S. V. Schmittou, Dickson; J. F. Sinclair, Dyer and Lauderdale; W. H. Shepherd, Hawkins; J. A. Taylor, Carter; L. M. Tharpe, Henry; G. W. Thompson, Bedford; D. G. Thornburgh, Greene, Hawkins, Hancock, and Jefferson; C. Underwood, Weakley; J. P. Walker, Rhea, Hamilton, and Sequatchie; W. L. Waters, Wilson; S. L. Warren, McNairy; William Wines, Montgomery; John Welsh, Sullivan; W. M. Woodcock, Macon; W. W. Woods, Carroll, Madison, Gibson, and Henry; William Wright, Sumner.

THIRTY-FIFTH GENERAL ASSEMBLY—*First Session*

Held at Nashville, October 7, 1867–March 16, 1868.

SENATORS—John Aldridge, Hardin, McNairy, and Hardeman; Eugene Cary, Davidson; A. M. Cate, Rhea, Bledsoe, Bradley, Hamilton, Marion, and Sequatchie; R. P. Eaton, Knox and Roane; Joseph Eckel, Hawkins, Hancock, and Jefferson; W. Y. Elliott, Rutherford and Williamson; Joshua B. Frierson, Maury, Lewis, Hickman, and Dickson; J. A. Fuson, Wilson and DeKalb; W. A. Garner, Giles, Lawrence, and Wayne; Samuel Henderson, Meigs, McMinn, Polk, and Monroe; George W. Keith, Morgan, Scott, Fentress, and Overton; A. V. S. Lindsley, Davidson; Berry Lyle, Robertson, Montgomery and Stewart; Stephen Matthews, Greene, Cocke, Sevier, and Blount; James R. McCall, Madison, Haywood, Lauderdale, and Tipton; P. P. C. Nelson, Johnson, Carter, Washington, and Sullivan; John Norman, Gibson, Carroll, and Dyer; Samuel Parker, White, Jackson, and Macon; H. S. Patterson, Smith and Sumner; John

B. Rodgers, Warren, Cannon, Coffee, Grundy, and Van Buren; D. C. Senter, Claiborne, Grainger, Anderson, and Campbell; W. J. Smith, Fayette and Shelby; C. Underwood, Weakley, Henry, and Obion; David Wilson, Benton, Humphreys, Perry, Decatur, and Henderson; W. H. Wisener, Sr., Bedford and Marshall; William Wyatt, Franklin and Lincoln.

REPRESENTATIVES–J. H. Agee, Campbell; R. J. Allen, Blount; John Anderson, White; J. W. Baker, Hancock; C. C. Bean, Williamson, Maury, and Lewis; G. M. Bloom, McMinn; John Bowles, Overton; J. W. Brown, Franklin; L. M. Blackman, Monroe; William Bosson, Rutherford; David Brewer, Benton and Humphreys; B. M. Carter, Stewart; J. C. Chiles, Anderson; John Carey, Lincoln; M. J. J. Cagle, Dickson; Faver Cason, Wilson; J. M. Cordell, Scott, Fentress, Morgan, and Cumberland; J. A. Doughty, Campbell and Anderson; Rufus Dowdy, Fentress, Morgan, Scott, and Cumberland; I. C. Dyer, Union; Geo. W. Dame, Marion; L. L. Faulkner, Warren; Robert Galbraith, Bedford and Rutherford; M. A. Graves, Jackson; J. T. Griffith, Polk, Meigs, and McMinn; Jeremiah Gilmer, Maury; J. W. M. Grayson, Johnson; James Hale, Hawkins, Greene, Hancock, and Jefferson; E. J. Hodges, McNairy; R. A. Hewatt, Obion; T. A. Hamilton, Shelby; J. M. Hammer, Sevier; T. S. Hunt, Smith; Newton Hacker, Washington; J. H. Hamilton, Lincoln, Marshall, and Giles; S. H. Inman, Cocke; Charles Inman, Knox and Sevier; Warren Jordan, Davidson, Robertson, Montgomery, and Cheatham; William Johnson, Hardeman; Thomas A. Kercheval, Davidson; A. F. Lillard, Marshall; Vincent Meyers, Claiborne; D. W. McFall, Williamson; Thompson McKinley, Sumner; J. M. Martin, Carroll; J. E. McNair, Gibson; L. M. Mynatt, Knox; T. J. Mason, Roane; J. A. Moore, Haywood; Hiram Morris, Cannon; Robert Medlin, Madison; W. T. Poston, Dyer and Lauderdale; J. N. Puckett, Hickman; J. J. Porter, Wayne; W. F. Prosser, Davidson; J. A. Prestwood, Weakley; Alfred Pitts, Hardin; J. O. K. Reeves, Fayette; J. P. C. Reed, Giles; R. S. Raulston, Marion; I. J. Roach, Carroll, Gibson, Madison, and Henry; W. T. Robinson, DeKalb; M. T. Ryder, Shelby; F. S. Richards, Fayette, Shelby, and Tipton; F. S. Singletary, Carter; W. H. Shepherd, Hawkins; T. A. Smith, Henderson; I. C. Stone, White; James Sparkman, Coffee, Grundy, and Van Buren; I. A. Taylor, Carter and Johnson; Jesse Taylor, Perry and Decatur; J. W. Thornburgh, Grainger; D. G. Thornburgh, Jefferson; G. W. Thompson, Bedford; W. P. H. Turner, Lawrence; W. O. White, Bradley; J. B. White, Greene; W. M. Woodcock, Macon; John Woodard, Robertson; John Welsh, Sullivan; J. P. Walker, Rhea, Hamilton, Bledsoe, and Sequatchie; Guy W. Wines, Montgomery; W. L. Waters, Wilson; E. S. Williams, Sumner, Smith, and Macon.

THIRTY-FIFTH GENERAL ASSEMBLY–*Extra Session*

Held at Nashville, July 27, 1868–September 14, 1868.

SENATORS–John Aldridge, Hardin, McNairy, and Hardeman; A. M. Cate, Rhea, Bledsoe, Bradley, Hamilton, Marion, and Sequatchie; Joseph Eckel, Hawkins, Hancock, Jefferson; R. P. Eaton, Knox and Roane; W. Y. Elliott, Rutherford and Williamson; J. B. Frierson, Maury, Lewis, Hickman, and Dickson; J. A. Fuson, Wilson and DeKalb; W. A. Garner, Giles, Lawrence, and Wayne; S. M. Henderson, Meigs, McMinn, Polk, and Monroe; G. W. Keith, Morgan, Scott, Fentress, and Overton; A. V. S. Lindsley, Davidson; Berry Lyle, Robertson, Montgomery, and Stewart; Stephen Matthews, Greene, Cocke, Sevier, and Blount; J. R. McCall, Madison, Haywood, Lauderdale, and Tipton; P. P. C. Nelson, Johnson, Carter, Washington, and Sullivan; John Norman, Gibson, Carroll, and Dyer; H. S. Patterson, Smith and Sumner; Samuel Parker, White, Jackson, and Macon; J. B. Rodgers, Warren, Cannon, Grundy, Coffee, and Van Buren; D. C. Senter, Claiborne, Grainger, Anderson, and Campbell; W. J. Smith, Fayette and Shelby; C. Underwood, Henry, Weakley, and Obion; William H. Wisener, Sr., Bedford and Marshall; William Wyatt, Franklin and Lincoln; David Wilson, Benton, Humphreys, Perry, Decatur, and Henderson.

REPRESENTATIVES—J. H. Agee, Campbell; R. J. Allen, Blount; John Anderson, Hamilton; J. W. Baker, Hancock; John Bowles, Overton; Jacob W. Brown, Franklin; L. M. Blackman, Monroe; G. M. Bloom, McMinn; William Bosson, Rutherford; David Brewer, Benton and Humphreys; B. M. Carter, Stewart; J. C. Chiles, Anderson; John Carey, Lincoln; M. J. J. Cagle, Dickson; Faver Cason, Wilson; J. M. Cordell, Scott, Fentress, Morgan, and Cumberland; G. W. Dame, Marion; J. A. Doughty, Campbell and Anderson; Rufus Dowdy, Fentress, Morgan, Scott, and Cumberland; I. C. Dyer, Union; L. L. Faulkner, Warren; Robert Galbraith, Bedford and Rutherford; J. T. Griffith, Polk, Meigs, and McMinn; Jeremiah Gilmer, Maury; J. W. M. Grayson, Johnson; James Hale, Hawkins, Greene, Hancock, and Jefferson; E. J. Hodges, McNairy; R. A. Hewatt, Obion; T. A. Hamilton, Shelby; J. H. Hamilton, Lincoln, Marshall, and Giles; J. M. Hammer, Sevier; T. S. Hunt, Smith; Newton Hacker, Washington; S. H. Inman, Cocke; Charles Inman, Knox and Sevier; Warren Jordan, Cheatham, Davidson, Robertson, and Montgomery; William Johnson, Hardeman; Thomas A. Kercheval, Davidson; A. F. Lillard, Marshall; Vincent Meyers, Claiborne; D. M. McFall, Williamson; Thompson McKinley, Sumner; Hiram Morris, Cannon; W. W. Murray, Carroll; J. E. McNair, Gibson; L. M. Mynatt, Knox; L. J. Mason, Roane; J. A. Moore, Haywood; Robert Medlin, Madison; W. T. Poston, Dyer and Lauderdale; J. N. Puckett, Hickman; J. J. Porter, Wayne; W. F. Prosser, Davidson; J. A. Prestwood, Weakley; Alfred Pitts, Hardeman; J. O. K. Reeves, Fayette; J. P. C. Reed, Giles; W. T. Robinson, DeKalb; I. J. Roach, Carroll, Gibson, and Madison; M. T. Ryder, Shelby; F. S. Richards, Fayette, Shelby, and Tipton; F. S. Singletary, Carter; W. H. Shepherd, Hawkins; T. A. Smith, Henderson; James Sparkman, Coffee, Grundy, and Van Buren; I. C. Stone, White; J. A. Taylor, Carter and Johnson; Jesse Taylor, Perry and Decatur; J. W. Thornburgh, Grainger; D. G. Thornburgh, Jefferson; G. W. Thompson, Bedford; W. P. H. Turner, Lawrence; W. O. White, Bradley, J. B. White, Greene; W. M. Woodcock, Macon; John Woodard, Robertson; John Welsh, Sullivan; John P. Walker, Rhea, Hamilton, Bledsoe, and Sequatchie; W. L. Waters, Wilson; E. S. Williams, Smith, Sumner, and Macon; Guy W. Wines, Montgomery.

THIRTY-FIFTH GENERAL ASSEMBLY—*Adjourned Session*

Held at Nashville, November 9, 1868-March 1, 1869.

SENATORS—John Aldridge, Hardin, McNairy, and Hardeman; A. M. Cate,

Rhea, Bledsoe, Bradley, Hamilton, Marion, and Sequatchie; R. P. Eaton, Knox and Roane; Joseph Eckel, Hawkins, Hancock, and Jefferson; W. Y. Elliott, Rutherford and Williamson; J. B. Frierson, Maury, Lewis, Hickman, and Dickson; J. A. Fuson, Wilson and DeKalb; W. A. Garner, Giles, Wayne, and Lawrence; S. M. Henderson, Meigs, McMinn, Polk, and Monroe; G. W. Keith, Morgan, Scott, Fentress, and Overton; A. V. S. Lindsley, Davidson; Berry Lyle, Robertson, Montgomery, and Stewart; Stephen Matthews, Greene, Cocke, Sevier, and Blount; J. R. Mc-Call, Madison, Haywood, Lauderdale, and Tipton; P. P. C. Nelson, Johnson, Carter, Washington, and Sullivan; John Norman, Gibson, Carroll, and Dyer; H. S. Patterson, Smith and Sumner; Samuel Parker, White, Jackson, and Macon; J. B. Rodgers, Warren, Cannon, Grundy, Coffee, and Van Buren; W. J. Smith, Fayette and Shelby; DeWitt C. Senter, Claiborne, Grainger, Anderson, and Campbell; C. Underwood, Henry, Weakley, and Obion; David Wilson, Benton, Humphreys, Perry, Decatur, and Henderson; W. H. Wisener, Bedford and Marshall; William Wyatt, Franklin and Lincoln.

REPRESENTATIVES—J. H. Agee, Campbell; John Anderson, Hamilton; R. J. Allen, Blount; J. W. Baker, Hancock; John Bowles, Overton; J. W. Brown, Franklin; L. M. Blackman, Monroe; G. M. Bloom, McMinn; William Bosson, Rutherford; David Brewer, Benton and Humphreys; B. M. Carter, Stewart; John C. Chiles, Anderson; John Carey, Lincoln; M. J. J. Cagle, Dickson; Faver Cason, Wilson; J. M. Cordell, Scott, Fentress, Morgan, and Cumberland; G. W. Dame, Marion; J. A. Doughty, Anderson and Campbell; Rufus Dowdy, Fentress, Morgan, Scott, and Cumberland; J. C. Dyer, Union; L. L. Faulkner, Warren; Robert Galbraith, Bedford and Rutherford; J. T. Griffith, Polk, Meigs, and McMinn; Jeremiah Gilmer, Maury; J. W. M. Grayson, Johnson; James Hale, Jefferson, Greene, Hancock, and Hawkins; E. J. Hodges, McNairy; R. A. Hewatt, Obion; T. A. Hamilton, Shelby; J. H. Hamilton, Lincoln, Marshall, and Giles; J. M. Hammer, Sevier; T. S. Hunt, Smith; Newton Hacker, Washington; S. H. Inman, Cocke; Charles Inman, Sevier and Knox; Warren Jordan, Davidson, Cheatham, Robertson, and Montgomery; W. M. Johnson, Hardeman; T. A. Kercheval, Davidson; A. F. Lillard, Marshall; Robert Medlin, Madison; Vincent Meyers, Claiborne; D. M. McFall, Williamson; Thompson McKinley, Sumner; Hiram Morris, Cannon; W. W. Murray, Carroll; J. E. McNair, Gibson; L. M. Mynatt, Knox; T. J. Mason, Roane; J. A. Moore, Haywood; W. T. Poston, Dyer and Lauderdale; J. N. Puckett, Hickman; J. J. Porter, Wayne; W. F. Prosser, Davidson; J. A. Prestwood, Weakley; Alfred Pitts, Hardin; J. O. K. Reeves, Fayette; J. P. C. Reed, Giles; W. T. Robinson, DeKalb County; M. T. Ryder, Shelby; W. B. Roddy, Jackson; I. J. Roach, Carroll, Gibson, Madison, and Henry; F. S. Richards, Fayette, Shelby, and Tipton; F. S. Singletary, Carter; W. H. Shepherd, Hawkins; T. A. Smith, Henderson; James Sparkman, Van Buren, Grundy, and Coffee; I. C. Stone, White; J. A. Taylor, Carter and Johnson; Jesse Taylor, Perry and Decatur; J. W. Thornburgh, Grainger; D. G. Thornburgh, Jefferson; G. W. Thompson, Bedford; W. P. H. Turner, Lawrence; W. O. White, Bradley; J. B. White, Greene; W. M. Woodcock, Macon; John Woodard, Robertson; John Welsh, Sullivan; J. P. Walker, Rhea, Hamilton, Bledsoe, and Sequatchie; W. L. Waters, Wilson; E. S. Williams, Smith, Sumner, and Macon; Guy W. Wines, Montgomery.

MINOR MESSAGES OF GOVERNOR BROWNLOW*
(Not included in Volume V)

Date	*Subject and Source*
May 1, 1865	Nominations of Trustees for Tennessee Hospital for the Insane. *Senate Journal*, First Session, 1865, 79–80.
May 19, 1865	Message *re* correspondence with Bank of Tennessee. *Senate Journal*, First Session, 1865, 142.
May 26, 1865	Communication *re* status of the Hermitage property. *Senate Journal*, First Session, 1865, 166–167.
May 31, 1865	Nominations of Inspectors for Penitentiary. *Senate Journal*, First Session, 1865, 182.
June 5, 1865	Message *re* salaries for Penitentiary Inspectors. *Senate Journal*, First Session, 1865, 194–195.
June 6, 1865	Nomination of Inspector for Penitentiary. *Senate Journal*, First Session, 1865, 202.
November 2, 1865	Appointment of Archelaus M. Hughes to Claim Agency in Washington City. *Senate Journal*, First Adjourned Session, 1865–66, 104.
October 24, 1865	*Re* Railroad Bonds. *House Journal*, First Adjourned Session, 1865–66, 82–84.
November 3, 1865	Five citizens of Greene County hanged. *House Journal*, First Adjourned Session, 1865–66, 112–113.
November 22, 1865	Increase in crime in Nashville. *Senate Journal*, First Adjourned Session, 1865–66, 151. *House Journal*, First Adjourned Session, 1865–66, 181–182.
November 25, 1865	Report *re* elective franchise, registration, vote by districts, etc. *Senate Journal*, First Adjourned Session, 1865–66, 166–170.
December 5, 1865	*Re* House Bill 293 relative to railroads. *Senate Journal*, First Adjourned Session, 1865–66, 195–196. *House Journal*, First Adjourned Session, 1865–66, 219–220.
January, 1866	*Re* Resignations of Penitentiary Inspectors. *Senate Journal*, First Adjourned Session, 1865–66, 235–236. *House Journal*, First Adjourned Session, 1865–66, 260–261.

* Author's note. Due to the large number of Messages issued by Governor Brownlow, it has been deemed advisable not to insert those documents dealing with rather minor topics. However, for the information of anyone who might be interested, a list of the omitted Messages is herewith inserted by date, subject, and specific citation as to where they may be found.

January 15, 1866   Increase in salary for Judicial officers.
                      Senate Journal, First Adjourned Session, 1865–66,
                      243.
                      House Journal, First Adjourned Session, 1865–66,
                      281–282.

January 24, 1866   Protection of military and civilian personnel from
                      suits against them for acts committed in military
                      capacity.
                      Senate Journal, First Adjourned Session, 1865–66,
                      275–276.
                      House Journal, First Adjourned Session, 1865–66,
                      297–299.

February 20, 1866   *Re* Directors of the Bank of Tennessee.
                      Senate Journal, First Adjourned Session, 1865–66,
                      374.

February 24, 1866   Message transmitting report *re* Tennessee Hospital
                      for the Insane.
                      Senate Journal, First Adjourned Session, 1865–66,
                      391.
                      House Journal, First Adjourned Session, 1865–66,
                      406.

May 10, 1866   *Re* Approval of Commissioners of the Penitentiary.
                      Senate Journal, First Adjourned Session, 1865–66,
                      508.

May 22, 1866   Nominations for Commissioners of Metropolitan
                      Police District of Shelby, State of Tennessee.
                      Senate Journal, First Adjourned Session, 1865–66,
                      576.

May 24, 1866   Nominations for Commissioners of Metropolitan
                      Police of the City of Nashville.
                      Senate Journal, First Adjourned Session, 1865–66,
                      591.

May 25, 1866   Nomination for Metropolitan Police Commissioner
                      for the City of Chattanooga.
                      Senate Journal, First Adjourned Session, 1865–66,
                      600.

July 9, 1866   Request for confirmation of appointment under
                      Metropolitan Police Law.
                      Senate Journal, Extra Session, 1866, 17.

November 15, 1866   Message transmitting letter from the Governor of
                      South Carolina *re* some valuable machinery.
                      Senate Journal, Second Adjourned Session, 1866–67,
                      25.
                      House Journal, Second Adjourned Session, 1866–67,
                      39.

November 17, 1866   Message transmitting important communication
                      from Rev. Thomas W. Humes, President of the East
                      Tennessee University at Knoxville.
                      Senate Journal, Second Adjourned Session, 1866–67,
                      32.

House Journal, Second Adjourned Session, 1866–67, 39.

November 20, 1866   Report *re* Bank of Tennessee.
Senate Journal, Second Adjourned Session, 1866–67, 40.
House Journal, Second Adjourned Session, 1866–67, 117.

December 10, 1866   *Re* Loan of the School Fund to a Memphis bank.
Senate Journal, Second Adjourned Session, 1866–67, 135.
House Journal, Second Adjourned Session, 1866–67, 149–150.

February 4, 1867   *Re* Appropriation to benefit certain railroads.
Senate Journal, Second Adjourned Session, 1866–67, 230.
House Journal, Second Adjourned Session, 1866–67, 233.

February 7, 1867   *Re* Vacancies in certain State offices.
Senate Journal, Second Adjourned Session, 1866–67, 252–253.

February 18, 1867   Difficulty at the State Capitol between the Superintendent and several officers of the General Assembly.
Senate Journal, Second Adjourned Session, 1866–67, 334.
House Journal, Second Adjourned Session, 1866–67, 289.

February 25, 1867   Message transmitting Report of the Superintendent of the Tennessee Insane Hospital.
Senate Journal, Second Adjourned Session, 1866–67, 346.

February 26, 1867   *Re* Disposition of valuable machinery shipped from South Carolina.
Senate Journal, Second Adjourned Session, 1866–67, 362.
House Journal, Second Adjourned Session, 1866–67, 341.

October 9, 1867   Joint Convention to count votes for Governor.
Senate Journal, 1867–68, 19.
House Journal, 1867–68, 27.

October 14, 1867   Message transmitting report of claims agent for the Tennessee National Bank of Memphis.
Senate Journal, 1867–68, 44.

November 4, 1867   Expenses relative to machinery shipped from South Carolina.
Senate Journal, 1867–68, 88.

November 6, 1867   Nomination for Metropolitan Board of Commissioners.
Senate Journal, 1867–68, 97.

November 8, 1867   Removal of Penitentiary Commissioner.
Senate Journal, 1867–68, 107.
House Journal, 1867–68, 152.

November 12, 1867	Meeting of teachers, county superintendents, and other educators. *House Journal*, 1867–68, 162.
November 12, 1867	Message transmitting Report of the Librarian. *Senate Journal*, 1867–68, 131. *House Journal*, 1867–68, 202.
November 20, 1867	Message transmitting Report of the Superintendent of the Insane Hospital. *Senate Journal*, 1867–68, 135. *House Journal*, 1867–68, 202.
November 26, 1867	*Re* Memorial from the lessees of the Penitentiary. *Senate Journal*, 1867–68, 156.
February 8, 1868	Employees of Memphis, Clarksville & Louisville Railroad on strike for back pay. *House Journal*, 1867–68, 582–583.
February 17, 1868	Nominations for Directors of the Bank of Tennessee. *Senate Journal*, 1867–68, 355.
February 24, 1868	*Re* Publication of legal notices in certain newspapers. *Senate Journal*, 1867–68, 385.
February 28, 1868	Nomination of additional newspaper for publication of legal notices. *Senate Journal*, 1867–68, 403.
March 4, 1868	Nomination of *Maryville Republican* for publication of legal notices. *Senate Journal*, 1867–68, 425.
March 4, 1868	Nomination of the *New Zeit* of Memphis for publication of legal notices. *Senate Journal*, 1867–68, 426.
March 12, 1868	Nominations of additional newspapers for publication of legal notices. *Senate Journal*, 1867–68, 487.
March 14, 1868	Nomination of the *Cookeville Times* for publication of legal notices. *Senate Journal*, 1867–68, 503.
July 29, 1868	Message transmitting letter and ordinance from Judge John M. Lea. *Senate Journal*, Extra Session, 1868, 71. *House Journal*, Extra Session, 1868, 44.
August 14, 1868	Nomination of the *Union Pilot* for publication of legal notices. *Senate Journal*, Extra Session, 1868, 108.
September 7, 1868	Nomination of the *Jackson Republican* for publication of legal notices. *Senate Journal*, 1868-69, 201.
July 28, 1868	Message transmitting Memorial from Maury County. *Senate Journal*, 1868-69, 90.
December 14, 1868	Nominations for Directors of the Penitentiary. *Senate Journal*, 1868-69, 92.

January 4, 1869	Nomination for Superintendent of the Metropolitan Police of Memphis. *Senate Journal*, 1868–69, 119.
January 26, 1869	Message transmitting letter and transcript in the case of Catharine Bigby *vs.* Jno. B., and Richard Hamilton. *Senate Journal*, 1868–69, 181–183.
January 26, 1869	Nomination of Director of the Penitentiary. *Senate Journal*, 1868–69, 183–184.
February 4, 1869	Withdrawal of nomination of Director of the Penitentiary. *Senate Journal*, 1868–69, 214.
February 20, 1869	Nomination of the *Clinton Independent* for the publication of legal notices. *Senate Journal*, 1868–69, 287.

LIST OF MILITARY OFFICIALS APPOINTED BY GOVERNOR ISHAM G. HARRIS FROM MAY 9, 1861 to OCTOBER 29, 1861.

"Executive Department,
Nashville, May 9, 1861. }

GENTLEMEN OF THE SENATE AND HOUSE OF REPRESENTATIVES:

I have nominated, and herewith submit for your confirmation, the following gentlemen:

For Majors General—Gideon J. Pillow and Samuel R. Anderson.

For Brigadiers General—Felix K. Zollicoffer, Benjamin F. Cheatham, Robert C. Foster 3d, John L. T. Sneed, and Wm. R. Caswell.

For Adjutant General—Daniel S. Donaldson.

For Inspector General—Wm. H. Carroll.

For Quartermaster General—Vernon K. Stevenson.

For Commissary General—R. G. Fain.

For Paymaster General—William Williams.

For Surgeon General—Dr. Paul F. Eve.

For Assistant Surgeons General—Dr. Joseph C. Newnan and Dr. John D. Winston.

For Assistant Adjutants General—W. C. Whitthorne, James D. Porter, Hiram S. Bradford, and D. M. Key.

For Assistant Inspectors General—J. W. Gillespie, James L. Scudder, John C. Brown, and Alexander W. Campbell.

For Assistant Quartermasters General—Paulding Anderson, George W. Cunningham, S. T. Bicknell, George W. Fisher, Thomas Marshall, Thomas Peters, John G. Finnie, W. P. Davis, and J. H. McMahon.

For Assistant Commissaries General—Calvin M. Fackler, John M. Brown, Miles M. Draughn, Madison Stratton, James S. Patton, James W. Duncan, W. W. Guy, and P. T. Glass.

For Assistant Paymasters General—Claiborne DeLoach, William B. Reese, and Thomas Boyers.

For Lieutenant Colonel of Artillery—John P. McCown.

For Military and Financial Board—Neill S. Brown, James E. Bailey, and William G. Harding.

By reference to your act of the 6th May inst., and the army regulations it will be seen that there are additional nominations yet to be submitted, the number of which it is impossible for me to determine until it is ascertained, with at least some degree of certainty, the number of troops that it may be necessary to call into active service, I have therefore nominated the heads of departments with such assistants as I considered necessary to the work of immediate organization, leaving the developments of the future to determine the additional appointments it may be proper to make.

Very respectfully,

ISHAM G. HARRIS."

"Executive Department, ⎫
Nashville, June 28, 1861. ⎭

GENTLEMEN OF THE SENATE AND HOUSE OF REPRESENTATIVES:

I herewith transmit for your confirmation the nominations which I have made since your adjournment on the 9th of May, under the provisions of the act of May 6, 1861, as follows:

Assistant Commissaries General.

May 17. Frank W. Greene,
" John R. Woods,
" Daniel F. Cocke,
" O. B. Caldwell,
" Lee M. Gardner,
" William C. Bryan,
" Jerome Ridley,
" Wm. H. Slover,
" R. H. Williamson,
" John D. Allen,
" Albert G. Ewing,

May 17. T. C. Ramsey,
" G. W. Menees,
" Samuel E. Barber,
May 22. J. W. Bennett,
" George D. Martin,
June 6. Wm. B. Deery,
" 14. Benj. L. Wilkes,
" 18. M. M. Henkle, Jr.
" 28. Felix Abby,
" W. F. Collins,
" James Glascock,
" W. J. Woods.

Assistant Quartermasters General.

May 17. Jesse B. Clements,
(vice Paulding Anderson, declined.)
May 17. E. Foster Cheatham,
" James Glover,
May 17. Jno. W. Eldridge,
" Jno. S. Bransford,
" John L. Sehon,
" John S. Hill,
" A. L. McClellan,
" Nathan Adams,
" H. T. Massengale,
" John W. Gorham,
May 22. Isaac Saffarans,
May 24. Ben P. Roy,
May 30. Moses Crues,
June 8. Owen H. Edwards,

June 14. R. M. Mason,
June 18. John Marshall, Jr.
June 21. James A. Wiggs,
" S. H. Ransom,
" Ben J. Lea,
June 21. S. L. Finley,
" Y. S. Patton,
" 28. Watt W. Floyd,
" Gilbert R. Campbell,
" Landon G. Oglesby,
" J. E. Rice,
" R. P. Crockett,
" L. F. Cabler,
" John F. Davis,
" A. W. Vick,
" E. A. Hornbeak,
" Jno. McLaughlin.

Artillery Corps.

May 17. John P. McCown, Colonel.
"   Milton A. Haynes, Lieutenant Colonel.
"   Alexander P. Stewart, Major.
"   Arthur M. Rutledge, Sr. Captain, 1.
"   James H. Wilson, Jr. Captain, 2.
"   Marshall J. Polk, Captain, 3.
"   Reuben R. Ross, Captain, 4.
"   William H. Jackson, Captain, 5.
"   Andrew Jackson, Captain, 6.
"   Smith P. Bankhead, Captain, 7.
May 22. William Miller, Captain, 8.
"   Fred Krone, Captain, 9.
"   Fred Werner, Captain, 10.

Ordnance Bureau.

June 15. Moses H. Wright, Senior Captain.
May 13. G. H. Monsarrat, Captain.
"   22. Wm. Richardson Hunt, Captain.
May 28. Nathaniel P. Chambliss, Captain.
"   25. C. P. Sengstack, Lieutenant.
June 28. George Grader, Lieutenant.

Assistant Adjutant General.

May 15. Pollok B. Lee,
June   7. Gustavus A. Henry, Jr.

Assistant Inspector General.

May 16. Henry W. Wall (vice John C. Brown, declined.)
"   Jo. G. Pickett,
"   C. H. Williams.

Engineer Corps.

"   B. R. Johnson, Colonel,
"   Achilles Bowen, Major,
"   W. D. Pickett, Senior Captain,
"   Montgomery Lynch, Captain,
"   Charles C. Rogers, Captain,
"   Thomas L. Estill, Captain,
"   J. A. Haydon, Captain,
"   J. G. Mann, Lieutenant,
"   E. W. Rucker, Lieutenant,
"   Felix R. R. Smith, Lieutenant,
"   Menefee Houston, Lieutenant.

Surgeon General.

May 10. Dr. B. W. Avent, (vice Paul F. Eve, declined).

Regimental Assistants.

May 10. Dr. Emmett Woodard, Surgeon, 1.

May	10.	Richard Butt, Assistant, 1.
"	17.	Samuel H. Stout, Surgeon, 2.
"	24.	W. T. Perry, Assistant, 2.
"	17.	William Nichol, Surgeon, 3.
"	17.	J. R. Buist, Assistant, 3.
"	23.	W. S. Bell, Surgeon, 4.
"	23.	Junius Williams, Surgeon, 5.
"	23.	L. P. Yandell, Assistant, 4.
"	25.	R. R. Dashiel, Assistant, 6.
"	25.	John S. Fenner, Assistant, 5.
"	27.	R. T. Clark, Surgeon, 7.
"	27.	F. F. Porter, Assistant, 6.
"	27.	J. M. Keller, Surgeon, 8.
"	27.	Charles McCormack, Assistant, 7.
"	28.	G. L. Robertson, Surgeon, 9.
"	28.	J. L. Fite, Assistant, 8.
"	28.	D. F. Wright, Surgeon, 10.
"	28.	James B. Murfree, Assistant, 9.
May	28.	John L. Baird, Assistant, 10.
"	31.	J. W. Gray, Surgeon, 11.
June	6.	S. W. Caldwell, Surgeon, 12.
"	6.	S. P. McGee, Assistant, 11.
"	6.	W. E. Rogers, Surgeon, 13.
"	6.	F. A. Kyle, Assistant, 12.
"	6.	J. M. Larkins, Surgeon, 14.
"	8.	W. B. Maney, Assistant, 13.
"	8.	J. F. Johnson, Surgeon, 15.
"	8.	J. D. Martin, Assistant, 14.
"	11.	Francis Rice, Surgeon, 16.
"	11.	R. W. Mitchell, Assistant, 15.
"	11.	A. H. Voorhies, Assistant, 16.
"	11.	George Blackie, Surgeon, 17.
"	12.	W. C. Cavanagh, Surgeon, 18.
June	12.	J. T. Reed, Surgeon, 19.
"	12.	C. K. Mauzy, Assistant, 17.
"	12.	J. T. Marable, Surgeon, 20.
"	12.	Geo. W. Conway, Surgeon, 21.
"	12.	A. B. Pulliam, Assistant, 18.
"	13.	Jas. E. Dulaney, Surgeon, 22.
"	13.	S. M. Carson, Assistant, 19.
"	14.	James A. Forbes, Surgeon, 23.
"	14.	B. F. Dickinson, Assistant, 20.
"	14.	W. M. Gentry, Surgeon, 24.
"	22.	H. W. Whitfield, Assistant, 21.
"	17.	Jno. W. Franklin, Surgeon, 25.
"	20.	J. H. Morton, Assistant, 22.
"	20.	John Patterson, Surgeon, 26.
"	20.	Isaac McGowan, Assistant, 23.
"	20.	Josephus Robertson, Surgeon, 27.
"	28.	L. P. Green, Assistant, 24.
"	28.	Gustavus B. Thornton, Assistant, 25.

All of which nominations are respectfully submitted.

ISHAM G. HARRIS."

"EXECUTIVE DEPARTMENT
Nashville Tenn., Oct. 29th 1861.

GENTLEMEN OF THE SENATE AND HOUSE OF REPRESENTATIVES:

Since the adjournment of the last Extra Session of the General Assembly, I have nominated the following Officers in the Provisional Army of Tennessee, under the provisions of the act of May 6th, 1861, to-wit:

SURGEONS.

July 4th. **Dr. Robt. J. Perry**, Surgeon, ordered to report to Dr. Avent at Memphis.

10th **Dr. Isaac S. House, Surgeon for Lt. Col.** McNairy's battalion of Cavalry.

12th **Dr. R. H. Taylor, Surgeon and Dr. J. H.** Nathall, Assistant Surgeon to Picketts regiment.

15th **Dr. W. P.** Massingal, Surgeon ordered to report to **Gen.** Caswell for East Tennessee Cavalry.

17th **Dr. J. B.** Lester, Assistant Surgeon for Col. Fultons regiment.

26th **Dr.** John Browning, Surgeon for Col. Blythe's battalion of Cavalry.

27th **Dr. W. W.** Herreford, Surgeon for Maj. Millers Mississippi battalion of Cavalry.

29th **Dr. R. S.** Green, Assistant Surgeon, and **Dr. W. T.** McClane, Surgeon for Col. Freeman's regiment.

19th **Dr. F. A.** Ramsey, Surgeon, ordered to report to **Gen.** Caswell at Knoxville.

31st **Dr. E. T.** Taliaferro, Surgeon, ordered to report to Medical Board.

August 8th **Dr. J. L.** Thompson, Surgeon, and Dr. E. A. McNight, Asst. Surgeon for Colonel Martins regiment.

9th **Dr.** James N. Bridges, Assistant Surgeon and Dr. W. M. Hatton, Surgeon for Col. Allisons regiment.

10th **Dr. D. B.** Cliffe, Surgeon for Col. Battle's regiment.

16th **Dr. R. E.** Fain, Surgeon, and Dr. W. A. Lightborn, Assistant Surgeon to Col. Stantons regiment.

28th **Dr. F. H.** Gains, Surgeon to Col. Brazeltons battalion of Cavalry.

30th **Dr. J. M.** Towler, Surgeon for Col. Jones battalion of Cavalry.

31st **Dr.** Joseph Sandek, Surgeon ordered to report to Maj. Alex P. Stewart at Camp Polk.

Sept. 12th **Dr.** John H. Callender, Surgeon for Col. Rains regiment.

17th **Dr. John H.** Cutter, Surgeon to Col. McClellands battalion of Cavalry.

30th **Dr. H. M.** Colquitt, Surgeon, ordered to report at Camp Zollicoffer.

Sept. 23rd **Dr. W. K.** Bowling, Surgeon, ordered to report to City Hospital, Nashville.

ASSISTANT COMMISSARIES GENERAL.

July 9th J. W. Dawson, assigned Col. Smith Regiment.

13th Thomas O'Keefe, assigned Col. Picketts Regiment.

19th Geo. P. Summers, assigned Col. Douglass Regiment,

27th Gideon S. Atkinson, assigned Jones Battalion,

Aug. 1st Robert Smith, assigned Freemans Battalion.
8th J. Q. Fare, assigned Martins Battalion.
14th Thomas H. Butler, assigned Stantons Battalion.
19th Geo. W. Cowan, assigned Allisons Battalion.
28th H. C. Green, assigned Brazeltons Battalion.
Sept. 13th J. B. Barnhill, assigned Williams Regiment.
17th James Munyhan, assigned McClellands Battalion.

ASSISTANT QUARTERMASTERS GENERAL.

July 13th T. V. Hyde, assigned to Col. Picketts Regiment.
August 1st M. A. Peeble, assigned to Freemans Regiment.
8th Saml. W. Morgan, assigned to Martins Regiment.
16th J. C. Freez, assigned to Stantons Regiment.
19th Jo. S. Green, assigned to Allisons Regiment.
Sept. 10th A. P. Hall, assigned to Williams Regiment.
17th J. F. Wise, assigned to McClellands Battalion.

ARTILLERY CORPS, CAPTAINS

July 12 James Hamilton.
July 12 William Keiter, vice James H. Wilson resigned.
July 20 Jesse Taylor, vice Reuben Ross resigned.
July 27 Walter Overton Crane.
July 27 Thomas K. Porter.
July 27 John P. Lynch.
July 27 John W. Stewart.
Aug. 1 Hugh L. W. McClung.
Aug. 16 Frank Maney.
Aug. 19 William R. Dunlap. (Since dead)
Sept. 17 G. H. Monsarrat, transferred from the Ordnance Department.
Sept. 19 S. H. D. Hamilton, vice James Hamilton deceased.
Oct. 21 Robert P. Griffith.
Oct. 28 J. G. Anglade.

ORDNANCE.

July 6 A. Wadgyman, Ordnance Sergeant.
Sept. 21 Arthur Wadgyman, 2nd Lieutenant.

ENGINEER CORPS.

July 29 W. F. Foster, 1st Lieutenant.
Sept. 2 Arthur W. Glouster, 1st Lieutenant.

All of which nominations are respectfully submitted for your approval and confirmation.

ISHAM G. HARRIS."

BIBLIOGRAPHY

PRIMARY SOURCES

Manuscript

Senate Bill No. 21 by J. J. Jones *re* Bank of Tennessee, 1857.
Senate Bill No. 37 by W. E. Travis *re* Regulation of Currency, 1857.
Senate Bill No. 117 by W. S. Munday *re* Regulation of Banking, 1857.
Bill by John Trimble *re* Erection of Monument to Andrew Jackson, 1859.
Bill by William H. Barksdale *re* Free Negroes, 1859.
Statement by Samuel D. Morgan, President of the Board of Commissioners for the Erection of the Capitol, 1859.
Statement by Capitol Commissioners *re* Capitol and Grounds, 1859.
Bill by George B. Peters *re* Emancipated Slaves and Free Persons of Color, 1860.
Substitute Bill by George B. Peters *re* Emancipated Slaves and Free Persons of Color, 1860.
Bill by R. W. Bumpass *re* Permanent Residence for the Governor, 1860.
Bill by B. L. Stovall *re* Leasing out the Penitentiary, 1860.
Memorial by Medical Faculty, University of Nashville, *re* Governor's Mansion, 1860.
Telegram by Governor Harris *re* President Lincoln's call for troops, 1861.
Bill by Pleasant Williams *re* Refusing Protection to Secession Ministers, 1865.
Bill by D. G. Thornburgh *re* Disfranchising Certain Persons, 1865.
Letter from William G. Brownlow to Andrew Johnson, May 19, 1865.
Letter from William G. Brownlow to Andrew Johnson, June 8, 1865.
Bill by William B. Lewis *re* Repeal of Elective Franchise Law, 1865.
Bill by W. R. Hall *re* His Vote on the Franchise Bill, 1865.
[Brownlow's] Proclamation Book.

State Publications

Acts of Tennessee, 1831, 1853, 1855, 1857–1861, 1865–1869.
Appendix, 1857, 1865–1869, 1879.
Constitution of Tennessee, 1835.
Frazier Impeachment Trial.
Senate Journal (Tennessee), 1857–1861, 1865–1869, 1879.
House Journal (Tennessee), 1857–1861, 1865–1869.
Public Documents, Tennessee Legislature, 1859, 1860.
Tennessee Reports, Yerger 6 (1834); Coldwell 3 (1866); Baxter 5 (1875).

U. S. Government Publications

Congressional Globe, Thirty-Fifth Congress.
Constitution of the United States.

Miscellaneous Documents, House of Representatives, Forty-First Congress, Second Session.
Ku Klux Conspiracy, Volume I.
Messages and Papers of the Presidents, (ed.) James D. Richardson, Vol. VI.

Newspapers

Brownlow's Knoxville Whig, 1861, 1866.
Brownlow's Weekly Whig, 1861.
Daily Morning Chronicle (Washington), 1866.
Daily Press and Times (Nashville), 1867, 1869.
Daily Times (Nashville), 1865.
Daily Union and American (Nashville), 1857, 1858, 1859.
Fayetteville Observer, 1866.
Knoxville Daily Free Press and Herald, 1868.
Knoxville Whig, 1861, 1866, 1867, 1869.
Knoxville Whig and Rebel Ventilator, 1866.
Louisville Journal, 1868.
Memphis Daily Appeal, 1861, 1867.
Memphis Daily Avalanche, 1862.
Nashville Daily Banner, 1861.
Nashville Daily Gazette, 1859, 1861.
Nashville Daily Union, 1865.
Nashville Patriot, 1860, 1861.
Nashville Union and American, 1859, 1860, 1861, 1868, 1869.
Nashville Union and Dispatch, 1867.
Republican Banner (Nashville), 1857, 1858, 1859, 1861, 1866.
Republican Banner and Nashville Whig, 1857, 1860.
Richmond Times, 1866.
Tri-Weekly Whig (Knoxville), 1859, 1861.
Union and Dispatch (Nashville), 1867.

SECONDARY SOURCES

Books

ALEXANDER, THOMAS B.: *Political Reconstruction in Tennessee.*
—— *Thomas A. R. Nelson of East Tennessee.*
BROWNLOW, WILLIAM G.: *Americanism Contrasted with Foreignism, Romanism, and Bogus Democracy.*
—— *The Great Iron Wheel Examined, Or Its False Spokes Extracted, and An Exhibition of Elder Graves, Its Builder.*
—— *Helps to the Study of Presbyterianism, Or An Unsophisticated Exposition of Calvinism, with Hopkinsian Modifications, and Policy, with a View to a More Easy Interpretation of the Same.*
—— and ABRAM PRYNE: *Ought American Slavery to be Perpetuated?*
—— *Sketches of the Rise, Progress, and Decline of Secession.*
CARMEN, BLISS: *The Joys of the Road.*
CLUSKY, MICHAEL W.: *The Democratic Handbook.*
COULTER, E. MERTON: *William G. Brownlow, Fighting Parson of the Southern Highlands.*
COX, S. S.: *Why We Laugh.*
DRAKE, JAMES VAULX: *Life of General Robert Hatton.*

FERTIG, JAMES W.: *The Secession and Reconstruction of Tennessee.*
FLEMING, WALTER LYNWOOD: *The Sequel of Appomattox.*
FOSTER, AUSTIN POWERS, and ROBERTS, ALBERT HOUSTON: *Tennessee Democracy.*
GRAVES, J. R.: *The Great Iron Wheel.*
HALE, WILLIAM T. and MERRITT, DIXON L.: *Tennessee and Tennesseans.*
HALL, CLIFTON R.: *Andrew Johnson, Military Governor of Tennessee.*
HAMER, PHILIP M.: *Tennessee—A History*, Volume II.
HENRY, ROBERT SELPH: *The Story of Reconstruction.*
History of Tennessee, by Goodspeed Publishing Company.
HORN, STANLEY F.: *KKK Invisible Empire.*
KROCK, ARTHUR: *The Editorials of Henry Watterson.*
LESTER, J. C., and WILSON, D. L.: *Ku Klux Klan: Its Origin, Growth and Disbandment.*
LOWELL, JAMES RUSSELL: *Poetical Works*, "The Biglow Papers."
MILLER, CHARLES A.: *Official and Political Manual of the State of Tennessee.*
MILTON, GEORGE FORT: *The Age of Hate.*
MOORE, JOHN TROTWOOD, and FOSTER, AUSTIN P.: *Tennessee—The Volunteer State*, Volume I.
PATTON, JAMES WELCH: *Unionism and Reconstruction in Tennessee.*
PRICE, R. N.: *Holston Methodism, From Its Origin to the Present Time.*
SAFFORD, JAMES M.: *Geology of Tennessee.*
The South in the Building of the Nation, Volume II, article by CAREY A. FOLK.
STRYKER, LLOYD PAUL: *Andrew Johnson.*
TEMPLE, OLIVER PERRY: *East Tennessee and the Civil War.*
———— *Notable Men of Tennessee.*
WELLES, GIDEON: *Diary of Gideon Welles*, Volume II.
WHITE, ROBT. H.: *Development of the Tennessee State Educational Organization, 1796–1929.*
———— *Messages of the Governors of Tennessee*, Volumes I, III, and IV.
WILLIAMS, SAMUEL COLE: *History of Codification in Tennessee.*

Magazines, Periodicals, Journals and Pamphlets

Journal of the Confederate Congress, Volume I.
GARRISON, WILLIAM LLOYD: *The Liberator*, July 4, 1856.
Legislative Union and American, 1857, 1859.
Remaines Concerning Britaine (1637).
Brownlow's Opinion of Colored People. (pamphlet)
Inaugural Address of Governor William G. Brownlow, 1865. (pamphlet)
Harper's Weekly, Volume X, 1866; Volume XI, 1867.
Tennessee Historical Quarterly, Volume XVII, 1958.

INDEX

TOPICAL INDEX

OF

GOVERNORS' MESSAGES

1857–1869

(CHRONOLOGICALLY ARRANGED)

Agriculture
Harris, Isham G.: activities of State Agricultural Bureau, 122–124.

Bank of Tennessee
Harris, Isham G.: nomination of directors, 34; liquidation recommended, 49.

Brownlow, William G.: report on captured assets, 467–468; recommendations *re* liquidation of, 539–540; dissatisfied with slow liquidation, 627.

Banking
Harris, Isham G.: status of, 43–49; prevailing customs and suggested recommendations, 108–120; existing regulations to continue, 347–348.

Brownlow, William G.: status of banking outlined, 1865, 419–420.

"Black Markets"
Harris, Isham G.: criticism of, 344.

Cattle Plague
Brownlow, William G.: recommended Tennessee participate in convention, 632–633.

Citizens, Loyal
Brownlow, William G.: recommended compensation for loss of property, 541; urged compensation for losses sustained by, 583–584.

Coercion
Harris, Isham G.: views and predictions of results, 265–267; usurpation and invasion by Lincoln, 279–280; refusal to comply with Lincoln's call for Tennessee troops, 283.

Confederacy, Southern
Harris, Isham G.: recommended affiliation with, 283–284; election of

Confederacy, Southern (*Continued*)
members to Confederate Congress recommended, 344–345.

Constitution of Tennessee
Harris, Isham G.: amendment to recommended, 49–50.

Constitution of United States
Harris, Isham G.: five suggested amendments, 263–264.

Brownlow, William G.: transmittal of Thirteenth Amendment to Legislature, 410–412.

Crime
Brownlow, William G.: severe penalties prescribed for certain acts, 413.

Education
Brownlow, William G.: school legislation recommended, 418; *re* East Tennessee University, 424; defeat of school bill lamented, 547; educational ideas outlined, 576–577; explanation *re* School Fund, 580–581; pleased with passage of school bill, 587.

Federal Relations
Brownlow, William G.: cooperation between State and Federal troops, 573–574.

Fourteenth Amendment
Brownlow, William G.: call for extra session, 510–511; analysis of provisions, 514–516.

Franchise
Brownlow, William G.: observations concerning, 420–421; law needed tightening up, 454–456; attempted justification of stringent regulations, 488–491; softened attitude toward Negroes voting, 532–533; required

709

GENERAL INDEX

Agriculture: Report of State Agricultural Bureau cited, 82; basic data concerning (footnote) 82; activities of State Agricultural Bureau, 122–124, 155; Address by Governor Harris at Fifth Annual State Fair, 1858, 242–246; Address by Matthew F. Maury at Sixth Annual State Fair, 1859, 230–242.

Alderson, William T.: Cited, 606.

Alexander, Thomas B.: Cited, 373; cited and quoted, 552; cited, 607; quoted, 659.

Anderson, Samuel R.: Appointed Major General, 301; re request for restoration of franchise privilege, 618–619.

Appendix: 665–705.
    Constitution, 1835, 665–680; Membership of General Assemblies, 1857–1869, 681–692; Minor Messages of Governor Brownlow, 693–697; Military Personnel appointed by Governor Harris, 697–702; Bibliography, 703–705.

Arnell, Samuel M.: Franchise restrictions proposed, 431; extract from speech on franchise bill, 434–435; submitted report of Franchise Committee, 480–481; proposal to violate Constitution of Tennessee, 519; pursued by Ku Klux, 608; "counted in" by Brownlow, 635–636.

Arnold, Thomas D.: Efforts to keep Tennessee pro-Union, 302.

Bailey, James E.: Appointed to Military and Financial Board, 301.

Bank of Tennessee: Directors nominated and approved, 34–35; extended comments by Governor Harris, 42–49; liquidation recommended by Governor Harris, 49; reply of Governor Harris to legislative inquiry, 62–67; proposed liquidation brought on spirited legislative battle, 140–151; Senatorial vote pro and con re liquida-

Bank of Tennessee (Continued)
tion of, 141–142; Senator Richardson's speech favoring liquidation, 142–150; effort to liquidate failed, 150–151; report on captured assets, 467–468; observations by Brownlow, 468–469; Brownlow's recommendations re liquidation, 539–540; slow liquidation unsatisfactory, 627.

Banking: Effort made to suppress circulation of small notes as currency, 52; a bill to regulate currency of Tennessee, 52–53; a bill to regulate the business of banking, 53; specific recommendations of Governor Harris, 54–55; newspaper criticism of legislative bickering, 55–56; sketch of fight between two legislators, 56–58; legislative delay chided by various newspapers, 58–60; provisions of law as enacted, 60–62; free banking law repealed, 83; survey of conditions and recommendations for improvement by Governor Harris, 108–120; public opinion shifted, 135–136; "Bob" Taylor's epigram, 136; nine recommendations submitted by Governor Harris, 137–138; newspaper comments upon Governor Harris' recommendations, 138–139; banking law enacted, 140; defeat of proposed constitutional amendment prohibiting State's assuming financial liability unless approved by popular vote, 151; status of, 1865, 419–420.

Barksdale, William H.: Author of bill to expel Free Negroes from Tennessee, 174–176; substitute bill re expulsion of Free Negroes, 178–180.

Barrow, Washington: Appointed Commissioner to confer with Confederate Agent, 289.

Bate, W. B.: Re request for restoration of franchise privilege, 618–619.